D1760375

Ill. 1. Igor Stravinsky

Stravinsky Dances
Re-Visions across a Century

Stephanie Jordan

DANCE BOOKS

To Howard

First published in 2007 by Dance Books Ltd
The Old Bakery
4 Lenten Street
Alton
Hampshire GU34 1HG

ISBN: 978 1 85273 125 0

A CIP catalogue record for this book is available from the British Library

Printed and bound in Great Britain by the Charlesworth Group

Contents

Acknowledgements

To remain undefeated by a topic of such complexity and magnitude, an author needs help and encouragement from a wide range of sources; in that, I have been wonderfully fortunate.

To begin with, one of the greatest pleasures of researching Stravinsky is to work at the Paul Sacher Stiftung in Basle, home of the Stravinsky Archive since 1983. My thanks to the staff who helped me through every stage of my journey, during the first unforgettable six months based with them (funded generously by a stipend from the Stiftung) as well as on many return visits, especially to Ulrich Mosch for his expert knowledge of the archive and continued support, and to Carlos Chanfón and Petra Kupfer for their tireless assistance as my designated librarians. I am also indebted to all the staff at the Jerome Robbins Dance Division of the New York Public Library for the Performing Arts, who have sustained me through numerous intense visits over many years, and especially to Monica Moseley and Charles Perrier for their friendliness and generosity in meeting my diverse and challenging demands. During 2001–2, I was honoured as John M. Ward Visiting Fellow in Dance and Music for the Theatre at Harvard University, and was consequently able to work through the George Balanchine Archive and other Stravinsky-related material in the Harvard Theatre Collection. My thanks to librarian Annette Fern for introducing me to these treasures.

Without the sponsorship of several other organisations, this project would never have come to fruition. The Arts and Humanities Research Council awarded a research leave grant that enabled its completion, and, before that, grants towards a Stravinsky chronology database and an analytical DVD on Ashton and the composer, both of which projects fed directly into the book. The British Academy offered financial assistance towards publication costs, including use of the photographs and notated examples that greatly enhance written argument in books such as this.

My own Roehampton University has also been a considerable fund of support, particularly in allowing me time to research and write. I am indebted to all my colleagues in Dance, who were especially understanding when something called the Research Assessment Exercise exerted a peculiar pressure of its own during the final preparations for publication.

My confidence was considerably boosted by a team of expert critical readers and Roehampton colleagues who between them covered convincingly the content range of the book: Carol Brown, Margarita Mazo, Helen Minors, Geraldine Morris (also my DVD collaborator), Christoph Neidhofer, Larraine Nicholas (also my database collaborator), Max Paddison, Nancy Reynolds, Bonnie Rowell, Marian Smith, David Vaughan, Georgiana Wierre-Gore and Lawrence Zbikowski. A particular thank you goes to Stravinsky's biographer, Stephen

Walsh, who not only closely examined the first chapter but also developed into my chief mentor. Ever encouraging and forbearing, he was immensely generous with advice on matters relating to the composer's life and work.

As endnotes demonstrate, many in the dance profession have assisted with this project, sending resources in the form of video/DVD material, providing valuable information in interview or through correspondence, contributing earlier to the Stravinsky database, and sometimes reading my writing. To them all, grateful thanks, and, specifically in connection with my choreomusical analysis, I acknowledge: Richard Alston, Marlis Alt, Gitta Barthel, Siobhan Davies, Sir Anthony Dowell, Suzanne Farrell, Robin Grove, Raimund Hoghe, Anne Teresa De Keersmaeker, Mark Morris, Susanna Della Pietra, Yvonne Rainer, Tero Saarinen and Jennifer Weber; Monica Mason, Anthony Russell Roberts, Christopher Newton, Robert Jude and Bennet Gartside of The Royal Ballet; Henk van Dyk (for material on Hans van Manen); Christopher Pennington of the Robbins Rights Trust; Ellen Sorrin of The George Balanchine Trust; Mei-Chen Lu of the Dance Notation Bureau; John Tomlinson of the Paul Taylor Dance Company; and Oliver Golloch, Barbara Hampel and Ed Kortlandt of Tanztheater Wuppertal.

Others who have offered valuable contributions as writers, scholars and dance enthusiasts include Henrietta Bannerman, Ramsay Burt, Drue Fergison, Millicent Hodson, Angela Kane, Marion Kant, Robert Kimber, Alastair Macaulay, Simon Morrison, Ann Nugent, Kimiko Okamoto, Natalie Raetz, Maria Ratanova, Lucie Rozmankova and Elizabeth Souritz. I also enjoyed full support from John Stravinsky on behalf of the Stravinsky Estate and from Stravinsky's publishers and those who work for them: especially from Claudine Murphy, Dale Wills and Mike Wood at Boosey & Hawkes, from Carolyn Fuller and James Rushton at Chester Music, and from Ben Newing at Schott. Nor do I forget the friendly and critical graduate students on whom I have tested my ideas over the years, those in my Music and Dance courses at Roehampton as well as the music students who attended my 2004–5 seminars at Princeton University.

The preparation of notated examples was a research project in itself, and in this I was amply supported by Paul Terry of Musonix, who, just for me, turned his skills to the documentation of dance rhythms as well as excerpts from Stravinsky's scores. It was both fun and illuminating to work with Karolina Romaniszyn-Tong on the analysis of dance excerpts from Nijinska's *Les Noces* and Bausch's *Sacre*, after which she took over most capably with the translation process into exquisite Labanotation.

I am of course greatly indebted to my Dance Books team, Rod Cuff, editor, Liz Morrell, designer, and indexer Helen Peters, who worked both swiftly and meticulously through the final pressured months. Most of all, thanks to David Leonard, whose dedication to publishing in the field of dance remains unmatched. He is truly a world leader in this respect, and once again, I have been very fortunate to enjoy his support.

As for my last two books, encouragement from family has played a crucial role. Thanks to my parents who have kept watch over my book progress for seven long years. And finally, to Howard, who, with immense generosity, read the entire manuscript, helped with musical matters large and small, proofread music and text with a keener eye than my own, and above all, believed in me. My next book won't be quite so long.

Stephanie Jordan
August 2007

A Note on Musical Referencing

For scores without rehearsal marks or cues, bar numbers have been used as the referencing system. Where a score uses rehearsal marks, the referencing system is as follows: [1]-1 refers to the bar preceding rehearsal fig. 1; [1] to the bar at [1]; [1]+2 the next bar; then [1]+3, and so on.

Introduction

It is hardly controversial nowadays to claim that Igor Stravinsky (1882–1971) is the number one dance composer of the twentieth century. He created more scores for dance (18 in total) or, more accurately, for theatre events with a significant dance element, than any other major composer of the century. These scores represent remarkable moments in music and theatre history: the huge-impact early Russian works *Firebird* (1910) *Petrushka* (1911) and *Le Sacre du printemps* (1913), the hard-edged, neo-nationalist *Les Noces* (1923) and warmly neoclassical *Apollo* (1928); then, breathing the air of serialism, *Agon* (1957), an instant and startling success and no less of a theatre event to mark the midpoint of the century. But a recent database 'Stravinsky the Global Dancer' (*SGD*)[1], the foundation to this book, provides stronger grounds for claiming the supremacy of the composer than we might ever have thought. It details over 1200 dances to his scores, revealing a mass of choreographers (so far over 680) who have been inspired by his music and/or who have used it to establish their credentials and their place in the grand tradition. For here was the legacy of 'the world's greatest living composer', as he was so often called; indeed, for many, Stravinsky's music stands for the twentieth century itself.

With countless evenings and festivals devoted to his work, Stravinsky 'events' have been considered eminently marketable, a route to success, his very name guaranteeing audiences. Such events have ranged from the occasional all-Stravinsky programmes presented by Diaghilev's Ballets Russes through the 1920s, to the extraordinarily ambitious week-long New York City Ballet Stravinsky festivals of 1972, the year after his death, and 1982, his centenary year. We can find more recent examples in the modern dance *Sacre* 'marathon' day in Rouen (2005) and the 'Sourcing Stravinsky' evening at Dance Theater Workshop in New York (2006), which included a commentary on *Agon* by the celebrated postmodern choreographer/film-maker Yvonne Rainer.

Stravinsky developed an impeccable dance pedigree, enjoying working relations with Diaghilev, who created twentieth-century ballet as an enterprise embracing the most exciting innovations across the arts, and with George

Balanchine, who, for a number of people, represents the pinnacle of twentieth-century choreography. In the context of Diaghilev and his Ballets Russes, Stravinsky was by far the most influential composer in the quest to raise the stature of musical composition and standing of composers in ballet, in establishing the compact one-act genre, and in creating a model for innumerable composers of the future. Choreographers soon flocked to stage Stravinsky's ballets, and with increasing rapidity as his new scores appeared. But as the years passed, these ballet scores gradually dried up. If the Diaghilev ballet commissions were formative, now Stravinsky turned more readily to other forms. The choreographers followed in hot pursuit. By today, practically all Stravinsky's scores, the concert works as well as the ballets, have been used for dance. Furthermore, there is no sign of a diminishing profile of new settings of familiar scores, even of *Firebird*, *Petrushka* and *Sacre*. Overall, there is every sign that Stravinsky choreographies will continue to be made, and across the planet. Stravinsky was and remains a truly global dancer as much as he was the prime global composer of the last century. Meanwhile, the composer's name rapidly became synonymous with ballet in the concert hall, where the ballet scores, suites, excerpts and arrangements have remained the most regularly performed of Stravinsky's works. Concert-goers can still thrill to the danger of *Sacre*, knowing the stories of its notorious premiere, or they can lose themselves in the exotic but safer *Firebird*, about a thousand performances of which the master conducted throughout his career.[2]

Stravinsky himself did everything he could to bolster the combined canon of the Diaghilev Ballets Russes and George Balanchine, a canon that represents virtually the entirety of his collaborations. It was a Russian émigré/American canon, and a classical ballet canon, and it has been the focus of most Stravinsky dance scholarship to date (for instance, on the Ballets Russes, by Richard Buckle, Lynn Garafola and Nancy Van Norman Baer; on Balanchine, by Charles Joseph).[3] There has long been the tradition in dance and music scholarship of privileging commissions and collaborations over settings of existing scores, whether dance or concert scores. But questions might now be asked as to whether the Diaghilev–Stravinsky ballets are the most interesting or important theatricalisations of those scores, at least from today's perspective. Collaborations create surprisingly strong mythologies. Even the Balanchine model raises the question of whether there is a direct relationship between interactive working processes and the success of a Balanchine–Stravinsky ballet. It also asks questions about the very concept of collaboration.

Using the qualifier 'even' for Balanchine raises the issue of his exceptional status. It is important to review this fact today, in terms not only of his Stravinsky work but also of its impact on other Stravinsky usage and its reception. For here, one choreographer's brilliance led to idolisation by critics and audiences, especially in New York. But whereas, on the one hand, Balanchine's work educated a generation of critics to see and write with unusual power, on the other it gave rise to a situation whereby some enthusiasts found it hard to recognise that there were other, radically different, ways of making musically interesting dance, and that formal musical training was not necessarily the route to the most 'musical' choreography. Balanchine's stupendous achievement had significant consequences for other dance.

It is timely now to look beyond the celebrated stories and allow those that are far less familiar to surface, from beyond the canon: the stories of those other Stravinsky choreographers and those other contexts in which his ballets have become known and in which he has become an institution. The *SGD* database confirms that Stravinsky's music inhabited a dance culture that included a wide range of modern dance,[4] as well as a wide range of ballet, and that the scores, once out of the hands of their composer, acquired a life of their own, with new connotations, styles and political implications. The database has also been a salutary reminder of our place in the world and our insular approaches to writing and reading dance history, which in Britain has been largely an English-language enterprise. We can now be aware of Western cultural tradition spreading worldwide through Stravinsky's music, but not only that: as cultures generally have become untidy, hybrid and dialectical in their workings, his music has become a site for negotiating identity. Although it is beyond the scope of this book and the limits of database research to more than touch on the issue of Stravinsky as global property, it is important to signal this larger context to the reader where possible. For, looking to the future, as much as we badly need more in-depth focused studies of dance, we also need more globally ambitious dance literature, referring to the spread of dance cultures and drawing comparisons between them.

The strategy described is in line with the more recently developed scholarly approaches to history, which seek to present the past in a more multi-layered fashion than before, positively embracing its complexities and ambiguities, and admitting the interplay of heterogeneous discourses. There is now a move away from the rigid historical model of straightforward cause and effect and linear continuity, away from the model of historical progress where events lead logically to other events, often within the terms of the art form, and where people act as agents of change, with teachers and choreographers passing on, adding to and breaking with tradition. Instead, in an approach that I find useful, the dance historian Linda Tomko argues for a dialectical approach that does not deny individual agency but that also takes fully into account a model, after Foucault, of 'conditions of possibility'.[5] Here, history operates as an interrogation of the particular social conditions in which artworks are made at a particular time.

No artist could better display the principle of heterogeneity of discourses surrounding his work than Stravinsky. He himself played an instrumental role in encouraging this. He could be playful, shrewd and deliberately misleading as well as passionately committed to the truth of the moment. What artist contradicted himself more in his statements? What artist more actively promoted a succession of ghost writers to speak for him? What artist has been more buffeted by the changing tide of judgement and value, and (apparently) switched artistic allegiance to work his own 'conditions of possibility' to his advantage?

Stravinsky's pronouncements on the non-expressivity of his music are perhaps the most famous site for debate of the discourses surrounding his work. The version in his *Autobiography* is the best known:

> Music is, by its very nature, essentially powerless to *express* anything at all, whether a feeling, an attitude of mind, a psychological mood, a phenomenon of nature ... The phenomenon of music is given to us with the sole purpose of establishing an order in things, including, and particularly, the coordination between *man* and *time*.[6]

Such thinking, however, which he later referred to as 'that overpublicized bit about expression (or non-expression)',[7] can be traced back to his manifesto 'Some Ideas about My Octuor' written in 1923, and there are even earlier hints of it in assertions about *Sacre* (1913 and 1920).[8] In 1965, the composer wryly admitted that 'music expresses itself, and very eloquently, *eloquently*.'[9] Had he finally mellowed?

Recent scholarship has dispelled the composer's self-driven myths about his break from the past during the years 1918–22. It was then that he embraced modernism (neoclassical modernism) and the values of Western European, as opposed to Russian, culture, while in retrospect, in a revisionist reading, absorbing into the new order the milestone *Sacre* of 1913. After this, the progress myth continued to take account of Stravinsky's turn towards serialism (the twelve-note compositional method) during the 1950s. We might now perceive a new set of continuities crossing and blurring the boundaries between Stravinsky's Russian, neoclassical and serial periods. Stravinsky's notion of an art removed from social conditions can be answered by arguing exactly the opposite – for instance, through contextualising his activity within a particular order-seeking political and artistic climate between the World Wars and by examining the composer as an artist who continued to betray his Russian roots after his apparent break from the past. We might also trace how some works, whatever he said about them, have been read in a number of ways: retrogressive, cutting-edge, elegantly fashionable, even politically subversive, according to the terms of the person reading them. Such is the power of recent writing by Richard Taruskin (the two-volume *Stravinsky and the Russian Traditions*), the two-volume biography by Stephen

Walsh, and the seminal work on the collaboration of Stravinsky and Balanchine by Charles Joseph.[10] Each of these scholars has rigorously interrogated the existing Stravinsky 'stories' whilst also uncovering new data on Stravinsky's life and work. Taruskin and Walsh have brought to light valuable dance information from Russian sources on the first half of Stravinsky's career.

New Stravinsky scholarship has also opened up the narrative interpretation of his work after years of favouring the decontextualised, abstract, formal mode of analysis of which Stravinsky himself would have approved – a mode eagerly embraced by twentieth-century musicology in general. This is amply demonstrated in the important *Cambridge Companion to Stravinsky* (2003) edited by Jonathan Cross, in which, at the end of 'Stravinsky's Century', leading international scholars, Stravinsky specialists and beyond, survey his contribution by examining context, the work itself, and its reception.[11]

My own book on Stravinsky and dance is hardly one that the composer himself would ever have contemplated – he might even have condemned the approach as too 'literary', too much about meaning and metaphor – yet, by its very nature, extending beyond the 'purely musical', it has to address such issues of narrative, meaning and interpretation. Recent Stravinsky scholarship has opened up the interdisciplinary field to encourage this kind of project. Nonetheless, it has, with a few notable exceptions, left the dance field relatively uncharted. Often dance information is sporadic; systematic treatment is needed that illuminates Stravinsky's complex connections with dance culture, his business manoeuvrings as well as his artistic endeavours. There is scope to draw him far more fully into the dance historical context and to reassemble existing information in a way that highlights the dance line through this career. The 'stories' that interest dance scholars are different from those that interest musicologists, just as Stravinsky's dance associates positioned themselves in their own particular way towards his music. Archive sources assembled in a new way can reveal a dance history that may disappear in the hands of a writer privileging the musical or Stravinskian angle. Take, for example, *Scènes de ballet* (1944) as it appears within the correspondence and documents held in the Paul Sacher Stiftung in Basle. When we put together, on the one hand, the original correspondence between the composer and his ballet business acquaintances and publishers and, on the other, the correspondence and documents filed under the name of the score, we discover an early history of this ballet that is absent from the published correspondence. Much of the latter was arranged by Stravinsky's assistant Robert Craft under the headings of separate authors and publishers rather than by topic.[12] It was also considerably edited by Craft, which raises another problem: Stravinsky's writings and the co-authorships involved.

Dance historians and musicologists alike have to be aware that they are not always reading the composer himself through his published writings, even when the material states that this is the case. Taking my position from Walsh, who has provided the most thorough account to date of the authorship problems, I assume first that the *Autobiography* is a largely accurate representation of Stravinsky. Walter Nouvel was a collaborator (though never formally acknowledged), but the composer invested a great deal of time and effort in the book. The subject of the later writings involving Craft is more complex, some officially co-authored, some published under the composer's name alone. (Craft was regularly associated with Stravinsky from 1948 and was instrumental in stimulating the composer's creativity during the last stage of his career.) The first of these writings, undertaken in 1957 (published as *Conversations with Igor Stravinsky* in 1959) is a sound reflection of Stravinsky's thoughts and memories, although the language betrays editing. But, within a few years, Walsh argues, Stravinsky began to recede into the background, as Craft, a very gifted writer, took on a steadily increasing creative role as spokesman for the composer. Not long after 1964, his physical health and mental stamina deteriorating, Stravinsky would probably have been incapable of writing anything himself – but the publications using his name continued: an overlapping trio *Themes and Episodes* (1966), *Retrospectives and Conclusions* (1969) and *Themes and Conclusions* (1972, the year after Stravinsky's death).[13] Vera Stravinsky's diaries, as published in *Dearest Bubushkin* (1985), pose another problem, for Craft interprets them as journals of events when they are sometimes plans that might never have happened (in the manner of an engagement diary), and he adds to the material contained in the originals.[14] Valuable as they are, it is imperative for the scholar to assess carefully all the writings bearing Stravinsky's name in relation to the period in which they were published and against other, often conflicting, historical evidence.

I have used archive sources extensively for analytical purposes and to release new historical data. Of primary importance is the Paul Sacher Stiftung (*PSS*), which houses the world's largest and most important Stravinsky archive and incorporates musical score sketches as well as publishers' proofs and final published material, primary source correspondence, programmes, reviews, interviews and a variety of secondary source material. This Stravinsky collection comprises a considerable body of material in Russian, German and French as well as in English. I had to make decisions about the boundaries of my project in the light of the Russian and German material, using translation assistance when it seemed important. Two major dance archives, the Harvard Theatre Collection (*HTC*) and the Jerome Robbins Dance Division of the New York Public Library (*NYPL*), have also been trawled for Stravinsky material, including dance films, videos and scores. These have been supplemented by the holdings of dance companies and music publishers, as well as by personal archives.

I thought it important that the book itself should release source material in the form of new charts and chronologies: hence the appendices, which include a chronology of Stravinsky's theatre visits, a compilation of his statements about dance, and various lists of repertory and stagings. The *SGD* database is intended to be used alongside the book as a chronology, including as it does brief descriptions of, and cast data on, a large number of entries. Likewise, my two analytical video/DVD documentaries on the Stravinsky works of Frederick Ashton and Balanchine should inform the chapters on those two choreographers.[15]

Choreomusical analytical research on Stravinsky dances is still in its early stages. In several instances, my analyses within this book constitute the first of their kind, yet they have been inspired by recent precedents, such as Joseph's work on Balanchine and Stravinsky and important studies of individual works (e.g. Robynn Stilwell on *Agon*, Julia Randel on *Agon* and *Movements for Piano and Orchestra*, and Andrew Wachtel's collection on *Petrushka*).[16] Taking a broader view, choreomusical studies is now a rapidly developing field. A spate of recent conferences has embraced the subject: *Sound Moves*, Roehampton University (2005); *Die Beziehung von Musik und Choreographie im Ballett* [The Relationship between Music and Choreography in Ballet], Hochschule für Musik und Theater, Leipzig (2006); *Tanz im Musiktheater – Tanz als Musiktheater*, Hochschule für Musik und Theater, Hanover (2006); and *Movimento et Volumina* (marking the 125th anniversary of Stravinsky's birth), University of Salzburg (2007). Also acknowledging the rise in activity, the journal *Opera Quarterly* has dedicated a full issue to choreomusical topics.[17] Increasingly, my own work is stimulated by colleagues working in the field who, like me, combine interests in historical and theoretical issues. They represent a range of periods and topics, but their ideas cut across these boundaries to inform my own: the work, for instance, of Rebecca Harris-Warrick, Carol Marsh and Kimiko Okamoto (baroque studies); Marian Smith (French romantic ballet); Roland John Wiley (Tchaikovsky ballets); Inger Damsholt (Mark Morris); Rachel Duerden (Morris and Antony Tudor); Deborah Mawer (Ravel ballets); Simon Morrison (Ravel and Soviet ballets); Beth Genné and Christian Matjias (Balanchine and American popular culture); and Barbara White (theoretical enquiry informing her work as a composer for modern dance).[18]

As regards the analytical aspects, this book represents theory in action rather than arguing in detail a new methodology as I did in my previous book *Moving Music* (2000).[19] However, I give a summary account here of my approach and the work by other scholars that it draws upon, refining the position that I presented in 2000.

Increasingly, choreomusicologists are using fluid conceptual models, theories of dynamic interaction between the media, which view the two juxtaposed media of dance and music as subject to change rather than static entities, operating within a mechanism of mutual implication and interdependence. The old, hard binaries of parallelism and counterpoint are rapidly disappearing. We are dealing with a composite form: music and dance. Although we might still be able to trace their separate development, especially in the case of music that already exists outside the dance and might preserve something of its original identity, these two sensory planes now meet to affect each other and to create a new identity from their meeting.

A number of theorists from outside dance have been directly useful to the development of this thinking about dynamic interaction between media, with an emphasis largely on semantic content. The film theorist Claudia Gorbman queries whether

> the music 'resembles' or ... 'contradicts' the action or mood of what happens on the screen ... Is there no other way to qualify film music which does not lie between these opposites but outside them? ... It is debatable that information conveyed by disparate media can justifiably be called *the same* or *different*.[20]

She notes too that the earlier film theorist Hanns Eisler (1947) had already recognised the inadequacy of the term 'parallelism', and made suggestions for a more multivalent (multifaceted) approach to description:

> From the aesthetic point of view, this relation is not one of similarity, but, as a rule, one of question and answer, affirmation and negation, appearance and essence. This is dictated by the divergence of the media in question and the specific nature of each.[21]

Instead, Gorbman proposes the concept of 'mutual implication, music and image working together in a *combinatoire* of expression.'[22] Similarly, Kathryn Kalinak uses the conceptual model of music and screen image sharing power in a mechanism of interdependence.[23]

Nicholas Cook's *Analysing Musical Multimedia* (1998) has proved an invaluable source, putting forward a general theory of how potentially *all* different media – music, words, moving pictures, dance – can work together in theatre, commercials, film and music video. In keeping with his emphasis on issues of denotation, Cook proposes metaphor as a viable model for cross-media interaction, with 'enabling similarity' at its root, the possibility of the 'transfer of attributes' that results in the creation of new meaning.[24] He draws from the literary theory first proposed by George Lakoff and Mark Johnson in 1980, according to which, given 'enabling similarity', we can map across two conceptual domains and understand a target domain in terms of a source domain. For instance, we can understand love (target) in terms of war (source) within the metaphor 'Love is war' because the two concepts have attributes in common: they involve more than one party, and, in certain circumstances, love can absorb from war the concepts of conquest, strategy and siege. But the metaphor, Lakoff and Johnson would say, 'gives love a new meaning'.[25] More recently, the theory of conceptual blending developed by the rhetorician Mark Turner and the linguist Gilles Fauconnier has extended the metaphor principle to account for coordinate mappings between two or more conceptual domains (several media may, for instance, be in operation). These work from a generic space and yield a new blended space, a further domain, all together forming a conceptual integration network (CIN).[26] This is also a more interactive structure, less determined by movement in one direction, from source to target. Lawrence Zbikowski has argued how the theory can be applied within music studies; his most detailed application is a study of relationships between text and music within nineteenth-century lied.[27] In my own work, the theory of conceptual blending has proved most useful in making me more aware of the possibilities for analogy between media, but systematic use of the method is an area for future research.

Aside from his application of linguistic theory in assessing a multimedia work as 'a distinctive combination of similarity and difference',[28] Cook puts forward three basic and potentially overlapping models of multimedia interaction:

- conformance, where there is direct congruence and no element of incompatibility, a concept associated with theories of synaesthesia;
- contest, a more dynamic concept indicating essential contradiction and potential for irony, the media 'vying for the same terrain, each attempting to impose its own characteristics upon the other ...each medium strives to deconstruct the other, and so create space for itself';[29] and
- complementation, a kind of mid-point between these two extremes.

In what he terms 'a relationship of contest', Cook proposes that there can be a sense of relationship through opposition, connection through a primary disconnection, as in punning (which is often introduced between visuals and music in commercials), but the issue of connection/disconnection can arise in far less connotationally loaded contexts, where there is loud music to very gentle dance, strong, 'bound' movement to soft sound and so on.

Cook also works with the useful concept of media acquiring qualities from each other. He provides examples from the *Sacre* section of Walt Disney's film *Fantasia* (1940). During the Mystic Circles of the Young Girls, from [97]+3, there is a reciprocal relationship, mutual implication. The lower string pizzicati draw out the 'balletic quality of the jogging dinosaurs' (but he admits that he could have put it the other way round just as easily), while the falling fifths in the flute and solo cello bring out the action of their heads reaching down to the water to drink.[30] In another example, the movement between media functions more clearly in one direction, visuals 'sopping up' rhythmic, kinetic or affective qualities from music.[31] During the transition into the Augurs of Spring section, from [12]+4, the volcanic explosions appear to take place in strict synchronisation with the pizzicato semiquavers in the strings – although when you look at the film with the sound turned off, the effect of rhythmic precision disappears.[32] Cook proposes too that there are different levels to cross-media relationships, both semantic and structural, deep and surface (and in between), and that matching and contradiction can occur simultaneously at different levels.

Within dance, the American modern dance pioneer Doris Humphrey was one of the first to acknowledge the important, active role of music in determining how movement is read. In her primer *The Art of Making Dances*, she explains that music can:

> ... distort the mood. Suppose the dancer has a sequence arranged which is quite serious, a small segment of one of life's major encounters. Accompany this by trivial music which patters along without any depth of feeling. The result is that the dancer does not become stronger by contrast; rather he seems empty, silly and pretentious. Such is the power of the sound to set the mood. This same sequence, accompanied by jaunty, slightly jazzy music, can make the dancer look cynical; he is pretending to be serious, but actually it is all bluff, and he believes in nothing. The variations on this kind of thing are endless.

But she also observed that in some circumstances the effect was more of separation or disjunction between music and dance, in other words, of two opposing voices, with music speaking from outside the dancer:

> If soft sound supports strong movement and vice versa, a curious effect is produced. The music seems to be antagonist; the figure of the dancer fights to be strong without encouragement; and in his more vulnerable moods the music seems to seek to destroy and dominate him.[33]

Prompted by his earlier book *Stravinsky: The Music-Box and the Nightingale* (1989),[34] which focuses on the composer's theatre pieces, the interdisciplinarian Daniel Albright uses the model of figures of consonance and dissonance among the arts in his *Untwisting the Serpent* (2000). Here, he examines modernist work where the media lose their identity and merge to create a total effect (in consonance, corresponding with mimetic principles) or where they retain their distinctiveness (through dissonance, following the principle of separate planes). He stresses a vertical, homophonic, chord-like (rather than horizontal, polyphonic) approach, although his method can surely be applied across moments in time and can accordingly demonstrate shifts through time. For Albright, the potency of the referent in carrying meaning seems crucial in securing the strongest effects of either consonance or dissonance. He also suggests both that over-emphasis on consonance can achieve the apparently opposite effect of drawing attention to the separateness of the media, and the antithesis, that major dissonance can result in our discovering startling, and therefore strong, points of media contact.[35] An example of the first effect is the cartoon or 'Mickey-Mouse' approach that *Fantasia*'s synchronised volcanoes demonstrate, when the cross-media contact is so emphatic (and silly) that it draws attention to the device of forging it from two separate planes. Albright's example of the second effect is the surrealist misnaming procedure – 'as when the husband in Apollinaire's *Les Mamelles de Tirésias* (1917) calls out "The violin" as he picks up a urinal'. He suggests that this might 'call attention to the solidity, the heft, of what lies beneath the flimsy constructs of language'.[36] It could also make us work so hard to establish the connection between two disparate concepts (as with puns to a lesser extent) that we register it especially strongly as the 'point' when we find it. Major strengths of Albright's work are the variety of interactive possibilities demonstrated, the wealth of examples ranging across many art forms, particularly music and literature, including many references to Stravinsky (who delights in crossing the borders between Albright's two primary categories), and the vivid manner in which he communicates distinctive effects.

As for the metaphor-based notion of 'enabling similarity', I would concur with Barbara White that there is always some kind of relationship when music and dance are put together.[37] We are also naturally inclined to find or work at finding coherence, although there may be times when this is so rarely possible that we lose interest in pursuing this line any further. There is always too an element of simultaneous opposition – congruence and incongruence, similarity and difference, various kinds of similarity and difference[38] – as well as occasions when words such as *similarity* and *difference* seem hopelessly inadequate.

But, to be reflexive about my own project: it is important to note that several of my analyses have been driven by a comparative approach, geared towards the examination of different settings of the same Stravinsky scores. This highlights the distinctiveness of different choreographic approaches, which illuminate different potential in any single Stravinsky score (including the potential for contest). Indeed, I have become especially attuned to how movement changes musical perceptions, how Stravinsky's scores 'change', at the same time as I acknowledge mechanisms of interdependence and mutual voicing. But does the visual usually override the aural? Some say yes, but others would claim that music can be more subversive, more secretive, in its power.[39] Does this depend too on our own backgrounds and experience? We as audience construct shape and meaning, just as music and dance construct shape and meaning from each other.

My discoveries are also about my expectations. During my work, I become accustomed to hearing music in one way, through one dance (and sometimes only one performance captured on film) at a time. Thus, any new musical component that I begin to hear from a new setting of a score seems especially striking. But also striking is a new choreographic treatment of musical repetition *within* the course of one particular dance. I literally hear new notes, or a particular instrumental line suddenly emerges more strongly. Movement seems to seek out related properties in the music and vice versa, and new meanings emerge from their points of contact. The consequence of or underside to this is that other aspects of the music and dance are hidden from view or erased. But it is my current conclusion that we have to go to precise examples within precise contexts in order to spell out these dilemmas and pleasures in any meaningful way, to go beyond the question of *whether* music and dance meet each other or not and to ask *where* or *how* they meet.[40]

In the area of structural processes of rhythm and formal organisation through time, I still find it useful to hold onto the notion of parallelism and counterpoint between music and dance. Here, I use the principle that music and dance are two simultaneous voices operating with and against each other through matching or crossing accents or metres (see p.14), with the term 'counterpoint' reserved for those occasions that I read in terms of conflicting accentual or metrical patterns. Again, I steer away from hard, binary opposition, acknowledging instead a continuum of possibility, of the weakening and strengthening effects of rapport and disjunction (according to the frequency and force of crossing accents). This notion of counterpoint is grounded in evidence from social dance traditions of the play between musicians and dancers that invites perceptions of tension, anxiety, chase and competition.[41] So it, too, contributes to meaning. I consider rhythm a logical basis for examining structural relationships between music and dance – especially so, given its particular importance as a structural agent in Stravinsky's music. Yet, when appropriate, I refer to relationships within the vertical spatial paradigm of pitch and movement level and between other components that contribute to tension and release. But I now restrict my use of the parallelism/counterpoint concept to this structural field, as I do with terms such as 'visualisation' and 'mirroring' (dance applied to music), which here refer only to clearly perceived structural mimicry rather than to any notion of equivalence between art forms.

Again, even within situations that might be interpreted as prime examples of rhythmic parallelism or 'music visualisation,' it is important to consider the distinctive manner in which music and dance operate. An example to illustrate this is the fluid arm movements that on two occasions 'duplicate' the repeating castanet rhythm in the Bransle Gay of Balanchine's *Agon* (1957): ♩♪♪♩

In considering these castanet/arm patterns, Rachel Duerden reminds us that the articulation of a musical event is by no means simple. A note is just a note, but a dance movement, by its very nature, has slowing and quickening built into it. The hand leaves an after-image that Duerden rightly says is

> at odds with the music's clear-cut, pristine edge ... an immediate tension is created: a clear correspondence in rhythmic terms, but at the same time a clear announcement of the divergence of media, an intimation of distance between the two. It is an invitation to notice and contemplate the difference between the two worlds, to acknowledge the autonomy of each ...[42]

In terms of the shared principles of beat and metrical framework, I am indebted to music rhythm theory as the basis of the system of structural categories that I propose for dance: the field is far more highly developed in music than in dance. Thus, I draw, for instance, from the work of Andrew Imbrie, Fred Lerdahl and Ray Jackendoff, as well as from theory dealing specifically with Stravinsky's metrics (as they interact with other formal constructs) by Pieter C. van den Toorn and Gretchen Horlacher.[43] My methodology also draws upon the practical approach tested out during research on Ashton and Stravinsky (for a project funded by the Arts and Humanities Research Board, 2003–5)[44] involving 'sketch' dancing – in other words, embodiment of movement to raise questions about dynamics, timing and relationship to music. Furthermore, as always in my work, developing and applying my method has proved a dialectical process, in other words, experiencing a dance through a framework leads to the refinement of that framework.

I have not ventured into the extremes of esoteric musical analysis, although my work is informed by existing musical analyses of the scores selected as case studies. Certain details of musical structure documented in musicological literature can be understood only after highly specialised analytical training. But I do not apologise for or skirt around technical discussion; rather, I attempt to provide an accessible route to understanding technicalities, whilst allowing readers to approach the topic of structure at a variety of levels. We have to address these issues in order to reveal the complexities of choreomusical relationships, to uncover the links, for instance, between formal device and meaning: accurately applied technical terms mean precision in communication. Thus, examples in music notation have been incorporated, as have examples that show dance-rhythmic information in musical notation, for easy cross-reference between the two media. A few Labanotation examples have been introduced, too, where they seemed especially important. But the analyses are written so that the line through them should be clear for those who read neither music nor dance notation systems.

To help the reader through the more technical aspects of the book, a summary follows of the rhythmic categories that I use in discussion of parallelism and counterpoint. These are explained in more detail in *Moving Music*.[45] The rhythmic categories can be divided into three strands, the less easy concepts being given more detailed explanation after this tabulation:

1   Categories that refer to duration and frequency: note or move (the basic unit of duration in dance and music); beat (or pulse); rubato/breath rhythm (the kind of rhythm that avoids or plays against a motoric beat); and speed – for instance, tempo (the rate of beats), the rate of consecutive notes or moves, harmonic rhythm (the rate of harmonic change), or the rate at which space is covered.

2   Categories of stress, or accent: the stress of single notes or moves – for instance, metrical accents (the accent of downbeat, the first beat of the bar, or strong relative to weak beat); rhythmic accents (when a movement or note stands out through lasting longer than those around it); and dynamic accents (accents produced by physical energy in both dance and music).

3   Categories referring to the grouping of sounds or movements through time, the interaction of items from 1 and 2: metre, metrical hierarchy, hypermetre, polymetre (the use of different metres simultaneously); units (of grouped notes or moves that are not necessarily congruent with metrical structure) – downbeat and upbeat units that are phrased to begin at or before the bar-line; and unit hierarchy (resulting from smaller units of notes or moves combining to form larger units, up to the level of the macroform, the first division, of a piece).

We make sense of music and dance in terms of patterns of linked or grouped beats, notes and moves. When we consider the linking of beats, we are dealing with the concepts of *metre* and *metrical hierarchy*. It is important that ostinatos, repeating melodic/rhythmic patterns, are characteristic of a great deal of Stravinsky's music and frequently define metre. An example is the 3/8 castanet pattern in the Bransle Gay of *Agon* (see p. 12), which occurs throughout that dance. Although the fundamental metrical unit is the bar (measure), which groups beats in twos, threes, fours and so forth, with a metrical accent at the beginning of each group, similar grouping and accenting is seen to occur at sub-bar and broader levels, the hierarchy extending from the length of the smallest note or movement values. Just as we often find shifting time signatures in Stravinsky's music, so we also find shifting lengths of beat – for instance, as crotchet, quaver or semiquaver, the time signature written accordingly as a number over 4, 8 or 16. But let us take as an example a bar of 2/4, which is a grouping of two beats (crotchets), and which contains two sub-bar groupings of two quavers. Several 2/4 bars may group together into *hypermeasures*, each bar lasting one *hyperbeat*. Metrical accents become stronger the broader the level in the hierarchy; in other words, they are strongest at the hypermetrical level. The following example shows metrical organisation in 2/4 time, with the grouping of bars into 3-bar hypermeasures.

Sub-bar counts:	1 2 1 2	1 2 1 2				
Metre beats:	1 2	1 2				
Hypermetre beats:	**1**	**2**	**3**	**1**	**2**	**3**

Hypermetre does not always exist in music and dance, but when it does, it is usually regular, and is perceived either as a result of regular notes or moves every two or more bars, or through successive units that group notes or moves, each unit being of equal length (two bars or more). The effect is strongest when dance and musical material repeats either exactly or with an element of variation. Hypermeasures can sometimes indicate units that we might call 'phrases'. In dance, the counts that dancers use in rehearsal demonstrate the grouping of bars into a hypermetrical structure, and these counts are sometimes marked in dance scores. As befits what is most useful to the particular medium, dancers and musicians customarily count differently, dancers at a slower pulse rate than musicians.

Grouping is also concerned with the processes of continuity and breaks in continuity that define units and articulate music and dance at various levels. *Return* is a particular form of *closure*. Signalling a concluding or terminal event, return articulates larger structural units and provides a major effect of closure, a sense of coming-home stability. We see this in simple ABA forms or in larger, more complex forms where return is sometimes referred to as *recapitulation*. Return can also be made more or less exact as repetition and therefore more or less emphatic.

Historical and analytical modes of writing co-exist within the book. Exploration of Stravinsky's legacy across time, geographical borders and genres of dance engages dialectically with analyses of examples representing a range of choreographic approaches. These analyses are in turn illuminated by discussion of other settings of the same score. The case studies (choreographers and musical scores) provide frameworks for further analytical work. As regards selection of works for the most detailed analysis, I have been led by choreographies that get inside the detail of the musical score and whose choreomusical relationships have sustained my interest after many viewings. This is not to deny the value of works that are less 'choreomusical' and more about other matters. Some choices have been encouraged by particular circumstances, as, for instance, with

Balanchine and Ashton, stemming from opportunities I have had to make ana-lytical video documentaries on their Stravinsky work. The policy has not been to ignore the canon, the most widely known productions, but rather to revitalise understanding of it, as well as to reveal the power of lesser-known dances. Avail-ability of film or video/DVD resources can be a problem, as it always has been for dance, and, in this respect, the more familiar choreographers and works natu-rally tend to fare the best. I have, as far as possible, selected works that I have seen in live performance and where multiple sources have been accessible, some-times including Laban and Benesh scores. Using the framework of contextualised case studies, the book is open-ended. I make no attempt to draw conclusions at the end and the chapters stand independently: they do not have to be read in the given order.

Historical and aesthetic issues highlighting the dance line through Stravinsky's career provide the logical starting point for the book. Chapter 1 draws from my new collection of Stravinsky's statements about dance and a new diary of his attendance at, and conducting of, dance events. It is important to examine Stravinsky's own perspective, because his stated intentions and dance aesthetics and the legal mechanisms of copyright and royalties operate in ten-sion with the take-up and interpretation of his music. Thus, I consider his experi-ence of dance beyond his ballet collaborations and his views on the theatrical realisation of specific ballet and concert scores. Research reveals that Stravinsky was a composer of hybrid scores involving spoken and sung text, a far more important aspect of his dance activity and legacy to future choreographers than is generally acknowledged. We might then ask: how do his broader conceptions of theatre interact with dance, and what challenges to choreographers (such as Ashton) do these hybrids pose, being so different from the 'pure music' with which Balanchine is primarily associated? And how, given Stravinsky's excep-tionally proactive nature, do his personality and business strategies impact on the nature of his collaborations, the dissemination of his scores and the profile of choreography made to them?

I begin Chapter 2 by posing general questions about the nature of Stravinsky's music as dance music. In relation to previous notions of music for dance, is his a new form of *musique dansante*? How do Stravinsky's own move-ment dynamics map on to his music, and how have dancers and choreographers responded to the physicality embodied in his music? In an overview of choreog-raphies drawn from the *SGD* database, I then reflect upon patterns of usage over time, including discussion of little-known settings. I consider which ballet and concert scores have been used when and where, by modern dance or ballet cho-reographers, the reasons for this distribution, and in relation to the general pat-tern of Stravinsky reception. The chapter concludes with a discussion of selected scores and dances, setting the scene for the later detailed case studies.

In-depth analytical research raises specific questions about the relationship between interpretations by choreographers and dancers and Stravinsky's own intentions, whether these were stated or not and whether as deliberate false-hoods or grounded guidance. In what ways have the boundaries been stretched recently (e.g. by Jérôme Bel) beyond theatrical interpretation of a score to its use as reference within a performative framework? For those using scores theatri-cally, there is also the notion of Stravinsky's musical style modifying individual choreographic styles, reflected in particular choices of movement vocabulary and dynamics, and approaches to structure, rhythm and phrasing. So, does Stravinsky sometimes bring the work of his choreographers closer together? And what are the distinctions between settings of the same score? We might also ask how the Stravinsky dance canon has been used and marketed. As a symbol of squeaky-clean high modernism or as raw, challenging commentary on hu-manity? As a source for further choreographers, using history overtly as part of their process? And how might understanding of the larger body of work illumi-nate understanding of the canon?

In Chapter 3, Balanchine's work is seen as the most marketed Stravinsky dance product, a symbol of Cold War apolitical purity and a quoted source (by, for instance, David Gordon and Yvonne Rainer). The chapter reflects on my own history: I have analysed the Balanchine–Stravinsky 'masterworks' in the past, and I deliberately do not examine in detail works that are very familiar, including *Agon*, which was subject to lengthy treatment in *Moving Music*. Instead, after surveying the range of Balanchine's Stravinsky ballets, I dedicate most attention to two works that represent extreme positions as radical statements: *Movements for Piano and Orchestra* (1963; a rare serial music setting) and *Divertimento from 'Le Baiser de la fée'* (1972; the score arranged by Balanchine).

Chapter 4 examines the work of Ashton, who, even if he set Stravinsky only four times, created one of the most complex choreomusical constructions of all, *Scènes de ballet* (1948); his style changed markedly in response to the composer's music. I also analyse his settings of two hybrid scores: *Persephone* (1961) and *Le Rossignol* (1981), involving spoken and sung text.

Noces and *Sacre* have given rise to the most diverse choreography over the years, fascinating examples of score renewal, with significant aesthetic implica-tions, themes of oppression, sexuality and human relations embodied within the most sophisticated structural detail or recalled through reference to a history that remains ever present. In Chapter 5, the *Noces* of Nijinska, Jerome Robbins and Anne Teresa De Keersmaeker are compared, the latter two productions us-ing the controversial 1994 Dmitri Pokrovsky recording that might be seen to have 'mis-translated' Stravinsky's intentions. No score attracts more choreogra-phers than *Sacre*, which also bears the greatest weight of mythology, and fea-tures increasingly in the work of the more conceptually oriented choreographers and performance artists. Thus, in Chapter 6, Raymond Hoghe's and Bel's settings are considered alongside those of Pina Bausch, Maurice Béjart, Vaslav Nijinsky and Paul Taylor. Amongst Stravinsky's scores, it is *Sacre* too that most readily invites discussion as global property, and I introduce the score as a presence within non-Western traditions and as a feature of cultural diaspora. In terms of dance currency, pointing to the future as well as the past more forcefully than any other score, *Sacre* signals the logical end to *Stravinsky Dances.*

Although it integrates two disciplines, this book is driven primarily from the dance point of view, with the emphasis on Stravinsky as a dance composer. Yet, it aims to be useful to scholars and students (both undergraduate and postgraduate) of dance, music and interdisciplinary studies as well as to a broader audience of dance and music enthusiasts. It is also intended to reach the profession, those interested in choreographing or dancing to Stravinsky and who are curious about how his music has 'worked' for choreographers and dancers in the past. But, however the reader is positioned and whatever the route chosen through this book, I hope there will be moments when Stravinsky dances off the page and into the imagination: for me, that was his major challenge.

1

The Composer's Perspective

Introduction

'Not an opera and not a ballet[1] ... Russian song (cantata, oratorio, or what?) with choreographic accompaniment[2] ... [a] divertissement[3] ... It's not strictly speaking a ballet, but pictures that I've tried to bring to life[4] ... a divertissement of the masquerade type'.[5] For years, Stravinsky wrestled with himself over how to describe his latest ballet *Les Noces* (1923). For the published score, he came up with 'Russian choreographic scenes'. But a glance at the Stravinsky chronology (see Appendix 1) demonstrates that creating subtitles to indicate the genre of a score was hardly ever straightforward. The list, which includes every work composed to include a dance component of any kind, large or small, reveals a very broad range of work. What can we learn from this? What kind of dance composer was he? In the first half of his career, at least, only some of his subtitles indicate 'ballet'. The early Diaghilev ballets were hardly conceived as ballets in the 'classical' sense of *danse d'école*, using the codified movement of training, least of all *Le Sacre du printemps*, but then, neither were *Renard* or *Histoire du soldat*, which were intended for far more modest resources outside the orbit of Diaghilev's Ballets Russes. Compare the chronology of Marius Petipa for the Maryinsky Ballet, which gave Stravinsky his early dance experience, with its narrow range of descriptors, always with 'ballet' included: 'fantastic ballet', 'anacreontic ballet', 'ballet-féerie', 'character ballet', and so on.[6] Nor was Stravinsky simply occupied with dance in his dance pieces. He had other notions of dance theatre in mind, and different weightings towards or against a dance component, as he embraced elements from other theatrical genres. Indeed, his theatre works, with or without dance, form a continuum and should be considered as a whole. It was only later in his career that Stravinsky returned regularly to the description 'ballet'.

The chronology reveals other variations. Although all the scores are relatively short by nineteenth-century standards, having a single act or being through-composed without intervals, they constitute a range of different structures to suit different conceptions. Then, looking beyond the titles and subtitles, there are different strategies for musical ensemble, large and small, markedly different orchestrations, and sometimes text, spoken or sung. The dates in the list also tell us of the time gaps between initial writing and completion of a score for performance. Stravinsky sometimes dropped a composition in progress for a new idea or in order to complete other work; conditions beyond his control sometimes delayed a premiere. Thus, by the time some works were premiered, his compositional style was no longer what it had been at their conception.

The background to this is that, to an unusual degree for a dance composer, Stravinsky himself was a major starting force behind his works. Led by both artistic and financial considerations, he clearly wanted to control the conception himself or to do so alongside a trusted collaborator. With George Balanchine generally an exception, the choreographer was often an afterthought. It is Stravinsky's power within dance culture that is largely responsible for the extraordinary diversity of his dance scores and the theatrical conceptions associated with them.

My aim here is to account for Stravinsky's contribution from his own perspective, plotting the story of his association with dance, surveying his approach to the artform, and tracing the development of his own aesthetic for dance and his sometimes changing ideas about specific pieces. The chapter is organised chronologically, and we can see how Stravinsky's association with dance changed and indeed lessened as his career progressed. Clearly it was at its peak during the Diaghilev period, when he was working closely with the Ballets Russes (1909-29) for extended periods of time and on numerous projects, although the number of newly conceived scores diminished rapidly during the second half of this period. After this, Stravinsky extended the scope of his composing into other fields, until dance appears to have become a relatively minor part of his life. Despite the composer's much-touted lifelong friendship and professional relationship with Balanchine, there are few ballet scores in his later career, and *Agon* (1957) took a long time coming.

The division into periods of Stravinsky's dance-making career has not been easy, and here I have been led by his changing perspective on and association with dance. My aim has been to create a structure for the reader, the number of divisions being deliberately kept to a minimum and the outline interpreted flexibly. Practices overlap the period boundaries, and Stravinsky's main moves from country to country or major turning points in style clearly relate to but do not precisely map onto these divisions.

It seemed logical to take 1909 to 1919 as one period, from the year of the *Firebird* commission to the year when Stravinsky was approached to write *Pulcinella*, both works for the Ballets Russes. Despite the lack of premieres and his exile in Switzerland during the war years, Stravinsky continued to develop dance conceptions that sprang from the early Diaghilev period. Some scholars have seen the stylistic shift from Stravinsky's 'Russian' to his neoclassical period starting with *Pulcinella*, where he began to rework, on his own terms, styles of previous periods and composers. This is encouraged by the composer's later statement that *Pulcinella* was his 'epiphany'.[7] But this has since been disputed. Others perceive the beginning of the new stylistic approach as happening earlier during the Swiss years, whereas Richard Taruskin and Stephen Walsh argue that the real turning point was the opera *Mavra* (1921–2): far more of a stylistic interaction than *Pulcinella* and showing a much more profound, self-conscious interest in the formal models and conventions of the past as a means of creating a new formalism.[8] The term 'neoclassicism' was first applied in the press in 1923 by Boris de Schloezer to the *Symphonies of Wind Instruments* (1920).[9]

The next period, from the commission of *Pulcinella* in 1919, covers most of the time when Stravinsky was living in France. His range as a composer broadened, and he began a new career as a touring conductor and pianist, as well as renewing creative contact with Diaghilev. Yet his experience with the Ballets Russes was now of a very different kind, far more diverse than earlier; hence, even if Stravinsky was the only composer to be associated with this company throughout its existence, the period division falls within the era of the Ballets Russes. There was a great sense of loss with Diaghilev's death in 1929, both financially and psychologically, but nevertheless there were continuities into the 1930s: for example, a second work *Persephone* (1934) for the rival ballet company of Ida Rubinstein, from whom he had also accepted the commission of *Le Baiser de la fée* in 1928. This period ends in 1937.

April 1937 was a significant moment of change within Stravinsky's career as a dance composer. There was the full-evening Stravinsky festival staged by Balanchine in New York, including the premiere of *Jeu de cartes* (the ballet entitled *The Card Party*), the opening up of a new dance culture to Stravinsky and the renewal of his most fruitful collaborative relationship. Now, he looked increasingly to America, moving there in 1939, and it was during this final period that the practice of using his concert music in dance became important. It was also during this period, in the mid-1950s, that Stravinsky's music underwent a stylistic shift to embrace the serial or twelve-note compositional method of the second Viennese school (Arnold Schoenberg, Alban Berg and Anton Webern).

The narrative of this chapter draws on a wide variety of primary and secondary source material, which includes new chronologies of Stravinsky's attendance at, and conducting of, dance across his career (see Appendix 2), and a new collation of his statements about dance (see Appendix 3). As always with Stravinsky, we need to read with great caution what he himself (or his ghostwriters) said. An opinion, given in the manner of a serious philosophical principle, might in fact reflect a quite different concern. For instance, the composer's need to distance himself from a particular choreographer might be the real reason behind a refusal to allow use of one of his concert scores. Or the need to promote his dance scores as concert music might lead him to downplay the importance of dance as part of the original conception of a score.

In highlighting the dance line, I draw especially from the writing of Taruskin and Walsh.[10] Likewise, I have supplemented Charles Joseph's work on the Stravinsky–Balanchine collaboration with an examination of the composer's broader connections with dance during the later part of his career.[11] If the narrative seems to contain a whistle-stop tour of Stravinsky's most famous dance scores, the approach nevertheless contains new inflections, and part of the reasoning was not to repeat documentation of what is already easily accessible, but rather to introduce information and examples that are fresher to the page.

Preparatory experiences in Russia: From the Imperial Ballet to the Symbolist avant-garde

As a boy brought up at No. 66 Kryukov Canal, St Petersburg, Stravinsky lived but a short distance from the Maryinsky Theatre, where his father Fyodor was an opera singer. Late in life, Stravinsky recalled that he became an experienced ballet-goer at that time and had been taken to see *The Sleeping Beauty* (1890) when he was seven or eight.[12] He also 'became aware that the ballet was petrifying, that it was, in fact, already quite rigidly conventional'.[13] Walsh describes his experience in the early 1890s of ballet matinees that consisted of 'processions of short vignettes danced to mediocre music shoddily played – a far cry from either the symphonic flights of Tchaikovsky or the brilliance and flair of the as yet unborn Ballets Russes'.[14]

Both Walsh and Taruskin use as evidence of Stravinsky's experience Prince Peter Lieven's recollections of the Wednesday and Sunday ballet performances: 'The half-empty auditorium contained a special public – a mixture of children accompanied by their mothers or governesses, and old men with binoculars.'[15] But it is worth considering whether these impressions may be misleading, even if it is clear that ballet did not have strong support in the intellectual circles of the times. For a start, there is the implication, although it does not come from Lieven, that ballet was merely the stuff of Maryinsky matinees, which is not true. Secondly, Stravinsky *could* have experienced what is now considered some of the finest ballet choreography and music, the nineteenth-century flowering largely associated with the choreographer Marius Petipa (1818–1910). There was not only *The Sleeping Beauty* (Petipa/Tchaikovsky, 1890), which was extremely popular in the repertoire, but also the other Tchaikovsky ballets *Swan*

Lake (Ivanov and Petipa, 1895) and *The Nutcracker* (Ivanov, 1892), as well as *Raymonda* (Petipa/Glazunov, 1894) and *Coppélia* (Petipa after St. Léon/Delibes, 1884). Stravinsky *might* also have seen *Giselle* (Petipa after Coralli and Perrot/Adam, 1884), *La Bayadère* (Petipa/Minkus, 1877), and other ballets with scores by Delibes, *Sylvia* (Ivanov and Gerdt, 1901) and *La Source* (Coppini, 1902, with musical additions by Minkus).[16]

During the early twentieth century, Stravinsky's accusations of petrification would have been more justifiable, for this was a much less artistically dynamic period, and the Imperial Theatres constituted a conservative, heavily bureaucratic institution. Besides, his activities led him away from any interest in the old ballet. The musical community into which Stravinsky entered in 1902 centred on his tutor Nikolay Rimsky-Korsakov, who had scorned ballet for years. Then, soon after Rimsky-Korsakov died in 1908, Stravinsky joined the league of radicals from the Maryinsky Ballet led by the choreographer with whom he first collaborated, Mikhail Fokine. They were to be key figures within the early Ballets Russes and they avidly sought freedom from the old strictures and a new kind of dance.

By the 1920s, however, Stravinsky was clearly a convert to the academic ballet. It is salutary to note the enthusiasm with which he became involved in the musical aspect of Diaghilev's 1921 revival of *Sleeping Beauty* for the Ballets Russes, which included the re-orchestration of two passages. There was a propagandist 'open letter' to Diaghilev that was later printed in *The Times*, which alludes to Stravinsky's attendance at an evening (not matinee) performance at the Maryinsky:

> This work appears to me as the most authentic expression of that period in our Russian life which we call the 'Petersburg Period', and which is stamped upon my memory with the morning vision of the Imperial sleighs of Alexander III, the giant Emperor, and his giant coachman, and the immense joy that awaited me in the evening, the performance of *The Sleeping Beauty*.[17]

Beauty was justification and inspiration for Stravinsky at this turning point towards neoclassicism in his career. Whatever he might or might not have thought back in the 1890s, he had now decided that his memories were golden. Ever after this, it was the tradition of Petipa that he, like Balanchine, upheld as his model for classical ballet. Yet, during this early period of his life, it is important that Stravinsky would have acquainted himself with the conventions of ballet music from the previous century, the established alternations between mime and dance, the standard dance rhythms, and also Tchaikovsky's development of a sense of musical coherence, breaking down the stylistic divisions between mime and dances and adding complexity to the rhythmic content.[18]

Before the Ballets Russes was established, Fokine worked on radical changes to the existing models for ballet, introducing a new, 'authentic' approach to the whole theatrical experience. He replaced the strict divisions between the two codified systems of mime and dance with unity of expression and movement that was appropriate to context – for instance, realist or naturalist vocabulary for the crowd movement and character dances in *Petrushka*, or classical vocabulary for the poetic milieu of *Les Sylphides*. He brought in new ideas about stage design and costume and introduced to dance new styles of music extending beyond conventional dance rhythms, often concert music.

Meanwhile, also in St Petersburg, a group of arts enthusiasts associated with the journal *Mir Iskusstva* (*The World of Art*, 1898–1904) began to take an interest in ballet. With Diaghilev in their midst, this led to the formation of the Ballets Russes. The artist-designer Alexander Benois, who later collaborated with Stravinsky, was their leader and the first real balletomane of the group. He met Fokine in 1907 and felt immediate kinship: 'We agreed with each other at once … wishing to save the ballet from cheapening influences and to give his art a new lease of life.'[19] Benois also felt that ballet was the perfect medium for the fundamental principle that the group espoused:

> The ballet is one of the most consistent and complete expressions of the idea of the *Gesamtkunstwerk*, the idea for which our circle was ready to give its soul. It was no accident that what was afterwards known as the Ballets Russes was originally conceived not by the professionals of the dance, but by a circle of artists, linked together by the idea of Art as an entity.[20]

Gesamtkunstwerk was the loosely applied Wagnerian term for synthesis of the arts, implying that each medium contributed equally to the whole, and that several highly creative minds were joined in close collaboration. The principle is questionable. Is it theoretically possible or even desirable to have true equality and synthesis of the arts? And how often did the Diaghilev ballets turn out to be truly collaborative in practice, or driven primarily by Diaghilev's directorial impetus? For those who spearheaded the early Ballets Russes, the concept gave new prominence to the visual element of design. Diaghilev's opera productions of Musorgsky's *Boris Godunov* (1908) and *Khovanshchina* (1913) demonstrated the new weighting towards what Taruskin has termed 'antiliterary esthetics'. Introducing many cuts as well as additions to the musical scores, Diaghilev placed maximum emphasis on theatrical pageantry, at the expense of words and their meaning, thereby lessening the prominence of ham acting prevalent in opera at the time.[21] Such aesthetics are precisely what drew Benois to ballet as the perfect medium:

Ballet is perhaps the most eloquent of all spectacles, since it permits the two most excellent conductors of thought – music and gesture – to appear in their full expanse and depth, unencumbered by words, which limit and fetter thought, bring it down from heaven to earth. In ballet one finds that *liturgical* quality of which we have lately come to dream so strenuously.[22]

Benois wrote as a member of the Symbolist movement, 'the rock on which *Mir Iskusstva* was built',[23] the movement that succeeded Realism. Now, there was concentration on evocation as opposed to recreation, essence of feeling, the poetic gesture, rather than literal representation. Lynn Garafola summarises the diverse ideas: 'themes of the beleaguered individual and the commedia dell'arte, notions of synaesthesia, suggestiveness, and subjectivity, the cult of beauty, fascination with eroticism, visions of poetic idealism'.[24] From the *Mir Iskusstva* circle and the Ballets Russes, two strands of Symbolist activity evolved: European retrospectivism (as in *Le Pavillon d'Armide*) and neonationalism (as in *Firebird*), work in the latter vein proving the particular delight of Paris during the early seasons, and leading to the pagan ritual of *Sacre*. But there were nevertheless links with the recent Realist movement – for instance, the careful ethnographic, empirical research into sources. As for Fokine, who was greatly influenced by the Symbolist movement, he sometimes found unstyled, 'natural' movement most appropriate to his cause. The concepts of Realism and Symbolism were both new to ballet. Artistic movements overlap, unsurprisingly where change happens fast, and no more so than in the Russian theatre at this period, where the highly influential Realism of Konstantin Stanislavsky, established with the founding of the Moscow Art Theatre in 1898, almost immediately led to a breakaway movement into Symbolism through the director Vsevolod Meyerhold. In 1902, *Mir Iskusstva* ran an article called 'Unnecessary Truth' by the poet Valeriy Bryusov attacking Stanislavsky's approach.[25] There were also crossover artists between theatre and Diaghilev's company (which performed opera as well as ballet), and with whom Stravinsky came into contact. Garafola has named several who were associated with both Diaghilev and Stanislavsky, perhaps most prominently Benois, who became artistic director of the Moscow Art Theatre in 1909 and later designed and produced for the company, but also Diaghilev's opera director Alexander Sanin, who later commissioned *Le Rossignol* from Stravinsky for his Free Theatre in Moscow (after the first act had been composed, see p. 33), and the designers Sergey Sudeykin and Mstislav Dobuzhinsky.[26]

Developments in theatre are crucial to the study of Stravinsky's work in dance, though via the theatrical experiments of Meyerhold rather than the Realism of Stanislavsky. Meyerhold moved from Moscow to St Petersburg in 1906. His project was to find a new artistic truth through what he called 'stylisation', the principles of which he outlined in an important essay of 1907: stage machinery and technical devices would be reduced to a minimum, with new emphasis placed on the actor, speech would be transformed into 'melodic declamation', diction and movement would be given a 'rhythmical basis', and there would be a new creative space for the spectators to employ their imagination and 'fill in those details suggested by the stage action'.[27] As early examples of his approach, Meyerhold directed two Symbolist plays by Maurice Maeterlinck, The Death of Tintageles (1905, Moscow) and Sister Beatrice (1906, St Petersburg), in which the actors moved and posed in the style of bas-reliefs or frescoes. This was a style that emphasised stasis and gave new weight to the visual, physical component supplied by actors. In marked contrast, later in 1906, Meyerhold staged the raucous commedia farce by Alexander Blok, The Fairground Booth, which satirised the Symbolists' seriousness and escape from everyday reality and drew upon the traditions of popular theatre. These were the beginnings of a career of theatrical experiment involving ideas gleaned from ancient Greek and Japanese theatre and from the traditions of preliterate folk theatre.

But Meyerhold was not alone in his endeavours. He was part of a wave of theatre people across Europe at the time who drew from Eastern as well as ancient tradition and fought against notions of Realism and the well-made play: from Adolphe Appia and Alfred Jarry to Gordon Craig,[28] Jean Cocteau and Jacques Copeau, then to Antonin Artaud, Bertolt Brecht and Luigi Pirandello. For all of them, linear plot was relatively unimportant. Human experience was better expressed through collage structures or distanced from the everyday, with actors going through the motions of ritual rather than persuading the audience of their agency as characters. A variety of tactics was employed to negate theatrical illusion: the narrator figure or chorus (or even the actor stepping out of role) removed from the protagonists and free to address the audience in the form of an intermediary; theatrical devices exposed to view, such as the process of changing scenery or costume; or musicians brought from the pit to the stage. On other occasions the human figure itself was distanced, not only through stylised forms of speech and movement, but also through the use of masks, and even through full-body transformation into the medium of puppets. These tactics were not fundamentally new. They were drawn from distant traditions to suit new modernist contexts.

There is little evidence of Stravinsky having direct contact with such theatre movements before he joined the Ballets Russes circle in 1909 or indeed during the early Diaghilev period before he left Russia to base himself permanently in the West. But he had contacts who did keep abreast of this scene and surely informed him of what they saw. There was Stepan Mitusov (a member of the Rimsky-Korsakov circle, with whom he was to write the libretto of Rossignol) who, from 1903, acted as 'a kind of literary and theatrical tutor to me at one of the greatest moments in the Russian theatre'.[29] Together, in St Petersburg, they saw a variety of Russian and modern French plays as well as Molière and Shakespeare. There was also Mikhail Gnesin, another member of the Rimsky-Korsakov circle: a part of the Symbolist crowd, he knew Meyerhold.[30] Stravinsky's Ballets Russes associates were also in touch with Meyerhold. In 1910, Fokine invited him to take the part of Pierrot in his *Carnaval*, and they collaborated on other occasions: in Russia, Oscar Wilde's *Salome* (1908) and Gluck's *Orpheus and Eurydice* (1911), and in Paris, for Ida Rubinstein, Gabriele D'Annunzio's *La Pisanelle* (1913).[31] Diaghilev invited the director to his St Petersburg soirées in 1910, a gathering of collaborators involved in his early Ballets Russes seasons.[32] In 1918, Meyerhold directed Stravinsky's *Rossignol* at the Maryinsky, after the composer had left Russia.

Stravinsky the dance composer

Period 1: 1909–19. To Europe: Russian ballets for Diaghilev's Ballets Russes

The modest job of orchestrating two Chopin pieces for *Les Sylphides* was Stravinsky's first professional contact with Diaghilev's Ballets Russes, for their 1909 season. In the same year, he was commissioned to write *Firebird*, in the one-act genre favoured by Diaghilev. The idea was to raise the musical standards of the company, seen as lacking during the 1909 season, with an exhilarating example of new Russian music. Thus, although only after both Nikolay Tcherepnin and Anatoly Lyadov had first been invited to compose *Firebird*, Stravinsky became 'staff composer' to the company for the first part of its existence, while in turn the company became his artistic family and main source of income. It was during this first period that he was closest to the company. He attended rehearsals and premieres of his own works, assisting the choreographers Fokine and Vaslav Nijinsky with his scores and keeping abreast of all the other new repertory during the key seasons in Paris. He also joined the company on tour, keeping tabs on performances and rehearsals of his ballets, visiting Monte Carlo, Rome, Berlin, Budapest, Vienna and London, before the war put an end to the expansive manner in which the company functioned.

Stravinsky had already settled in Switzerland, and he remained there until 1920. The connections with Diaghilev and his itinerant company continued for a while during the war years and there was regular correspondence. When the company were eight months in residence at Ouchy, beside the lake at Lausanne, from May 1915, Stravinsky would cycle from his house in Morges to visit them all. In December 1915, Diaghilev also gave him his first two opportunities to conduct ballet: both were of *Firebird*, first in Geneva as an entr'acte during a gala, and then nine days later in Paris, with dancers, for a gala in aid of the

British Red Cross. The impresario invited Stravinsky to join the company as it toured Madrid, Rome and Naples in 1916–17. But the May 1917 Paris season, the first there since the beginning of the war, did not feature a Stravinsky premiere. After that, Diaghilev and Stravinsky did not see each other again until September 1919. Relations resumed, with Stravinsky's work still greatly prized, but by the 1920s Diaghilev was commissioning much more broadly and the composer's association with the company had changed.

It is well known that, although they forged a very productive artistic collaboration – and Diaghilev was, after all, responsible for establishing Stravinsky as a major composer and giving him his seminal dance experience – the business and personal relations between these two protagonists were often troubled, the friction increasing as time progressed. They enjoyed a longstanding friendship, but both were egotistical, canny and jealous: they fought most bitterly over money. Diaghilev's financial position was frequently at crisis point and he constantly delayed or forgot about payments. He took advantage of the fact that Stravinsky's copyright claims were precarious, asking him for exclusivity on his early ballets but then denying his obligation to pay royalties at all on works that were, like *Firebird*, unprotected by international law (the Berne Convention).[33] Meanwhile, Stravinsky was stretched, supporting a large family, with his publishers' activities effectively halted during the war years.

Walsh and Joseph have slightly different takes on the relationship. Walsh observes:

> The curious thing – and it is a profoundly Russian trait – is that even at the height of mutual recriminations, the deep artistic sympathy and warm personal affection somehow remained intact ... Like cartoon Russians, Stravinsky and Diaghilev could hug and get drunk together by night and still wrangle over money and contracts by day ...[34]

Joseph weighs more readily into the animosity between the two men, perceiving that, by the 1920s, it was Diaghilev's 'whims and ploys', together with a distrust of his artistic intentions and standards, that drew Stravinsky away from the impresario and closer to Balanchine.[35] For Diaghilev also interfered artistically, threatening cuts to both *Sacre* and *Apollo*, the latter ballet provoking a bitter quarrel that was left unresolved at the point of Diaghilev's death in 1929. A few weeks earlier, the two found themselves on the same train, but did not speak. It is important to note this troubled relationship between the composer and his employer because the experience, especially its financial aspect, defined the cautious, even aggressive nature of Stravinsky's business negotiations throughout his later career and in his ballet business.

As for Stravinsky's composition for dance during the period 1909–19, there were not only the three staged ballet scores, *Firebird, Petrushka* and *Sacre*, but also *Histoire du soldat, Renard* (completed but not staged until 1922) and *Noces* (completed but for its instrumentation, which was finalised in 1923). The opera *Rossignol* became a hybrid with dancing when it was staged. This was Stravinsky's most productive period of all in terms of dance. Equally impressive is the development in his thinking about dance theatre, its forms and subject matter.

Fokine presented Stravinsky with a fait accompli scenario for *Firebird*, agreed by Diaghilev's artistic committee. The libretto about the magical bird that enables Prince Ivan to marry the imprisoned Princess represented a conflation of elements from various Russian tales. To Parisian audiences, its visually exuberant exoticism made it seem excitingly avant-garde, the music introducing sonorities, harmonies and rhythms to which both they and the dancers were unaccustomed. In accordance with Fokine's principles, there were no applause breaks and the ballet vocabulary was replaced, except for the Firebird herself, by a far more realist and folk-derived style. Prince Ivan, for instance, seems more ordinary and rustic than characteristically noble. Yet the theatrical conceit was fundamentally traditional, a tale simply told, drawing on the long Russian musical tradition in which human characters were represented diatonically and otherworldly ones chromatically. The final coronation scene was Stravinsky's idea, replacing Fokine's more conventional one of a divertissement. Walsh pertinently observes that this already reflects Stravinsky's feeling for ritual.[36] As ballet music, this first score diverges from tradition in one other key respect. If, for Fokine's dramatic purposes, the score usefully retained a distinction between mime sections and dance, the music dealt with the convention operatically rather than balletically. There is 'gestural' music, but from Wagnerian music drama comes the free-flowing recitative technique, transitions, and use of leitmotifs to distinguish different characters and their worlds. Stravinsky himself referred to the score as 'leit-musique'.[37] Indeed, there is a larger proportion of narrative music and, concomitantly, fewer set dance numbers than in many of the traditional ballet scores that preceded *Firebird*. Prince Ivan's long pas de deux with the *Firebird* is also the only pas de deux in the ballet and is not the standard love duet. Taruskin notes Stravinsky's innovation here as a ballet composer. The composer himself was later embarrassed by the operatic derivations, and *Firebird* was his only ballet score to employ descriptive music to such a degree.[38]

Fokine gave Stravinsky strict instructions as to the construction of the *Firebird* score. Commenting on a compositional draft of the ballet, Joseph notes that Stravinsky made many concessions.[39] The choreographer was a notoriously difficult collaborator, and the music was created in the spirit of an accompaniment to the choreography; it is telling that the composer never again put up with such a power relationship. Soon his opinion of Fokine soured on other accounts. Although Stravinsky had at first considered him highly progressive, by 1912 he had decided that he was out of date. 'I consider Fokine *finished* as an artist', he wrote to his mother in Russia. 'It's all just *habileté* [skill], from which there's no salvation ...'[40]

Fokine was musically conservative after all. In his autobiography, he deplores the lack of 'danceability' in *Petrushka*, questions the need for complex musical rhythms and asks for a more repetitious, more authentic, musical style for national dances. He also criticises the *Petrushka* finale, which had presented major hurdles to the Ballets Russes dancers, who were totally unused to this level of musical difficulty.[41] Yet perhaps *Petrushka* is Fokine's finest work, and in terms of the sheer level of achievement of all three collaborators, the truest of all Stravinsky's ballets to the concept of *Gesamtkunstwerk*. Here, the composer and Benois led the collaboration, devising together the scenario and theatrical framework, and it is this ballet, probably through Benois's involvement, that led Stravinsky into a totally new world of theatrical conception.

Originally, it was Stravinsky's idea to base a ballet on a *commedia dell' arte* theme centring on the character Petrushka. But it was probably Benois, with his greater experience of theatre and Symbolist art, who came up with the signal component of a two-tiered scenario, action split between the planes of the St Petersburg crowd and the three puppets, Petrushka, the Ballerina and the Moor, within a fairground booth, behind two prosceniums, inner and outer. Between the two collaborators, the libretto was formed from a broad range of sources: *commedia* filtered through Russian experience, which included Shrovetide carnivals, Symbolism and contemporary theatrical retellings of *commedia* themes such as Blok's *Fairground Booth.* They adopted for the Petrushka figure the soulful, pathetic lineage of Pierrot rather than the more usual extrovert one of Punch.[42] Theatrically, this second ballet moves far more boldly than *Firebird* into the terrain of stylisation, asking us as audience to consider how we position and reposition ourselves in relation to the planes of activity on stage: as spectators watching the crowd who watch the puppets, or simply us watching the puppets, or even us watching the crowd through the eyes of the puppets, with whom we come to identify as they demonstrate their superior expressive powers. Such is the play between planes. We are also transported from the large Realist theatre picture of the first tableau to the close-up, unreal, Symbolist space inhabited by the puppets.[43] If we believe Stravinsky's memoirs (and whether he thought this in 1910–11 we do not know), he had had at least one idea about extending the artifice still further. He entertained the notion of amplifying the concept of watching through the eyes of the puppets by having Petrushka actually seen watching the dances of the Fourth Tableau through a hole in his cell.[44]

Stravinsky's memoirs may well demonstrate the more advanced thinking of later years, possibly encouraged by other people's imaginative wanderings. Yet at the time of *Petrushka*'s creation, Stravinsky was new to such an experimental theatrical conception. He was still thinking literally. There is the story that he and Benois both had doubts about the repetition between subsequent tableaux (to enable the scene shifts) of the drum roll device that introduces the puppets during the first tableau, although they eventually agreed to go ahead.[45] The initial drum roll was meant to invite the crowd's attention, within the world of the carnival. How could it then switch to us, the audience? On the other hand, Stravinsky's eagerness to learn and experiment may have galvanised Benois to work more imaginatively than usual.[46] Benois was essentially conservative in artistic temperament and, as soon as the *Petrushka* collaboration was over, he turned back from Symbolism to Realist staging and design for the Moscow Arts Theatre. Stravinsky certainly demonstrated his own progressive powers within his musical operations, devising a stylisation that Walsh has termed 'fractured realism'.[47] Mime and dance distinctions in the score are blurred, if they exist at all. There is toytown realism, presented as a non-stop collage of distinct identities: the appearance and disappearance of characters and situations out of the crowd music in the first and last scenes, the two street dancers, the bear, the coachmen, the masqueraders. Touches such as these, which include urban cultural reference, took the audiences of 1911 into a world well beyond the ballet music conventions of the time. So did the 'expressionist' violence and anguish of the music for Petrushka's Cell scene, with its unpredictable mood swings between paroxysms of fury and lament.

If Stravinsky might have delayed immersing himself fully in the ideas of the new theatre, probably the experience of working with Benois on *Petrushka* (1910–11) was decisive. By 1911, he was enthusing about an article by the experimental theatre director Georg Fuchs attacking literary theatre and calling, in Walsh's words, for 'a new approach to theatre in which dance and the cult of the body played a pre-eminent role alongside music'. Fuchs was not talking about classical ballet, but about dance that would be 'a sacred, ritualistic expression of the whole community'.[48] With his development of rhythmical movement and advanced notions of two-dimensional staging using a narrow strip of stage space, Fuchs had been an important influence on Meyerhold. Theatre was coming closer to dance; indeed, Meyerhold had proclaimed that stylised theatre 'hopes to bring about the revival of the *dance*'.[49]

While he was working on *Petrushka*, Stravinsky already had in mind his next ballet, *Sacre*, which was to be a close collaboration with the painter and ethnographer Nicolay Roerich. Yet again, there was a major step forward in terms of theatrical conception. The work is fundamentally in two parts, a ceremony paying homage to the earth and a sacrifice – a young girl has to die for the sake of her community – the ritual on stage, nothing more, nothing less. In a September 1912 interview in St Petersburg, Stravinsky called it a 'mysterium':

There is practically no plot to it, there is only a series of dances or action in dance. How do I conceive of classical ballet at present? In general, I am an adherent of so-called choreodrama, which is bound to replace the contemporary type of ballet.[50]

Two days later in St Petersburg, his description was even more daring in its abstract emphasis:

Like everything I write, this is not a ballet, but simply a fantasia in two parts, like two movements of a symphony.[51]

Certainly, without any mime music, and hardly any pockets of musical realism of the kind that still asserted themselves in *Petrushka*, *Sacre* came closer to Stravinsky's later 'pure dance' conceptions, thus, as Taruskin argues, initiating the dismantling of the *Gesamtkunstwerk*. Without the narrative element embedded in the music, and with ritual and ceremony displacing discourse, the separate media could be seen to operate separately rather than in fusion.[52] Or at least the music could. There was no need to make a suite out of *Sacre* for concert purposes. It already was one. Yet, at the same time as the new work looked forward to Stravinsky's later dance structures, its subject matter looked backwards to the nineteenth century. As the dance scholars Lynn Garafola and Joan Acocella have argued, the primitivism of *Sacre* had its roots in the nineteenth century, and the subject of sacrifice was certainly no stranger to classical ballet (viz. *Giselle* and *La Sylphide*).[53] Another layer of ambiguity: if the media drew further apart on one level so that the music could become self-sufficient, on another level they seemed closer than ever before. By dint of force, the *Sacre* music announced for the first time in ballet the real weight and physicality of the body (rather than its representation or virtual denial), a new image of dancers being totally and simply 'in the body', doing, dancing, ritual on stage.

The colossal impact of *Sacre* on dance since the Nijinsky premiere is the subject of the final chapter of this book, which also touches on the peculiar status of this work within Stravinsky's mind: its relations with the past and with dance that he did all he could to deny. Suffice to say here that the composer's very positive view of the original choreography was subject to gross revisionism soon after the premiere, at the expense of a choreographer now believed to be one of the most innovative of the twentieth century.

We might reflect at this point on just how far Stravinsky had come within four years: from a new kind of dance music that borrowed from operatic forms, to an even newer modernism shorn of neat literalism, from folk sources as exotic colouring to folk as a secret source of musical style, and to rampant primitivism, a dance music that sounded dangerous and engulfed the dancing body. The rhythmic techniques that would form the basis of his later musical style had also evolved over these years. These are discussed in more detail in later chapters.

Meanwhile, spanning the whole of this period, another work had been brewing: *Le Rossignol*, begun as a straight opera pre-*Firebird* in 1908 and completed after *Sacre* in 1914, when it was staged as a hybrid form with a considerable movement component. The setting of this 'kind of opera' under the auspices of the Ballets Russes is not as strange as it might at first sound, for Diaghilev had already staged operas as well as ballets, and used his resources to explore various guises of cross-genres.[54] Looked at another way, this was Stravinsky's first 'ballet with singing'.[55]

The work told the Hans Christian Andersen story about the Nightingale, a personification of Nature, who restores to life the dying Emperor of China. By the time *Rossignol* was premiered by the Ballets Russes in 1914, Stravinsky's stance towards opera was quite different from what it had been when he initially conceived of the work in 1908 with his friend Mitusov (see p. 26). The genre no longer interested him. In March 1913, Alexander Sanin, familiar for staging most of Diaghilev's operas to date, commissioned Stravinsky to complete the work for his adventurous but short-lived Moscow Free Theatre, an organisation that promoted 'synthetic' theatre and allowed considerable genre freedom:

> You need not limit the character or form; employ prose, opera, dance, and mime all together as you wish in a single work.[56]

The commission never came to fruition. Instead, Diaghilev billed *Rossignol* together with his production of Rimsky-Korsakov's opera *Le Coq d'or*. In fact, the latter work set an important and immediate precedent in terms of production style, with its roles aurally and visually divided between singers ranged up the sides of the stage and dancers miming the action in the space between them. It proved a major success and, interestingly, the separation of voice from body did not necessarily create a sense of disjunction for some viewers at the time: quite the opposite. It did not dismantle the fusion principle behind the *Gesamtkunstwerk*, but instead reinforced it. Prince Sergey Volkonsky, the former director of the Imperial Theatres, enthused:

> Only for the first minute was one's attention divided. Thereafter the complete merger of visual and auditory impressions took over.[57]

... as did the ballet critic N. Minsky:

> I have no doubt that this time the inspirers of the Russian Ballet have hit upon a new form of theatrical art, one that has a huge future. It is neither ballet

illustrated by music nor opera flavoured with ballet, but a union of two hitherto separate art forms: a union that takes place not on the stage but in the
viewer's soul.[58]

It is as if the new device of divided roles foregrounded the very issue of relationship; so connection was reinforced, as it were, through disconnection.

Benois took credit for conceiving the staging idea for *Coq d'or* even if he did not
design the piece himself,[59] and he also both designed *Rossignol* and produced it
alongside Sanin, brought over from Russia now that the Free Theatre had folded.
As in *Coq d'or*, there were singers 'offstage', this time in the pit. The Nightingale
was represented by a prop on stage, a tiny bird; the role of the Fisherman who
frames the work was divided between a singer and a dancer.

Once again, Benois worked very closely with Stravinsky, probably entering the
Rossignol collaboration in January 1914.[60] Together he and the composer exploited their interest in a spectacle devoid of what they saw as the tired old
operatic mannerisms, creating instead one that was artificial, predominantly
visual in emphasis and ironic in its 'fausse-Chinoiserie'.[61] Stravinsky and
Mitusov had already devised a reduced libretto for Acts II and III. Here at
work were the same antiliterary aesthetics that had determined Diaghilev's
earlier cutting of the operas *Boris Godunov* and *Khovanshchina* (see p. 24).
The choreography was by Boris Romanov, a dancer with the Ballets Russes,
who had choreographed Florent Schmitt's *La Tragédie de Salomé* the year before
(see p. 317).

In 1917, Stravinsky turned the opera into a symphonic poem/ballet, *Le Chant
du rossignol*, according to Diaghilev's particular requirements, though, interestingly, the composer and writer Virgil Thomson felt that he could still spot the
cross-genre origins in the texture of the music:

> The opera version is almost a ballet. And the ballet is almost an opera ... The
> ballet version, nevertheless, still yearns to sing, just as the opera version
> strained toward the dance.[62]

Two more theatre works that did not materialise were projected around the
time of *Rossignol*. In 1914, there was a plan for *David* with a libretto by Jean
Cocteau, a crucial Stravinsky contact during the Diaghilev period. Cocteau's
idea was an event juxtaposing the Old Testament story of David alongside fairground imagery, including the notion of action outside a booth drawing people
inside. He explains:

> An acrobat was to do the parade for 'David', a big spectacle which was sup-
> posed to be taking place inside; a clown, who subsequently became a box, a

theatrical version of the phonograph at a fair, a modern equivalent of the mask of the ancients, was to sing through a megaphone the prowess of David and implore the public to enter to see the piece inside. It was, in a sense, the first sketch of *Parade*, but uselessly complicated by the Bible and a text.[63]

Another fairground piece, another dual-plane conception, within a few months the project was dropped. This was the case too in 1915, when Diaghilev proposed *Liturgie*, a ritual based on the Mass with *a cappella* chorus, another dance project with text.

By this time, increasingly confident about developing his own theatrical conceptions and much in the spirit of a director, Stravinsky was wholly committed to theatrical forms that involved text and extended the traditional terms of ballet. Turning to ritualistic and popular strands of theatre, the texted pieces constitute a more important part of his dance work in the first part of his career than is generally recognised in dance scholarship. There has always been a tendency to overlook text unless it is as strong and autonomous a component as in *Histoire du soldat*, especially when in a foreign language or hard to absorb alongside other theatrical aspects. But it is especially noteworthy that the decision to embrace these new theatrical forms sprang mostly from the composer himself, and that he created his own texts, based on folk sources, for both *Renard* and *Les Noces*. As we shall see, he also introduced his own idiosyncratic approach to word setting. In 1962, reminiscing on the *Histoire du soldat* and the particular role of the Narrator standing outside the action in that work, Stravinsky confirmed: 'I am always attracted by new conditions and those of the theatre are, to me, a great part of its appeal.'[64] This interest in stylised theatre with text remained with Stravinsky throughout his career, until his television piece *The Flood* (1962).

In 1915, Stravinsky began work on a conception entirely of his own, the twenty-minute *Renard*, a work important enough in his theatrical career to merit special discussion. For a start, it was never conceived for Diaghilev or a ballet company context. One of the impresario's wealthy backers, the Princesse de Polignac, paid for the work, contracted at Christmas 1915 after composition had begun during the summer, with the aim of presenting it at her house in Paris. There are contradictory accounts of Diaghilev's attitude on hearing the music in 1916. Stravinsky said that it 'left him completely indifferent (naturally, as does everything I write that is not for him)'.[65] But the conductor Ernest Ansermet reported to Stravinsky that Diaghilev had found it 'a splendid thing and the one thing I reproach Igor for is having used up there the best of what he could have kept for *Noces*'.[66] In fact, it was Diaghilev who staged the work for the first time in 1922, taking advantage of the fact that he did not need to pay for the commission.

It is important to note that, since 1914, Stravinsky had been driven by a new interest in setting Russian folk texts. His 'rejoicing discovery'[67] was the particular manner in Russian folk song of distorting normal verbal stress. This was naturally allied to his anti-expression aesthetic and was a further weapon against the concept of *Gesamtkunstwerk*: words in this instance have a new value as sounds beyond and separate from their original meaning.[68]

The premise of *Renard* was a piece of traditional street theatre, likely to have been an invented conception rather than something that had really existed.[69] Strolling players arrive, introduce themselves, get into role to tell the story of the Fox and the Cock, and of the Cat and the Goat who prevent the Fox from killing the Cock, and then get out of role to ask the audience for money before leaving the stage. The tale is from the Alexander Afanasyev anthology of Russian folklore, and Stravinsky's idea of a theatrical rendering that used his own libretto gradually took shape by the end of 1915. The work had begun as song settings. The second development was to divide singers from movers, which, Walsh maintains, was not clear from the start,[70] and the notion of doubling emerged. The preface to the score indicates:

> *Reynard* is to be played by clowns, dancers or acrobats, preferably on a trestle stage with the orchestra placed behind. If produced in a theatre, it should be played in front of the curtain ... The roles are dumb. The singers (two tenors and two basses) are in the orchestra.[71]

Cross-purpose through stylisation abounds in Stravinsky's *Renard* conception. As Walsh points out with regard to the *Pribaoutki* songs (completed in 1914), words stressed 'incorrectly' hold a particular dual perspective for Russian speakers, who understand them both for their meaning and their distortion.[72] (In the event, *Renard* was premiered by the Ballets Russes in French.) Then, the doubling relationship of participants is by no means straightforward, as the singers do not match exactly the four named characters on stage. The singers do not hold on to specific roles in the score, and there is no simple unity in the doubling, unlike that of the 'two' Fishermen (one sung, one danced) in *Rossignol*.

The established norm is for the two tenors to sing the Cock and the Fox respectively and the two basses the Cat and the Goat, but these identities are destabilised from time to time. The Fox, who arrives in disguise as a nun, is a tenor, but playing himself, a bass, who wheedles in falsetto. There is even less reason for both tenors to join up as one character, as they do for the Fox offering confession:

> So that you be spared
> The risk of dying in sin

... or soon afterwards as the Cock:

Oh-oh-come to my aid![73]

Equally illogical is the Cock's begging the Fox not to eat him, first by a tenor, then a bass, then two basses. Voices associated with characters later become musical instruments, the *gusli* carried on stage by the Cat and the Goat. Releasing his imagination to relationships between all the theatrical components, the interdisciplinarian Daniel Albright delights in the fact that

> Stravinsky continually challenges the boundaries ... So the sound of the onstage actors comes not from the actors themselves but from a little knot of singers standing amid trumpets, flutes, violins, and so forth; and the sound of the onstage *gusli* comes not from the *gusli* but from the nearby cimbalom – or, still more confusingly, from the larynxes of the singers who are the tentative surrogates for the dancers.[74]

Later still, voices identify with the body parts of the Fox – his eyes, feet and tail. But by this time, cross-media identities have become strained to the limit, the verbal imagery more and more diffuse, until the actor-dancers step out of their roles and the singers simply sing themselves as exiting strolling players. As for us, in such circumstances we grasp the links between singers and dancers when they occur, a perception that in turn highlights the moments when they do not.

Shortly after the premiere, the musicologist André Schaeffner wrote about the lack of a clear narrative from the words, yet he still admitted dramatic purpose, a kind of edge arising from the oddity of their mixture.[75] On the other hand, the Soviet music critic Boris Asafyev and Taruskin consider that the music ultimately dominates, even overpowers, the text in *Renard*.[76] But it could be that Stravinsky, rather than concerning himself simply with the issue of story within his own musical/textual medium, actively chose to give power to the visual plane to clarify the story *as part of* his larger conception. Or, when Taruskin writes that the music is 'absolute', the words 'literally and indispensably *a part of the music*', we might argue that the real theatrical point is about counterpoint between aural and visual, and mutual 'troubling'. But musicologists naturally tend to privilege the aural component.

There is a also a huge repetition in the action – the ensemble go through the operation of the Fox seducing the Cock off his perch and needing to be rescued, not just once but twice. Elliott Carter wrote that 'the characters on stage and the audience are dealt with as if they had no memory, as if living always in the present and not learning from previous events'.[77] The repetition occurs in the original Afanasyev story itself,[78] but it shaped and suited Stravinsky's abstract predilections. So *Renard* too turns out to be a kind of ritual, within a pseudo-folk theatre frame, through its various devices for upsetting theatrical illusion. It is a story that is anti-story. But we can also look at *Renard* as a double 're-enactment', to borrow Walsh's term for the concept of the underlying relationship between audience and stage wherein the interest lies in anything but the story and its outcome.[79] First, the actor-dancers inform us of the 're-enactment' as they put on their masks. Then there is the false repetition, the 're-enactment', of the story. In his 1969 production for the Royal Ballet Choreographic Group, David Drew had the Goat and the Cat exchange roles with the Cock and the Fox for the 're-enactment', which not only highlighted the artifice of the repeat in the story but also outdid Stravinsky in ensuring an unstable relationship between dancers and singers.

Yet Stravinsky's conception was already fundamentally a tease, a queasy kind of ritual. As Albright sees it:

> Stravinsky manufactures hieroglyphs – bits of picture-music – but instead of claiming that these cross-media entities have any prestige or expressive value, he handles them with tweezers, pieces them together like a collage of butterfly wings.[80]

Back in 1915–16, all this eccentric theatrical thinking was Stravinsky's. There was no one yet from the theatre to put his ideas into practice or to collaborate with his vision. He would have to wait for Bronislava Nijinska and 1922, and alas, her choreography has been lost forever.

Likewise, *Noces* awaited Nijinska, and this *was* conceived for a ballet company. Stemming from 1912 but only completed for premiere in 1923, this was the work that Stravinsky worried over for longer than any other that he made. It may have been inspired by Sanin's concept of 'synthetic' theatre;[81] the theatre director had been interested in the composer's 'wedding' idea before his *Rossignol* commission. With Diaghilev thoroughly committed to *Noces* from the start, serious composition on this Russian wedding ritual began in 1914, the year of the 'rejoicing discovery'. The short score was completed in 1917, yet Stravinsky kept changing his mind about its instrumentation. To summarise and simplify: his imagination ranged from string quintets and wind (1914–15); a scoring that weights the wind far more heavily and includes a cimbalom (1915–17); six instrumentalists – harmonium, two cimbaloms, pianola and percussion (1918–19); and finally, for the 1923 premiere, to four pianos and percussion.[82] More anarchic than in *Renard*, the text, which uses Wedding Songs from the anthology of Pyotr Kireyevsky, was formed to sound like nonsense chatter.

In common with *Renard*, there is conjunction and disjunction between aural and visual. Singing voices sometimes match the characters on stage (the Bride,

Groom and parents), but often do not, and even named persons in the text do not find their counterparts in the choreography. These techniques will be discussed more fully in the chapter on *Noces*, but here we can draw comparisons with *Sacre*. Like the earlier work, it is a ritual, a choreodrama, but it is of a new order. In theatrical manner, it is an experiment that blends the most human imagery – the anxiety, pathos and exuberance of a peasant wedding – with the most post-human. Consider where Stravinsky left the work in 1919 in that odd orchestration: the two cimbaloms give it the most 'of the people' colouring of all the versions, and yet it is surely also the most technological view of *Noces* of all, with that extraordinary array of musical machinery, including pianola. How far Stravinsky's thinking about dance theatre had developed in just ten years!

But Stravinsky was already aware of a changing aesthetic in Paris, from the hedonism of Russian Symbolism to the mechanisation reflected in Diaghilev's revolutionary production of *Parade* (1917, a collaboration between Cocteau, Picasso and Satie). And there was no new Stravinsky work in that 1917 Paris season. He needed to update himself. As Margarita Mazo writes in her preface to the recent *Noces* study score: 'To live up to his self-vision as the premier international composer, he had to get to the forefront again', and she tells us that his discourse now was about the cinema and cinematographic rhythm, 'the association of the sound of the pianola with silent film, and the non-diegetic relationship between music and the action on the screen'.[83] The 1919 scoring already looks forward to the ethos of the 1920s when the composer would once more be centre stage. Yet it was only in 1922 that Stravinsky finally settled on his orchestration. The identity of *Noces* lies in both early and late Diaghilev periods: the matter of sonority is as important as the matter of form.

On the other hand, the very popular *Histoire du soldat* (1918) is a throwback, although its retrogressive nature may not be apparent at first. Again based on Afanasyev, it is the last work involving dance from the period 1909–19. This is the closest Stravinsky ever came to 'rough theatre'[84] – *Histoire* was intended as a modest travelling show during the war. It employed the distancing device of a narrator who functions as intermediary between audience and stage, and, as in the final version of *Noces*, the musicians were meant to be part of the stage picture. Later, in Weimar Germany, the stark manner of staging, the distancing techniques and the removal of illusion encouraged viewers to think that *Histoire* had foreshadowed Bertolt Brecht. Written from an entirely different political standpoint, the Brecht/Weill *Threepenny Opera* (1927) owes a lot stylistically to the Stravinsky work.[85] Yet, 'to be read [not sung], played and danced', with C.F. Ramuz's libretto, *Histoire* recalls elements of the traditional literary theatre that Stravinsky had tried to remove from his most recent texted works.[86] The dance component for the Devil and the Princess was slight – we know that Lyudmila Pitoëff, the Princess, was not a ballet dancer, so the style was probably quite free – and it was hardly a thoroughly considered aspect of the original production.[87]

During the period 1909–19, Stravinsky began to articulate strong ideas about ballet in his correspondence and to the press. At first, enamoured of his new position at the forefront of the star ballet company in Europe, he sided eagerly with the pro-ballet, anti-opera league. In 1911, he tried to persuade his unconverted friend Vladimir Rimsky-Korsakov (son of the composer) that all the arts are equal, but that ballet reaches the greatest heights of expression. He sounds like a true Symbolist:

> I love ballet and am more interested in it than in anything else ... For the only form of scenic art that sets itself, as its cornerstone, the *tasks of beauty*, and *nothing else*, is ballet ... I think that if you would attend the ballet regularly (artistic ballet, of course [meaning not the old ballet repertory of the Maryinsky]), you would see that this 'lower form' brings you incomparably more artistic joy than any operatic performance (even the operas with your favourite music), a joy I have been experiencing now for over a year and which I would so like to infect you all with and share with you.

For the purposes of ballet, in the same letter, Stravinsky even excuses the introduction of a new story to a score by Vladimir's father that already had a programme. Interestingly, he would hardly have condoned this in later years for his own music (see pp. 77-79):

> The main thing here is not the subject, but the divine spectacle, which transports you utterly into the atmosphere of *Scheherazade*'s stupendous music.[88]

Soon, there was a string of anti-opera statements, about not marrying music to gesture and words at the same time – 'Music can be married to gesture or to words – not to both without bigamy'[89] – and about the advantages of ballet stylisation and artifice:

> Opera does not attract me at all. What interests me is choreographic drama, the only form in which I see any movement forward, without trying to foretell its future direction. Opera is falsehood pretending to be truth, while I need falsehood that pretends to be falsehood. Opera is a competition with nature.[90]

By 1914, Stravinsky had started to show concern that the musical component should not be diminished within a theatrical or mixed-media work. Noting this danger when he met the writer Romain Rolland, he still entertained the possibility of movement and music collaborating successfully. There was the proviso of a more artistic approach than that of the Swiss music pedagogue Emile Jaques-Dalcroze, originator of the eurhythmics movement technique that Nijinsky had used in *Sacre*:

> He agrees that theatrical performance, such as it is today, diminishes the music, reduces the emotion or motion expressed, enclosing these within too precise a character image. However, there is value in performance through gesture and movement (a kind of rhythmic gymnastics, but more artistic than those of Dalcroze), broad, generous, sweeping lines in motion.

At this juncture, Stravinsky is much harder on the design element of production, which he considers far more likely than dance to overpower the music, probably as a result of his recent *Rossignol* experience with Benois:

> He resents designs and costumes that are too rich and too individual, that detract from the spirit of musical emotion. The painter seems to him to be the musician's enemy. The Wagnerian dream of the artwork in which all the arts would join together is mistaken, he said. Where there is music, it must be sovereign! It is not possible to have two masters at the same time. Suppress colour! Colour is too powerful; it is a kingdom in itself, a music of its own.[91]

Earlier than this, by June 1912, Stravinsky had begun to be critical of the Diaghilev repertoire. He complained to Benois of generally poor music and too much 'Greek' ballet with Bakst designs.[92] And by 1914, to Benois again:

> Oh! How I feel this [Diaghilev] business isn't for me. Precisely because its artistic life is over, and is now pure commerce – which is the one thing that stops me (since I survive on it) from breaking with this international soldier's club.[93]

Stravinsky had moved on artistically. When he 'returned' to the Ballets Russes in 1919, he discovered that Diaghilev had moved on too.

For most of the period 1909–19, dance and the Ballets Russes were central to Stravinsky's experience. Apart from his ballet scores, what did he come up with? Songs and piano pieces mainly, crucial to his development as a composer even if not to his livelihood; they brought him little money or exposure. Meanwhile, his dance acclaim paid dividends. There were concert performances of his *Firebird* and *Petrushka* in suite form. There was also the reverse, towards the end of the period, a trickle of concert scores transformed into theatre by choreographers outside the Ballets Russes: Léo Staats at the Paris Opéra, *Scherzo Fantastique* (music 1908/choreography 1917); and two early 'modern dance' women choreographers – in Paris, Loie Fuller, *Fireworks* (1909/1914), and in London, Margaret Morris, *Pastorale* (1907/1917) and *Spring* (set to the *Three Japanese Lyrics*, 1913/1917).

Table 1. Stravinsky ballet premieres for Diaghilev's Ballets Russes in the 1920s.

1920	*Le Chant du rossignol* – Massine;
	Pulcinella – Massine;
	Le Sacre du printemps (version 2) – Massine
1921	*The Sleeping Beauty* (2 orchestrations)
1922	*Renard* – Nijinska; *Mavra* – Nijinska staging
1923	*Les Noces* – Nijinska
1925	*Le Chant du rossignol* (version 2) – Balanchine
1927	*Oedipus Rex* (opera-oratorio)
1928	*Apollo* – Balanchine
1929	*Renard* (version 2) – Lifar

Period 2: 1919–37. The European composer: Diaghilev and beyond

The second instalment of this story of Stravinsky's career in dance reveals much greater diversification. *Pulcinella* (composed 1919–20/premiered 1920) was Stravinsky's first major ballet premiere since *Rossignol* in 1914, and he naturally accepted the commission, even though, as we shall see later, it was an odd one. He maintained regular professional contact with the Ballets Russes, but his relationship with the company during this, its final decade, was very different from that of the early years when he had been, to all intents and purposes, 'staff composer'. The company had entered a different phase artistically, driven predominantly by a Western rather than Russian cultural outlook, with Diaghilev now commissioning far more broadly, embracing fashion and current issues, work termed by Garafola 'lifestyle modernism' and in tune with Cocteau's 'art of the sophisticated commonplace'.[94] Stravinsky continued to attend rehearsals and performances in Paris and London, occasionally visiting the Ballets Russes at its base in Monte Carlo, and acquainting himself with Diaghilev's new list of choreographers: Leonid Massine, Nijinska, Balanchine and Serge Lifar.

For Stravinsky, there were no more new ballet commissions from the Ballets Russes after *Pulcinella* so far as we know – at least, none agreed to. *Apollo* (1927–8/1928), which dates from this period, had been premiered and paid for in the USA (see Table 1). But there was the task of assisting with productions of pieces that had already been completed during the previous period (*Renard*), or completed but for the final orchestration (*Noces*), and he was occasionally called upon to conduct his own scores. Another important task now was checking on revivals of old works and on new choreography to old works. Stravinsky's scores continued to be well represented in the repertory of the Ballets Russes throughout its final period. There was the Stravinsky evening in 1922 and the festival in his name in 1928; and in the Paris season of 1923, four of the eight works had scores by him: *Petrushka, Pulcinella, Sacre* and *Noces.*

In another major change, the composer wrote two opera-style works specially for Diaghilev during this period: the one-act opera bouffe *Mavra* (1922), a commentary on the models of Russian popular opera-cum-cabaret, and the opera-oratorio *Oedipus Rex* (1927). No longer was there a need to justify ballet over opera, and during the Swiss years Stravinsky had found his own idiosyncratic, artificial solution to the problem of text setting in musical theatre. In any case, it was opera according to the new terms of neoclassicism. And who staged *Mavra?* The experimental choreographer Nijinska. *Oedipus,* a collaboration with Cocteau, received only three concert performances with the Ballets Russes. It was supposed to be a surprise gift to Diaghilev, but he was unimpressed.

With *Oedipus* again, the genre title 'opera-oratorio' betrays its crossover nature. No dance element was intended here, yet within the conception of this 'monumental' theatre piece, we find stylisation at an extreme: the masked characters and chorus who move only arms and heads; the distancing effect of the Latin text (translated from Cocteau's French); the narrator who frames the work into a series of tableaux and 'expresses himself like a conférencier, presenting the story with a detached voice',[95] in French, a second language; the two-dimensional setting, not to mention the collage of disparate musical types, 'a Merzbild, put together from whatever came to hand'.[96] In a 1952 production of *Oedipus,* the first performance of which Stravinsky conducted, Cocteau wanted to introduce the missing dance element. Initially, Stravinsky rejected his idea: he felt strongly that dance or mime would detract from his music.[97] Yet there was mime in the end, seven *tableaux vivants,* and the composer later admitted that, although it contradicted his intentions, this was his favourite staging.[98]

Stravinsky's career now extended well beyond the Ballets Russes. He had to build financial independence from Diaghilev, especially as, during this period, his personal life became both complex and expensive, and this independence served him well after the impresario's death in 1929. Early on during this period, his mother and his wife Catherine's relations arrived from Russia and needed support, and from 1921 he had a mistress, Vera Sudeykina (whom he met through the Ballets Russes), who was later to become his second wife. There was much geographical dislocation and various house moves: from Switzerland to Paris (1920), to Biarritz (1921), to Nice (1924), to Voreppe near Grenoble (1931) and back to Paris (1933), with a studio for Stravinsky himself in Paris (where Vera was based) along the way (1921–33).

There was now a rival ballet company on the horizon, run by the wealthy dancer-actress Ida Rubinstein. When she commissioned a ballet score from Stravinsky in 1928, *Le Baiser de la fée*, he accepted, much to Diaghilev's disgust. He did so again when she came back to him in 1933 with the idea of *Persephone*. It was also during the 1920s that Stravinsky developed a performing career for himself. Serious international touring featuring the composer both as conductor and pianist began in 1924, and later he formed strategic partnerships, first with the violinist Samuel Dushkin, for whom his *Violin Concerto* (1931) was written, and with whom he toured as a violin/piano duo from 1932, and, from 1935, with his pianist son Soulima. Stravinsky composed accordingly for these new contexts: piano pieces, arrangements and new works for violin and piano, as well as a concerto for two pianos. He toured extensively in Europe, and in the US, which he visited in 1925 (a visit that made him financially comfortable for seven years), 1935 and 1937. As the Second World War approached, touring opportunities in Europe declined, as did his financial stability. Meanwhile, he was hard at work getting his music transcribed to piano rolls and recorded on disc, a new source of income, as well as addressing the increasing business arising from his dealings with publishers, including proofreading, royalty issues, rights and so on.

At last Stravinsky witnessed the premieres of works written during the previous decade: *Renard* (1915–16/1922), with Nijinska's circus buffoon choreography, *Les Noces* (1914–23/1923) in Nijinska's austere, monochrome setting that has become a repertoire classic. There was even a second *Renard* by Serge Lifar with double doubling (1929), the dance roles of the Cock, Goat and Cat now magnified by three corresponding acrobats. A further work was *Le Chant du rossignol*, a telescoped version of the 1914 opera without voices, in two versions by Massine (1920) and Balanchine (1925). Parisian audiences of the early 1920s must have been astonished, witnessing in rapid succession a series of Stravinsky premieres in wildly divergent musical styles – the overwhelming force of *Sacre* in Massine's new version, then the new terse energy of *Renard* and *Noces* juxtaposed with the 'sophisticated' *Pulcinella* and *Mavra* and the chinoiserie of *Le Chant du rossignol*. At the same time, they might have read his manifesto in *Le Figaro* (1922) proclaiming the virtues of Tchaikovsky and *Sleeping Beauty* (see p. 23).[99] Supporting the new classicism also meant supporting the heritage of dance classicism.

The idea behind *Pulcinella* was presented as a fait accompli to Stravinsky by Diaghilev and Massine. Designed by Picasso, the ballet was an immediate success, but hardly the kind of work that Stravinsky would have attempted off his own bat, either musically or theatrically. A complex web of intrigue based on Neapolitan *commedia dell'arte* characters and a plot about fathers opposing the love affairs of their children, it was, as Stravinsky said years later, more an *action dansante* than a ballet.[100] As was customary by this time, the demarcation lines between mime and dance sections were not strongly drawn. Stravinsky had the musical sources handed to him as well: a series of instrumental and operatic pieces by Pergolesi and other eighteenth-century composers, which he was asked to arrange, following the pattern of other recent Ballets Russes repertory, such as Tommasini's work on Scarlatti for *The Good-Humoured Ladies* (1917) and Respighi's on Rossini for *La Boutique fantasque* (1919). As it happens, Stravinsky was sufficiently inspired to go further and update the Pergolesi pieces, investing them with his own authority. Interestingly, as in *Renard*, the three singers stood offstage, but White suggests that, even though their words in this 'ballet with singing' now had no clear connection with the narrative on stage:

> In performance the effect of this device is to hint at a further musical dimen-
> sion behind the instrumental score and behind the danced action on the
> stage.[101]

In fact, the general sentiments of love, as well as anguish in love, in the arias are not far removed from the content of the ballet plot. Nevertheless, as a theatre conception, apart from the disjunctive feature of 'time travelling'[102] back to the Baroque period, *Pulcinella* was much more conventional than *Renard* or *Noces*.

As for Massine's contribution, Stravinsky remembered it as 'on the whole ... very good'.[103] For some time, he was also far more complimentary about Massine's version of *Sacre* (premiered later in 1920) than he was about the original Nijinsky (see pp. 421-2). The composer retained professional contact with Massine over many years, wary of some of his schemes, but nevertheless rating him a respected colleague from the Diaghilev days.

The notion of a ballet score as a series of distinct, separate 'numbers' or sections links *Pulcinella* with several of Stravinsky's later ballets. In more general terms, its use of material from Western tradition as opposed to Russian folklore links it with the neoclassical tendency in Stravinsky's work that developed during the 1920s.

Early in that decade, Stravinsky began to adopt a new philosophy of art that became the subject of his published manifesto 'Some Ideas About My Octuor' (1924).[104] He had read *Art et scolastique* (1920) by the Catholic philosopher Jacques Maritain,[105] a book that attempted to create an aesthetics for modern art. Maritain saw himself assisting in the recovery process from the destructive intellectual tendencies of nineteenth-century romanticism. In his opinion, the antidote to individualism and emotional expression was for art to reflect the values of order, restraint and objectivity. But he also subscribed to the notion of artistic autonomy, with the composer as 'humble provider who must neverthe-less insist on the integrity of his work and its freedom from outside moral and

emotional pressures'.[106] All these were values that suited Stravinsky well: they operated in a dialectical relationship with his reaction against the notion of expression in music (see p. 4). They certainly make good sense in relation to the *Octet* (1923) itself, the *Concerto for Piano and Wind Instruments* (1924) and *Sonata for Piano* (1924), all pieces that represent a 'hardboiled'[107] kind of neoclassicism at the same time as they participated in the 'return to Bach' movement that lasted through the mid-1920s. These are also values that fit the conservative tendencies within France at the time, an outcome of the war years, demonstrating a new rapprochement with non-resistant, playful avant-gardism and classical cultural values. Diaghilev and Stravinsky slipped easily into membership of the conservative cultural elite, their leanings perhaps most obviously manifest in their enthusiasm for the revival of *Sleeping Beauty*, which referred directly to the classicism of the Louis XIV era. But the values of restraint and objectivity, directness and plain speaking emerged earlier, certainly in the dryness and hardness of *Renard* and *Histoire du soldat*, and in other smaller works of the war years.

The matter of a neo-'classicism' is complicated, too, by the independent question of stylistic dissociation. Here, an existing style (or sometimes more than one juxtaposed) becomes subject matter for new composition, in other words, the devices and conventions that gave the old style its identity become substance for a new rhetoric. Such formal allusions to the past intensify the formalism and objectivity of the music of the present.[108]

In the light of the values of this inter-war period, it is fascinating to see that *Noces*, finally premiered, was now read as a return to Greek classicism. In 1923, Jacques Copeau, director of the experimental Théâtre du Vieux-Colombier in Paris, proclaimed that, of all works produced during the last decade, it was the one that represented the possibility of renewal within dramatic tragedy.[109] Copeau, a pioneer of theatrical non-realism himself (see p. 26), was one of the most important modernist theatre directors and theorists working in France in the period before the Second World War. In his 1924 article 'Une nouvelle forme dramatique: Les chanteurs dans la "fosse"', Schaeffner agreed. With *Noces*, the essentially non-realist Greek chorus had returned to the centre of the theatre event, and, aligning the theatrical concept with Nietzsche's vision for tragedy, he asked, 'Now what could be closer in matter and spirit to the primitive dithyramb?'[110] During the years 1914–17, when the substance of *Noces* was essentially composed, would anyone have been so ready to make the connection with Greek classicism? But Stravinsky had updated *Noces* according to the terms of a new era (see p. 39).

For Stravinsky, political and aesthetic stance related to religious belief, and in 1926, encouraged by his reading of Maritain, he returned to Russian Orthodoxy, neoclassicism now making peace with the spiritual side of his life.[111] Diaghilev once suggested, and perhaps we should not believe him, that religion was the reason why Stravinsky would not give him a ballet for his 1927 season. He had given him the opera-oratorio *Oedipus Rex* instead. Ballet, Stravinsky had supposedly said, is 'the anathema of Christ'.[112] Perhaps there had been thoughts of another ballet commission after all. But there could have been other reasons why Stravinsky might not have been interested in writing a ballet at this time. Nicolas Nabokov, friend and spokesman for the composer, suggests that Stravinsky began to find the form wanting in the early 1920s. Having originally applauded ballet because it allowed autonomy for its constituent media and a level of abstraction that music drama or opera did not, Stravinsky now felt constrained by its theatrical demands and by the need to provide a 'danceable' style of music. According to Nabokov, he also felt that choreographers (other than Balanchine) misused his music: they would employ it as mere 'expressive background' or 'count up beats and measures and base their choreography on the durative elements of music' – which might be a reference to Massine's approach (see pp. 440-41).[113] Whatever the case, in 1927 Stravinsky did accept the *Apollo* ballet commission from the USA, a work in which musical values would not be constrained by external requirements.

Also, on a practical, financial level, the composer downplayed his collaborations because they involved sharing royalties, even if the stage brought in more money than concerts. Walsh maintains that Stravinsky actually obstructed stage performances of *Histoire du soldat* because of a grievance over Ramuz's earnings from the work. He also resented the share of earnings that Fokine and Benois got from *Firebird* and *Petrushka* performances.[114]

Stravinsky's published statements during both the 1920s and 1930s betray further concerns about the use of music in ballet. After all, he moved philosophically towards severe abstraction during this period. He continues the thread of argument that Rolland noted in his 1914 diary – music should not be a servant or an accompaniment to a visual spectacle – and he stresses the need for the independent identity of the media involved; the *Gesamtkunstwerk* is a concept of the past. Even the ballet scores conceived as programmatic theatre works are now supposed to make sense purely musically, and there are extraordinary falsehoods about his earliest practice:

> I have never tried, in my stage works, to make the music illustrate the action, or the action the music; I have always endeavoured to find an architectural basis of connection. I produce 'music itself'. Whenever 'music itself' is not the aim, music suffers ...
>
> I have always felt the same. I have never made 'applied music' of any kind. Even in the early days, in the *Firebird*, I was concerned with a purely musical composition ....

The *Rite* exists as a piece of music, first and last.[115]

Hence, with purely musical values assured, the next stage is to claim that the 'narrative ballet' scores are entirely effective in concert – which Stravinsky did in an interview to the New York press during his 1925 tour, by going one stage further, trying to persuade listeners that his music came across *best of all* without dance attached. Several versions of this interview were published, but this one printed in *Musical America* makes the point most strongly:

> His ballets, Stravinsky says, are more effective in concert than on the stage ... Of course the music loses when it is given with the ballet. The eye gets impressions more easily than the ear. Either the music detracts from your enjoyment of the ballet or the ballet from your absorption in the music. And then, ballets are not the perfect instruments that orchestras are. There is not the exact coordination between the movement and the music that is essential if it is to be an artistic achievement.[116]

Debates about whether his ballet scores should be performed in concert dogged Stravinsky for much of his career. Some listeners needed persuading, even when the scores were in suite form, the narrative passages that seemed to need the stage edited out of them. But they were driven by the old notions of mutual dependence between media.[117] Others, such as Jaques-Dalcroze, got round the problem by claiming that audiences imagined or physically felt the dance as they listened to the early descriptive scores: dance was already built into the music.[118] Stravinsky's aesthetic position meant that he brooked no arguments of this kind. Undoubtedly there were other reasons too. Why not perform his ballets in concert if he thought the choreography was lacking, or if such performances gave him extra income and fame?

Yet there are also several statements from the 1930s onwards proclaiming the supreme virtues of the classical ballet tradition (the *danse d'école*), the most famous of them in his *Autobiography* (1936):

> The evolution of the classical dance and its problems now seem much more real to me, and touch me more closely than the distant aesthetics of Fokine ...
> And if I appreciate so highly the value of classical ballet, it is not simply a matter of taste on my part, but because I see exactly in it the perfect expression of the Apollonian [as opposed to Dionysian] principle.[119]

It was always to classical ballet that Stravinsky referred from now on when speaking about dance – the grand tradition – and *Apollo* had affirmed this in several ways. After his *Sleeping Beauty* experience, it was his next nod to

Tchaikovsky. With its sublime lyricism and fundamental serenity, the work can be seen as a metaphor for the reconciliation of the various tensions in Stravinsky's life, and also as a signal of his renewed religious faith and need to return to dance on new terms of his own. Furthermore, as with much neoclassical art of the time and like *Oedipus* of the previous year, it appealed to the cultural authority of Greece, an authority magnified by the distance of time. Ballet turned out to be the principal medium through which Stravinsky chose to explore this interest: after *Apollo*, in *Persephone*, *Orpheus* and *Agon*.

It hardly needs repeating here how important *Apollo* was to the careers of both Stravinsky and Balanchine and how seminal a dance theatre work of the twentieth century it is now considered. Stravinsky called the collaboration 'among the most satisfying in my artistic life'.[120] For both artists, it was an exercise in elimination: an essay in the 'ballet blanc' tradition, gestures selected according to 'family relations',[121] a strings-only score. Diaghilev, although he had the effrontery to propose a cut in the score, watched a ballet rehearsal and pronounced, 'What he [Balanchine] is doing is magnificent. It is pure classicism, such as we have not seen since Petipa's.'[122]

In fact, the first *Apollo* happened in Washington, in a tiny auditorium within the Library of Congress, commissioned by the well-known arts benefactor Elizabeth Sprague Coolidge and choreographed by Adolph Bolm for an ad hoc assortment of dancers. Stravinsky never saw the result, chose to forget all about the Washington part of the story, and probably all along had his mind set on a Ballets Russes Paris production as the first 'real' premiere. He was clear in his contract that he should be 'free to offer the ballet to Europe and South America immediately after the American premiere'.[123] Although the original concept of the ballet was the composer's, Joseph maintains that Balanchine was involved in discussions in Nice and Monte Carlo and was even beginning to choreograph *Apollo* before the score reached Bolm in the USA.[124] Whatever the truth, Stravinsky imparted very clear directives to Washington, even conveying choreographic ideas and stipulations as to costume and design.

The musical form suited Stravinsky's interest in abstraction, with generic dance titles from the nineteenth-century lexicon: prologue, variations, pas d'action, pas de deux, coda and apotheosis, a suite of dances but without conventional dance rhythms. Walsh has described the style as 'immobility rendered mobile',[125] which matches the style of the 'story', if indeed it can be called thus. Slight as it is – the birth, the choice of Terpsichore as the ideal amongst the three Muses, the procession to Parnassus – what happens on stage happens as if frozen in time, as if the action has already taken place and is now recalled. The time tone is essentially the same as in *Scènes de ballet*, which has no real story at all (see pp. 265-6).

Stravinsky was pleased not only with *Apollo* but also with his next ballet score for Rubinstein, *Le Baiser de la fée.* He wrote a 1929 New Year greeting to Ansermet, citing the two ballets and confirming that the previous year had been one of the best and most important for his creative development.[126] There were conceptual links between these two works. *Baiser* was an overt homage to Tchaikovsky, the score dedicated to the composer, borrowing many themes, mostly from the composer's songs and piano music, although there were a number of allusions to the ballet scores as well. Theatrically, too, it was to be presented 'in classical form, after the manner of *Apollo*' with the 'fantastic roles ... danced in white ballet skirts',[127] and it adopted too the nineteenth-century tradition of an apotheosis. But, with a running time of 45 minutes, it was much longer than *Apollo*. It also returned to the nineteenth-century tradition of narrative ballet, with character transformations and disguises, and to the multi-act grand ballet, but in précis form with four linked scenes, for a twentieth-century context. In characteristic fashion, Rubinstein took the leading role of the Fairy for herself.

Benois, who designed the production, came up with the idea of the Tchaikovsky sources and may also have prompted the use of Hans Christian Andersen's *The Ice Maiden*, with its theme of the Muse's fatal kiss. Together, he and Stravinsky agreed a Swiss Alpine setting, Interlaken in the 1850s, in the manner of the original story. By the time his score was published, Stravinsky's own views on the staging were very clear, about where he was willing to be flexible and where he was not. In the note to his piano score, he insisted:

> The strict and precise indications for the movements of the characters in this ballet as given in my score are intended to form *a fixed basis* for the producer.

Yet he was far more flexible about the context of the staging:

> On the other hand, the vagueness and imprecision of my directions concerning the place and period of the action are meant to give designer and producer full freedom to construct a choreographic spectacle directly on the character and style of the music.

The surprise is Stravinsky's opinion of Nijinska's contribution, indeed, his whole approach to this 'collaboration'. It is worth digressing here because the documentary evidence reveals especially strongly Stravinsky's determination to be in control of a theatrical conception and possibly, too, what he really thought of the status of a choreographer. His tone in correspondence is domineering and mistrusting and, dangerously late on during the collaborative process, he even discouraged his publisher Païchadze from releasing his score to her:

It is necessary for people such as they are – not particularly initiated – that I play the music for them myself ... Nijinskaya will howl, but do not pay any attention to that.[128]

He soon had to relent and send the score in stages from the Haute-Savoie to Paris, but he demanded through Païchadze that Nijinska should strictly observe the metronome indications, betraying his anxiety about choreographers' tempi.[129] A week later he asked Païchadze to insist that the bride should not appear in the third and final Scene, as had been initially proposed.

I am informing Nijinskaya about this particularly ... for fear that she would not pay attention to the text and take the absence of the bride's last appearance as an omission, or as forgetfulness on my part.[130]

Perhaps Stravinsky's tone betrays his considerable unease at not being involved in the staging of the production, which was his normal procedure by this time. In this case, the race against time to complete an exceptionally lengthy score kept him away. Increasingly as his career progressed, and to the point of obstinacy, Stravinsky was confident of his own theatrical conceptions and dismissive when his own plans or ideals were not adhered to. Typically, too, he distanced himself from failure, absolving himself of responsibility, setting himself above the event and, as we shall see in relation to Balanchine (see pp. 221-2), *Baiser* was always to be a problem ballet score. After the premiere of *Baiser*, Stravinsky would surely have been sore about the cool reception and lack of appreciation for what some critics viewed as his retrogressive pastiche. In his *Autobiography* he writes:

I found some of the scenes successful and worthy of Nijinska's talent. But there was, on the other hand, a good deal of which I could not approve, and which, had I been present at the moment of their composition, I should have tried to get altered. But it was now too late for any interference on my part, and I had, whether I liked it or not, to leave things as they were. It is hardly surprising in these circumstances that the choreography of *Le Baiser de la fée* left me cold.[131]

Other evidence clarifies that Stravinsky *did* believe in Nijinska's talent. We do not hear of any problems between them before this, and by 1960 he appears to be positively enthusiastic: 'her choreography for the original productions of *Renard* (1922) and *Noces* (1923) pleased me more than any other works of mine as interpreted by the Diaghilev troupe'.[132]

They pleased him more than *Apollo*? This is indeed doubtful, but what about the contractual note stipulating that Stravinsky wanted to be 'free to offer the ballet [*Apollo*] to Europe and South America immediately after the American premiere'? Nijinska was working at the Teatro Colón in Buenos Aires at the time, 1926–7, and she had reported to him the success of her *Noces* revival there.[133] It sounds as if he rated her highly enough to be a serious contender for another *Apollo* production. Stravinsky's writings are typically contradictory and, even if he heaped high praise on *Renard* and *Noces* at one moment, at others he clearly stressed again that he did not like to see his own intentions thwarted. He never let go of the fact that Nijinska had gone her own way with *Noces* – his own theatrical vision was of a more hybrid piece with musicians as well as dancers on stage (see p. 336).[134] Perhaps it was her cavalier attitude then – and perhaps her choreographic success increased his irritation – that contributed to his petulance when the *Baiser* collaboration came along.

Persephone was Stravinsky's second Rubinstein commission and another of his hybrid dance works to include words. Rubinstein was already celebrated as a theatrical entrepreneur promoting hybrids that required extensive resources.[135] Here, there was a speaking dancer-mime in the title role, further dancers (soloists and a chorus), a solo tenor (as narrator who addresses both us and the stage protagonists), a singing chorus supplemented by a children's choir in the third and final scene, and an orchestra. 'Neither opera, nor ballet, but rather, if you insist on a label, melodrama', was Stravinsky's verdict on the genre of his new piece,[136] the score comprising sung sections, often in a declamatory style, recitation and instrumental interludes. *Persephone* was another Greek work, with the libretto commissioned from André Gide, who had come up with its topic. It was based on the Homeric myth about Demeter, the corn goddess, and her daughter Persephone, who is fated to commute between the underworld, where she is married to Pluto, and the earth, where she is married to Demophoon/Triptolemus (he is given two names in the text), following the seasonal cycle. But Gide inflected the original story in a particular way that would have attracted Stravinsky, as a Christianised reading with Persephone demonstrating free will and compassion for those in the underworld, not merely raped and abducted by Pluto, not passive, rather redeemed through her act of renunciation. The section in the third scene, when the chorus celebrates Persephone's return to earth, Stravinsky called 'Russian Easter music'.[137] Stravinsky worked closely with Gide on the libretto. Again, Rubinstein took the speaking/dancing (or rather miming) title role for herself in the new work.

Stravinsky was pleased to have as director Jacques Copeau, whom he already knew and admired, the one-time director of the Théâtre du Vieux-Colombier (see p. 46) who had read the whole text of *Histoire du soldat* in a 1929 performance in Paris.[138] Copeau shared the Christian convictions of the other collaborators and an interest in ancient Greek drama. The programme note for *Persephone* explained that it was conceived in the manner of a religious celebration (another Stravinsky ritual), with the characters on stage acting as if they were officiants of the Eleusinian cult of Demeter. Copeau chose the designer André Barsacq, who provided a set of Greek-style columns and arches, and possibly also the choreographer Kurt Jooss.[139] Stravinsky had already turned down the idea of Fokine as choreographer, although he had then insisted that either Balanchine or Massine should be invited to do the job.[140] Instead, Jooss arrived, from the German modern dance tradition, still fresh from winning the first international choreographers' competition in Paris in 1932 with *The Green Table*.

Gide was notably absent from both rehearsals and performances, because of disagreements with Stravinsky. These were partly a result of differences in their aesthetic and philosophical outlooks – the composer was suspicious that Gide, a declared communist, wanted to convey a political message[141] – but particularly an outcome of Stravinsky's modifying the syllabic structure of the French libretto to suit his own musical purposes, just as he had modified Russian texts in the past. Before the premiere, the composer wrote one of his typical manifestos on abstraction, asserting the importance of the syllable and sound over the word that carries thought.[142]

Persephone might well be another instance of Stravinsky's feeling of being removed from the development of a production and, possibly as a result of that, finding it unsatisfactory. He wrote economically in his *Autobiography*:

> My participation was limited to conducting the music. The scenic effects were created without consulting me. I should like here to express my appreciation of the efforts made by Kurt Jooss, as master choreographer, and my regret that the poet was absent both from rehearsals and the actual performances.[143]

The event of the premiere was recent, and Stravinsky would say no more. By the time of *Dialogues and a Diary* (1963), Stravinsky remembered the first production as 'visually unsatisfactory', and did not even bother to mention Jooss.[144] As a theatrical conception, *Persephone* does not demonstrate any of the ingenuity and network of theatrical tensions that we find in *Renard* or *Oedipus Rex*, but it is marvellous music, its lyricism and serenity aligning it with *Apollo*. The first production will be discussed in more detail in relation to Frederick Ashton's version (see pp. 299-301).

Stravinsky conducted the premieres of *Apollo*, *Baiser* and *Persephone*, and for *Apollo* he undertook a full run of performances in Paris and then London. Before this, Diaghilev had given him only occasional opportunities to conduct his ballets once they were in the repertory. There were also guest conducting opportunities abroad during this 'middle' period of his career, for instance three *Petrushka* productions: in Copenhagen, revived by Fokine for the Royal Danish

Ballet (1925); in Milan (four performances), a version by Boris Romanov, his colleague on *Le Rossignol* (1926);[145] and in Los Angeles at the Hollywood Bowl, *Petrushka Suite*, a spectacular staging after Fokine by the ex-Diaghilev dancer Theodore Kosloff (1937). He conducted four performances too for the Teatro Colón's Stravinsky Festival in Buenos Aires and Montevideo (1936), of *Firebird*, *Petrushka* and *Le Baiser de la fée*, which Nijinska revived (and possibly reworked) especially for the occasion.

The chronologies of Stravinsky's attendance at performances up to this point in his career suggest that his knowledge of and involvement with dance was almost entirely ballet-based, broadly defined as 'ballet' was by companies such as the Ballets Russes. But the chronologies are admittedly incomplete, with little reference to the popular entertainment or theatre including dance that Stravinsky might well have seen from time to time. His experience of European modern dance seems to have been slight. He had practical experience of Jooss's work on *Persephone*. Other than that, we know only that he visited the Bauhaus Exhibition in Weimar in 1923 and saw Oskar Schlemmer's *Triadic Ballet* (1922 – the title mentioned in Vera's diary[146]), the famous experiment exploring the abstract, masked body and its relationship to space. But he was in Weimar ostensibly to catch a performance of his own *Histoire du soldat*. He also saw the Swiss choreographer Max Terpis's *Petrushka* at the Berlin Staatsoper (1928), although the original *Petrushka* was inherently so unballetic that it may not have occurred to him that he was watching something by a modern dance choreographer. Here, the main attraction was *Oedipus Rex*, conducted by Otto Klemperer, the first stage performance that Stravinsky saw of this work.[147] The triple bill also included *Mavra*.

Still, the occasional proposal for a ballet came his way, without coming to fruition. One is especially interesting, hitherto unrecorded in the dance literature and worth quoting in full. It is a request dating from 1931 on behalf of the Camargo Society in London, the organisation that was instrumental in the formation of the Sadler's Wells (later Royal) Ballet. The signature is impossible to decipher:

> I have by me the typescript synopses of several I, II and III act Ballets which have been considered by the Committee of the Camargo Society for the Production of Ballet and am informed by the secretary that production cannot be contemplated in the absence of musical settings. One among them to which special reference is made is built upon a theme having Tartini and 'The Devil's Trill' as the central motive and the entire mise en scène is designed to represent a wild frolic of witches and demons.
>
> I am convinced that no living composer could interpret a theme of this kind with greater distinction than yourself, sir, and I am writing to ask

whether I may send the typescript for your perusal. It is not without diffidence that I make this request to a master in connection with what is only a small matter but should you feel disposed to look at the M.S. I should greatly appreciate your kindness in doing so and will forward it wherever you may direct.[148]

The proposed theme of 'a wild frolic of witches and demons' says more about the culture of British ballet at the time than anything about Stravinsky. There seems to have been little comprehension of the composer's current interests. The Basle archive files suggest that the composer did not bother to reply.

Period 3: 1937–71. The American composer: Balanchine as collaborator, and all Stravinsky becomes ballet music

Apart from *Persephone*, Stravinsky wrote nothing new for dance in the early 1930s. *Jeu de cartes,* commissioned for the American Ballet and premiered in 1937 within a full-evening Stravinsky Festival in New York, signalled a new beginning and a renewal of professional relations with Balanchine, following his work on *Le Chant du rossignol* and *Apollo* during the Diaghilev period. At this time too, America started to offer the composer concert commissions, and Harvard University invited him to take the Charles Eliot Norton Chair of Poetry (between 1939 and 1940), for which he was required to give a series of lectures. Meanwhile, as the political situation worsened, the scene in Europe became increasingly difficult. And there were family tragedies: the deaths of his eldest daughter in 1938, and of both his wife and his mother in 1939. That year, Stravinsky left Europe without knowing that it would be for good; in May 1940, he and Vera, now his second wife, made their permanent home in Hollywood.

It was during the American period that the Stravinsky–Balanchine collaboration firmed up into a virtual institution. Balanchine was always the first choreographer to spring to the composer's mind if a project involving dance was under discussion. Balanchine stands out as unique amongst Stravinsky's choreographer collaborators: there are absolutely no reservations about him in the Stravinsky literature, and in no other collaboration with a choreographer is there the sense of a developing equality in the relationship. They became very close friends too, sharing their common Russian heritage, socialising as frequently as their schedules permitted in New York and Los Angeles, with Balanchine a regular guest in the Stravinskys' Hollywood home. For the composer, Balanchine's companies, Ballet Society and its later development as New York City Ballet, became something like family. He entertained an affectionate relationship with several Balanchine dancers, including those who became his wives, Vera Zorina, Maria Tallchief and Tanaquil Le Clercq; the Basle archive files also contain warm letters from Diana Adams and Suzanne Farrell. After *Jeu de cartes*, the commissions involving dance from this period were *Orpheus*

(1948), *Agon* (1957) – the most brilliant score of the period, *The Flood* (1962) and a miniature curiosity ballet, *Circus Polka* (1942), which Balanchine conceived for fifty elephants, with Zorina riding the leading 'ballerina'. *Scènes de ballet* (1944) was the one ballet score not commissioned for Balanchine, being destined instead for the unusual circumstances of a Billy Rose Broadway revue 'The Seven Lively Arts.'

Yet, if we look at Stravinsky's American period as a whole – some thirty years – this is not a big output for dance, compared with what he achieved in his earlier career. He had developed broad creative interests by this time, and he maintained that breadth throughout his late career. This is one reason why, apart from the collaboration with Balanchine, which has been especially well covered by Joseph, Stravinsky's association with dance during this period is far less well documented than it is for the earlier years. But there is an additional story to tell.

Stravinsky's decision to live in Hollywood with his second wife Vera meant that, for much of the time, he lived away from the dance mainstream. Another explanation was that, alongside his composing, he was a globetrotting conductor and major musical celebrity. During the 1940s, including the whole of the Second World War, his tours were almost exclusively within the USA. Later, he travelled abroad, often extensively, until 1967, when illness finally ended this way of life. Aside from their regular visits to Europe, which included the Eastern bloc countries (and the USSR in 1962), the Stravinskys visited South and Central America on numerous occasions, Israel (twice), Japan, Australia, New Zealand and South Africa.

Nonetheless, despite their hectic travelling schedule, their visits to New York became increasingly frequent annual events, often lasting a month or more and often over the Christmas and New Year period. There, the composer could catch up on the artistic scene, and dance remained an important part of this. The chronology for the years 1950 and 1951 gives an example of their attendance at New York City Ballet. There were at least seven performances during four weeks in February–March 1950, and 'many ballets' during their month in New York in November–December 1951. Vera reports that they saw Balanchine's 1951 premieres of *Swan Lake*, *La Valse* (Ravel) and *Tyl Eulenspiegel* (Richard Strauss), and that they found performances at the Metropolitan Opera much less interesting.[149] Stravinsky lived the last nineteen months of his life in New York; he died on 6 April 1971. Vera's diary tells us that she still attended dance performances during this period, but it is highly unlikely that he would have felt well enough to join her.

Especially noteworthy is the importance Stravinsky attached to keeping in touch with dance contacts from the past and to maintaining his close circle of Russian émigré friends associated with dance. On the whole, he respected their opinions. In Hollywood, there was Eugene Berman, the Russian designer, who came to the USA in 1937, and Adolph Bolm, the dancer/choreographer. Bolm had emigrated after a distinguished dancing career with the Ballets Russes and had settled in California in the 1930s. He proved a valuable ally in promoting the work of his composer friend, also helping him to acquire American citizenship in 1940. Although Stravinsky had reservations about his creative skills,[150] Bolm developed a considerable reputation as a choreographer and ballet master in the USA. At the Metropolitan Opera House in New York, he staged *Petrushka* (1919), and for Washington he choreographed the original American *Apollo* (1928). Later, he was responsible for settings of both the 1919 and 1945 *Firebird Suites*, the first version for the Adolph Bolm Ballet in 1940 (another spectacular at the Hollywood Bowl, where Bolm was resident choreographer), the second for Ballet Theatre, New York, in 1945 (see p. 135). Other close friends from the 1920s Diaghilev period now resident in the USA were the Russian Nicolas Nabokov (composer of *Ode*, 1928) and the Italian Vittorio Rieti (composer of *Barabau*, 1925, and *Le Bal*, 1929). Stravinsky referred regularly to Pavel Tchelitcheff (designer of *Ode*) as a potential designer for his ballets.

Stravinsky's dance contacts extended into the larger professional arena. We read in the diaries that he attended a dinner party in Los Angeles in 1952 hosted by Ludovic Kennedy and his wife Moira Shearer (of the Sadler's Wells Ballet, and by then famous from the 1948 film *The Red Shoes*), at which Frederick Ashton was also present. He met Ashton again in Copenhagen in 1955 when the British choreographer was creating *Romeo and Juliet* for the Royal Danish Ballet. According to Vera in her diary,[151] this encounter took place in a hotel foyer, with the dancer-teacher Vera Volkova present, although Julie Kavanagh, Ashton's biographer, describes a friendly meeting at the theatre. They embraced, and Ashton recalled saying, 'What are you doing tonight?' to which Stravinsky replied, 'I'm having dinner with you'. It seems that they developed a friendship.[152] Stravinsky met Ashton at least once again in London in 1961, after conducting *Persephone* in concert but before the choreographer's setting of the score (see p. 312). At some time in the 1950s, the composer also met Robert Helpmann, another *Red Shoes* star.[153] Then, in 1967, Fonteyn and Nureyev called by; Craft reports that 'after trying to avoid the visit, I.S. was especially lively during it'.[154] And there was contact with the Soviet ballet community after the thaw that had allowed Stravinsky's music to be heard once more in the USSR. In 1966, the Bolshoi Ballet choreographer Yuri Grigorovitch came to dinner, although there is no record that the Stravinskys attended a performance by his touring company. In 1968, the Bolshoi dancer Maya Plisetskaya also paid a visit.

Several of the companies that we know Stravinsky saw touring the West Coast of America or in New York had strong connections with Diaghilev's Ballets Russes. There were the repertory companies drawing from the work of the Diaghilev choreographers Fokine, Massine and Balanchine: the Ballet Russe de

Monte Carlo and Original Ballet Russe of de Basil, the two successors to Diaghilev's Ballets Russes. There were also the companies led by Balanchine, promoting above all his own choreography, but also showing occasional works by Jerome Robbins or other company choreographers: American Ballet, Ballet Society and New York City Ballet. Lucia Chase's Ballet Theatre, later named American Ballet Theatre, opened in 1940 and introduced Stravinsky to the work of Antony Tudor and probably that of Agnes de Mille, as well as earlier Robbins choreography. The composer also went to see Balanchine's choreography for the commercial theatre: the Broadway musical comedies *Cabin in the Sky* (1940, with Katherine Dunham and her dancers and an all-black cast)[155] and *House of Flowers* (1955), and, in Los Angeles, the operetta *Song of Norway* (1944).

Stravinsky had professional links with all these ballet companies, but it was the Balanchine organisations and Ballet Theatre that held sway and sometimes competed for him. Joseph has documented in great detail the rivalry between Chase and Lincoln Kirstein, the business mind behind Balanchine's operations.[156] As early as 1941, Stravinsky had dealings with Chase, arranging the 'Bluebird' pas de deux from *Sleeping Beauty* for her use, and later conducting the company (in 1948, back-to-back with Kirstein's organisation, conducting *Apollo* for Chase the evening before the premiere of *Orpheus* for Ballet Society). For a while, she even entertained the idea of a Balanchine setting of *Scènes de ballet* (see p. 261). Stravinsky was willing to respond to her courtship: in 1947, he agreed to join the Board of the Ballet Theatre Foundation, although wording his response with typical caution, absolving himself of any responsibilities. He would not 'assume definitely and absolutely any obligations or participation' in financial or artistic matters.[157]

In 1965, now a composer of serial music, he wrote Chase a twelve-note row as a gift to mark the 'Silver Wedding' of her company.[158] As well as promoting Balanchine, New York City Ballet and Ballet Theatre showcased the work of Robbins and Tudor. This is important because, from what the Stravinsky literature suggests, these were the only 'new' choreographers he came across in the USA whose work genuinely interested him.

Robbins danced and choreographed for Ballet Theatre in the 1940s, creating for them his sensationally successful *Fancy Free* (1944), seen by Stravinsky, after which he divided his time between Broadway and the ballet world, gaining worldwide attention with *West Side Story* in 1957. He became associate artistic director of New York City Ballet 1949–59, returning to the company as ballet master from 1969 until his retirement in 1990. As Robbins was frequently pursuing a musically-based kind of work that was complementary to Balanchine's neoclassicism, the association with City Ballet was logical. On a number of occasions, as we shall see, Stravinsky turned down Robbins's requests to use his music (see pp. 78-9), but they entertained considerable mutual respect – the composer may well have been impressed by the choreographer's artistic and commercial success – and Robbins was meticulous about sending him regular birthday greetings. After Balanchine, Robbins is the most cited choreographer in Vera's diary. In 1953, when he originally considered staging *Noces* for La Scala, Milan, he wrote to Stravinsky for advice about the technical aspects of the score, and visited him on the West Coast to discuss this (see p. 389). Stravinsky attended an early performance of the American Ballet Theatre production in 1965 and enjoyed it. He had looked forward to seeing the work and, in an out-take from a CBS television documentary on Stravinsky, mentioning his curiosity about the forthcoming production, the composer praised Robbins as 'a very talented man', referring to him as a pupil of Balanchine. The choreographer had enthused, 'It's extraordinary because Robbins is an American and he understood so well the Russian gestures ... not the official Russian gestures but the musical gestures.'[159]

The association with Balanchine was important to Stravinsky. Another City Ballet choreographer, Todd Bolender (who set *Pulcinella Suite* as *Comedia Balletica* in 1945), he referred to as 'un de ses [Balanchine's] jeunes et brillants emules [sic]'.[160] So Bolender was seen as a Balanchine 'emulator', in the school of the great master whom Stravinsky admired so much, and perhaps that very fact encouraged the composer to be sympathetic to his work.

The Stravinskys saw a number of works by Antony Tudor at Ballet Theatre: *Jardin aux lilas* in 1940 (1936, Chausson), in 1943 *Pillar of Fire* (1942, Schoenberg), *Gala Performance* (1938, Prokofiev) and *Romeo and Juliet* (1943, Delius), and in 1948 *Shadow of the Wind* (1948, Mahler). Vera's diaries suggest that they much enjoyed *Jardin* and *Pillar*; both are among Tudor's most celebrated works.[161] Compliments of this kind are sparing in the diaries, mostly being reserved for Balanchine, and are all the more remarkable given that Tudor himself never set any Stravinsky and worked from a very different, narrative-expressionist aesthetic: he was in no way part of Balanchine's neoclassical school. But Tudor was one of the outstanding choreographers of the century, and his name emerges in the archival files on a couple of occasions as a potential collaborator, a tentatively suggested alternative to Balanchine for film and theatre proposals (see p. 70). It is interesting too that, although they both declined, Tudor and Ashton were the only choreographers outside the New York City Ballet circle invited to contribute to its 1972 Stravinsky Festival.[162]

Maurice Béjart is another choreographer whose name regularly appears in the archive files, if for very different reasons. Since the premiere of his 1959 *Sacre*, Béjart had become the most celebrated choreographer operating in continental Europe: he represented a new contemporary radicalism within ballet and developed an ecstatic, youthful following wherever he toured, including the USA. The high point of his international success was the 1960s. More than with any other work, Béjart was associated with Stravinsky's *Sacre*. No wonder then that Stravinsky took notice of his progress, and listened to what his friends had to say about his work, especially as he had a close working relationship with Pierre Boulez, a composer-conductor whose career Stravinsky also followed. Stravinsky met Béjart at least once. He was in the Stravinsky entourage in 1966, attending a screening of the CBS documentary on the composer for French critics in Paris.[163] In terms of his work, Stravinsky was unimpressed; he despised Béjart's twisting of the original libretti of his ballets and the tone of his programme notes. In the Basle archive is a 1959 *Sacre* programme sent to the composer, which included a lengthy note about the sexual union of man and woman as symbolic of the act of creation, in the manner of a 'universal' message (see p. 445). Stravinsky was alarmed from the start by the new take and, according to Mario Bois, the manager of Boosey & Hawkes's Paris office, he even pushed for the work to be banned.[164] In the margin next to Béjart's note, Stravinsky wrote 'Quel idiot!'. In 1968, as he criticised the legal arrangements behind the Belgian film of *Sacre*, he prejudged the work on hearsay: 'I did not see Béjart's choreography, but reliable opinion says that it is very bad.'[165] When he did eventually get to see it at the Paris Opéra a couple of months later, he left the theatre in good spirits, nonetheless dropping the cryptic remark, 'the problem with *Sacre* is the music'.[166] *Sacre* was probably the only Béjart work that Stravinsky actually saw.

Before *Sacre*, Béjart had created a *Pulcinella* (1957), for which he had likewise hatched a new plot, set in eighteenth-century Naples, about a duke who falls in love with the leading actress of a travelling troupe (of which Pulcinella is director). It was a farce involving various disguises and ending in the reconciliation of the duke and his duchess. Here, Stravinsky wrote in the margin of the programme note, 'Why not use one of the better Italian [*commedia*] plots involving Pulcinella like we did with Diaghilev?'.[167]

The Stravinsky archive sheds little light on his experience of Ashton's choreography and the Sadler's Wells/Royal Ballet. This company enjoyed a big reputation in the USA, following its first appearance there in 1949. The Stravinskys saw it three times in Los Angeles in 1953, performing *Swan Lake*, *The Sleeping Beauty* and Ashton's *Sylvia*.[168] Stravinsky had already got to know something of Ashton's work through New York City Ballet, for which company Ashton made two ballets in the early 1950s, both of them of a literary kind. He certainly saw the premiere of *Illuminations* (1950), using Benjamin Britten's song cycle and based on the life and poems of Arthur Rimbaud. During a later trip to New York, he might well have seen the ballet again and also *Picnic at Tintagel* (Bax, 1952), about a party of tourists who find themselves transported into a re-enactment of the Tristan and Isolde story. Perhaps Stravinsky took a special interest in Ashton and his company partly because of this recent connection. Yet we know that the

Stravinskys were in Los Angeles when the Royal Ballet returned (regularly every two years), although there is no longer any record of their attendance. Perhaps working professional links were all-important to Stravinsky, or perhaps Vera simply omitted to note Royal Ballet performances in her diary. Occasionally, she mentions other performance visits that are out of the ordinary: to a company called the 'Ballet Nègre' (1949), and to the 'Ukrainian Ballet' (1966), Pavel Virsky's then internationally popular Ukrainian Dance Company.

One other organisation, the Santa Fe Opera, deserves mention for its promotion of two of Stravinsky's hybrid dance theatre pieces during the annual summer seasons at its new open-air theatre. The association with the composer began in 1957 with a staging of the opera *The Rake's Progress*. Stravinsky himself became unusually involved and attended performances annually during 1958–63. In 1961 he conducted *Persephone*, with designs from sketches by Vera, and, later that year, the same company again in Berlin and Belgrade. *Persephone* was kept in the repertoire for the following season, and revived in 1968. Meeting the dance critic Walter Terry in Santa Fe, Stravinsky was enthusiastic: 'This was the *Perséphone* I always dreamed of and never saw until now.'[169] The choreographer was Thomas Andrew, a dancer/choreographer with the Metropolitan Opera in New York, and the title role was taken by Balanchine's ex-wife, the dancer/actress Vera Zorina, whom the composer much admired (see pp. 313-14). In 1962, Stravinsky turned 80, and John Crosby, director at Santa Fe, proudly promoted his prize connection with a Stravinsky Festival. The plan was to present Stravinsky's complete operatic works for the Festival, and, had there been a resident ballet company, many more of his ballets would have featured.[170] Balanchine had been invited to direct *Rossignol*, but was unable to undertake the task.[171] Once again, the composer himself conducted the new production, of *Renard* (another choreography by Andrew), and the 'Stravinsky and the Dance' exhibition that had opened in New York in May moved over to Santa Fe. In an interview printed in the Festival programme, Crosby surely overstated his case, apparently oblivious to Stravinsky's longstanding relationship with Balanchine and his associated organisations:

> Words cannot express Santa Fe's great fortune of having the honor to be associated with Igor Stravinsky; it is notable that his participation in Santa Fe Opera productions since 1957 seems to be the longest Stravinsky association with any one organization since the Diaghilev era which ended in the 20s. And the two and one half months which Stravinsky will have spent in Santa Fe last summer and this summer probably represent the longest time in one place for him during the past several years.[172]

But Crosby was right about the strength of the connection with Stravinsky, for,

as well as the two dance theatre productions mentioned above, Santa Fe presented *Rossignol* (Balanchine's absence notwithstanding), *Mavra, Oedipus Rex*
and *The Flood* during 1962.

Stravinsky undertook other ballet conducting during this period, maintaining a lasting connection with Balanchine's companies over the years, but making additional appearances with the Original Ballet Russe, Ballet Russe de Monte
Carlo, Ballet Theatre and London Festival Ballet. He was also responsible for the
premieres of *Jeu de cartes* and *Orpheus*, but neither *Scènes de ballet* (first performed
within Billy Rose's revue) nor *Agon*. Kirstein could not afford him for the immensely successful *Agon*, and, extraordinary as it now seems, he even went
home to the West Coast and missed the premiere in New York.[173] Appearances
with Ballet Theatre (1943–4) and London Festival Ballet (1954–5) were promoted by Sol Hurok – excellent opportunities by ballet standards, each company
offering Stravinsky a whole series of performances and good money. They also
contribute significantly to the statistic that the composer conducted *Petrushka*
more than any of his other ballets (at least twenty-five times, far more frequently
than *Firebird*, which was his most frequently conducted score in concert). The
norm was for Stravinsky to take charge of just one piece, to his own music, on a
ballet programme. Perhaps, after a while, the ballet world could no longer afford
the expensive composer, or he was dissatisfied with the performance standards
of their orchestras (see pp. 75-6). His final appearance as a ballet conductor
seems to have been in Santa Fe in 1962, whereas he stopped conducting
concerts in 1967. In 1965, however, he did go to Hamburg, where he made a
notoriously fast recording of *Apollo* before the televising of Balanchine's ballet.

Taking an overview of Stravinsky's association with dance during his American years, there seems to have been a peak period of involvement during the
1940s and early 1950s, but the grounds are very different from those of the
Diaghilev period, and new commissions were not the reason for this involvement. Perhaps Stravinsky saw ballet as a vital means of promoting his work in
his new home country, a useful financial prospect during the early, leaner years;
perhaps he welcomed the professional contact that it afforded as he entered a
new phase in his life (before the foreign tours began in 1951), but probably
equally, he maintained a genuine interest in the form.

Quite apart from the connections with the various ballet companies already
mentioned and the two commissions (*Orpheus* and the little *Circus Polka*),
Stravinsky was now actively involved in the new stagings by Balanchine of his
existing scores, attending ballet rehearsals in New York and assisting with musi-
cal direction. He worked on *Renard* (1947)[174] and *Firebird Suite* (1949) for
Kirstein's organisation, and *Apollo* (1943) for Ballet Theatre; a restaging of
Balanchine's *Le Baiser de la fée* for the Ballet Russe de Monte Carlo in 1946; and
Balanchine's settings of his concert works, *Balustrade* (1941, to the *Violin Con-*

certo) for the Original Ballet Russe and *Danses Concertantes* (1944) for the Ballet Russe de Monte Carlo.

Meanwhile, Stravinsky must have been aware of the burgeoning American modern dance tradition – it certainly knew about him – but, surprisingly, there is no evidence that he had any direct experience of it at all. While he was touring in the USA in February 1940, Vera took herself to a performance by Martha Graham, describing her in her diary as a dancing 'skeleton', although acknowledging her considerable technical expertise.[175] But we do not hear that Stravinsky ever got to see Graham. In 1944, the choreographer herself toyed with the idea of commissioning a score from him, another Coolidge commission to be premiered in the tiny Library of Congress auditorium that had hosted the first *Apollo*. Coolidge had suggested Stravinsky's name amongst others. Aaron Copland, who had already been commissioned to write *Appalachian Spring*, encouraged Graham to choose Stravinsky. But, although Graham was enthusiastic, she was also realistic, her response to Coolidge saying it all:

> I do know that Stravinsky is interested only in the Ballet. I think he has never seen any performance of modern dance, either mine or any one else in that field ... Of course his music is magical for dance and theatre performance. And I am greatly excited by it.[176]

Graham waited until 1984 before setting Stravinsky for the first time: her *Sacre*. Writing for Minna Lederman's *Stravinsky in the Theatre*, Nabokov relays Stravinsky's highly conservative stance on modern dance. As the tone of Lederman's collection of essays is overwhelmingly one of tributes, with friends and colleagues flattering the composer, we can assume that Nabokov is acting here as spokesman:

> [Stravinsky] recognized that if ballet were to deviate from its rigid classicism it would become that nebulous form of entertainment we now call modern dancing, which so often has neither canon nor form.[177]

On the other hand, the Stravinskys did get to see a range of dance in the commercial world of musicals and films, partly because of the Balanchine connection again, but also because they liked to keep abreast of their local Hollywood scene. However, no doubt about it, the composer's personal creative horizons for dance had narrowed over the years. The considerable accomplishments of his later years lie entirely within the field of dance classicism, canon and form, and particularly Balanchine classicism with its shared tendencies towards frozen narrative and abstraction.

Conservatively, the term 'collaboration' refers to the situation where two or more people share ideas in creating a new work (whether in early discussion or later work in the dance studio) and all involved allow their personal vision to be changed: in other words, there is a dialectical process. The term is used more liberally here to cover not only the pieces for which a score was especially commissioned, but also ballets to existing scores. Joseph favours this more open definition and makes the case that the composer was actively involved during Balanchine's setting of several existing scores, from the first time he played the piano at rehearsals of *Le Chant du rossignol* through to the 1960s and the serial scores, readily discussing the technical details of the music and offering advice on how to handle them.[178] In other words, Balanchine was likely to have been influenced by Stravinsky's opinions. But who knows – he might not have been aware himself – how many ideas the composer might have picked up from his respected friend and put on hold for future use? Joseph also charts a working relationship between the two men that developed over time.

For the first Balanchine premiere, *Jeu de cartes*, Stravinsky made many decisions before Balanchine became creatively involved: the scenario based on the three deals of a poker game (worked out with the assistance of Nikita Malayev), the length, stage design and even the size of cast. In an illuminating account of rehearsals, Kirstein recalls his 'detailed and exactly plotted plan' – for Stravinsky had scored in great detail a series of dance events and complex confrontations between characters – but

> for all questions of interpretation within his indicated limits of personal style or private preference, he has a respectful generosity. He is helpful in a wholly practical sense.[179]

In other words, the composer was intensely involved in the matters of theatre, offering choreographic suggestions – for example, the elimination of pirouettes and the occasional introduction of repetition rather than new material.[180] The phrase 'indicated limits of personal style or private preference' suggests Stravinsky's clear boundaries on what he considered suitable. Yet the composer was willing to compose some additional music at one point to suit the developing choreography. There are numerous records of Stravinsky literally demonstrating dance moves in such studio situations, and this was not the first occasion. It was a sign of his theatrical confidence as well as his own urgent sense of physicality, both of which in turn imbued his music (see pp. 93-6).

Orpheus was the brainchild of Balanchine (strongly supported by Kirstein), and a ballet based on the myth of the musician who descended into Hades to recover his wife Eurydice. Yet, once the basic idea had been established, it marked the beginning of a more conversational relationship between composer and choreographer from start to completion. Developing an increasing admiration for

Balanchine, Stravinsky would defer more frequently to his ideas. Again, it is well known that Stravinsky lengthened passages in his *Orpheus* score to suit the choreographic demands, most famously the moment of Eurydice's death, where four counts got added to the score.[181] The *Orpheus* collaboration set the pattern for the two works that followed: *Agon*, a plotless ballet referencing seventeenth-century dance types, and *The Flood*, a dance drama for television based on the story of Noah. In each case, the initial idea came from Stravinsky, although, crucially, *Agon* was prompted by Kirstein sending him a period dance manual by François de Lauze. The gestation period for the latter work was unusually long, Kirstein in 1948 having asked for an Act III to complete a trilogy that opened with *Apollo* and *Orpheus*. But, by then, Stravinsky was preoccupied with other work, most importantly his opera *The Rake's Progress* (1951). He began to write the new ballet score in 1953. Still, with Balanchine closely involved in discussions about the structure and nature of the piece, it took him until 1957 to complete the score, and thus some parts of it are serial-phase music (see p. 21). In the meantime, Kirstein had other plans for the use of existing Stravinsky ballet scores, none of which came to anything. There was the idea for a *Petrushka* with Tchelitcheff designs in 1951.[182] Correspondence between Stravinsky and Kirstein continued for years (1948–57) about a possible *Pulcinella*, which Balanchine and Robbins eventually choreographed jointly in 1972.

One additional score needs introduction, *Scènes de ballet* (1944), commissioned for a Broadway revue as a vehicle for the star dancers Anton Dolin and Alicia Markova. Dolin initiated the idea behind the work, which drew from nineteenth-century sources, although there was no libretto in the conventional sense. Three sections labelled 'Pantomime' suggest a story element, but they are hardly descriptive music: *Scènes* is fundamentally a plotless ballet, a suite of dances. Indeed, the ballet scores of the American period as a whole clearly demonstrate a move towards abstraction and suite form, drawing from the tradition of *Apollo*. Although about a poker game, *Jeu de cartes* already points in this direction: the score is distinctly formal, comprising three sections (the three deals), each of which contains discrete set numbers, no mime sections, and some named dances, such as Pas d'Action, Variation, March, Waltz-Minuet. This was a light-hearted, easy-on-the-ear kind of score – a number of Stravinsky's American works of the 1930s and 40s were popular in tone, even commercially driven – with lots of references to the nineteenth century, and even some quotations from Rossini, Johann Strauss and Ravel. After *Jeu*, we have the little elephant ballet (a polka), then *Scènes*, and finally *Agon*, which bears a Greek title meaning 'contest' but is in actuality the most abstract conception of all: no more than a suite of movements bearing dance titles (including those representing a period, such as the Bransles, Saraband and Gailliarde). After all, leaving aside the polka, some kind of 'story' activated Stravinsky to start all the other ballet scores. *Orpheus* is a hybrid dance theatre work, the style mainly pantomime and prop manipulation, with luscious dramatic entwinement in the pas de deux for Orpheus and Eurydice, but not so much classical dance – indeed, very little dance momentum at all save in the choreography for the Bacchantes. Yet even here we see far more of an episodic, suite structure than in most of Stravinsky's early ballets – a series of dances as framework for a story; after *Apollo*, it was another mythological essay in mobilised immobility (see p. 49). Contradictions surround Stravinsky's *Danses Concertantes* (1942) as to whether or not it was actually conceived for dance (see pp. 79-80). It was premiered in concert and later set by Balanchine. Certainly, it confirms Stravinsky's predilection for structuring dance in suite form during this period.

The Flood, a late, serial score, is very different in kind from the other dance scores of the American period. According to Stravinsky's own account, it represented a return to the texted theatrical conceptions of the European period. After discussion with Balanchine, he wrote to the television producer Robert Graff:

> I do not yet see the exact *form* of this work, whether it will employ a chorus, what kind of instrumentation, whether or not a narrator, but I do think it might be theatrically, if not musically, closer to my *Oedipus Rex* and *Persephone* than to any other works of mine.[183]

Stravinsky had originally wanted T.S. Eliot to write the text, but in the end the libretto was shaped by Craft and based principally on the Book of Genesis and the Chester and York Miracle Plays. Subtitled 'dance drama', *The Flood* included sung sections and spoken melodrama by actors, as well as two dance interludes, 'The Building of the Ark' and 'The Flood'. The thorny question persisted as to what the new work really was and how to pigeonhole it in such a way as to be comprehensible to media and press. Was it an opera or a ballet for television? Together, Stravinsky and Balanchine countered both descriptions.[184] But when they knew better themselves what form the work was taking, they wrote to Graff admitting:

> We have worked out a choreographic visualization ... and your earlier publicity releases about *The Flood* calling it a Stravinsky–Balanchine ballet are now more precise than we at that time thought. It is in fact a 'choreographic allegory' ...[185]

As for the television aspect of the work, Stravinsky went into print with some high-sounding comments about the new form of musical writing that it prompted:

The saving of musical time interests me more than anything visual. This new musical economy was the one specific of the medium guiding my conception of *The Flood* ... So far I have not been able to imagine the work on the operatic stage because the musical speed is so uniquely cinematographic.[186]

In fact, Stravinsky's vision was considerably mediated throughout the process, by Craft, by Balanchine (who already had television experience), and most importantly by the medium itself. The result has gone down in history as a failure, showing misjudgement of the medium and its public by all concerned, the 'work' drowning in television gimmickry, dark lighting and masks that submerged the dancers and the choreography, framed awkwardly by shampoo commercials and pre- and post-performance commentary. The British actor Laurence Harvey introduced the programme with references to the importance of high art and allusions to various flood myths and the current threat of The Bomb. Rehearsal footage featuring Balanchine and Stravinsky followed the event. If *Flood* referred back to the challenging theatrical conceptions of Stravinsky's past, it failed to address the possibilities of the medium of the future.

For years, Stravinsky had despised the commercial media. He never completed a contract despite several aborted attempts to get into film, yet remained interested in what the media might offer him. Of one thing he was clear: the principles behind any musical composition for the media. This links with the discussion of his dance activity.[187]

During his American period, Stravinsky's published statements on dance continue to demonstrate his commitment to classicism. In 1945, he talked about the recent *Scènes*:

Ballet is the purest form of theatre art ... [I want] to return to the classical dance in all its beauty and purity. These Ballet Scenes are in the nature of music that would be composed today if the classical ballet dominated as it did at that time.[188]

And later, in 1954, there is affirmation of a tradition cast in stone:

Movements of all sorts may be introduced into the dance, but on the condition that the canons of the dance and its immutable laws are respected.[189]

But some of his most detailed thoughts on dance classicism, as well as on relations in general between music and dance, emerge in a 1946 interview with Ingolf Dahl that is ostensibly about film music. The frame is a diatribe about the commercial film world, its poor musical standards and pandering to the masses.

Stravinsky explains that the days of his descriptive, narrative music such as *Petrushka* are long past, but then he claims that abstraction is at the root of all ballet, even the nineteenth-century narrative ballet. Baldly stated like this, the assertion seems rather absurd, but Stravinsky's main point that ballet stories are principally an excuse for dancing merely accords with his own ahistorical, 'objective' terms, and thus, again, he bolsters his commitment to the movement values of ballet classicism:

> The ballet consists of movements which have their own aesthetic and logic, and if one of those movements should happen to be a visualization of the words 'I Love You', then this reference to the external world would play the same role in the dance (and in my music) that a guitar in a Picasso still-life would play: something of the world is caught as pretext of clothing for the inherent abstraction. Dancers have nothing to narrate and neither has my music. Even in older ballets like *Giselle*, descriptiveness has been removed – by virtue of its naivete, its unpretentious traditionalism and its simplicity – to a level of objectivity and pure art-play.

Continuing in the same vein, using recent plotless ballet examples, he advocates that form should drive music and dance and their relationship, and he uses the image of two arts living side by side as if 'happily married':

> In *Scènes de Ballet* the dramatic action was given by an evolution of plastic problems, and both dance and music had to be constructed on the architectural feeling for contrast and similarity ...

He writes approvingly that, when Balanchine choreographed *Danses Concertantes*, he worked from the structural foundations of the music:

> He approached the problem architecturally and not descriptively. And his success was extraordinary for one great reason: he went to the roots of the musical form, of the *jeu musical*, and recreated it in forms of movements.

But Stravinsky's main point in this article is that music should stand 'for itself', not as an accompaniment, and not in the role of explaining, narrating or representing through underlining action and characters: it should be self-sufficient. He also acknowledges the crucial fact that something new is created when media combine, as if he welcomes an element of clash or struggle between two different entities. He encourages us to continue drawing analogies with dance as we read his points on music and film:

Put music and drama together as individual entities, put them together and let them alone, without compelling one to try to 'explain' and to react to the other. To borrow a term from chemistry: my idea is the chemical reaction, where a new entity, a third body, results from uniting two different but equally important elements, music and drama; it is not the chemical mixture where, as in the films, to the preordained whole just the ingredient of music is added, resulting in nothing either new or creative.[190]

All this sets the stage for the now famous manifesto about counterpoint that Stravinsky framed with Craft in 1960, which emerges as perhaps the composer's strongest statement of all about choreography. However, it is quite clearly couched in the rhythmic, formal terms of Balanchine style, and it is just as likely that the choreographer fed the ideas to the composer, whether through his dance or his discussion, as vice versa:

Choreography as I conceive it, must realize its own form, one independent of the musical form though measured to the musical unit. Its construction will be based on whatever correspondences the choreographer may invent, but it must not seek merely to duplicate the line and beat of the music. I do not see how one can be a choreographer unless, like Balanchine, one is a musician first.[191]

If Balanchine remained Stravinsky's first-choice choreographer throughout this period, this did not stop the flow of requests to the celebrated composer from other quarters. Many of these are noted in the Stravinsky archives, though often scantily documented; we usually do not know why they never came to anything, whether for artistic or financial reasons or merely from pressure of other work. In the composer's late career, a secretary or publisher would often act as intermediary in such correspondence, sometimes sending standard letters of rejection.

Three proposals came from his old Diaghilev contact Massine. The first of these they discussed in Paris in 1937 at the suggestion of the choreographer, a ballet based on Shakespeare for the Ballet Russe de Monte Carlo, of which he was at that time artistic director. But Stravinsky's idea was much more complex, to undertake a project inspired by several of the tragedies – 'Shakespeariana' – with a narrator standing outside the action in the manner of *Histoire du soldat* or *Oedipus Rex*. But no funding for the project was ever forthcoming.[192] In 1942, the choreographer suggested the idea of a ballet using Donizetti themes for the Ballet Russe de Monte Carlo, but took so long finding the musical sources that Stravinsky abandoned the project.[193] In 1962, Massine came up with another plan for a ballet based on American-Indian songs and dances and was all set to send recordings as raw material for Stravinsky to work with. Stravinsky wrote in the margin, 'Received this absurd letter.'[194] It is hard to imagine such an ethnographic basis interesting Stravinsky.

Just as unsuitable was a request in 1957 to create a score based on the ballet-pantomime scene in Jean-Jacques Rousseau's pastoral *Le Devin du village* (1752). This was projected for the 1958 Brussels International Exposition, the score to be choreographed at the Théâtre Royal de la Monnaie by the resident choreographer J.J. Etchevery (predecessor of Béjart). Stravinsky was invited to create an adaptation of the original score in a manner that appealed to him, working very freely or borrowing directly from Rousseau, but presumably at least using the existing libretto.[195]

Stravinsky's reputation as a composer of hybrid forms brought him a number of such proposals. In 1946, enthused by his work with Balanchine and Stravinsky on *Danses Concertantes*, the designer Eugene Berman wrote to his collaborators about two further possible projects. A letter in the Stravinsky archive suggests that they had first discussed one based on Molière, but now he was hoping to interest them in an adaptation of the Medea drama by the American poet Robinson Jeffers for the Theatre Guild, New York. The celebrated actress Judith Anderson had asked if Stravinsky would be interested in writing the music, and Berman was confident that the collaboration would be useful in generating interest in their Molière project. But, Berman asked, if Stravinsky and Balanchine were too busy, could they suggest another composer or another choreographer? Tudor's name was raised as a possibility.[196]

Film proposals involving dance attracted Stravinsky, who knew that they could be lucrative. Remarkably, for several months in 1952, Stravinsky entertained the odd idea of writing a score for a film about an English window cleaner who goes to America and becomes a millionaire, 'based on pantomime and ballet' and called *A Fable of Fortune*. Stravinsky immediately warmed to the idea of Balanchine as choreographer, though Valerie Bettis, Agnes de Mille and again Tudor were suggested as alternatives. Stravinsky wrote to David Adams at Boosey & Hawkes:

> I just read the script [by Robert Shapiro] you sent me. It is a rather pleasant, gay, and surrealistic affair which should allow for a fairly interesting film.[197]

Was this faint praise? Balanchine claimed to have too much pressure of work, and Adams informed Stravinsky that Tudor had been contacted, at which point the archive files on this proposal run dry.

In 1952, the eminent British director Michael Powell put forward an idea for a film about the *Odyssey* with a libretto by Dylan Thomas and songs, dances and 'an Overture and a couple of Hymns' by Stravinsky, but he eventually realised that this was unlikely to attract sufficient funding. Instead, the next year, Powell suggested a film consisting of a series of Tales, using music, singing, dance, narrative, mime and speech, and that the Nausicaa scene from the original *Odyssey* could be one of these Tales.[198] In his excitement, Stravinsky started a plan for twelve minutes of music: a prelude, songs and dances, but this idea too came to nothing, and Thomas, who was again asked to write the libretto, died later that year.

The director Sam Wanamaker wanted to book the composer for a dramatised production of *The Iliad*, using a libretto by Robert Graves based on Graves's own translation of Homer. It was to be a grand, all-star, multi-media event at Lincoln Center in summer, 1968. Arnold Weissberger, Stravinsky's lawyer, met Wanamaker in 1966, and reported that the work was to be 'total theatre', including film projection, and that the director would approach Balanchine, Martha Graham and Paul Taylor for the choreography. There was also an idea that Marlon Brando would play Achilles.[199] But, by this time, Stravinsky's composing career was rapidly drawing to a close.

Meanwhile, Stravinsky continued to take an active role in business matters concerning what he *did* take on as a composer. Hardened by his business difficulties with Diaghilev and driven by the knowledge of what he was worth, he remained forever watchful of contracts. Never one to strike a soft bargain, his manner of dealing with Kirstein's *Orpheus* commission is instructive. Kirstein had asked in 1946 for exclusive choreographic rights for five years[200] and should have known better than to imagine Stravinsky would accept that. The composer wanted the exposure and dissemination of his ballet scores to choreographers and audiences worldwide once Balanchine's prize premiere (1948) was out of the way. Joseph notes Kirstein's worry that Stravinsky, if he sensed a real profit was at stake, might offer his score to Lucia Chase.[201] Soon Hawkes was busily at work selling the forthcoming score to ballet companies in Europe, although with the compromise that no productions would premiere until at least four months had passed after the Balanchine opening, 'to give Lincoln Kirstein plenty of time to get over his premiere'.[202] Meanwhile, Kirstein had complained to Hawkes about possible concert performances interfering with Ballet Society performances.[203] Stravinsky's tart reply sent via Hawkes was: 'my contract or rather agreement with Lincoln Kirstein concerns only his exclusivity of its stage premiere'.[204] By this time, Stravinsky was getting used to having his new ballet scores released for concert use immediately after the theatre premiere.

Stravinsky was keen to conduct *Orpheus* too. The idea had been mooted when the ballet was commissioned, but later we find him angling for a contract via his concert agent Bruno Zirato, asking him to contact Kirstein on his behalf, without mentioning that he had made the suggestion.[205] In this instance, he allowed a reduction in his usual conducting fee (to $750), knowing that his presence would enlarge the public scale of the event, and matched the deal when Chase asked him to be generous in his *Apollo* appearances with her company immediately before the *Orpheus* premiere.[206] Remarking upon the various commercial recordings and TV and radio performances generated by the new ballet score, Joseph writes: 'More than for any previous ballet, the publicizing of *Orpheus* became big business for the composer.'[207]

But Stravinsky could be inconsistent. The debate about exclusivity arose again with *Agon*, and once more the composer was fully involved, this time fuelling an already confusing situation. As before, it was agreed that the score could be offered to other companies outside the USA after the Balanchine premiere. Soon after the news broke that La Scala, Milan, had signed the ballet, Balanchine apparently tried to 'prohibit' the idea, and Ernst Roth of the London Boosey & Hawkes cabled Stravinsky in dismay.[208] Stravinsky, writing in defence of his friend, now claimed that the choreographer had 'a moral right to enjoy at least some stage exclusivity for, say, one year ... I find it fair to recognize the City Center's exclusivity and not only for the USA' – after all, City Center had paid for the score and, unusually, even allowed a concert premiere before the ballet premiere. In addition, there were artistic reasons: 'having arranged with Balanchine a well-established choreographic construction for this plotless ballet, you can easily imagine my complete lack of interest for a staging of *Agon* by strangers of a La Scala in a total ignorance of my ideas and how we realised it with Balanchine'.[209] If this was an atypical stance for Stravinsky, perhaps it was because Balanchine was involved. Understandably, with several contracts signed, Roth forced Stravinsky to back down, at which point the composer made light of the whole affair: 'The worse that can happen is that La Scala will have a lousy performance of *Agon* if they perform it, what is quite possible, but here we can do exactly nothing. I am trying not to think about it and advising you to do the same. Don't worry!'[210] In fact, La Scala never did undertake a staging of anyone else's *Agon*.

The composer was also watchful of prompt payments. In 1947, in the early days of his signing with Booseys, Stravinsky wrote to Hawkes pressing him to get up to date on what the ballet companies owed him. Chase's agreement on *Apollo* had expired and needed renewal. From Serge Denham, director of the Ballet Russe de Monte Carlo, he had never received any money for the uses of his *Pulcinella Suite* (for Bolender's *Comedia Balletica*, 1945) and of his *Baiser de la fée* (the Balanchine ballet, staged for Denham in 1940).[211] He dealt cleverly and firmly with Denham's request to lower his price on *Danses Concertantes*. In 1945, Gretl Urban of Associated Music Publishers told Stravinsky that Denham was currently paying $1200 for thirty guaranteed shows per year, and $30 for each additional show (seventy-two performances in fact had taken place during the last season, the total bill coming to $2460). Denham pleaded inability to continue at such a high price, asking if Stravinsky could now simply guarantee seventy-two shows per year for $1200 (about $16 per show). When Urban suggested a compromise of $20 per show with a guarantee of $1200 (the same number of shows bringing in $1440), Stravinsky took command and advised her in no uncertain terms:

> a. I don't see any reason to change the agreement for the past year. What is agreed and signed must be paid.
> b. For the forthcoming year you could ask him for 25 dollars per show – maybe a guarantee too?[212]

Denham agreed to Stravinsky's conditions, but the composer could not refrain from adding just one more point of pressure. He wrote to Urban:

> I'm sure that he won't relinquish it [*Danses Concertantes*]: he's simply trying to intimidate you. Now the clever strategy would be: before allowing him to continue with performances, make him pay what he owes you for the last year or season; only after that ...[213]

Stravinsky was confident of his position. Performances of *Danses Concertantes* carried on up to and including the 1947–8 season.

On another occasion, Stravinsky suspected that Leeds Music Corporation was not keeping up with royalty payments on his 1945 *Firebird Suite*. For years, he enlisted the friendly assistance of the New York City Ballet administration (Betty Cage and later Barbara Horgan) in documenting their use of the score.[214] Here, another bone of contention was the sloppy production of musical parts. Leeds brought out the *Suite* ready for Adolph Bolm's *Firebird* production (1945) at the Metropolitan Opera House. The hurriedly copied orchestral parts were seriously unsatisfactory, yet remained in circulation alongside a much better set used by New York City Ballet after Balanchine choreographed the score in 1949.

The composer also kept a close eye on his foreign business and checked carefully through the records that his publishers sent to him. In May 1966, he wrote to Rufina Ampenoff, his Boosey contact in London:

> I have noticed that the fees resulting from the performances of my grand right works in England are rather low and that certain theatres are not paying enough ... Will you please confirm that you will make sure that you obtain the full and not reduced amounts. Otherwise, I do not wish you to allow the performances to take place.[215]

The point to emphasise is that the dance world was not accustomed to composers who were so astute and demanding in business affairs, and expensive. Stravinsky set his own standards; he took the lead for a twentieth-century breed of composer. In certain circumstances, too, we can be sure that his high fees prohibited the choreographic use, or at least legal choreographic use, of his scores.

Issues of copyright were a constant worry. Many of Stravinsky's early scores, including *Sacre* and *Petrushka*, were ineligible for copyright protection in the USA (see p. 111), which was one of the reasons why he arranged the publication of revised versions in the 1940s, when he became a US citizen. The original 1911 version of *Petrushka*, for instance, could be performed freely in the USA, even if not in any other country of the world. There was an interesting case in 1950, when Stravinsky urged Booseys to shame the Grand Ballet de Marquis de Cuevas into using, and paying to use, his new edition of *Petrushka*. He resented the company escaping payment of royalties by using the American Musicus Edition, especially as this was an arrangement for greatly reduced orchestra. As he had no legal rights, artistic reasons were given to pressure the company, and they agreed, possibly because they did not want to jeopardise their chances of performing the ballet in Europe in the future.[216]

Musical standards were a major concern in Stravinsky's dealings with the ballet world. On more than one occasion, he indicated his disapproval of Sol Hurok's habit of cutting down the number of players when Ballet Theatre toured his *Petrushka* (1943–4). He heard word in 1945 from his composer friend Rieti that the same was happening to *Apollo*. Balanchine had communicated his disgust. Hurok had provided just enough strings to cover the various parts, even though he had promised the extra numbers that the score required.[217] Stravinsky used his spies. Rieti's observations prompted Stravinsky to check the detail with Chase through his lawyer.[218] Ballet Theatre duly responded, anxious to regain Stravinsky's approval, and assuring him that all would be well under their control, now that the Hurok contract had been terminated.[219]

The following year, Massine pressed for permission to use a reduced orchestra for the *Petrushka* performance in the 1946 play *A Bullet in the Ballet* (the dramatisation of a murder-mystery novel by Caryl Brahms and S.J. Simon that was going to be staged in England). Stravinsky might have been partly tempted by financial gain, but, disapproving of the way in which *Petrushka* had been handled 'by such enterprises as that of Hurok', he wrote sternly to the choreographer:

It is not the number but the way the instrumentation is made which is really important thing. 35 years ago I wrote *Petroushka* for one hundred musicians and now I succeeded in reducing the size of the orchestra to 68 without the distortion of original combinations and balance. It was a very difficult work. That is why I am puzzled how anyone can do it with 45.

And he demanded an equally stern programme note absolving himself of all responsibility, in capitals:

IN VIEW OF THE LIMITED SITTING CAPACITY IN THE ORCHESTRA PIT THE PRESENT REDUCED ORCHESTRATION OF *PETROUSHKA* IS MADE WITH THE PERMISSION OF THE COMPOSER BUT WITHOUT HIS KNOWLEDGE AND WITHOUT HIS ACTUAL PARTICIPATION IN THIS ARRANGEMENT.[220]

The *Petrushka* issue arose again in 1963. London Festival Ballet now cited the Massine precedent for the small orchestration, producing as evidence Stravinsky's original letter to the choreographer. This time, Stravinsky flatly refused permission.[221] He had done so too in 1960, when Robbins requested the right to perform *Sacre* with a reduced orchestra at the Royal Danish Ballet, the reason there being that the orchestral pit was too small for the required number of players. The choreographer enclosed a letter of request from the General Administrator of the Royal Theatre asking for a version of the score for approximately sixty-six musicians, but Stravinsky would not hear of it.[222]

In 1941, Stravinsky had undertaken his own arrangement of the 'Bluebird' pas de deux from *Sleeping Beauty* for Ballet Theatre, perhaps because the full score was not available in America at the time, and large orchestral resources could not be assembled during the war.[223] It is interesting how carefully he justified himself to Richard Pleasant, administrative director of the company, taking the opportunity to caution him that ballet companies should not build whole repertoires at music's expense. The problem, he perceived, with many touring companies was that, with insufficient orchestral resources, they deceived the public into thinking that they were hearing the real thing.[224]

Standards of orchestral playing and conducting for ballet also concerned Stravinsky. Another composer acquaintance and musical spy, David Diamond, reported on the poor orchestra for *Danses Concertantes* in 1944: the trumpet could have been better, the horns were slightly 'feeble' and the strings 'disinterested'.[225] On one occasion, in a 1949 newspaper interview, Stravinsky even blamed the troubles of ballet on its musical standards:

'You can't have good ballet if the music is bad', he exploded. 'Nearly all we hear now – it is wretchedly played. The only dance company in the United States with good music is Lincoln Kirstein's Ballet Society in New York, and it doesn't travel. The Ballet Russe? Many excellent dancers, but the music – ?' He spread his hands in despair. 'Who could make music with that orchestra?'

When asked whether he approved the performance of *Danses Concertantes*:

> At the premiere in 1942 they did it right, he said. 'Never since. I heard it in Los Angeles recently and I took my head in my hands.'[226]

As well as involving himself in business matters related to the ballet, Stravinsky demanded high artistic standards from the ballet world.

Given all this evidence, it is hardly possible to imagine that Stravinsky ever condoned cuts in his ballet scores. He had rowed with Diaghilev over this (see p. 28). But on at least one occasion he acceded, for the Billy Rose premiere of *Scènes de ballet*, and for sound reason. Wily as ever, he stipulated the billing as 'Excerpts' from *Scènes de ballet*. This, the conductor Maurice Abravanel recalls, allowed the New York Philharmonic concert performance to be announced as a 'world premiere'. Stravinsky also agreed to a reduced orchestration for the occasion, knowing that the work would otherwise be dropped and that a long season was likely if he agreed to this.[227]

One other important dance matter increasingly occupied Stravinsky's attention during the American years, the restaging of his existing scores. Records suggest that the composer was relatively easygoing about new settings of his *ballet* scores, provided that they were performed as written. There are a few exceptions. In 1938, he turned down a proposal from Jacques Rouché, director of the Paris Opéra, to allow Serge Lifar to set his *Jeu de cartes*, but the context for this refusal was his lack of respect for Lifar and a strained meeting with Rouché that Stravinsky had reported in the press: he felt it was high time that the Opéra staged a whole evening of his well-established scores instead, *Baiser*, *Pulcinella* and *Firebird*.[228]

An unusual proposal that Stravinsky welcomed came from Jack Cole, a well-known Broadway and Hollywood jazz dance choreographer who had trained with the early American pioneers of modern dance Ruth St Denis and Ted Shawn. It was agreed that he would choreograph *Apollo* for the California Ojai Festival in the summer of 1954. This was remarkable on two accounts, because of his jazz background and also because in so doing he would have set himself against the Balanchine version in the USA (although this did not achieve classic status until the 1960s). Stravinsky might well have been impressed by Cole's high standing in the commercial theatre. In April that year, he attended his celebrated Middle Eastern extravaganza *Kismet* in New York. However, Cole sustained an injury during rehearsals, and the project never happened. Vera reported her grave disappointment to Stravinsky, then on tour in Europe: she and Lawrence Morton, director of the Festival, put it down to Cole's anxiety about choreographing a ballet for the first time.[229]

Even though he had enthusiastically justified Diaghilev's appropriation of

Rimsky-Korsakov's *Scheherazade* (see p. 40), Stravinsky regularly turned down requests to use his own *concert* scores in dance performance. Such uses brought in money without involving him in any actual work, but Stravinsky was wary, and his rejections included choreographers he respected. Of course, he had to address this issue more frequently than any other composer. Noticing this developing market, and aware too that theatre brought in more money than concert performances (grand rights), Boosey & Hawkes suggested adding a clause to the composer's main contract, to the effect that royalties would be distributed in accordance with the use of, rather than original intention for, a score:

> Thus a work written for concert orchestra and subsequently adapted as music for a ballet or stage performance, should be treated as a theatrical work so far as royalty payments are concerned.[230]

The earliest recorded use of a concert score in the 'Stravinsky the Global Dancer' database is a setting of *Fireworks* in Paris (1914) by the American modern dance pioneer Loie Fuller, famous for her use of lighting on billowing silks that enveloped her body. There is no evidence that Stravinsky was aware of the performance. But he was fully aware of Léo Staats's 1917 *Les Abeilles* at the Paris Opéra, set to his *Scherzo Fantastique*. The composer sanctioned this and would probably have conducted the production, save for an illness that kept him away. This was a *ballet blanc* based on Maeterlinck's book *The Life of the Bee* (1901), which was also the origin of the score, although later Stravinsky struggled to deny any such programme. The story was about life in a beehive, featuring the famous Carlotta Zambelli as the Queen Bee.[231]

Only a few years later, Stravinsky began to exercise his authority over use of his scores. He heard about Massine's 1922 *Ragtime*, a duet he performed at Covent Garden with Lydia Lopokova without informing the composer. The composer went to the press, claiming that the score was only suitable for concert performance, but it was just as likely in this case that he simply wanted payment for the use.[232] Soon, however, he began to develop a specific policy on the theatricalisation of scores that were non-programmatic and 'symphonic' in intent. Comte Etienne de Beaumont, patron of the arts, wanted Stravinsky to allow him use of his *Octet* for his Soirées de Paris in June 1924, with Picasso in charge of a 'représentation plastique'. Stravinsky's response is one that he repeated later on several occasions: his *Octet*, like all his symphonic compositions, was self-sufficient and not yet well-known enough in its intended form to be presented as 'plastique'.[233] The composer's concerns were about protecting, or at least establishing, the original identity of his symphonic scores, and he was not out of kilter with the spirit of the times. Diaghilev had led the field in promoting the use of existing music, usually in arranged form, but considerable controversy arose over the later use of symphonic scores and absolute music, and this extended into the 1940s.[234]

Thus, in 1930, Stravinsky turned down Lifar's request from the Paris Opéra to use his *Capriccio* for piano and orchestra (1929) and the *Symphony of Psalms* that he was currently completing, although he also suspected that Lifar was really angling for a new ballet score. Just as he would to Rouché several years later, he suggested *Baiser* as an alternative (see p. 76).[235] For the same reason, in 1947 Stravinsky rejected a proposal from Todd Bolender and the designer Corrado Cagli to use his *Symphony in Three Movements*, a score that eventually proved one of Stravinsky's most popular with choreographers (see p. 115). The pair were too shy to ask the composer directly, so the request came via his composer friend Rieti. Stravinsky's response was polite; Bolender was a Balanchine dancer, and he wanted both artists to know that he was aware of their work and liked it.[236]

Robbins received a similar rejection when he too asked for the *Symphony in Three Movements* in 1953.[237] In a letter to Kirstein explaining his rejection of the idea, Stravinsky expanded, citing Robbins's celebrated *The Cage* (1951) as the work that confirmed his opinion. This was a setting of the *Concerto in D* commissioned for the Basle Chamber Orchestra. Yet, as always with Robbins, Stravinsky is highly respectful and most careful to admit the merit of his work:

> I always feel uneasy at the idea of using my straight symphonic forms on the stage. I let the experiment be tried with the *Basler Concerto* and, to tell you the truth (*confidentially*), I feel somewhat unhappy and uncomfortable about it.
>
> Not that Jerome Robbins has not done well. On the contrary, I think he is a very talented man and he is still proving it in *The Cage*. But it is simply a matter of 'plastic' incompatibility. This one experience has only confirmed me in my opinion and cautiousness.[238]

With *The Cage*'s tale of an animal- or insect-like tribe of females that preys on males, it is indeed astonishing that Stravinsky ever allowed his *Concerto* to be used in this way. He had already refused to conduct *The Cage* for New York City Ballet the previous year. This would have been tantamount to 'sanctifying' the work, he said, which he could not do, citing exactly the same reason that he had given de Beaumont back in 1924.[239]

There is a surprising number of records of Robbins, or someone on his behalf, approaching the composer and being turned down – for instance, a proposal for *Sacre* with the reduced orchestration (see p. 75) and a 1947 request to use the orchestral *Suites* in a Ballet Theatre production, dismissed without clear reasons.[240] Yet Robbins still did not give up. He wrote again to Stravinsky in 1956, pressing to use 'either or both' the *Symphony in Three Movements* and the *Capriccio*. Balanchine eventually got both these scores, the *Symphony* after Stravinsky's death; Robbins never did.[241]

We do not know what Stravinsky thought of a plan for Agnes de Mille to choreograph the *Concerto in E-flat* (*Dumbarton Oaks*) for a 1952 Stravinsky Festival at New York City Ballet. Kirstein wrote to the composer with his own sketch of a possible scenario. He had in mind an evening party at Dumbarton Oaks, the house of Mildred Bliss, a wealthy diplomat's wife and music-loving friend of the Stravinskys.[242] This was yet another project, and a Festival, that never happened. And there were, as usual, the requests from far less established figures that also came to nothing. Remarkably, in 1952 he took time to reply to a woman from Tonawanda, New York, asking if she could apply an allegorical theme to his *Capriccio* and perform the piece in a reduced orchestration. True to form, the answer was, politely, no.[243]

By the 1950s, Stravinsky's views on choreography to symphonic music had undoubtedly begun to change, at least as far as Balanchine was concerned, for the practice went hand in hand with the trend towards plotless dance that had been led by Balanchine, gaining momentum during the 1940s. Joseph has suggested that *Balustrade*, Balanchine's 1941 setting of the *Violin Concerto* for the Original Ballet Russe was a turning point for Stravinsky.[244] Even though it received only three performances, Stravinsky was around for rehearsals with Balanchine and Samuel Dushkin, the violinist for whom the work had originally been written, and he went on to conduct the premiere. *Balustrade* was fundamentally a plotless piece in neoclassical style, even though it expressed contrasting moods and had surrealist designs by Tchelitcheff. Balanchine went on in the same year to create the plotless and symphonic *Concerto Barocco* (Bach) and *Ballet Imperial* (Tchaikovsky), though there is no evidence that Stravinsky saw these ballets at the time. But the composer needed further prompts before he was ready to conceive of writing a new ballet score without being led by a libretto or literary idea of some kind.

Meanwhile, Stravinsky embarked on a new work of his own, *Danses Concertantes*, which was premiered in concert in 1942. However, the score had originated as a ballet score. Balanchine remembers asking the composer to write something for him: 'just start with something – a variation – anything ... so he wrote *Danses Concertantes*'.[245] On another occasion, the choreographer recalls suggesting that Stravinsky compose a theme and variations.[246] For some reason, Stravinsky always publicly denied this starting point – for instance, in the programme note that he prepared for concerts after the ballet had been premiered in 1944. Perhaps with no story or theme and no further collaboration during the writing process, Stravinsky simply stopped thinking about and gearing his writing towards the theatrical context. Perhaps, like most audiences too at the time, he was still not entirely ready to think of a dance without any narrative pretext, despite what he said in interview with Dahl about stories being no more than an excuse for dancing. After all, for his last ballet *Jeu de cartes*, he had himself con-structed a highly detailed scenario. So he used dance forms and rhythms in *Danses Concertantes*, but otherwise felt totally free from theatrical constraints. In the following explanatory notes written before the Balanchine premiere, Stravinsky clearly equates normal theatre dance tightly with plot, and there is a sense of overkill in his emphasis on structural principles and parallels between the forms of music and dance. The ballet *Danses Concertantes* was still excep-tional during this period:

> *Danses Concertantes* is a suite of instrumental pieces composed in the form of a Sonata, or better still, in the form of a Concerto Grosso.
> The two parts entitled 'Pas de deux' and 'Pas d'Action' borrowed from the choreographic terminology are none but the two principal movements of a Sonata, its allegro and its andante constituting the kernel of a Symphony, a Concerto, a quartet etc.
> In applying choreographic titles to pieces composing my *Danses Concertantes* I emphasized the close relationship of the structural principle on which both arts are based namely the architectural, inherent to music as well as to choreography.
> In spite of the fact that this work was composed without any idea of a dramatic action be it ballet or pantomime this music nevertheless by its dance and structural character lends itself naturally to a classical choreography stage presentation.[247]

As for the collaboration with dance, once the score had been finished, Stravinsky seems to have been enthusiastic about the project. Joseph claims that 'the com-poser and choreographer met more frequently during the preparation of *Danses Concertantes* than for any previous collaboration'.[248] Afterwards, Stravinsky at-tended several performances and conducted the ballet on at least one occasion, in 1944. But again, in the programme note written subsequent to the ballet premiere, the composer equates theatre dance with plot, insisting:

> Though it has served admirably as a ballet, it was not conceived as a stage work and is without plot. The use of choreographic terms – Pas de Deux, Pas d'Action – merely emphasizes close structural relationships between dancing and music.

By 1953, with *Agon* in mind, Stravinsky *was* ready to be committed to writing a ballet without a narrative starting point. He wrote enthusiastically to Kirstein:

I will compose a 'Concerto for the dance' for which George will create a matching choreographic construction. He is a master at this, and has done beautifully with Bizet, Tchaikovsky, Bach, Mozart in music not composed for the dance. So, we can well imagine how successful he will be if given something specially composed for the ballet.[249]

He used the old definition of the term 'concerto', as an instrumental rather than formal concept, and likewise when he shifted to the metaphor of 'symphony' in a newspaper interview early in 1954. The choreographer had 'done so well adapting dances to symphonies that I would like to write a special symphony with the dance in mind. It will be a dancing symphony.'[250] But Stravinsky was by then far more open to the use of his existing symphonic scores as well, and now, with Balanchine's approach well established, the general furore over using symphonic and absolute music had also died down. Of course, the odd thing about *Agon* is that, even if it was the most abstract of his dance scores, it hardly turned out to be 'symphonic' or 'concerto'-like in the manner or scale of the works he alludes to by other Balanchine composers. It was also a one-off: *The Flood* was a return to narrative and hybridity.

As the database 'Stravinsky the Global Dancer' demonstrates, Stravinsky's concert scores hit the ballet repertory in a major way in the 1960s. By then, most of the scores that choreographers wanted to use were well established in the concert repertory, their intended identity as concert pieces secure, and Stravinsky appears to have been approving. Aurel Milloss was the first choreographer to set the *Symphony in Three Movements*, in 1960, and Stravinsky happily gave him permission to use his *Violin Concerto* in 1965. Still, there was at least one piece that Stravinsky felt uncomfortable with as a ballet, the *Symphony of Psalms*, possibly because of its religious theme (see p. 78). When the Deutsche Oper in Berlin requested to set the score in 1962, Stravinsky immediately instructed Boosey & Hawkes, 'Inform Berlin Psalm idea absurd and impossible.'[251] Significantly, when the piece was performed at the end of the 1972 Stravinsky Festival of New York City Ballet, one year after the composer's death, it was not danced; the company sat on stage. But it *has* been choreographed elsewhere, the first time in 1969, by Fernand Nault for Les Grands Ballets Canadiens, and at least fourteen times since.[252]

We should understand the limits of Stravinsky's interest in the take-up of his existing scores. It does not follow that he was particularly concerned about how they might be used for dance. He probably did not have much time to be concerned. Indeed, he knew almost no details about this broader Stravinsky choreographic culture – except that it existed – and what mattered was that the royalties came in. Compiling the first chronology of Stravinsky's theatre works in 1947, Lederman asked if Stravinsky had any factual information to give her about Russian, German and Italian productions. He did not, and he was una-shamed about having 'so little interest' in what went on 'outside my milieu', which was Diaghilev and Balanchine.[253]

But this shows the blinkered Stravinsky who would not have wanted to know what he would surely not have liked – recall his controlling personality and the boundaries he placed on the premiere productions of his scores. As time pro-gressed and his music spread to wider and more diverse audiences (and choreog-raphers and dancers), the composer's own vision for dance narrowed.

Yet, in so many other respects, the breadth of Stravinsky's dance experience is impressive, and likewise his contribution to the tradition of composing for dance. There is the range of his theatrical conceptions involving dance and there is his intense practical involvement in the creative process, from initiating a number of works to contributing to, even controlling, the studio process. He also brought a new respect to the job of composing for dance, the composer as proactive leader ensuring high standards of musical performance. The quick transference of ballet score to the concert hall became routine with him, be it in suite form or complete as for the original theatre production. And there is the composer as business man, entrepreneurial, adhering strongly to artistic princi-ples, yet at the same time determined to see the spread of his music to the widest possible audience, with fees paid to him at an appropriate level and promptly. Stravinsky was not the 'greatest composer of the twentieth century' for nothing. And we see him as both affectionate and generous towards choreographers and dancers and arrogant, a feared collaborator, a control freak.

In the next chapter, I examine the evidence of the spread of Stravinsky's work through the dance world, the huge repertory surrounding his name and of which he actually saw only a mere fragment. Here, he is distinctly out of control.

2

From Stravinsky to Choreography:
Musique Dansante and a Century of Dance

Introduction

With well over a thousand dances known to have been choreographed to his music, we now find Stravinsky and his music distinctly 'out of control'. This is the irony for an artist with unnaturally strict views on the interpretation of his product: to confront the broadest and biggest choreographic assault to face any composer. In this chapter, I consider what choreographers and dancers have wanted from Stravinsky, *their* perspective. Stravinsky was compelled to face up to the fact that a new tradition of use was flourishing, and his music was at the forefront of it. On the one hand, he made dance scores according to new rules: most scores were led by his own dictates, without his being subservient to a choreographer, director or impresario (see p. 20), and they were conceived as intact, complete entities, not, as so often had been the case in ballet, to be broken up and re-arranged at the whim of anyone else. On the other hand, he could see that his dance scores had the potential to be set in many different ways, and he had to come to terms with the notion of his scores being freestanding, no longer tightly locked into any agreement regarding his own intentions. We are now so used to the bigger, freer exchange of culture affecting all composers that we need reminding of the fact that the advent of radio and recordings was responsible for a major increase in accessibility to music. Furthermore, in Stravinsky's case the explosion of activity has been greatly enlarged, as it had even in his lifetime, by the general plundering of his concert music alongside the scores specially written for dance. Even though he knew what was happening in his own lifetime, he could never have contemplated the diversity of ways in which his music has been 'choreographed'. But he would surely have been delighted by his staying power.

Stravinsky arrived on the dance scene at a time of major shifts in thinking about the nature of dance music and about relations between music and dance. Diaghilev was committed to the new thinking, and his choreographers responded in tune with him. But there were many complementary developments outside Diaghilev's immediate circle during this period: for instance, in the work of the Swiss music pedagogue Emile Jaques-Dalcroze, founder of the music/movement eurhythmics system that informed Nijinsky's *Sacre*; Fedor Lopukhov, the Russian ballet choreographer, now celebrated for his *Dance Symphony* of 1923 and theory of dance modelled on music; and the American modern dance pioneers Isadora Duncan (who was highly influential in Europe) and Ruth St Denis and Ted Shawn, the latter partnership through their so-called 'music visualisations'. First-rate music was now used to enhance the quality of dance. It was also seen as a guide, a liberating force to choreographers, as its structural principles could be borrowed to enable non-narrative forms of dance, including large-scale symphonic forms. At the same time, choreomusical relationships could encompass counterpoint alongside models of synthesis and music visualisation.

Stravinsky's own scores, sophisticated in their structural content, contributed to the new climate, but have in turn been required by choreographers to face the challenges of further developments in dance/music practice and theory that the composer never knew. His work became an extreme example of challenge, with so many choreographers wanting to use him, and some in radical ways. Even some choreographers who have used Stravinsky's most clearly identifiable 'dance music' have not used it in any conventional sense as dance music driving the dance and supporting the dancer rhythmically. After all, from the Nijinsky of *L'Après-midi d'un faune* (1912) through to Merce Cunningham and beyond, still more radical questions have been raised as to whether music used for dance should necessarily drive the dance, whether it needs to be of the kind that urges us to move or supports the dancer rhythmically, questions bound up with the agency and autonomy of the dancer and the dance.

But the twentieth century also highlighted the potential for reference in scores, as an access route to history, reference to the early dance and musical history of a score. With Stravinsky, there came plenty of history. There is the music, the dance and the total theatre event that in several instances has developed iconic status over time: original choreography stapled to a famous ballet score, offering opportunity for comment, dance and music feeding from dance and music. There is also the intertextual notion of a musical score developing its own tradition. It bears a mass of historical and cultural reference (including references to choreographies created along the way) to be used and negotiated with by choreographers and dancers. But it is also subject to freedom from the composer's supposed intentions and renewed through each choreography set to it, informed by new dance contexts and social conditions. Thus, *our* perceptions of the music are changed.

At this point, the issue of intention needs teasing out, along with its relationship to interpretation. The model I use for engaging with music (a network of relations between author, musical work, performer and listener) uses the notion of authorial intention in a particular way: not in the simplistic sense of what the author had in mind or said, which Wimsatt and Beardsley famously critiqued in

'The Intentional Fallacy' (1954),[1] but, working from Arthur Danto's theory of art embodying ideas (1981),[2] in the sense that contextual information is part of the work of art. We can presume, for instance, that an author might intend something, such as irony, because of what we already know about the context of the work. Thus, there is the possibility of an inappropriate interpretation even though, from the point of view of the reader (or performing musician) reading from different contexts, interpretations can broaden or shift with time: for instance, certain kinds of reading may seem particularly significant in some periods, but not in others.[3]

However, choreography to music raises separate issues of interpretation. We do not experience choreographic interpretation of music as such, even though some choreographers and viewers might think or hope that we do, and even though choreographers surely went through the business of interpreting the music before and/or during their own creative process. For us, watching choreography to music, we are no longer simply engaged in the act of seeking to understand and evaluate what the music is about. The notion of a separate musical identity and past does not disappear entirely, and sometimes this might come into focus very positively. But, to refer back to my interactive choreomusical model (see pp. 7-12), we are primarily engaged in the act of interpreting a new, composite artwork (the new model for engagement: authors, composite work, performers, spectator/listener). Of course, we may still work with the notion that the new *Sacre du printemps* that we watch (titled thus in our programme) is intended to be a *Sacre du printemps*, and thus proposes a hugely significant and traditional connection between score and choreography. But at the same time, it could well be that the choreography subverts aspects of the music (not just its story), and that the two media combined might, for instance, create a new shape through time.

Is there then notionally an inappropriate choreographic 'interpretation' or use of Stravinsky's music? Over the years many people have complained that there is, when they disliked what they saw. But perhaps what they were really saying is that the choreography made them hear the music in a manner that contradicted their preconceptions of it. Stravinsky's situation is complicated by the fact that, for his pieces, he had very clear, narrow ideas about what the whole dance theatre experience should be like. Arguably the first composer regularly to initiate his own theatre pieces and to have his concert music so often transformed into dance, he liked to occupy the whole territory of theatre. And yet, quite clearly, ignoring his views on dance matters has usually been considered entirely acceptable by those evaluating Stravinsky dances. I can only sympathise with the theatre director Phyllida Lloyd when she once complained about the restrictions on modern texts by those who control dramatists' estates, such as the regulations on producing the plays of Samuel Beckett and Noël Coward: 'By placing a preservation order on a certain way of producing a work it may atrophy and refuse to speak to the audience of the moment.'[4]

This brings me to the point that boundaries have been stretched further in recent years with postmodern choreographers and performance artists (overlapping fields), extending beyond any notion of theatrical 'interpretation' or use of a score (such as creating a new *Sacre)* to its use as reference or image within a performative framework. The increasing use of reference and history as a creative resource over the years eased the way to the new approach. But now the performers perform 'themselves' (a complicated concept in itself – see pp. 491-7), bearing the past with them, their experience of Stravinsky included, rather than dancing roles within the programme schema that the composer originally envisaged or indeed any other programme schema dreamed up since to go alongside the music. Sometimes a complete score might be used, sometimes a fragment or two from a score, and sometimes Stravinsky is part of a collage soundscape embracing other music by other composers, even noise; often, there is no sense of 'dancing to' the music in the traditional sense.

It is the purpose of this book to embrace such a Stravinsky enterprise in all its variety and exuberance; but as Stravinsky himself thought in theatrical terms when he wrote for dance, I shall begin the current survey chapter from this standpoint. It is not fair to call these terms traditional; we hardly have to look far to find plenty of examples of theatricality that were radical for their time. Yet it is pertinent to consider Stravinsky's contribution *first* according to the fundamental tenet of the dancing body responding directly to the music's presumed physicality. After all, this still represents the norm in Stravinsky usage, and it supports his own aesthetic, as Hanns Eisler in *Composing for the Films* (1947) appears to have recognised when he claimed the physical or gestural element as the key function of music, in both film and dance:

> The concrete factor of unity of music and pictures consists in the gestural element ... The function of music, however, is not to 'express' this movement ... but to release, or more accurately, to justify movement ... At this point music intervenes, supplying momentum, muscular energy, a sense of corporeity, as it were. Its aesthetic effect is that of a stimulus of motion, not a reduplication of motion. In the same way, good ballet music, for instance Stravinsky's, does not express the feelings of the dancers and does not aim at any identity with them, but only summons them to dance.[5]

The chapter is in three main parts. After discussion of the physicality of Stravinsky's music, I undertake a broad survey of choreographic usage, based on the database 'Stravinsky the Global Dancer' (*SGD*), an international chronology of his works. Then I discuss selected scores and dances that raise especially interesting questions about Stravinsky 'interpretation' through choreography, setting the scene for the more detailed case studies in later chapters.

Rhythm, dynamics and the body

Both Balanchine and Roland John Wiley, the authority on Tchaikovsky's ballet music, have referred to Stravinsky's music as *musique dansante* or, using the Russian term, *dansantnost'*. Both think of dance music as ballet music and in relation to nineteenth-century tradition. Balanchine famously said that, like Delibes and Tchaikovsky, Stravinsky 'made music for the body to dance to. They invented the floor for the dancer to walk on.'[6] Balanchine stressed rhythm as key in Stravinsky's music. Wiley agrees about the importance of rhythm, but emphasises melody as the key element in *musique dansante*: "*dansantnost'* connotes in part a melody more substantial in its identity than mere accompaniment, a melody memorable in content, ripe with eloquence and implication. Something about *dansantnost'* is akin to physical gesture ..."[7] And he tells us that this something is less apparent in *The Firebird* and *Petrushka*, with their emphasis on mime – though, of course, nineteenth-century ballet scores also contained mime sections – than in *Apollo* or *Agon*.

I would agree with both Balanchine and Wiley that the physicality of Stravinsky's music is clear, although I contend that, whatever the case with earlier ballet music, Stravinsky's rhythmic content far outweighs any melodic impetus in creating this sense of physicality. Try to encapsulate what is key to Stravinsky, and nearly everyone thinks of rhythm first, and an outstanding vibrancy in his rhythmic content.

But neither Wiley nor Balanchine make much of the fact that there is an important distinction: Stravinsky's music is rhythmically quite different from nineteenth-century-style ballet music with its sense of ebb and flow, swing and breath, within and across the bar-lines. Rather it emphasises motor rhythm and a more equal accentuation or attack of beat between. As Nicolas Nabokov, Stravinsky's spokesman, put it in 1944:

> Look at any one of [Stravinsky's] bars and you will find that it is not the measure closed in by barlines (as it would be in Mozart, for example), but the monometrical unit of the measure, the single beat which determines the life of his musical organism.[8]

The effect is of insisting on the present moment, a holding-in of energy rather than its release with breath, until the jolt of an unexpected accent or shift into new material, and then the sense of the present re-establishes itself once more. That pulse can be heavily presented, as in some parts of *Sacre* and *Noces*. Or it can be far lighter of touch, as in much neoclassical Stravinsky – after nine-teenth-century ballet music tradition – but nevertheless powerfully felt, even during the rests. These are generalisations, of course, but they nevertheless help us make sense of a new kind of *musique dansante*.

Beyond pulse, a new concept of rhythm as a whole evolved with Stravinsky (*Sacre* blasting it into the foreground). Through techniques of immobility and abrupt discontinuity, it too centred on the notion of an emphatic present or state, rather than a process or development towards and away from a goal. Taruskin has been especially perceptive in his explanation of typical devices: on the one hand, the rigid, hypnotic ostinato, such as the famous chords in Augurs of Spring (see Ex. 2.1), here one repeated event (pulse laid bare), and on the

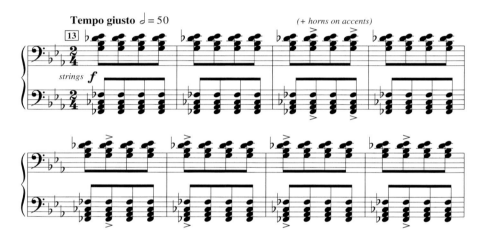

Ex. 2.1. *Le Sacre du printemps*, The Augurs of Spring.

other, the pattern of irregular downbeats defining changing metre in the score. Sometimes both these devices join, two or more metrical systems moving along-side each other as fundamentally inert activity – for instance (at the start of Mystic Circles of the Young Girls), the passive 4-quaver ostinato in the cellos under a tune that is in a persistently variable metre (4/4, 2/4, 4/4, 3/4, 4/4, 5/4) (see Ex. 2.2).[9]

Then, sometimes, there is a whole composite 'system' of different rhythmic layers or cycles set in motion and going nowhere. Large tracts of *Sacre* are based on ostinato structures. But then, when will these tracts end? We cannot predict when, we can only predict that they will. There is no sense of transition towards the moment, to provide expectation of when it will happen. As the Russian musi-cologist Irina Vershinina observes, it 'can only be stopped, interrupted, broken

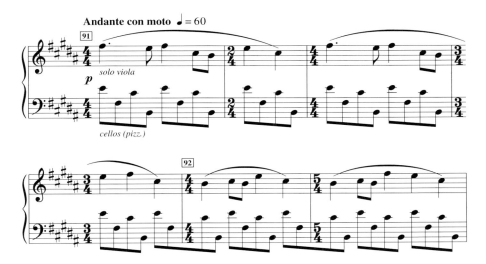

Ex. 2.2. *Le Sacre du printemps*, Mystic Circles of the Young Girls.

off by outside interference'.[10] The same sense of going nowhere and being cut off arbitrarily appears in passages of highly irregular metre where there is no ostinato, the most flamboyant example of all being the opening section of the Sacrificial Dance. Here, the construction is a mosaic formed from a limited number of cells, the shifting permutations of which establish metrical irregularity and together form blocks of material, while the registral and instrumental content of the individual cells remains static. Example 2.3a (accompanied by the opening of the music to which it refers, Ex. 2.3b) is a diagram of the opening large block of the Sacrificial Dance, and is a simplified form of the analysis by Pierre Boulez.[11] There are three cells, A, B and C, which vary in length (Boulez's division into units of semiquaver beats is shown next to the cell identification) and pattern of succession. The original barring that Nijinsky would have known is shown here: current scores reflect Stravinsky's later revisions.

The foregoing discussion fits Pieter van den Toorn's typology for the characteristic rhythmic structuring devices in Stravinsky's music. He outlines two main types of construction. Type 1, based on foreground and perceived metrical *irregularity*, predominates, reaching its most extreme manifestation in the Sacrificial Dance, where the complexity derives partly from rhythmic coordination occurring at the level of sub-tactus, semiquavers, a quicker rate than we actually perceive as beat. Type 2, based on foreground and perceived metrical *regularity*, is the 'system of different rhythmic layers', their motifs repeating according to cycles that vary independently of each other. Van den Toorn notes the static nature of these two types in registral and instrumental content, but also proposes how a sense of 'development', movement or change can take place: for

Ex. 2.3a. *Le Sacre du printemps*, opening, Sacrificial Dance, diagram of cell structure.

Ex. 2.3b. *Le Sacre du printemps*, opening, Sacrificial Dance, in four-hand piano reduction.

Type 1, 'from the lengthening, shortening, or reshuffling of the blocks and their internal subdivisions upon successive repeats' and, for Type 2, 'from the synchronization and non-sychronization of the stable or unstable periods as defined by the reiterating fragments and with the vertical or harmonic implications of these shifts in alignment'.[12] But this is hardly 'development' in the traditional sense of progress in a more or less clear direction.

Again, it would not be fair to make a generalisation and claim that this typology works equally well for Stravinsky's output as a whole. Scores such as *Pulcinella* and *Le Baiser de la fée* draw from sources that respect traditional Western tonal and rhythmic procedures far more obviously than *Sacre* does. Nevertheless, there are plenty of examples of neoclassical works that subscribe to the fundamental conception of static time – plenty of ostinato passages, for instance – as well as block construction.[13]

Now, if we turn to the impact of such rhythmic systems on dance, we shall find any number of examples of choreography similarly rooted in time, as if compelled according to the same principles: the intense weaving of step patterns within one phase or block of material, 'in-the-groove' phrasing, before being 'told' to break off, at which point another phase begins. For movement, the added tension is that the old symmetries, defined by the organisation of the human body, are disrupted. Stravinsky's music does not function according to the old principles of balance and equality, which, in choreographic terms, means repeating a phrase exactly, or dancing a phrase on one side of the body and then on the other. Furthermore, such rhythmically insistent music seems to command the dancer (and choreographer likewise) to conform to its insistence on the moment.

Taruskin admits one kind of process, that of accumulation, as the sole principle of process within the new rhythmic scheme:

> Prime movers in *The Rite* are the mounting tension caused by the expectation of imminent change after prolonged unmodified activity and the sonic crescendo resulting from the gradual piling-up of individually unaffected elements.[14]

We might draw an analogy with the mounting tension in choreography stemming from similar repetitive elements. Using *Sacre* as the example, pounding the ground with fervour, building a sense of hypnotic frenzy and ecstasy through repetition of pulse and pattern, makes the awful event happen. Yet repeating ostinatos can achieve effects of accumulation in much quieter ways. Whatever the case, the rhythmic terms are quite different from those of the nineteenth-century classical ballet, even when, as in *Scènes de ballet* (1944), Stravinsky uses this as a source.

Stravinsky's is also a kind of music for dance that suggests different dancing dynamics and attitudes to the body from those of the previous century. Even when a score contains reference to nineteenth-century ballet tradition, there is a tendency towards a new boldness and blatancy about the physicality, a body with more weight and force than the earlier classical ideal. Many choreographers have responded accordingly, showing the body as real, strong, a working mechanism, rather than an idealistic image of something beyond its capacity, which is in line with modernism's focus on the materials of the medium. For Louis Danz, an American critic reflecting on Stravinsky's work in 1935, physicality totally dominates the experience, and choreographers seem to have responded in similar spirit:

> Stravinsky's music is iconolatrous – a frontalistic music – it always faces you;
> like the friend who always faces you. You cannot look behind him nor into
> him. You may understand him as biology – but not as biography.
>
> Stravinsky's music is not autobiographical. It is music of the body – the
> human body. One cannot separate this music from body.[15]

Here, a digression is needed, returning briefly to consider Stravinsky himself as a physical being, because this relates to his musical style. A composer's physicality is not necessarily transferred to the music, but in the case of Stravinsky a link has regularly been perceived. Perhaps especially when conducting, composers betray the physical qualities embodied in and suggested by their music and that they want to reanimate in performance. Descriptions of Stravinsky's way of moving in daily life, as well as his movement when playing or conducting his own music, fit descriptions of his musical dynamics. Given that his strong association with dance might well have encouraged people to see him 'dancing', which they did, there is nevertheless a surprisingly large body of literature on the subject of Stravinsky's physicality and its relationship to his music. Has any other composer attracted so many comments of this kind? Roger Shattuck was moved to summarise a number of examples in his article 'The Devil's Dance: Stravinsky's Corporal Imagination'.[16] He refers, for instance, to the librettist Charles-Ferdinand Ramuz trying to persuade Stravinsky to dance the Devil's last Triumphal March in the original *Histoire du soldat* production – possibly mere fantasy, but nonetheless recorded in Ramuz's letter: 'Dance the last scene yourself; you will liven it rhythmically and save everything.'[17]

Robert Craft, who came to know Stravinsky as well as anyone, saw him this way:

> ... a physical creature first, the rare escapee from 'that violent severance from
> man's animal past' which bothered Nietzsche. In I.S., physical appetites and

body gestures are apparent long before the mind comes out of hiding, which may be why the self-identification and the personality of the physical gestures in the music are so immediate. Or, to put it differently, with I.S., 'abstract thought' – for which he has an unlimited capacity, no matter how contemptuously he regards it – is never dissociated (or prescinded) from physical instinct.[18]

So it comes as no surprise that Stravinsky relished the physical act of performance, and that he always composed at the piano, needing physical contact with the instrument to provoke ideas – he once said that 'fingers are not to be despised: they are great inspirers, and, in contact with a musical instrument, often give birth to subconscious ideas which might otherwise never come to life'.[19] Exercise was an important part of his daily life: we know that he practised a daily gymnastics routine from the early 1920s until 1953, becoming a follower of the method devised by the Hungarian Siposh in 1941.[20] Balanchine recalls an unusual and extrovert physicality early in their friendship:

> I could see he was very interested in dance. He was very lithe himself, very agile. He could walk on his hands like an acrobat, and he liked social dancing ...[21]

We are reminded here too of Stravinsky's passion for being close to the movement in dance rehearsals, and joining in with physical ideas of his own.

Descriptions of Stravinsky's body attitude and dynamics in daily life are vivid, the designer Tchelitcheff likening him to a 'prancing grasshopper', Cocteau seeing him as an 'erect ant' at the conductor's podium, whilst, for his composer friend Nabokov, he was 'much more like a bird – one of those small birds with large, sturdy beaks, like cardinals or love birds, whose movements are quick, electric and nervous'.[22] In the terminology of the movement theorist Rudolf Laban, the analogies are clear: a small body favouring direct, sudden movement qualities, manifesting a light touch (as economical use of force), bound-flow punctuations and defiance of gravity. At other times, Stravinsky is metaphorically a dancer, but the language betrays the same dynamic qualities. At the piano, his fingers fly

> ... like a group of dancers on a stage. He leaps from the keyboard to the conductor's podium and back to the piano with the agility of a dancer, and, at the end, stepping down in youthful waltz-like movement, lights another cigarette.[23]

Now we find the composer Elliott Carter observing the qualities of directness, suddenness and economy again, injected into Stravinsky's style as pianist. He notes his

> remarkable piano playing, filled with electricity ... What impressed me most, aside from the music itself, was the very telling quality of attack he gave to piano notes, embodying often in just one sound the very quality so characteristic of his music – incisive but not brutal, rhythmically highly controlled yet filled with intensity so that each note was made to seem weighty and important. Every time I heard him play ... the strong impression of highly individualized, usually detached notes filled with extraordinary dynamism caught my attention immediately – and this was true in soft passages as well as loud.[24]

Each note he played, Carter says, was 'a "Stravinsky-note", full of energy, excitement, and serious intentness'.[25]

Naturally, conducting allowed Stravinsky more physical freedom as a performer. Although, according to Eric Walter White, some considered his conducting 'too mechanical and too inhibited',[26] the literature from the 1920s and 1930s describing rehearsals and performances reveals a tantalising array of body imagery:

> He underlines the design of the music with the movement of his body ... According to the character of the passage, he dances lightly, or rebounds, and groans like a wounded man after a detonation from the brass. He pounces like a feline, and, full of Slavic ardor and spirit, mimes his music, now violently, now caressingly ...[27]
>
> Rhythm is made flesh in the form of a little man who bends his legs like a fencer taking guard, who splays his thighs like a horseman, who snaps his elbows back like a boxer on the attack, who looks alternately, or all at once, like a bird, an engineer, a Kobold, and a surgeon.[28]
>
> When he conducts, there isn't a part of his body that doesn't participate in the action, from head to toes ... Stravinsky's whole body laughs, and plays, and dances, and pirouettes ...[29]

Here, a reviewer spots a direct link between Stravinsky's physicality and his particular rhythmic quality:

> It was enough to watch him, to observe his brusque jerkings, to understand the animating role played by rhythm in this music.[30]

Most film footage of Stravinsky conducting stems from the 1960s and shows him in his later years. By this time, the movement range is diminished, but we can nevertheless recognise the features poeticised in the literature, Stravinsky's physical *habitus*. The style is idiosyncratic, untaught and unmediated by conventional conducting technique. Good examples are two 1965 recordings, one of *Firebird Suite* with the New Philharmonia Orchestra at the Royal Festival Hall, London (which Craft rates as the best example available of Stravinsky's conducting), the other of an *Apollo* rehearsal in Hamburg captured on the film *A Stravinsky Portrait*.[31] There is the familiar incisiveness, sometimes in a dramatic gesture, like a snatch at the air or a beheading action, direct, sharp. The approach to beat in the rhythmic sections is telling, too – with the emphasis so often *up*, shoulders raised, and the sharp rebound from the down impulse cut short, a taut, clipped finish – not a jot of energy lost. In an outtake of Tony Palmer's 1982 Stravinsky documentary *Once at a border ...*, Craft suggests that Stravinsky's music and his body operated in mutual definition: the musical emphasis upbeat, his conducting beat upbeat. Except for very late in life, it seems that the composer-conductor lived up on his toes.[32]

I am also interested in how powerfully the fact of musical embodiment can be communicated through the act of performing Stravinsky's music. There is no better example than my hearing/seeing the four-hand piano version of *Sacre* played by Fiona and John York at the Wigmore Hall in 2004.[33] Here, the movement dynamics of the two pianists conveyed with total conviction the notion of movement in the music, and an impression of feelings expressed through that motion. Through the tension in the shoulders in a crouch over the keyboard, the letting-out of massive force down through the arms, the weighty rocking motions of the body, I sensed anger, needling anxiety, collective hysteria, shrieks, screams, the bravado of battle. Of course, there is the argument that the performers must have been aware of the huge, painful mythology surrounding *Sacre*, which might well have infiltrated their performance in some fashion. Yet, even so, such was the authenticity of their performance – there was no inkling of their consciously 'adding' anything to make the show more exciting – the effect of physicality seemed to spring directly from their engagement with the music and the body in the music.

The effect of musical embodiment is especially strong in this version of the score because the connection between performer and sound is so elemental – it is about just two people at work on one piano. It is pertinent that Vaslav Nijinsky first confronted *Sacre* through its piano rehearsal score, and at least once with the composer playing, providing a similar elemental, raw rendering of the music. The choreographer only heard the orchestral score just before the premiere.

Given my reading of this four-hand piano performance, it is interesting that Stravinsky made a point about the virtues of seeing musicians playing, the extra vitality of physical presence. He was anxious about passive listening without a visual element, one reason why he wanted the small orchestra on stage for *Histoire du soldat*:

> I have always had a horror of listening to music with my eyes shut, with nothing for them to do. The sight of the gestures and movements of the various parts of the body producing the music is fundamentally necessary if it is to be grasped in all its fullness. All music created or composed demands some exteriorization for the perception of the listener.[34]

The Adorno question

Most of the cited comments so far, by those who saw Stravinsky in action or tried to put in words the impact of his rhythmic discoveries, register fascination, even delight and pleasure. But there have been significant exceptions along the way, critics who have viewed the rhythmic element in Stravinsky's music as essentially problematic. One of these was the influential philosopher-musicologist Theodor Adorno, notorious for his damaging assessment of Stravinsky, especially within *Philosophy of Modern Music* (1949),[35] when he set the composer in dialectical opposition to Arnold Schoenberg, thereby polarising the traditions of serialism and neoclassicism against each other. The problems posed by Adorno's 1949 account of Stravinsky are widely recognised, including the quality of the published translation of this book. My summary here of the issues relies to a large extent on the thorough and carefully argued scholarship of the Adorno specialist Max Paddison.[36]

Adorno approaches art as political statement and offers a sociological critique, maintaining that its content lies within the musical materials themselves. But his is also an aesthetic of modernism, wherein he perceives a dilemma in, on the one hand, the need for 'unity and integration (the harmonious relationship between part and whole) and, on the other hand, the loss of faith in any overarching unity on both individual and social levels in the face of the evident fragmentation of modern existence'.[37] Art, he believes, should nevertheless maintain the presence of the Subject, revealing self-awareness and critical edge in its view of the human condition, and, according to these terms, Adorno seems to subscribe to a notion of art as an expression of the Subject's position in the world. This self-reflection he found more evident in Schoenberg than in Stravinsky, whose music, he felt, fell readily into the category of commodity or entertainment. For Adorno, Stravinsky's avoidance of the developmental, progressive structural tradition (which Schoenberg promoted in an atonal idiom) was a symbol of the liquidation of the Subject and of denial of individual freedom. The repetition structures that Stravinsky preferred represented lack of individual agency or will for change.

Paddison points out that Adorno's view of Stravinsky shifted over time, suggesting that he was responding to a changing political landscape. The essays 'Die stabilisierte Musik' (1928) and 'Zur gesellschaftlichen Lage der Musik' (1932)[38] were written during the relatively liberal period of Weimar Germany, and *Histoire du soldat* is hailed in them as a landmark critical reflection upon the position of the Subject through irony. By the 1940s, Adorno would have been all too aware of the literal annihilation of the individual in the concentration camps. He would also have been aware of Stravinsky's anti-expression philosophy and possibly sensitive too to Stravinsky's anti-semitism and admiration for the Italian fascist Mussolini.[39] Now, according to Adorno, the Subject is sacrificed in Stravinsky's music. This can be a programmatic enterprise. For instance, the music is complicit with the sacrifice of the victim in *Petrushka* and *Sacre*, in both cases by a crowd or tribe, and with no hope of redemption suggested. But, for Adorno, this is also the 'content' of plotless concert works, the Subject likewise 'disappeared'.

As Paddison has pointed out, the devices of modernism in Adorno's eyes 'risk losing their critical edge in their regression either to a mythic past through distancing from the real world, or [especially in the case of the neoclassical works] to a cartoon-like mimicking of an unacceptable reality as protection from it'.[40] In *Philosophy of Modern Music* (1949), Stravinsky is depicted at best as heartless, mocking, a trickster, at worst as authoritarian, marked with irresponsibility like the totalitarian regimes of recent times.[41]

As the title of his 1962 essay 'Stravinsky: A Dialectical Portrait' suggests, Adorno's third critique of Stravinsky is less damning, and Adorno is quick to point out that he has been misread: he had meant that the unwholesome aspects of the music that he had described are inherent in the music, not in Stravinsky the man.[42] He still rejects Stravinsky's non-developmental compositional technique and remains suspicious of Stravinsky's urbane manner in disguising a state of affairs that is intolerable through technical virtuosity and by using the mask of fine taste. But by this time, Adorno had read the work of Samuel Beckett, and read similarities to Stravinsky in Beckett's use of devices of repetition. Now, Adorno seems to admit to glimpses of truth in Stravinsky's work, a movement between entertainment and cover-up on the one hand and, on the other, showing us the horror of the void at the heart of experience.[43]

Today, Adorno's political reading of Stravinsky has been discredited by many Stravinsky scholars, who do not believe that expressing barbarism necessarily means being complicit with barbarism.[44] We might argue, for instance, that music presents an image of the world in which it was made, showing us ourselves, warts and all. Yet Taruskin is clearly tormented by his own mixed reaction – the tension between interpreting monstrous content as signalling despicable politics and a positive reading stemming from the complex interior of the scores.[45] Adorno's criticism of Stravinsky's non-developmental approach to form has likewise been dismissed in the light of re-evaluations of Stravinsky according to Russian as opposed to Austro-German structural models. Adorno critiqued Stravinsky's music for its exclusive attention to rhythm and colour, indeed the 'fetishisation' of rhythm, at the expense of what he considered the developmental agencies of harmony, melody and counterpoint. Can he really be so dogmatic and authoritarian himself as to suggest that only the Austro-German tradition allows space for the free Subject?[46] And is there no room for manoeuvre, allowing for Stravinsky's purposeful and integral use of heritage and musical components other than rhythm?

Yet, on the other hand, what Adorno has to say about Stravinsky and physicality is revealing, and to date scholars have not drawn out this aspect of his writing or analysed it in relation to Stravinsky's particular quality of *musique dansante*. We may find Adorno elitist, dogmatic and narrow in his view, but the physical subtext of his writing may make more sense than at first appears. It might point to an ambiguity in Stravinsky as a dance composer, that, as much as we 'experience' vitality from his music, we also experience an element of discomfort or pain – although, unlike Adorno, I would not claim that this means Stravinsky (or his music) is complicit with discomfort or pain.

Interestingly, on one occasion Adorno seems to allow dance the opportunity to contain the Subject where it is absent from the music, so there is a sense in which the body on stage offers some hope of redemption. The dancer's body is, in reality, an alien object, but at the same time, the 'feeling of the ego' can be projected upon it. Music, on the other hand,

remains alienated; it stands in contrast to the subject as being-in-itself.

Thus, the physical operates as 'a transcendent factor' and adopts, metaphorically, the role of melody:

Even in Stravinsky's earlier ballets there is no lack of passages in which the 'melody' is by-passed, in order that it might appear in the actual leading voice – in bodily movement on the stage.[47]

Perhaps this betrays a sympathetic engagement with dance movement. Here, Adorno says, in the early ballets, the melodic element finds itself elsewhere, on stage.

Elsewhere, Adorno writes disparagingly of dance as a negative influence on Stravinsky's music. He believes in the ideal of a 'spiritualised' music in an 'expressive-dynamic' mode, reflecting the 'subjective and psychological experience of time', Bergson's *le temps durée*. Dance aficionados are likely to take issue with him, but he catalogues dance as a fundamentally spatial and pictorial rather than time-based art, subscribing to *le temps espace*.

> True dance – in contrast to mature music [viz. sonata form, the model for progressive, developmental structure] – is an art of static time, a turning in a circle, movement without progress.[48]

For Adorno, Stravinsky's crime was to make music spatial too, encouraged by his early experience of ballet. Hence, with an inflexible machine pulse taking over his work, Stravinsky's rhythm represents stasis, not directed motion, and now it is problematic that the body, even the heartbeat, is the true basis of music.

> The concentration of [Stravinsky's] music upon accents and time relationships produces an illusion of bodily movement[49] ... The physical aspect of music, however ... accords with the retrogression of society.[50]

Thus dance is ultimately damned and the body banished from serious music. Time and time again in Adorno's writing, dance is used as a metaphor for music that fails to meet his ideals. The *Symphony in Three Movements* (1945), which held more promise for Adorno than most of Stravinsky's works, probably because its programme content of 'tragic symbols' had been publicised (see p. 141), in the end disappoints:

> Symphonic pathos is nothing but the obscure countenance of an abstract ballet suite.[51]

The Adorno of 'Stravinsky: A Dialectical Portrait' refers to dance in much the same way.

Yet Adorno had a body and it is patently obvious that he experiences Stravinsky's music as symbolising a devastatingly powerful physicality. We might acknowledge, as Paddison suggests, that Adorno's writing stems from a 'long German literary tradition of using the extremes and the rhetoric of exaggeration, irony and the grotesque, as strategies for revealing underlying truths',[52] but, as we shall see later, his writing about the body in Stravinsky's music is not without parallel. It is not merely hysterical. And here is the pain. Adorno uses language that signifies brutality to the body: 'convulsive blows ... electric blows ... attack ... shock ... irregular, jolting accents ... pounding into the head ... stomping and hammering ... sado-masochistic pleasure'.[53]

It is such shocks that drive out the Subject: here is a mindless body in spasm. Language of the body is not what Adorno chooses to use for Schoenberg. Furthermore, the brutality of *Sacre* haunts Adorno's entire Stravinsky portrait in

Philosophy of Modern Music. His vision of the composer's work as a whole, including his neoclassical music, allows no space for the light touch, the 'incisive but not brutal' manner, that Carter remembered from Stravinsky the pianist.

Thus Adorno responds to Stravinsky's physical music. For him, it is neither vibrant nor uplifting, it is not expressive of a horror that we should know about and learn from – it is a signal of totalitarianism, assault on the body, intended brutality to the person most evilly cast as a joke. Did he respond thus so strongly because of his philosophical ideals for mature music? Or because he had lived through Nazism, and knew something of Stravinsky's personal politics? Or perhaps the strength of the physical discomfort that he clearly felt symbolically through Stravinsky's music helped to define his distaste for the composer's music? In considering the power and nature of Adorno's physical response, we should now turn to other writing on the subject of Stravinsky's rhythm.

For different reasons, two British music critics, Cecil Gray and Constant Lambert, contemporaries of Adorno, felt similar disturbance from Stravinsky's new kind of rhythmic content. This emerges from their writings published before Adorno's most influential critique of Stravinsky came out, writings that are now considered misguided, but were not so at the time when Stravinsky's neoclassicism was barely appreciated in Britain. Like Adorno, both criticise Stravinsky for his celebration of rhythm at the expense of melody and harmony. Gray, in *A Survey of Contemporary Music* (1924), bemoans the loss of the balance shown in the classics between these three components so that, in the end, rhythm itself is 'inert, lifeless, mechanical, metrical ... Rhythm implies life, some kind of movement or progression at least, but this music stands quite still, in a quite frightening immobility. It is like a top or gyroscope turning ceaselessly and ineffectually on itself ...'[54]

In his brilliantly acerbic book *Music Ho!* (1934), Constant Lambert, who was also a composer and conductor, claims that, without the strength of melody and harmony, there is no emotional significance. For him, *Sacre* is the first problematic work, its brutality resonating with the deeply unsettled political landscape that led to war. Here is intensification of expression and nervous effect, yet an element of mockery is also observed as content: 'This is barbaric music for the supercivilized, an aphrodisiac for the jaded and surfeited.'[55]

Lambert saves his most cutting remarks for the detached experiments of the neoclassical Stravinsky. Now he refers to 'the jolt he gives the machine [*Pulcinella*] ... the objective juggling with rhythm [*Histoire*] ... the niggling use of rhythm in Stravinsky's nursery-rhyme period ... the essentially marionette works'.[56] And he ridicules the 'wrong' asymmetries forced on to the dance music which, in *Histoire*, 'acquire a new perversity when attached to the left-right-left and the one-two-three hop of the wooden soldier's march and the baby's polka ... To dance to these movements is really as absurd as it would be to read the news in the sections of *Le Journal* incorporated by Picasso or Juan Gris in one of their "abstracts"'.[57]

Minus Adorno's approach to art as political statement, Lambert turns the neoclassical Stravinsky into a facetious, superficial parodist who borrows from heritage in the absence of original ideas, a 'time traveller'[58] who promotes a rhythmic content that is more irritation than galvanising force of propulsion.

Of course, Adorno, Gray and Lambert lived through periods of political and human turmoil, and one could argue that this has affected their reading of Stravinsky. But it is interesting to find the American ballerina Gelsey Kirkland fundamentally in tune with their experience, years later, and now compelled to visualise the rhythmic impetus literally, in her own body. In her autobiography, Kirkland complains bitterly of the rhythmic domination of Balanchine and Stravinsky when she took on the title role in *Firebird* in 1970. Her natural inclination was to 'interpret', to phrase material with freedom, and she yearned to escape from the rigid framework of pulse, reading Stravinsky's music as an attack on the autonomy of the dancer performer. She felt dehumanised and mindless, the epitome of the victim encapsulated in Adorno's prose:

> According to their [Balanchine and Stravinsky] aesthetic code, the human condition was reflected primarily through animal and mechanical imagery, to be realized through the senses by way of instinct and imitation ...
>
> As a dancer I rebelled against rhythm. I did not care for its effects. Rather than an expression of freedom or release, I felt rhythm obscured meaning and constrained my movement. In longing to tell a story through my dance, I was frustrated by music that appealed only to my sense of time and tempo. I needed more than the propulsion of a beat.
>
> Stravinsky replaced the thematic development of classical music with a range of sensations that alternately jolted or lulled the mind.[59]

Firebird may not be the strongest example of Stravinsky's rhythmic pain: I read Kirkland's words as referring to her much wider experience of the Stravinsky–Balanchine repertory.

Many, of course, have read Stravinsky's rhythmic language much more positively, and for some it has even made excellent sense from a political standpoint. Writing in communist Russia during the 1920s, the music critic Boris Asafyev considered that the intellectual depth of Stravinsky's music prevented it from being mere commodity music – 'it offers more than mere hypnotisation of our feelings'.[60] Quite the reverse of Adorno's thinking! Yet, despite such intellectual demands, he says, Stravinsky is still close to the people, the masses who constitute the great hope for the future. Using *Renard* as his example, Asafyev maintains that Stravinsky is alive to the authentic folk heritage, to its most energetic roots, and also to the dynamics of contemporary urban life, his music reflecting 'the impetuous current of our lives, with its elastic rhythms, its fast tempi, and its obedience to the pulsations of work'.[61] The tone of Asafyev's rhythmic language is Futurist or Constructivist.[62] For Asafyev, Stravinsky's Subject seems to have agency despite the requirements of the new order. The one who is lost is the one who fails to rise to the new requirements.[63]

Many dancers, too, have been positive about the composer, like Suzanne Farrell, Balanchine–Stravinsky dancer par excellence. Her language suggests a remarkable freedom, a passion in her response to music, quite the opposite to Kirkland's experience:

> I ... felt in tune with his music, even when there was no tune in the score. He made sense in my body, not because I had figured him out – that was an intellectual fantasy exercise for others to enjoy – but because I listened and, energized, let my body ride the waves. If I had had to stop and think, I wouldn't have danced a step.[64]

And on dancing the Chosen One (L'Elue) in Maurice Béjart's *Sacre*:

> It was still Stravinsky's ecstatic music that I so loved.[65]

Many other Balanchine soloists have spoken about the pleasure, after an initial stage of counting, of forgetting the mathematics and feeling the music 'in the body'.[66]

The choreographer Siobhan Davies who, although she has never used the composer's music herself, applauds what he has achieved for dance, *is* fascinated by the new intellectual element in his scores, and their sophisticated construction:

> All that rhythm, all that excitement and innovation has helped dance ... become a brainier aspect of the arts. Stravinsky made us think in an extraordinary way ...

Yet Davies also understands that the music is

> visceral, urgent rhythm as well as lucid mental musical games ... I don't just imagine my body changing when I listen to *The Rite of Spring*. It *does* change. My gravity shifts so that I am ready to whip round, turn and run. My breath is higher in my chest, pulse irregular, a deep feeling of disquiet and urgency. I feel part of a group and then horrifyingly alone. I am rootless, pushed beyond myself ...[67]

When asked the reason why she has not choreographed any music by Stravinsky herself, Davies alludes to the huge power of his music:

> In the past, I was not ready to use music that was so strong. Now, in the present, I don't want to be dominated by the excellence of the music. I need my dance to stand up by itself, with its own phrasing, logic and grammar.[68]

So, today, Davies admires Stravinsky's power and achievement, but as a composer for other choreographers to use: dance autonomy, not being driven by music, is an issue for her.

The Finnish dancer/choreographer Tero Saarinen would agree with her stance on dance, yet he *has* used Stravinsky's music. At the same time, in his 2007 programme article 'Why Stravinsky?', he avoids totally the issue of rhythmic content. Writing 'positively' of *Sacre*, *Petrushka* and *Noces*, all of which he has choreographed, he stresses that:

> The brutality and the sense of a personal, individual voice make the works moving on a human level. For me they are like agonised screams from the unconscious – and hence fascinating.

As we shall see later (pp. 477-8), he, and some other artists today, have undertaken an entirely new approach to the physicality in Stravinsky's music.

Yet many of those who respond positively to Stravinsky's music betray something of the physical disturbance and tension described by Adorno et al. Davies clearly appreciates the dangerous implications of Stravinsky's music. Aaron Copland claims that Stravinsky was unique for his rhythmic 'jolt'.[69] Carter suggests that the particular rhythmic intensity through regular beat causes a kind of body 'stiffening'.[70] We stumble upon that interesting and contradictory phenomenon of rhythm as agent of both control and vitality. Could this be connected to the mixed feelings about the machine in early/mid-twentieth-century culture, feelings of both fascination and horror, the machine read as either Utopian and a symbol of freedom, or dangerous to the notion of subjectivity and oppressive, or as a fundamentally ambiguous phenomenon?

Stravinsky's repetitive rhythmic constructions are machine metaphors themselves, not only his emphatic beat, but also those complex multi-layered systems, 'mindless', set in motion and simply repeating until cut off. Consequently, it is no surprise that a common element in descriptions of Stravinsky's music is machine imagery, which Asafyev, as we have seen, favoured as a positive metaphor. So, it seems, did T.S. Eliot. Listen to what he wrote in 1921 about *Sacre*, which seemed to him to reflect the commonalities between primitivism and the contemporary period, to transform the rhythm of the steppes into the scream of the motor-horn, the rattle of machinery, the grind of wheels, the beating of iron and steel, the roar of the underground railway, and the other barbaric noises of modern life.[71]

Stravinsky himself was fascinated by matters mechanical. Around this time, he was busy experimenting with the musical machine baby of the age, the pianola, and relishing its metronomic precision and capability to allow him full control over the performance of his work.

Mapped directly onto the body, the Stravinsky machine symbolises the properties of channelled force, punctuation by bound flow, and automatic response. We might image in our bodies the thrusting of pistons and regular pulsating, the occasional judder or shift of gear, and with all this a kind of 'stiffening'. Human-style irregularities in alternating dynamic patterns of tension and release, breath models, are overruled. If choreography conforms to such a musical spirit, it lets the music control the dancers, shape their movement and subdue human impulse. Just how exciting, just how awful is this?

Daniel Albright has devoted a whole book to the thesis of the machine as integral: *Stravinsky: The Music Box and The Nightingale*. He views the fundamental dichotomy in the composer's music as

the deep equivalence of the natural and the artificial. At the center of his dramatic imagination is the desire to juxtapose in a single work two competing systems – one of which seems natural, tasteful, approved alike by man and God, the other of which seems artificial, abhorrent, devilish – and to subvert these distinctions as best he can.[72]

Such a dichotomy feeds Stravinsky's programme for the objectification of music and for the stifling and suppression of the human Subject in his stage works. Thus, in Albright's view, artifice wins. Petrushka is a doll, which is already another kind of Stravinsky machine, one that demonstrates an ironical attitude towards the Subject, even if the doll is invested with human emotions. *Sacre* is even more an 'assault on subjectivity' and representation of a 'pre-human' vista,[73] objectification on stage and in the music. As for *Le Rossignol*, Stravinsky was really more interested in the mechanical nightingale than the real one: 'the triumph of Nature over Art, described in the libretto, is reversed in the depths of the music'.[74] And *Noces*, Albright suggests, represents the ultimate art-machine, constituted by rhythm and caught up in Stravinsky's pianola experiments: the instrument was included in an early scoring plan. People are negligible, with speeches misfitting the dancers on stage, and Nijinska's emotionless masses highlighting the manner of the music.[75]

Unlike Adorno, Albright does not suggest that this frightening metaphor represents what Stravinsky really thought about humanity, which is a major intellectual distinction; indeed, he finds the questions Stravinsky poses positively stimulating. Yet the language of dehumanisation and physical brutality certainly brings the two theorists together. As much as we may now find Adorno's philosophy untenable and argue that there is still human space in Stravinsky's music, his point about rhythmic force and its effect upon the body rings unnervingly true. As much, too, as we can find examples of Stravinsky works that hardly foreground the machine at all, machine rhythm is undeniably a strong tendency in his music.

Balanchine once said that what he 'mainly' expects from a composer is 'a steady and reassuring pulse which holds the work together and which one should feel even in the rests'.[76] He wants a machine to drive him. So it comes as no surprise that he so often singled out the tautness of pulse-driven rhythms in his appreciation of Stravinsky, 'an architect of time':[77] the silences pregnant because the pulse continued through them – 'life goes on within each silence'; the strictly pulsed fermata, 'always counted out in beats'; and rubato, 'notated precisely, in unequal measures'.[78] Balanchine is right. Stravinsky, more than any other composer, prompted rhythmic prioritisation from his choreographers, and Balanchine jumped at the opportunity. The composer once joked, 'What he needs is not a *pas de deux* but a motor impulse.'[79] Jerome Robbins too referred to the 'tremendous motor', concentrating on its power of propulsion: 'It almost carries you, takes you along with it. It's almost irresistible.'[80]

It was that motor impulse that most disturbed Kirkland about Balanchine's choreography. Discussing rehearsals of his *Concerto Barocco* (Bach, 1941), she refers to his

> mechanical interpretation of the score. It was as if he were constructing a clock on the stage, each of us keeping time like a cog in the mechanism.[81]

Balanchine probably represents the most extreme choreographic parallel to the Stravinsky machine. Yet, unlike Farrell and many other Balanchine soloists, Kirkland does not recognise that there is still room for an individual performer's rubato, for active rather than purely passive response to the motor. As the choreographer once wrote: 'A good instrumentalist, Milstein, for instance, or a resourceful dancer, can give the feeling of rubato in Stravinsky's music ...' – then he added, 'without blurring the beat'.[82]

A final word here on the sheer weight of Stravinsky's 'Russian' dance scores, be that through orchestration, volume, use of low registers, rhythmic accentuation, or metaphorical weight in relation to other theatrical elements.

This was a new phenomenon for *musique dansante* at the time. Hearing *Petrushka* in concert – he had never seen the ballet – was enough to convince the Moscow music critic Nikolai Kashkin that the centre of gravity had moved away from the dance to the music.[83]

The perceptive Russian ballet critic André Levinson, who might well have seen all of Stravinsky's Diaghilev ballets, either before or after he settled in Paris, decided that the music was wonderful but simply not right for dance: too heavy, too powerful. For him, *Firebird* was not *dansante*: it was a hybrid between a symphonic poem for the concert hall and a ballet, and its rhythms were too complex.[84] *Sacre* and *Noces* simply overwhelmed the dance with their huge vitality and power. Levinson changed his mind on *Petrushka* from 'it renders the ballet itself superfluous'[85] to 'the balance between the ear and the eye is perfect ... [it is] incomplete outside of the theatre',[86] only to return to his original opinion:

> Stravinsky is sufficient unto himself and neither demands nor permits interpretation through the dance.[87]

Levinson was a conservative who maintained traditional values on *musique dansante* that Stravinsky flouted. He believed that music should be 'appended to the dance ...' and asked for 'the formation of dance music from within the spirit of the dance itself',[88] meaning classical dance, the *danse d'école*. Stravinsky would never have agreed with Levinson about such musical subservience. However, after he had opened up the possibilities of a new, weightier, more dominant form of *musique dansante*, he turned towards the *danse d'école* himself and his musical textures became more spare.

Already we have seen that choreographers, dancers, spectators and listeners have variously estimated Stravinsky's music as a source of liberating contemporary excitement or expressive symbol of menace and control, as mere irritation or full-blown assault, or even something to keep well away from. Now we take a look at the multiple choreographic uses of these new kinds of *musique dansante*.

Choreographing Stravinsky: Tales from a chronology

At the time of going to print, the *SGD* database, a record of premiere information on potentially all the dance works choreographed to Stravinsky's music, numbered 1218 entries from all over the world, featuring 682 choreographers and 99 different scores, indeed nearly all the scores that Stravinsky wrote (*www.roehampton.ac.uk/stravinsky*, see Ex. 2.4). A project that Larraine Nicholas and I began in 2001, this bank of data reveals many patterns and raises

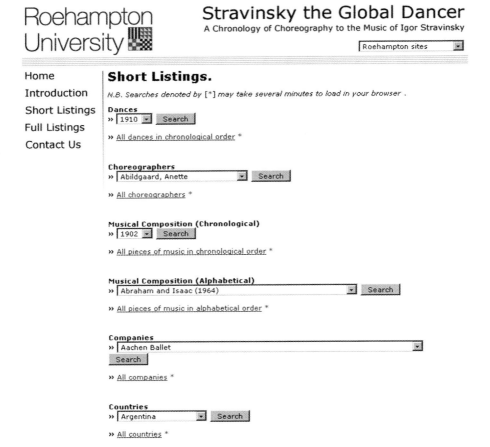

Ex. 2.4. Sample web page from the 'Stravinsky the Global Dancer' (*SGD*) database.

many issues. The database is clearly the place to begin a survey of multiple choreographic uses.

First, it is important to consider our criteria for creating this database, its coverage and its limitations. A *comprehensive* database of choreographies to the music of Stravinsky? Although we never believed that such a thing was a possibility, we had no idea about the sheer number and complexity of entries that we would have to make. So often, initial research led not only to one work for entry but to an array of others, a culture of Stravinsky dances by a choreographer of whom we had barely any knowledge and perhaps in a part of the world for which we had little access to information.

There are not only far more entries today than we imagined when we started the project, but also far more categories of entry than we expected. Original database fields and methodologies were established and later modified, as we turned up works using several Stravinsky scores or involving several choreographers. We had to find ways of expressing the use of selections from scores and of collage soundscapes by a variety of composers, as well as Stravinsky's inclination to re-arrange his work for new instrumentations.

An important point is the provisional nature of the database as a foundation for analysis. It does not, and cannot, tell us the whole story. That issue has been addressed more fully in the database Introduction, included on the website. In summary here, it is important to acknowledge the limits of what could be achieved within time and geographical constraints: a project centre in the UK and funded blocks of time in selected archives and libraries abroad, including the Jerome Robbins Dance Division of the New York Public Library for the Performing Arts and Paul Sacher Stiftung in Basle. It soon became obvious that our geographical spread was uneven, and our data particularly strong where it represented the English-speaking world, with Western Europe next in line for strong coverage. Information on Stravinsky dances has become increasingly globalised in recent years; nevertheless, beyond the bounds of the UK, North America and Germany, what we had access to in the libraries and archives used was often disappointing. Despite the good holdings of foreign language dance journals in the major British and American collections, the solid primary source base was missing. Furthermore, the systematic collecting and recording of data ended in December 2002 and works premiered after that date have been included on a more ad hoc basis.[89]

Even for the central geographic domain of this project, there are surely some omissions. The major listing *Stravinsky on Stage* (1982) by Alexander Schouvaloff and Victor Borovsky covers itself with the reference to 'major productions'.[90] We decided that it was important to get beyond the very public picture and well beyond established canons of work, and thus to welcome the inclusion of student and non-professional productions: for instance, the 1964 *Pulcinella* by John Begg for the Ballet Guild of Cleveland, Ohio, which was performed in a hospital and a community centre; Jennifer Jackson's 1991 *Les Noces*, a youth project stemming from the Education Department of Birmingham Royal Ballet; and, in 2003, Pamela Walsh's *Stravinsky Ballet Music* project with the Jackdaws Educational Trust (using excerpts from *Firebird*, *Petrushka* and *Sacre*), for students from two local middle schools and a group from Chernobyl. These enterprises too have interesting points to make about the spread of Stravinsky's music.

But if there is no review available of a work or other document to merit its appearance in the more established Stravinsky choreography listings, how could we find out about such a production? In this regard, Stravinsky's publishers' records have proved useful (those of Boosey & Hawkes, publishers of the main body of Stravinsky scores, Schott and Chester). The publishers hold lists of performances for which copyright fees have been paid, potentially the most complete charting possible of the history of a dance work across the years and around the world, although, in actuality, their listings are not complete. Sometimes copyright fees have not been paid, so no record appears. There has been a particular problem, for instance, with stagings in the Eastern bloc,[91] but there are other occasions when dance companies have not registered usage: for instance, if a musical recording is used rather than live music, and no hire fee – of orchestral parts – is documented. In other cases, publishers' files tantalise us with records that a performance took place, but without confirmation of the choreographer's name. Having said that, we have every reason to believe that our records are less complete for non-professional productions and small companies where the work is less broadly 'public'.

The invaluable input to the database by contributors from around the world, as well as my own opportunities to visit new countries, have naturally shaped the profile of data. *Sacre* is the clearest example of this. It is by far the best-documented work in the database, because of the groundwork already carried out by other scholars. Thus, it has been possible to annotate an unusually high proportion of *Sacre* productions, and to synthesise trends as regards type of setting. The Internet has become an increasingly important tool in database research.

In summary, Nicholas and I recognise the time and geographical restraints on our achievement to date, yet I am convinced that we have gained enough information to suggest certain trends with confidence. Future expansion of the database will enable me to refine my view of these trends.

Early on, we made a decision to limit our project in terms of what we believed a dance database should prioritise. A number of Stravinsky's ballet scores have been used as opportunities for jugglers, puppets, marionettes and animation (Walt Disney's *Fantasia* (1940) being the most celebrated example of the latter) and other movement forms allied to dance. We have not included these, yet it is important to recognise these associated disciplines. We did include oddities such as Balanchine's 1942 *Circus Polka* for fifty elephants, fifty 'beautiful girls' and a ballerina, and *Triptyk*, a 2000 staging of *Le Sacre du printemps* and *Symphony of Psalms* by Bartabas for the Zingaro troupe (premiered at Expo in Hanover), which introduced horses alongside the dancers. Where the borders between dance, mime and theatre are blurred, we happily strayed across them. Also included is work made for film, television and opera. In the case of opera, the weight of choreography has often been considerable, going beyond the traditional incorporation of incidental dances (see pp. 113-14).

The full-theatre piece *Histoire du soldat* (as opposed to the *Suite* drawn from it) holds an unusual place in the repertory. Partly because of its modest resource requirements, it has received hundreds of productions, ranging from full staging to concert performance with a token gesture towards theatre. Many of these minimised the dance component that was a part of the original conception and it is not always possible to distinguish dancers from actors in cast lists. We did not attempt documentation beyond what readily appears in the standard dance listings.

A note with regard to publishing and copyright issues is in order, because several factors beyond the choice of choreographers influence the spread of productions. First, there is the issue of exclusivity, which is a contractual agreement that may prohibit the use of a score for a fixed period after the premiere. Next, publishers (if contacted according to the correct procedures) monitor the usage of scores in accordance with the wishes of the Stravinsky estate, *Sacre* being especially carefully protected.[92] There has been a notably freer approach in the USA than elsewhere to Stravinsky's early works, because they have not enjoyed copyright protection there. For dance, this has had the strongest implications for *Sacre*, *Firebird* and *Petrushka* (see p. 74). As an example of freer approach, we find use of the *Sacre* orchestration/arrangement by Robert Rudolf (by, for instance, Martha Graham and Millicent Hodson, for the original Joffrey Ballet production of her Nijinsky reconstruction), and also other, much more radical score manipulations. The rules for copyright protection in the USA have now changed, and all Stravinsky's works published since 1923 are protected there for 95 years from the date of publication.[93]

The summary that now follows, based on analysis of the current database, derives from the short listings (chronologies organised by dance, choreographer, musical composition, company and country of premiere) and full records for individual dances, which have themselves prompted further research. Readers are encouraged to cross-reference the database, to use it to illustrate the points made. Occasionally, examples are discussed for which there is currently insufficient information to generate a database entry, but which have important things to tell us.

The general distribution of productions

A look first at the distribution of new Stravinsky productions over the years confirms several expectations. The anniversary years 1962, 1972 and 1982 are especially important for new productions, most of all 1982 (the Centenary), with a total of 69 new works recorded. Such anniversaries occasioned the largest Stravinsky Festivals, such as those of New York City Ballet in 1972 and 1982. 1997 stands out as another high point, with 32 new productions in total. Anniversaries of individual scores seem to have been far less significant, although it remains to be seen what impact centenary years will have for *Firebird*, *Petrushka, Sacre* and *Noces*, which are still very popular scores.

After a marked growth of Stravinsky usage towards the end of the 1920s, there was a contraction, the nadir being during the Second World War. Usage increased during the mid-1950s and, as to be expected, faster still during the latter part of the century.

From the mid-1960s, we see a trend towards collages of several short Stravinsky scores, alongside the increased use of excerpts from scores, probably an attempt to move beyond the well-known, well-worn repertoire, whilst also conforming to the standard time length of a dance within a triple bill. Collages of this kind proved especially popular during Centenary year 1982. Most examples from 1982 are mixtures from concert works: Michael Smuin's *Stravinsky Piano Pieces* (San Francisco Ballet), for instance, drew from as many as eight scores, with some individual numbers barely a minute long (for instance, from the *Easy Pieces* and *Les Cinq Doigts*).

Over the years, there has also been increased use of Stravinsky's music within collage soundscapes involving a number of other composers. For 1992, unusually, seven examples of collage are recorded in the database, encompassing rock as well as other classical music and text, from choreographers as diverse as Maurice Béjart and Peter Martins from ballet, and Stephen Petronio and Michael Clark from modern dance. Outside mainstream dance, many choreographers today (or performance artists allied to dance) are neither led by nor inclined to negotiate an interpretive, theatrical relationship with existing music. Rather, they use music primarily according to their own needs, and perhaps a famous fragment – from *Sacre*, for instance – first and foremost for its connotational values.

The ballet scores

So often, writers have declared surprise that choreographers should want to make yet another *Firebird*, *Petrushka* or *Sacre*. But they do, and now *Noces* as well. The flow of new versions of these ballets appears, if anything, to have increased towards the end of the twentieth century. There is no sign of a diminishing profile. Indeed, there is every sign that Stravinsky choreographies to such scores will continue to be made across the planet. This is partly choreographic choice, but also an indication that these scores are extremely popular with audiences.

The narrative ballet scores written for Diaghilev have been by far the most popular with choreographers, most of all *Sacre*, for which the global demand seems unrelenting. The database so far records 181 uses of the score, over 90 of which have been premiered since 1990. Nearly all of these probably use the score in its entirety and some others that do not are still *about Sacre*. Next in order of popularity are *Firebird, Petrushka* (the dance traditions of these two scores are examined later in this chapter), *Pulcinella, Noces* and *Renard*. The production profiles of these scores shift over the years, each with individual peaks of popularity during different periods. Detailing the reasons for these differing profiles is a topic for future research, such as, for instance, why, according to the database:

- *Petrushka* was especially popular in the 1920s and 1930s, after which the number of productions decreased, usage picking up again from the 1970s to the present;
- there were no new productions of the full *Pulcinella* score during the 1940s, but just one of the *Suite* by Todd Bolender in 1945. The score was at its most popular during the 1980s;
- figures for *Orpheus* drop suddenly to no productions at all during the 1990s (with one in 2000).

Noces received few settings during the early decades of its existence, probably because it required cumbersome musical resources, including four pianos, a chorus and percussion. The availability of recordings reduced that problem in later years, and the figures for *Noces* suddenly soared in the 1990s (see p. 330).

The figures for settings of the ballet scores written after the Diaghilev period are all in the tens or twenties, except for *Orpheus* (31 settings recorded) and *The Flood*, which proved the least popular of all of Stravinsky's scores conceived to include dance. Balanchine made a stage setting of *The Flood* (originally a television piece) for the 1982 Centennial Celebrations. Only two other versions are recorded in the database: a production by Günther Rennert with choreography by Peter van Dijk (Hamburg, 1963) and one incorporated within a collage of Stravinsky's sacred choral works entitled *Biblical Pieces* (Netherlands Opera, 1999), bringing together actors and dancers, directed by Peter Sellars.

Any discussion of Stravinsky productions needs to take into account the issue of revival and the presence of a work 'in the repertory', which partially determines whether a new production is needed. Most significant has been the sustained presence around the world of the Fokine classics *Firebird* and *Petrushka*, and there are, in addition to those productions attributed directly to the choreographer himself, any number of versions 'after Fokine'. Indeed, for this reason, it could well be that the number of performances of these ballet scores in the theatre is larger than that for all the *Sacres* put together. But the tradition of *Sacre* is quite different, as we shall see later.

Those Stravinsky theatre scores not originally intended to have a dance component have also been staged. His flexible approach to theatre seems to have caught the imagination of those wanting to choreograph his work. His most clearly operatic works, *Mavra*, *Oedipus Rex* and *The Rake's Progress*, have all been choreographed, and *Rossignol* and *Histoire du soldat* often more extensively than in their original productions. It is doubtful that this kind of thing has happened to such a degree with any other composer's 'operas' and theatre pieces. Perhaps Stravinsky's original enquiring attitude gave permission to others (whatever he himself might have thought of specific productions). Or perhaps it is simply that a dance presence makes itself felt in the style of every work that he wrote. *Mavra* has been set five times (four of these productions in Italy, the first by Aurel Milloss, 1942), featuring dancers or mimes on stage and singers in the orchestra pit or on view at the side, similar doubling techniques to those intended for the original *Renard* and *Rossignol*.[94] *Oedipus Rex*, which Stravinsky stipulated should not be danced, has been 'choreographed' on at least six occasions. There was the 1952 Cocteau production, consisting of seven *tableaux vivants*, which Stravinsky later decided was his favourite staging (see p. 43). Perhaps the most choreographed of all is Julie Taymor's production for the Saito Kinen Festival in Japan (1992),[95] which included a large dancing chorus and also the Butoh dancer Min Tanaka (see p. 477) as an alter ego for the singing Oedipus. *The Rake* was choreographed by Andrew de Groat (1995) for his own company at the Lyon Opéra, and once more used doubling techniques for the three main protagonists.[96]

Finally, we should consider the issue of exclusivity agreements. Both *Firebird* and *Petrushka*, for instance, were covered by five-year contractual agreements with Diaghilev, extended further in the case of *Firebird*, so that when the Russian Imperial Theatres asked for these ballet scores (with Fokine's choreography attached), they could not get them as quickly as they wished.[97] There are no new productions of these scores in Europe until after the First World War. The major Russian theatres waited until 1920 when, in Petrograd, Leonid Leontiev set *Petrushka*, modelled in some fashion after Fokine (who began staging the work in 1918, but never completed the task), although today's version of this production reveals many major differences. Then, in 1921, Vladimir Riabtzev staged *Petrushka* after Fokine at the Bolshoi in Moscow. The same year, in Petrograd, Fedor Lopukhov created his own *Firebird*, the first since Fokine's. There is just one *Petrushka* between the Fokine and Leontiev productions, at the Neighborhood Playhouse, New York, in 1915 (see p. 133), currently the earliest example in the database of a second choreography to a ballet score. The first rechoreography with which Stravinsky was directly involved was Massine's *Sacre* for the Ballets Russes (1920, the second *Sacre* after Nijinsky). In later years, the businessman in the composer became adept at agreeing far less punitive exclusivity arrangements (see pp. 71-72). Choreographers even signed up to stage his ballets before the Balanchine premiere had taken place.

The concert scores

For many years, Stravinsky had reservations about the choreographic use of his concert scores, particularly the 'symphonic' scores (see pp. 77-9). Loie Fuller began the tradition in 1914 with her setting of *Fireworks* in Paris. However, the use of concert scores became noteworthy in the 1960s, and they were strongly featured after Stravinsky's death during the anniversary years 1972 and 1982.

Stravinsky's most popular concert scores, featuring at least 20 settings apiece, are the two orchestral *Suites*, *Ebony Concerto*, *Symphony in Three Movements* and *Ragtime*. Indeed, there have been more productions of these scores than of some expressly written for ballet, more for instance than of *Agon*, *Jeu de cartes* or *Scènes de ballet*. Choreographers have frequently made non-narrative work to the concert scores, as they often do not suit narrative timing; often, in neoclassical ballet tradition, they have borrowed the musical title, emphasising that their choreography is primarily a statement about the music.

Soon after Stravinsky wrote them, in the 1910s and 1920s, choreographers began to be drawn to the *Three Easy Pieces* and *Five Easy Pieces* for piano (perhaps because they contained dance numbers), the two *Suites* for small orchestra (orchestrations of sections from the *Easy Pieces*) and *Ragtime*. Pairing the *Suites* became a particularly popular option. They are short, each comprising a series of brief numbers. But they could also be assembled in different ways, or selected numbers chosen, and, in later years, as with the short *Ragtime*, we find items from the *Suites* introduced into collages involving other scores. Amongst choreographers attracted to the jazz and vaudeville associations of *Ragtime* were Balanchine, Massine and Nijinska, their choreography appearing in contexts outside the Ballets Russes. Interestingly, Nijinska's *Jazz* (1925) was a black-face duet danced by herself and Eugene Lapitzky, inspired by black American culture, with designs by the constructivist Alexandra Exter; the piece was presented by her Théâtre Chorégraphique and premiered at the Winter Gardens Theatre, Margate, England.

Later, the trend towards using the wider range of concert scores was led by Balanchine, who moved increasingly into this repertory once the collaborations had dried up (after *The Flood* (1962)). Yet there are examples of choreographers pre-empting him, indeed, using scores that later became Balanchine 'classics'. The *Capriccio* was used by Massine (1948) for a story about a young man who has visions and falls prey to the power of the grotesque,[98] and later by Herbert Ross (1950) and Alan Carter (1957), before Balanchine's 1967 *Rubies* setting. *Symphony in Three Movements* was used by Aurel Milloss (1960), Hans van Manen (1963) and Kenneth MacMillan (1968) before Balanchine's 1972 setting.

Perhaps choreographers perceived drama in *Symphony in Three Movements* and were attracted by its suggestions of conflict, struggle and major mood shifts (see p. 141). *Ebony Concerto* is accessible and light-hearted, a popular concert piece with a jazzy rhythmic liveliness that has made it an obvious choice for plotless dance. Here, Jiří Kylián is well known for his *Nomaden* (Nederlands Dans Theater, 1981), which drew movement ideas from Australian Aboriginal dances; the score was played twice through, with the male/female roles reversed on the repeat. The *Concerto in D* for string orchestra (1946) was the last concert score to receive frequent treatment and has, like the *Symphony*, tended to inspire mood or narrative content. Unsurprisingly, there is a dearth of choreography to Stravinsky's 'difficult' serial music from the 1950s onwards, other than for the (partially serial) ballet score *Agon*. Balanchine dominates the field with his use of the serial scores.

In terms of dance use, the concert scores as a whole have never matched the popularity of the ballets. The data for the late 1990s and the first years of the twenty-first century suggest a tailing-off. It may be too early to make a firm judgement as to whether this is really an indication of a changing culture, or rather a signal of incomplete data.

Choreographers

The listing by choreographers shows which of them used Stravinsky most frequently and the profile of their musical choices. As expected, Balanchine more than any other choreographer turned to Stravinsky, indeed as his most regular choice of composer, setting a total of 39 pieces to his music (see Appendix 5). In fact, having staged so many Stravinsky ballets, and with so many of them celebrated, Balanchine's legacy has probably deterred some other, would-be Stravinsky choreographers from setting the same scores.[99] New pieces to Stravinsky appear almost throughout Balanchine's career, with a peak of 9 for the New York City Ballet Stravinsky Festival in 1972. Unusually amongst the choreographers who most frequently used Stravinsky, Balanchine did not set any of the best-known full ballet scores – *Firebird* (although he set the 1945 ballet suite in 1949), *Petrushka*, *Sacre* or *Noces*.

Aurel Milloss, the Hungarian-Italian choreographer whose career spanned Germany, Italy and Austria, is the next most prolific Stravinsky choreographer. Again, the works spread across his career, 18 in all. Inspired by the idea of making new versions of the ballets for which scores were commissioned, drawing ideas from the originals as part of his choreographic process,[100] he staged nearly all the ballet scores, but notably not the partly serial *Agon*. His output includes a few plotless ballets to concert scores.

The other main Stravinsky choreographers can be grouped according to whether they favoured the ballet scores (usually the early ones with story content, up to *Pulcinella*), or whether they worked with concert scores in the tradition of plotless dance. The statistics are as follows after Milloss: Maurice Béjart (13 works); John Taras and Hans van Manen (12); Peter Martins and Erich Walter (11); Jerome Robbins (10); John Cranko and Heinz Spoerli (9); Kenneth MacMillan and Uwe Scholz (8); Todd Bolender, Nils Christe, Michael Corder, Yvonne Georgi, Tatiana Gsovsky, John Neumeier, Irene Schneider and Renato Zanella (7).

Apart from his setting of the *Violin Concerto* (1982) and a collage of 'jazz' pieces (*Crucifixion* (1992)), Béjart favoured the narrative ballet scores up until the 1928 *Baiser*, usually disrupting the original scenarios in a manner that disturbed Stravinsky (see p. 60). Other choreographers who favoured the narrative ballet scores are Georgi, Gsovsky, Neumeier, Schneider, Spoerli and Walter.

Choreographers working primarily within the tradition of neoclassical plotless dance are Corder, Christe, van Manen, Martins and Robbins. Van Manen's *Sacre* (1974) programme note quoted Stravinsky himself on the fundamentally abstract, architectonic nature of the score (see p. 417), but much of this choreographer's plotless work suggests anxiety, even menace, between people, especially between men and women. Martins has often used short pieces, such as the *Tango*, *Instrumental Miniatures* and *Easy Pieces*, and he created a ballet to the orchestral *Suite* version of *Easy Pieces* called *Eight More* (1985). Robbins would have set more Stravinsky if only he had been allowed (see p. 78).[101] As well as neoclassical dances, he created three 'story' ballets, *The Cage* (to the *Concerto in D* for strings), *Les Noces* (1965) and, with Balanchine, *Pulcinella* (1972).

Cranko and MacMillan also mixed interests in narrative and plotless ballet, Cranko's *Jeu de cartes* (1965) becoming well established across the international repertory, MacMillan's profile ranging from a *Sacre* (1962) to a setting of *Agon* (1958) (see pp. 243-4). Taras's work relates closely to the Balanchine tradition, although he demonstrates greater interest than his colleague in the early narrative scores. It is interesting that he set one score three times, the *Concerto for Piano and Wind Instruments* (1963, 1972 and 1982).

To establish a profile in terms of dance style is a virtually impossible task, except that choreographers from ballet tradition – as broad a range of meanings as that term can withstand – easily outweigh those from outside it. The exception is *Sacre*, with a far larger proportion of non-balletic treatments than any other score. Yet it is interesting to note several concert score settings by pioneers of modern dance in the early years before the Second World War – and there are probably more that have not come to light – partly because this was a more economic option than commissioning new music, partly because music not written for dance was welcomed as a fresh source of inspiration. Such settings include the Loie Fuller and Margaret Morris miniatures of 1914 and 1917 already mentioned (see p. 42) and Penelope Spencer's *Pastorale* (1922); and several uses of *Easy Pieces* for piano and the orchestral *Suites* in continental Europe, by Valeria Kratina (1925), Gertrude Bodenwieser (1926), Harald Kreutzberg and Yvonne Georgi (1927), Ruth Loeser (1929) and Gertrud Leistikow (1930), and in the USA, by José Limon (1935). Working with live music, modern dance choreographers have tended to favour the small chamber pieces: they have rarely enjoyed the large instrumental resources of the ballet companies.

Dance companies

Certain dance companies, or rather ballet companies, stand out for featuring new Stravinsky productions especially prominently. It goes without saying that Diaghilev's Ballets Russes made the largest contribution of its time to Stravinsky production history (12 works to 9 scores). This company and its later offshoots also constitute an interesting case study in assessing longevity in repertory. Although life in repertory over the years is frequently overlooked and not nearly as easy to trace as the history of premieres, it is quite as significant, indicating the staying power and presence of a work. The extraordinary record books of the ballet *régisseur* Sergey Grigoriev (in conjunction with further programme information) make a systematic survey of repertory possible for these companies. Held in the Harvard Theatre Collection, the record books set out to document every single performance of the Diaghilev company (1909–29), and of the Colonel de Basil/René Blum Ballets Russes de Monte Carlo (1932–52), which in 1940, under de Basil, was retitled the Original Ballet Russe. (De Basil and Blum split in 1935.) The repertory of the rival Ballet Russe de Monte Carlo (1938–62) has been documented by Jack Anderson in his book on the company, although he does not give specific numbers of performances.[102]

Unsurprisingly, Fokine's *Firebird* and *Petrushka* are particularly prominent in the repertory from 1910 to 1952, but perhaps we would not predict that *Petrushka* performances easily outnumber those of *Firebird*: almost 350 in Diaghilev's Ballets Russes, nearly 250 in the Original Ballet Russe (about 200 more than their combined *Firebird* total), and further *Petrushkas* in the repertory of the rival Monte Carlo company. In the opening years of the de Basil/Blum company, from 1932, both Fokine ballets were transferred from the Diaghilev repertory and supervised by Grigoriev himself, with some assistance from Leon Woizikowsky.[103] In 1937, Fokine took over their supervision at de Basil's company. He had arrived from Blum's interim company Les Ballets de Monte Carlo (1936–7), the repertory of which was absorbed into the new Ballet Russe de Monte Carlo in 1938 and included *Petrushka* (for the seasons 1938–42). Hence *Petrushka* appeared in the repertory of both rival companies.

Pulcinella was regularly performed by Diaghilev's Ballets Russes (in the Massine choreography – just over 60 performances), but only three times by the de Basil company in Boris Romanov's production (1932), which was taken over from the repertory of l'Opéra Russe à Paris. Todd Bolender choreographed his 1945 setting of the *Suite* for the Ballet Russe de Monte Carlo, entitling it *Comedia Balletica*. Within the Diaghilev company, only two works did not hold their own beyond one season, the two *Renards* – Nijinska's, which was dropped, and Lifar's, which was short-lived because Diaghilev died the same year and the company disbanded. *Rossignol* enjoyed just 6 performances, its costumes and sets perishing during the war in the cellars of Drury Lane Theatre. *Sacre* made 31 performances, 8 of these in Nijinsky's choreography, 23 in Massine's. The era of outstanding popularity for *Sacre* was yet to come.

New York City Ballet, together with its predecessors American Ballet and Ballet Society, has been responsible for the largest number of premiere productions overall (56 in total). Led by Balanchine, who dominated the three Stravinsky Festivals in 1937, 1972 and 1982, these companies represent canonic Stravinsky tradition after Diaghilev's Ballets Russes. The majority of ballets by choreographers other than Balanchine were made for the company's packed festivals of 1972 and 1982, but most of these rapidly disappeared (see Appendix 4). Hardly any new Stravinsky works appeared between these two festivals, possibly because the 1972 event had made such a major statement, with the exception of Willi Christensen's *Norwegian Moods*, premiered on San Francisco Ballet, then brought to New York City Ballet in 1976, and Martins's *Eight Easy Pieces* (1980) and *Suite from Histoire du Soldat* (1981).

A surprising number of scores, 17 in total, were re-used by Balanchine and his 'family'. Perhaps, after a while, the company felt that it had exhausted the Stravinsky music considered acceptable for dance. Sometimes the same choreographer returned to a score after a time gap, sometimes a choreographer made his own realisation of a score that had been set by a colleague.

New York City Ballet productions can also be seen as repertory items. Fortunately, here there are full company records in card files and on database, indicating how each ballet fared, lived on into our own times or for a number of years, or died a rapid death. The overwhelming evidence is that Balanchine and Martins as ballet masters maintained the place of their own work in the repertory, to a degree far above that of their colleagues. This is partly because of the quality of work as judged by critical and audience success, but also because of their power within the company hierarchy. Of the 39 Balanchine works to Stravinsky's music, 13 still hold a regular place in the repertoire of New York City Ballet (and a number of these have been staged internationally – see p. 161); a few more are occasionally revived or have been reconstructed; others were lost irrevocably from the early years when Balanchine did not have the stable, regular support of a company of his own. This is an outstanding statistic for any choreographer, over a third of the Stravinsky works that he produced. Robbins's celebrated *The Cage* is the only other Stravinsky ballet to have enjoyed such continuity in the New York City Ballet repertory, from 1951 to the present. However, his 1965 *Les Noces* for American Ballet Theatre has also become an international 'classic;' it entered the New York City Ballet repertory in 1998.

Balanchine called the shots to a considerable degree, it seems, getting the first pick of scores, designating at least some of the other acceptable scores to individual choreographers, in 1982 declaring that there would be absolutely no place for settings of the Diaghilev 'Russian' ballets *Petrushka*, *Sacre* or *Noces* (nor were these pieces shown in 1972).[104] The New York City Ballet revival of Robbins's *Noces* waited until after Balanchine's death. Significantly, San Francisco Ballet also promoted Stravinsky scores (14 premieres, as well as taking on existing Balanchine repertory). Enjoying an especially close relationship with Balanchine and New York City Ballet tradition, the company has also emphasised the concert scores; it presented 5 new Stravinsky works during Centenary year 1982.

Another company with an especially strong Stravinsky tradition is Nederlands Dans Theater. Presenting 24 new productions overall, the company has showcased the work of two Stravinsky 'specialists', Hans van Manen (12 works) and Jiří Kylián (5 works), both of them emphasising the concert scores. After NDT come three German companies, the Stuttgart Ballet, Bavarian State Opera Ballet and Hamburg Ballet. Their respective repertories feature several Stravinsky choreographers, each responsible for between one and four works, and demonstrating the rapid increase in interest in the composer after the Second World War. The cluster of Vic-Wells/Royal Ballet/Sadler's Wells British companies also creates a considerable Stravinsky presence (20 new productions), enlarged by repertory including both the Fokine classics *Firebird* and *Petrushka* and a number of Balanchine ballets.

It might seem odd that the Paris Opéra Ballet has staged so few Stravinsky premieres, given that the city hosted all the early ballet premieres by the companies of Diaghilev and Rubinstein, including several at the Opéra itself. After Léo Staats's *Les Abeilles* (1917), there is a gap in premieres until Serge Lifar's *Firebird* (1954), then Béjart's *Renard* (1965) and *Firebird* (1970), after which there is only Douglas Dunn's *Pulcinella* (1980). Recall Stravinsky's anger at being overlooked by the Opéra director Jacques Rouché for many years (see p. 76). As regards existing productions, the imports began with Balanchine's residence at the Paris Opéra in 1947, when he set *Apollo* and *Baiser*, and a year later Fokine's *Petrushka* entered the repertory. Later re-stagings included more choreography by Balanchine and ballets by Béjart and Robbins, as well as Nijinska's *Noces* and, extraordinarily, four *Sacres*, by Béjart (in 1965), Paul Taylor (in 1984), Nijinsky (or rather after Nijinsky, the Hodson/Archer production in 1991) and Pina Bausch (in 1997).

One remarkable discovery is that Les Grands Ballets Canadiens boasts no fewer than five different productions of *Noces*. Two of these were by their founder Ludmilla Chiriaeff (1954, for television, when the company was still named Les Ballets Chiriaeff, and 1972), there was a 2002 setting by Stijn Celis and there were also stagings of existing productions by Lar Lubovitch (1978) and Nijinska (1987).

Countries

Any systematic survey of Stravinsky use by country is impossible at this stage of the database, yet certain trends and interesting country histories already emerge from the current documentation. The countries that have hosted by far the most Stravinsky production premieres are Germany and the USA: almost 300 works are so far recorded for each, together comprising almost half the total database entries, collating the figures for the unified Germany and for East and West Germany during the period of two zones (1949–89). Explanations for these large figures must include size of country and its economy, and dance/music culture: the leading New York City Ballet/Balanchine tradition, which spread to other American companies, and the strong German musical culture, tradition of meticulous documentation of data, and unusually extensive network of opera houses with their own dance companies. American use of Stravinsky accelerated with the arrival of Balanchine and the early Stravinsky Festival in New York in 1937, but the 1929 *Les Noces* under the auspices of the American League of Composers in New York, conducted by Leopold Stokowski and choreographed by Elizaveta Anderson-Ivantzova, can be seen as a landmark event (see pp. 379-80). Current data for these early years in the USA also suggests a slighter Stravinsky presence than in Europe amongst modern dancers. The general 'rule' for pioneering, and often politically motivated, modern dancers was that twentieth-century and traditional American music should be used, but their stance was also to be independent of European tradition; Stravinsky might well have been associated with carrying too much intellectual baggage from Europe and, indeed, classical ballet.

Britain is next in line statistically (97 works), with a number of choreographers each making several works to Stravinsky's music. But we need to be cautious: it is relatively easy to access data in the home country. We can note, however, that choreographic interest in Britain got going relatively late. Although there are occasional examples from the early years, the boom in interest starts in the 1950s, when Ninette de Valois introduced the 'safe' Russian period ballets *Firebird* and *Petrushka* into the Royal Ballet repertory in 1954 and 1957 respectively. Kenneth MacMillan created *Danses Concertantes* for the Sadler's Wells Theatre Ballet in 1955. It used a neoclassical score, but was received rapturously by both critics and audiences and moved to Covent Garden in 1959.

Britain had taken longer than other Western countries to reveal its interest in the later Stravinsky. Whereas his earlier Russian period music was much acclaimed, especially *Firebird* and *Petrushka*, problems with regard to this turn to neoclassicism were immediately perceived by many, including Ernest Newman of *The Sunday Times*, the most influential critic of the period. Stephen Walsh claims that:

> On the whole Stravinsky's London press of the twenties and thirties has a persistent and depressing 'what can you expect of foreigners' air.[105]

Eric Walter White writes that Stravinsky's reputation reached an all-time low immediately prior to 1939, but this attitude lingered on in some quarters well into the 1950s:

> Many of the critics (especially in England) stigmatised much of his neo-classical music as 'the artificial product of a cock-eyed aesthetic' [the words of *The Times* critic, April 4, 1952], and considered that almost the only qualities of his instrumentation deserving of notice were its aridity and brittleness. [Stravinsky's new works] though listened to with a show of politeness, were usually shelved by concert promoters as soon as seemed decent.[106]

When Stravinsky conducted *Agon* at the Festival Hall in 1958, the *Times* critic declared that the new work had no rhythm. William Glock rushed to the composer's defence in *The New Statesman*, referring to 'pronouncements which always follow the performance of any recent work of Stravinsky in this country'.[107]

The *Dancing Times* also reflected conservative attitudes to Stravinsky. The music and dance critic Dyneley Hussey entitled his 1946 review of Ballet Theatre's London season 'The Tragedy of Stravinsky'. He heaped high praise on this American company's production of *Petrushka*, describing its score as 'the signal masterpiece of modern ballet', while asking how its composer could possibly have come to compose a work 'so lacking in life and humanity' as the neoclassical *Apollo*:

> It is true that the music of this work has a certain arid charm, which is pleasing in the way that an excessively dry sherry is sometimes pleasing to the palate. But music so lacking in warmth and emotionally so sterile could hardly stimulate a choreographer's invention, and, in effect, Balanchine's

choreography is uniformly dull and even ugly to watch. How, one can only repeat, came it that a composer gifted with so much dramatic genius, could throw it all away, and devote himself to the fabrication of a lifeless pseudo-classicism?[108]

In 1962, the composer himself welcomed the change in the English music world:

The open-door policy to new music in England in the last few years was made possible to a great extent by the accession of an intelligent younger generation in the musical press. In consequence, London has become a great capital of contemporary music.[109]

The same year, Richard Buckle reported on a new all-Stravinsky programme at the Royal Ballet and its position within the larger Stravinsky repertory:

When Frederick Ashton first made *Scènes de ballet* in 1948 there was no other work with music by Stravinsky in the Royal Ballet's repertory. Now there is hardly a ballet given at Covent Garden which does not have music by Stravinsky – and what could be nicer?
    Last Saturday we were given a whole Stravinsky programme, made up of *Le Baiser de la fée* [MacMillan], *Scènes de Ballet* and *The Firebird*. They could make another if they wished, choosing from *Petrouchka*, *Persephone* [Ashton], *Danses Concertantes* and *Agon* [MacMillan] ...[110]

MacMillan's *Rite of Spring* was premiered later the same year, and for a while there was a plan for Jerome Robbins to choreograph *Noces* (see p. 387). In 1966, after Ashton had succeeded de Valois as Artistic Director of the Royal, he introduced Nijinska's *Noces* and Balanchine's *Apollo*. In a relatively short space of time, late in the day as this may seem, Stravinsky became a major presence within the Royal Ballet repertory.

Given the extent of Stravinsky production in Germany, it is surprising how little information about it is available in the English-language dance literature. But the German story of Stravinsky dance production is especially interesting and worth considering here in some detail. In 1923, the music historian Hans Joachim Moser claimed that there were about fifty opera houses preserved by the state.[111] But there is a production tradition here that extends throughout the twentieth and into the twenty-first century and reflects not only the strength of the opera house culture but also the sustained commitment to Stravinsky's music – to his neoclassical and serial, as well as early Russian, scores, a far greater commitment than in other countries.[112] The notion of a musical score carrying the event is also unusually strong in Germany. It would seem, until mid-century at least, that a Stravinsky ballet score was often produced simply as an expected part of the repertory, no matter who the choreographer. There was a framework to fill, and the house choreographer's job was to carry out the task of staging, rather in the manner of opera. The comments of the British critic Clive Barnes about Heinz Rosen's all-Stravinsky evening in Munich in 1963 are telling about another kind of culture from his own:

> The presumptuousness of such a proceeding never seems to occur to them. It is typical of the bad old view of German ballet, that a German ballet director would have no more hesitation in giving his own choreography to an old work, than an opera director would have in reproducing a standard opera. In fairness, enlightenment of the differences between opera and ballet is nowadays slowly dawning on Germany – but slowly is still the operative word.[113]

Another indication of the German passion for Stravinsky's music was the rush to produce his new ballet scores, to be ahead of the game as far as possible. Even if they never staged the first production of a ballet score, the Germans were regularly in hot pursuit. The series of new *Firebirds* and *Petrushkas* began outside Germany in the 1920s. But soon, German productions were next in line after the premiere, as the following list demonstrates:

- After the respective Diaghilev Ballets Russes premieres of *Pulcinella*, *Renard* and *Les Noces*, the next productions were by Heinrich Kröller (*Pulcinella*, Munich, 1925), Franz Hörth (*Renard*, Berlin, 1925), and Marion Hermann (*Noces*, Königsberg, 1929). The first *Sacre* after the Nijinsky and Massine productions for Diaghilev was by Lasar Galpern (Cologne, 1930).
- After its Swiss premiere, the first *Histoire du soldat* production took place in Frankfurt (1923).[114]
- After the respective Ida Rubinstein company premieres of *Le Baiser de la fée* and *Persephone*, the next productions were by Alice Zickler (*Baiser*, Magdeburg, 1932) and Hans Macke (*Persephone*, Braunschweig, 1937).
- After Balanchine's initial settings in the USA, the next *Jeu de cartes* was choreographed by Valeria Kratina (Dresden, 1937) and the next *Agon* by Otto Krüger (Dusseldorf, 1958).

Again, the list above does not account for the longevity of Stravinsky productions in the German repertoire, a subject for future research. A telling statistic, however, is provided by the music historian Fred Prieberg. Between 1935 and 1940, during the Nazi period, no fewer than 18 productions of *Firebird* could be viewed around Germany.[115] An interesting footnote is that Rudolf Laban made early proposals to stage *Petrushka* and *Pulcinella* for the Mannheim Nationaltheater in 1921, although these projects never materialised.[116]

Stravinsky attracted the full range of German choreographers, from ballet to Ausdruckstanz (early German modern dance) to Tanztheater and beyond. Unusually, a phenomenon extending beyond mid-century, we find many opera-house choreographers trained in both modern and ballet styles, and even some choreographers whose backgrounds were primarily in modern dance but who embraced ballet in the opera houses. For example, Valeria Kratina and Yvonne Georgi, both trained in Dalcroze eurhythmics and with Mary Wigman, turned neoclassical when it was appropriate, reflecting the stylistic change in Stravinsky's music: Kratina choreographed the first European *Jeu de cartes* (Dresden, 1937) and Georgi made her own versions of *Apollo* (Dusseldorf, 1954) and *Agon* (Hanover, 1958 – see p. 239). The German modern dancers responded to need. They were first employed to revitalise dance in the opera houses in the 1920s and 1930s, though often inheriting a traditional corps de ballet;[117] later, those who remained in Germany acquiesced in the aesthetic preference for ballet of Nazi leaders and, later still, of audiences in the post-war period (see p. 241).

Yet evidence suggests that modern dance choreographers constituted something of an alternative force within the opera house sector before the Nazi period. As examples, we might follow the fortunes of the Swiss-born choreographer Max Terpis and the Germans Harald Kreutzberg and Georgi, all students of Mary Wigman, the latter two especially renowned concert dancers in the USA as well as Europe.[118] Hanover was a forward-looking opera house, Terpis directing dance activities there in 1922–4 and Georgi taking over in 1926. She had already danced with Kurt Jooss in Munster (1924) and been 'ballet mistress' in Gera (1925). Her first major dance evening in Hanover (1926) included *Petrushka* and *Pulcinella*. Kreutzberg joined her, and in 1927 they presented their experimental *Marsch, Polka, Galopp und Walzer: Groteske Tanzszene* using numbers from the *Suite No. 2 for Orchestra* that were already conceived as parodies of dance forms. They revived this work at the New Theatre, Leipzig, in 1929. Terpis meanwhile had gone to take charge of dance at the Berlin Staatsoper, where he created *Pulcinella* (1925) and *Petrushka* (1928). These modern dance choreographers did not merely promote the new music of Stravinsky, encouraged undoubtedly by theatre Intendants, but sometimes presented unconventional readings of his ballets (see p. 133).

During the Third Reich, Stravinsky had somewhat less of a presence in Germany.[119] If, during the experimental Weimar period of the 1920s, his work symbolised an exciting radicalism, he was to be branded a musical Bolshevik by the Nazi regime in the early 1930s, *Histoire du soldat* and *Sacre* being singled out as especially dangerous (see p. 412). Although his profile had significantly improved by the mid-1930s, pockets of opposition still existed and he was not fully rehabilitated as a safe modernist. For instance, to his considerable dismay, he was featured in the 1938 'Entartete Musik' (decadent music) exhibition that opened in Dusseldorf and travelled to other German cities, included alongside such composers as Schoenberg and Paul Hindemith. Yet Stravinsky had no qualms about pressing for acceptability within Nazi Germany, for financial as well as artistic reasons. Stravinsky was unencumbered by political scruples, and the story of how he willingly disregarded totalitarian politics at this stage in his life in the furtherance of personal gain makes uncomfortable reading.

Recently, Joan Evans has argued that *Jeu de cartes* was 'composed as much for Germany as for Balanchine's newly formed American Ballet'.[120] Years later, in the original *Themes and Episodes* (a passage drastically cut in the second edition), Stravinsky claimed that this was the most German of his works, although 'I cannot say to what extent I may have been aware of this at the time, *or to what degree (unconscious, in any case) the music may have been designed for German tastes and German audiences.*'[121] Evans proposes that Stravinsky wrote *Jeu* at a time when he was very anxious to re-establish his position in Germany, the country that had given him an outstanding share of his royalties. She suggests too that his stylistic conservatism of the 1930s may have been partly due to this desire to reinstate himself in Germany. *Jeu* would have been viewed as nicely accessible music. Stravinsky's publisher Willi Strecker wrote encouragingly of a prospective European premiere in Dresden, saying that the production there would be of better than average standard for Germany and that Kratina had full official support. The circumstances were propitious, both politically and artistically.[122] The performance was conducted by Karl Bohm and was the 'crowning event' of the regional arts festival, which had Nazi party support.[123] After the premiere, Strecker reported on a huge success, and that all the key critics considered the event Stravinsky's artistic rehabilitation in Germany.[124] Later, during the Second World War in Germany, performances of work by all composers of enemy lands were banned. After the war, political manoeuvrings of a totally different kind brought Stravinsky back into full focus, and it was helpful that he had maintained contacts throughout the Nazi period. There was the embrace of neoclassicism in Germany (and, with it, the Balanchine tradition). The new Tanztheater movement from the early 1970s (including Bausch) also used his music.

The most telling gap in dance production to Stravinsky's music occurred in the Soviet Union from the late 1920s, lasting about thirty years. In the 1920s, the era of the New Economic Policy and a spectacular period of experiment in Russian arts, Leonid Leontiev and Vladimir Riabtzev both staged *Petrushka* (in 1920 and 1921 respectively), followed by Lopukhov's modernist settings of *Firebird* (1921), *Pulcinella* (1926) and *Renard* (1927). All of these (except for

Riabtzev's *Petrushka* for the Bolshoi) were for GATOB, acronym for the Petrograd State Academic Theatre of Opera and Ballet, formerly the Maryinsky. *Firebird* visualised musical detail very closely and stressed the power of reason in overcoming evil and Slavic, rather than Orientalist, source material. *Pulcinella* and *Renard* were contemporary treatments of folklore, using as models the Russian buffoon play.[125] Mary Grace Swift has published a fascinating repertoire index indicating the ballet scores accessible to Soviet choreographers in 1929. The index is classified with ratings, and all six Stravinsky works – including *Noces* and *Histoire du soldat*, which do not appear to have been choreographed during this period – are rated A: 'the best works ideologically; universally recommended for presentation'.[126] Of course, Soviet Russia never saw the original stagings, never being part of the touring circuit of Diaghilev's company. Testimony that Stravinsky's work met with wholehearted approval during this period is that Anatoly Lunacharsky invited him to Russia, an invitation that he declined.[127]

By 1933, all had changed, and as the system of Socialist Realism hardened under Stalin and his successors, Stravinsky's modernism was considered unacceptable by the ruling regime and characterised as formalist, empty, elitist, unforgivable in its 'mockery' of Russian folk material. This state of play lasted for three decades. The composer's anti-Soviet views, published in his numerous writings over the years, did not help the situation.

Then, in 1959, Leonard Bernstein took the New York Philharmonic on tour to Leningrad, Moscow and Kiev, performing *Sacre* and the *Concerto for Piano and Wind Instruments*. The Stravinsky thaw had begun. By the early 1960s, there was a clear move to open up the repertory in Russia. A review in *Sovietskaya Muzyka* of a 1962 New York City Ballet Stravinsky evening is entirely favourable about the music, and Stravinsky made his first return visit to his homeland since 1914 in September/October that year.[128] Konstantin Boyarsky was a step ahead in choreographing a new *Orpheus* for the preceding March, in a programme alongside the Fokine *Petrushka* and *Firebird* (which had been produced in 1961 and 1962 respectively). But in 1958, the experimental choreographer Leonid Jacobson had already come up with a merry divertissement-style setting of Augurs of Spring from *Sacre* (*Troika* – see p. 498). The film was entitled *Choreographic Miniatures*, after Jacobson's Leningrad company, for which he went on to create a new *Firebird* (1965), following this in 1971 with settings of concert music: the orchestral *Suites*, *Danses Concertantes* and *Ebony Concerto*. Georgii Aleksidze set four Stravinsky works in Leningrad and Tblisi: *Baiser* (1970), *Pulcinella* (1978), *Fireworks* (1986) and *Scherzo à la Russe* (1997). Today, the modern dance choreographer Tatiana Baganova enjoys an international reputation through her setting of *Noces* (1999); she has also staged a highly choreographed production of *Le Rossignol* (2004).

The major public breakthrough for Stravinsky's reception in Soviet ballet came with the 1965 *Sacre* of Natalia Kasatkina and Vladimir Vasilyov. An interesting communication from the dance historian Marion Kant implies that, even if the handling of the narrative smacked of Soviet dogma – the proletarian hero reveals the falsity of gods – the very fact of using this radical score made an important statement. *Sacre* invited experiment:

> The ballets staged in the East German theatres were mostly the 'Grand Russian/Soviet ballets', like *Gayane, The Fountain of Bakhchisarai, The Stone Flower*, the Tchaikovsky ballets. Prokofiev was probably the most modern [composer heard] … That's why *Sacre* had to be a sensation, in [the] way Stravinsky was allowed to enter the stages from then on. Stravinsky's music had been played in concerts before, of course, but having *Sacre* in the State Opera was a *state* decision, it was a symbol, a sign of changing cultural politics.[129]

This Soviet *Sacre* seems to have opened the door to Stravinsky stagings elsewhere within Soviet Russia and the Eastern bloc. *Sacre* was staged in East Berlin, for instance, in 1967. Yet some of these countries staged *Sacre* before the Russians. We know that Imre Eck produced the work in Hungary in 1963, and in Czechoslovakia two versions appeared in 1964, by Luboš Ogoun and Karol Tóth. Data on the latter country is especially interesting. Remarkably, before the Second World War, when the country was still in contact with Western European dance traditions, the woman choreographer Máša Cvejičová staged four works by Stravinsky in rapid succession, for the National Theatre at Brno: *Firebird* (1931), *Petrushka* (1932), *Apollo* and *Noces* (both 1933) (see p. 242). Over the years, a variety of theatres across Czechoslovakia (in Prague, Bratislava and Brno, amongst other cities) staged a range of Diaghilev ballet scores, at least eight productions of *Firebird* and thirteen of *Petrushka*.[130]

The database has drawn attention to close links between South America and the dance traditions of Europe and the USA. Argentina is the most interesting country in this respect, representing both ballet and modern dance, and hosting the work of several Stravinsky choreographers who moved to or simply visited the country. The Teatro Colón in Buenos Aires appears early on the map, a massive European-style opera house that had strong links with the major Western European and Russian ballet traditions. Adolph Bolm staged *Petrushka* there (probably after Fokine) in 1925, and Fokine himself staged *Firebird* in 1931; then Boris Romanov created a *Pulcinella* (1928) and a *Sacre* (1932), and later, in 1948, Margarethe Wallmann, the Austrian choreographer, expanded the repertory with her *Histoire du soldat* and *Jeu de cartes*. Nijinska also visited on several occasions, and staged her *Noces* in 1926 and *Baiser* in 1933 (revived in 1936). Balanchine was guest director in 1942, when he staged his *Apollo*. During and after the war, several modern dancers from Europe took refuge in South America, especially in Argentina. One of these was Renate Schottelius, who premiered *Renard* in Buenos Aires (1958): she came from Germany, having studied Wigman technique and danced with the Berlin Opera and Ballets Jooss, then learnt the Humphrey–Limon method in the USA before arriving in Argentina in the early 1950s to found her own dance group. The Chilean-born choreographer Ana Itelman also studied a range of modern dance techniques in the USA, returning later to Buenos Aires and choreographing an *Agon* there in 1963 (see p. 245). But the diaspora works in reverse in the case of the Argentinian Oscar Araiz. At home, he created an *Orpheus* (1964), a *Sacre* and an *Ebony Concerto* (1966), becoming director of the San Martin Municipal Theatre Contemporary Ballet in Buenos Aires in 1968. After that, he enjoyed an international career, as director of the Geneva Ballet, setting *Pulcinella* (1980) and *Baiser* (1981), although he eventually returned to work in Buenos Aires.

The database is not strong in its representation of Stravinsky premieres beyond 'Western' countries, but it does highlight a recent surge of interest in setting the composer's music in the Far East. Outstanding is the profile that has developed from Japanese choreographers since 1972, mostly outside ballet culture: nine works premiered in Japan, four in Europe, with nine of these being uses of *Sacre* (partially or in full). Choreographers have included Carlotta Ikeda, Saburo Teshigawara and Min Tanaka (see Ch. 6). Yet in South Korea – and here, my visit to the country helped generate information – the database stresses the ballet companies that have presented his music. First, there was a traditional *Firebird* by Mansur Kamaletdinov (1989) and a *Pulcinella* by the ex-Balanchine dancer Roy Tobias (1990), both for the Universal Ballet Company. Later there were two settings of *Noces*, by Geungsoo Kim for the Geungsoo Kim Ballet Company (2000, revived for the Korean National Ballet Company in 2003) and James Jeon for the Seoul Ballet Theatre (2003), both drawing upon Korean tradition, in ballet and modern dance styles respectively.[131] There was also a *Sacre* (1993) by Sooho Kook in Korean-style modern dance. So indigenous traditions are incorporated in recent Stravinsky settings by Korean choreographers. The database lists two *Sacre* productions under China, by Xing Liang (1997) and Li Hangzhong and Ma Bo (2001), for the Guang Dong and Beijing Modern Dance Companies.

Renewing Stravinsky: Some preliminary dance examples

Moving now to the dances listed in the Stravinsky database, to film and video material and live performance, there are a number that, although not fitting later chapters, deal with central issues relating to Stravinsky as a dance

composer and suggest a frame for the later debates. First, there are the dances
that have used the narrative ballet scores *Firebird* and *Petrushka* across the century. After *Sacre*, these are by far the most popular scores with audiences. They
carry the heaviest weight of the past within them, choreographers can hardly be
unaware of their colourful Ballets Russes origins, and their respective traditions
both as scores and ballets prompt especially interesting questions. But these
scores also exist in concert arrangement, more formal, less strongly narrative
accounts of the ballet originals – *Firebird* in suite form, *Petrushka* in a three-
movement piano version – inviting debate about the new kinds of
theatricalisation that they propose.

Related issues arise with scores that originated in concert form. How can
choreography to these (or rather the dance-music composites) be read in relation to Stravinsky's developing anti-expression philosophy and his neoclassical
approach, or in relation to how he has been read and reread by musicologists?
Examples of choreographed concert scores range from the second of the *Three
Pieces for String Quartet*, possibly the only music by Stravinsky inspired by a
specific person's movement, to the *Symphonies of Wind Instruments*, a work that
bears probably a larger history of abstract, un-bodied structural theorisation
than any other by the composer. I refer back to the earlier discussion of
Stravinsky's aesthetics and the rhythmic style and physicality of his music,
while expanding further the concept of *musique dansante*. My examples also
introduce choreographers whose musicality is exceptionally interesting, such
as George Balanchine (a preview item before Chapter 3), Richard Alston and
Mark Morris.

Firebird *and* Petrushka: *Ballet scores and ballet suites*

In the case of both *Firebird* and *Petrushka*, the original Fokine versions
(and versions after Fokine) have remained here and there in the global repertory,
alongside the new versions that soon sprang up. But there is overwhelming evidence from the database that new choreographers, with rare exceptions, have
respected the original stories, even if sometimes introducing modifications. The
power of good over evil, the movement from darkness into light with a Firebird
figure as saviour, is a constantly recurring theme; likewise, the love triangle and
figures of outsider and oppressor return regularly in the series of *Petrushkas*. In
both cases, the music is programmatic and amply illustrates the forces at work,
so it comes as no surprise that the scores of these two ballets have been used with
their programmes stapled firmly to them.

Firebird is overwhelmingly balletic, the province of ballet companies, with a
ballet kind of story, mime as well as dance, even though the terms of ballet were
renewed by the original (see p. 29). It revels in its own mystery and glitter, a

spectacle about magic and enchantment, with the image of a bird itself suggesting the flight from gravity inherent in the *danse d'école*, and the musical style
of Stravinsky's bird has proved persuasive enough to speak ballet to most
choreographers. There is the fantastic light scherzo orchestration that connotes
elevation, and the shimmer of the Berceuse (Lullaby) that has often conjured
forth bourrées. The lyrical episodes for the princesses readily suggest an upward
flow that can be augmented through pointes, even though Fokine's original
princesses wore heeled shoes. Indeed, for some choreographers, updating the
Firebird ballet has meant making it more balletic than the original.

It is significant that *Petrushka*, although again principally a ballet company
production, has attracted a larger cohort of choreographers than *Firebird* from
outside ballet tradition, since the early years of the score. Is this because it carries with it more of an aura of experiment and less old-style baggage? It is not a
spectacle of enchantment, and the distinctions between mime and dance music
are more blurred than in *Firebird*. Through the medium of the puppet, it references the person with 'feeling moments' from the start. Parts of the score, such
as Petrushka's cell, are openly expressionist (see pp. 138-40). Furthermore, the
ballet content, embodied in the two street dancers and the Ballerina, is musically
stilted, a parody of the real thing.

For both scores, there has been an increasing tendency from mid-century
onwards to open up treatment of the music and its accompanying scenario and
setting. Quite apart from modifying cultural settings, some choreographers have
given a modern twist to the scenario. Looking first at *Firebird*, we find psychological developments. Brian Macdonald's 1967 setting for the Harkness Ballet had a
'cast of Freudian characters'; the Firebird was like a 'mother figure', with the
'erotic side' of the Prince's character suggested by a female snake. The setting
was exotic but unspecific.[132] Or in Eske Holm's controversial but well-received
1972 production for the Royal Swedish Ballet, the Firebird absorbs the role of
the Princess; she is Kastchei's prisoner, is raped by him, and gives birth to a child
of evil. The enamoured Ivan is distraught and rejects her: the lovers' future
remains in doubt and there is no happy ending.[133] Meanwhile, John Neumeier, in
his 1970 version for the Frankfurt Ballet, used the outline of the original scenario but introduced a science-fiction theme: his Kastchei was a huge robot with
a TV screen for a face, and his hero a space explorer.[134] His 1983 version for the
Vienna Staatsoper Ballet featured a dancing machine tyrant. The original scenario was reworked into a metaphor for the regeneration of a darkened waste-
land and, at the end, the sun shone once more, renewal symbolised by the flowering of a potted plant into a tree.[135] In Uwe Scholz's 1986 version for the Zurich
Ballet, revived on several occasions for other companies, the Firebird character
introduced gender into the discussion, being embodied by a man, a deliberately
androgynous personality.[136] James Kudelka's 2001 *Firebird* for the Houston Bal-

let was much closer to the traditional scenario, but made a point about quoting familiar choreographic imagery, such as Fokine's characteristic Firebird arms and her kneeling pose in fear of Prince Ivan. At the end, in postmodern fashion, Kudelka stepped outside his frame of reference to include a Nijinska *Noces* body pyramid, marking the moment of considerable likeness between these two Stravinsky–Diaghilev works, both of which present the slow, ordered climax of a wedding ritual.[137]

Glen Tetley's *Ildfuglen* (Royal Danish Ballet, 1981) stands out as one of the most radically altered approaches to the original story. Indeed, he made a relatively abstract work, delving into the mind of a young girl trapped within a starchy nineteenth-century community, who dreams of freedom, is metamorphosed into a lycra unitard Firebird (symbolising freedom for herself, rather than portraying her as saviour of others) and eventually finds love and fulfilment. In this world of dreams, there is no clear narrative logic, but the basic theme of opposing forces, good and evil, is still there, and the musical gestures are still used to underline 'feeling moments', indications of anger, force and threat.[138] We might ask, does Stravinsky's music simply expand into a new time and place with these new realities, or, given that we might well be familiar with the original, do we still hear the old exotic world behind the new?

Exceptions to classical ballet company treatments include settings by Amanda Miller for her Ballet Freiburg Pretty Ugly (2003) and the Indian choreographer Dasappa Keshava's 2004 production for his company Kalasri (Basle, Switzerland). Miller's dance theatre piece about the desire to get out of a barren earthly domain featured a red-feathered alien wearing grotesque masks, and referred to the moon and outer space as symbolic goals of aspiration. At the same time, she made clear allusions to the original *Firebird*.[139] Keshava used the original scenario, unusually mixing Bharatanatyam and modern dance movement styles to suit a cast with various dance backgrounds.[140] Meanwhile, in New York, Jennifer Weber's *Decadance vs. the Firebird – A Hip-Hop Ballet* (2004) invaded Stravinsky's own domain. She selected about ten minutes from the score for a 'mash up' creative collage, as the word 'vs.' indicates: straight samples (for instance, the opening two minutes of his music), and shorter samples with added beats as transitions into sections of straight hip-hop. The dance also 'remixes' the Russian fairytale for an all-female cast, which 'challenges the ballet convention of a "handsome prince" and instead creates a world where women battle for the right to rule the dance floor'. Iva (female version of the Prince) meets her sequinned, baseball-capped Firebird saviour in a twenty-first-century urban setting.[141]

Petrushka has likewise been updated on several occasions, portraying the titular hero as rock star (Michael Uthoff, Hartford Ballet, 1988), drug addict (Ricardo Fernando, Chemnitz Ballet, 2000) or young thief amongst the clothing in a stylish department store (Mauro Bigonzetti, Compagnia Aterballetto, 2002). The statement about oppressor and oppressed has also been made more overt or grounded in relation to a contemporary political reality. In Germany (1930), the modern dance choreographer Jooss modified the denouement so that the Charlatan and Petrushka exchanged roles. His Dancer, not billed as a ballerina, wore high boots.[142] For Scottish Ballet (1989), the Kirov's Oleg Vinogradov turned the work into a statement against the by then moribund Soviet regime; indeed, one costume design was named for the character of Leonid Brezhnev. Here, Petrushka rebels against politicians and police alike, dies for his cause, and then becomes a symbolic hero for his people.[143] Later still, for the Gothenburg Ballet (1998), Brian Macdonald introduced the situation of a young soldier as Petrushka returning from war in Afghanistan to a *ménage à trois* with a Mafia boss and his moll.[144]

Most striking is the group of *Petrushkas* in which women have taken over the title role, all of them from outside the ballet establishment. The second *Petrushka* after Fokine's original production was probably the one staged by the sisters Alice and Irene Lewisohn, community arts workers and directors of the Neighborhood Playhouse in New York, the dances arranged by Louis Chalif. Alice recalls that her sister played the puppet (even though an Ivan Litvinoff was mentioned in the programme) and that they premiered the work in 1915 just before the Diaghilev company brought the original version to America. She also maintains that they visualised the score differently from the original production that they had seen in London the previous year: 'in terms of a purely folk experi-ence'.[145] The acclaimed Austrian modern dancer Rosalia Chladek staged two versions in rapid succession, the first following the original scenario (Basle, 1929), the second, *Figuren aus Petrushka*, cast as a series of three solos for the three puppets (Vienna, 1930). She danced the title role in the first version, and all three solos in the second. John Martin, dance critic of *The New York Times*, saw the second work during a visit to the Dalcroze-based Hellerau–Laxenburg School in 1932, and singled out her Petrushka characterisation as 'an exciting piece of dramatic psychology, good theatre as well as good dance – and, inciden-tally, good acrobatics'.[146] Since Chladek created these pieces herself, we may speculate that she wanted to give herself challenging dance opportunities, or they might have been proto-feminist statements containing an element of cri-tique. Assuming this political stance years later in *Fokiniana (Part I: L'Autre)* (London, 1997), Jacky Lansley used the *Three Movements from 'Petrushka'*, with the piano on stage; according to the programme note, it was a solo exploration of 'themes of survival and oppression, psychologically and choreographically con-structing her female Petrushka'.

The smaller dance ensembles, rather than ballet companies, have tended to favour *Petrushka* arrangements. As well as the *Three Movements from 'Petrushka'*, the database records several settings of the four-hand piano reduction of the complete score: by Chalif (1915), Chladek (1930) and Senia Gluck Sandor (1931). Yair Vardi's quartet setting for English Dance Theatre (1985) used an arrangement of parts of the piano score for the jazz group Full Circle. While two men and one woman enacted the love triangle of the original scenario (Company Toothpick, 2001), the Finnish choreographer Tero Saarinen had two onstage accordionists playing an adaptation of the Stravinsky score. A pianola recording was used for the American Paul Taylor's *Le Grand Puppetier* (2004), its vicious jangle perhaps a reminder of what attracted him to the piano score of *Sacre* (1980 – see p. 484); both Taylor dances were dark-humoured commentaries on corruption in society, at the same time putting into sharp relief a particular mechanical component in the music.[147]

On a number of occasions, as we have seen, Stravinsky's *Firebird* and *Petrushka* scores have been used as vehicles for political or radical statement, and in their early as well as later history. It is interesting too that the early American *Petrushka* (1931) by Gluck Sandor featured an African-American dancer Randolph Sawyer as the Moor, alongside a white woman as the 'ballerina', daring for its time.[148] One of the earliest American *Firebirds* is especially interesting in that it was presented by the American Negro Ballet, the country's first black modern dance company. *Firebird* was the last item on its opening programme in 1937. The company had been established by the German Eugene von Grona, who had studied modern dance with Wigman as well as Swedish gymnastics, and who deplored the fact that black dancers in the USA at that time were limited to performing jazz and ethnic dance.[149] According to the programme note, his idea was to show 'the deeper and more intellectual sources of the race', through alternative barefoot dance styles. So this was not a ballet *Firebird*. Martin, one of several critics to respond in what were, in hindsight, uncomfortably patronising tones, relayed the interesting fact that the group itself 'fell in love with the music and story of Stravinsky's *Firebird*, when it was played for them as part of their training in music and dance background, and decided that this was to be one of their productions'.[150] The American Negro Ballet performed to Stokowski's recording of the score.

The fact that both the *Firebird* and *Petrushka* scores have more than one identity also merits discussion. There are three different *Suite* versions of *Firebird* dating from 1910, 1919 and 1945, the last two of which have dance entries recorded in the database.[151] The *Suite* trend established itself first in America, with the 1945 version, which Stravinsky created partly because he wanted to copyright his music and receive royalties for the first time in the USA, partly because the illustrative recitative music in the old score was anathema to his mature aesthetic approach (see p. 29). Some choreographers too sought opportunities for more compact storytelling and a higher level of abstraction;

the reduction of mime music allowed them more freedom. Although Balanchine was intended to be the first choreographer of the 1945 *Suite*,[152] Bolm was hastily brought in instead to create the production for Ballet Theatre, with Alicia Markova as the Firebird and designs by Marc Chagall. He had already staged the ballet on his own company in Los Angeles (1940), according to the programme, using a 'symphonic suite' (the 1919 score). It seems that Stravinsky was paid to tailor the new pantomime bridges of the 1945 *Suite* specifically for the Bolm production.[153]

But it was Balanchine's setting of the readymade *Suite* in 1949 (for New York City Ballet, using the Chagall designs again), a personal triumph for Maria Tallchief as the Firebird, that proved far more successful. The choreographer himself seems to have been unconvinced. Perhaps he wanted to help his friend financially by using the new copyrighted score, and Stravinsky certainly took an interest in the progress of his staging. But Balanchine always disliked complex stories,[154] and the numerous choreographic and design modifications over the years (including new material by Jerome Robbins for the Monsters introduced in 1970) are a sign of his own dissatisfaction with the work. Robert Garis described the unusually formal emphasis of Balanchine's *Firebird* production, like his *Swan Lake* (1951) with radically reduced mime, the drama emerging through 'what is structurally a suite of dances'.[155]

As a whole, the ballet remains unconvincing, but the 1949 Firebird/Prince Ivan pas de deux and the Berceuse/Lullaby are interesting choreography, and here we also see the new formal emphasis in the detail of the movement. Comparison with the Fokine original is illuminating, using the 1951 film of these dances with Tallchief and Michael Maule.[156] There is overt reference to the original choreography (and thus the history of the score) in the bird arms, the pulling away from the Prince in arabesque, the images of entrapment, and later the endless bourrées of the Berceuse. Yet both dances reveal pattern more clearly than in the Fokine version. The pas de deux demonstrates a sharper body line and outline of phrase units in their varying proportions (the smaller unit of the bar, as well as longer units). It begins with a step forwards into penché arabesque, and back into a massive arch of the torso, the seesaw repeated, cleanly printed steps culminating in shapes firmly etched on the memory, unlike Fokine's movement, which seems to escape or flutter away from the body. The recapitulation of the main tune is set as a dangerous promenade, the Firebird pulling out centrifugally from the Prince, à la seconde, carving a huge circle. The image is exceptionally enlarged through temporal extension and the sheer number of rotations, six in all (more than in some contemporary performances), and an extra turn with which Tallchief steadies herself, filling a 4-bar phrase unit. The pas de deux ends with the famous image of interlocked right angled arms, the Firebird, weary and imprisoned, standing on pointe and then hanging, wriggling gently to the floor three times, each wriggle clinging tightly to its own (one-bar) musical gesture. So, as well as drama, and with Tallchief's extraordinary, driven grandeur and animal sensuality, design is emphasised, shape in space and (musical) time. Balanchine's pas de deux is also much more about rhythm than Fokine's, the treatment more bracing, the tempo faster, articulation of beat and bar more defined. Balanchine's Berceuse too, where the main emphasis is on serene flow, is much more closely related to musical form than its predecessor, articulating rise and fall in pitch as well as rhythm. Thus, the score is reread by Balanchine according to the terms of a new Stravinsky era, highlighting his special rhythmic, formal rapport with Stravinsky's music (see Ch. 3). This *Firebird* was also strategically important in drawing new audiences to the ballet: it became New York City Ballet's first box-office hit.

Whereas the 1945 score (28 minutes long) still contains short Pantomime sections, the 1919 version (22 minutes long) cuts these out completely: including some further abbreviations within the selected dance sections, it comprises the Introduction, Firebird Variation, the Princesses' Round Dance, Infernal Dance, Lullaby and Finale. This total freedom from pantomime led Ferenc Barbay to create an extremely economical *Firebird* at the Bavarian State Opera Ballet (1981) for just two men (the Sorcerer and Firebird), stripped down to dance belts and on a bare stage. Barbay introduced the 1976 synthesiser version of the *Suite* by Isao Tomitas.[157] Another setting of the 1919 *Suite*, by the dance theatre choreographer Angelin Preljocaj (Bavarian State Opera Ballet, 1995), removed all vestiges of the original tale. He claimed that it was simply the danger and fascination of fire, and not birds, that interested him. Here, a fire breaks out in what might be a factory, symbolised by two female Firebirds flickering and flaring up, and a band of workers and firemen storm the stage.[158]

But it is Béjart's choreography to the 1919 *Suite* (Paris Opéra Ballet, 1970) that is the most widely known, and it demonstrates well the problems of imposing a new narrative on any score, suite or otherwise. Described in his programme note as an 'abstract' production, there is no discursive narrative action as such, but there is a clear 'story' element, of a totally different kind from the original ballet. As usual, the choreographer was impatient with the original scenario, and he worked with what he called

the two major elements that startled at the creation.

– STRAVINSKY, RUSSIAN musician

– STRAVINSKY, REVOLUTIONARY musician

Let the dance become the abstract expression of these two elements that are always present in the music: a profound feeling of Russia and a certain rupture with traditional music, translated above all by an inhabitual rhythmic violence.

– The Firebird is the Phoenix reborn from ashes.

– The Poet, like the revolutionary, is a Firebird.

In his programme, Béjart also noted the group of avant-garde artists who banded together under the title 'Firebird' just before the Russian Revolution.[159]

Thus, in a reworking of the original theme of good overcoming evil, Béjart's ballet shows a group of nine young partisans stirring into action; a young man who becomes their leader and discards his dungarees to don a red unitard (becoming the Firebird figure); their ritual of union, involving the passing of a symbolic kiss between the hands (to the Princesses' Round Dance); a kind of battle dance of revolutionary fervour, which ends with the leader struck down (the Infernal Dance); the Firebird's final fight against death (Lullaby); and, last of all, rebirth through the figure of another man in red, the Phoenix, with a huge ensemble of Firebirds and the eight remaining partisans crowding the stage at the end.[160] Such a spectacular modern rendering, danced with full-out commitment, proved an immediate success and the ballet has since received numerous international stagings.

Yet, even if removal of pantomime might have released the choreographer from certain constraints, there are moments when the music seems to fight awkwardly against Béjart's vision. The Lullaby cannot be a lullaby here – it does not fit Béjart's new 'story' – and it is a dance of spasm and struggle, fast and punchy alongside this gently swaying music. The opening phrase, for instance, is packed full of information: a tentative développé to the side abolished by contraction and contortion, a pirouette climaxing in arabesque, a body shake, flow constantly punctuated by rapid spurts of motion and jagged accents. When the same music returns, the movement phrase quickens, embellished with ronds de jambe and a couple of cabrioles. In one especially flamboyant moment, the Firebird lies face down and beats his legs overhead. There are no seamless bourrées here, and the spasms continue until the closing moment of death. Interesting choreomusical statements can result when music and dance speak in different tones, but Béjart's overall approach is fundamentally conventional in *Firebird*, broad brushstroke compliance, and there seems to be no reason why this should change. The Lullaby music is neither erased nor a force of contradiction: it is simply a negative contribution, a bit of a nuisance. As he tends to throughout his *Firebird*, Béjart rides over many of the more subtle distinctions in the music, with a large measure of strong, bound movement dynamics, gestures and single or multi-body configurations presented as striking poses, all tactics that still the progressive energy and line in the music.

Béjart also radically revised the scenario when setting *Petrushka* in 1977 for his Ballet of the 20th Century, turning it into a ballet about personal identity. According to his programme note, it was about a Young Man, his Friend and young lover (The Young Girl) enticed by a Magician to don the masks of the three puppets of the original ballet. But the Young Man undertakes further masking in a labyrinth of mirrors, which results in his enslavement to the Magician and the destruction of his relationship with his former world.

In 1921, for the virtuoso Artur Rubinstein, Stravinsky created the *Three Movements from 'Petrushka'* piano arrangement, which was described as 'a sonata made of the material of *Petrushka*',[161] 'sonata' being read as a prime example of musical abstraction. Later, the composer argued that the new work had its own musical form 'in which dramatic line was no concern'[162] – he used just the Russian dance, the scene in Petrushka's cell, and the final Fairground scene with a shortened ending (which was published as the concert ending in the 1947 orchestral score revision). Stravinsky wanted to give his music a new identity, to distance it from the orchestral score. The piano scoring also got rid of the drama of orchestral colour. The term *espressivo* was edited from the score – though at one point *Furioso* is added (bar 34 of the second movement) – and there is a brittle brilliance to the sound. Stravinsky once asserted to Rubinstein that 'the piano is nothing but a utility instrument and it sounds right only as percussion'.[163]

In 1976, John Neumeier seems to have taken Stravinsky's stated intentions at face value in his *Petrushka Variations* for the Hamburg Ballet, a plotless work, although it incorporated everyday gesture. John Percival reported that

> In spite of the humorous overtones, the work is primarily a suite of dances to be enjoyed for their own sake, the distinctive character coming from the droll style and often explosive nature of the music out of its dramatic context.[164]

Yet it is not easy to erase the serious dramatic line, given the dancegoer's familiarity with the ballet and ballet score, and the British modern dance choreographer Richard Alston made an especially interesting point about reference when he created his own *Movements from 'Petrushka'* (1994). In a dance that works more successfully as a whole than either the Balanchine or Béjart *Suites*, relinquishing all sense of narrative continuity, Alston absorbed the strategy of neoclassical double coding, accessing materials from the past to be reworked for the present. But he felt that the music was undeniably 'about something' and that, if Stravinsky had simply wanted to make 'a nice neoclassical suite, he'd have avoided the second movement, that very strange, dissonant, expressive music'. He also confessed in interview to being inspired far more by the image of the person than the puppet.[165] The programme note signals reference to the great dancer who suffered mental breakdown as much as to the dance that featured him. Alston's starting point was the famous 1929 photograph of Nijinsky meeting his old company after watching a performance of *Petrushka*: he 'looks away, smiling blankly, distantly ...'

Onstage, it is hard not to read the man who dances the 'cell' music and becomes part of the action in the final scene as a kind of Nijinsky/Petrushka figure: he returns during the last group scene, highlighting the sinister 'outsider' musics of both the original bear (shortened in this piano score into a rude excrescence) and masqueraders. Increasingly isolated, he crouches on the floor. One of the group approaches him, he starts up, then they all look sharply away in one final statement of rupture. Movement images are transferred from the original Fokine to the new solo: the holding onto, even clutching, a body part, like a gesture of self-protection; hands held, restrained, behind the back or crossed in front; arms opening out from the body in jerky beats or wheeling fast one after the other. But the new manner is especially poignant – far more so today, I feel, than when I first wrote about this work six years ago. It is offset by the relatively simple yet rhythmically sophisticated group work of the outer movements, which references Nijinska's *Noces* in working blocks of four men and four women with and against each other.[166] How can one not be moved by those despairing falls and the exertion of superhuman will to combat such despair? Darshan Singh Bhuller, on whom the solo was created, danced razor sharp and elastic, at two extremes. Ben Ash got into the weight of the piano chords and breathed and softened into a state of vulnerability. Like most Alston dancers, both listened and embodied.[167]

This Petrushka has been given a rich dance language: not the laconic repeating gestures of Fokine's actor-dancer, but a range of vocabulary, sometimes exposed as fragmentary utterances, sometimes formed into long convoluted sentences. So meaning, character and emotion are achieved differently, and, in his movement and its relation to music, he shows intelligence, a wild imagination and depth of experience. This is a different personality from the Fokine Pierrot puppet, not only a victim, more robust, nervy and explosive, giving us a real 'shout', which relates to Stravinsky's initial concept of the hero's characterisation within his music.[168] But is this a statement that is also appropriate to recent positive re-readings of Nijinsky's creative achievements?

The presence of the piano stage centre – as it was at the premiere, forming an obstacle that the dancers have to circumnavigate – is a device that works against the convention of music as the non-visual sound world inhabited by Fokine's characters, which became a kind of ballet realism. It foregrounds the fact of the choreography being about music, a concept of media separation (because it draws attention to the device) as much as of integration. But perhaps the piano, the music, also becomes a protagonist in its own right, especially so when

Nijinsky/Petrushka is on stage. The gesture of hands over ears suggests an op-pressive clamour from the piano's immediate proximity. Sometimes the piano is simply to be listened to quietly in stillness, but its motor pulse is also used to provide energy for spirited dancing, and it constitutes a force that sparks at times a virtuoso sweep of feeling, at others, thoughtful, collected conversation. For instance, if we look at the early part of the big solo, we can compare the gesture-to-gesture response of Fokine with the freer articulations of Alston, who does not pick up on every moment, just on *some* moments, such as the desperate flurry of arms to a cadenza passage, or a sudden meeting of brutal accents. This Nijinsky/Petrushka is not simply set in motion by sound.

Yet we also see a paring-down, a removal of emotion, specific situation and through-narrative: the piece is like a meditation on personality and isolation of the individual from the group. Named characters and facial expression are ab-sent, and the costuming is plain black T-shirt and trousers for Nijinsky/Petrushka, black and white for the group. In this new context, the familiar im-ages from the Fokine work have become frozen. The clear, often angular, outlines of Nijinsky/Petrushka's body are like a hardened account of the original puppet.

As usual in Alston's work, structure too is a highlighted part of the content, contributing to meaning. We read devices of restraint as moves suddenly return, perhaps angled differently, contextualised differently, or, most formally and 'un-realistically', recapitulated. The manner of structuring movement also creates character. Just at the furious fortissimo moments when the old Petrushka railed against the Charlatan with manic stuttering steps, gestures and jumps of anger and anguish repeated as if to emphasise futility, the new Petrushka turns into a long phrase that is later recapitulated, almost exactly. In contrast to the original Fokine, it grows, shifts, twists and turns, and comes to a sharp halt, with a closing of the feet like a door slamming shut, a complicated, multi-faceted argu-ment in movement. On the repeat, it is differently nuanced by different music, and shows a higher grade of anxiety, an even sharper stop.

Thus, as much as formal devices are like a straitjacket, a hardening device, they highlight the turbulence within, operating in tension with emotion. Indeed, Alston's dance as a whole is a metaphor for this combat between restraint and emotional vigour. Alston shares Stravinsky's post-Russian-period inclinations as a formalist and classicist, interested in the language and structures of the art medium, but he has not been just that for some years: for him, form is definitely not everything, even when Stravinsky says so.[169]

Concert scores as choreography

Stravinsky's concert scores are far less burdened than the ballet scores by myth, tradition and familiar narratives, and many of them were served up by the composer with an exaggerated account of their abstraction. Yet choreographers, even if they can hardly have been unaware of Stravinsky's neoclassicism and aesthetics, go largely by what they hear and in relation to their previous musical experience. Like Alston, they have not let Stravinsky get away with the idea of 'form is everything', and the concert scores have inspired a surprising range of treatments, including narrative treatments.

The two works to which clear subject matter or reference has most often been applied are the *Symphony in Three Movements* and *Concerto in D* for string orchestra, and accordingly many of these settings do not borrow the musical title. For once, Stravinsky was uncharacteristically clear about the reference contained in his *Symphony*. In his programme note, he admitted that the music could be read according to the time when it was written (1942–5): 'our arduous time of sharp and shifting events, of despair and hope, of continual torments, of tension, and at last cessation and relief'.[170] In *Dialogues and a Diary* he tells us that each part of the *Symphony* stemmed from concrete images (usually from film) of the war. The first movement was inspired by 'a documentary of scorched-earth tactics in China', and the third was 'a musical reaction to the newsreels and documentaries that I had seen of goose-stepping soldiers. The square march-beat, the brass-band instrumentation, the grotesque *crescendo* in the tuba – these are all related to those repellent pictures.' The fugue exposition and end of the *Symphony* he saw as 'the rise of the Allies'.[171]

Choreographers have read the dramatic tension in a variety of ways. Aurel Milloss's *Gezeiten (Tides)* (Cologne Ballet, 1960), in the mode of 'synthetic' dance, was plotless but driven by feeling: tides as metaphor for opposites, active/passive, tension/relaxation.[172] Kenneth MacMillan's *Olympiade* (Ballet of the Deutsche Oper, Berlin, 1968) was based on sports activities, gymnastics, tennis and marathon running,[173] whilst Uwe Scholz (Stuttgart Ballet, 1984), omitting precise reference and deciding in the end to keep the musical title, characterised the outer movements with an antagonistic mechanical staccato.[174] In Australia, Gray Veredon read the score as symbolising initiation into sexuality in his ritual trilogy *Inner Circles* (1981), following it with *Sacre* (the sacrifice) and *Les Noces* (the union).[175] There were other collage settings: Jochen Ulrich staging the *Symphony* next to *Pulcinella* and *Firebird* in *Geschichte von Pulcinella* (Tanz-Forum Cologne, 1982), Charles Lisner including sections of the *Symphony* together with orchestral music by Webern and Berg alongside a setting of *Oedipus Rex* (Queensland Ballet, 1969).

The *Concerto in D* for string orchestra (1946) has likewise tended to inspire mood or narrative content, although in this instance nothing Stravinsky said supports this. Several settings have explored sexuality, but the range of mood suggested by, or imposed upon, the music has been considerable. By far the most well-known setting is Robbins's *The Cage* (1951), about an animal- or insect-like tribe of females that preys on males and a 'Novice' whose rite of passage is to kill two male invaders by strangling them between her legs.[176] Robbins makes the strings buzz more ferociously than any other choreographer. We know that Stravinsky had reservations about his setting (see p. 78). *Tilt* (1972) by van Manen, for Nederlands Dans Theater, was another combative piece, a comment on male/female power exchange, but with a formal twist: it used a repeat of the whole score to show reversals in male/female roles, facing directions and partner exchange.[177] Michael Corder's *Party Game* (Royal Ballet, 1984) was fundamentally lighthearted, but still with competitive, sexually charged connotations.[178] Other settings have pursued quite different topics, such as Werner Ulbrich's *Attis und die Nymphe* (Stuttgart Ballet, 1959), which used a Greek theme. It is especially interesting that Dore Hoyer, a leading figure in German modern dance, set the score on the Hamburg Ballet, which she directed during 1949–51. Hers was a group work, *Vision* (1950), about a woman and her soul.[179]

Excentrique

The second of the *Three Pieces for String Quartet*, written in 1914 and re-orchestrated in 1928–9 as one of the *Quatre Etudes*, is interesting because it was inspired by actual movement, the famous English music-hall artist Little Tich whom the composer saw in London in 1914: 'the jerky, spastic movement, the ups and downs, the rhythm – even the mood or joke of the music – was suggested by the art of the great clown'.[180] Little Tich specialised in moving in a greatly elongated pair of shoes that enabled him to tilt forwards at a perilous angle. The database records fourteen settings to date of this piece, which is just over two minutes long. When he orchestrated the original three pieces, Stravinsky added a fourth to make *Quatre Etudes*, at which point he gave them descriptive titles: 1. Danse; 2. Excentrique (the piece after Little Tich); 3. Cantique; 4. Madrid. Before this, the composer appears to have been in two minds about committing himself to any programme, except that, for at least one of the first performances by the Flonzaley Quartet in the USA (1915), the three pieces were grouped as 'Grotesques', and the point about the contrasting moods and reference was made clear by Daniel Gregory Mason, who introduced the work.[181]

It was on this occasion that the American imagist poet Amy Lowell wrote a poem about each of the quartet pieces. For the second:

> Pale violin music whiffs across the moon,
> A pale smoke of violin music blows over the moon,
> Cherry petals fall and flutter,

And the white Pierrot,
Wreathed in the smoke of the violins,
Splashed with cherry petals falling, falling,
Claws a grave for himself in the fresh earth
With his finger-nails.[182]

For later London performances in 1919, we assume that Ernest Ansermet, to whom the pieces are dedicated, wrote his programme note according to Stravinsky's wishes. He noted that the second piece 'represents an unhappy juggler, who must hide his grief while he performs his feats before the crowd'.[183]

In both instrumental versions (the Etude being sparsely orchestrated), this is a very strange little number, a series of isolated, 'jerky' statements, recurring in unpredictable patterns, from the opening falling two-note 'push' (heard six times) to a perky fragment (labelled in a sketch 'Dancing Girl: Bareback Rider'),[184] a lazy sighing breath, an angry stutter and fierce shrieks (see Exs. 2.5a–e). In the centre, there is a brief cadenza, and when scored for piano (as an Etude), it is reminiscent of Petrushka's desperate fist-banging as he races round his cell.[185] Then the music settles into a repeating 'oom-pah' that becomes accompaniment to a jaunty tune, before returning to earlier material. So the little piece reaches towards expressionism and *Petrushka,* while also having the terse, disjointed quality of Webern. Considered physically, this is essentially gestural music, but broken, without Stravinsky's characteristic dance momentum.

Two settings of *Excentrique* (using the orchestral Etude version), one by Marie Marchowsky and James Waring and one by Pina Bausch (using the string quartet version) make us hear these gestures in contrasting ways. Marchowsky had danced with Martha Graham and Anna Sokolow in the 1930s and later branched out to perform solo or with her own group, as part of the experimental wing of modern dancers who presented at the 92nd Street Y in New York. Her setting (1952) called *After Toulouse-Lautrec* was a sequel to *Odalisque* (to Bartok), the pair of dances together called *Two Portraits.*[186] The choreographer-dancer is a woman of a certain age (out of Lautrec's *La Buveuse* (1890)), we presume under the influence of drink, in bare feet and the old modern dance uniform of torsohugging long dress.[187] The statement is bitter and darkly humorous, with exag-

Ex. 2.5a. *Excentrique* from *Quatre Etudes* (re-orchestration of *Three Pieces for String Quartet*), two-note 'push'.

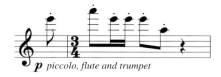

Ex. 2.5b. *Excentrique*, 'Dancing Girl'.

Ex. 2.5c. *Excentrique*, 'sighing breath'.

Ex. 2.5d. *Excentrique*, 'angry stutter'.

Ex. 2.5e. *Excentrique*, 'shrieks'.

gerated acting, possibly a sly joke about the seriousness of pioneering modern dance. Her table and chair are her anchor: she thrusts herself way across the table with chin jutting, swings a leg over the back of the chair, or goes for a trip round the table, only to land splat on the floor (at [5]+3). Picking up her skirt, she imagines that she has a dancing partner (to the oom-pah section), and then, prompted by the music, returns to movement from the opening of the dance. Marchowsky does not respond tidily to every musical moment – she goes her own way a lot of the time like any wavering drunk, and thus we find her lolling back even before the music begins, indulging in a strange stirring action with one foot in the air. She also slaps the table, creating her own sound during a couple of musical rests. Being with the music, especially with the recurring 'push', indicates a routine stability. But the harshest musical accents whip her body into violent twists and torso wrenches. She is both a tough old bird and a source of pathos, with that awesome, hot-tempered gutsiness of early modern dancers, magnifying greatly the grotesque properties of the music.

James Waring occupied an unusual position in American dance, a ballet- and modern-trained choreographer who retained an interest in ballet and theatricality, but who was also an important avant-garde figure, associated with the postmodern Judson Dance Theater of the 1960s, which incorporated pedestrian movement. Waring set *Excentrique* within a piece called *Arena*, alongside other numbers selected from the *Etudes*, orchestral *Suites* and *Instrumental Miniatures*. *Arena* was made in 1967 for Manhattan Festival Ballet and remade in 1975 for the modern dancers of New England Dinosaur: different choreography but wrought according to similar principles, using the same combination of three women and two men, the same musical selection, and dressed in unitards.[188] Both settings are about the ritual of performance: the preparation for it, the act itself (dance or circus) and the aftermath.[189] There is a certain sadness about their 'show', and also an enigmatic quality: you sense the presence and power of private movement symbols without fully understanding them. Both versions of *Arena* are full of movement jokes, hand and arm gestures from daily life, as well as simple ballet steps – balancés, échappés, ballonnés – and at one point during the 1967 piece a bit of cancan. Sometimes these moves are timed not to fit the music precisely, as in the nature of preparation or warm-up, and some of *Excentrique* is like this. All the material is like 'found movement', gestural objects performed blankly without expression, in a kind of nonsense collage. Performed by the three women, slow shuffle steps with a twist and curve to the side mark the two-note 'push' gestures in both versions of the piece. Later, with the change in musical mood, the women's gestures become frantic and, in the 1975 version, they step out bluntly to the oom-pah, jabbing their heels into the ground and beating their elbows on their chests. Waring employs more musical mimicry than Marchowsky, but here, the gestures are not 'acted out', and they refuse to add up to anything: they have a life of their own and escape... like butterflies, or petals. There are no convulsions, and the music can still sound pale. Waring is closer to Dada, Cunningham and Cage.

The German Tanztheater choreographer Pina Bausch likewise explores the fragmentary nature of *Excentrique*, her setting situated within a twenty-minute piece, *Der zweite Frühling* (*The Second Spring*), that was part of her 1975 Stravinsky programme alongside *Sacre* (see p. 449), and an early foray into the dance theatre that became her specialism.[190] The larger piece is about a Husband and Wife musing on the past, on what they might once have been, in search of renewal (a second spring) of their relationship. As they eat supper together at table stage left (in formal dress, high heels, suit), other characters (billed as Memories) enter their consciousness: an innocent Bride barefoot in white, a romantic young man (perhaps the image that the Husband has of his past) and two seductresses, one young, sweet and a bit daft (her home base is a chair stage right) and an older, more worldly-wise vamp who presides from a sofa throne upstage before emerging for a fierce tango with both men. Displacements, collisions and invasions of another's territory make the dance both funny and tragic. Husband and Wife are both in search of alternative identities, for themselves and for their partner. The perennial questions are: who am I, what was I, what have I become, can I make real human contact with someone else and, if so, whom? The Husband, especially, seeks out other kinds of women: his Wife is far more lost to herself. But he is not unsympathetic: he wants to give her love. There is heartbreaking tenderness near the end as the older couple gently remove each other's shoes, but then the whirl of domestic duties takes over, the Wife refuses closer contact, and they end separated once more across their dinner table. The clockwork of the Andante from *Easy Pieces for Piano* (Stravinsky's bracing motor again) sets the scene and closes *Der Zweite Frühling*: other selections are from *Three Pieces for Clarinet Solo*, *Instrumental Miniatures* and *Three Pieces for String Quartet* (*Excentrique* and *Cantique*), all early proto-neoclassical, except the *Tango* (1940).

More than any other section of *Der Zweite Frühling*, the dance quartet to *Excentrique* epitomises fractured identity, in Bausch's scheme as part of an imaginary surreal situation. The point is made with exceptional clarity when all four characters find themselves in a cluster: the young seductress lying across the lap of the young man, the Wife perching on his knees in a deliberate move to get in between the younger model and the Husband, who stands facing them all. But the fragmentary nature of the music contributes to the confusion of subjectivities. The young seductress, who is the main focus of this dance, plays a number of roles herself, taut and sophisticated (to the perky motif), languorous (to the legato sigh), playful dancer (she takes the oom-pah 'dance music' literally as Marchowsky did) or voracious eater (the big accent at [5]+3 when Marchowsky landed on the floor marks her thrill as she tucks into a bowl of cream). Other fortissimo stutters and shrieks mean sudden starts and reactions from the rest of the cast that dart our eye round the stage, fragmenting the visual focus as much as Stravinsky fragments aural focus between different timbres.

All three choreographers discussed make the Stravinsky music more specific in its resonance and express a pathos tinged with humour that makes sense in relation to the early musical programme (though they are hardly likely to have been aware of this). In her analysis of the music, Marianne Kielian-Gilbert argues for the rhythmic connections underlying its disconnections, the 'rhythms of form'. Like the work of Picasso and Gertrude Stein, she says, the music evokes 'not only our powerful and painful isolation as humans but also our fundamental interrelatedness and interdependence as well'.[191] Whereas her purely musical plan makes no sense once dance is added and new choreomusical forms have been created, it is possible to see that Bausch's social statement is complementary to Kielian-Gilbert's vision. On the other hand, Marchowsky and Waring are less concerned with the issue of interdependence and more with the fragmented nature of the individual human Subject. Marchowsky strives towards a unified character or Subject, towards the coherence of sound fragments as she struggles to manage the tatters of her identity, whereas Waring skirts playfully around the whole issue of Subject and is content to leave those sound fragments in teasing disarray.

Mark Morris marks Stravinsky

Mark Morris is hardly known as a Stravinsky choreographer, having only used his music in three pieces, and his is an unusual musical selection: the *Symphonies of Wind Instruments* (1920, choreographed as *Frisson*, 1985); the three short unaccompanied sacred choruses, *Ave Maria*, *Credo* and *Pater Noster* (1926–34, revised 1949, choreographed for the Netherlands Opera as part of *Biblical Pieces*, 1999 – see p. 113); and the *Serenade in A* for piano (1925, choreographed as *Candleflowerdance*, 2005). Video recordings exist of *Frisson* and *Candleflowerdance*. In interview, Morris observes that choreographers often hear dissonance in twentieth-century music (including Stravinsky's) and think that they should contract or flex a foot in a kind of angst response.[192] Morris himself is more likely to choreograph such moves to Purcell or popular music, yet, at the same time, he totally dismisses any claim that Stravinsky's music is not expressive. This is crucial.

The *Serenade* is a tight, twelve-minute work in four movements, Hymn, Romanza, Rondoletto and Cadenza Finale, bearing allusions to Bach, and dedicated to the composer's wife Catherine. But Morris took no notice of biographical detail when he choreographed the piece: for instance, the fact that Catherine was unhappily involved in a triangular relationship including Vera at the time of composition. *Candleflowerdance* is just 'a piano ballet', he said. But it is not just a piano ballet. Morris clearly heard darkness in the music, at the same time refusing to pin down the nature of his own expression in discussion or to over-dramatise the sadness: 'It's still noble ... It's not a walk to the gallows.'

Lit candles and a vase of flowers border the stage and hint at a modern, secular shrine; but only after the dance was made did Morris decide that it was the right piece to dedicate to his late friend Susan Sontag. Why then is the choreography so moving? It takes place within a square of white tape centre stage, which looks as if it could have been marked out for a sports activity. There are six dancers, 'normal' Morris dancers, not glossy ballet or stylised modern dance people, straightforward in their manner, in variously coloured shirts and trousers. Their steps often seem to have a disarming hop, skip and doodle simplicity, in the unaffected manner typical of Morris, picking up very accurately on rhythmic detail, including the crazy syncopations of the Rondoletto when, in pairs, they rock merrily out of kilter with each other. The dancers are free to leave the square and the stage. Yet, for some reason they always return, drawn back, and small disturbances hint at high drama: a solo gesture to no one in particular or a moment of being stopped by another person's whispered secret or sudden contact.

At the start, standing in a huddle in one corner, an arm sequence climaxes with all six pointing straight upwards. Why this gesture? It is declamatory, like the opening music, and also the only way out of the square (Morris's own point). It returns at the musical climax in the centre of the last movement, and here as an image of enormous stress. As the music swells towards the end of the Hymn, two men ripple their arms from side to side as if needing to catch the feeling behind the surge. In the Romanza, one woman and then another in front of her slap their arms round their torsos, an impulse to reach diagonally upwards, after which they draw their arms down across their faces like tears. Thus, in turn, the two women exaggerate the first two notes of the main melody (see Ex. 2.6). The slight bluntness achieved by the mutual underlining of musical sound and gestures, the effect we get of 'overhearing' the notes, reduces sentimentality, and makes these gestures as strange as they are deeply troubled. The pianist Steven Beck told me that, waiting for the women's cue, he might articulate those two notes more strongly than he would outside the theatre.[193] The Cadenza Finale is all about falling, very simply dropping to the floor, again and again, with the falling melody. Collapsing is especially upsetting when people seem unable to muster any resistance. The ending is shockingly bleak, a woman in yellow, supported but struggling to stand at the corner, hair strewn across her face, arms outstretched, as if opening to an image of catastrophe before her.

Ex. 2.6. *Serenade in A* for piano, Romanza.

In *Candleflowerdance*, poignancy is largely the result of the exaggerated split between private anguish and public normality, the former set off by the latter and brought into sharp focus at singular moments of concurrence between sound and visual gestures. Morris says rightly, 'You suffer by watching it',[194] whatever Stravinsky might have thought. Morris convinces us of what he feels to be latent in the score.

Ian Spink set the *Serenade* on the British group Second Stride in 1982 as *There Is No Other Woman*, pairing it with the *Piano Sonata* and extending it with further dancing in the gaps between musical movements. It is illuminating to make comparisons with Morris's piece. In Spink's setting, there is more motion than emotion, more pattern than personality, a kind of *moderato perpetuum mobile* accentuating the Bach in the music, with the occasional enigmatic human touch. In 1982, I called this a 'dense, cerebral piece'.[195] Looking at it now, it recalls for me a period when we could take a stronger dose of abstraction than we can today, and one in which time moved more slowly.

Morris's *Frisson* (1985) to the *Symphonies of Wind Instruments* is hardly recognisable as a Morris piece, and neither is the music in any sense traditional *musique dansante*: even if it accords strictly with metronomic indications, it generates no sense of rhythmic momentum. Perhaps it is not surprising, then, that the database records only seven uses of the *Symphonies*. Small dance groups also find its resources hard to manage: Morris himself, insisting as he does on live music, has rarely been able to meet the needs of the orchestration. He used a recording for the premiere at Dance Theater Workshop, New York, although the full live wind ensemble was available for performances at the Théâtre Royal de la Monnaie in Brussels (1988) and in Tanglewood (2003). On the other hand, the *Symphonies* is one of the most often analysed musical scores, 'a structural paradigm for the twentieth century', it has been called,[196] regularly considered key to Stravinsky's own style while also looking forward to the new conceptions of musical time that were prevalent after the Second World War. In 1923, it was the first work to be described in the press as neoclassical, by Boris de Schloezer.[197] Given its huge musicological importance, then, some attention to its use in a dance context would seem justified. Besides, Morris's choreography creates a fascinating conversation with the score.

It is beyond the needs of my project to discuss the detail of the *Symphonies* or the analytical issues that it gave rise to, but a broad understanding of its structural principles is helpful. Walsh tells us that Stravinsky first wrote the ending, what has come to be called the Chorale, and then rapidly assembled the nine-minute score 'from back to front' as it were, in a kind of patchwork manner, not as a linear process.[198] The decision to use a wind band was 'cool', the emotional warmth associated with strings avoided. Stravinsky revised the work in 1947; the following choreomusical analysis uses the 1947 score.

In a seminal article, 'Stravinsky: The Progress of a Method' (1962), Edward T. Cone used the *Symphonies* to illuminate the principle of block construction, and with it the fundamental discontinuities on the surface of the composer's style – breaks or disruptions, some like shocks, some more subtle as one block of musical material gives way to the next.[199] He goes on to explain how what he refers to as stratification or layering through time is complemented by two other modes:

first, the interlock, as musical lines or blocks operate in alternation, like a counterpoint through time; second, synthesis, as a process of unification is applied to
successively introduced musical ideas. Cone's summary table indicates six strata
functioning as musical continuities within the *Symphonies* and resolved within
the Chorale. Put another way, what we hear is a series of musical blocks or
fragments differentiated by various means (melody, harmony, timbre, articulation and tempi – three different metronome markings recur across the work).
New ideas gradually emerge, old ones gradually disappear, and one (a motif
spanning the interval of a fourth, first heard five bars after [1]) pervades the
entire work (see Ex. 2.7). Are these fragments interpolations or structural 'pillars'?[200] They might be either, in different contexts, and the progress of the piece
complicates the issue by uncovering relationships between them. As for the Chorale, although it refers to what has gone before and feels like a culmination, its
rhythmic simplicity combined with homophonic texture make it sound like a
new beginning; there are two short anticipations of its arrival that Stravinsky
added retrospectively (at [42] and [56]) and that link it into the overall formal
scheme of alternating blocks.

Ex. 2.7. *Symphonies of Wind Instruments.*

Since Cone, many musicologists have argued about issues of continuity and
discontinuity within the *Symphonies*. As much as we might or might not want
the piece to cohere (and opinions differ on that fundamental point too), how
much does it propose either continuity or discontinuity and what are the processes involved in effecting these different strategies? Broadly, views range between the linear model and organicist approach, which uses cellular analytical
techniques to discover processes of crossing the divide between blocks (László
Somfai), and the non-linear model, in which form-giving durational ratios between temporal units (Jonathan Kramer) preserve the entity of separate blocks
as 'moments'. Other views reflect mixtures of these two models, and include an
argument for a 'logic of discontinuity' (Alexander Rehding).[201] So do we sense
that the work 'progresses' or not, or do we feel this only in retrospect because the
final Chorale seems so final? Furthermore, do we experience the work in a few
larger divisions, within which nest the many fragments?

Until very recently, nearly all musicological discussion has been about the
radical form of the *Symphonies*. Yet it is interesting to point to a couple of excep-

tions along the way. Even though he fights to eliminate the non-musical, which accords with what Stravinsky was about to express in his manifesto 'Some Ideas About My Octuor' (1924),[202] de Schloezer was clearly moved in 1923, and did not know how to handle it. With 'but' and 'nevertheless' (in translation), his argument twists and turns upon itself:

> This genial work is only a system of sounds, which follow one another and group themselves according to purely musical affinities; the thought of the artist places itself only in the musical plan without ever setting foot in the domain of psychology. Emotions, feelings, desires, aspirations – this is the terrain from which he has pushed his work. The art of Stravinsky is nevertheless strongly expressive; he moves us profoundly and his perception is never formularized; but there is one specific emotion, a musical emotion. This art does not pursue feeling or emotion; but it attains grace infallibly by its force and by its perfection.[203]

It is relevant that de Schloezer was similarly ambiguous about *Noces* later the same year, moved by rigorous construction and stylistic purity and form in French, but to his Russian readers, who were less concerned with the new Western values, 'Actually, what is particularly striking … is its emotional meaning; it disturbs and affects one … I would call it the most human of all Stravinsky's works.'[204]

Even if his actual analysis of *Symphonies* is now largely forgotten, Eric Walter White came up with descriptive terms that clearly indicate affective and referential content: the 'Bell' motif (the opening fanfare); 'Russian popular melodies' (oscillating melodic sequences, at [6] and [8]); 'Pastorale' (flute and clarinet dialogues, at [15]–[21]); 'Wild Dance' (at [46], a quick staccato episode leading to a climax at [54]–[56]).[205] Although he does not discuss their reference, it is interesting that, in his recent analysis, Alexander Rehding still borrows White's terms.

As for what the composer himself said about *Symphonies*, there are the hardly unexpected contradictions. His 1920s programme note referred merely to 'tonal masses … sculptured in marble … to be regarded objectively by the ear'.[206] Yet, in his *Autobiography*, he gives a clue as to alternative intentions: he refers to 'an austere ritual' unfolding as a series of 'short litanies between different groups of homogeneous instruments' and a 'liturgical dialogue' between clarinets and flutes.[207]

Taruskin latches on to the statement in the *Autobiography*, and makes a case for a parallel between the *Symphonies* and the Russian Orthodox rite for the dead, thus showing that the work looks backwards to the composer's Russian roots as much as it looks forwards. There is the halting quality of Slavonic liturgical chant, and also correspondences between particular sections of the score and the chant – for instance, the Kanon hymn (from [46], when material in the fast Tempo III becomes pronounced) and the repeated Eternal Remembrance utterance (the Chorale).[208] Arnold Whittall is convinced of the allusions to 'song, dance, celebration, lament – whose presence, far from the accidental results of the composer's failure to enforce his own logic of abstraction, are essential aspects of the music's integration of form and content'.[209]

Morris himself undertook no formal reading of the musicological literature. What is more, *Frisson* is one of the rare dances where he did not work with the musical score.[210] If he always choreographs primarily from sound, in this case it was only from sound, a procedure that turned out to be key to the particular style of this work. Unusually too, the movement was created in blocks (perhaps forming a subconscious link with Stravinsky's structure here), its tempo and distribution then adjusted to fit the music. There is none of the usual attention to musical detail that we expect from a Morris piece: movement between his specified cue points is not nailed to sound. But those very tactics allow for the spaciousness of the composite work: opportunities, sound spaces for us literally to hear the dance, the thud of a step in an awkward manoeuvre or of a landing from a fall – and the opposite, many visual pauses that then turn our attention full on to the music. Like the score, the time sense of the choreography is mainly static: it leads in no clear direction.

A limited number of movement ideas recur many times in different contexts – distinctive positions and clusters of activity – but Morris organises them quite differently from the musical structure. The movement fragments are like kaleidoscopic particles rather than either structural interpolations or pillars, and none of them conspicuously drops out to give more space to others. Nor do we associate particular moves with particular musical ideas. Again, sound and movement coexist with plenty of 'air' between them. Relations with the score are a good deal more specific and planned than in Merce Cunningham's work, famed for its intentional independence between music and dance, but the freedom from sound detail is strikingly similar in effect. (It seemed apt to look at the choreography by itself, and proved instructive occasionally to watch the video material in silence.)

Many other aspects of the choreography are reminiscent of Cunningham. There is the factual performance manner and non-linear structuring of time, the decentred use of the stage and multi-directional facings, the autonomy of each of the five performers (three women and two men in silver unitards), operating alone or in shifting combinations. Morris describes the attitude behind the execution: 'Report over there and do this. When you're done with that go over there and do this.' The movement style is chunky, sturdy, and sculptural, with emphasis on angles within body designs – not a curve or soft wrist to be seen –

Ill. 2. *Frisson*, choreography by Mark Morris, left to right Tina Fehlandt, Teri Weksler, Donald Mouton, David Landis and Jennifer Thienes, Mark Morris Dance Group.

but with an element of suspension and precariousness as well (which the title *Frisson* complements nicely; see Ill. 2). One or two images are plain and stable, such as a wide second position (arms and legs, straight or in plié), often an occasion for tentative matching across the group. But most moves are uncomfortable; there are many versions of standing on one leg and getting into the position fast with no time to find balance, for instance, one knee raised at a right angle in front of the body and an arm covering it with a parallel line, or the lower leg bent up behind the body, the opposite arm straight forward, while the head twists an awkward 90 degrees to the side. Morris sought 'wrongnesses' to extract a particular intensity of concentration, and that intensity gets conveyed to us, the audience. We also see lifts in which a woman is held flat and floating like a table top, and a couple of allegro movements: a series of three jumps with legs in parallel and arms swung back into pre-dive position, and dramatic backwards falls to the floor ending with the body in a plain straight line. Sometimes several moves together repeat as clusters. Transitions from one place to another are simple walks, on the toes, which 'gives a tension'; they become jaunty, even a trifle sneering, during the 'Wild Dance'.

The opening of *Frisson* is striking and energetic. A woman is somersaulted forwards down centre stage to the audience and back, and forwards again, her four *porteurs* gradually dropping down to one man, on his back and hoisting her up on his feet. She sits, legs apart, with her feet flexed, iconic, all right angles – one of the motif second position plié positions in the air. This final image returns fleetingly at the very end of *Frisson*, but without the same spatial symmetry, off centre, against one of the floating flat-body lifts, and with an extra man jumping on the outside, still moving as the lights go down. Perhaps it is a tease about closure that does not quite happen, just as some musicologists have proposed about the score.[211] It makes us contemplate the larger structure of the piece. So does the point two-thirds of the way through the dance at [56], the one major stasis, fully committed punctuation, with four of the dancers lying flat and just one facing away to an upstage corner, sitting tilted forwards, her arms stretched above her. The ensemble stays like that for all of ten bars.

With that major stasis, Morris imposes his own clear large shape, two parts, his point of division neither the one at [65] when the Chorale proper begins, nor the one that Kramer makes at [42], at the first of the two anticipations of the Chorale.[212] Morris's moment of punctuation is instead the second premonition at [56]. His choice is to maintain pace, increasing it for the climax of the 'Wild Dance', where there is more action than at any other point in *Frisson*. Events happen in rapid succession and keep our attention over the full width of the stage, three of the dancers do the 'three jumps' and all but one ends up falling flat, a couple, a third, a fourth. Then the big halt, unequivocal shift of gear, enhanced by white/blue lighting, the coldest yet in the piece: in the video of the 1988 performance at the Théâtre Royal de la Monnaie, there is a steady cooling towards this point in the dance. After a kind of breather that has all five in unison in a strange animalian rolling and circling with necks as fulcra, the concentration of the main Chorale begins, and we are calmed by its new cosmic resonance. There is a dance canon bathed in a golden glow, when many of the notes of the melody seem to be dispersed across the ensemble (perhaps a passage of detailed musical articulation at last), fleeting unisons or almost unisons, a sense of easy communion and a glimpse of wholeness, before the teasing final asymmetry.

Morris takes up the musical suggestions of experiencing or living the 'moment' of a particular block of material, and of change as disturbance or point of recognition: he adds further changes of this kind. His tactics evoke the practice of looking at a sheet of paper overlaid by a transparency and contemplating their marks both separately and in combination through each other. This means that, although Morris's large two-part division is clearer than in the music alone, he seems to have increased the jangles and jolts at a more detailed level. But most of the connections between musical cues and changes of movement speed are not exaggerated. More of these connections are apparent in the

Monnaie film than in the earlier one shot at Dance Theater Workshop, but sometimes we cannot be sure that they are meant to exist at all.

There is one other kind of cross-media connection in *Frisson* that is fundamental, creating shape and meaning within the composite work. What I call
here 'feeling moments' pierce the frame of the piece from time to time like darts,
surprising and especially strong in emotional impact, and there are more of
them towards the end of the dance. If we agree with Morris that the main tone
of the choreography is 'dry ... sober ... sciency', he is still telling us only half the
story. One such moment is the big halt, a desolate moment like a death symbol,
with so many floored bodies, plus the withdrawal of the woman who sits turned
away from us. Another, spectacular in its brevity and the coincidence of our
aural/visual intake, occurs during the Chorale, when a man puts his arms
around the waists of two women on either side of him and stretches forward
between them, a big effort of striving to straighten into a line, at a perilous angle.
He makes contact with the most poignant harmony in the whole score, the moment of expanded pitch span reached by melodic ascent to E against bass line
descent to C (four bars after [70] – see Ex. 2.8). The effort sets off a flurry of
activity, his torso contraction and the women's panic arm gestures, then another
contraction and ricochet reactions from the other dancers, crossing the music,
which has already returned to calm. At the end, it is the same man who is
exposed, jumping, the lone mover.[213] Image and sound combined signal a surprising humanity, and the cosmic becomes earthly. Serenity is close cousin to
sorrow in the Chorale. There is the ritual that Stravinsky talked about in his
Autobiography, but it is not always an austere ritual.

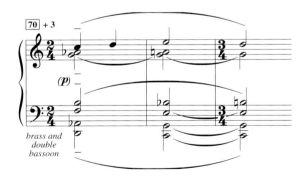

Ex. 2.8. *Symphonies of Wind Instruments.*

Despite the suggestion of the walks, which once or twice seem to go with the
music, there is definitely no motor in Morris's piece. The Stravinsky of *Frisson* is
not the composer who encourages smart attention to rhythm and a battery of

dance counts. Far more than usually, he encourages physical spontaneity. But, after all, this is a very different kind of *musique dansante* from what I described earlier in this chapter.

The 'feeling moments' in *Frisson* remind me of an image that still stands out amongst the hundreds of Stravinsky works that I have scrutinised live or on video: *Clone* (1997) by the Slovenian choreographer Matjaz Faric.[214] The dance is long and fails to sustain interest (using most of the *Concerto for Piano and Wind Instruments* [1924] and a lot of material from at least five other neoclassical pieces). But it contains one wonderful, unforgettable moment. In the slow movement of the *Concerto*, the full musical resources declaim a big chord theme. One man, his back to us, simply jumps to the slow, weighty beat, two feet to two, straightforward jumps, legs in parallel. It is hard to know why such a stark image was so moving, but it was one of those sudden, astonishingly expressive Stravinsky moments that dance – one body, diminutive in proportion to the sound – can make even more human.

Morris bucks the trend in all his Stravinsky choices and the handling of those choices. As for *Symphonies* and *Frisson*, there could hardly be a more unlikely or irregular example of a Stravinsky dance score or dance treatment of a Stravinsky score. Indeed, *Frisson* is a marvellous testament to how a composer's legacy to dance continues to expand both our imaginations and how we hear his music, well beyond his own dreams and directives.

To complete the story of dancing the *Symphonies*, it is instructive to find the music sounding quite different in the hands of other choreographers. Alvin Ailey's *Myth* (1971) is about a woman's various encounters with three men in a forest setting, and the music here is used primarily for its gestural content and timbre.[215] Ailey picks up on the series of pressure chords that follow the opening fanfare, an opportunity for a Graham-style contraction as the woman pushes the men back. The wind scoring connotes breeze and nature (recall White's 'Pastorale' title), and also shifts in emotional tone, with curlicues on flute/clarinet and strident brass simulating playfulness and threat respectively. Another American modern dance choreographer, Paul Sanasardo, placed his 1979 setting within a larger work, *Rotaring: The Stravinsky Dance Circus* (Batsheva Dance Company), incorporating selections from the orchestral *Suites* as well as the whole *Concerto in D*. Largely free from musical detail and driven by the circus theme, his version was divided sharply into two at the first anticipation of the Chorale: the first section for three quirky, melancholic clowns, the second for a couple of acrobats, who progress towards a state of serenity.[216] According to the programme note, Peter Sparling's ambitious *The Second Space* (2004) for twenty-three student dancers (the University Dance Company, Michigan) describes a community 'moving towards a collective ideal'. At first, jagged choreography reinforces the rhythmic definition of phrases, and, unlikely as this may seem after the other versions described, Sparling even finds a motor in the score.[217] The Chorale signals departure towards a new, more hopeful space where movement can flow more freely through the music. Sparling's setting is the most emphatic about musical detail that I have seen, and, in its own different way, it makes very good sense.

More recently still, there is Anne Teresa De Keersmaeker's setting within an evening-length work, *D'un soir un jour* (2006), which combines Stravinsky (his *Fireworks* too) with Debussy (*Prélude à l'Après-midi d'un Faune* and *Jeux*) and music by the contemporary British composer George Benjamin. Of all these scores, which mix hedonistic thrill and turbulence, the *Symphonies* is the most architectural, but De Keersmaeker sets to it a dance that has to go its own way outside this architecture for most of the time. The central figure Cynthia Loemij responds to the clarion call of the opening and its recurrences, her refuge a table top, but she cannot stop tumbling from vertical into the arms of colleagues below, her long dress falling untidily around her; her dance is prompted by emotional need and gravity, not musical structure. During the Chorale, Loemij still twitches and convulses, despite the serenity of sound. Only at the very end, she suddenly stretches out flat, as if on a tomb: the *Symphonies* were, after all, Stravinsky's '*tombeau*' tribute to Debussy.[218]

* * *

To reflect from a twenty-first-century viewpoint, the Stravinsky dances that are perhaps hardest to swallow are those that straightforwardly equate his dissonance with angst or fury or revolution or striving towards an ideal. We live at a time when reading Stravinsky is about being knowing rather than innocent of resonances and games, expecting irony and a multi-layered experience. Thus, Béjart's *Firebird* now looks like a huge, if well-intended, over-indulgence of emotional fervour. Robbins's *The Cage*, on the other hand, is plain uncomfortable, taking such pleasure in presenting women as harpies, and strangling the score as much as its victims. Both these works are, in their different ways, one-dimensional spectacles, and Stravinsky's music seems now to be anything but one-dimensional. But I also react with impatience to the busy-ness of many recent Stravinsky choreographies, the rhythmic legacy of Balanchine–Stravinsky to both ballet and modern dance over-read and gone awry, with choreographers finding so much detail in the music that they stifle it. Anything for a telling, simple moment, as with that man jumping! We have come a long way since the generalised characterisation of Stravinsky's rhythmic style, physicality and *musique dansante*. I now turn back to review what is more familiar, alongside what is again less familiar, and over to Balanchine.

3

George Balanchine's Stravinsky:
Collaboration as Challenge

Introduction

Reviewing Charles Joseph's monograph *Stravinsky and Balanchine: A Journey of Invention* in 2003, the New York dance critic Nancy Goldner dared to suggest that very little outcome of this collaboration was top-drawer Balanchine – in fact only *Agon* (1957) in its entirety, with just 'passages' from, she suggests, *Apollo* (1928), *Stravinsky Violin Concerto* (1972) and *Monumentum Pro Gesualdo* (1960). Top-drawer Stravinsky was much more in evidence. She also proposed that the work that these two artists undertook together (including Balanchine's use of existing Stravinsky scores) might not be the kind that showed his most sophisticated choreography, even if it showed his musical sophistication. The dance language of most Balanchine–Stravinsky was fairly 'generic', she claimed, and it prioritised rhythm.[1] This was a daring evaluation indeed, with the additional irony that Goldner herself had edited and contributed generously to the other most substantial book on their work together, *The Stravinsky Festival of the New York City Ballet*,[2] a celebration of that key event of 1972. For years, after all, Stravinsky and Balanchine have been touted as an exemplary composer-choreographer collaboration, perhaps the most distinguished in dance history, their partnership an institution from the mid-twentieth century onwards. Surprising as Goldner's evaluation might seem, it is certainly worth further interrogation, partly because of the distinction that she draws between musicality and choreography, but also for the weightier reason that it is timely in the context of this book to review the whole collaboration and to reconsider the aura that has grown up around it.

Meanwhile, much has been written elsewhere about the shared aesthetic belief of these two artists in order, precision, economy and classicism, also a tendency to play down expressive values, a practical, no-nonsense creative approach, a common Russian cultural background, and an affinity for the other's art. Much too has been written about Balanchine's possibly unique depth and breadth of musical knowledge as a choreographer, knowledge gained through practice and theory as well as listening, and which warmed him to Stravinsky. Alongside his studies at the Petrograd Theatre Ballet School, he had trained at the Conservatory of Music in piano, composition and music theory, and he remained an active pianist throughout his life. He was able to play from short scores (abbreviated versions of orchestral scores) and to compose the odd song and piano miniature, and was well equipped to converse with musician colleagues in sophisticated musical terms. Soon after arriving in America in 1933, he was still 'freshening up on counterpoint and harmony'[3] with the Russian composer Nicolas Nabokov, a mutual friend of both Stravinsky and Balanchine. He also made his own piano transcriptions from orchestral scores for his own try-outs. The Stravinsky transcriptions include *Monumentum*, the *Violin Concerto* (Aria I), the *Choral Variations on Bach's 'Von Himmel Hoch'*, and pieces that Balanchine never choreographed: *Scènes de ballet*, the first movement of the *Three Pieces for String Quartet*, and part of the *Symphony in E flat major*.[4] But I have argued elsewhere, comparing the musical styles of Frederick Ashton and Balanchine, that musically exceptional choreography is not always seeded in formal musical training.[5]

Other generally accepted facts about Balanchine and Stravinsky require review. Regularly, the choreographer showed deference to music as the superior art:

> The composer is able to give more life to a bar, more vitality and rhythmical substance than a choreographer, or a dancer for that matter. The musician deals with time and sound in a highly scientific way ... The choreographer will never be able to achieve such precision in the expression of movement as the composer through sound effect.[6]

Specifically, Balanchine was fond of stressing the rhythmic component of his own work and the useful temporal foundation that music provided, at the expense of other aspects: 'Music is time. It's not the melody that's important but the division of time ...'[7] Music puts a time corset on the dance.'[8] For him, Stravinsky was 'an architect of time'.[9] For Stravinsky, equally deeply committed to the rhythmic component of his work, Balanchine was the choreographer who best understood his time architecture. He also supported Balanchine's rhetoric nicely in 'Eye Music', the famous essay on his *Movements for Piano and Orchestra*, by saying (through Craft), 'What he needs is not a *pas de deux* but a motor impulse.'[10] But I will deconstruct that statement later. For now, is all this rhetoric misleading, an exaggeration of the truth? Is the time-corset style of rhythm driven by beat and motor as constraining as that description suggests? Is motor too simplistic a concept for what Balanchine creates? As much as the rhythmic component is important, should we integrate other choreomusical aspects? In the same essay on the *Movements*, there is the statement about Balanchine revealing to the composer the detail of his own music, relationships and stylistic aspects, and using a metaphor from architecture:

To see Balanchine's choreography of the *Movements* is to hear the music with one's eyes; and this visual hearing has been a greater revelation to me, I think, than to anyone else. The choreography emphasizes relationships of which I had hardly been aware – in the same way – and the performance was like a tour of a building for which I had drawn the plans but never explored the result. Balanchine approached the music by identifying some of the more familiar marks of my style, and as I heard him fastening on my tiniest re- peated rhythm or sustaining group, I knew he had joined the work to the corpus of my music, at the same time probably reducing the time lag of its general acceptability by as much as a decade.[11]

But what does this really mean? Was Stravinsky only talking about structure and rhythm and architecture? Or was it about his music suddenly becoming new and refreshed, in the new circumstances of choreography, differently stressed per- haps in terms of accent or texture, or more radically, with new meanings result- ing from the new composite? Let us take this further. Given all the talk about deference to music, and the younger choreographer to the composer twenty-two years his senior, we can now open up for debate the younger man's challenge to the older, which happened in the composer's presence and absence (especially after his death), altering the perspective on his music, even in ways that Stravinsky himself might not have accepted.

The present chapter addresses all these issues in a new assessment of the Balanchine–Stravinsky collaboration; it is also a reworking of ideas in my *Mov- ing Music*, written seven years ago and including a detailed analysis of *Agon* in its chapter on Balanchine. After a survey of the collaboration (like Goldner, I use this term broadly to include work to Stravinsky's concert scores), I examine in detail two case studies that are hardly canonic and are not obvious choices from amongst the Balanchine–Stravinsky list, but which instead represent extreme positions. The plotless *Movements* is an example of Stravinsky's most uncompro- mising serial music, and it provoked a pronounced shift in choreomusical style from Balanchine. For *Divertimento from 'Le Baiser de la fée'* (1972), which draws from the story ballet *Baiser*, the choreographer forged his own score arrange- ment from Stravinsky material, a bold creative musical act after the composer's death, to create a fundamentally unstable work that reflects on its history in an elusive, fragmentary manner. As a Coda, I discuss the world-wide impact of Balanchine–Stravinsky and particularly of the two prime representatives of the canon, *Apollo* and *Agon*. Reflecting upon other *Apollos* and *Agons*, I discuss exam- ples where not only the scores but also the choreomusical composites have con- stituted a challenge.

A survey of Balanchine–Stravinsky: The choreographer's musical choices

The statistics are compelling: a total of 39 settings of Stravinsky's music are listed in Appendix 5 (Balanchine used more Stravinsky than he did any other composer and more often than any other choreographer). Of these, 5 were commissions (*The Card Party* – Balanchine's title in English for *Jeu de cartes* – the very brief *Ballet of the Elephants*, *Orpheus*, *Agon* and *Noah and the Flood*); 9 were substantial reworkings of earlier settings; and 13 works (asterisked in Appendix 5) are still flourishing in the repertory (of New York City Ballet, and several have featured in repertories across the world). The full list in the Appendix reveals that the Stravinsky ballets extended across Balanchine's career, from the *Ragtime* (1922) of his Petrograd days, when he also embarked upon, but never brought to the stage, a setting of *Pulcinella* (1924), until 1982, the year before he died. There was a peak in production in 1972 with 9 new works created for the Stravinsky Festival (6 of these are still in the repertory, and, perhaps a significant marker of their style, 3 of them are practice-clothes ballets). There was a drop in production during the 1950s, with *Agon* the only new ballet, then another, hardly surprisingly, before the 1982 event, given the sudden large influx of new works mounted for the 1972 Festival, which had covered a generous proportion of Stravinsky's output. Balanchine's various companies over the years staged in total three Stravinsky festivals, in 1937 as well as 1972 and 1982, not to mention numerous Stravinsky evenings. Perhaps unsurprisingly, all of these were dominated by Balanchine's choreography.

There are a few instances of pieces premiered outside his own company, such as the *Ballet of the Elephants* (1942, for circus) and *The Rake's Progress* (1953, the Metropolitan Opera production, directed for the stage by Balanchine, without any actual dances); the second *Elégie* (a solo) and *Ragtime II* (a duet – his third setting of this score), both premiered during a concert as part of 'A Festival of Stravinsky: His Heritage and His Legacy' (1966) in Philharmonic Hall, New York. These last two short works both featured Suzanne Farrell, one of Balanchine's most important muses. She became especially important in the Stravinsky repertory, although not in any of the 1972 Festival works: relations with Balanchine, who was in love with her, became impossible when she married a company dancer in 1969, soon after which she left New York City Ballet for five years. The *Elégie* for solo viola Balanchine staged for her twice, after setting it first in 1945 as a piece for two women, their bodies interlacing; the second solo for her, a lament, he created for the 1982 festival. Likewise, he set the *Variations Aldous Huxley in Memoriam* twice for her, in 1966 and 1982. None of these works stayed in the repertory, although Farrell restaged the 1982 *Variations* for her own company in 2001; it seems that these solos were vehicles that demonstrated her considerable performance range and charisma, rather than strong, self-standing choreography.

The stories behind these statistics and the schedule of premieres are interesting. In an article 'Balanchine and Stravinsky' that, like Goldner's, deconstructs received views, the New York critic Robert Garis suggested that there were fundamental differences in opinion between the two artists about what constituted ballet music and composer-choreographer collaboration. Their professional relationship could well have been trickier than we might suspect. In Chapter 1, I highlighted Stravinsky's reluctance to come to terms with the new concept of ballet without narrative pretext. Alluding to Stravinsky's controlling personality, Garis's thesis unfolds as follows:

> ... there developed a quiet disagreement between Balanchine and Stravinsky about the relationship between music and dance, if only the simple one that Stravinsky thought it correct, and more fruitful, for the music to come first as a kind of assignment to the choreographer, while Balanchine preferred to hunt up his own music and do what he wanted with it.[12]

At one point, Garis suggests something beyond gentlemanly disagreement, describing the misjudged revisions to *Firebird* in the 1970s as an act of destructive anger. But, perhaps more importantly, he claims that Stravinsky did not regard the position of choreographer, or rather ballet master – even Balanchine as choreographer or ballet master – as one of independent authority until *Agon*. The shift in attitude with *Agon*, he claims, was reflected in the later, generous statement about *Movements* (a ballet that, ironically, Garis never liked himself). Meanwhile, he gives *The Card Party* and *Orpheus* short shrift, citing non-programmatic concert music as the music that Balanchine especially favoured and that best suited him. But he understands certain advantages well:

> Even the most intimate and actively detailed collaboration is unlikely to yield this natural gestation of a ballet that comes from a long attachment to the music.[13]

Perhaps the surest scenario is that Balanchine simply wanted for his purposes more than Stravinsky wanted or was able to give him, more quantity and more breadth, the old as well as the recent or new Stravinsky, the large- and the small-scale, the symphonic and the suite structure, more abstraction and narrative – for, despite the plotless ballets, Balanchine retained an interest in narrative throughout his career.

Certainly, *Agon* could not have been a happier collusion of minds. Balanchine wanted and got a plot-free suite of dances, not a dramatically based Act III of a Greek trilogy beginning with *Apollo* and *Orpheus*, but just a series of dances about dances. In Kirstein's words, he had asked for:

> ... a competition before the gods; the audience are statues; the gods are tired and old; the dancers re-animate them by a series of historic dances ... It is as if time called the tune, and the dances which began quite simply in the sixteenth century took fire in the twentieth and exploded. It would be in the form of a *suite de danses*, or variations ...[14]

But Balanchine never had such an opportunity again. The only collaboration that ensued was a return to narrative in a hybrid with text and singing, *Noah and the Flood*. From mid-century, the composer was too busy with other kinds of composition – and besides, proposed straight after the success of *Orpheus*, *Agon* had taken nine years (1948–57) to come to fruition. Just once more, in 1968, Stravinsky, now old and frail, agreed to write something for the choreographer, an instrumental prelude to lengthen his already complete *Requiem Canticles*. At the time of Martin Luther King's assassination, Balanchine wanted to respond quickly with a ballet in his memory, but Stravinsky was unable to finish the writing ready for the premiere, and the choreographer went ahead with the existing score.[15] The ballet was performed only once, a religious ritual with barefoot dancers in long robes, and Arthur Mitchell, as King, raised aloft at the end.

Thus, after having favoured Stravinsky's scores written for ballet, either specially for him or for other choreographers, and wanting more from Stravinsky that was not already well-used by others, Balanchine had no option but to trawl his concert music, the pattern that he followed for so much of his other work. He did this with particular enthusiasm in the 1960s and 1970s. It is also obvious that in the 1960s he favoured recent Stravinsky: he premiered *Monumentum* within two months of the concert premiere. When he diverged from this principle, he was clearly restrained by circumstances: *Ragtime I* in 1960 for an evening of ballets shared with colleagues and collectively titled 'Jazz Concert'; *Ragtime II* and the second *Elégie* in 1966 for the chamber concert context of 'A Festival of Stravinsky'; and the *Capriccio* (1929) as the right choice for *Rubies* (1967), the centrepiece of *Jewels* (between *Emeralds* and *Diamonds*).

Balanchine's enthusiasm for the serial scores is especially striking. These represent a very different kind of Stravinsky sound, a new terse, condensed manner, highly dissonant, built on particular orderings and permutations of all twelve notes of the chromatic scale, but without the familiar foundation or orientation of tonal centre or, in many cases, ostinato structure. The choreographer had been introduced to serial music (especially that of Arnold Schoenberg and

Anton Webern of the second Viennese School) by Stravinsky and Craft, perhaps in 1952, when the composer himself began to explore the method. Led in this direction by Craft, Stravinsky had welcomed the capacity of serialism to revitalise him at a difficult moment in his career. As such a close associate of the composer, Craft got to know Balanchine well; he continued as advisor on Balanchine's Stravinsky projects well after the composer's death, for instance, conducting *Noah and the Flood* and *Persephone* during the 1982 Stravinsky Festival.

Arlene Croce has suggested that Balanchine might have been alarmed about 'losing Stravinsky the dance composer to Stravinsky the serialist', and, 'as if to reassure him further, Balanchine launched his own investigation of twelve-tone theory' with his 1954 setting of Schoenberg's *Music for a Film Scene* Op. 34.[16] Apparently, Craft had nominated this work, Balanchine and he having talked with Schoenberg's widow about the possibility of a ballet.[17] The choreographer responded with a work in which the score was played twice, a procedure that Stravinsky also used (repeating in concert some of his short serial pieces). His comments about his ballet *Opus 34* betrayed a sense of mission to help audiences appreciate this difficult music:

> I decided to use the music twice in my ballet. The first time, I hoped would focus people's eyes enough for them to hear the music better and the second time it was played maybe they would understand.[18]

The first time round was a 'white abstraction', incorporating non-classical movement; the second, more pantomimic, was a highly theatrical expression of morbid horror, complete with hospital imagery, medical instruments and blood-stained bandages. The *New York Times* critic John Martin suggested that Balanchine's work evoked the world of German expressionism around 1930, when the music had been composed.[19] But Balanchine's main 'serial period' began in 1957 with the supremely successful *Agon* (a transitional, partly serial work), drawing from Stravinsky's much drier aesthetic. His strategy now was to chase new (serial) Stravinsky and to choreograph just about everything he could, understanding the difficulty of taking on too much that was very short (during this period, Stravinsky wrote seven miniatures, each of only a few minutes duration), or was weighted towards the vocal (although he choreographed five vocal pieces by Stravinsky across his career, few by other composers) or was liturgical (perhaps he knew Stravinsky's doubts about setting his *Symphony of Psalms* – see p. 81). The problem was that most new Stravinsky was like this. But Balanchine was willing to stretch his boundaries, and he also wanted to be challenged by difficulty. He too was ready for a new direction. The difficulty for audiences confronting serialism seems to have been the last thing to put him off

and, indeed, he proved instrumental in bringing music of this kind into public view.

After *Agon*, Balanchine's serial Stravinsky was the hybrid *Noah* and three
more concert pieces, all of them small-scale. *Movements* (1963) was 10 minutes
long, and it made *Agon* seem positively lyrical. Balanchine had rejected the idea
of using this score when it was first mooted by Nabokov in 1958 before its premiere,[20] but clearly changed his mind when he heard the music. Stravinsky attended a rehearsal of the ballet during its creation in 1963. Then there was the
5-minute *Variations Aldous Huxley in Memoriam*, which Balanchine set in 1966 –
played three times, celebrating the number twelve and its divisions in versions
for twelve men and six women and then the solo for Farrell. Stravinsky supported his colleague by sending a tape and a short score, also discussing the work
with him.[21] This ballet was dropped from the repertory after the 1968/69 season, and when Balanchine re-choreographed the music for the 1982 Festival as
a solo for Farrell, the music was played just once through. Finally, there was a
work that was both vocal and liturgical, the 15-minute *Requiem Canticles*
(1968), which again they discussed together.[22] Along the way, sharing the complete orchestral works of Webern with the modern dance pioneer Martha
Graham, Balanchine choreographed *Episodes* (1959). Perhaps from the same
period stems his undated piano transcription of sections from the *Lulu Suite*,
music by Alban Berg, another member of the second Viennese School, although
this never resulted in choreography.[23] Balanchine's other 'new Stravinsky' ballet
was *Monumentum pro Gesualdo* (1960), a result of Craft's persuasion, it seems,
and Stravinsky seems not to have been directly involved this time.[24] But it is
important that the score demonstrated the link between the pretonal music of
the Renaissance – it was a re-composition of three Gesualdo madrigals for instruments – and serial music, which Balanchine picked up on when deciding to
pair the piece regularly as a preface to his *Movements* (see p. 195).

For Balanchine, serial music demanded a new kind of choreography, a new
Spartan look, usually with practice clothes and no set, and a new kind of programming. This was the era of the New York City Ballet's 'Twelve-Tone Nights'
at City Center, always sold-out occasions and fascinating as hypermodern spectacle. Croce describes the style aptly as 'increasingly microscopic, cellular: tight
phrases exploding like crystals in a confined space ... These were richly concentrated, high-protein ballets, with more "grip" per measure than anything that
had been seen up to that time.'[25] *Agon* was all-in-an-instant pressure, witty,
erotic, but also, as Kirstein put it, like an 'I.B.M. device, but one that thinks and
smiles' and an 'existential metaphor for tension and anxiety'.[26] *Movements*, as
we shall see, was more aggressive still in its modernist assault. The first *Variations*
continued in the same scientific, technological, high-octane spirit, with Farrell's
solo a final concentration of fragmented information within one body, ending in

a walkover. (The 1982 *Variations* ended similarly, but Farrell has described it as much more pared down than before, underplaying the music.[27])

But it is worth remembering that Balanchine was also interested in work of quite a different kind during his 'serial period', frequently charging his batteries by choosing opposite tactics between one work and the next. For instance, in 1958 there was *Gounod Symphony*, in 1960 the romantic *Liebeslieder Walzer*, set to Brahms, as well as *Donizetti Variations*, in 1962 the full-evening narrative *A Midsummer Night's Dream* to Mendelssohn, not to mention *Meditation* in 1963 (Tchaikovsky) – a love pas de deux and a totally different perspective on Farrell. The 'Twelve-Tone Nights' were but one aspect of the choreographer's work.

No one was prepared for the sudden explosion of inspiration on display during the 1972 Festival. It also marked Balanchine's 'return' after a period of relative creative dormancy usually ascribed to Farrell's marriage and departure from New York City Ballet. Most interesting of all, it marked the beginning of Balanchine's shift in attitude towards Stravinsky's music. Now that the composer was dead, there were no new works to chase, and we find the choreographer looking back again across a broad span of Stravinsky's career before the 1960s, from the hitherto lost Sonata movement of 1904 (set as a pas de deux), through *Pulcinella* of 1920 and the works of the 1930s (*Duo Concertant*) and 1940s (*Symphony in Three Movements* and *Scherzo à la Russe*), to the *Choral Variations* of 1956 based on Bach. (Incorporating children from the School of American Ballet, with solos and duets leading to a *grand défilé*, *Choral Variations* was performed only once, during the Festival.) There were also his repeat settings of the *Violin Concerto* (after the first, *Balustrade*, in 1941) and *Danses Concertantes*. The Festival ended with a concert performance of *Symphony of Psalms*, the dancers seated at the side of the stage and behind the singers.

Balanchine also felt a new creative freedom and security in dealing with Stravinsky's music after the composer's death. Two works demonstrate radical manipulation of the composer's scores. The choreographer's bold reworking of the music from *Le Baiser de la fée* for the 1972 Festival will be discussed later: a highly stimulating experiment, although obviously we will never know what Stravinsky himself might have thought about it.

What Garis described as the 'decapitation' of *Apollo* in the late 1970s[28] has stood up to scrutiny far less well. He was referring to Balanchine's removal of the Prologue and the final rising to Parnassus, beginning the score with the last section of the Prologue as overture and ending the choreography with the fan of arabesques from earlier in the original Apotheosis (dropping Apollo's first solo for one season, too). The large shape of the music and some of its motivic cross-references disappeared, likewise the sense of loss that came with the protagonists' 'departure' at the end of the ballet. Perhaps the choreographer was bored with the work – he dropped it entirely from the New York City Ballet repertory

between 1973 and 1979 – and perhaps it did not suit the move from the company's original home at City Center to the larger stage of the New York State Theatre. There is also the suggestion that when Mikhail Baryshnikov assumed the
title role during the 1978 International Dance Festival in Chicago, Balanchine
was concerned that he would add inappropriate virtuosity to the Prologue pirouettes.[29] If there is a thread of logic to Balanchine's act, it must be that over the
years he had reduced the narrative component, radically simplifying the design
and removing the word 'Musagète' (alluding to the Muses) from the title, thereby
increasing the stress on the components of 'pure' music and dance. Whatever
the reason, he made his unpopular decision at the time when Baryshnikov was
learning *Apollo*. Croce makes the interesting suggestion that Balanchine now
thought of the work as a 'concert' piece, like his other 'abstract' practice-clothes
ballets. Although she too had serious doubts about what he had done, she much
admired Baryshnikov's performance, and it is noteworthy that she found stimulating the increased 'radical intensity' of the compressed version: 'The performance is a synoptic miracle; it's as if everything that we don't see had been taken
into account in everything that we do see.'[30] Craft reports simply that
Balanchine 'consulted with me about his experimental cuts'.[31]

For the 1982 Festival, after choreographing no Stravinsky for ten years,
Balanchine's most substantial achievements were hybrids, *Persephone* (see pp.
314-15) and his first staging of *Noah*. Both works had been considered for
1972,[32] but now, as his own life drew to a close, they reflected a special commitment to the ritual and spiritual concerns that he shared with the composer. On
the last night of the Festival, he included a concert performance of the cantata
Zvezdoliki (1912), a setting of the Symbolist Konstantin Balmont's poem about
the Last Judgement. None of Balanchine's 1982 works has become a 'repertory'
work, but it is nevertheless significant that their music was important to him at
the end of his life. It is also significant that, in 1982, Balanchine's working
pattern was very different, much more collaborative than before. He needed help
with his choreography, his health having increasingly deteriorated after his first
heart attack in 1978.

At this point, it is interesting to review the Stravinsky works that Balanchine
did not choreograph. There was very little Russian-period music, except *Firebird*
(the 1945 *Suite* choreographed in 1949), *Renard* (a character dance work for
Ballet Society, 1947) and *Le Chant du rossignol*, a Diaghilev commission (1925)
eagerly undertaken by Balanchine at that early stage in his career. Given his
well-known statement that *Sacre* should not be choreographed (as well as
Petrushka and *Noces* – see p. 120), it comes as a surprise that Balanchine was
enthusiastic about the opportunity to stage this ballet in collaboration with the
composer for Nabokov's 1952 Paris festival *L'Oeuvre du XXe siècle*. The idea was
for a 'non-russe' version of the ballet. Balanchine recommended that Picasso

should be the designer, although Nabokov was quick to point out that the artist's activities as a communist rendered him wholly unsuitable for the Festival (see pp. 239-40).[33] In the event, the project did not materialise. Charles Joseph learnt from Balanchine's personal assistant Barbara Horgan that he was very interested in staging the two-piano version of the ballet in the late 1960s and early 1970s.[34] In an attempt to encourage a production at the time of the 1972 Stravinsky Festival, Craft showed to Robbins the original 1913 piano rehearsal score containing Stravinsky's choreographic notes (see pp. 420-1), 'for guidance, not reconstruction'. There was brief consideration of a production in which Balanchine might choreograph the solo and Robbins the group sections.[35]

Although there is no evidence that Balanchine wanted to stage *Noces* at any point in his career, the ferocity of his reaction to other stagings is fascinating. For a 1965 television documentary at the time of the Robbins *Noces* premiere, Stravinsky recalled Balanchine talking to him admiringly about the forthcoming event, praising Robbins's understanding of Russian cultural symbols (see p. 59).[36] Yet in a public lecture in Memphis shortly after the premiere, Balanchine went out of his way to insist that the score could not be choreographed.[37] Interviewed in *The New York Times* prior to his company's 1982 Festival, he declared the Nijinska 'impossible to do' and that those who take on the score 'will be punished in the other world'.[38] Nobody at the time seemed to think that he was joking. Bearing in mind too his changing views on *Sacre*, was he jealous? Was he anxious about seeing others choreograph (and well) what he might have wanted for himself one day? Remember that he took over the *Symphony in Three Movements* from Robbins during preparations for the 1972 Festival (see p. 551, note 241): the reasons may not have been entirely practical. So the stories behind Balanchine's choices of what to do and what not to do are more complex than at first meets the eye.

Before moving on to assess Balanchine's use of Stravinsky, it is illuminating to look back over the list of works and consider the huge range of styles and genres that they exemplify. And what do these represent as *musique dansante*? Three scores are symphonic in scale – the *Capriccio* for *Rubies*, *Violin Concerto* and *Symphony in Three Movements*; many more are built up of short sections, as suites of dances or theatrical episodes. Some are heavyweight conceptions, both in structure and tone, but others are in Stravinsky's more popular American, even commercially driven, style. *Danses Concertantes* and *Jeu de cartes* (for *The Card Party*) are witty, sophisticated in the mode of enjoyable ballet music, updating familiar dance rhythms; *Circus Polka* and *Scherzo à la Russe* are positively lightweight. The *Scherzo*, Stravinsky claimed, started life as music for a Samuel Goldwyn film about a Nazi attack on a farm in the Ukraine; it ended up as a jolly Russian folk-style number for the Paul Whiteman jazz band.[39] The earlier *Capriccio* led the way in the more popular direction with its jazzy cosmopolitanism. The

serial works, as we shall see later, uproot the dancer from any stable foundation for movement, as Farrell has said: 'it [the music] just forces you to move
differently ...',[40] and perhaps they are the greatest advance of all in terms of a
musique dansante.

The music in action

Such a great range of Stravinsky music presented Balanchine with
the challenge to explore a variety of choreomusical methods and meanings,
prompted by the music but also by his own independent authority. The
choreographer's full imaginative scope was put to the test.

Apollo, as we shall see, was in many respects atypical in relation to later developments, although it was the earliest in the line of Balanchine–Stravinsky works
with a basis in ritual, leading to *Orpheus*, *Requiem Canticles* and *Persephone*. Such
was the serenity of its music – written soon after Stravinsky's reconversion to
orthodoxy – that the critic Boris de Schloezer wrote, 'Logically, after *Apollo*, he
can only give us a Mass.'[41] Balanchine described its rhythms as 'simple' in his
article 'The Dance Element in Stravinsky's Music',[42] probably referring to the
lack of radical syncopations at the most detailed level; yet other aspects of
rhythm are sophisticated, and significant as regards the meaning of the piece.
Apollo shows how, within a 'frozen' narrative and next to music that has been
described as 'immobility rendered mobile',[43] dance movement can develop in
continuity and drive while also showing the power of stasis. The 'story' is about
the birth of Apollo, the God of Music, his growth to maturity, and the choice and
celebration of Terpsichore, Muse of Dance, as his ideal, over Calliope, Muse of
Poetry, and Polyhymnia, Muse of Mime. The ballet is also about the forging of
classical dance. The actual celebration is a joyous, galloping jig, which is the
Coda, the single occasion of developed rhythmic impetus and momentum in the
ballet before the harmonious Apotheosis, a return to the timeless pace of ritual
before the ascent to Parnassus. The dance critic Edwin Denby observed the importance of the link between dance energy and the developing classicism:

> [*Apollo*] grows more and more civilized. But the rhythmic vitality of the
> dance, the abundance of vigor, increase simultaneously, so that you feel as if
> the heightening of discipline led to a heightening of power, to a freer, bolder
> range of imagination.[44]

Along the way, the choreography constantly teases us about the distinctions
between the still and the mobile, for it is full of pictures that etch themselves
upon the memory, photo opportunities, sculptures and friezes. These arrive out

of nowhere and are quickly gone, many of them extraordinary, seen as odd or gauche back in 1928, when they proclaimed a new kind of movement language. Some are famous, with evocative names such as the 'wheelbarrow' (one handmaiden pushing forwards another who bears Apollo's lute), the 'swimming lesson' (Apollo carrying Terpsichore on his shoulders), the 'troika' (when he drives all three Muses like horses in the Coda) and the 'sunburst' or 'peacock' (the fan of arabesques at different heights in the Apotheosis). In the slower sections of the ballet, these pictures are gently mobilised by music that caresses them like waves. They are marked acts within ritual, an equally gentle hardening against the temptation to indulge in Stravinsky's string sound. As Kirstein put it, Balanchine 'deliberately inverted an ideal academic idiom against some of Stravinsky's most mellifluous measures'.[45]

Yet, when the rhythmic impetus begins to emerge in the solo Variations, after the Pas d'Action, the still moments continue as hiatus points, now more often prompted by the phrase structure of the music, with its complementary pauses and fermatas.[46] Announcing herself, Calliope runs across to Apollo, with a mimed flourish of the pen upon her tablet, and she halts, focus down, runs again, sweeps her arm overhead, halts, focus up: she shows us the start and stop pattern of the music, and also how its statements shift in pitch. After she puts down her tablet, her dance begins, but immediately there is an interruption, now a musical event causing a break in flow: a deep D minor pizzicato chord (at [40]), like a thud. She contracts and clutches her heart, a violent emotional reaction. Later, the flow of Terpsichore's variation is suddenly punctuated by 'four huge sustained *attitudes*' (from [55]),[47] when she crosses one leg over the other, gesturing one arm up, the other pressing down, thrilling to her personal power. Just before the four protagonists set off for their final jubilant unison in the Coda, there is one last hiatus for all of them (at [86]-1), bent over and poised like runners ready for a race, a light-hearted moment, like a joke.

The pause is one of the features that betray the literary roots of *Apollo*, before the literary principle gives way to dance and music as superior art forms. The music encouraged Balanchine to choreograph dance phrases like verbal statements, with stressed pauses as in poetic speech, and moments of suspension rather than dead stoppage. It is well known that the score was based on poetic models taken from the seventeenth century of Louis XIV, themselves derived from Greek precedents, and Balanchine incorporated these models into his source material. Calliope's Variation is the best example, prefaced in the score as it is with alexandrines theorising on alexandrines by Nicolas Boileau (from his *L'Art poétique* (1674)). The twelve-syllable concept that can be transferred into musical notes or movement impulses is clear, as is the dual notion of suspension (motion continuing) and rest (motion stopped) during a pause:

Que toujours dans nos vers le sens coupant les mots
Suspende l'hémistiche et marque le repos.

Although Calliope's rhythms do not match those of Boileau's writing, her introduction could be read as marking out the two halves or hexameters of an alexandrine, using the poetic model as the original source.[48] Later, we find her literally dancing short–long iambs, at [41]-4 and in the concluding bars, and anapests, short–short–long runs on pointe, from [41], precisely coordinated with the pizzicato accompaniment to a cello melody. In Calliope's concluding bars, the pressure to step most of the notes as a series of piqués, with subtle shifts of movement direction and brief breaks to crouch (in a down–*up*, short–long pattern), checks her progress, also conveying her anxiety about failure.

Baryshnikov's unusual attention to poetic metre was one of the features that made his interpretation of *Apollo* especially interesting. He articulated the patterns by pushing the balls of his feet into the floor, supplying what Croce described as 'the percussive dimension that is absent in the score'.[49] Again, his flow was blunted; he danced his rhythms in the manner of a self-imposed trial or tricky thought process, with the hesitation of a primitive god learning about nobility. More than any other Apollo I have seen, he stressed the sustained moments in his solos with particular intensity and fervour. But thought process is also silent speech, and in *Dialogues and a Diary* Stravinsky pointed out how the violin cadenza in Apollo's first variation relates to the poetic principle, as 'the initial solo speech, the first essay in verse of Apollo the god'.[50]

Indeed, the concept of words and vocal sound infuses *Apollo*. The Prologue leads as mime drama, exposing the lack of narrative in the main part of the ballet, and when Leto gives birth, we virtually hear her screams from the stage. Calliope writes words and opens her mouth wide as she gestures. Her opening dance phrase is all but literal utterance. Suki Schorer, who danced the role, describes an array of verbal/vocal allusions:

> You have speech that comes from deep inside you [referring to the contraction and clutch at the heart] ... When you run forward, you speak a little, addressing yourself to one side, then to the other, as if in a Greek amphitheatre. Speech grows weaker and weaker; finally there's nothing. Then you get an idea [at [41] to the pizzicato]. As you start running, you regain your strength. The idea is that you're going to write.[51]

Polyhymnia, Muse of Mime, holds a finger to her mouth throughout her solo in a stylised 'Shh!' – that is her 'still picture', the block on her freedom to move – carried above non-stop allegro feet and legs. Thus, she symbolises absent speech, until she suddenly opens her mouth at the end and is summarily dismissed. It is the whole point of Terpsichore's solo that she is the one who can move from literary metaphor to dance and musical expression, and her pauses look different, more like experiments in physical thought. She too reflects a learning process during her solo, the act of putting herself through a series of tests. Then, by contrast, in her final approach to Apollo, the directness and authority of her high kicks culminating in a stupendous arch of her back make her totally irresistible, outright winner of the contest. *Apollo* is not only a particular kind of Stravinsky but also a particular kind of Balanchine–Stravinsky, and the early piece that taught the choreographer so much did not teach him the basics of motor drive as much as other things, about the potential links between the rhythms of dance and speech and large-scale rhythmic structure.

Orpheus is even less concerned with motor drive, stressing speech and song again (Orpheus is a musician who sings), and speech here is more direct, less led by conventional models of poetic structure. Unsurprisingly, Stravinsky was ready for his opera *The Rake's Progress* on completion of the ballet. Croce places the ballet in its period, citing the hieratic style of mime prevalent in the 1940s, 'an unemphatic narrative style', and describing the work as 'an ashen meditation permeated by the sweetish odor of death'.[52] There are dances, but they are driven by dramatic timing as the story unfolds continuously. There are also long stretches of mime, involving the manipulation of props such as Orpheus's lyre and mask, musical interludes, and slow processions as the Angel of Death guides Orpheus to Hades and back to earth with his wife Eurydice. Time moves slowly.

From the start, characters mime or evoke speech through dance, with musical utterances regularly underlining the vocal nature of such movement. Orpheus gestures to his wife's grave and beseeches her to talk to him through his lyre hanging over her grave (to the flute at [6], [10]+2 and [24]). Later, in the underworld, she dances a solo with metaphorical gasps and interruptions reminiscent of Calliope's variation and, in the happy allegro centre of the pas de deux, she delights in drawing sounds from her mouth to the 'breath' instruments: to the oboe (at [110]), then to the clarinet (at [114]), after which she plays her pipe (the flute).[53] Orpheus sings his way to her release from Pluto in the underworld (through the voice of the oboe) and, during the Apotheosis, after her death (the moment when she removes his mask) and his own at the hands of the Bacchantes, there is reference to his song once more. Apollo enters carrying the masked, severed head of Orpheus and tries without success to draw song from its lips before offering the head to the heavens. Stravinsky explained to Nabokov that he interpolated two short passages of solo harp into the Apotheosis as a reminder that Orpheus was dead: 'It sounds like a kind of ... compulsion, like something unable to stop ... Orpheus is dead, the song is gone, but the accompaniment goes on.'[54] The idea of the lyre (orchestrated here as the harp) as accompaniment to Orpheus's voice resonates especially strongly through the absence of voice.

There is very little conventional dance drive in *Orpheus*, save for the Bacchantes, whose very tight, cartoon-cut adherence to irregular musical accentuations is unusual amongst the Stravinsky–Balanchine collaborations. The women's job is to taunt Orpheus and then tear him to pieces, and you can never predict the next arm strike or foot slam, enlarged musically to frightening proportions, musical gesture to dance gesture: this is the loudest part of the entire score. Towards the end, though, as they exit (from [141]), the Bacchantes start to march the beats on pointe, and you hear the pulse during the musical silences like the clack of stilettos, a technique that, we will discover, became common in Balanchine's settings of new, especially serial, music in the 1950s and 1960s.

The centre of gravity of this score is the pas de deux for Orpheus and Eurydice, their intertwining, or rather her passionate wrapping around and pressure of limbs upon him, which is heightened by the full-throttle searing espressivo of string counterpoint. 'Eurydice writhes at her husband's feet like a mountain lioness in heat,' wrote Denby of the weighty and deeply erotic interpretation of Maria Tallchief to Nicholas Magallanes's Orpheus.[55] The work had massive impact at its premiere in 1948, since when it has surely lost some of this power. But we are unaccustomed to this kind of ritual mime as a way of moving to music nowadays, and so are dancers, and this is not the Balanchine we have come to know and expect. He it is, after all, who got us into the habit of equating dance and its music with rhythmic propulsion.

By the time of *Orpheus*, however, Balanchine was already accustomed to using music that provided him with a tight time corset, and, when using nineteenth-century scores, tightening them up more than usual for dance performance, ensuring that in them, too, the pulse was firmly established and retained. Balanchine's extreme manifestation of propulsion is the simple, regular articulation of beat through dance steps, and it is surprisingly easy to find examples of this across his career. The tick-tick-tick style of rhythm, as if the dancers have been 'plugged in', like 'cogs' in a 'mechanism' (see p. 106), is especially common where the musical accents are already irregular and provide variety. The fast outer movements of *Symphony in Three Movements* are prime examples in simple walking, marching and jogging, the kind of movement that is usually transitional and that here becomes dance substance. Perhaps this was an unconscious reference to the war music origins of the score (see p. 141),[56] a fact that rubs unkindly against the Busby Berkeley line-ups and spatial manoeuvres and presentation of the 'girls' in white and pink with swinging ponytails.

The outer movements of *Stravinsky Violin Concerto*, most notably the last, are similarly loaded with pulse-step choreography. Here, borrowing style tips from

Russian folk dance, Balanchine uses the corps to map out pulse in many different ways behind the soloists, not just in prances and pointe steps with fidgety folk decoration but also in knee-wags, wrist-flicks and arm-waves. Through rein-forcement, the choreography heightens the effect of Stravinsky's chugging mo-tor current. All this does not bear too close attention and is easily seen as jigging to little purpose, yet the buoyancy of some of the choreography can be thrilling. This is especially the case when Balanchine picks up on the ambiguities and shifts between 2/8 and 3/8 characteristic of the score, and the dancers surge across the musical boundaries and, literally, the stage, with their own independ-ent metrical patterning. One section of this dance is perhaps Balanchine's most ambitious choreomusical/metrical experiment ever, three layers of movement in all ([116]-[118]; see Exs. 3.1a and b): the soloists in the centre in a slow, Rus-sian-style lilting and intertwining dance counted in 4s (or 8s), framed by blocks of kneeling men working a pulse half as fast in an 8-count dance ostinato (rather like semaphore, one arm swinging across the body so that the hand clasps the shoulder (1), swinging up and out again (3), the knee turning in (5), and then out (7)), and backed by blocks of standing women moving in canon with the men. All the groups start up at different times, nobody with the music (written in 3/8) and everyone keeping more or less to one spot.[57] The effect of this passage is curious, as if the work had suddenly veered off course, the groups of dancers strangely disconnected both from each other and from their music, in a kind of static nowhere-land. But the mechanical puzzle barely lets us into its secrets before the full flood of folk jollity takes over again. Cross-metre patterns are typical of Balanchine, and occur most frequently to music that is already irregular.[58] With Stravinsky's music he undertook his most extreme explora-tions, especially in the works of his later career.

In *Rubies*, the pulsing conveys meaning and purpose more obviously, and its trotting-jogging motifs are appropriate to the circus showdance frame of the piece. There is a particularly delicious passage near the end of the first move-ment (from [31]), when the corps look on as the woman soloist undertakes high-extension adage to a legato wind melody, surrounded by four cavaliers. The corps women, divided into two groups, step and stab their pointes into the floor, creating a 4/4 metre, one group syncopating between the beats of the other to the off-beat musical pulse, as if they are at odds with or trying to get the better of each other. Then the soloist starts up, pointe-stabbing too, as if taunting her cavaliers, before embarking on an eccentric exit that ends up in wide-legged pliés and, now unescorted, arabesques penchées. There is one additional complica-tion: against all this, what is *heard* here is a 3/4 metre articulated as an ostinato, on timpani, piano, cellos and basses. Balanchine clearly decided to follow the look, rather than sound, of the score.[59]

In *Duo Concertant*, to the eponymous violin and piano duet, Balanchine is

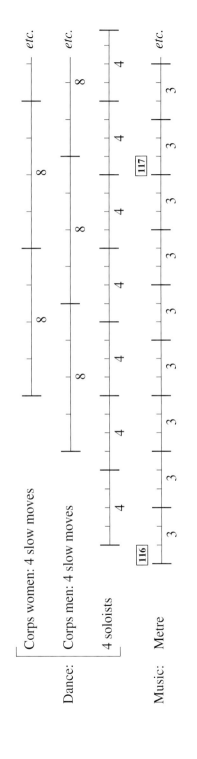

Ex 3.1a. *Stravinsky Violin Concerto*, excerpt from third movement, Capriccio, diagram of metrical structure including beats/counts.

Ex 3.1b. *Stravinsky Violin Concerto,* Capriccio movement. 'Meno' (meno mosso) is the hand-written tempo mark (not the composer's) added to the piano reduction accompanying the Labanotation score.

reflexive about the relationship between dance and music. During the opening musical movement, the Cantilène, a man and woman simply stand and listen at the piano; they enjoy a few listening breaks later on as well. This is like an exaggeration of the choreographer's famous manifesto about not hiding the music, not interfering with music, but rather 'subduing' the dance:

> As in modern architecture [he paraphrases the high modern architect Mies van der Rohe], you rather should do less than more.[60]

So he starts out in *Duo Concertant* by getting our ears attuned. The beginning of the dance proper is a witty essay about different metres and pulse rates, using the steady perpetuum mobile of the music with its 4-semiquaver ostinato accompaniment figure as a ground for these playful manoeuvres. The choreography is structured as a series of blocks (see p. 149), each containing its own repeating, 'in-the-groove' ostinato motif. First, the man and woman stand side by side, each stepping with one leg swinging in and out, in canon; then an arm makes a slow pulse, with a fast decoration at one point (a 6-count unit), followed by a quick 4-count arm phrase, still as a canon; finally the woman performs three moves in 3 counts (at the slowest pulse rate of all), turning her body from one side to the other and twisting her arms into different shapes, while the man draws a quick, staccato circle with his arm as a frame behind her, called 'clock' in the piano rehearsal score. At one point during the canon, the piano score reads 'Boy plays violin', which is a cheeky suggestion that her quick staccato 4-count arm phrase, smoothed out by him when set to a violin as opposed to a piano, turns rhythm into melody. So this is at once a canon and not really a canon – the dynamic articulation has changed. It is a registral shift that provides a moment of recognition, drawing attention to a structural device and its relation to the music. *Duo Concertant* moves back and forth many times between foregrounding melody and rhythm as it progresses, a formal conceit that in no way interferes with the projection of a joyous romance. But then, for the last movement, Balanchine transforms the work into something extraordinary and urgent, a love duet dramatically spotlit on a darkened stage, a painful commentary on need, adoration, distance and thwarted desire.

Balanchine shows his choreomusical skill and wit in the most modest circumstances. Stravinsky's *Scherzo à la Russe* is just four minutes long and very simply structured, a scherzo section heard three times in alternation with two trio episodes, constantly tripping itself up with its rhythmic ingenuities. Choreographing the score very speedily for the 1972 Festival as a Russian folk dance for two bands of women, Balanchine decided to go for simplicity during the scherzo sections; the rhythm patterns are far squarer than those in the music, although he enlivens the texture with canons between the groups and occasional divergences from the two group leaders. The automatic result is a constant criss-crossing of the musical accentuations. Looked at one way, the choreomusical texture is highly unstable, but looked at again, we sense the physical balance within the choreography, and a visual simplicity, another means by which Balanchine 'subdues' his dances. The overall result is lightweight, yet lively and sophisticated, its effectiveness achieved almost entirely through choreomusical means.

Another work that relies heavily on choreomusicality for its effectiveness is *Danses Concertantes*, and, from first-hand experience of the second, 1972 setting, the work is more intricate and sophisticated than any of the examples so far described. The 1972 setting incorporates simple pulse steps, but much more: a rhythmic elasticity and variety that adds up to major theatrical vitality. Indeed, here Balanchine's ebullient energy often seems in advance of what the music itself suggests: he takes its unrest several stages further. Yet, for some reason, the

1972 *Danses* has often been rated as minor Balanchine, and many critics have written about it in terms of loss, remembering or hearing tales of the sparkling personality, wit and invention of the 1944 work for the Ballet Russe de Monte Carlo, which had been led by the stars Alexandra Danilova and Frederic Franklin. Some, however, clearly thought very highly of the second version. Kirstein and Robbins both prompted the revival of the work in 1989. Before a change of schedule prevented him, Robbins even offered to supervise rehearsals.[61]

As for Balanchine himself, he seems not to have cared too much about either version of the ballet. The first was dropped in 1948, perhaps because it was too hard for orchestral players when the Ballet Russe was out on tour (see pp. 75-6), perhaps because Balanchine was by then no longer a resident choreographer looking after his own work. The second he let go only a couple of years after its premiere, and alongside *Firebird* (another problem work) it was his only reviv-able Stravinsky piece not staged for the 1982 Festival. Perhaps there is some truth in a 1966 statement, purportedly by Stravinsky, in *Themes and Episodes* – 'the ballet is not among my Balanchine favorites' (Craft expunged this comment from the 1972 edition) – and the work held bad memories for him.[62]

Both versions of *Danses Concertantes* were playful ballets, with *commedia dell' arte* and circus flavour, the same colourful, glittering designs against a black background by Eugene Berman (which now look fussy and old-fashioned) and the same organisation: an introduction to the soloists on the stage apron, then the main part of the work – framing large ensembles, a series of trios each for two women and one man (in green, blue, purple and red), and a duet for a couple in yellow. The large ensembles are fine, the trios extraordinary, so perhaps the relatively flaccid pas de deux is one of the reasons why the work has never achieved the success it deserves.

The rhythmic content of both Balanchine settings has attracted the attention of perceptive writers. Coming from a very different aesthetic, the chance-procedures composer John Cage dubbed the early work 'exceptional' when it was hot off the press. He was writing about the clarity of rhythmic structure and phrasing in ballet as opposed to modern dance.[63] At the same time, Denby, trained in eurhythmics and unusually observant about rhythm and musicality, noted the effective interplay between the small- and large-scale:

> The changes from staccato movements to continuous ones, from rapid leaps and displacements to standing still, from one dancer solo to several all at once follow hard on one another. The rhythm is unexpected. But the shift of the figures and the order of the steps is miraculously logical and light, and so even fitful changes have a grace and a spontaneous impetus. What had first seemed separate spurts, stops and clipped stalkings turn out to be a single long phrase or impulse that has risen and subsided in a group of dancers

simultaneously. The line of the large phrase is seen in their relations to one another ...[64]

It is interesting that Tobi Tobias wrote in very similar vein in 1989 about a revival of the second *Danses*. It too had the capacity to build a larger picture from a mosaic of small contributions:

> The choreography looks eccentric because the movement is everywhere fragmented – stopped short just as its energy peaks or shattered into glittering shards, the action passing from one member of the cast to another like an electric impulse. No single figure in the ballet holds the key to its 'meaning' or sums up its contents. It's rather as if *Danses Concertantes* reveals Balanchine raising a multifaceted jewel to the light, playfully yet methodically angling it this way and that so it can finally be understood in its entirety, its full coherence.[65]

An especially fine example of group rhythm is the opening line-up of the green trio, the dancers all holding hands, but each doing something different (see Ex. 3.2). The woman stage left takes the lead with a piqué arabesque accent, the beginning of a 6-count unit, the man in the middle toe-tapping and wagging a knee in and out (a 4-count unit), while the woman stage right starts a beat later (another 6-count unit) with a patter of bourrées reflecting the semiquaver decoration in the music. (My analysis here incorporates my own breakdown of counts.) The sequences for the women zigzag as they change legs for each repeat.[66]

Stravinsky plays rhythmic mayhem against this, as he does during all of the trios. Although he wrote the score in a regular 3/4 metre and the melody winds around a limited number of pitches, it is impossible for the ear to perceive a secure metre. The overall choreomusical effect is oddly tipsy, the dance energy driving in several directions simultaneously, although there is a semblance of order from the repetition of movement patterns. But by the time you think you have worked out what is going on, the trio is on to something else. (There is a chance to see the opening material again at the end: like all the trios, the form is a loose ABA.) The exuberance of the dancers is unstoppable. Soon, at [79], there is a musical hiatus of sustained chords, syncopated and gradually developing a sense of urgency towards release of tension, but the dancers carry on, showing the same quick beat as before, filling in 'the gaps' (see Ex. 3.3); you literally hear their autonomous patterns unencumbered by sound impulses. They pursue their own course of accentuation, progressing into allegro moves and even adding saucy triplet patterns across the flow. They seem on top of the world.

Balanchine uses similar tactics choreographing 'against' the musical Lento in an earlier ensemble section. He begins with adage, the solo woman in yellow answered by the female ensemble, dancing the same phrase, but this is now

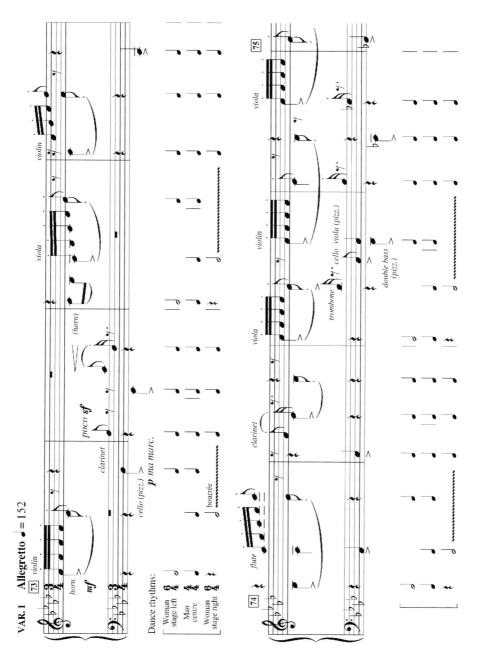

Ex. 3.2. *Danses Concertantes*, Variation 1, Green Trio.

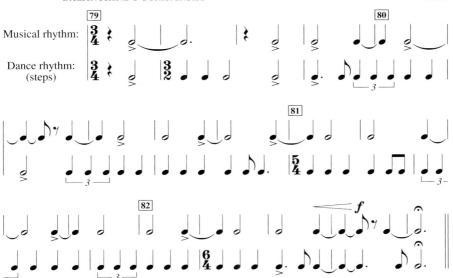

Ex. 3.3. *Danses Concertantes*, Variation 1, Green Trio. The dance rhythm was notated from a video of the New York City Ballet performance of 25 June 1993 (Miriam Mahdaviani, Roma Sosenko, Tom Gold), *NYPL*. Slight variations exist between performances examined on video.

inflected differently by different music. Then he gets the women mobilised, a stealthy progress initiated by the man in yellow (at [66], followed by the other men toe-tapping and knee-wagging – the motif already described), easing into little runs and later (at [69]+2) embarking on a nifty jazz move nicknamed 'chug' in the piano rehearsal score. The dance pulse is now fast – notes on the piano score indicate twice the speed that it was before – and again perceptible to the ear in the 'gaps'. The effect is restless, especially as the whole cast gradually joins in the 'chug', the men falling into canon with the women: group allegro energy has taken over. Yet the relaxed Lento spirit of the score remains unchanged; the dancers push on despite the music.

Balanchine introduces plenty of other choreomusical tricks in *Danses*, 'visualisations' that suddenly emerge like sparks, and dotty rhythms that scurry over Stravinsky's already buckled patterns. Examples are the opening signature steps of the blue and red trios, based on different versions of a big pas de chat and, on both occasions, these steps are timed differently when they return. My example is the red trio. Here, the pas de chat is of the rumbustious, galumphing sort, feet tucked up under the body (2 counts), before dissolving into a series of limping 'step–ball–change' sequences (three 4-count units). At first the choreography fits the regular duple-time elephant-jig rhythm (Stravinsky's melodic patterns again run riot above). But to the recapitulation of the opening music (at [131]) Balanchine cannot resist introducing more galumphs and fewer limping steps, making a 5-count pattern – step, pas de chat (1–2), limping steps (3, 4, 5) – all of which is repeated three times in total and crosses the musical metre. In the centre of the little dance, lifts and high legs yawn to a series of musical yawns and pointe steps pick out pizzicato chords (once a group of 7, from [125]-3, next a group of 4, from [130]-2), highlights that suddenly fix our attention on surface interruptions in the score. *Danses Concertantes* is alive with such intricate engineering, which means that it can hardly be described as subduing the dance and not interfering with the music. Nor is it possible in these circumstances to divorce notions of musicality from those of first-rate choreography. The ballet *is* its musicality, and does very well by it.

At the other end of the spectrum is Balanchine's intimate adagio choreography privileging melody line and timbre, and pushing rhythm and pulse into the background. Indeed, extended passages of this kind are not always grounded in hard counts, even when first taught. It emerges that Balanchine was especially drawn to the solo violin (or viola), adagio writing for which prompted some of his most poignant work, as in the Bach *Double Violin Concerto* for *Concerto Barocco* and Stravinsky's *Duo Concertant*. He was also moved to choreograph two Stravinsky string pieces a second time: the *Violin Concerto* (first as *Balustrade*) and the *Elégie* for solo viola. String instruments can be made to sound percussive, but they also have a lyrical, singing quality that a more percussive instrument like the piano cannot match. Given this vocal quality, a solo string instrument can project a sense of embodiment in the theatre, conveying that a dancer is both possessed by and in possession of (spoken by and empowered to speak through) its sound, enjoying an especially intimate relationship with music.[67]

There is no more compelling example than Balanchine's 1972 setting of the *Violin Concerto* (which he later called *Stravinsky Violin Concerto*), the one piece where the choreographer said he would never change a step: he allocated it some hundred hours of rehearsal during the 1972 Festival, more time than for any other ballet.[68] It seems that in both this and the earlier setting of 1941, which was dressed in surreal designs by Pavel Tchelitcheff, the central Aria movements attracted most interest, and above all Aria II. In the earlier version, the first Aria was scored for a couple, two supporting soloists and eight women, the second for a ballerina and two men: in the later version, both Arias are pas de deux. In both cases, the outer movements are public dancing, the inner ones private dialogues, and in the 1972 ballet, the solo women remove their short black skirts and appear in their black leotards and tights for the two inner pas de deux. Writing of the earlier version, Denby noted the 'wonderfully sensual acrobatics of the middle section that delighted one part of the audience and shocked another'.[69] Silent film fragments of *Balustrade* reveal interweaving limbs, a crab position, Tamara Toumanova trapping a man between her pincer legs, all images that could have seeded the later work. My analysis is based on the second setting and primarily on two television films of the performance made during the 1970s. Both films feature the original cast, Karin von Aroldingen and Jean-Pierre Bonnefous (Aria I) and Kay Mazzo and Peter Martins (Aria II), with the exception that Bart Cook replaces Bonnefous in the second film.[70]

It has often been said that Aria I is about struggle, a fundamental incompatibility merged with an irrational need for partnership. When the woman dances with the man, she cannot look at him; when they dance apart and faster, their energy always seems to propel them in opposite directions and, at a climactic juncture, they form the image of mutual imprisonment and acute tension. The music contributes significantly to this impression. The legato after the opening exclamatory chords sustains itself only briefly, even if Balanchine helps us to register its effect by dropping the written tempo and increasing the effect of adage – from Stravinsky's crotchet=116 to crotchet=104 (according to the Labanotation score, but as low as 92 in the later Dance in America film). Soon the solo violin is off into nervous, rapid staccato and, during the accelerating centre of the pas de deux (both musical Arias are in ABA form), it sounds more and more spiky and vicious, like the devil's instrument (of *Histoire du soldat*). Other subtle textural and timbral features are useful for Balanchine's purpose. Stravinsky's opening 'vocal' duet, the solo violin in counterpoint with cellos, becomes a metaphor for a couple at odds. Their push and pull come fully into focus during one of the strangest passages of all, when von Aroldingen exits from this difficult emotional entanglement by reverting to the inverted and grotesque. She bends over backwards into crab and, by turning over sideways, walks herself round in a semicircle while Bonnefous looks on, tracing a line of steps that follows her trajectory. It is as if, Garis wrote, she 'had revealed herself to be a powerful insect from another planet'.[71] The music here is a series of harmonics on the solo violin, a repeating 3-note crotchet pattern with occasional rests interspersed, accompanied by other strings syncopating between the notes (see Ex. 3.4). Joseph has aptly described the sound as 'eerily glassy, unearthly', and he also notes the additional unsettling impression of duple working against triple metre.[72] Balanchine also uses rhythmic means to reinforce the incongruity of the pair, creating a pattern that is always at odds with itself. Bonnefous's steps mark the onbeats, von Aroldingen's hands and feet the in-between offbeats.

There is just one passage near the end of Aria I when Balanchine gets us to hear the violin as a warm, sympathetic sound, at [75], during a series of four legato, sighing, 5-note phrases scored for emphasis with the instruction *poco a poco allargando*. Or, perhaps, it is the other way round, and the violin colours our impression of what the dancers do. In any case, the effect is far more pronounced in the later Dance in America film, with Cook partnering von Aroldingen. Having met in a frightening interlock of arms stretched across and through each other, they both appear to experience something of a change of heart: he takes

Ex. 3.4. *Stravinsky Violin Concerto*, Aria I.

her into a promenade, cradling her with his arm and then, even if she still looks away into the distance, she softens, more willing than before to take his support. The violin sounds sweeter here than at any other part of the Aria, and Balanchine grasps the opportunity, looking ahead to the different kind of expression and the bittersweet sighing song-lines of Aria II. But the woman here trashes the opportunity as she turns into a walkover, ending the pas de deux in a huge arch backwards, focused in the opposite direction to her partner.

In Aria II, cantilena-style melody is much more pronounced, in neo-baroque style or, as Garis puts it, 'embroidered, perhaps tortured, by astringent ornamentation',[73] though perhaps he was already reading into it Balanchine's choreographic vision. Aria II also stands apart from the other musical movements as the only one not clearly in D (major/minor): it shifts between F-sharp minor and A major. The relationship between the couple here seems much closer than in the earlier pas de deux: theirs is a love that is ardent, too ardent, also painful, even cruel, and the woman as the main focus of attention is vulnerable, passive rather than competitive. If she embodies the violin as her voice, it is not words that are the utterance, but unspeakable feeling. On a couple of occasions, she

opens herself boldly: a striking X-shape to sharp declamatory gestures,[74] arms
and legs stretched apart, on pointe so she is larger and more open still *and* ready
to fall. Notably, Balanchine does not let us see this startling signature motif at
the beginning of the pas de deux when we first hear the gestures (see Ex. 3.5, bar
1), but only later, timed as sudden brutal interruptions rather than preliminary

Ex. 3.5. *Stravinsky Violin Concerto*, Aria II.

calls to attention or moments of comfortable recognition or closure. However,
Mazzo's dominant body action is introverted, most expressively with the pressure of her thighs joining, in the turned-in position that is the resolution of the X
– Martins rushes to grasp her knees (see Ill. 3) – or in taut stepping, one pointe
across the other, like a closing off from the threat of intimacy. Apparently,
Stravinsky had written this Aria as an apology to his first wife about his extra-
marital relationship with Vera: indeed, he was once moved to weep when listening to a performance by Samuel Dushkin, for whom the concerto had been written. Balanchine knew this story and could make use of it, even though he never
discussed it publicly.[75] Stravinsky too preferred to keep information of this kind
well away from public consumption, but perhaps he would have wept again had
he known Balanchine's choreography.

One of the principal movement motifs of the pas de deux is a kind of tortuous
entanglement, her stepping action as described, or their arms forcefully wrapping and re-wrapping around each other in a manner that suggests inability as
much as unwillingness to escape from partnership. These ideas constitute a visual
counterpart to the astringent, florid ornamentation in the violin line. On other occasions, Balanchine stresses a 3-note sighing motif, which we first hear when it
completes the opening melodic phrase (see Ex. 3.5; bar 3, beat 3, E-sharp, F-
sharp, C-sharp). Melodic descent is the predominant style of Aria II, through the
opening chords, then most of the first melodic phrase until the sighing motif, indeed
across Section A as a whole; such descending patterns bear strong associations

Ill.3. Nikolaj Hübbe and Alexandra Ansanelli in *Stravinsky Violin Concerto*, Aria II, choreography by George Balanchine, New York City Ballet.

of darker moods such as sadness, even death.[76] Balanchine complements the contour of the first phrase, Mazzo's crossing legs taking her into a fall, after which Martins scoops her up and settles her beside him, a curved trajectory that complements the rise before the stressed fall, the sigh motif. Thus Balanchine marks out for us key choreographic and musical material. Then, for a while, he simply lets this musical motif pass him by choreographically, and visual and aural strands co-exist in a weightless ebb and flow of connection and disconnection.

The sigh motif projects particular emotional force when we hear/see it as a release from climax at the close of Section A (at [81]). While she continues with still more crossing steps, he holds her off-centre and rotates her, for ever it would seem, a recollection of another famous turning, turning off-balance in the last movement of Balanchine's *Serenade* (Tchaikovsky, 1935), finally releasing her from danger into a deep curve forwards. During the turning, we first hear the sigh pulling her down against her resistance, then finally she folds over into safety and allows the rich low violin registers to embrace her, as if letting go her repressed sob. The sighing motif becomes the focus once more at the end of the pas de deux, at which point the pair seem resigned to dance no longer. Reflecting a plaintive trio, two flutes enmeshed with the solo violin line, Martins and Mazzo stand locked together (from [85]-1), he behind her with his right arm over her shoulder, rocking her, closing the arm across her as they sway to the left, opening it as they go to the right. Then, to the sigh in the penultimate bar, stated quietly but twice, and thus clearly registered, they bow modestly, and it looks as if his arm has become hers. Again, the point of contact is far more pronounced in the later of the two films. We could argue that this is just another occasion when Balanchine consciously held back, determined not to interfere with the music, but the starkness here stresses the image of a couple who love, but with difficulty. On two other occasions, the choreographer reinforces the abrasive sound of double-stopping, the only moments during the pas de deux adagio when Mazzo's pointes suddenly turn into flexed feet, an anxious inversion of her normal manner. Thus, again, Balanchine draws our attention to selected moments within the music, seeking out qualities compatible with his drama. As stresses, these moments also structure the choreomusical composite, as moments of special focus, special poignancy.

The insider interpretative points that are most often cited about this pas de deux are mundane and not at all about a romantic relationship. Balanchine told Martins about his right arm gesture: 'Make it look like an elephant trunk, and then move out your hand as if you're asking for money.'[77] Then, for the bow, understanding the Russian nostalgia in the music, he explained: 'I made a gesture as if to say, "How do you do, Stravinsky?"'[78] But perhaps he spoke like this because he wanted to avoid overstatement of emotion, though I find it hard to understand Martins's rationalisation of the final gesture of blinding Mazzo as looking 'almost sentimental'.[79] This is one of the most heart-rending and disturbing pas de deux that I know. Some critics have read the woman's state of being more positively than I do, suggesting that, if she suffers, she also glows, or she takes comfort in the knowledge that, like Balanchine the choreographer, the man will make her look beautiful.[80] Croce was on to something when she described Martins as 'both benevolent and authoritarian'.[81] The manner in which he closes his right arm across her is barely comfortable: as much as it is tender, it also hints at strangulation. There is a big moment in the final duet of *Duo Concertant* (significantly, it is for Martins and Mazzo again) that is much the same, half protective and framing her beauty, half deadly dangerous, and, once again, a hold round the throat metamorphoses into blinding. Choreomusical reading has supported my especially dark reading of this pas de deux, making it seem quite as tortured as the one that precedes it. The jolt into jollity that follows is hard to take.

But the jolt reminds us that *Stravinsky Violin Concerto*, despite the private intensity at its core, is a formal work with public outer movements. It also demonstrates ways of harmonising structural argument with a dramatic theme about relations within couples, commencing with a movement where the soloists of the central duets dance as individuals against the landscape of their community, concluding with the entire cast as ten unison couples. Furthermore, Balanchine felt the need to resolve the unusual 'problem' of two central pas de deux rather than one, and, as Croce put it, during the last movement 'we seem to be watching two ballets moving toward each other like sliding mirrored doors'.[82] But choreomusical large structure is also telling in this work: Balanchine goes out of his way in every movement to avoid the association of blocks of musical thematic material with dance material and the comfortable sense of heightened recognition that this affords. Instead, he constantly pushes us on into new territory, challenging us with new information. So, for instance, in both pas de deux, he does not duplicate the recapitulation in the music's ABA structures.

The outer musical movements, the Toccata and Capriccio, are both loosely structured, witty celebrations of the violin's virtuoso capacity, the first a patchwork of sixteen episodes, the second a free, through-composed form. Nevertheless, both contain points of recapitulation. The musicologist Lynne Rogers makes a case for three-part form in the Toccata, with the main musical thematic material reiterated several times during the opening section, giving way after reiteration at bar 76 to more diversity in a central section, before its recapitulation at bar 172.[83] But, important for choreomusical analysis, it is always the music, never the dance, that contains the device of structural recapitulation. The Toccata is an especially imaginative example of Balanchine meeting the needs of his choreography with and against an existing musical structure, forging a fascinating composite interlocking pattern of structural counterpoint. Here, I read the musical recapitulation as beginning at bar 184, with bar 172 (Rogers's point of recapitulation) parallel to the opening of the Toccata, as an anticipatory account of the main, repeating theme. The recapitulation then extends for 45 bars before the Coda (at bar 229). Across the sixteen musical episodes, Balanchine scores eight dance sections, all of them cast differently. He presents each soloist in turn accompanied by four dancers of the opposite sex; then next time round, they are of the same sex. The ordering is almost totally schematic, and is especially predictable if you have glanced at the cast list in your programme beforehand; after the half-way point at bar 134, the key structural division in the choreography, you can begin to foresee who will dance next, and also when the movement is likely to end.

Part 1:

Group 1: Mazzo and four men 1–53	Introduction and Music sections 1–2
Group 2: von Aroldingen and four men 54–85	Music sections 3–5
Group 3: Bonnefous/Cook and four women 86–106	Music sections 6–7
Group 4: Martins and four women 107–133	Music sections 8–9

Part 2:

Group 5: Mazzo and four women 134–159	Music section 10
Group 6: von Aroldingen and four women 160–183	Music sections 11–12
Group 7: Bonnefous/Cook and four men 184–203	Music section 13 (recapitulation)
Solo: Martins 204–228	Music sections 14–15
Group 8: Martins and four men 229–250	Music section 16 (coda)

Joseph points out that there is an uneven distribution of musical episodes per dance group.[84] My reading of the interlocking musical and choreographic structure is that Balanchine arranged matters so as to provide a semblance of democracy, but all the same to give prominence (simply through allocation of time and number of bars) to his most 'important' couple, Mazzo and Martins. However, for someone who does not know the work, their importance will not become clear until later. (He does the same in the last movement.) So here, Mazzo comes first, simply standing and waiting with her group of men for 14 bars: plenty of time to register her presence before they launch into dance. Martins comes last, and when he returns at the end of the Toccata, he develops into the authority figure that we see in Aria II. He is even given a solo, which is like a structural tease, the only break from the scheme, and gets us anxious and asking, 'Where are the boys?'. Perhaps it is significant that his solo is to music that Mazzo danced to earlier. It also contains a strange moment that looks rather like mime (bars 221–22, immediately before [46]), a quick writhing motion of the arms that reverses itself and hints at trouble in the future – a quick, inverted account of one of the moves that he later performs entangled with Mazzo. Interestingly, the moment is made more strange still by the sudden ritardando at this point (emphasised by commencement one bar earlier than Stravinsky indicated). Balanchine ignored this score-marking at the corresponding point near the beginning of the Toccata, when Mazzo danced this music.[85] Perhaps he wanted to make Martins's solo gesture stand out more by saving the slowing-down for him. The end of the Toccata is celebratory, with increasingly jubilant reiterations of the main musical theme: the male backing group devour the space with leaps marking the boundaries of the stage, leading to a coalescence of forces in a final pose with Martins out front.

Yet, if the progression of the Toccata choreography is highly schematic, it is subverted by its constantly shifting relations with the music, which is either new, or familiar but choreographed in a new way. Even the block of material at the important point of musical recapitulation sounds different the second time around. When first heard, the choreography was as quiet as the dynamic marking in the score, and Mazzo, literally with her pointes, identified some striking isolated violin notes played as harmonics (bars 24–26, [4]+5-[5]). Perhaps this passage foreshadows the attention to the isolated harmonics in Aria I (see p. 183). Second time around, Balanchine decided to build dance energy with big travelling jumps, large-scale male allegro. Although we may entertain memories of the earlier visualisation, we are now more likely to hear the continuity of the supporting orchestra, which seems more compatible with what we see, and to grasp the sense of impending climax. Balanchine enjoyed the overspill of invention characteristic of this musical movement as a whole, and added more of his own.

The Capriccio is a more unwieldy musical construction, with two 'codas' after the main 'shape' of the music has been completed. There are five sections:

Bars 1–54 led by von Aroldingen and Bonnefous
Bars 55–107 led by von Mazzo and Martins
Bars 108–174 (recapitulation) beginning of Grand Finale
Bars 175–204 Coda 1
Bars 205–285 Coda 2

Balanchine starts to assemble his full cast of twenty at the point of recapitulation, and the piano rehearsal score that accompanies the Labanotation score marks 'Grand Finale' as recognition of this moment. This is a conventional choreographic response to an important structural division in the music, and we might well be persuaded to think that the end is near, but it is not.

Perhaps it was because he was faced with the problem of dealing with a false ending that begins less than half-way through the movement that Balanchine decided to veer off course for a while: he introduced his ambitious metrical experiment (see pp. 174-6) almost precisely at the half-way point of the Capriccio. That strange departure into disconnected activity, three separate dance machines operating simultaneously, is underlined by a slowing of tempo, another occasion where he took licence with indications in Stravinsky's score. The composer marked the bar 153 (at [116]) with a ritardando followed by an instruction to return to tempo within the same bar. On film, Balanchine exaggerated the effect by sustaining the drop in tempo over twelve bars (the Labanotation score indicates *poco più* after seven bars). The staged deviation into suspended time reinforces by contrast the fusion of forces and increase in exuberance towards the final climax of the ballet.

In *Violin Concerto*, Balanchine was confronted with relatively loose large-scale musical forms, unlike, for instance, those of *Concerto Barocco* (to Bach, 1941), *Symphonie Concertante* (to Mozart, 1947) and *Symphony in C* (to Bizet, premiered as *Le Palais de cristal* in 1947). He responded to these tighter baroque and classical forms by respecting the conventions of musical return and closure: in other words, with far more regular association between choreography and music. Yet he handles other Stravinsky symphonic scores very differently from the *Violin Concerto*; their movement content is also simpler to read and more limited in scope.

In the earlier *Rubies*, there is a clear sense of recapitulation of dance together with its music in the first two movements, where the musical forms themselves are more conventionally shaped. *Symphony in Three Movements* is of quite a different order both musically and choreographically, often described as Dionysian (a rare epithet for Stravinsky), explosive and almost out of control. Its greatest choreographic strength lies in the use of a mass cast of thirty-two as a kind of ironic ballet army, operating as unison fronts and phalanxes that shift formation in the manner of military manoeuvres, while perpetually hyperactive in their motor patterns. The first movement Stravinsky structured with a declamatory Introduction, then an exposition that can be divided into two distinct sections, which return in the form of a much-telescoped recapitulation, and a Coda containing material from the Introduction. A line of sixteen women in white leotards, hair in ponytails, declare war at the outset: with the ascending rush of the orchestra, they swing their arms around and up into a flat wall and strike threatening arabesques tendus. Such choreomusical imagery acts as a firm clamp around the first movement. In between, a series of groups of various sizes and gender-mixes amass and splinter. Balanchine treats the musical recapitulation with some of the dance moves that we saw earlier to similar music, although obliquely, very differently organised and using different formations of dancers.

The pas de deux in the centre of *Symphony* offers a period of quiet. The movement has an 'Eastern' flavour; Balanchine pointed out that there was 'a little Balinese-type gesture' honouring Stravinsky, who, he said, 'loved' that culture.[86] Responding to the arch form of the music, the dance pushes further and further towards a semblance of immobility, akin to searching for a still centre. When the music that opened the movement returns, Balanchine delays the choreographic response, and then gives us just a brief glimpse of his past. The last movement is more like a free discourse in music and choreography, through-composed, offering image memories in sound and movement from the earlier part of the work but no structurally significant recollections of the familiar. The ending is one of the most powerful in ballet, the entire ensemble, crouched and standing, in frozen confrontation with the audience, handing over the last word to the furious music.

It is hard to disagree with Goldner: *Agon* remains exceptional. Suddenly, with that 1957 work, like no other, Balanchine's level of invention rose several notches in one go, inviting us to react likewise with our listening and watching. There was a new intensity of delivery – no time for transitions, only contrasts – that seemed to take him beyond what any choreographer had achieved before. *Agon* also proved a rich source, a model for the ballets that followed in terms of interface between choreography and the melodic, timbral as well as rhythmic aspects of music.

My analysis of *Agon* as a case study in both *Moving Music* and the analytical video *Music Dances* drew special attention to structural and rhythmic features and how these contribute to meaning: what I then called 'music visualisation', simultaneous duplicating patterns as well as dance echoes and anticipations of the music, and a virtuoso display of contrapuntal rhythmic strategies, crossings, canon devices, and dialogues at the level of larger structure. Still now, what I enjoy most is *Agon*'s indomitable power to shock and to tease: to provide an image of balance and then to destabilise it, to pose tantalising questions but not to answer them, to promise closure but then to revoke the offer, to draw our attention to landscape only the next instant to concentrate it on the tiniest movement detail, all at the same time suggesting a wide range of human behaviour and mood. As I wrote in 2000, 'the final statement is that the contest continues'.[87]

Writing about *Agon* since then, Joseph has revealed Balanchine's careful response to Stravinsky's serial segmentations and the interplay of canon structures in music and dance, whilst reflecting upon the seventeenth-century models underlying the composer's dances and the complex generative process behind the work.[88] In her doctoral thesis, Julia Randel considered gender issues: how orchestration, texture and the choice between diatonicism and chromaticism demonstrate particular associations with male or female dancing. She also pointed out references to the conventions of nineteenth-century ballet and the concept (through association with chromaticism) of woman as Other.[89] I return to her ideas later in this chapter.

In hindsight, returning to rhythm, my earlier analysis treated the pulse of *Agon* as a more rigid phenomenon than it really is, as if it grounded the rhythmic impetus and overlooked the dancers' invasion of the larger space around and above them, their buoyancy and capacity to hover dangerously. 'They hang in the air like a swarm of girl-size bees ...', Denby wrote of the arrival of the women,[90] but it is when we later discover the dancers as individuals that the piece takes off. The firm print of pointes and steps acts as a launch for rhythms with a spring in them, an escape from beat that finds its apex in the grand breath of the Pas-de-Deux.

Stressed moves in a downward direction that overtly mimic the music become acidic jokes: the women caving in at the end of an immaculate deep plié during their entry dance or the first trio jerkily bumping shoulders and bending into a huddle. But these moments merely play against what is of primary importance, as do the curious endings during the first Pas-de-Trois that all unexpectedly point to the earth (in a bow, a kneel, or a stretch down along a leg in tendu). On the other hand, the endings in the second Pas-de-Trois celebrate the journey into space, pushing the energy upwards and outwards, with an arm (the Bransle Gay) or with the focus (one man looks up and away from the other at the end of the Bransle Simple). The woman caught in mid-air escaping skywards at the end of the Bransle Double provides the perfect link to the Pas-de-

Deux. According to these terms, the rules of the time corset and motor are only there to be broken.

In 'Three Sides of *Agon*', perhaps his most brilliant piece of writing about rhythm and musicality, Denby betrays that he too felt the air in *Agon:*

> ... take the canonic imitations. At times a dancer begins a complex phrase bristling with accents and a second dancer leaping up and twisting back an eighth note later repeats it, then suddenly passes a quarter note ahead. The dissonance between them doesn't blur; if you follow it, you feel the contradictory lift of the double image put in doubt where the floor is. Or else you see a phrase of dance rhythm include a brief representational gesture, and the gesture's alien impetus and weight – the 'false note' of it – make the momentum of the rhythm more vividly exact. These classic dissonances (and others you see) *Agon* fantastically extends. The wit isn't the device, it is the surprise of the quick lift you feel at that point.

Denby secures his impression within the style of the music. Whereas conventional tonality shows the force of gravity pulling us downwards and grounding our experience within a planned time frame of proposals and expected completions, the peculiar lift in *Agon*

> ... relates to the atonal harmonies of the score – atonal harmonies that make the rhythmic momentum of the music more vividly exact.[91]

Meanwhile, there is the impatient style of structuring material in blocks or modules, without transitions, another example of choreography following musical principles. The dance phrases

> fit like the stones of a mosaic, the many-colored stones of a mosaic seen closeby. Each is distinct, you see the cut between; and you see that the cut between them does not interrupt the dance impetus.[92]

It is the air in *Agon*, enabled by Stravinsky's serialism and in tandem with its special intensity and density of dance information, that makes the ballet seem perennially modern. For those occasions when the 'Greek trilogy' was programmed as a single ballet evening, Stravinsky and Craft had different ideas about which ballet should come last. Stravinsky apparently wanted *Orpheus*, whereas Craft wanted *Apollo* (as in Hamburg in 1962).[93] But Balanchine was right (in the 1972 Festival) that *Agon*, choreography free at last of all literary allusions, should have the last word. Yes, 'the gods are tired', and the old dances that took fire and exploded in the twentieth century explode with just as much vigour in the twenty-first.

But there is one ballet that extends even the boundaries of *Agon* for charge and intensity: the *Movements for Piano and Orchestra*.

Movements for Piano and Orchestra

It starts with an explosion. A rocketing minor ninth from a flute sets off an abrupt chord and a pointillist helter-skelter on the piano. A man and woman, both in the same confrontational wide second position of modern dance, feet parallel, backs facing, swing their arms in a furious circle and twist sharply towards each other. Two framing trios of women, stretching out into space in an image of considerable tension, draw closer, the woman in the centre of each threesome opening into a wide-legged plié on pointe (see Ill.4). It is an assault on the senses and before you can take in what you have seen, all eight dancers have moved into the future and the soloists are engaged in a dense pattern of stop-start steps and gestures, like a set of agreements and arguments.

Suzanne Farrell, who took over and premiered the role of the woman soloist in 1963 when Diana Adams became pregnant, recalls how, before every curtain-up, her partner Jacques d'Amboise would brace himself and growl like a

Ill. 4. Suzanne Farrell and Sean Lavery in *Movements for Piano and Orchestra*, Movement 1, choreography by George Balanchine, New York City Ballet.

tiger: 'Animals', she said, 'are always on their toes like that and not sitting back on their heels ... in order to be ready to pounce.'[94] Thus, audiences in the early 1960s were thrown headlong into an alien world of animalian aggression, risk and sensuality, a new kind of Balanchine–Stravinsky, this one dressed in all-white leotards (except for the man in *Agon*-style black and white), and the score a new kind of *musique dansante*. At the same time, *Movements* was instantly acclaimed as the next Balanchine masterpiece, far more warmly received than Stravinsky's score had been in concert since 1960,[95] and its premiere was also a key moment in the career of the 18-year-old Farrell. The ballet has since become a regular part of New York City Ballet repertory and has been staged on a handful of other companies. Since 1966, it has been consistently paired with the courtly, 7-minute *Monumentum pro Gesualdo*, which offers a number of parallels, brevity, white practice clothes (with the addition of short skirts for the women), geometrical formations and similar casting, except for the addition of male partners for the six women. The same ballerina normally takes the leading role in both ballets. The quiet exaltation of *Monumentum* settles the audience in readiness for the concentration and focus required for its partner ballet.

Movements has also excited radically varying comment over the years, which is important to choreomusical analysis. At the time of the premiere, Balanchine's biographer Bernard Taper stressed cool and abstraction in his description of the ballet as

> rarefied, remote, beyond good and evil, with an impersonal, godlike serenity.[96]

So did Donal J. Henahan, adding a touch of science:

> At times one had the feeling that d'Amboise and the rubber-spined Farrell had solved a geometry theorem or successfully traced through an electrical circuit.[97]

Farrell finds particularly relevant Walter Terry's idea that the ballet celebrated

> the almost clinical but spectacular creed of the Spartan ... The designs and the movements are spare – not sparse.[98]

Meanwhile, observing the piece in London in 1965, the dance critic of *The Times* noted an anti-gravitational force at work. He characterised the ballet as

> an essay in suspended motion. Its appeal is at once musical and spatial, and its dancers seem like a mobile caught in the breath of the music. The air is full of pauses.[99]

Yet, in the twenty-first century, while presenting a choreomusical perspective, Julia Randel found something far more personal and concrete. She saw *Movements* as a love story, working through the strategies of the *ballet blanc* tradition, expressing the conflict between intimacy and the elusiveness of the beloved (the ballerina):

> In spite of their practical attire and businesslike approach to dancing, the women of *Movements* are the modern, athletic descendants of sylphs and swan maidens.[100]

In 1985, halfway through the history of *Movements*, watching the now mature Farrell in action, Jennifer Dunning adopted something of an intermediary position:

> The lead dancers ... have been let loose to prowl, hinge and thrust through the ballet's pure world, which presents those who move through it as if they were preserved in pale amber. Throughout, Miss Farrell and Mr. Lavery [Sean Lavery] danced with an air of mysterious privacy that gave them the look of being engaged in prayer.[101]

How can such diverse readings be possible? Do they all make sense? Stravinsky and Balanchine simply reinforce the contradictions. The Stravinsky–Craft essay on *Movements* assumed that 'the dramatic point is a love parable – in what ballet is it not?'[102] while, on the other hand, suggesting that a good alternative title would have been *Electric Currents*. Balanchine is well known for countering claims about his abstract approach: 'Put a man and a girl on stage, and there's already a story.'[103] However, when creating and rehearsing *Movements*, he said nothing whatsoever about romance or human relationships. I will attempt to rationalise these conflicting accounts later, during the course of the choreomusical analysis.

Turning first to Stravinsky's score, *Movements* marked a huge step forward after *Agon*, a totally new sound and approach to serial structure, ferociously modern (perhaps a reason why only three other choreographic uses are recorded in the 'Stravinsky the Global Dancer' [*SGD*] database). *Memories and Commentaries* reports him saying that this was 'the most advanced music from the point of view of construction of anything I have composed'.[104] Observing this sudden shock within Stravinsky's career, Walsh suggests that it was as if the music 'breathed the rarefied atmosphere of the extreme post-Webern European avant-garde'.[105] There were many noteworthy developments: extreme compression and concision, aphoristic, aerated gestures, sudden outbursts rapidly quelled, transparent textures shot through with silences, super-short notes and super-wide intervals, and, with the single exception of the opening (bars 1–22), a canvas totally devoid of the comfort of letting you hear something more than once. The score is just 9–10 minutes long, in five movements, with four short interludes (see Table 2, p. 207), which operate as introductions to the movements that follow them.[106] Kirstein vividly described a new aggressive leanness in the composer's aesthetic:

> Stravinsky made sharp distinctions between ordinary clock time and other dimensions of encapsulated or concentrated metrics through an imploded intensity of musical ideas which permitted no fat or rhetoric upon the fluid structure of his motor process.[107]

There was indeed a new attitude to rhythm, the effect highly unsettled, especially in the outer movements. We find Stravinsky's familiar changing metres, with changing base units, of quaver, semiquaver, even demisemiquaver (bar 4), but the major change is that the new method rarely provides any sense of security through pulse or motor. Christoph Neidhöfer, who has examined Stravinsky's working process through his sketches, notes that he 'systematically removes audible metric pulses from the musical surface. Metric pulses then merely survive at the background level as notated yet inaudible metre.'[108] There is also a marked absence of the composer's characteristic ostinatos, and instead a rich variety of complex rhythmic asymmetries and polyrhythmic combinations, fives and sevens as well as the familiar threes (triplets) and twos.[109] (Similar principles and a similar volatility lie at the heart of the *Variations for Orchestra*.)

What with all this, and furthermore without the use of traditional musical forms and tonality, it is difficult to find and hold on to temporal bearings in *Movements* and to predict what will happen in relation to clear, established markers. So, when Garis watched the ballet, it is hardly surprising that he blamed the music.

> I usually know where I am in a ballet by knowing where I am in its music ... Because I never know where I am in the music of *Movements*, I've never gotten to know the ballet either ... In *Movements* I miss what I think of as continuity in dance, and for me that is to miss the sine qua non, not only of the art of ballet but of all art.[110]

I sympathise, but *Movements* is a different kind of art, the sort that disrupts the traditional continuities that give us confidence. Audiences, at least concert audiences, needed help. Stravinsky wanted to have his work played twice at the concert premiere (although the plan fell through). Balanchine once said to his co-author Francis Mason, 'I seriously think that the best preparation for seeing this ballet is to listen to Stravinsky's recording of it a number of times.'[111]

Movements was also a major step in Stravinsky's departure from his hallmark tonal/serial compromise (as in *Agon*) with its clear references to traditional harmony. Put simply, the method involves use of the twelve notes of the chromatic scale as a fixed template governing the melodic and harmonic content of the piece, but as well as playing it in its original form (O), it can be inverted (I) or played backwards as retrograde (R), the inversion can be played backwards (RI) and the retrograde can be inverted (IR). Example 3.6 demonstrates these options for *Movements*.

Ex. 3.6. *Movements for Piano and Orchestra*, the twelve-note row in its five basic forms, each divided into hexachords.

Any of the above versions of the row can also be transposed to begin at any position on the scale, not just on E-flat. To make matters far more complicated, Stravinsky was interested in working with half-rows (hexachords) as well as full and, by the time of *Movements*, with rotational array systems that he had learnt from the composer Ernst Krenek. Example 3.7 demonstrates use of the original form of the row (untransposed), divided into two hexachords (alpha and beta) and showing rotation by one position in row I, two positions in row II and so forth.

Now, having summarised the framework of row options, we can turn to their application. The serial structure of Stravinsky's *Movements* can often be read linearly, though with some notes forming chords. There are some very simple examples: at the start, the twelve notes of the row in its original form (bars 1–2), and likewise at the end of the whole work (bars 187–193 – see Exs. 3.8a and b), but the effects here are totally different, the abrupt, noisy start, a quick-fire exposition of the row contrasting with a more drawn-out, gentle, and mysterious conclusion.

Then, at the end of the first movement, we find statements of the four basic forms O, IR, R and I (all in bar 42 – see Ex. 3.13, p. 212), mainly as a flurry of single notes, a monodic texture, on the piano. Movement 4, serially the simplest of the five, is similarly constructed around these four basic forms of the row, presented in a mainly linear fashion. Sometimes the row is fragmented: the flute

Ex. 3.7. *Movements*, example of Stravinsky's rotational array, derived from the original form of the row (O). The manuscript document is housed in the Paul Sacher Stiftung.

passage in Movement 1 (bars 13–17) is a prime example, ten fragments of 3, 4 or 5 notes each. There are also far more complicated superimpositions of different rows and half-rows, like chords. Look at the four forms of the row written so that all the first notes coincide, all the second notes and so on, then divide each row into two hexachords, superimposing the notes from column 1 upon those in

Ex. 3.8a. *Movements*, opening, Movement 1, bars 1-2, using the twelve notes of the row in its original form.

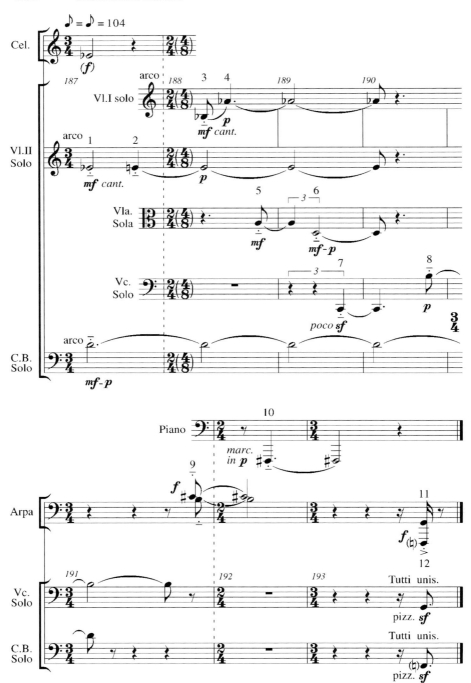

Ex. 3.8b. *Movements,* end of Movement 5, bars 187-93, using the twelve notes of the row in its original form.

column 7, those from column 2 upon those in column 8, and so on, and we have an 8-part array structure, rather like 8-part harmony (see Ex. 3.9a). This is the structure of the opening bars of the piano part in Movement 5 (bars 141–144), while the trumpet, clarinet and violins play the retrograde of the row in simple linear form (see Ex. 3.9b). A similar technique lies behind the wind scoring in the previous interlude (bars 137-140), but here transposed up four semitones (so that the original row begins on G instead of E-flat).

Such techniques gave Stravinsky useful limits within which to work, a launch pad for his ideas; they are not obvious to the ear. Balanchine took a keen interest in serial procedures, but would surely not have been able to grasp the full complexities of this score, which has continued to tease music theorists over many years. When it came to choreographing, even though he once described *Movements* as his most 'in-the-music ballet' to date,[112] Balanchine appears, sensibly, to have put most of the theory aside. If a precise 'visualisation' of rows were attempted, then as Randel puts it, 'the dancers would spend half the ballet walking backwards on their hands'.[113] Techniques such as forming chords from separate versions of the row would be virtually impossible to illustrate in dance as convincing, perceptible choreomusical connections. Yet, there are a few occasions when the presence of a row appears to have prompted visualisation. At the end of *Movements*, the group of six women embark on a series of bourrées into the

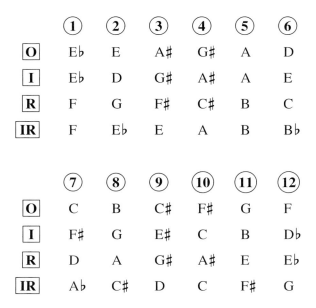

Ex. 3.9a. *Movements*, diagram of eight-part array structure in Movement 5.

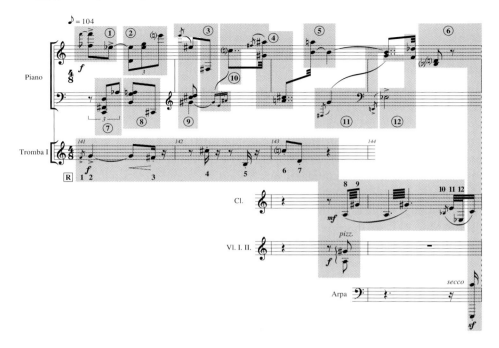

Ex. 3.9b. *Movements*, opening, Movement 5, eight-part array against the row in retrograde.

centre, in turn, to each note of the row; they gather like a storm cloud behind the soloists who then begin to move, first into a lift, the woman drawing herself into a tight ball, after which she is the one who strikes the final dominant position, the only one left standing (see Ex. 3.10).

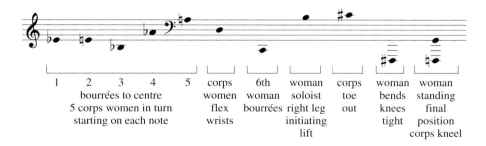

Ex. 3.10. *Movements*, end of Movement 5, diagram of choreography to the row in its original form.

Balanchine himself went public about the dancers marking this final statement. He had responded before to serial structure in setting Webern's *Symphony*
for *Episodes*, when the women are upturned by their partners to a row inversion.
But, he said, 'These certain things I do, naturally, but as little as possible. I don't
imitate the notes of a piece.'[114] There are only two other examples of visualisation in *Movements* that I find plausible. The most striking occurs during a retrograde inversion in the flute part in Movement 1 (bars 40–41), when the man
upturns the woman in a lift, moving her backwards to stage right – she pitches
forwards over his shoulder, holding her left foot in her right hand – then he
reverses back again to centre and sets her down, her right leg descending to
carve a huge arc through space.[115] Later, the female group retreat from centre to
the retrograde at the beginning of Movement 5 (bars 141–44 – see above). Yet
even these two brief moments could be merely chance coincidences within musical structure rather than planned events.

Balanchine discovered much more potential for choreomusical relations from
other parameters that *are* discernible to the ear. Even if his attention to serial
structure was limited, his interest in other kinds of structuring device remained
as consuming as usual. There is rhythm, although in *Movements* it is very different from what he had been used to from Stravinsky, and this aspect will be discussed later. There are also the block structures and stratification devices that
have already been mentioned in relation to the *Symphonies of Wind Instruments*
(see pp. 149-50) and that constitute the strongest linking points between *Movements* and Stravinsky's previous practice. Theorists have noted connections between the blocks of musical material in *Movements*, such as transitions, overlaps
and pivot notes.[116] Nonetheless, many components join to make them clearly
discrete: serial structure, contour, rhythm and, above all, orchestration. Craft
tells us that it was the organisation of instruments in 'groups or blocks' (as
layers or strata) that had particularly interested Balanchine in setting
Monumentum earlier,[117] and the layout of both written scores draws attention to
this organisation. Balanchine in turn could use this organisation as a reference
point for his own choreographic orchestration. In *Movements*, this block structure goes well beyond separation of the solo piano from the rest of the orchestra.
Edward Cone concluded his seminal article on the *Symphonies* with some observations about *Movements*, where, he agrees, 'instrumental differentiation becomes the chief source of stratification'. He finds the practice especially clear in
Movements 3 and 4 (see pp. 206-11). He also notes that the four interludes
emphasise different instrumental groups in turn: woodwinds, strings, and brass,
and then all three together, the single orchestral tutti of the work. Here is a
'climactic synthesis' before a decomposition of the orchestra once more into
layers in Movement 5, where even the harp tone has been divided 'into a harp
and celesta component' (bars 183–186).[118]

In the following discussion of choreomusical issues and of how Balanchine addresses particular musical parameters, both video and written sources ground my analysis. I used a number of video recordings of the full ballet, most importantly three featuring Farrell, in rehearsal and in a televised performance at Lincoln Center, both from 1963 (with d'Amboise as her partner), and again in performance in 1982 (partnered by Sean Lavery); a Dutch National Ballet recording (1984) led by Coleen Davis and John Wisman; and material for a George Balanchine Foundation Interpreters Archive video in which Farrell coaches the solo roles. I also scrutinised the Benesh score of the ballet completed by Jurg Lanzrein at New York City Ballet during 1973, and the New York City Ballet piano rehearsal score with its various count and cue annotations.[119] Both scores were useful in clarifying material that was hard to read on film. Of paramount importance was the 1963 rehearsal film, to piano, under the jurisdiction of Balanchine himself. In her book *Holding On to the Air*, Farrell recalls the shock of making this film, suddenly, without warning, in the presence of Stravinsky himself (for the West German documentary *A Stravinsky Portrait*): 'I was stone cold from not having had class that morning ... The rehearsal was terrible. I made a lot of mistakes that upset me ...'[120] Yet she herself returned to this important documentation when she revived the ballet for The Suzanne Farrell Ballet in 2001, and has spoken of the particular 'aliveness', 'eagerness' and 'vulnerability' that exists before a first performance.[121] The film records aspects of style that have since disappeared, and, quite as important, it shows the choreographer conducting, finger-snapping and foot-tapping the pulse, demonstrating his close rhythmic analysis of the score and the rhythmic precision that he demanded of his dancers.

In all the films, it is clear that the music prompted Balanchine to use the more radical end of his vocabulary (a far remove from 'proper' classicism), actions that are made additionally distinctive by the music accompanying them. But his extreme 180-degree arabesques penchées and splits do not look like tricks or virtuosity in this context. It is as if they belong to a distant world of meaning, or perhaps some vertiginous world of the future. Coinciding with a leap to a high note, especially when this is marked out as an eerie harmonic, the pointe at the end of an extended leg looks like a needle puncturing the skyline (bar 73). At the end of Movement 2, the female group slowly descend into splits, in unison but all facing out into the beyond in different directions. They end folded up, hugging their knees. The effect is doubly bleak with the mutual reinforcement between the choreography and the stark musical texture at this point: the call of a muted trumpet symbolises distance and emptiness. During the next Movement, the women turn into eccentric creatures of the earth: they kneel on one knee and look at their hands, palms-down on the floor (marking the downbeat of bar 85), pause; bend the leg on the floor to a difficult angle (the next downbeat, bar 86), pause; and shift their hand positions (a third downbeat, bar 87).

Farrell writes about her earliest struggle to learn the ballet: 'There were enough steps to fill a four-act *Swan Lake*, only they seemed to be danced backward and upside down.'[122] The lifts are wild, like aerobatics: not just the pitch over the man's shoulder near the end of Movement 1, but also the cartwheel lift out of a penchée during the second part of Movement 2, a slow process involving a re-angling of her body so that, Farrell says, it looked as though she were 'showing different clock times' with her legs.[123] Like Stravinsky's music, Balanchine's choreography breathed a new atmosphere. The *Times* critic was right with his image of 'suspended motion', the 'mobile caught in the breath of the music'. There is an exuberant travelling variant of this lift in Movement 5. Perhaps, after all, even if direct structural parallels are rare, Balanchine had found a way of reflecting the serial principles of retrograde and inversion. But some of the extreme movement finds itself at stage level, such as the woman's giant flexed-foot split in second position over the man's thighs to a sudden, clamorous piano gesture (in Movement 3, bar 83). There are also awkward, grating, off-balance supports when the woman lets one of her legs (on pointe) drag across the ground. During one such doublework challenge, after the man suddenly reverses their direction, the woman viciously locks her raised right knee over his supporting arm (the brutal end to the repeating exposition of Movement 1). Another time, to a landmark clarinet tremolo in Movement 3 (bars 85–91), he wields her across the floor so that her pointe traces a swirling pattern, uncomfortable manhandling that eventually leads her into a pirouette outburst, then a gentle body fold (still poised on one pointe), while he holds her from behind in a tight embrace.[124]

Balanchine mirrors the large structure of Stravinsky's score, not only in terms of its five main sections and interludes but also in its dynamic shape, which is of a traditional kind. After the explosive opening, the work quietens during the central Movements, the fourth being the most simply structured and 'legible' of all. Meanwhile, the interludes exert their own increasing pressure (through orchestration rather than indicated volume changes), and Movement 5 is another explosion as 'decomposition', aggressive reverberations that end quietly. To Stravinsky's big repetition during the first Movement, Balanchine repeats the material of his dance exposition – the dancers race back to their starting positions in the manner of rewinding a film. As with the music, this is the only marked choreographic repetition in the whole work, although a few movement motifs reappear sporadically. The female group becomes more assertive as the ballet progresses: the women start to share the territory of the soloists, and the interludes, all four of which Balanchine allocated to them, become correspondingly more mobile and forceful, contrapuntal textures turning to unison for the final climax before Movement 5. Balanchine enlarges the pattern of contrast and development that Stravinsky offered him.

Table 2 illustrates in outline how Balanchine reflects the interior block structure of individual Movements. For instance, the most simply sectionalised Movements 2 and 3 are both divided into two parts by clear breaks in music and dance events. I will use Movements 1 and 4 as detailed examples, both illustrated in the analytical video *Music Dances*. They contrast, but at the same time both reveal two distinct choreomusical methods. First there is what Stravinsky referred to as Balanchine's 'fastening on my tiniest repeated rhythm or sustaining group',[125] in hard-to-catch footwork, gestures and wrist- or ankle-flexions. Then there is the reflection of the larger sweep or outline of a musical unit through ambitious doublework and adage.

Movement 4 is the most legible: it is easier here than anywhere else in the ballet to grasp a relationship between Stravinsky's score and Balanchine's organisation of material and 'orchestration'. There are three stanzas, related through the parameters of orchestration and rhythm, and Cone characterises their orchestral stratification and block structure as follows:

> ... one level always opened by flutes and sustained by chords in string harmonics. Each statement of this area is answered by one of the piano, but each phrase of the piano is in turn introduced and interrupted by an orchestral interjection. The interrupting area is always the same: solo cellos or basses. The introductory area [after the flutes and string chords] constantly changes: from cello harmonics (m. 98) to clarinets (m. 111) to trombones and bass clarinet (m. 125).[126]

Balanchine's detailed response to the first stanza can be tabulated as follows (see Ex. 3.11):

1 The introductory block opened by flutes and followed by 'chords in string harmonics': (4 bars) 2/8 3/8 4/8 5/8, a 14-count group phrase led by two women in canon centre front marking the pulse in a series of steps and leg gestures. The other women respond with port de bras to the pedal chord (an example of 'larger sweep', and a note in the Benesh score refers to painting the sky).

2 Piano answer: (6 bars) 3/8 3/16 2/8 3/16 3/8 5/16, the man's solo, two turned-in steps followed by a jump on the high chord (last beat of bar 100), after which he reflects each bar division, and for the 5/16 bar, a stretch upwards and a drop into a crouch, arms crossed over his front thigh, during the

Table 2. Diagram of structure: *Movements for Piano and Orchestra.*

The two soloists work as a duo unless otherwise indicated. The group is symmetrically organised in two trios, with the dancers like sculptures or statues for short periods, and sometimes for longer time spans (e.g. at 27–30 and 165–169).

Movement 1: 1–42

1–26 repeated (up to 22): both music and dance repeat
From 27: Meno mosso
42: woman's solo, with punctuating chords and moves by other dancers

Interlude 1: 43–45 Female group: two matching trios in mirror symmetry

Movement 2: 46–67 (a slower rate of musical and dance events than in surrounding Movements)

46–51 Part 1: man's solo (to tremolos and flutter-tonguing), followed by
duet 52–55; group move towards front of stage
56–57 Interruption: 'Flower' (description from piano rehearsal score),
visualisation of three staccato notes
58–67 Part 2: a more stark, open musical and choreographic texture; group
retreat upstage

Interlude 2: 68–73 Female group: two matching trios

Movement 3: 74–91

74–84 Part 1: supporting trios emerge as two couples and two matching
sub-soloists
85–91 Part 2: to a clarinet tremolo, a slower rate of events

Interlude 3: 92–95 Female group: two trios as three unison couples

Movement 4: 96–135 (3 stanzas: overlapping and alternating soloists and group, the woman starting front stage left)

96–109 Stanza 1: man's solo from 100
110–122 Stanza 2: woman's solo from 113
123–135 Stanza 3: duet from 127

Interlude 4: 136–40 Female group: two trios in mirror symmetry/ unison

Movement 5: 141–93 (overlapping and alternating soloists and group, the man starting front stage right)

141–154: solo woman
155–186: duet
187–193: slow Coda

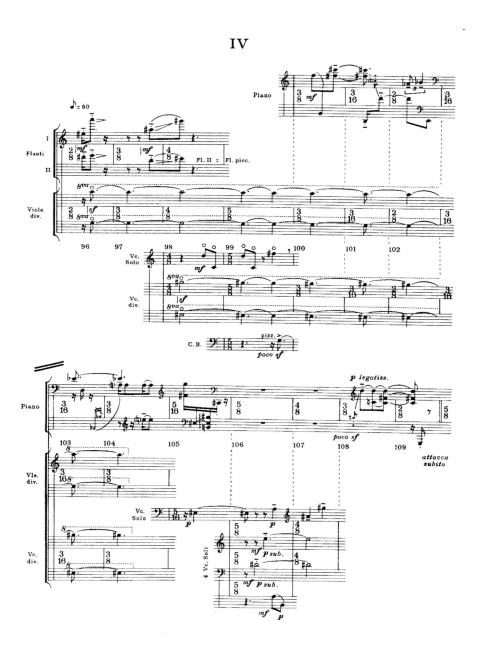

Ex. 3.11. *Movements*, Movement 4, stanza 1.

musical silence, count 5 (the piano rehearsal score indicates 'fast five', referring to the five-semiquaver span of the bar).[127]

3 Interruption by solo cellos: (2 bars) 5/8 4/8, the female group, with the
addition of the woman soloist, a 9-count pulse-based phrase of pointe steps
and heel drops.

4 Piano continuation: (2 bars) 3/8 2/8, the end of the man's solo, four moves
timed to 'visualise' the four musical events, the last on the offbeat.

The following two stanzas demonstrate not only certain similarities in orchestration with the first, but also rhythmic parallels: from the entry of the piano, the
third stanza is identical in rhythmic (but not pitch) pattern to the first, and the
second, middle stanza is a variation (with the same 'fast five', for instance) (see
Ex. 3.12). Comparing the initial piano entries of each stanza illustrates the
point.

Balanchine reinforces and clarifies this structure for us by introducing his
own stanza features. There is the same introduction and interruption by the
female group, although their pulse-based material changes for each stanza, becoming less extended, with breaks during which we, the audience, take the responsibility for maintaining the continuity that has been established. The
woman is the soloist in the second stanza, and both soloists lead the third. All the
initial solo statements begin with the same pattern of two turned-in steps (beats
1–2) and some kind of open, extended movement on the third beat of the bar;
they end in a similar crouch, one leg in front of the other. Otherwise, the soloists
perform different material in each stanza, but it relates rhythmically to the music
in a similar fashion each time.

Movement 1 is a much more anarchic construction, beginning with the repeated exposition (the most complex section, very fragmented, stop-start and
wide-ranging in movement scale and dynamics), which is followed by a second
section that is Meno Mosso and easier to read. The soloists lead the exposition
along with the piano, although the group perform the orchestral interjections
and take the lead for the whole of the flute solo (bars 13–17). The piano score
indicates this flute solo passage as the '7s', and the choreography reveals the
7/16 metre: the ends of most dance bars match, a wide version of Balanchine's
familiar 'B minus' position, the legs parallel, one foot resting on pointe. The
exposition ends with the woman lifted in a second-position split, reversed into
the drag and knee-lock (see p. 205), an example of Balanchine showing the
musical sweep rather than the 'tiniest' rhythm. When the tempo drops for the
next section, the soloists continue their doublework to the piano, later joined by
the orchestra and group, all then building to the main climax of Movement 1:

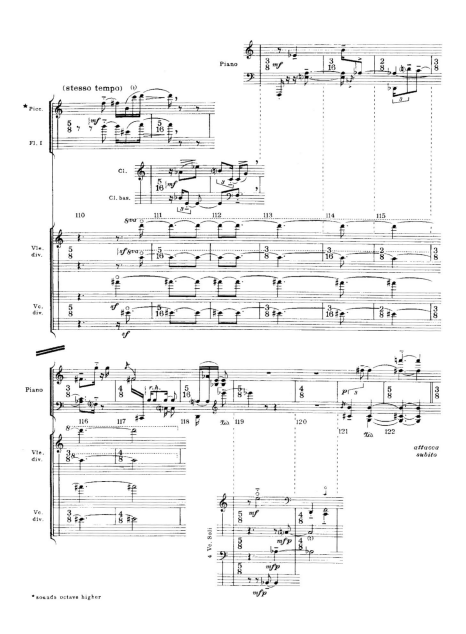

Stanza 2

Ex. 3.12. *Movements*, Movement 4.

Stanza 3

Ex. 3.12 continued. *Movements*, Movement 4.

another, even larger sweep to legato flute and strings (bars 40–41 – see p. 203). Finally, there is the piano solo (bar 42), and the woman prints out all the notes as rapid steps, on flat foot and pointe, with the punctuating reinforcement of chord fermatas and staccato moves by her partner and the female group. There are eleven steps up to the first fermata, then eight to the next, then nine, then quick pairs of moves to end (see Ex. 3.13). She visualizes rise and fall in pitch too, the final upward leap accentuated by another high lift.

Ex. 3.13. *Movements,* end of Movement 1, woman's solo, as in the New York City Ballet piano rehearsal score, showing 'D's [Diana Adams] steps' and counts.

Throughout *Movements*, Balanchine firmly maintains the association between solo dancers and the solo piano, just as he established clear associations between soloists and solo instruments and between group and orchestra in his concerto ballets of the past, such as *Concerto Barocco* (1941, to the Bach *Double Violin Concerto*), *Ballet Imperial* (1941) and *Allegro Brillante* (1956) to Tchaikovksy's second and unfinished third *Piano Concertos* respectively. There are just a few occasions when he very obviously relaxes his hold on this association, although, as Randel observes, there are further more subtle instances of overlapping, imprecise relationships.[128] The flute turns into an interesting protagonist in the first movement, during the climactic lift (bars 40–41), and again in two places during Movement 5 (bars 161–162 and 175–179). These are all occasions where the couple's movement seems especially pressured. The lack of the piano proves eloquent, speaking of an absence of security or ground: it is as if the breath of the flute urges them to be airborne and then, through mutual reinforcement, we hear that breath more vividly through the dance. There is a similar effect of departure from the known when the couple respond to the clarinet tremolo in Movement 3.

Despite these occasional 'larger sweep' forays, however, detailed articulation is a strong feature of the ballet. Sometimes Balanchine highlights notes or chords – examples include:

- the fermatas during the woman's first solo;
- the man's rocket jump to the piano's first melodic leap in Movement 4 (bar 100);
- the three piano bass notes that form the dividing line between the two parts of Movement 2 (visualised as one pointe touching the floor, B minus position; transfer to the opposite leg; break the hands open like buds, a moment called 'flower' in the piano score);
- the three staccato steps to the three punctuating gestures in Movement 5 (bars 155–156), Stravinsky's example of 'fastening on' the 'tiniest repeating rhythmic figure'.[129]

Sometimes Balanchine visualises quieter musical events. The effect is of mutual highlighting, music and dance. But he chooses which moments to stress: his behaviour is unpredictable. More often, he applies himself to the rhythmic content of the score, not the asymmetrical patterns of fives or sevens, but rather pulse and metre. It is crucial to the analysis that these components are visible in the score but rarely heard in concert. Indeed, Richard Moredock, a rehearsal pianist with New York City Ballet, thinks that the famous remarks about Stravinsky touring his own 'building' for the first time really referred to Balanchine's illumination of this secret technical layout of the musical score.[130]

There is a very unusual moment at the beginning of Movement 5, where an element of rhythmic repetition does allow us to hear not only a regular pulse, taken over directly from the spectacularly reinforced pulse of the previous interlude, but also the written 4/8 of the woman's solo. Elsewhere, metre, like pulse, is often hard to fathom via the ear – for instance, in Movement 3's unusual kneeling sequence (bars 85–87 – see pp. 204-5), where the written and danced downbeats occur within such rhythmically irregular music that they are hard to perceive as such.

Short bursts of dance pulse, instances of choreography clarifying the musical pulse, occur throughout the ballet. I have already noted several examples from Movement 4, where the female group dance the quaver pulse. But Balanchine also choreographed steps to the very rapid semiquaver pulse: for the woman (her solo in Movement 1 and isolated bars in Movement 5, 166 and 172), and during the group's '7s' to the flute solo in Movement 1 (on film you can catch glimpses of him beating at this rate). Each dance interlude offers a stronger pulse than the previous one, so that it becomes a symbol of power, group power. The last interlude shows a different action on every pulse (24 in total), with a thigh slap to conclude, seen and literally heard during the musical silence. Indeed, though there are occasional instances of arm-gesture pulses, the actual sound of steps or jabbing pointes becomes important, the quirky marching of the fourth Movement an especially lively example.

This clarification of pulse is probably the reason why the original *Movements* pianist Gordon Boelzner talked of Balanchine 'scanning' the music:

> That's one piece that is very tight, where everything has *got* to be nailed down. To put it somewhat naively, Stravinsky was writing shorthand rhythmic phrases; that is, they're not what you'd call scannable, really, to the ear. But they could be made scannable without the dreariness of following a score because Balanchine can visually clarify the meter. Of course there's a lot of silence in that score, but Stravinsky never gave up rhythm even though you don't hear it so much in this sort of shattered, twelve-tone music. But you can see it. It's all being ticked away for you on the stage.[131]

In fact, the dance pulse comes and goes – again, Balanchine's approach is unpredictable – and the soloists are never as preoccupied as the group with it. Yet it is insistent enough when it is present to affect your grasp of the entire piece.

Movements asks the question again as to whether Balanchine's choreography underplays the music. True, he is very selective about highlighting musical detail – there is no overplaying of that kind – but he makes the dance extremely assertive in another sense: he makes it bear the burden of the continuity that is so hard to find, and that Garis worried over so much, in this 'shattered' music.

Denby suggested that the especially 'fierce impetus' of New York City Ballet 'makes some scores [for *Opus 34*, *Agon* and *Episodes*] unexpectedly "listenable" – scores whose momentum is unforeseen by the public'.[132] He wrote this before Balanchine's *Movements* was born. I suggest that *Movements* was no longer a case of unforeseen musical momentum, but rather one of dancers creating the momentum themselves and developing a new autonomy as a result. Far less encumbered than usual by music or reliant upon it, they became superhuman, larger than usual, forcing a new, pristine physical presence into our conscious-ness. It is pertinent that another late serial Balanchine–Stravinsky dance inhab-ited a similar world, another white-leotard dance, the brief Building of the Ark scene in the 1962 television film *Noah and the Flood*. Here was another spiky, high-modern number, with a hidden musical pulse and a movement language that filled 'gaps' with dance momentum. Balanchine's working notes indicated that 'The dancers' movements must be as mechanical as a watch, and the build-ers' arms should work like semaphores.'[133] So is this late serial style *musique dansante*? Yes, because Balanchine made it so, and, without ever admitting or even knowing it, he moved a step closer to the aesthetic of a choreographer he probably had little time for, Merce Cunningham.

There were, of course, fundamental aesthetic differences between Balanchine and the radical American modern dance choreographer. By the 1960s, Cunningham, influenced by the philosophy of John Cage, famously operated with total structural independence from music, during both creative process and performance. Balanchine, on the other hand, elected to use Stravinsky's late serial music, which was pressured, driven in a manner that the music of Cage and like-minded composers was not. Yet it is tantalising to speculate that some-thing of this contemporary mode might have rubbed off on Balanchine. He would have seen Cunningham's *The Seasons* (to Cage) in 1949 (premiered 1947 by Ballet Society), and Tanaquil Le Clercq, his wife from 1952 to 1969, danced his work on more than one occasion and was positive about the experience.[134] Her recollections of *The Seasons* are especially significant here as regards dance autonomy:

> So many choreographers are swamped by their music; not Cunningham. He really knew his business. He gave you the counts and they worked. It was a pleasure ...[135]

Another link with Cunningham is the practical, anti-theatrical element within *Movements*. There is the break in dance energy before each interlude when the dancers simply walk to their next starting position. A similar break occurs before the big repetition at the opening, the moment made far more obvious than usual by the device of run-back-to-the-beginning film rewind.

The approach to time in *Movements* also suggests a relationship with Cunningham. There is the ironic juxtaposition of high speed and insistence upon the present: the impossible tension between the hyperactivity of often large movements achieved in what Farrell calls Stravinsky's 'split-second timing ... doing something in one hundredth of a second'[136] and time stopped in held shape or sculpture (highlighted by the all-white leotards). Clarity of the moment is sacrosanct, profoundly visible even if for an instant. When Croce wrote that, in Balanchine's 'Twelve-Tone' ballets, the dancers 'moved one muscle and froze the time they moved it in, as if time, by catching up, might force it to move by itself', she was talking about the urge to control time, to become superhuman.[137] *Movements* presents this as an image of anxiety as well as thrill.

In this respect, placing *Movements* in the historical context of the early 1960s is instructive. The concept of the superhuman was in the foreground of public consciousness at the time, what with the recent developments in computer technology and rapid progress in space exploration. *Agon* had already been labelled an IBM ballet (see p. 165), responding to that company's momentous computer innovations during the 1950s, and at least two of Stravinsky's scores (*Agon* and *Variations*) had been labelled Space Age music, which, Joseph suggests, meant that most people thought they were inaccessible.[138] The USSR's Sputnik I was launched in 1957, and in 1961 Yuri Gagarin became the first man in space. Soon after *Movements*, in 1965, at the time of the first space walks, Frederick Ashton in Britain choreographed his celestial trio *Monotones*. All this is especially relevant to *Movements*. White is the colour of outer space film footage (and white leotards also featured in *Monotones*), and the upturned aerialism of Balanchine's ballet could well be interpreted as a metaphor for an expanded, interplanetary world in which life operates without the customary gravity force, and beyond known means of communication. Perhaps something akin to this was behind Taper's early description of the ballet as 'rarefied, remote, beyond good and evil, with an impersonal, godlike serenity' (see p. 195).

But allusions to outer space do nothing to remove the human charge in *Movements*, and this totally different way of looking at the ballet makes it anything but straightforwardly impersonal. Although offering a vision of something much larger than themselves, the *Movements* dancers still represent a community. The female group demonstrate that they become more oppressive as well as more active, and the soloists scatter copious clues about feelings and situations. When the same woman soloist reappears after the even more human *Monumentum*, I fancy that something of her personality goes with her into this new world. The man's back-up role has always been more one-dimensional, with some good steps, a tiger fascinated by the woman, but fundamentally reactive, protective, available for use.

Perhaps it is significant that Diana Adams was originally selected for the woman's role. Lamenting that Balanchine's ballet was made up of 'pinheads', the literary critic R.P. Blackmur said that she was the only one in the company 'with a proper face'.[139] Farrell also had a face, a human side from the start, sensual, voluptuous, sometimes vulnerable, willing to be manipulated; but in sharp contrast to this, most of the time she was hugely wilful, ambitious beyond belief, with a colossal stride. As the years progressed, she increased in authority and determination, showing even more bravery in this uncompromising environment, as the occasions of baby vulnerability metamorphosed into a kind of considered closing-off from the world and from her partner. Thus, her pleading arms (in the rehearsal film) as she folded her body at the end of Movement 3 transformed in the later film into arms that wrapped tightly around herself, a withdrawal into privacy, and the clarinet tremolo seemed to shift from sympathetic warmth to ice. But Farrell was always ready to burst out of any given situation and when, in Movement 1, she dropped like a stone across the man's extended arm and hung there like a rag doll (end of bar 30), there was still an intensity of presence that augured her next shock wave. Farrell embodied the stop-start, volatile character of the score: she was truly 'in-the-music'. Yet, when asked about what was most difficult about the ballet, she simply said, 'It was a lot of fun.'[140] Specific interpretive information she never discussed with Balanchine, nor does she do so herself with new dancers today. So what is the particular take on humanity within this work?

Randel has drawn up a detailed case for reading the *Movements* woman as modern sylph or swan maiden within the tradition of the nineteenth-century *ballet blanc*. She finds a series of hints, even if not a consistent narrative, that confirm the familiar ballet drama about a man's 'amorous pursuit of an elusive female' and an otherworldly group of women who come between them and, by the end, turn menacing like wilis or sylphides. Finally, the 'elusive female' breaks free of them all.[141] To summarise, Randel equates musical lyricism with the intimate aspects of the couple's relationship, and staccato with the ballerina's independent streak.[142] I would not say no to her scenario, though Farrell does, most vehemently. Rather, *she* speaks of the straightforward issues of space, time and energy, how the size of a dancer affects the look of movement and its musical timing, how the early or late completion of one step or gesture affects the dynamic of the next and, as a result – it is not calculated – how it feels to the dancer in the act of discovery and might be read by the audience. There is an admission of dancer temperament – d'Amboise more 'animal' than Lavery – but not as a dramatic component specific to this piece. In similar fashion, Farrell explained the pas de deux in *Agon*: 'The movement is the story' – the pas de deux was not about sex or power play.[143] Her case is well made – however, I would rather say yes to the possibility of several scenarios in *Movements*. It is intriguing that there has been such a diverse range of readings over the years – incidentally, none of these that I have found is like Randel's – and I have purposely injected yet another story about outer space into my own text. These various readings of course speak to some degree of the background and period of the reader, but the sheer range is significant in itself.

For the multi-vocal nature of *Movements* seems to be one of its most pronounced characteristics. Balanchine constantly subverts himself, with his anti-theatrical devices (which Randel admits), with the huge swings of movement dynamics that can be read as mood swings, with his allusion to contemporary consciousness as well as to the dance tradition and its familiar casting hierarchy. All this is supported by the fact that he himself offered no firmly stapled, articulated meanings to the performer. An example is the last of the five movements, the choreographic equivalent of musical decomposition. It starts with a solo, the woman charging towards the audience, and ends up (from bar 180) with a rapid series of conflicting images involving the man, although the focus is still on her. There is a violent outburst, a few playful steps ending with a dramatic flourish, a brisk pirouette, a sudden turn towards her partner and a big embrace (held while the group gathers behind, from bar 187), her curling into a ball in his arms, her dominant final standing position over him. The delay before the last low thud in the score would in more traditional circumstances encourage us to sense finality and catharsis when the thud arrives, but instead, in this context, we are left uncertain as to the significance of this pose, or even of any larger story that we might attach it to. For Farrell, the ending changed over the years. In her 1963 televised performance, there was gentleness; she looked down at d'Amboise as he curled his wrists up and around hers. In 1982, she struck a position over Lavery, and their arms never met. She was imperious. Neither version confirmed closure. As for the group, they simply do the movement, wearing the impassive facial expression that distances them from feeling, and that makes you question the very nature of role: do they really gather like a storm cloud, do they really crowd the soloist, are they really oppressive, or are these just light-touch changes of choreographic tactics? All in all, we are faced with shards of narrative possibility, like 'found' movement, meanings that attach and detach themselves, that happen without logical introduction or follow-through, that refuse to add up to a coherent whole, and that contribute to a profound effect of uncertainty.

For me, the one sure, all-absorbing feature is the physical energy and athleticism of the whole endeavour, the super-body that takes on challenge, with pleasure, determination and more than a touch of anxiety, that enjoys the enlarged possibilities of risk and size afforded by doublework, with a female backing group that reinforces the behaviour of the woman soloist. As for the couple presenting a metaphor for love, or sexual play, I just as much interpret what they do as if it were the joint effort of partner explorers.

The fragmented musical structure and its highly unsettled surface presumably prompted this choreographic approach. It refused closure, and Balanchine respected that fact, though he knew that the presence of people next to this music would automatically suggest specific meanings that the music alone could not provide. He and his dancers went out of their way to keep the dance open, and he may or may not have been conscious of the meanings that developed from his response to the music. In 1963, d'Amboise explained the dancers' role at the filmed public presentation at the Lincoln Center: 'We visually embody the music.'[144] Hardly the full story, but he is still right about the music here having the power – to undermine story at every turn.

As for music and choreography making these various meanings together, we are dealing with a subtle situation that involves the creativity, choices and, in the case of Farrell, changing perspectives of performers, as well as the choreographer's contribution, and again a great deal left unsaid. It is important to consider the dancers' learning process. Farrell's early experience was extraordinary. Initially she had no access to the music, and rehearsals took place in Adams's tiny living room and in silence. In her autobiography she recalls

> Jacques' and Diana's grunting, clapping, and singing ... I did learn the important counts, but most of the ballet was uncountable, and I was told to listen for 'the big boom', 'the second crash', 'the sixth silent note', or 'the sort of pretty music after the messy music'.[145]

So Farrell started out doing a lot through listening to verbal sound, although elsewhere she recalls most of all developing a strong sense of pulse: she went back to learn the counts when she had to revive the work. A few of these can be found in the piano rehearsal score that documents cues for 'Diana' (see Ex. 3.13) and 'Jacques'. Like Farrell, dancers today, partly because of the nature of the music, are still most likely to learn their movement through counts and percussive sounds rather than by careful listening to the score. (At the 1963 filmed rehearsal, the dancers apparently surprised Stravinsky and Craft by repeating a section to counts without the music.[146]) Later, through Nicholas Cook's concept of 'enabling similarity' (see p. 8), they might start listening and discover connections with musical sound that feed back as subtle changes to their movement. These are their own discoveries, not necessarily those of the choreographer. By doing this, they too structure the music in a new way and give it more specific meanings than it has in concert.

But do dancers necessarily listen and feel the dance pulse strongly enough? As early as 1971, Croce wrote about the 'sting' disappearing from some of Balanchine's serial ballets;[147] in that respect, the physical force, daring and precision of everyone involved in the 1963 rehearsal film of *Movements* is a revelation. But is anyone today snapping and tapping with the vigour of Balanchine on that film? Farrell recalls that he did not always rehearse like this, but, in those days, it seems, the dancers held that charge within their bodies and shared it. She also maintains that it is important to get the full group rehearsing together as soon as possible, sensing their combined energy: today's common practice of coaching the couple and the six women separately has its down side. It seems that both listening (which counts can prevent) and being utterly secure in knowing where the hidden pulse lies are crucial. Dancers need both to hear what can be heard and hear the unhearable, in order to articulate (without overplaying) the landmarks that Balanchine noted in the score, the convergences as well as the clever echoes and reverberations between media, and in order to sting as they did in the 1960s. It is a subtle game, but this is what makes *Movements* a distinctive statement, a more extreme vision than any other Balanchine leotard ballet; this is what enables us both to experience its fragmented stories and join Mr B 'in-the-music'.

Divertimento from 'Le Baiser de la fée'

With the *Divertimento from 'Le Baiser de la fée'*, we move into the very different world of Tchaikovsky–Stravinsky, but Balanchine looks back in time according to the terms of his late career, as a review or rearticulation of a past that is still present. A consideration of the tradition that a work creates about itself will be the focus of my analysis, and the resonances between it and other work of the past – memories, traces, even ghosts. Balanchine had already made a real, full *Baiser* for the American Ballet in 1937. This was a ballet in four scenes, 45 minutes long, reflecting the manner of the nineteenth-century ballet. Yet, after this, he kept going back to the work, clearly both fascinated and worried by it, reviving it for the Ballet Russe de Monte Carlo in 1940 and 1946, for the Paris Opéra in 1947 and for New York City Ballet in 1950, finally letting it out of the repertoire in 1951. Stravinsky demonstrated his approval by conducting not only the 1937 premiere, but also the 1946 revival and a performance in 1951 of the New York City Ballet production. Then, for the 1972 Festival, after the composer's death, Balanchine took the bold step of forming his own score arrangement and came up with the much more economical work that we still see today. Its title referred to the *Divertimento* concert suite that Stravinsky himself concocted in 1934 from the full ballet score.

Stravinsky used Hans Christian Andersen's tale *The Ice Maiden*, with its theme of the muse's fatal kiss, to compose a homage to Tchaikovsky. His score was dedicated to this composer:

As my object was to commemorate the work of Tchaikovsky, this subject seemed to me to be particularly appropriate as an allegory, the Muse having similarly branded Tchaikovsky with her fatal kiss.[148]

Stravinsky also borrowed many themes, mostly from Tchaikovsky's songs and piano music.

Set in the Swiss Alps in the 1850s, the ballet was initially choreographed by Nijinska for the Ballets Ida Rubinstein in 1928, with the following scenario:

The Fairy implants her magic kiss on a child at birth. When the child has grown to young manhood and good fortune and is about to be married, the Fairy reappears [first in the disguise of a Gyspy fortune-teller at a village fete, later as his Bride at the Mill where his real Bride lives] ... repeating the kiss she leads the young man (the artist in allegory) to abandon his bride and dwell with her forever.[149]

As indicated in the score, the four Scenes were:

1 The Lullaby in the Storm
2 A Village Fete
3 At the Mill
4 The Lullaby of the Land Beyond Time and Space.

The critic André Levinson recognised that the ballet prototype for the story was *La Sylphide* (1832), and indeed the whole style of the Nijinska ballet referenced the romantic ballet era. There was a wealth of action and characters, with the young man and bride named Rudi and Babette as in the original Andersen tale.[150] Stravinsky had reservations about Nijinska's choreography, and the reception at the premiere was cool, with his own contribution criticised as retrogressive pastiche (see p. 51). Yet she revived the piece for the Teatro Colón in Buenos Aires in 1933 and 1936; the Basle Stravinsky archive contains several positive reviews of the 1936 revival, also marking the occasion when Stravinsky conducted the ballet.

Balanchine's 1937 *Baiser* was a long-tutu ballet, neoclassical for the most part in movement style, a modernisation of nineteenth-century idioms, with local colour in the Village Fete Scene, elements of folk dance, a brass band, a shooting competition and even some yodelling. Famously assertive that ballet should make sense through dance alone, and concerned that this ballet of transformations and complex relationships between characters was not readily understandable, he kept tinkering with it. The scenario invited a number of questions: Who is the grown man at the Village Fete, and how do we know his relationship to the baby in the first Scene? Why should the Gypsy/Fairy lead the Young Man to his Fiancée, her rival for his attention? Do we see the Young Man as an artist figure, and how can this allegorical level suggested in Stravinsky's programme be made clear?

There were technical problems too, sets that needed to be changed between scenes. Balanchine decided to choreograph the long, original curtain-down interludes, thus taking liberties with Stravinsky's strict score directives (see p. 50). Between Scenes 2 and 3, the Fairy led the Young Man on his journey to his Bride, and between Scenes 3 and 4, the Bride searched for the Young Man, now taken from her.[151] Balanchine was also dissatisfied by what seemed to be an overlong, quiet theatrical ending, with a lot of music in Stravinsky's typical timeless style of musical apotheosis – a point of agreement with a number of critics. Here the Fairy metaphorically glided with him into the water, sucking him into her power or, in another version, seen at a great height, she forced him to climb up a colossal net to reach her in her Ice Kingdom.[152] Critical reactions were mixed, but many saw or at least came to see great things in the ballet as Balanchine undertook his revisions, despite the structural problems.

The writer Minna Lederman was one of the ballet's most ardent supporters, and her eloquent description of the 1946 revival is worth quoting in detail:

At the opening it was wonderful to see how Tallchief, young, grand, implacable, carried off the central role. And how Danilova danced the mill scene with delicate, contorted grace and the look of a tender Modigliani.

Le Baiser is not major Stravinsky yet it is one of the great ballets of our time. Year after year Balanchine's Alpine Fairy, the terrifying nature deity out of Andersen's fable, looms larger as a conception of genius. Among choreographers Balanchine alone projects such forms. His images evoke no time or place, they have no atmosphere. Their force is naked and direct; they seize on the mind and become basic matter to which one refers more transient experiences. In several passages *Le Baiser* exhibits this power at its highest intensity.

First there is the Fairy's glittering appearance with her black Shadow. She swoops over the baby in devouring benevolence and the figure beside her moves ominously through the same arc of space – a device that fills the theatre with instant mystery and dread.

Later she is herself her Shadow, prowling through the village. She descends on the Boy in a series of constricting rectangles to wrestle for his soul. Rough and brutal, she thrusts him from left to right until she seizes his head in triumph and forces it to the ground.

And finally there is the searing encounter in the mill. She confronts him suddenly, a towering apparition and, helpless, he embraces and carries her rigid form away with him. Raising her veil, he rushes off in panic but returns in painful submission. Dragging one knee after another, he pulls the Fairy from behind him, down over his body in an extreme arabesque penchée. Her head seems to touch the ground. She draws back and we see them both tense and anguished. So, their hands locked, they move in an open-and-shut diagonal across the stage with an effect of mounting, cruel sensuality. The Fairy then glides with her prey into the sea and the allegory fulfils itself. By soft, underwater cuffing (a version new this season), she beats out his last breath, his last resistance …

Lederman stressed the dark qualities that infused the ballet:

> For me this work has none of the charm and gaiety that endear it to many others. The hard sunlight, the yodelling Swiss peasants, seem blatant, a coarse relief for its central theme, the despair of human fate.

She was also struck by the 'tension of the … Tchaikovskian phrases' and 'spare sound of every instrument' under the composer's baton:

> His beat permits no swooning retards to soften one up, no brilliant telescoping of allegro measures. The ballet then takes on a truly spacious proportion.[153]

Despite the problems posed by the full *Baiser* and scenario, Balanchine was only one of many to choreograph this score. Fairy stories are, after all, a strong part of ballet tradition. The *SGD* database records twenty-six settings (other than Balanchine's edited version) and three more of Stravinsky's *Divertimento* concert score. For the full setting, all the evidence to date reveals a heavy reliance on the original scenario, with the most marked deviations dating from after the composer's death. A strong signal is that the score title has almost always been retained, or, to much the same effect, the Andersen title 'The Ice Maiden' has been substituted. There is also the tendency to refer to neo-romantic/classical nineteenth-century style, with a folk element where appropriate. For instance, within the British repertory, there is Kenneth MacMillan's setting for the Royal Ballet (1960), a homage to Frederick Ashton, and unusually romantic-classical for MacMillan, although he pursued his regular theme of alienation, focusing on the plight of the girl, not the Young Man or Ice Maiden. Lynn Seymour, who danced this role, explained: 'he identified with the betrayed bride who is left in the lurch'.[154]

James Kudelka emphasised in the programme note for his 1996 Birmingham Royal Ballet setting that he had been inspired by Petipa's romantic ballet themes and classical ballet structures. Within a pared-down production that favoured swift lighting changes rather than the cumbersome shifting of sets and props, he slightly modified the story to make the seductive Gypsy a separate character and dancer in her own right, even though clearly a memory of the Ice Maiden, and her kiss too was a fatal stab. In the third Scene, both the Gypsy and the Bride beckoned and taunted the Young Man before he succumbed forever to the power of the Ice Maiden.[155]

Supporting information about the ballets listed in the database indicates that a few choreographers enlarged upon Stravinsky's idea of the Artist and his Muse. In his *Le Baiser* (1981) for the Geneva Ballet, Oscar Araiz's central figure was the Artist as outsider, negotiating between his Muse and a woman from everyday life. He removed the Swiss locale, making his ballet a study in black and white.[156] In 1989, for Tulsa Ballet Theatre in the USA, Peter Anastos took the allegory into a different direction, referring in the programme note to the 'mystery' of Tchaikovsky and Stravinsky, then to 'the artists who are born (awaken), who die (leave the world), and who are resurrected in the creations they leave us and in the "kiss" they bestow on our own imaginations'.

For Frankfurt Ballet (1972), John Neumeier employed the character names Rudi and Babette from the Andersen (and Nijinska) original and returned to the Swiss setting, but introduced further layers of meaning, including a psychological complication in the form of Rudi's Sehnsucht, another dancer, 'his subconscious yearning self' or 'longing', who draws him towards the world of dreams and memory. There was additional story and music: a prologue that was the beginning of the Wedding Celebration, and where a stranger sings 'Nur wer die Sehnsucht kennt' (in English translation, 'None but the lonely heart', the Tchaikovsky/Goethe song that Stravinsky uses when the Fairy leads the Young Man to her kingdom), and then gives Rudi a kiss. That is the fatal kiss, and she is the Fairy in disguise. Not only the song was introduced: there was also a short piano piece from Tchaikovsky's *Feuillet d'Album*, Op. 19, No. 3, so Prologue music related referentially to both the real and unreal world that featured later in Stravinsky's part of the ballet. Was this an allegory about the fated artist? The programme note says that it was,[157] but it was also about Neumeier, for his ballet was in part homage to Balanchine, as if he were seeking inspiration through another person's work. His Scene 1 Remembrance (a *ballet blanc*) was a step back in time to Rudi's childhood; it was neoclassical and dressed in Balanchine-style white practice clothes. Here, the Fairy makes her first appearance, and she kisses the child Rudi at the end, a kiss that is also 'felt' by the grown Rudi and his Other. The critic Anna Kisselgoff noted actual quotes from *Apollo* later in the ballet.[158] Scenes 2–4 continued the story in Stravinsky's vein, but with Rudi's Sehnsucht becoming increasingly powerful as he led Rudi to his doom.

In 1985, Maurice Béjart introduced a still more radical development from the original *Baiser* scenario, without getting rid of the basics. Opening with a verbal explanation of the subject matter and sprinkling the Stravinsky with Tchaikovsky interpolations, Béjart made his Young Man a chosen artist as star dancer, who needs to sacrifice living in the real world in order to fulfil his genius potential. One scene shows him in a St Petersburg ballet studio, which links him neatly with the Tchaikovsky/Maryinsky tradition. The three central characters are still recognisable. The Young Man becomes part of a mass ending where everyone holds up baby dolls, perhaps as a reminder to him of how his fate was sealed at birth.[159]

The *Divertimento* concert suite settings include Peter Martins's *Sinfonia* (1993), choreography to the violin and piano transcription of the first two movements, those parts that Balanchine did not use for *his* Divertimento. But it was a homage to the earlier choreographer, set for three women and one man, a neoclassical ballet that made reference to *Apollo*. Mark Baldwin set the whole of the orchestral piece for Scottish Ballet and called his ballet *Ae Fond Kiss* (1996), after Robert Burns's poem about loss of a first love. It was a plotless, neoclassical piece and the programme note tells us that 'the women control the action', but their domination was not serious, and the tone was playful.[160] So was the title and the programming, alluding to the kiss of the fairy but also to the original story's link with its nineteenth-century model: Baldwin's work was billed before a performance of *La Sylphide* on the same programme.

Balanchine's 1972 *Divertimento* was a radical new version, if indeed it can be called a version at all, of his former full ballet – I shall return to that point many times. For now, if we do call it a version of the full ballet, it is certainly vastly more stripped down than most other *Baisers*. It is an odd construction, using only 23 minutes or so of the full ballet score, mostly from its second half, with no overt narrative and no identified characters. On the surface, it is a typical, plotless Balanchine ballet about its music. Croce was one of several critics inspired to write most eloquently about the work, and her fascination with, but doubts about, the new piece are significant. The *Divertimento*, she says:

> has always been something more than a divertissement and something less than a drama .... [it] is one of the most superbly crafted pieces that have come from Balanchine in recent years, and McBride [Patricia McBride], Tomasson, and the girls always perform it with exceptional polish, but it's basically footnote material, a collection of thoughts about a lost work of art.[161]

The 1972 structure was fundamentally an expanded pas de deux: first an ensemble dance for thirteen women (including the leading woman and two other soloists), then a central pas de deux (adagio, then solos for the man and woman), and finally an allegro ensemble Coda including brief sequences for the soloists. Balanchine had doubts about this ballet too. In 1974, he added a new pas de deux with ensemble at the end, an elegiac statement about the separation of lovers to balance the tone of the man's solo. It did not convince Croce:

> The new scene matches Tomasson's solo in mood; the question is whether it's just a bit of tacked-on drama or an extension into new territory that resets the proportions of the *Divertimento* as we've known it up to now.[162]

A number of viewers felt that there was something of the old piece left in the new one, but what? First, of course, there is the ghost of Tchaikovsky, perhaps even more than a ghost, in the music. But ghosts abound in the *Divertimento* choreography too: it is thoroughly haunted. It has proved extremely enlightening to analyse both the music and the interplay between the music and the choreography in Balanchine's *Divertimento*, and with a glance back to his full *Baiser*, for this has revealed many points of resonance and cross-reference between the early and late ballet.

The main video resources that I have used and compared are:

- a reconstruction from the original ballet of the two pas de deux (the Young Man, with the Gypsy and then with his real Bride-to-be) and of the Bride's solo (1996–7 reconstructions by Maria Tallchief and Frederic Franklin, who danced in revivals of the original ballet);
- Peter Boal dancing the 1972 man's solo, which used the Gypsy/Young Man pas de deux music;
- a video of Tomasson coaching that solo (this solo will be my main focus for analysis);
- silent film footage from the early Ballet Russe de Monte Carlo and New York City Ballet productions.[163]

First of all, the *Divertimento* represents Balanchine boldly shaping a score, in a sense 'composing' it for his own ends. The extent of Balanchine's musical editing in general is not widely known,[164] but my point here is that *Divertimento* is perhaps his boldest reconception, and the composer was not in a position to complain. For it is not simply a matter of using largely the second half of the ballet score; nor is it a matter of using Stravinsky's *Divertimento* concert suite. This was one of the big surprises of my research, for every source, including recent New York City Ballet programme notes, claims that Balanchine drew his score from Stravinsky's *Divertimento* and the full ballet score.[165] So do the recommendations to today's City Ballet audiences for follow-up listening – in principle, wonderfully useful handouts at performances. Only recordings of Stravinsky's *Divertimento* are listed. Eager audiences must end up rather confused. In fact, Balanchine's arrangement proves that Stravinsky's concert suite *Divertimento* had nothing whatsoever to do with Balanchine's thinking: *his Divertimento*. Table 3 shows the format of Stravinsky's *Divertimento* concert suite in relation to the original ballet score, and next to it Balanchine's own score construction.

Balanchine used nothing from the first and second scene of the ballet score except the pas de deux for the Gypsy and the Young Man, which is not included in Stravinsky's suite, and he recontextualised this within Scene 3 material. He constructed his score as follows. He commenced with Scene 3 music, but made his own edited version of the beginning of this – the cutting is quite different from Stravinsky's in his *Divertimento*. He included the Entrée that was omitted from Stravinsky's suite, followed it with an insertion of the Gypsy/Young Man pas de deux from Scene 2 as the man's solo, and continued with the rest of the Scene 3 pas de deux music until the end. Then, he made his own ending! Perhaps he felt that Stravinsky's concert suite ending with the Coda was insufficiently 'happy', with too much *tranquillo* and *espressivo* and too few triumphal chords, so he cut some of the quiet music and reiterated a passage of six loud chords to make a strong ending. (This ending is recorded in a 1973 Berlin film, incidentally, one of fifteen ballets filmed that year under the auspices of Reiner Moritz Productions.) In 1974, Balanchine restored the ballet-score ending of the Coda, and added music from the final Scene, none of which was in the concert suite. But again, he edited the music as he saw fit, making an extensive cut in fact, perhaps with a view to the overall proportions of his work.

One might well ask why Balanchine called his work *Divertimento* at all. It was not Stravinsky's *Divertimento*. *Divertimento* is a musical title generally implying a lightness of character, and Stravinsky got rid of most of what I would call the 'anxious' music, while Balanchine went out of his way to keep this in. Perhaps the title worked better in 1972 with the 'happy' ending, although this obviously did not satisfy him, and, as we have seen, he went on to add more material and changed the tone of his ending. But the old title, ill fitting and misleading as it may seem, remained.

Now, looking at the 1974 work, what does this new Balanchine construction signify? I shall look broadly across the whole piece first. The drama, if we believe there is one to talk about, and I do, is telescoped: there is still the crux situation of a search for happiness ending tragically, the bonding and separation of lovers, and a sense that the outcome is governed by the hand of fate (now somewhere up above, outside the dance). Several writers have observed that the corps de ballet seem to be villagers who turn into messengers of fate or 'agents of doom' who remorselessly divide the couple during the final section. But there are hints of trouble even during the opening ensemble with its squalls, flurries and concentration of uneasy rhythms, Balanchine adding to Stravinsky's flighty example. There is also the briefest glimpse of a gesture of desperation, the women's parallel arms flung forward from arabesque tendu, an image that shows its full

Table 3. Diagram of score structures: *Le Baiser de la fée* and *Divertimento.*

Stravinsky: **Ballet Score** ***Le Baiser de la fée*** **(1928)**	Stravinsky: ***Divertimento from Le Baiser de la fée*** **concert suite (1934)**	**Balanchine Score:** ***Divertimento from Le Baiser de la fée*** **(1972/74)**
Scene 1 The Lullaby in the Storm	Sinfonia: Scene 1, lacking [27]–[39]	
Scene 2 A Village Fete	Danses Suisses: Scene 2 up to [96], omitting music of Pas de deux for Young Man and Gypsy that ends Scene 2	
Scene 3 At the Mill (including Pas de deux for Young Man and Bride: Entrée, Adagio, Bride's Variation, Coda)	Scherzo: slightly shortened version of Scene 3 opening	Scene 3: opening edited by Balanchine, then: Entrée and Adagio from Pas de deux for Young Man and Bride
	Pas de deux: Adagio, Bride's Variation, Coda (with concert ending). Entrée omitted	Insertion: Scene 2 Pas de deux for Young Man and Gypsy (edited by Balanchine) – set as man's solo Pas de deux for Young Man and Bride: Bride's Variation, Coda (latter edited by Balanchine, end of 1972 version)
Scene 4 Epilogue: The Lullaby of the Land Beyond Time and Space		Scene 4: edited by Balanchine, an extensive cut (end of 1974 version)

impact at the climax of the lovers' final private meeting. Writers have observed too the parallel between the Young Man/Groom of the original and the un-named leading male soloist in the 1972/74 piece, because there is also a notion of the leading female soloist being both Bride and Fairy. They have begun to sense presences and ghosts. Croce wrote tellingly about the female 'character':

> The bride of the original tale becomes the fairy, and this, too, recalls a tradi-tional Balanchine theme – the heroine whose aspect flickers between vampire and goddess.[166]

On a number of occasions, we see her lock him in her embrace or pull him towards her, images that read ambiguously, of love and need, but also of danger and threat.

At the same time, there is clearer reference than in the early full ballet to Petipa/Tchaikovsky-associated conventional formal structure, in a pas de deux with a separate male as well as female solo. There are references too to Petipa/Ivanov-style framing ensembles that are both formal *danse d'école* and devices for hiding and separating a pair of lovers, as in *Swan Lake* and the vision scene in *The Sleeping Beauty*.

The tension between conventional form/abstraction and narrative content certainly exists, identified as a concern by Croce in the 1970s. For me today, it refreshes the notion of tale, and the awkwardness of the juxtaposition is in itself compelling. Balanchine played with this tension tentatively in *Firebird* in 1949, formalising the original concept of the ballet to match Stravinsky's *Suite* ar-rangement of his score, then again in *Swan Lake* (1951), a development of Act II of the original four-act ballet with the mime removed, and even more boldly with his exact formal recapitulation (of dance and music) during the 'narrative' slow movement of *Scotch Symphony* (1952, Mendelssohn).[167]

Divertimento is another work full of odd twists and turns, continuing in the line of Balanchine's abstract versus narrative experiments. The man's solo is strange and substantial, weighed down with potential content. The woman's solo is unusually lightweight in juxtaposition with it. This is the wrong way round, and especially in terms of what we had come to expect from Balanchine at the time when he made this piece. The solo material for the man here and in *Duo Concertant* (1972) represented a new direction for Balanchine, the first in a series of substantial choreographies for men (especially Peter Martins and Ib Andersen) made during the 1970s. Nothing is straightforward in the applica-tion of convention, but again, the subversion of convention, the resulting awk-wardness, holds meaning.

There is more to say about the effect of Balanchine's musical shaping and editing processes. His tendency is to make the music more compact, to give a

greater sense of urgency to a score that demonstrates less of Stravinsky's modernist manipulation of sources than usual. Balanchine, as we have already seen,
does the work instead, and now we can see that he also made the link between
some of the numbers far more abrupt than did Stravinsky. The insertion of the
man's solo music into a new context demonstrates this. Originally, after the
Swiss dances in bright D major in the Village Fete Scene, there was a lengthy
transition to A minor (during which the Fairy entered); A minor was the key of
the Gypsy duet, and the note A was the link note into the Mill Scene. Then,
during the Mill Scene, there was a transition passage between the Adagio (E flat
major) and the Bride's solo (G minor). In Balanchine's 1972 score, there is an
abrupt shift from the E flat major of the Adagio to the A minor of the man's solo
– a distant tonal relationship without any transition – and equally, after his solo,
another abrupt harmonic shift into the G minor of the woman's variation.

We could interpret the new construction as simply a matter of Balanchine not
wanting actually to compose any transitions himself. Speculation apart, now,
our job is to examine the *impact* of what he did. In effect, he highlights the
separate components of form, pulling, as I have already said, against narrative
implications.

In the analytical documentary *Music Dances*, the man's solo is examined in
terms of structure and phrasing in relation to music and reference to nineteenth-century characteristics. Here, in a rereading, the 'narrative' layer is
added to the discussion, though not, I hasten to add, 'narrative' in any traditional linear sense.

A number of writers singled out this solo as the centre of gravity or emotional
heart of the 1972 work. It had a sense of mystery. It intrigued them. Nancy
Goldner observed:

> The solo emits the tension of uncertainty, as when the stage darkens before
> something happens. Balanchine and Stravinsky take you to the brink of
> Event. The choreography becomes more febrile and unpredictable, and the
> music becomes more pressing and anticipatory.[168]

She explains most persuasively how the effect is achieved solely through modifying the classical vocabulary, not through literal gesture or facial expression.

After the bright opening ensemble dance and the grand romance of the Adagio, the man finds himself alone. This was always a dangerous situation in the
earlier ballet, and his disturbance emerges again in 1972. Sometimes he waves
his arms curiously, as if under a spell or casting a spell. He begins moving simply
on and around a spot upstage centre. The choreography later expands into circles around the stage, each one bigger and longer than the last. We associate
some of the movement with virtuoso nineteenth-century male solos, but with a

Ill.5. Peter Boal in *Divertimento from 'Le Baiser de la fée'*, man's solo, choreography by George Balanchine, New York City Ballet.

difference: potential symmetries are disrupted. A striking turn centre stage finishes just as the next musical phrase begins, so there is no stop: the effect is of overlapping, seamlessness. Later, the man pulls back briefly into a tightly spaced pirouette and petit jeté sequence on the diagonal, facing downstage left, allowing a brief lull in the tension. He moves boldly out into space again on a new horn melody (see Ex. 3.14), before getting trapped into an obsessive series of pirouettes that keep turning back on themselves, oddly placed and balanced.

Ex. 3.14. *Le Baiser de la fée*, music used for the man's solo in Balanchine's *Divertimento from 'Le Baiser de la fée'*, horn melody.

Then the music shifts gear, giving way to a series of rising-scale gestures and, as Paul Gellen writes,

> In a series of croisés assemblés élancés that cleave the air, he falls in a broken motion to the knee.[169]

Indeed, most poignantly, the man's action is half grace, half stumble. This is the last of the circles. The tension between earth and sky is unusually exaggerated in this solo, signifying an outside presence that drives the man and yet curtails his freedom. He can soar, but he also shows the burden of weight and the effort of striving.

An examination of the music and of choreomusical relations tells us more. There are three cuts by the hand of Balanchine, and their effect is to increase the sense of urgency. Two of the cuts remove what seems in retrospect to be transitional material. In the original Stravinsky, after the opening gurgling tune, a new motif is heard at [104], which is later slowed down and played at increased volume (see Ex. 3.15). Balanchine chooses not to let us hear how this motif begins, but jolts us straight into the enlarged, loud version at [105]-1.

Later, at [109], he cuts out another six bars, and again there is a sense of abrupt change. At [110], the horn melody begins (see Ex. 3.14), the start of an 8-bar passage that Stravinsky wanted to have repeated, but Balanchine omits the repeat and rushes us on towards the musical climax. The treatment matches that of Balanchine's arrangement of the score as a whole. He emphasises twentieth-century modernist, abrupt shifts and dislocations, urgency, more than Stravinsky does in this particular score.

At the same time, Balanchine crosses the musical phrasing with aplomb. The pirouette and petit jeté sequence mentioned earlier (at [108] in the score) is structured as a 9-count dance unit shown twice and riding boldly against the musical material structured regularly in 2s and 4s. The circles around the stage begin without the prompt of any phrase beginning in the music. These instances of rhythmic cross-relation combine to create an effect of instability, floating, or swimming dangerously, and often one of extended continuity between moments

Ex. 3.15. *Divertimento from 'Le Baiser de la fée',* man's solo, as in the New York City Ballet piano rehearsal score, showing a passage cut by Balanchine.

of resolution. The reference points in the music and dance are separate and work against each other. Moments of combined, accented articulation are rare, and when they do occur, they stand out emphatically as moments of power.

It is impossible not to consider meaning, even when focusing on structural detail. But we can now consider the connotational values of this solo from other standpoints, references within the musical score, and references back to the lost ballet. We go in search of ghosts.

First, within the musical score, Stravinsky's two borrowings from Tchaikovsky are not straightforward. The opening gurgling melody is from the song *What sadness, what sweetness*, one of *Six Romances* (Op. 6, 1870) that might have been written in the wake of a love affair, addressed to the lost love.[170] Transformed from A major to A minor, it now takes on sinister overtones, appropriate signal for the Gypsy in the original ballet, even more so for the dangerous figure in the ether for whom the male soloist in Balanchine's *Divertimento* might be yearning. Later, at [113] (developed from a hint at [111]), there is a reference to Tchaikovsky's fifth symphony, which has long been read as a piece about foreboding – for instance, by Massine when he choreographed the symphony in 1933 and called it *Les Présages*. Stravinsky quotes from the symphony's slow second movement (bar 46), a theme that has been interpreted as an outpouring of personal longing.[171] But in Stravinsky's hands, it becomes, on the violins, a warning (with the flutes, piccolo, oboes and trumpet bearing it in counterpoint, see Exs. 3.16a and b). It is interesting that it links organically with motifs from the first scene of the original ballet, at the point of the Fairy's first fateful encounter with the Young Man as a child.

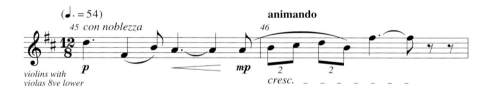

Ex. 3.16a. Tchaikovsky *Symphony No. 5*, slow movement, theme quoted by Stravinsky.

Other, timbral echoes from Scene 1 of the ballet score are telling. Balanchine's second cut ends with the break into the horn melody (see Ex. 3.14). In the first scene of *Baiser*, the horn is clearly the Fairy's instrument: she owns two broad horn melodies, the second indicating her tenderness as she gathers the child within her embrace. At this precise point in the man's solo, the man starts to show the will to soar, pulling up to relevé, arching upwards, even if he is to be repeatedly broken, doomed. Coaching the solo, Tomasson is emphatic about

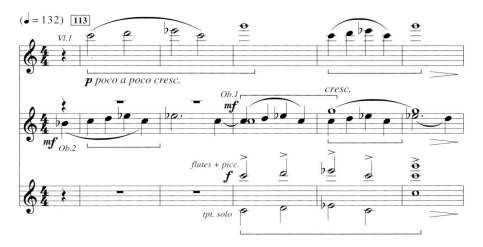

Ex. 3.16b. *Divertimento from 'Le Baiser de la fée'*, man's solo, Stravinsky's contrapuntal treatment of Tchaikovsky's theme.

getting up 'on top of your leg right away'[172] – the urgent call of the high note is physically articulated again and again. This is already a high point of anxiety in the choreography; considering the connection with the lost ballet ghosting behind it focuses the moment even more. It is this passage that leads to the warning violins. Another example: just after the pirouette and petit jeté sequence (at [108]+6), cackling bassoons, flute, oboes and horn remind us momentarily of Carabosse in *The Sleeping Beauty*.[173] This is another timbral feature borrowed from Scene 1, when the Fairy's attendant spirits pursue the mother until she relinquishes her child – another whiff of another world.

We can trace yet more ghosts by comparing the choreography of the original Gypsy pas de deux with that of Tomasson's solo. In short, the Gypsy gets the Young Man increasingly into her power, and then, during the soft scalewise gestures at the end of their pas de deux, drives him towards his destiny. It is interesting to compare the spatial arrangement of the original and 1972 choreographies. Both start upstage centre and expand from that point, there are circles, there is a diagonal passage facing the same downstage left corner, and both dances end with a departure via the downstage right corner. In the 1937 setting, there is the powerful image of the Gypsy coming up behind the Young Man and pushing him towards his exit point by extending her pointed finger over his shoulder, again and again. But there are repeating gestures still today, during the final circling of the stage, even if they are not so literal. At one point too, the Gypsy waved her arms to and fro as if making mayhem, not unlike the curious arm-waving of Tomasson years later. Finally, the arrival of the horn melody was also dramatically important in the original pas de deux: another striking image, the moment when the two became fiercely locked together, and they walked forwards jabbing their toes into the floor as they went. Balanchine simply told Tomasson that he could not remember the original, but that this was the music for the fortune-teller Gypsy and that he was after something 'a little mysterious'.[174] So Tomasson embodied something of the old ballet through embodying the music.

Whether these parallels between the two *Baiser* choreographies were part of Balanchine's consciousness or subconsciousness hardly matters. I find the connections compelling for anyone who knows the full Stravinsky score, and indeed perhaps for those who have seen and remembered Balanchine's early ballet. It is fascinating that other *Baisers* have likewise singled out the horn tune in this dance, as a special moment recalling the Fairy and her power. In MacMillan's ballet (1960), the Gypsy/Fairy dances a solo passage at this point. In Kudelka's 1996 setting, the Gypsy (a separate dancer in this production), suddenly becomes a memory of the Ice Maiden: her four servants, introduced in Scene 1, suddenly return, to hold the Gypsy aloft, towering above the Young Man.

There are plenty of examples of ambiguity and anxiety elsewhere in this ballet. Goldner described the odd effect of Tomasson's return in the ensemble Coda of the Pas de deux with the Bride, a short solo that was 'over in a flash' (at [189]):

> Again, Tomasson's role sends the ballet soaring. This time he does a series of low grands jetés around the stage. Instead of springing off the front foot into a jump, he pushes off the back foot. Momentum comes not from a forward drive, but, it seems, from an unseen propeller pushing Tomasson from behind. Instead of facing the circular line of direction, this body is at an oblique angle to it. His weight pulls away from the center of the circle in which he travels, yet he stays in orbit defying centrifugal force.[175]

A number of force lines are implied: backwards and forwards, into the circle and out. I would add to these up and down, because that strange arrangement of body weight increases the sense of downward pull, a grounding force, and an exertion to counter it. I would also add that the sense of awkwardness is greatly increased by the arrangement of the sequence, which dancers would describe as in 7 counts against the clear 2, 4, 8 count structure of the musical rhythm. The man's Coda solo arrives in the midst of an otherwise merry part of the ballet, bringing with it a tinge of discomfort, but perhaps those corps de ballet women are also reminders of an army of Wilis, implacable with their hops in arabesque and marching piqués?

Even the least anxious parts of the *Divertimento* hide ghosts. It is fascinating to trace the history of the woman's solo that was originally the Bride's solo in the Mill Scene of the full ballet. We have records of what amounts to three 'versions':

Franklin's 1996/97 reconstruction on Nichol Hlinka of the solo as he remembered it from the Ballet Russe de Monte Carlo production of the 1940s, a 1951
performance on silent film by Tanaquil Le Clercq of New York City Ballet, and
the 1972 choreography that we still see today.[176] The 1951 performance is incomplete: the film does not show the choreography to the musical recapitulation. (It was shot at Jacob's Pillow, and, with Franklin as supervising artist, a
piano part was added in 1996 by Nancy McDill. A note accompanying the 1996
film states that the choreography was 'modified for this performance to accom-
modate the size of the stage at Jacob's Pillow'.)

Hardly surprisingly, the two early versions are very similar in terms of actual
steps. The big surprise is that the Le Clercq performance (but not the Hlinka)
clearly shows signs of 1972 developments, in terms of body and spatial attitudes, aspects of movement style that in many ways forge a more compelling link
than mere steps. Both the 1951 and 1972 versions feature a number of sequences of steps rooted around one spot. Towards the end (from [179], bars 23–
26), there is a passage where the very vivacious Le Clercq shifts forward and
back, changing diagonal facing, eight shifts in all (16 counts), almost like playful
doodling, and the movement of her upper body and arms is free, as in extempori-
sation. (Hlinka covers much more space at this point.) At exactly the same place
in the 1972 ballet, the woman similarly doodles forward and back, changing
facing and arms, and it is interesting that McBride, who premiered this role,
refers to it as her '"arm" variation. ... Mr. B didn't set any arms, although he gave
me some suggestions. You have freedom to do what's most natural with the
arms, but, of course, the variations are very classical, so that's a guide.'[177] So, we
might ask, was the doodling effect only the result of a smaller space at the Pillow? Again, are there ghosts of earlier choreographies, or at least the unforgettable memory of Le Clercq, to be found in the last of Balanchine's settings of this
music too? Furthermore, all three versions cross the musical phrasing and metre, touches of choreographic waywardness, at exactly the same points in the
music. In the first half of the solo (from [176]+5; bars 11–18), Balanchine rides
over the 3+5 bar musical structure, continuing with regular 8-count (2-bar)
dance units over the musical division. Then, for what became the doodling section, he ignores the shifts between 4- and 6-count units – he maintains the 4-
count patterning that he establishes at the start.

The multiple layers of reference in *Divertimento from 'Le Baiser de la Fée'* make
it curious and untidy, and the viewer could well feel insecure in their presence. I
am reminded of Croce's fascinating 1974 judgement on this work, and of how,
faced with a structurally diffuse *Mozartiana* (Balanchine–Tchaikovsky) in 1981,
she similarly willed its unity and coherence.[178] But today, surely there is less
demand than there used to be for organic wholeness and coherent form, and
more ready acceptance of instability, being left in a state of disarray, wonder-

ment, even hovering dangerously. Writing about the *Divertimento*, Croce longed to see the full ballet again, believing that Americans were now culturally ready, now far more familiar with the full-length Tchaikovsky classics and able to believe in transformations and relationships that were not wholly explicable in visual terms.[179]

But Balanchine was already one step ahead, asking still more of his audience, hoping perhaps that we would consider inheritance, and learn to read and accept a ballet that is as much about what is not immediately perceptible in it as much as what is, hoping to share something of what clearly haunted him, and even hoping that some of the traces of the past might affect the way we perceive the detail of his new work. Music was the pivotal component in his quest, the medium through which the past could be embodied. I could suggest too that Balanchine was looking to the future, interested in mixing conventional, even conflicting, modes of ballet delivery, and understanding that we might not always have the same demands for unity and for the tying-up of loose ends. The strategy is modernist/postmodernist, but I would not want to end with that kind of reductive statement. I would rather stress that Balanchine used the newer conventions of a newer era to make one of his most poetic and tantalising statements.

Coda: Deconstructing the Balanchine–Stravinsky canon – The challenge of other voices

The *SGD* database prompted the Coda to this chapter. Returning to the notion of a Balanchine–Stravinsky canon, it underlines the fact that Stravinsky's *Apollo* and *Agon* represent production histories that contrast starkly with those of the other big ballet scores such as *Noces* and *Sacre*, the case studies of later chapters. More than any other Stravinsky score, *Apollo* and *Agon* are marked indelibly by the hand of one choreographer, Balanchine, and they are used here as focus for an examination of the distribution of Balanchine–Stravinsky and the status and image of this collaborative institution around the world. *Apollo* also became by far the most popular Balanchine ballet in the international repertory, with *Agon* and *Rubies* next in line. During the course of the analysis, I shall raise questions about canonic status, also asking what it does to our understanding of Stravinsky's music, whilst reviewing the contributions of other contestants, other choreographers who have dared to use *Apollo* and *Agon*.

Balanchine–Stravinsky ballets were not always so tightly associated with Balanchine. Early on, after *Apollo* (which was first staged by Adolph Bolm – see p. 49), the pattern was rapidly established that the Balanchine ballet premiere of a Stravinsky score took place first, and then other choreographers followed. Two interesting points flow from this. First, as time went on, those other choreographers moved in with increasing rapidity as soon as a new ballet score was announced. Looking at a two-year time-span after the Balanchine premieres, the database reveals the following pattern of productions:

1 after Balanchine's *Jeu de cartes*, New York, 27 April 1937, two more settings: Valeria Kratina, Dresden, 13 October 1937; Pia Mlakar and Pino Mlakar, Zurich, 1938;

2 after Balanchine's *Orpheus*, New York, 28 April 1948, three more settings: Aurel Milloss, Venice, 9 September 1948; David Lichine, Paris, 16 November 1948; Rudolf Kölling, Munich, 17 September 1949;

3 after Balanchine's *Agon*, New York, 1 December 1957, four more settings: Otto Krüger, Dusseldorf, 27 January 1958; Tatiana Gsovsky, Berlin, 3 May 1958; Yvonne Georgi, Hanover, 21 May 1958; Kenneth MacMillan, London, 20 August 1958.

This acceleration towards new ballet scores could have reflected Stravinsky's growing status as 'the world's greatest living composer'; it could also have reflected the international swing towards neoclassicism, which his scores championed. This leads to the second point, which is one about possession. Within a short time after the first five *Agon* productions had taken place, the alternatives to both Balanchine's *Agon* and his *Apollo* start to dry up. The number of new productions of both these ballets diminishes dramatically during the 1960s. We are left with only eleven uses of *Agon* recorded in the database, the smallest number for any Stravinsky ballet score. But why this change?

The answer lies in the Balanchine presence, which profoundly affected European ballet at this time. Within Europe, during the middle years of the twentieth century, major changes took place in ballet taste and ballet business. Balanchine's neoclassicism symbolised optimism and idealism in the aftermath of the war, and represented American work at a time when American money and culture were seen to be important to the regeneration of a torn, older continent. It must be remembered too that this was the early Cold War period when America became particularly active in cultural diplomacy and in funding the export of its arts.[180]

A prime example of such American activity was Nicolas Nabokov's 1952 international music festival in Paris, *L'Oeuvre du XXe siècle*, with which both Stravinsky and Balanchine were involved. Nabokov, who was a friend of both artists, and particularly important to the composer as a promoter of his work, had organised the one-month festival as Secretary General of the Congress for Cultural Freedom. The result was that, although nowhere stressed, the Festival was clearly a statement of American imperialism.[181] It only became public in the mid-1960s that the Congress had been partly funded by the CIA. Yet the rhetoric used in publicity and programmes was clearly anti-Soviet; the festival aimed to demonstrate that the apparent creative freedom within the West was a direct result of political freedom. France was the logical target for such a festival because of its mid-way 'neither-nor' position, there being a broad suspicion of American economic imperialism via the Marshall Plan with cultural imperialism following suit. The 1952 festival brought these anxieties into focus, also for the more radical artistic community (the young Pierre Boulez included), especially as the festival's stance was highly conservative, proclaiming the traditional values of the by now well-established neoclassicism, stability and objectivity. Many of the largest, most prestigious events took place at the Théâtre des Champs-Elysées. Stravinsky was paraded as the star neoclassical composer to illustrate such traditional values, and a range of his works was performed across the month. An extra touch of glamour was provided by Balanchine's New York City Ballet, which arrived for a week, opening at the Opéra and including in its repertoire *Firebird*, *Orpheus* (the composer conducted one performance) and Robbins's *The Cage*. (Jean Cocteau's *tableaux vivants* production of *Oedipus Rex* was also included during the festival – see p. 43). It was for this festival that Balanchine's *Sacre* with Picasso's designs had been mooted (see pp. 167-8), but, with the artist being a communist, this would have been quite out of place, and instead *Sacre* was performed safely, in concert.

We could infer that composer and choreographer were being used for the political purposes of the festival. Did this even cross their minds? It was hardly in Stravinsky's or Balanchine's nature to have wanted to ask too many questions. Balanchine would have done the work as part of his normal business and was undoubtedly delighted to be taking part in an event with his friend. Stravinsky was intent on getting reinstated in Europe as a celebrity composer, during what was only his second visit after the war. It is pertinent that later, when Willi Brandt was mayor of West Berlin in the early 1960s, Nabokov became his cultural advisor and was made commander of the Grand Cross of Merit of the German Federal Republic. Stravinsky and Balanchine were to become important figures there too.

Balanchine had already been back to Europe of his own accord after the war. He had been in residence for six months at the Paris Opéra in 1947. Now, from the 1950s onwards, he was invited at regular intervals to stage his ballets in Europe. Meanwhile, the New York City Ballet undertook a series of extensive European tours, in 1952, 1953, 1954 and 1956; after visits to the Far East and Australia (1958) and Canada (1961), the company returned for more European tours in 1962 and 1965. In 1959, by which time Balanchine enjoyed unmatched status on the American ballet scene, the spread of his repertory to other companies became official, arranged through the Department of State; it was agreed that he would 'give his ballets to state-supported national companies in Europe; first companies to benefit are La Scala, Netherlands Ballet and Royal Swedish Ballet'.[182] The most popular ballets were *Serenade* (Tchaikovsky, 1935), *Concerto Barocco* (Bach, 1941), *The Four Temperaments* (Hindemith, 1946), *Symphony in C* (Bizet, 1947) and *Apollo*. In the 1960s alone, *Apollo* was set on the Hamburg, Dutch National, Norway, Royal, Stuttgart, Vienna, Berlin and Geneva companies. Interestingly, this was only just after the work had achieved masterpiece status in the USA itself, thirty years after its premiere.[183] Now it was considered the perfect ballet.

Nowhere was Balanchine's influence felt more strongly than in West Germany, which, for a time, promoted ballet at the expense of its own modern dance tradition. In an official atmosphere of cultural conservatism during the Adenauer era, neoclassical ballet was seen as politically clean, despite its having had a role under the Nazis. The years after the war have been viewed as the period of 'the "Americanization" of daily life', and of '"Restoration" and "classicism" in the arts'.[184] Jochen Schmidt, an advocate of the later German Tanztheater movement, writes:

> Quite obviously Ausdruckstanz was, after 1945, not what the West Germans wanted. Perhaps to a generation rebuilding a new world from the ruins it seemed too heavy, too oppressive, too close to the ground, even too realistic in its form of expression and possibilities. They wanted something lighter, the art of the danse d'école, aspiring to heaven, defying gravity.[185]

West Germany featured especially prominently in the New York City Ballet tours of the 1950s and 1960s. The company's first appearance there was at the 1952 Berlin Cultural Festival, funded by the American government, and it received rave reviews.[186] Balanchine himself made further visits to support the Hamburg and Berlin companies, and filmed fifteen of his works there too.[187] He had many disciples amongst the ballet masters in Germany's vast network of municipal opera houses. In the 1960s, John Cranko and Kenneth MacMillan from Britain joined this German neoclassical movement, making works for companies in Stuttgart, Munich and Berlin, a number of which betrayed the influence of Balanchine. Hamburg became a major stronghold of Balanchine-style neoclassicism: the opera house director there since 1959, Rolf Liebermann, was a friend of Stravinsky. In 1960, Hamburg acquired *Serenade* and *Concerto Barocco*. In February 1962, billed as ballet company *régisseur* and choreographer, Balanchine directed and choreographed Tchaikovsky's opera *Eugene Onegin*; later, in June, for Stravinsky's eightieth birthday celebrations (a coup for Hamburg), he staged his *Orpheus* and *Apollo*, but made the condition that he bring over New York City Ballet dancers to perform *Agon* as part of the triple bill.[188] German choreographers also made neoclassical Stravinsky ballets for the Hamburg repertory: Werner Ulbrich, an earlier *Apollo* (1959); Gustav Blank, *Concerto for Two Solo Pianos* and *Jeu de cartes* (both premiered in 1960); and Peter van Dijk, *Scènes de ballet* (January, 1962). In 1963 van Dijk choreographed the first stage version of Stravinsky's *Flood*. Fuelling the enthusiasm for Balanchine's *Apollo* and *Agon* was the fact that Stravinsky's music was enjoying a general renaissance in post-war Germany.

Let us now go back in time to trace the early history of *Apollo*. The score enjoyed a steady flow of productions into the 1950s, but there is a striking decline in numbers during the 1960s and 1970s (twenty-nine uses of the score in total over the years).[189] Most settings followed the outline of the 'scenario' indicated in the score, with local modifications. The first post-Balanchine *Apollo* recorded in the database is a surprise newcomer to Stravinsky listings: a 1933 production by the Czech Máša Cvejičová for the Ballet of the National Theatre in Brno, which enjoyed progressive policies during the inter-war period. Photographs of her *Apollo* reveal a blatant debt to Balanchine's version, which Cvejičová must have seen: there is a shot of the famous 'swimming' image, Terpsichore on Apollo's back in the Pas de deux, and another of the final staircase to Parnassus, the rising line of muses (but in long tutus here) led by Apollo.[190] In some settings, the birth scene with Leto, Apollo's mother, and handmaidens was removed: even in the Bolm world premiere, in which the Greco-Roman reference was possibly at its most overt.[191] (In 1978, Balanchine, as discussed on p. 166, also decided to edit this scene, removing with it the first part of the score.) In 1951, Françoise Adret modernised the ballet for Strasbourg, using a bare stage, literalising the birth of Apollo so that it took place in a *chambre d'accouchement* with a surgeon and nurse present.[192] Other choreographers have enlarged the scale of the ballet. In Australia (1963), Robin Grove omitted Leto but introduced a cast of nine Muses, from whom came the three principals. The last ensemble was 'a bigger event, as Apollo drove his human chariot in circling sweeps around the stage, until the formation disappeared with the final pizzicato chords, leaving the three main muses to farewell him in the epilogue'.[193]

Nearly all these early productions featured a neoclassical style of movement. It is curious, then, that the 1972 Kimie Sasomoto production for the Japan Ballet Association moved back in time to the nineteenth-century roots of the Balanchine ballet. This was an entirely academic production in the manner of Petipa's *La Bayadère*, with the women in tutus, a hierarchical community of dancers (nineteen in total) and virtuosic elements including fouettés for the three Muses. It emphasised the Tchaikovskian strains in the music.[194] It is significant that there are currently so few database entries from the 1960s and 1970s. There was one *Apollo* by Lothar Höfgen in 1966, in West Germany. Other than this, the database shows just two Australian productions – the one by Grove, another by Charles Lisner (remarkably, there was a third Australian *Apollo* in 1951 by Margaret Scott) – and the Sasomoto production in Japan: there was no Balanchine 'invasion' in these two countries.

Eight of the *Apollos* listed in the database were German productions. It comes as no surprise, then, that four out of the ten *Agons* were also German. After its Los Angeles concert premiere on 17 June 1957, the music received its European premiere in Paris on 11 October, followed swiftly, on 19 October, by the German premiere in Donaueschingen (both European performances conducted by Stravinsky). Then Balanchine's ballet appeared in New York on 1 December 1957. There were three German productions in 1958 (by Krüger, Georgi and Gsovsky), and, indicative of the excitement that the new score engendered, apparently more were announced for the 1958–9 season, though they were never carried out.[195] Georgi was invited to stage her production in Vienna in 1959, and Gsovsky took hers in the same year to Frankfurt when she became the new ballet director there. The fourth and last German *Agon* by Heino Heiden in Mannheim premiered on 5 April 1962, two months before Balanchine showed his own version on his own dancers in Hamburg. This was Europe's first sighting of the Balanchine version: the Germans had all choreographed without knowledge of it, although news had spread fast of its rapturous premiere reception. Then the flow of new German productions stopped sharply.

All these early *Agons* were neoclassical and abstract in style, dressed in short tunics or sketchy tutus. They followed the outline of the dances and casting indications in the score (the total of twelve dancers, eight women and four men, subdivided in various ways), except that Gsovsky introduced a cast of fourteen, with a maximum of twelve onstage at any time. One interesting aspect is that Krüger and Georgi took the score indications of Prelude and matching Interludes literally, absenting the action, believing this to be what Stravinsky intended, and replacing it with lighting changes (Krüger) or blackouts (Georgi), which must surely have interrupted the momentum of the piece. The fact that Gsovsky *did* choreograph these sections, as, it turned out, Balanchine himself did, the critic Horst Koegler considered a divergence from the score! He also criticised her musical pedantry in the Bransle Gay solo (in the second Pas-de-Trois). There is a castanet ostinato throughout (see p. 12), and the female soloist had to perform 'a series of head movements synchronised with every single clatter of the castanets'.[196]

In August 1958, MacMillan premiered his neoclassical *Agon* on the Royal Ballet in London. He too had a cast of fourteen, because he added two 'extra' dancers to introduce the twelve and to form links during the Prelude and Interludes. The Diaghilev conductor Ernest Ansermet maintained that this was 'the first truly abstract ballet he had ever seen'.[197] Although the audience reception at the premiere was highly enthusiastic, critical reception was wide-ranging. For Clement Crisp in the *Financial Times,* MacMillan demonstrated the

> mastery of his craft ... Superimposed on the movement are overtones of sly humour, and what may be considered satiric comments on the conventions of dancing ... The dance vocabulary is extremely rich ... by turns astringent, lyrical and declamatory.[198]

A review published in the Parisian paper *Arts* proclaimed MacMillan's *Agon* an exceptional achievement, given the difficulties posed by the music. But more than this, it proved to the author the interesting point that this score needed to be brought to life by dance, in contrast to Stravinsky's *Firebird, Petrushka* and *Sacre*:

> *Agon* demands to be danced ... One 'hears' this score better when it is danced, which is an unusual phenomenon in ballet tradition.[199]

Negative criticism seems to have stemmed from difficulties with the score and uncertainty about the message of the work, at a time indeed when dance viewers in Britain did not take naturally to abstraction. There were questions regarding the nature of the 'contest' (translation of the Greek *Agon*). Was it between men and women? Was it between the dance, the music and the design? Clive Barnes felt that there was a kind of story: the setting suggested a bordello,[200] and perhaps the group of figures overlooking the stage action in Nicholas Georgiadis's backcloth encouraged literal interpretation. For Barnes, the two 'bordello keepers' (the extra pair of dancers) were also Greek Fates who separated the pas de deux couple at the end of the ballet. At later Covent Garden performances, a deputy orchestra, the London Symphonic Players, took over – a 'fiasco' according to the reviewer for the *Glasgow Herald*.[201] The work received nineteen performances, at Covent Garden and on tour, and lasted only one season. In spring 1959, MacMillan's much safer Stravinsky ballet *Danses Concertantes* (1955, for Sadler's Wells Theatre Ballet) was revived for the Covent Garden company.

Stravinsky's *Agon* was considered hard to play, hard to choreograph and hard to dance. These are all reasons why *Agon* productions have been few, but the presence of the brilliant Balanchine version was probably the most important reason of all. For here was yet another 'perfect ballet', and this time with the added frisson of high modernism and instant popular and critical success in America. The stagings of Balanchine's *Agon* began in the 1970s, Balanchine feeling that European companies were now ready to take on this especially demanding choreography. The following companies acquired the ballet during the 1970s: Geneva, Hamburg, Stuttgart, Royal, Dutch National, Paris, Berlin, Zurich and Hungary. In 1991, William Forsythe, as director of Ballet Frankfurt, took the radical step of renewing the look of this iconic work by introducing costumes designed by Gianni Versace, the women's black leotards shaped like soft body corsets.[202]

Once Balanchine's *Agon* began to travel, alternative settings of the score have been very few. The Chilean-born, modern dance choreographer Ana Itelman staged the piece in 1963 at the Teatro Colón in Buenos Aires, following the outline of dances and casting indicated in the score.[203] There was an Eske Holm production for the Royal Danish Ballet in 1967, which featured a 'fighting' competitiveness alongside humour.[204] Just one other full setting is recorded in the database, a 1993 production by the Australian Chrissie Parrott, which again followed Stravinsky's outline in the score. There was an element of circus, with crinoline hoops and ostentatious ostrich-feather headpieces possibly alluding to the Louis XIV court dance references in the music.[205] The Queensland Ballet had wanted to stage the Balanchine version, but did not get permission from the Balanchine Trust. Parrott stepped in.[206] Australia came late to Balanchine, its own tradition stemming from the de Basil Ballet Russe via the Borovansky Ballet and from Britain's Royal Ballet.[207]

Meanwhile, settings of *Apollo*, a much 'easier' score, have continued, albeit sporadically. Trends since the 1980s have been to use excerpts from the score or to incorporate it within a musical collage. Although altering the 'story', the manner was often to make reference to the legendary Balanchine production, for Balanchine haunts the score. The American Murray Louis's *Stravinsky-Montage* (1982, Hamburg Ballet, later staged on his own modern dance company) used excerpts from several scores and worked 'provocatively against other associations with the composer's music'.[208] The central Apollo solo was now an opportunity for an oppressive acrobatic duet for two men. (The Firebird's Lullaby was a ritualistic solo for a woman with a 'claw'.) In 1997, the French choreographer Jean-Jacques Vidal made a modern dance work about an Apollo who is sent to earth (an urban ruin) to found a new human sex with one of four muses, urged on by an alter ego. But he is half-hearted about the prospect and chooses to remain single.[209] He again introduced two men into his cast, here as two Apollos, and removed the original emphasis on male–female union as a symbol of artistic idealism.

In Britain, Michael Clark began what he now calls his unfinished *O* (1994) with a punk music prelude as well as movement material from his earlier setting of *Sacre*, called *Mmm …* (1992). Then, to the complete score of *Apollo*, he represented a birth (from his real-life mother Bessie seen in bed – he danced the God himself), and made dance movement that borrowed images from the Balanchine. Here was the application of a distancing technique to renew the familiar. His second version of 2005, prefaced again by punk (Iggy Pop and

Wire), drew more heavily still on the Balanchine original. (This work was the beginning of Clark's three-year Stravinsky project, which continued with new settings of *Sacre* and *Noces* in partnership with the Barbican Theatre, London.) There was clearer reference to the 'characters' of Leto (as mother, now a dancer) and the three Muses, as well as many sculptural moments, although the end seemed to suggest a return to nature rather than a passage to Parnassus.[210] In Ireland in 2006, Liz Roche presented her modern dance *Sweet Apollo*, inspired by the Balanchine, but reinterpreting the myth with an especially unruly, knowing and sexually manipulative group of Muses; at the end, all four protagonists struck the famous 'sunburst' fan of arabesques. David Turpin 'treated' excerpts from the Stravinsky score electronically; the work also incorporated songs from Bob Dylan, Maria McKee and, at the end, The Beatles.[211]

Meanwhile, in *Eidos:Telos* (Part 1, 1994) for Ballet Frankfurt, Forsythe referenced the classic *Apollo* by merely incorporating fragments of the Stravinsky into a new, partly electronic, partly improvised score by Thom Willems. Thus, he used the former work primarily for its connotational values. An onstage solo violinist, Maxim Franke, played a few treated, interrupted excerpts from the cadenza of Apollo's first solo and the Apotheosis. Apart from one brief moment when a woman extends her leg in second position supported by the kneeling violinist, which perhaps alludes obliquely to the opening of Balanchine's Pas de deux, there are no obvious choreographic references. Yet, because of the iconic nature of the early ballet, its memory soon begins to hover over Forsythe's new work.[212]

It seems unarguable now that the Balanchine *Apollo* and *Agon* restrained other impulses to set the score, especially to set *Agon*: they frightened off competition and became Balanchine's 'possession' as they became widely recognised as masterpieces. But that is not the whole story. There are other reasons to do with the huge presence of these Balanchine ballets across the international repertory: Balanchine's supreme position within American ballet, which led to his work being chosen for the purposes of American cultural diplomacy during the post-War years (toured by New York City Ballet and eagerly devoured by other company repertories); the needs of war-scarred Europe for a politically clean classical ballet culture; and finally, powerful contacts, not least that Balanchine was marked out as the favourite of Stravinsky himself. The energy of the Balanchine tradition continues today, strengthened indeed by the excellent organisational skills and expert marketing of the George Balanchine Trust and Foundation.

But is it blasphemy today to suggest that it would be interesting to see other *Agons*, to consider new questions asked of the Stravinsky score by choreographers, indeed to be asked to hear the music differently? Some would prefer *Apollo* to be left alone as well. And here is an irony: as works play off and against each other, alternative settings of the music might renew our conception of the two iconic originals. Perhaps we know too well these exceptional, 'perfect' ballets, and they can benefit from refreshment and debate? Two settings, one of *Apollo* by David Gordon, the other of *Agon* by Yvonne Rainer, are especially interesting in undertaking conceptual interrogation of the musical as well as dance values of the originals. It is important that both choreographers had been part of the radical 'postmodern' Judson Dance Theater movement in New York in the 1960s, which asked fundamental questions about the nature and status of dance, including its use of music.

Apollo *as autobiography*

Trying Times (1982) was David Gordon's statement about an emblematic moment in ballet classicism; he created it in Stravinsky's centenary year soon after Balanchine had shocked the dance world by removing the opening of his *Apollo* (see p. 166). Perhaps that act was especially pertinent for the critic Deborah Jowitt, who suggested that *Apollo* could be considered 'an exercise in autobiography in art – a first chapter titled "George Hits on His Credo"; and Balanchine keeps altering it to accord with his current views'. She added: 'That's like Gordon.'[213] For *Trying Times* was a reflection on Gordon's own role as an artist, and the whole business of labelling – postmodernist or classicist? – as this affected his relationship with his public. With Gordon a central figure on stage, Balanchine's own quiet identification with the eponymous god became an enlarged and witty conceit, with more than a touch of self-mockery attached. But Gordon has spoken of his admiration for the original: 'the best kind of irony also has some kind of reverence in it, some kind of battle between distance and seduction'.[214]

Created for the David Gordon/Pick Up Company, *Trying Times* is about 70 minutes long, and much of its first half is given to talking, relaying situations where people do not communicate, relationships break down and words tie people in knots, and nothing is solved through the desperate attempts to clarify with: 'You know ... I mean ...'[215] The trying relationship within one couple becomes a focus. Meanwhile, the performers manipulate a variety of screens into framing and masking devices – arches, pens and doors – a relentless series of nonsensical tasks. At the end of the work, as we hear Stravinsky's Apotheosis, the talk turns into a mock courtroom trial with Gordon on the stand and questions being asked about his identity and purpose: 'How can we tell it's his signature when we can't read his handwriting? ... Is he on trial for what he does or does not do? ... He does not deny postmodern you-know-what ... He doesn't know what it is. Is he guilty of playing hide-and-seek when we all want tag? ...' Immediately before this trial scene, Pick Up Company danced the whole of the *Apollo* score up to the Apotheosis – the clarity and legibility of Gordon's movement and, through him, Balanchine's, signifying that choreography can speak of grace and simplicity where words fail hopelessly. Movement to music, like Terpsichore herself, wins outright.

There are clear references to Balanchine's *Apollo*, most obviously near the beginning when we can immediately identify Gordon (Apollo) with this three Muses. He extends a hand, which they all take so that he can bring them up to standing, they daisy-chain, and go into a low, modest version of the 'sunburst'. At the end of the work, Gordon, Valda Setterfield (his partner and in real life his wife) and the 'judge' are arranged on and beside the screens that now emulate the final stairway to Parnassus. Less direct references, the components of counterbalance and leverage, so important in the original choreography, infuse *Trying Times*, and not just the part set to Stravinsky.

In the Stravinsky section, the setting of movement to music confounds all expectations. You see a solo woman dancing to the beginning of Apollo's first variation, and think: is this Apollo? Is she a Muse? But this pigeonholing makes little sense, as what were once solo variations are now often sextets and four-somes and the dances overlap the edges of many of the musical sections. As for the movement to Stravinsky, it is like a private meditation: simple falls, slides, stretches, in the manner of undertaking tasks, not theatrically phrased, not forced, not 'presented', and definitely not 'with' the music in any traditional sense. There are just light-touch connections. The warmth of the strings is invasive; for the Terpsichore/Apollo duet, the stretchy doublework of two couples seems especially tender, caressed by the timbre of the music. An occasional small jump or skip echoes a quicker impulse. The group definitely shifts up a gear for the celebratory pre-Apotheosis Coda. But the larger effect is of complementary voices simply coexisting in harmonious juxtaposition. Disrespectful to Stravinsky? After Merce Cunningham, we know that we do not *have* to hear dance movement underlined; when media simply coexist, we have space to choose, room for manoeuvre. In the manner of other postmodern, post-Cunningham choreographers, Gordon wanted to show the dancing body freed from the statues and abrupt halts of the original and from motor pulse, whether driven by music or, as in the case of much Cunningham, by an internal body metronome. So, instead of Gordon's *Apollo* being yet another 'trying time', we can relax and take pleasure.

Stravinsky as 'Pink Panther'

Rainer's 2006 commentary on *Agon* is titled *AG Indexical, with a little help from H.M.*, 'indexical' indicating the referential, analytical-academic aspect of the work and H.M. being the initials of the composer Henry Mancini, whose 'Pink Panther' music she had first used in 1969 for *Performance Fractions for the*

West Coast.[216] The circumstances of the new work were a commission from Dance Theater Workshop, New York, and specifically from choreographer Annie-B Parson, curator of an evening titled 'Sourcing Stravinsky'. Six artists had been invited to use the composer's music as a starting point in whichever way they chose. One piece, for instance, was a hip-hop treatment of a section from *Sacre* (*Heaven*, by Rennie Harris). Another was a deliberately incompetent lecture with film and dance (*Track 11*, by Dayna Hanson and Linas Phillips), using *The Essential Igor Stravinsky* CD, and presenting him as a much-loved contemporary commodity. A pivotal concept was homelessness, Stravinsky being an émigré, with an actual homeless man (or someone posing as such) reporting on having once met him over lunch. In her introductory note to the programme, Parson noted the secret impact that the two bastions of the ballet world, Balanchine and Stravinsky, had had on her own independent work, and when Rainer, a founder member of Judson Dance Theater, agreed with alacrity to take part and to make a piece about *Agon*, no less, it was as if 'a very strangely shaped circle feels like it is closing for a moment'. After all, back in 1968, Rainer famously said, 'I am a music-hater. The only remaining meaningful role for muzeek in relation to dance is to be totally absent or to mock itself.'[217] But manifestos set out to clear the air, and Rainer has since moved on and, for much of her later career, away from dance into film.

Rainer has spoken about her 're-vision' of what had always been one of her favourite Balanchine works,[218] which means, as we shall see, from video reconstruction and with the help, partly musical, of dance colleagues (Pat Catterson and Taisha Paggett), using some of the actual choreographic detail of the original work. She says that she liked *Agon*'s 'rigour', 'athleticism' and 'abstraction' (similarly, she admired Balanchine's *Episodes* to Webern).[219] But she had no need for men here – her piece was for four women of varying shapes and sizes and aged from thirties to sixties, modern/postmodern of dance background: Catterson, Patricia Hoffbauer, Sally Silvers, and one ex-New York City Ballet dancer, Emily Coates, who had never danced in *Agon* when in the company. They wear practice clothes: they did in the original, Balanchine's standard black and white smart version. Here that means unmatching loose trousers and tops, although Coates adopts a sleeker unitard version (which is, after all, her background), and wears pointe shoes.

The new piece is what it is because the old one is an icon, and knowing the original, as many present at DTW did, is important, not crucial, but it certainly adds a brilliant layer of resonance. The 'presence' of the original and the play between connection with and disconnection from it are very important to my discussion here, and are also signalled by the presence of a recording of the ballet on an onstage monitor during part of the dance.

While respecting Balanchine's work, Rainer does still recall some of the issues that prompted her earlier clearing of the air, especially the handling of women in ballet, illustrated, as we shall see, by the extreme manipulatory element in the Pas-de-Deux:

> As he [Balanchine] allegedly said, the ballerinas were the flowers and he was the gardener. To make my 'flower' even more dependent and powerless, I upped the ante and refused her even more agency than in the original pas-de-deux.[220]

The programme merrily (and ironically) announces 'four girls' for the new gender line-up at the opening. The fact of such a diverse group of performers doing some of the original choreography also highlights that performers, to some, often unacknowledged, degree, make their own dance. In Rainer's work there is a different kind of performance persona from what we see in ballet, and plain facial expression (despite the considerable humour in the piece), relating to her interest in performance as task. Prompted by an observation from a *New York Times* reporter in the audience, Rainer said that Coates 'dances these steps much differently than she would if she were in a ballet company. She didn't use this expression, but it would be a much harder sell ... a much more flamboyant presentation. And here she just does them [the steps].'[221] But, at the same time, Rainer realises that many features of the original, and the performance tradition stemming from the original, can be read in more than one way, both as appealing and as disconcerting and ripe for critique.

Rainer's project also makes us see and hear the music and the dance more clearly, and differently, both in the passages that borrow most from Balanchine and in those where the opposite is the case, because we are likely to make comparisons. The dynamics and spatial forms of the borrowed movement have to be different on modern dancers: their manner tends to be more relaxed and fluid and less academically positioned, even though the timing of material remains admirably accurate. Indeed, some of the step rhythms come across more clearly than before, more precise patterns that are not pulled out of shape by the effort of high-level accents; nor is our attention diverted by performance 'presence'. Again, we perceive in more than one way: something is gained, something lost. Then, when the choreography is not Balanchine, we are inclined to home in on the music as a rescuing device in order to remember what should be happening, or to shift gear and notice that the music sounds different against new movement.

Table 4 illustrates Rainer's use of the score in relation to the original: she cuts it down to make a shorter overall piece, 17 minutes long as opposed to the original 20 minutes indicated in the music score (Balanchine's ballet often takes slightly longer than 20 minutes), and she also undertakes a certain amount of

Table 4. *Agon* layout, Balanchine and Rainer.

Original Balanchine	Rainer Re-vision
Rainer Re-visionPas-de-Quatre 4m	Pas-de-Quatre ('four girls') – Catterson, Coates, Hoffbauer, Silvers (Balanchine choreography)
Double Pas-de-Quatre 8w	
Triple Pas-de-Quatre 4m, 8w	Double and Triple Pas-de-Quatre (Taisha's solo) – Hoffbauer solo (new choreography next to original on video monitor), Coates solo (music on monitor stopped early)
[First Pas-de-Trois]	
Prelude 1m, 2w	Prelude – Coates, Hoffbauer, Silvers (Balanchine choreography)
Saraband-Step 1m	Bransle Gay – Catterson (music and Balanchine choreography taken out of order from the second Pas de Trois section)
Gailliarde 2w	Sarabande – Silvers (learning Balanchine choreography alongside video shown on monitor)
Coda 2w	
[Second Pas-de-Trois]	Gailliarde – Catterson, Coates (new choreography)
Interlude 2m, 1w	Bransle Double – Catterson, Hoffbauer, Silvers (a compilation of Balanchine's Coda from the first Pas de Trois and Bransle Double)
Bransle Simple 2m	
Bransle Gay 1w	
Bransle Double 2m, 1w	
Interlude 1m, 1w	Interlude/Pas-de-Deux – Catterson, Coates, Hoffbauer, Silvers (variation on Balanchine choreography)
Pas-de-Deux 1m, 1w	
Four Duos 4m, 4w	
Four Trios 4m, 8w	
(Coda: recapitulation of opening Pas-de-Quatre) 4m, 8w	Pas-de-Quatre (Variation: 'four girls') – Catterson, Coates, Hoffbauer, Silvers (repeat of Balanchine choreography to Henry Mancini's 'The Pink Panther')

reordering. I have drawn information directly from the Dance Theater Workshop programme, but have added comments on her approach to each section of the music. This falls roughly into two categories: first, what is fundamentally, but never entirely straight, Balanchine (or attempted Balanchine), incorporating what Rainer calls her 'interventions'; second, new Rainer material, most of which is peppered with recognisable allusions to Balanchine.

To take examples from Rainer's choreography, the solos to the Double and Triple Pas-de-Quatre are a major remove from the original (these were called 'Taisha's solo' because Taisha Paggett had helped Rainer work out the moves for these two sections).[222] Hoffbauer stands next to the monitor in a strange fidgety-feet number with legato arms starting up independently and gradually taking over almost entirely. She highlights the two distinct dynamic qualities in the musical texture here – nervous string gestures and sweeping wind – and the contrast between what she does and what we see on the box. Next, Coates runs about, constantly changing direction and getting nowhere, and the music turns urban busy-bee. The Gailliarde duet begins with quotes from various parts of Rainer's signature piece *Trio A* (1966), such as the oily shoulder-circle while standing in profile in a fourth position plié on the toes, and the hands patting the air like paws. We hear the sustained flute and string lines more readily than in the original: the spiky mandolin and harp fade from the surface. There is also a hand-across-the-breast gesture from Rainer's earliest solo *Three Satie Spoons* (1961). After material that references the Balanchine very loosely, the duet ends, as in the Balanchine, with a series of nine quick, staccato unison arm gestures in the silence, continuing the established pulse.

The Sarabande looks like a mere sketch of the Balanchine because we see it in the process of being learnt from the monitor now turned away from the audience – Silvers was asked not to study it outside performances. The fact of learning draws attention to the constantly shifting, irregular and independent rhythms of music and dance, to the choreomusical complexity of the dance. Another nice intervention comes in the Bransle Gay, where Catterson suddenly stops dancing the real Balanchine, walks to a new place to pick something up off the floor, and then links in to where she should have reached in the choreography. The Bransle Gay was the one occasion when a performer was allowed to adopt a specific facial expression: 'I told her to smile at the end of it,' says Rainer, 'because at that point a smile is like a challenge – "OK, I dare you stuffed shirts out there to compare me to Wendy Whelan".'[223]

The Pas-de-Deux also looks like real Balanchine, although it is expanded into a Pas-de-Quatre. In the introductory Interlude of the original there is a wonderful moment when the ballerina pitches forwards from a turn and lops her attitude leg across the back of her partner behind. In Rainer's version this looks more like a stranglehold, while the two extra women, of different statures, deco-

Ill.6. *AG Indexical, with a little help from H.M.,* Interlude before Pas-de-Deux, choreography by Yvonne Rainer (after George Balanchine's *Agon*), left to right Patricia Hoffbauer, Emily Coates, Sally Silvers and Pat Catterson.

rate the clinch on either side, producing a composite effect like a lop-sided candelabra (see Ill. 6). The audience laughed and the big musical accent here seemed especially big, the broad chord even broader. During the long Adagio, Rainer has amplified the manipulations of the original by giving her 'ballerina' three escorts instead of one, so that intertwinings are enlarged and more complex, and new multi-body sculptures arise during the process. The manipulation of Coates is exaggerated and amusing: at the beginning even her simplest leg movements have to be made by one of the other women, and there is a marvellous promenade engineered by all three, one turning her, another supporting her leg, a third beckoning to the leg in the manner of guiding a car as it reverses. But this strangely complicit and absurd idealisation of the ballerina by three women is also poignant. It reveals gentle, careful group endeavour and, Rainer has pointed out, there is literal reference to Balanchine's working on the paralysed legs of his wife Le Clercq, who had been struck down by polio only shortly before he choreographed *Agon*.[224] As for relations with the score, the whole Adagio takes longer than the original, spilling over into the music for the solo Variations. The effect is not as strange as this might seem, because the original was already free from detailed correspondence with the music, and both versions to some degree reveal the choreography as a series of tasks without Balanchine's usual dance continuity between them.

The main choreomusical excitement emerges with the opening and closing

Pas-de-Quatre. First time around, the 'four girls' swing into it straight, except for a couple of interventions when suddenly Balanchine breaks out into Rainer, a brief foray for two of the women in a canon for four, including a bent-legged handstand, later a couple of 'lifts' downstage that explode out of line; Rainer lets on that she incorporated a fingers-to-the-cheeks move from *Three Satie Spoons*. But the real fun starts in the last section when Coates exchanges her pointe shoes for a pair of sneakers and all four bounce through the Balanchine choreography, now to Mancini. With a slight retard before the final gesture, the choreography fits its new music miraculously. Rainer explains:

> In response to Sally's question: 'Is it alright if we groove a little during the Pink Panther?' I gave them a little leeway to relax while maintaining the precision of the first pas de quatre.

Part of the pleasure is that the movement appears as if rephrased by the music and looks different because of the music, its jazziness enlarged. It is as if Rainer reminds us that, as much as we take pleasure in the interactions between Balanchine and Stravinsky, there is an autonomous strength to this movement that allows it to work perfectly well without the Stravinsky or, rather, to music different from that which gave birth to it. Unlike the original music, the Mancini also makes the regular pulse that underlies the whole dance a consistent hearable presence. Looked at another way, Rainer's choice of Mancini is significant, for she referred to him as an exemplar of cliché in her 1968 diatribe about 'muzeek'. The 'Pink Panther' is also a reminder of the sharp, hard motor cliché that has come to be associated with Balanchine–Stravinsky, but through subversion, marked absence, opposition and that 'little leeway to relax'. Writing about Rainer and her films, Douglas Crimp claims that our subjection to cliché in film is unavoidable, but that, through Rainer, we can at least 'become critically aware … we can learn to experience it differently next time, to change its meanings, alter its form'.[225] Similarly, in the case of the very familiar Balanchine–Stravinsky, we might also learn through her – witness the music at this point in *Agon* – that elasticity and rhythmic unrest are crucial to the success of their choreomusical collaboration and that the tick-tick motor cliché is often overdetermined and unfairly exaggerated.

Rainer's *Agon* turns out be a postscript (in capitals) from a choreographer whose earlier battles with the fundamentals of dance included questioning its rules of choreomusicality. Although I am not sure how much she was aware of it, her new work, even though no longer the composition of a music-hater, emerges as a fascinating commentary on listening as well as on watching. She has referred to her work as a 'pedagogical enterprise'. I hope too that she is pleased by its excellent theatre and the drama of its constantly changing tactics.

Her re-vision inspired me to look at Mr. B's dance once again, and with refreshed eyes and ears. Now, I would like to see the two versions performed in sequence on the same programme. In principle, this tactic of musical repetition, which, after all, Stravinsky and Balanchine used themselves (see p. 164), could be a very illuminating one.

* * *

While considering how Balanchine–Stravinsky has now become source material for current enquiring choreographers and is released from the possession of just one, it is especially important that the act of closing the 'very strangely shaped circle' has not diminished the power of the original *Apollo* and *Agon*. It is also important that Rainer, particularly, tells us in a new way about the rigour and abstraction of the original *Agon*, ingredients that her own re-vision respects above all. For structure, including choreomusical structure, was central to Balanchine's thinking, and probably because he was a trained musician, even if it is now unfashionable in some circles to admire or spend analytical time on such matters. Furthermore, although it is beyond the scope of this chapter to prove the point, the range and brilliance of his Stravinsky techniques are probably unmatched elsewhere in his repertory: the dance motor, whether autonomous and held in the dance or shared with music; the *play* with motor (as drama, time-filler, undercurrent for elasticity or primary force of momentum); the counterpoint with music; the embodiment of melody and timbre; and the virtuoso interlocking with large musical structures.

Balanchine's own comments were often misleading and reductive about choreomusical relations within his work. As we have seen, his motto about subduing the dance in order not to interfere with the music is a gross over-simplification, and his account of his musical needs likewise. He hardly ever talked about the expressive or idea content of his work, and never, so far as I know, about musical meaning and its interface with his choreography. But this is an area that I have tried to emphasise in my analyses, in observations about music and dance connecting through common attributes. These are not necessarily interactions that propose unity or stability, one simple, primary story embodied in the work. Indeed, I have chosen case studies that propose quite the opposite and that are some of the most open work that Balanchine ever produced. At the same time, absurdly deferential as he could be about what music could do and dance could not, Balanchine can be seen to challenge Stravinsky, not always as obviously as in the *Divertimento*, where he shaped a musical score to suit his own ends, but also through taking responsibility for new structures and meanings, mutually driven highlights and, sometimes, musical erasure.

Let us return now to Goldner's radical assessment, that Balanchine–Stravinsky may reveal the choreographer's musical sophistication but rarely his

most sophisticated choreography. She may well be right that musical sophistication is sometimes the most intriguing feature about Balanchine's choreography.
However, in his case, I am unable to separate the two concepts. Perhaps we are
really talking here about a different balance of power where, in the shift towards
a no-plot, no-design, concert-based genre, the dramas emerge from choreomusical relations – and are structural and intellectual as well as emotional –
rather than the other way round. Perhaps one of Balanchine's most important
contributions as a Stravinsky choreographer was to demonstrate that choreomusical relations can sometimes take on a major burden of responsibility within
choreography and, in doing so, surprise and delight those who listen.

4

Frederick Ashton:

Unlikely Stravinsky Choreographer?

Introduction

'If God said, "you have one left" – that would be it.'[1] It was in these terms that Ashton spoke of his 1948 *Scènes de ballet*, a work that critics likewise, certainly within the UK, have come to regard as one of his finest. It is indeed perhaps the most brilliant construction Ashton ever made. Yet it is strangely atypical of him. Furthermore, if we look beyond *Scènes* and think of Stravinsky, Ashton's name is unlikely to race to mind, for he set his music on only three other occasions: *Le Baiser de la fée* (1935), *Persephone* (1961) and the dancing roles of the Nightingale and Fisherman in the opera *Le Rossignol* (1981). These other works are no longer in the regular repertory, existing largely in the form of rudimentary recording (although *Rossignol* was revived in New York in 2003), and in the case of *Baiser* only a couple of fragments survive. Yet all four Stravinsky settings together form a fascinating group, demonstrating a tantalising range from the more familiar languorous, lyrical Ashton to the extremes of cool classicism, from hybrid forms of dance theatre, with narrative made concrete through text, to the most formal geometry and frozen allusion. At the same time, it is interesting to consider how Ashton, in many respects an unlikely Stravinsky choreographer, might have been moved in particular ways by his music – literally, even his dance vocabulary affected – not only in *Scènes*, but also in the other lesser-known works. I will also examine Ashton's Stravinsky settings in relation to other settings of the same scores.

There was no doubt of Ashton's admiration for the composer, as he wrote at the time of the *Scènes* creation:

> Stravinsky has always been a favourite composer of mine, because I feel that he is among the few composers of today who thinks in a really contemporary way. He also has a greater understanding of the problems of ballet than any other living composer ...[2]

In the last interview of his life, discussing the importance of rhythm in his work, Ashton cited Stravinsky as his model:

I immediately get the rhythm: it's almost the first thing. Pulse: you see it's like Stravinsky ... [you must get] the drive and the force of it.[3]

Given Stravinsky's seminal role as a ballet composer, there might well have been something of an aura attached to the act of setting his music. Ashton particularly admired the work of Balanchine and Nijinska and their Stravinsky ballets. He had seen Balanchine's *Apollo* (possibly first in London in 1928, soon after its creation) and Nijinska's *Les Noces* (when it came to London in 1926, three years after its Paris premiere), and had danced in the premiere of Nijinska's own *Le Baiser de la fée* (in 1928, when he was a member of Ida Rubinstein's company). It was after 1925, during his formative years as a young dancer and choreographer and when he regularly attended performances of Diaghilev's Ballets Russes in London, that he established his primary conception of the composer as a neoclassicist, in the middle period of his career but very much a part of the bracing, youthful world of the 1920s.

Piecing together data from a variety of sources, we discover that Stravinsky and Ashton enjoyed more of a social and professional relationship than is generally recognised. It was at the time of Nijinska's *Baiser* premiere that Ashton first came into direct contact with the composer, who conducted the event and played the piano at rehearsals. Ashton remembers one occasion when Stravinsky appeared especially engaged at the piano, chanting 'I-da-hache! Et-da-hache!'[4] Was this a manifestation of his celebrated physicality when playing his music? It was around this time too that he noted how Stravinsky (and Ravel) would flatter Rubinstein about her own performance. She was a poor dancer, but, as director of her own company, she gave herself key roles, and Stravinsky's duplicity disturbed Ashton.

After this, there is nothing in the literature about Stravinsky and Ashton meeting again until the 1950s, by which time there is evidence to suggest that they enjoyed a comfortable relationship as fellow artists (see p. 57). Meanwhile, the anglophile Lincoln Kirstein was working hard on Anglo-American exchanges between his and Balanchine's New York company and the Sadler's Wells Ballet, and had offered early on to buy *Scènes* for Ballet Society, though Ashton turned him down.[5] Preparing for *Persephone* in 1961, Ashton took Svetlana Beriosova to a concert performance of the piece at the Royal Festival Hall with Stravinsky conducting. Beriosova was to dance the title role. They went backstage, and A.H. Franks reported in *The Dancing Times*:

The composer congratulated him with great warmth and assured the choreographer he was content in the knowledge that the British presentation of the ballet *Perséphone* was in such brilliant and sensitive hands. In substantiation of that compliment he then invited Ashton to make a ballet in connection with Stravinsky's eightieth birthday celebrations in Germany early next year.[6]

But was Ashton the source of Frank's information, and how much can we trust such hearsay? And just how much of a compliment to Ashton was such a proposal, which was surely as much self-enhancing on Stravinsky's part? It is hard to say. Certainly, no Ashton contribution materialised for the 1962 Hamburg celebrations, in which only Balanchine featured as invited choreographer. Stravinsky never suggested collaboration with Ashton, who in turn would probably have never dared to initiate such a thing. Neither is there any record of Stravinsky ever seeing any of Ashton's settings of his own scores.

The four scores that Ashton used had all been written for the theatre. *Le Rossignol* (1914) was created for Diaghilev's Ballets Russes, with choreography originally by Boris Romanov, later reworked in the adapted ballet version *Le Chant du rossignol*, by Massine (1920) and Balanchine (1925). For the Ballets Ida Rubinstein, as well as Nijinska's *Baiser* (1928) there was *Persephone* (1934) by Kurt Jooss. *Scènes*, a cut version of the score, was originally set by Anton Dolin as a showpiece for himself and Alicia Markova to open the second half of the Billy Rose Broadway revue 'The Seven Lively Arts' (premiered in Philadelphia on 24 November 1944 and later that year taken to New York). Ashton never used any of Stravinsky's concert scores. In October 1931, the *Dancing Times* announced that for the Camargo Society he would set the two orchestral *Suites*, which had already proved very popular with choreographers: they were short, each a series of brief numbers.[7] But this project never came to fruition.

It might seem surprising that Ashton turned to the composer's music on so few occasions. However, there are several possible reasons why this was so. The ballet conductor Constant Lambert, his early musical mentor, disliked Stravinsky's post-Russian period music and undoubtedly would have dissuaded Ashton from using it in the 1930s and 40s (he died in 1951 – see pp. 101-2).[8] Apparently, Ninette de Valois was against the *Scènes* project.[9] Perhaps she was nervous of audience reaction to its acerbic qualities, perhaps guided by Lambert himself. As we shall see, initial critical reaction was mixed, and the music was considered a problem. The music was also more complex than the Sadler's Wells Ballet dancers were used to at the time and the work could not be staged without meticulous rehearsal. *Baiser*, with its mildly disruptive absorptions of Tchaikovsky's themes and style – in other words, it was hardly 'fashionably' disjunctive – might not have been considered so controversial, but Lambert had already been somewhat grudging about this too. Only a year before Ashton's setting, he wrote in *Music Ho!*:

The neglected element of melodic charm is exploited with all the mechanical solemnity of *Oedipus*, though the necessary element of chic and time travelling is provided by the sour and deliberate harmonic distortions of such a saccharine melody as 'None but the Weary Heart' [*sic* – see p. 224] . The effect is like a collaboration between Marcus Stone and Picabia, and *Le Baiser de la Fée* is perhaps the most surrealist of his works, combining the nationalist charm of *L'Oiseau de Feu* with the neo-classical solemnities of his later period … At the same time the very fact that the thematic material is drawn from the always fecund Tchaikovsky gives to *Le Baiser de la Fée* a certain character, which is lacking in the later works …[10]

But there were broader problems with Stravinsky's reception in Britain during this period (see pp. 121-3), and *Scènes* for a while proved to be an isolated example in the repertory of the Royal Ballet (the name of the Sadler's Wells company from 1956). The situation changed only after de Valois brought *Firebird* and *Petrushka* into the repertory in 1954 and 1957 respectively.

We might now ask just what Stravinsky music Ashton might have used other than the four scores that he did choreograph. His predilections were generally for scores written for dance, or music with programmatic content, or short pieces that might be arranged to suit a story line. His leanings were rarely towards the 'abstract', symphonically contructed kind of work that suited Balanchine and those who followed closely within his tradition. On the other hand, he excused himself from setting *Sacre*: 'I didn't do it because it seemed to me so Russian, and I felt I was not sufficiently acquainted with that.' But he also tended to steer clear of scores that were already in the regular repertory, and kept away from scores set by Balanchine. Ashton would not have wished to be seen in direct competition with his fellow choreographer – Balanchine, though much admired by Ashton, was his rival – and increasingly scores were seen to be 'used up' by him:

We never really encroached on each other. I tackled *Persephone* and *Scènes de ballet*, which he never did [in fact Balanchine part-choreographed *Persephone* in 1982 – see pp. 314-15]; but I would never have done *Agon*, which is considered one of his best things; it was much too dry for me. He was very in accord with Stravinsky, and those ballets were among his best …[11]

It is extraordinary, therefore, that in January 1948 Ashton made a bid to set the new *Orpheus* score, originally commissioned for Balanchine and eventually performed by Ballet Society in April 1948, only a month before the premiere of his *Scènes*. There was a plan for the Sadler's Wells company to take Balanchine's setting into its repertory, but Ashton proposed giving the company his own production later the same year. It might have been something of a defiant gesture or simply a show of massive enthusiasm on Ashton's part.[12] In the event, the Sadler's Wells company performed neither version of *Orpheus*, and Balanchine brought his choreography to Covent Garden with the New York City Ballet in 1950.

Perhaps it was by some measure of chance that Ashton managed to secure for himself instead of Balanchine the first opportunity to set *Scènes* for a major ballet company repertory. For *Scènes* had, after all, been marked out for Balanchine. Right at the start, Dolin, unhappy with what he himself had come up with, suggested that it would be better if Balanchine took over.[13] Then there is a record of Stravinsky, Balanchine and the designer Eugene Berman (a friend of Stravinsky) meeting on 24 June 1946 to plan a new version of the ballet for Ballet Theatre, at the director Lucia Chase's request, but the money for the project was not forthcoming.[14] The Harvard Theatre Collection houses Balanchine's own piano reduction of the score, two-thirds completed: he must have thought seriously about the project. A letter from Kirstein to Stravinsky mentions that Chase still wanted this ballet from Balanchine in autumn 1947.[15] Then, in 1950, after Kirstein had angled unsuccessfully for Ashton's work to come to Ballet Society, there is a letter from Stravinsky to Kirstein declaring his own continuing eagerness to see a Balanchine setting of his score.[16] In the meantime, Berman, whose pre-planned designs Ashton had to use in *Devil's Holiday* (1939, Ballet Russe de Monte Carlo), had seen his *Scènes* production in London and had thoroughly damned it in a vitriolic letter to Stravinsky. Measuring the work solely against the gold standard of Balanchine, Berman admitted that there were very occasionally some good things about it – when in the manner of recent choreography by his favourite – but concluded that as a whole it was nonsense, worthless, and totally lacking in interest.[17]

Was Berman put out that he had not had his chance to design the ballet? Even though Stravinsky's son Soulima and his wife Françoise had spoken highly of the work to him,[18] did the composer take note of what Berman told him? Again, in 1953, Stravinsky would not let the matter rest. Writing to Kirstein about his next ballet, which was to be *Agon*, he did not miss the opportunity to suggest that it would work well in between *Scènes* and *Pulcinella*.[19] *Scènes*, it turns out, is one of the few Stravinsky ballet scores that Balanchine never set. For once, might the Ashton precedent have stemmed his enthusiasm?

Scènes de ballet

Ashton's *Scènes* setting was a major step forward for him in terms of construction techniques and expression. In these respects, the ballet alludes to Ashton's model Stravinsky choreographers Balanchine and Nijinska, but it extends in directions that are his own. The music made Ashton examine the technical interior of the score in detail[20] much more than he was used to, as he did not read music. Thus he approached structure in a new way. Yet one of my most surprising discoveries during analysis of *Scènes* was an increased perception of the ballet's connotational values, which emerged directly in tandem with a developing understanding of its structure.

The familiar story is that Ashton heard the music first on the radio and then got to know it from a gramophone recording. His acquaintance with the score must have come from the only recording available at the time, Stravinsky conducting the Philharmonia Symphony Orchestra of New York in 1945.[21] The ballet was created for Margot Fonteyn, Michael Somes and a further four men and twelve women, with scenery and costumes by André Beaurepaire. The layout of the score is as follows. Reference numbers are included, and the notes in brackets indicate additional information about Ashton's casting:

Introduction: *Andante* [the five men]
Danses (Corps de Ballet) [5]: *Moderato*
Variation (Ballerina) [42]: *Con moto*
Pantomime: *Lento* leading to *Andantino* and *Più mosso* [54]
    [the corps and leading couple]
Pas de deux: *Adagio* [69] [the ballerina attended by all 5
    men, accompanied by the other 12 women]
Pantomime: *Agitato ma tempo giusto* [82] [corps de ballet]
Variation (Dancer): *Risoluto* [89] [originally for solo male dancer,
    in Ashton's ballet accompanied by the other men in a group dance]
Variation (Ballerina): *Andantino* [96]
Pantomime: *Andantino* [103] [leading couple and 3 corps women]
Danses (Corps de Ballet): *Con moto* [106] [full cast]
Apothéose: *Poco meno mosso* [119] [full cast]

The score, which, according to performance tempo, ranges in duration from about 16 to 19 minutes, was short by Sadler's Wells standards, and Ashton asked whether Stravinsky would be willing to extend it. The request was turned down.[22] The premiere programme shows that the ballet was immediately preceded by a 'symphonic interlude', like an overture, standard Lambert practice in those days, but which must here have had an impact on readings of the ballet that followed. This was the $3\frac{1}{2}$-minute Rondo finale of Stravinsky's *Concerto in D* for strings (written in 1946), an interesting choice for its highly abrasive, 'insectoid' buzzing quality (it was the score that Jerome Robbins later used for *The Cage* (1951)) and for being the most up-to-date Stravinsky composition on offer at the time.[23] In later performances of *Scènes*, the Introduction music of the ballet score has always been repeated, its initial appearance used as an overture and adding almost one minute to the total length of the ballet.

A considerable bank of source material on Ashton's ballet is available for analysis, including nine videos of Royal Ballet performances and rehearsals over the years until the present day, the earliest an Edmée Wood film from the 1960s featuring Annette Page and Brian Shaw.[24] I had access to two further 1992 videos of the Dutch National Ballet production, which uses Ashton's original ending, the twelve corps women having left the stage, with just the main couple in the centre and the four other men back in the sculptural poses that they held when the curtain went up. For the Royal Ballet, Ashton changed the ending, so that the twelve corps women remain on stage. Together the videos demonstrate some minor choreographic changes and shifts in movement style. I also used Benesh scores and, as well as the full published musical score, an arrangement for piano prepared by Geoffrey Corbett, the conductor at Ashton's premiere.[25] Besides all these sources, 'sketch dancing' the material to the music myself proved revealing, highlighting choreomusical connections and suggesting further possibilities. The opportunity to watch parts of the ballet coached and danced by former and current members of the Royal Ballet for the analytical video *Ashton to Stravinsky* (a collaboration with Geraldine Morris)[26] also opened up many new perspectives.

Turning now to the hermeneutics of Stravinsky's score, we find that it leads us in a number of different directions. The referential bias is of course central to much of Stravinsky's neoclassical writing. We are led by the composer himself, who reminisced with Robert Craft in *Dialogues and a Diary* (1963) about his 'portrait of Broadway in the last years of the War' with its allusions to 'blues' and 'jazz'.[27] It was undoubtedly the popular reference that hastened comments that the score was vulgar, dubious Stravinsky with no part of it more guilty of this than the Pas de deux. Not all critics found this a problem. Desmond Shawe-Taylor wittily pronounced that the trumpet melody of the Pas de deux answered by the horn in imitation

> sounds like a tune played outside a celestial pub and gives one the same sort of pleasure as one of Sickert's paraphrases on Victorian oleographs – the pleasure of the commonplace transformed by the magic of style.[28]

Lawrence Morton offered an acute analysis of this passage according to its original revue setting. The trumpet tune is

> of almost incredible sentimentality. I know nothing quite like it anywhere else in Stravinsky's music. Remove from it the marks of genius, make it four-square, give it a Cole Porter lyric, and you have a genuine pop-tune. As it stands, however, it is a solemnisation of Broadway, a halo for a chorus girl, a portrait of Mr. Rose as Diaghilev. Why should it be? Merely because *The Seven Lively Arts*, for which it was written, was a pretentious production, rich in

snob values. This could not be said; but it could be sung, especially by Broadway's most expressive instrument, the trumpet.

Importantly, he added, to reflect the subtlety of Stravinsky:

> No critic could have written a sharper commentary on the show than did Stravinsky. But it was a gentle ribbing, the storm was tempered to the shorn lamb, for the composer is as humane as he is discerning.[29]

So we note hints of irony and wit as part of Stravinsky's treatment of Broadway paraphernalia.

There are also nineteenth-century allusions in the score. Sources that Stravinsky used include *Giselle*, *Swan Lake*, *The Sleeping Beauty* (he borrowed Dolin's piano scores) and *Coppélia*.[30] Nineteenth-century balletic features of the score, and particularly Tchaikovskian features, include the repetitive, terse staccato figurations in dance rhythms (a natural link with Stravinsky's personal style), the use of hemiola (3/4 across 6/8 in the first variation of the ballerina), the intimate solo violin for her solo section in the Pas de deux, and other passages of feathery strings and filigree frills for flutes and piccolos, not to mention the layout of solo variations, pas de deux, corps dances and pantomime sections. The apotheosis, such a common Stravinsky feature, is likewise a feature of the nineteenth-century grand ballet.

But it is worth bearing in mind that *Giselle* (not one of the Tchaikovsky classics) was the principal source ballet behind *Scènes* in the first instance. There is a hint of it in a sketch outline of *Scènes* in the Basle Stravinsky archive, where the ballerina's first variation is referred to as 'l'entrée de Giselle'. Craft went further in *Stravinsky in Pictures and Documents*, adding a line of references to specific pages in the various nineteenth-century ballet scores, *Giselle* most prominent in the list.[31] Yet, processes of transformation have left any decisive link to these original sources far behind. The following plan draws from Stravinsky's sketch outline, showing the casting and pantomimic indications. I have added Craft's paginations from the source ballets in square brackets.

	[Overture – *Giselle* p. 67]
1 Corps de ballet	[*Giselle* pp. 55–6]
2 'Entre de L'Etoile' and Variation	[*Giselle* p. 65]
('l'entrée de Giselle')	
3 Pantomime: he looks; she disappears,	[Pas d'Action *Coppélia* p. 119
comes back, and they join for the Pas de Deux	(Aurora)]
4 Pas de deux	[*Swan Lake* p. 131]
5 Man's Variation	[*Giselle*]
6 Woman's Variation	

7 Corps de ballet   [*Giselle* p. 87]
8 Finale   [*Giselle* pp. 90–2]

Originally, when Stravinsky was involved with contractual arrangements for the ballet, he hinted at 'a general literary and psychological idea' behind it and a 'romantic character', with Dolin as 'the author of the idea and its choreographic realization'.[32] He admitted that there was no libretto in the conventional sense, but that the occasions of pantomime suggested a story element. The sketch outline for the ballet confirms the element of story in the Pantomime that follows the ballerina's first variation. For some, the 'romantic' tone of the music was prevalent, witness the critic Edwin Denby responding to the Broadway ballet. While suggesting that the revue was the wrong setting for 'a serious Stravinsky', he observed that the score

> has a good deal of nineteenth century expressively and buildup and reaches a sonorous, beautifully tragic climax.

He was undoubtedly influenced by the style of the choreography and its nineteenth-century reference:

> much of the time Markova and Dolin are doing choice bits from *Giselle* anywhere on the stage ... Dolin, in his part, can't resist gazing impressively at one of his hands in what is meant as a tragic pose.[33]

Mercedes de Acosta, a writer friend of the Stravinskys, reported to them (Stravinsky never saw the ballet) that Markova danced as if she were the 'reincarnation' of Pavlova, in other words, the Dying Swan.[34] Markova did wear a short tutu after all, although Stravinsky recalled that he had in mind for her not a white swan tutu, but a black one 'with diamond sequins'.[35] Initially, the ballet was to be called *L'Etoile* after her.

But Denby conveyed one crucial insight. He understood that the music had the potential to represent more than one thing, and that choreography can profoundly affect our reading of the music and what it appears to represent:

> The dancing 'interprets' it [the music] as if it were formless mood-music, a sort of Wagnerian yearning, and blurs its shape ... For the choreographer who can discover the rhythm under its brass surfacing, it would make an excellent ballerina vehicle, touching and grand.[36]

So the discovery of rhythm might have radically changed our perceptions of the music and led to a different kind of ballet. What would Denby have made of Ashton's setting, we might well ask?

There is also in the score a tendency quite the opposite of romanticism, the 'bright, wide-awake beauty'[37] that is far more regularly associated with the Stravinsky aesthetic. For many modernists, like Stravinsky, the disorder of the early years of the twentieth century marked the death-knell of the 'vitalist' romantic movement, with its emphasis on art as a language of the emotions. Instead, there was a call for emotional detachment, order and precision, a lightening of tone and an irony that Ortega calls 'the ban on all pathos ... first consequence of the retreat of art upon itself'.[38] This is more the spirit of Petipa–Tchaikovsky divertissement than of their ballet narratives. Both were artists of the utmost importance to Ashton and, just recently, in 1946, he had renewed his acquaintance with *The Sleeping Beauty*, for the revival of which he created several new dances. There are a number of pronounced references to *Beauty* in *Scènes*.

For Stravinsky himself, no sooner had he completed the score than he changed tack entirely and emphasised abstraction in his programme note for concert performance of his score. He distanced himself from the Billy Rose revue and what it stood for:

> This music is patterned after the forms of the classical dance free of any given literary or dramatic argument. The parts follow each other as in a sonata or a symphony, in contrasts or similarities.

In any case, Stravinsky had been working in the neoclassical tradition of *Apollo*, *Jeu de cartes* (1937) and *Danses Concertantes* (1942), building a score from a string of dances that used the formulae of classical ballet. André Boucourechliev characterises the tradition for *Scènes* with an exquisite elegance that is best left untranslated:

> *Comme les 'pointes', cette musique tourbillonne en cercle clos dans la marge d'une histoire arrêtée.*[39]

In scores such as these, any hint of story is presented without pressure or motivation, as if recalled, frozen in time, rather than as immediate experience (see p. 49). In any case, 'pure dance' is now the most important component. Stravinsky's concert programme note accompanied Ashton's ballet. The critic Richard Buckle had originally developed for him a psychological, metaphysical plot about a hero journeying through life and in a process of self-discovery, even if there was to be no specific characterisation, and the ballet was to be in the 'grand manner', performed in 'conventional ballet costume'. He also had the idea that 'every end is a beginning'.[40] But Ashton abandoned Buckle's theme in order to be in line with Stravinsky's new abstract conception, even if not with all the details of casting indicated in his score.

The musical performance manner in *Scènes* is bracing, and it is enlightening to consider the particularly brisk account of the score with which Ashton first familiarised himself, the Philharmonia Symphony Orchestra of New York recording conducted by the composer and lasting a mere 16 minutes 8 seconds. Then there is the choice of the relentlessly busy, fiercely articulated Rondo of the *Concerto in D* as overture to the premiere of Ashton's ballet. Denby, always musically astute, noted in *Scènes* the rhythmic precision, drive and emphasis on motoric beat that are so often central to Stravinsky's style: 'Stravinsky rhythm' he called it. Ashton, as we shall see later, certainly responded to it too. This indeed was the only feature that the 'Sitter Out' *Dancing Times* critic could grasp. In an oddly perceptive article, he criticised this rhythmic emphasis as a shortcoming – the root of the dryness then widely considered a problem with neoclassical Stravinsky – while congratulating Ashton on his successful interpretation of the music:

> The rhythm allows only one statement, as do classroom exercises ... Stravinsky's music marks only the duration of the step in its academic form and hard as Mr. Ashton may try to make his dance patterns light, gracious and joyous, the lack of melody holds him back. Just when the movements begin to flow harmoniously onward and outward, they have to be abruptly curtailed and brought down to earth before they can even complete a formal pattern. The rhythm allows no more, with a result that the dances seem to be chopped into little pieces.[41]

The full import of this commentary will emerge later. For now, bringing 'down to earth' can be read as a kind of negation of feeling that was unfamiliar to British ballet audiences at the time. Ashton, after all, included elements of romanticism within his work. Philip Hope-Wallace, although very positive about Ashton's new ballet, nevertheless realised that some would find it 'chilling, meaningless and quite heartless'.[42] But Ashton was fully aware of his new expression, describing:

> a hidden beauty ... a cold, distant, uncompromising beauty which says I am here, beautiful, but I will make no effort to charm you.[43]

Years later, he emphasised in an interview, jabbing the air with his fingers:

> The dancers must be staccato. Not at all the usual English business.[44]

Aged only 22 when he saw the new ballet in 1948, the German composer Hans Werner Henze proved remarkably insightful about the aesthetic position:

> Getting away from direct human feelings, concentrating on the abstract ... It was modern, cool ... this music: like steel, the dancers: like apassionate [sic] appearances, the prezision [sic] of the movements, and this absolute beauty ...[45]

The impersonal aspect of the ballet extends beyond vocabulary and dance style to casting and the arrangement and symbolism of dance forms drawn from Petipa. Alastair Macaulay observed:

> Ashton takes up the theme of ballet as a code of forms and ceremonies and occasions – of entries, vision scenes, supported adagios, solo variations, grand pas ... [and he made] a dense and intricate précis of all that ... [The dancers function] as official balletic personae ... there are no particular characters and no emphasis on human intimacy and private personality ...[46]

My own view is that these impersonal qualities lie at the core of this particular Ashton work: in terms of dance style, the brittle staccato dynamics and emphasis on taut vertical stance (and returning to it after bending the torso), the sharp needle pointes and stark, angular designs of tutus and hats. But any primary quality is a matter of emphasis; it is not the whole story. Certainly, heard through Ashton's choreographic vision, it is hard to understand why some critics perceived vulgarity in Stravinsky's score, but the pleasure of the work is that it hints at a number of different qualities and is at heart ambiguous.

There are the qualities of wit and irony that stem readily from choreographic ideas such as the head nods and twists from side to side, the passing of material like messages between dancers, and the marionettish dynamics. Stravinsky's Pas de deux is now a mock 'Rose Adagio', referenced thus in Corbett's piano arrangement, with the ballerina waited on not just by one man, but by all five (see Ill. 7). The trumpet tune reminds us wryly that the ballet is a comment: atypical orchestration, not the real thing. Removed from Broadway connotations here, we sense radical opposition to the scoring conventions of the Petipa grand ballet – none of the emotional warmth of string presence here – and we set out distanced, a touch amused as if we are viewing the event from some secret off-centre position.

Visualisation of musical patterns is another route to wit (amply demonstrated by the work of Walt Disney and Mark Morris), although Ashton introduces this so lightly that it is barely apprehended or so tartly that he eliminates any sense of cliché. Again, he makes us look anew at classical language. At the opening of

Ill. 7. Lesley Collier in *Scènes de ballet*, 'Rose Adagio,' choreography by Frederick Ashton, Royal Ballet.

the ballet, two male couples form sculptures at opposite corners of the stage. On Stravinsky's 'blues' chords, they switch smartly to other 'statues'. In their later dance to stark brass accompaniment, they match the short–long musical rhythms with brutal simplicity in sissonnes fermées. Rather like the three male athletes of Nijinska's *Les Biches* (1924), stepping and jumping on Poulenc's gruff chords, they are almost doll-like in their false academicism. In the first Pantomime, the women perform bourrées side to side, marking the accents and intervallic leaps on flute and piano with retirés, head twists and wrist flicks, looking up on the high note, down on the low note (there is an especially spiky, shrill account of this in the 1945 recording). Even the ballerina, in her first Variation, responds to the taut melodic rhythm with an exactitude that seems to question, if not reduce, her flesh-and-blood physicality.

In the Apotheosis, Ashton uses this visualisation technique to double ironic and brilliant effect, with the commencement of a series of soaring lifts, up and over, side to side, the ballerina and her partner gradually drawing in more and more of the cast. The lifts begin just at the point when the melody line begins a pattern of sighs (up–down motion). With the effect of riding cumulus clouds, the women progress downstage in tandem with the deepening musical sighs, their motion enlarged by the women of the corps, who step to duplicate the second arabesque line of the landing. After three sighs, the melodic gestures start to take an upward turn in opposition to the lifts, and each landing suddenly looks uneasy, effortful. But there is added complication in that other women further from centre stage are stepping into arabesque but reaching upwards; so, if the central women oppose the direction of the melodic line, those on the side match it, and vice versa.[47] As your eye moves around this complex texture, you sense a multitude of oppositions, both spatial and between eye and ear, and Ashton makes a small distance in pitch seem vast. On and on continue the lifts to melody and bass oscillating anxiously up and down in semitone steps and for longer than seems comfortable. Pressure is finally released when the directional thrust turns vertical. The five men hoist their partners up on to their shoulders to new clamorous chords, and continuity breaks.

In a sense, the Apotheosis as a whole represents a major change in the ballet, both musically and choreographically, an escape from the brittle vitality and acute rhythmic tension that hitherto predominated, into long lines, lifts and brilliant tableaux. Macaulay refers to the new 'guiding momentum'[48] discovered at this point. Apparently, this was Stravinsky's favourite section, and he had composed it on the day when Paris was liberated: 'I interrupted my work every few minutes to listen to the radio reports. I think my jubilation is in the music.' He had envisaged the choreography as 'a stage full of groups twirling and mounting "*delirando*"'.[49] The final moment in Ashton's ballet is dazzling, but relatively contained, with the ballerina's supported arabesque penchée and flourish of the arms, the men back in their initial sculptural pairs, and the twelve women kneeling behind the central couple, alternating between arms overhead and upright or stretched out over the front leg, switching positions smartly on the final musical blast. Originally, the ending was even quieter, after the twelve women had left the stage. The main tone of the piece is about reining energy in, not about letting it escape. We tauten our muscles once more. Ashton's *Scènes* is fundamentally brilliant, but also icy and anxious.

There have been earlier, briefer diversions from the primary tone of the ballet. It is always the ballerina who exerts a force that threatens the frozen image, and she introduces more progressive dynamic contours to the ballet. Her first Variation, which surely parallels Aurora's arrival Variation in *Sleeping Beauty*, is an emphatic crescendo leading to a rush down the diagonal into a high supported lift. The second is rounded, blooms gently and ends quietly. The Rose Adagio expands like its Tchaikovsky–Petipa predecessor into a more active use of the stage, a vibrant full circle of dancers from which the ballerina finds her cavaliers to support her (a soft shape within this straight line and angle ballet), back to centre for the fullest orchestral rendering of the main theme, before a diminuendo into the next part of the ballet. The Rose Adagio is also a rare moment when the ballerina can 'sing' with the music, swooping and soaring to the broad legato of the trumpet. It is hard to imagine how Stravinsky's intentions as articulated in *Dialogues and a Diary* could possibly have made sense in a classical Adagio: his idea was for the woman to be associated with the comparatively unobtrusive sound of the contrapuntal horn line, and the man with the trumpet.[50]

There is also an element of darkness and mystery in Ashton's *Scènes*. He once described the ballerina in her langorous second Variation as a dark pearl conjuring up spirits.[51] Then there is the strange moment in the first Danses when the full corps of sixteen suddenly assembles into a phalanx and quietly retreats towards an upstage corner (the 'block step'[52]). Joan Acocella found the moment particularly vivid and curious:

> We can't see their faces, their 'story'. We only see their lovely backs and thighs, moving away from us, leaving us behind, and the sight is tremendous. Things don't have to be warm in order to be moving.[53]

The decor is a construction of pillars hiding sinister, shadowy corners. Buckle described the arches as 'seen through the eyes of a northern pupil of the early Chirico';[54] at one point during the third Pantomime, three women emerge from behind them, strike poses, 'just sort of peep and look pretty' according to the Royal Ballet Benesh score, retreat to re-emerge further along, then exit as if they have briefly engaged in stylised eavesdropping. This happens at the point when the ballerina rushes to embrace her partner and throws herself into his arms, the only apparent outburst of passion in the piece, and it seems strangely out of context here: the three women distance the moment further and make us feel like voyeurs. The ensemble Danses that immediately follows, called 'Samba' in the Benesh score, negates all romance with its insect-like pointe-walk entrance and mechanical adherence to beat.

The reason for the strange corps retreat in the 'block step' is perhaps the now familiar one, that Ashton explored the theorems of Euclid when creating this ballet. One section (a series of brisk changements and relevés at [66]) was actually called 'Geometry',[55] but otherwise, perhaps the Euclid source was most influential in suggesting new facings and travelling directions to Ashton. Evidence of a direct relationship between Euclid and the choreography is hard to find. But the concern here is to explore the effect of the choreographer's exploration within the ballet that we see on stage. In many ways it is the score that gives the key to Ashton's constructional techniques in the ballet, whether or not the choreographer was ever fully conscious of this.

Structural business

Stravinsky's score is a tightly knit symphonic construction, based on clearly connecting motivic material. He refers in *Dialogues and a Diary* to the 'melodic-pull' in the Introduction (at [1]), a seed idea for the whole work (see the

5/8 bars in Ex. 4.1a).[56] It generates the melody of the ensuing Danses. Its intervals later expand (Ex. 4.1b, at [15]), and it is rhythmically manipulated in various ways, re-shaped with internal repetition on its immediate repeat (the 7/8 bar in Ex. 4.1a), then at [117] foreshortened as its opening note is removed (or rather placed at the end), to become the beginning (and end) of the next full account of the motif (Ex. 4.9d, p. 283). The stepwise ascending upper line of the opening 'blues' chords (A, B then A, B, C) is the root of the melody heard in the final ensemble Danses (Ex. 4.9a) and Apotheosis; it is also a 'filled-out' version of the melodic-pull motif. Ashton, in not untypical fashion, also builds a tightly knit language for the ballet, a mosaic of movement ideas, some of them hallmarks of this particular work, like the sharp head and hand movements, flicks of wrists, and frozen poses based on Cecchetti arm positions, and other cliché steps given motivic status, like piqué in attitude and arabesque, sissonne fermée or ouverte followed by coupé assemblé.[57] The Apotheosis is particularly strong in its recapitulatory features, the sideways bourrées to retiré with turning heads and wrists, the women lifted up to sit on the men's shoulders (a moment from the first Danses), the men's sculptures from the Introduction. Nowhere in the Ashton repertory is there a more intricate network of relationships across his movement material.

Ex. 4.1a. *Scènes de ballet*, Introduction, 'melodic-pull'.

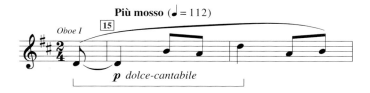

Ex. 4.1b. *Scènes de ballet*, first Danses, 'melodic-pull'.

There are, however, other Stravinsky techniques that are not typical of Ashton and yet have been borrowed by the choreographer for this piece. One of these is what the musicologist Edward T. Cone has referred to as 'block' construction, the discontinuous formal process for which *Symphonies of Wind Instruments* is the paradigm example (see pp. 149-50), and which involves interlock, with blocks in counterpoint through time as well as synthesis and unification of disparate ideas.[58] The case for the latter in *Scènes* has already been made. Suffice it to say that stratification is also a clear feature of this score, and Ashton readily adopts it for himself. The first ensemble Danses features lines or square formations of dancers interrupting each other, each with its own distinctive movement statement or block of movement material. Three 'layers' of women are arranged according to their respective heights. There is the line of four women who enter across the front to the horn breaking in at [8], in 3/4 over 5/8 strings: soubresaut, soubresaut, step jeté en avant, relevé in attitude and extend into arabesque (see Ex. 4.2). They take the attention away from the square wedge of four women who open the Danses and who, though Ashton could surely not have known this, accord with Stravinsky's apparent 'plan' (remembered in *Dialogues*) that the four violas should be danced by four women.[59] They all halt as a third group of women enters across the back of the stage, but memories of their material linger on. Stratification operates spatially as well as through time as groups of dancers occupy distinctive territories. Ashton introduces synthesis towards the end of this Danses as he places on top of each other the three layers first seen successively.

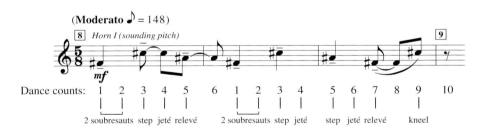

Ex. 4.2. *Scènes de ballet*, first Danses, second women's group.

Part of the effect of discontinuity arises from the abrupt and often apparently arbitrary manner in which Ashton's phrases end. The dancers perform their phrases with flat dynamics as if performing a task: they just do a phrase and stop, sometimes even with the air of automata (for example, the first two groups of women halting in the early Danses). There is no breath pattern, no move towards a climax or from dynamic flowering to repose, with arms gracefully delaying the point of rest. The latter are the customary phrasings practised by dancers, even in their day-to-day class, and that had found full expression in Ashton's recently created *Symphonic Variations* (1946). It is interesting, therefore, that Michael Somes, in a 1979 rehearsal video of *Scènes* (led by Jennifer Penney and Michael Coleman), urges the men to clip their arms to bras bas, refusing to allow any sense of breath delay. The performance here is more rhythmically taut than on many later videos. Analogous to this, effects of crescendo and diminuendo are relatively rare in the music: as in Stravinsky's usual style, dynamics tend to shift abruptly. No wonder, then, that the *Dancing Times* reviewer referred to movements that

> have to be abruptly curtailed and brought down to earth before they can even complete a formal pattern ... [and dances that] seem to be chopped into little pieces.

Another form of Stravinskian discontinuity stems from rhythm pattern, asymmetries that disrupt expectations. The symmetries of traditional ballet, two or four presentations of a movement unit, have no place here, and would not fit the music either. Single and odd-number appearances of ideas defy any sense of balance or expectation. The manner in which movement units are constructed contributes to this effect of asymmetry. Musical motifs often expand or contract through internal repetition, for instance the 'melodic-pull' discussed earlier. This is also the case in the choreography (though not necessarily in simultaneous relationship with any matching musical motif pattern). There are many examples, and several have been recorded on the *Ashton to Stravinsky* video. For instance, after their opening sculptures, the four men perform a 7-count unit of simple steps, ronds de jambes, half-turns; they dance it twice, and each time hold still on counts 4 and 5. Two of the men move on the spot; the other two edge away to make a square formation. Beat is pronounced, whether heard or seen or both. The effect of the sequence is like a clock ticking. The third time, the unit is telescoped to fit 5 counts (see Ex. 4.3). The 7-7-5 structure rides across the written 5/8 musical metre until the last bar, but here, you nevertheless perceive the 7-7-5 outline in the music. As he usually does, Ashton responds to what you hear rather than to the appearance of the score, even if, for *Scènes*, Ashton employed counts for the sake of rhythmic precision, a rare procedure for him. Likewise, the material is asymmetrical for the wedge of four women who open the Danses that follows. They perform a sequence of two phrases: one, phrase *a*, leading to relevés in arabesque, the next, phrase *b*, to hops on pointe with the working leg extending from attitude devant, the whole sequence then repeated (see Ex. 4.4). The form of the material is *a b a b* but in a count structure 10-10-13-9, in harmony with the thematic organisation (repetition or varied repeti-

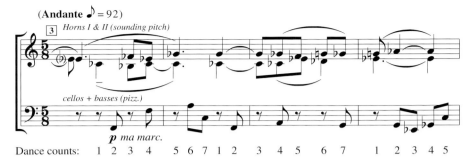

Ex. 4.3. *Scènes de ballet*, Introduction, men's phrase.

Ex. 4.4. *Scènes de ballet*, first Danses, first women's group.

tion) and phrase lengths in the music. Units expand and contract. The second *a* is longer than the first, 13 counts instead of 10, because the original opening pas de basque has been changed to two pas de bourrée. When *b* is repeated, one of the little hops near the end is removed, so 10 counts become 9. Again, the dancers hesitate on the silent count 1 of the bar and then make their first step with what you hear, as the melody starts on count 2.

When the second group of women enter to the horn at [8], they repeat their opening phrase (see Ex. 4.2), adding an extra step jeté that spreads them right across the front of the stage, after which they kneel to finish (a 6-count phrase becoming 10 counts). The insertion of an extra jeté might well have been led by the need to cross the stage, but here, as often elsewhere, Ashton does not duplicate the structure of musical repetition. The principle of expansion and contraction has been borrowed from Stravinsky and then adopted to independent choreographic ends by Ashton. Again, driven by the timing of their arrival at the side of the stage rather than by the music, at [16] a group of women start up a pattern of piqués derrières and then a drawing to fifth on pointe (3, 5 then 1 piqués). Such asymmetries are evident in other, quite different ways in the ballet: in the choreographic formations, for instance, or in Beaurepaire's pattern of arches.

Repeating 'pieces' of material like ostinatos, on or around one spot or in a simple spatial pattern, are another feature of Ashton's construction. The 'clockticking' men near the opening present the seed of this principle. Later, in the men's Variation, they perform sissonnes fermées backwards and forwards and side to side, all within a strictly limited territory. In the second Danses, they carry a repeating jumping sequence in a line-up at the backcloth while the women progress repeatedly in channels up-, down- and across the stage. It is perhaps not a coincidence that Stravinsky runs an ostinato in the bass line right through this Danses. But this is his familiar technique of immobility, complement to that of violent discontinuity through abrupt change. Pedal notes or chords as well as ostinatos create a static effect over a period of time, likewise melodic lines oscillating around a centre (as in the original 'melodic-pull' – see Ex. 4.1a). The jubilant ending of the piece on the chord of C major is effective through reiteration rather than as expected culmination or resolution. In another sense then, the ballet is frozen in time.

The *Ashton to Stravinsky* video reveals that some of the wittiest recognition of and play with musical procedures lies in the ballerina material. Her first Variation is already formally playful, its three main sections driven by the statement and re-statement of the main musical theme, but at the same time a sense of balance and hence two-part division is suggested by the two similar crescendos when the ballerina bursts down the diagonal in a series of grands jetés.[60] At the rhythmic level, a predominant characteristic is the shift in both music and dance between 2- and 3-count units. However, reference to melodic or pitch-related procedures also creates tension. When she starts dancing, she not only stops and starts with the main musical theme, she also moves up to pointe and down to flat-foot with its contour, the long–short–long motif characteristically outlining a drop in musical pitch (see Ex. 4.5). Soon, in a series of jumps on pointe and sharp relevés with retiré, she first articulates the top of the melody with the retiré and lift of the matching arm, and then the downward trajectory with a stabbing pointe.

Ex. 4.5. *Scènes de ballet*, opening, the ballerina's first Variation.

In the middle section of the Variation, the reading of the main theme is subtler, although now the steps often match the dotted-note motif exactly. Several phrases end in a flat-foot fourth position with one arm raised above the head, a grounded action in tension with a pull upwards (see Ill. 8). First, the drop in pitch draws our attention to the grounded action. Along the way, Ashton gives us a step unit ending on relevé with a pull of the body and arms down to one side: up and down have switched between body parts, but again the emphasis on down – now in the arms – is most forceful, with the drop in pitch. Now, the musical theme, in a kind of inverted form, demonstrates its relationship with the stepwise *ascent* of the opening chords of the score (a form of the 'melodic-pull'), and we see another account of the flat-foot fourth position ending with one arm raised. But how do we reconcile aural and visual perceptions here, where surely the pull upwards is most forceful, an effect 'enabled' by the music? By now, we feel drawn in many directions. Certainly, we never feel settled, just as we sense shock when the pitch and contour of the lifts in the Apotheosis move out of synchronisation (see pp. 269-70). Ashton also marks this special moment in the ballerina's Variation with a wry interpolation of his signature 'Fred step' – the beginning of it, posé en arabesque, coupé dessous, small développé à la seconde, pas de bourrée, before a kind of straight-legged turning pas de chat and the flat-foot fourth ending. The Fred step is also a legato insertion, quite different in dynamic character from the rest of the Variation. In the final section of this dance, for the last statement of the main theme in the music, the ballerina almost falls over her feet in excitement, no longer in time with the clipped musical motif, no longer drawing attention to pitch contour, racing ahead, with the up-

Ill.8. Lesley Collier in *Scènes de ballet*, first ballerina Variation, choreography by Frederick Ashton, Royal Ballet.

Ex. 4.6. *Scènes de ballet*, opening, the ballerina's second Variation.

beat phrasing typical of Ashton, anticipating the downbeat arrival of the melody.

In her second Variation, the most liquid, legato part of the ballet, the ballerina connects and reconnects with different aspects of the music at different times. Sometimes, she selects the 6-count ostinato rhythm that we hear throughout (3/4 in the music), tapping it out, for instance, with her pointe at both the beginning and end of the solo (see Ex. 4.6). Sometimes she connects with the underlying metre but not specifically the ostinato rhythm, sometimes with the sweep of the melody. But she draws particular attention to pitch contour in the central part of the Variation, where two upward moving intervals in a clarinet line are singled out. The ballerina cancels out the musical gesture on both occasions, at [99] and [100], a développé to the side emphatically folded down across behind the body into tendu (see Ex. 4.7).

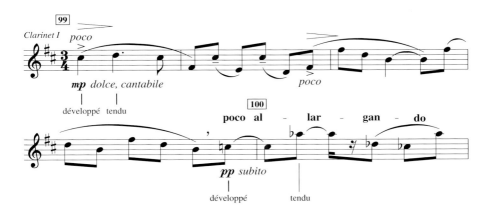

Ex. 4.7. *Scènes de ballet*, central section, the ballerina's second Variation.

The second occasion needles with particular irony, with its wider interval in the music (the initial note breaking in before the bar-line) and checked tempo around this point. The centuries-old semiotic significance of moving upwards in pitch, meaning idealism, aspirations heavenwards, overcoming earthliness, or literally just going upwards, and matched by choreographers for years, has been deftly deconstructed. In the final section of the Variation, the ballerina takes her freedom and swims across the musical metre in a fast waltz (3-count units across the back) and then several series of little hops in arabesque. The latter have been counted in different ways across the years. For the *Ashton to Stravinsky* video, Antoinette Sibley counted the sequence irregularly as 5-4-7 with a relevé just *after* the peak note in the melody, but Benesh notation scores indicate that for a while this diagonal settled into plain 5s with the relevé *on* the high note. Both versions cross the metre of the music, and here they do not fit neatly with what is heard, either. The difference hardly matters, although a measure of irregularity achieved by some means or other, within the choreography or between the choreography and the music, is probably crucial to the effect of waywardness. Perhaps important too is the sense of being 'with' the peak note as culmination, although the process of creating the video revealed that sometimes a dancer's 'with' means being led or lifted by the note (in other words just *after* it), sometimes it means simultaneous response. Such metrical irregularity, incidentally, is unusual for Ashton.

We see Ashton responding again to melodic organisation in the third Pantomime, which immediately follows the ballerina's second Variation. There is a retrograde version of Stravinsky's 'melodic-pull' at the end of this section (see Ex. 4.8). Ashton produces a kind of retrograde, too: his motif of arms pressing down into an inverted V-shape (over arabesque) reversed, so that the ballerina now goes from the V to the 'preparatory' position of arms overhead in fifth position and ends with the arms overhead. But this is yet another demonstration of Ashton going against the grain of the melody: the arms are pressed down as the pitch rises and raised overhead to the low notes. He makes you see up and down against the contour of what you hear. The fact of opposition is brilliantly clear.

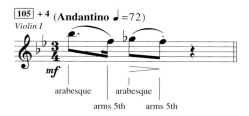

Ex. 4.8. *Scènes de ballet*, third Pantomime, retrograde of 'melodic-pull'.

Ashton writes that he 'set out to merge the rhythmic subtleties with the visual counterpoint'[61] in *Scènes*, and his analysis of different rhythmic lines is particularly striking in the last Danses (see Ex. 4.9). Here is another mode of stratification in the ballet. Stravinsky writes the score in 3/8, although he also lets us hear a touch of 3/4 like a hemiola across two bars of 3/8. A 4/8 bass ostinato running throughout emerges more and more strongly from the texture as the dance progresses. The dancers all start out in 3/8 or 3/4 time (6–count units – Ex. 4.9a). However, the three intermingled groups – women, men and solo couple – create three different rhythmic strands, the quaver motor very prominent across them all, but each with accents sparking out of the texture at different times. Later, at [113], most of the dancers begin to respond to the 4/8 ostinato (in units of 8 counts, estimated at a crotchet rate – see Ex. 4.9c). This is reinforced for a while by the melody. However, there are still flashes of 3/8 dance material. The four men forming a line across the back mark this metrical system against every-thing else, including what is heard, with a 6-count ostinato unit of little jetés and temps de poisson on count 5 (across two musical bars still written in 3/8). Here, very unusually, Ashton reflects only the written metre, the look of the score. Straight after this, we hear the 4/8 ostinato especially starkly isolated on the piano, but suddenly there is nothing in the choreography to go with it. The men continue doggedly in 3s with a 9-count sequence towards us, sissonne coupé assemblé once to each side, then on the spot, changement and entrechat six, three 3-count units, the sequence then repeated. But they start the sequence on count 2 of the bar, prompted by the horn line (Ex. 4.9d). There has been some doubt about the timing of this last sequence over the years. In some of the video performances examined, the jump forwards occurs on the bass note on count 1 of the bar. During the making of *Ashton to Stravinsky*, the rehearsal director Christopher Newton taught what he remembered as the earlier version. The fact that Newton got to his feet with such lack of hesitation, hummed a bass note and prepared with a plié before the first jump forwards on the first note of the horn line was highly persuasive. His memory also confirmed Ashton's more usual style of being led into a dance phrase by melody, not by the bar-line.

Such detailed textural and metrical analysis of music and contrapuntal activity are rare for Ashton, though he did show some inclination towards visualising melody and accompaniment in *Symphonic Variations*. Likewise, if we examine his other work, it is very hard to find the same singular attitude to dynamics and phrasing. In *Cinderella*, created later the same year and which borrows a number of movement ideas from *Scènes*, there are examples of asymmetries in Prokofiev's phrasing, but Ashton's phrases follow his more usual patterns of motion directed towards climax or repose. There is no doubt that *Scènes* is a work in which Ashton shows an exceptional approach to music, prompted, I suggest, by the fact that he was choreographing to Stravinsky. Significantly, in the one part of Hans Werner Henze's *Ondine* (1958) that is closest to neoclassical Stravinsky, we again see signs of Ashton's most motoric style of choreography. It is the wedding divertissement music in Act III, a miniature piano concerto, and *Symphony in Three Movements* comes readily to mind. In the last section particu-larly – a 'sinister waltz' for the full ensemble of entertainers – the musical syncopations and accents stride freely across the regular 3/4 framework, but Ashton continues to clarify for us the 3/4 in waltz steps, plain and clear against the musical complications.[62] These tactics are very similar to those that Balanchine often adopts when he works with a rhythmically complex musical passage: keeping the motor going and the choreography simple (see p. 173).

It is interesting to go further with speculations that Ashton might have adopted some ideas in *Scènes* from Balanchine and Nijinska and especially from

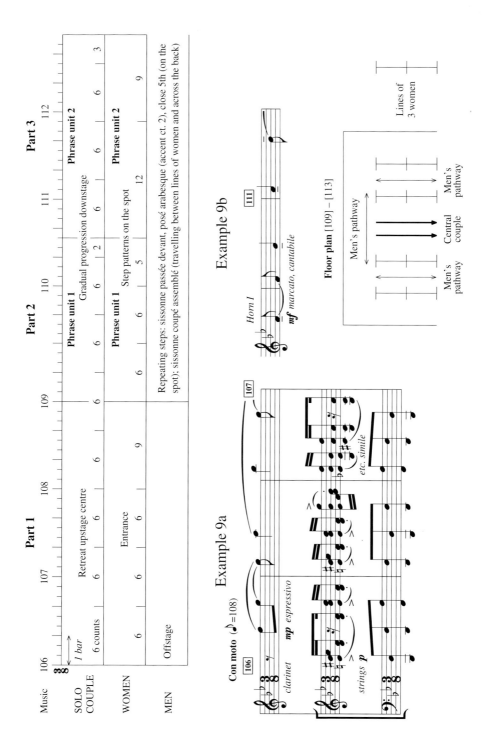

Exs. 4.9a and b. *Scènes de ballet*, second Danses, diagram of metrical structure including counts.

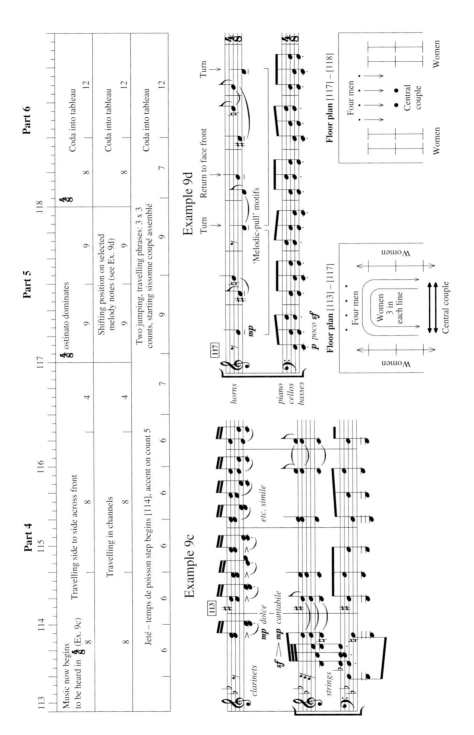

Exs. 4.9c and d. *Scènes de ballet*, second *Danses*, diagram of metrical structure including counts (continued).

their Stravinsky ballets. Critics, especially in the USA, have consistently drawn the comparison with Balanchine. Ashton might have heard the hints of both *Apollo* and *Les Noces* in this score. There are the sculptures at the beginning and end of *Scènes*, with one man partly in view behind his partner, reminiscent of both these other ballets,[63] or the sitting and kneeling poses, reminders of Apollo observing his muses. The phrasing is not unlike that of Nijinska's *Noces*, with its unexpected accents, asymmetrical phrase lengths, sudden halts and shifts of gear. Common to both Balanchine and Nijinska are the *Scènes* techniques of immobility and abrupt discontinuity.

In Ashton's analysis of the texture and rhythmic content of Stravinsky's *Scènes*, there are clear links with Balanchine. Yet Ashton's use of music differs in certain important respects. He is driven far more by melody than by the appearance of the score. Indeed, a significant component of the second Danses is Ashton's exposure of the conflict between melody and bar-line. There are occasions when he is clearly led by a melody that does not match the bar-line – new dance material starting, for instance, with the onset of melody on beat 3 (two bars before [111] and immediately before [113] – see Exs. 4.9b and c). Similarly, in the early, 5/8 Danses, Ashton regularly choreographs to bring out the melody, beginning after a rest on the downbeat of the bar. I suspect that Balanchine would have been moved to choreograph such silent downbeats. That is often his approach: he does so, for instance, at the start of *Agon* (1957). But it is also worth noting that Ashton's structural complexity in this ballet surpasses anything that Balanchine had attempted by this point in his career, and possibly afterwards. This tendency is perhaps why *Scènes* has been criticised for being too fussy and dense, too cool and cerebral. Some reviewers of the 1948 Sadler's Wells Ballet European tour (when Henze saw *Scènes*) were interested in its complexity; others worried over its lack of humanity, an interesting observation after the trauma of the war.[64] The ballet was first taken to the USA in 1955, although press releases indicate that there were originally plans to include it in the repertory of the first triumphal visit of Sadler's Wells in 1949.[65] American opinions were mixed then and have remained so ever since.

We have seen, then, that Ashton's techniques link closely with those of his composer, even though it is unlikely that he was aware of the degree to which this was so. There are many structural devices common to choreography and music, particularly noteworthy in that this ballet is in many respects unique in Ashton's output. The ballet also shares with Stravinsky a sophisticated, double-edged commentary on tradition. There is nostalgia, but treated with dry humour; there is satire, but gently offered. Mystery and shadows have their place, but there is also glitter. Yet Ashton nuances the expressive content of the score in a particular way. Stravinsky comments on Broadway and nineteenth-century ballet. Ashton ignores the former, but draws on his experience of nineteenth-century Petipa and twentieth-century Balanchine and Nijinska, and in these sources lies the aesthetic weighting of the choreography: in Henze's terms 'modern, cool … like steel', the weighting of bright, wide-awake Stravinsky modernism. It has also been illuminating to see how detailed relationships between music and dance contribute to the force of expression in Ashton's *Scènes*: there is an extraordinary density of moment throughout the ballet, with both melodic line and rhythm as sources for Ashton's interactions. Now, perhaps, analysis has increased our understanding of that perceived concentrated experience. Having watched the ballet, we are left astonished that we have travelled so far so quickly.

Sharing Scènes

The 'Stravinsky the Global Dancer' (*SGD*) database reveals that there are at least fifteen other settings of *Scènes*, most by far created in the 1950s and 1960s, celebrating the post-war swing to neoclassicism and no doubt, too, the absence of any Balanchine classic to this music. The Ashton ballet did not travel until MacMillan brought it in a no-costume, no-décor version to the Ballet of the Deutsche Oper Berlin in 1968.[66] Unsurprisingly, West Germany features most strongly within the group of ballets made in the 1950s and 1960s, including, for instance, Peter van Dijk's setting in 1962, part of a major flowering of interest in Stravinsky in Hamburg at the time, which culminated in the eightieth birthday celebrations for which Balanchine presented his *Orpheus, Apollo* and *Agon* (see p. 241). There were also several settings in the USA and, interestingly, one by David Dupré in 1961 for the Teatro Municipal in Rio de Janeiro.

The general impression from the database of a neoclassical, plotless response is hardly surprising. Given the dictates of the score, what room is there for any linear plot? Only one setting does not borrow the musical title: Robert Rodham's allusive title *Pas de Poissons* for Pennsylvania Ballet (1966) speaks for itself. Boris Kniasev's *Scene di Balletto* (1955) for La Scala, Milan, introduced a kind of theme through a set of allegorical characters: La Gelosia, La Speranza, Il Destino, Il Dolore and L'Angelo. Gustav Blank's *Scènes* for the Ballet of the Städtische Oper Berlin (1952) featured six performers as audience ('Zuschauer') to the three soloists and female corps of eight 'Damen'.

John Taras set *Scènes* on two occasions, for the Netherlands Ballet (1954) and for the New York City Ballet Stravinsky Festival in 1972. In contrast to Ashton, Taras found the music 'a digest version of a romantic ballet' (his own words). Reporting on the 1972 setting, Nancy Reynolds recalled chiffon-clad creatures in a moonlit woodland, and a couple in shifting relationship – 'happy meetings, sad partings, ominous warnings … without, however, resolution or development'. She also noted that some reviewers saw touches of *Giselle, Swan Lake* or *Sylphide* in the ballet, perhaps 'a bit of an overreaction to the quasi-narrative aspects of the work',[67] although it is fascinating that their observations resonate with the actual sources of Stravinsky's score. The general impression we are left with is of a mild, charming response to the music. Some American critics compared it with the 'canonic' Ashton version, their readings of the music governed by his. Taras's *Scènes* was 'gracious enough', wrote Jack Anderson. 'But Stravinsky's music is more than gracious. It is a heady mixture of sentiment and irony. When Ashton choreographed it for Sadler's Wells, he stressed the irony and produced a quirky marvel.'[68] When Clive Barnes (the British dance critic who had moved to New York) saw Nicolas Petrov's earlier 1972 setting for Pittsburgh Ballet Theatre, he wrote:

> To rechoreograph *Scènes de Ballet* after Ashton's version – regrettably less well-known in America than it deserves – is tantamount to re-choreographing *Apollo*. There are some scores that have found their definitive choreographic interpretation and this is surely one of them.[69]

He repeated the opinion even more forcefully a few months later when reviewing the Taras choreography:

> To attempt a second version is like attempting a second version of *Apollo*. Gallant, but profoundly idiotic.[70]

I have been able to look in detail at four further versions of *Scènes* on video, and the process proved especially illuminating in relation to the potential within the score itself, as well as highlighting what is particular to Ashton's response. At the same time, it is clear that Ashton's *Scènes* is not an iconic work like *Apollo* or *Agon*: it does not appear to have restrained choreographers, nor has it stimulated a series of commentaries upon itself.

Christopher Wheeldon would probably be the first to admit that his *Scènes de ballet* (1999) for the School of American Ballet (SAB) is not one of his major works, and I for one found it oversweet, too pink and too cute when I saw it live.[71] Yet it did receive appreciative reviews and, on a closer viewing – aware that I first watched it through the lens of the Ashton ballet (how could I not?) – an intriguing musical sophistication became apparent. The ballet was revived in 2006.

Wheeldon was in the unusual position of knowing the Ashton work, having danced with the Royal Ballet for many years and trained at the Royal Ballet School before moving to New York City Ballet, but this did not deter him from staging the music in a country less familiar with or impressed by the Ashton precedent. There may be a couple of sly references back to the early work, most notably to the motif of waving the arms gently overhead from the second ballerina Variation, but Wheeldon's setting is in marked contrast to the Ashton in almost every other respect.

The fundamental premise of the ballet had considerable bearing on the response to, as well as original choice of, the music. It is about the process of becoming a dancer, moving from childhood up through the hierarchy to the status of professional ballerina (or male dancer) and it involved dancers from SAB at various stages of training, a cast of fifty-two in all (one reason why it has received few performances), including just two professionals from the corps of New York City Ballet. Naturally, Wheeldon had to keep much of the movement material relatively simple, likewise the spatial arrangements. For good reasons, he did not employ Ashton's range of movement. There is also whimsical reference to the Russian ballet tradition in the designs by Ian Falconer (who had once worked with David Hockney): a dance studio setting, with a cityscape of onion domes seen outside the windows, and portraits of dancers on the walls. A double barre, slightly slanted on the diagonal, upstage right to downstage left, gives rise to the most important structural feature of the whole piece, exact reflection between the two sides of the stage, as if one of the barres is attached to a mirror. So one dancer becomes two, two become four, and at the end 26 become 52. Consequently, there is no notion of a single glittering ballerina as the recurring personality within the ballet. This has a direct effect upon how we experience its shape.

The only ballerina moment is the Pas de deux – a real one (unlike in the Ashton ballet), and the one specially marked point in the ballet (not one of several). One side of the stage darkens – this is the main occasion on which the reflection device disappears – and a small girl watches from the barre as if her dreamworld is on the other side. Made strange, even arch by the 'public' timbre of the solo trumpet and horn, this is a duet of grand lifts, arabesques penchées, one very high leg extension to the side, and the embellishment of early ideas for the musical recapitulation. For the biggest climax of all, at [79], the ballerina sits across her partner's thigh and they embrace passionately. Just before that moment, the ballerina and young girl bid farewell graciously to each other, as if the latter should not be witness to such a private or adult event, but then, abruptly after it, the stage lights brighten again and the statutory reflection couple enters, immediately releasing the tension. So this magic centre, this brief glimpse of stardom and major romance, signalled as especially significant, is nevertheless rapidly dispensed with. The ballerina and her partner dissolve back into the ensemble (she in a pink dress, he in black practice tights like the other older girls and boys). And, if their movement once looked fresh and personal when they began the Pas de deux, some of it now gets borrowed and formalised by the ensemble. Even the solo ballerina Variations are not solos – there are two soloists for each and an accompanying ensemble of 3+3 or 6+6. The male Variation (scored by Ashton for 1+4) is danced by eight men (4+4).

For the following analysis, the reader might wish to cross-reference parallel points in the analysis of Ashton's *Scènes*, and also in the *Ashton to Stravinsky* video. In Variation I, Ashton treats us to a high impact 'Aurora'-style arrival, and his solo moves from relatively contained movement grounded in flat fourth positions to two explosions, grand jeté sequences down each diagonal, creating the effect of closure at these points (and a hint of two-part form against another division into three sections – see p. 276). The second explosion is vastly bigger than the first and ends in a high lift. Thus, the ballerina immediately shows that she operates somewhere outside and above the common denominator of Ashton's setting.

Wheeldon shapes Variation I differently. He adopts a lively approach but without extremes. The first solo step is piqué attitude devant, and joyous skip rhythm runs into a flying grand jeté. For the first explosion music, the soloists perform relevés on the spot, unfolding the leg devant, a comparatively static response. For the second, they run, leap and escape downstage right and upstage left respectively (the exit releasing tension); the accompanying trios perform simple soutenu turns, one dancer after another in a line (showing the three beats in a bar), and kneel to finish (another release of tension). Wheeldon's dance is more overtly in three-part form than Ashton's, without ambiguity – broadly speaking, the soloists enter, progress downstage, upstage, downstage and then leave. It is also a less intense experience. But this is not meant to be a value judgement. Ashton makes us feel the rise and fall in a melody, but both uses and contradicts it, as well as exploiting tensions, between the pull of gravity downwards and the pull upwards against it, and between stasis and motion. Wheeldon's dancers' generous jumps articulate the simpler pleasures of being airborne, mobile and liberated, not having to work against resistance.

Wheeldon emphasises flow and ease in the ballet as a whole, dynamics that are perhaps more achievable for dancers in training. This affects how or indeed whether we perceive musical staccato. For instance, at [58] in the first Pantomime, the isolated flute notes are treated with luscious arm gestures or piqué arabesques with the line of motion streaming up through and beyond the body, not curtailed. Ashton emphasised the isolation of these notes, with wrist flicks, sharp retirés and turns of the head, motion held within the body. During the section called 'Geometry' in the Ashton ballet (at [66]), Wheeldon's women perform lunge runs, marking each quaver beat; but their circling arms, alternating up and over the head and dissolving into port de bras over bourrées, draw our attention far more to the wispy phrases of the upper strings than to the pizzicato bass revealed by Ashton's changements and relevés. Ashton treated the pompous gesticulations of the male Variation music with additional pomposity as irony: clipped sissonnes and abrupt halts. Wheeldon's men move with equal power, but their steps flow on, an effect enhanced by canon textures continuing the motion across the musical punctuations. Again, the overall effect is much more legato.

On the other hand, Wheeldon's ballet is full of simple polymetrical effects, far more of them than in Ashton's. Near the beginning of Danses I, for instance, when the horn strides in 3/4 across the 5/8 in the strings (at [8] – see Ex. 4.2), two small boys enter with a 3-count sequence: step–glissade–assemblé. Meanwhile, two little girls dance a 2-count sequence: run, run, run and hold (short–short–long). Such effects are reminiscent of Balanchine's musicality, decorating the texture and adding buoyancy. But Wheeldon's treatment of Danses II (for the more advanced group of students) is much simpler than Ashton's, with no attempt to show different rhythmic lines simultaneously. Perhaps Wheeldon felt that the score already held enough rhythmic ingenuity within it.

Wheeldon's Apotheosis is simply wrought but highly effective, an accumulation led by the smallest girls in procession. A final burst of mobility culminates in a tableau featuring the entire ensemble on stage, with lifts to the shoulder included, a much bigger climax than in the Ashton, and after a continual process of enlargement, without any closing down or reining-in of energy.

Wheeldon's *Scènes* fulfils the task of challenging young dancers musically as well as technically. Yet his musicality is quite different from Ashton's. Wheeldon's is a more sympathetic, less anxious or wry response to Stravinsky, and his account does not have the energy and speed of Ashton's, despite the fact that both choreographers favour the quick musical beat. Ashton's much more consistent use of full-grown academic ballet steps with staccato impetus makes all the difference.

Some choreographers never hear the quick beat. That is perhaps the most interesting observation that can be made about Nicolas Petrov's 1972 setting of *Scènes*.[72] Of Yugoslav origin and with a professional career background in Europe, Petrov founded Pittsburgh Ballet Theatre in 1969. Attracting big-name support from Leonid Massine, Vitale Fokine and Frederic Franklin (who became co-artistic director), he built a repertory of established ballets, including classics, and also created story ballets himself, including the first production in the USA of *Romeo and Juliet*. In 1972, he also created a *Sacre* with a huge cast. By comparison, his *Scènes* is small-scale, featuring various combinations of twelve women, five men and a solo man and woman (one more than the 'normal' casting, and we can guess that the fifth man might have been an afterthought), neoclassical and dressed in practice clothes. Adding prestige to the premiere, Violette Verdy and Edward Villella led the cast. Clive Barnes commented on their 'simple and beguiling' Pas de deux and the 'exultant panache' of Villella's Variation.[73] But it is an odd piece, the women combining simple academic steps with

stretchy adage, while the men seem to operate in another world of standard virtuoso beats and turns.

Even though there is some allegro dancing, particularly for the men, Petrov's *Scènes* is fundamentally an andante dance. The music of Danses I he read as just two step-impulses per bar. Ashton's basic pulse is twice as fast. Likewise in Danses II, after much posing interspersed with fluttering bourrées, Petrov's women settle into plain unison, marking each crotchet beat with a step or body shape: Ashton created a three-part texture and choreographed to the quaver and semiquaver divisions. There is nothing inherently amiss about using Stravinsky's slower musical pulse – the legato lines in both his Danses can make you sense a lazier heartbeat. It is the manner of use that is crucial. Petrov reminds us that Ashton had choices.

In his *Ballet Scenes* (1985), Hans van Manen also tends to hear a slower tempo than Ashton, but the reasons here make more sense.[74] He made his ballet for Nederlands Dans Theater, the hybrid modern dance/ballet company; hence there are plain steps and no fleet academic allegro or pointe work. (Dutch National Ballet acquired Ashton's *Scènes* in 1992.) But there is also a dramatic theme, typical of van Manen, with male–female antagonism across the cast of ten, either as five men (bare-chested and in tights) massed against five women (in knee-length dresses and sandals) or as five couples. One man is an outsider to them all, although occasionally merged with the group or linked with a partner. The group express their feelings bluntly, without the encumbrance of busy movement or attention to the structural detail of the music. Van Manen all but ignores the choreographic outline as indicated in the score. All the solo Variations are full ensemble dances, and the one solo for the outsider is danced to the first Pantomime. Only the Pas de deux is a pas de deux, although it too admits group power and soon starts to give way to an ensemble of couples.

The outsider emerges early in Danses I, where the main theme, recapitulated like the music, is a convulsive tumbling towards the audience, after he drops out of a tight clump of dancers centre stage. His companions alternately withdraw and return to crowd him. The same tumbling and regrouping recurs to the third Pantomime music. Van Manen hears the weight in Stravinsky's score and stresses it; the ballet is full of floorwork and falling, partners dragging each other down. As in the Ashton and Wheeldon settings, van Manen treats the Pas de deux and Apotheosis as occasions for liberation. But the final statement is most definitely a closing-down, and sinister. In the silence immediately following the end of the score, the group collapse to the floor, the outsider left alone standing. At the same time, van Manen's ballet appears to pay tribute to Balanchine's *The Four Temperaments* (1946), and perhaps indirectly via this to the Balanchine–Stravinsky collaboration as well. The outsider's solo recalls the famous Melancholic solo for a man and accompanying group menace in that ballet. Numerous doublework manoeuvres elsewhere recall the choreography of the earlier work, including a glimpse of the travelling grand jeté lifts to freedom in van Manen's Pas de deux. There are occasional touches of humour: for instance, the men suddenly rush in and light up cigarettes for their partners just before the first ballerina Variation music begins. Later they leave the women to take a puff lying flat on their backs. This is a push and pull doublework dance, only obliquely revealing the structure of the music. In Pantomime II, the dancers suddenly become robots, absurdly stiff and jerky, literally punching out the pulse.

The outsider's solo to Pantomime I represents one of the most striking alternatives to Ashton's reading of the score. In this dance context, the muted horns sound acidic (one bar after [57]). His movement hugs the floor, and, to the flute and horn notes that once inspired wrist flicks and sharp head turns, tiny movements over tiny bourrées or, for Ashton's ballerina, needle-sharp retirés, he flings his head from side to side, showing you the powerful action of his neck, or exaggeratedly displaces a hip – all big, strong action. Shrill sound seems to linger with this kind of movement. The man communicates disturbance, driving towards an angry stamp and sharp thrust of both arms to the floor when a trombone suddenly shouts out a single note G [60]; the stern arm-gesture repeats to each of the succeeding three trombone exclamations as the dominating choreomusical motif of the passage. None of the other choreographers makes a point of these trombone notes, and in the Ashton version (after the first, which simply marks a structural division in the score) they 'disappear' amidst a dance phrase that has nothing to do with them. Nor was it appropriate for the other choreographers to use them in *their* ballets. *Ballet Scenes* treats the anxiety in the music in a quite different way.

'Stravinsky's Broadway Baby' was the title of Birmingham Royal Ballet's programme note when the company revived Ashton's *Scènes* in 2005, and I imagine that this is what Uwe Scholz had in mind when he made his own version in 1993 for the Leipzig Ballet: commercial theatre welcomes the ballet dancers mocking their own classics – again (responding to the musical hints) the Tchaikovsky ballets.[75] There is a Rose Adagio sequence down a line of men and a joke about the Swan Queen adagio in the Pas de deux, when a woman ripples on the floor to the introductory viola/cello triplets, and then rises with a cigarette in her mouth. A smoky pub image perhaps, and yet another cigarette *Scènes*! It is a ballet for five couples, the women in leather leotards and net tights, engaging in various tiffs and flirtations with their partners: showy and sexy, mixing classical steps with plain behaviour, and often going for the fast beat except when the movement dissolves into acting. The 'Geometry' section here is a hard-nosed pattern, a percussive jump on to pointe rapidly breaking down into flat-foot walking. Given his theme of heavy mockery, Scholz elected not to stress the light-touch Stravinsky.

Le Baiser de la fée: *Fragments*

Hints of the movement style of Ashton's *Scènes* lie within his first Stravinsky ballet, *Le Baiser de la fée* (1935), which was also his first ballet for Margot Fonteyn (as the Bride, then aged only sixteen) and an important collaboration with his favourite designer, Sophie Fedorovitch. But it is not safe to assume strong links across the two ballets, for the *Baiser* score is much more heavily weighted towards Tchaikovsky than is *Scènes,* drawing actual themes from the earlier composer and suggesting nineteenth- as well as twentieth-century dance conventions far more broadly, in narrative sections as well as divertissement. Details of the score and story, based on Hans Christian Andersen's *The Ice Maiden,* have already been given in Chapter 3. Ashton set the various scenes (which he called Tableaux) in different dance styles. He introduced an earthy modern dance approach (which could have been of Central European or Martha Graham origins) into the Prologue Storm scene, the movement itself creating the effect of tempest. Social dance was the style of the Village Fete: the women wore long dresses and heeled shoes, the men Alpine-style shorts and long socks, and there was a maypole dance.[76] The choreographer felt that this was the weakest part of the ballet, partly because the piano rehearsal reduction had disguised the reality of the orchestration. The Mill Scene was neoclassical ballet and contained Ashton's first major (and well received) pas de deux, for Fonteyn and Harold Turner. Ashton told David Vaughan that he was pleased with his solution to the problem of the final scene

> with the dancers grouped behind a gauze curtain, and Turner carrying [Pearl] Argyle as the Fairy, in slow, floating lifts, or dragging her along the floor; at other moments she would jump over a group of dancers lying on the stage, and he would catch her. Finally she was carried along a line of dancers and off into the light, as though into eternity.[77]

It is the dances for the Bridesmaids in the Mill Scene that Margaret Dale (who was in the company when *Baiser* was in the repertoire) recalls as foreshadowing *Scènes,*[78] but we may be able to extend the connections still further into the Bride's Solo. These are the only *Baiser* dances that have survived, although photographs give us valuable supplementary stylistic information.

The key to *Baiser* lies in Ashton's own comments on the music and his approach to it in the *Old Vic and Sadler's Wells Magazine*:

> Since the music is based on Tschaikowsky, the score is in a more lyrical vein than is usual with Stravinsky, and has all the brilliance of his masterly orches-

tration, yet at the same time giving an edge to the melodiousness of Tschaikowsky.[79]

'Edge' is the crucial word here as we consider Ashton's indelible memory of the 1920s aesthetic, which he literally embodied when dancing Nijinska's work in Paris:

> At the end of the Twenties, no one wanted Romantic, emotionally-charged music, everything was Bach, Mozart, Poulenc, simplicity of orchestration, Stravinsky and all that.[80]

But Ashton also announced that he would be taking 'the necessary liberties for the construction of a choreographic spectacle emanating directly from the character and style of the music'.[81] Perhaps here he was referring to the stylistic diversity, which would include, amongst other things, the 'classical basis of dancing', just as Stravinsky had referred back to Tchaikovsky classicism.

Perhaps the 'edge' can be seen in the photographs of modernist Nijinska-like groupings, usually asymmetrically arranged on the stage, with often-straight lines of arms and legs duplicated across a closely packed cluster of dancers and forming mass (as in her *Noces*). A striking photograph of the fourth Tableau shows a cascade of arabesques (on eight dancers) that elongates the physical image of one dancer's line into frightening proportions. Photographs of Fonteyn in supported arabesque behind or in front of Turner emphasise straight line and angle at the elbow, her short tutu doing little to soften the image.[82] Before she dances the Pas de deux, Fonteyn wears a jagged headdress from which her bridal veil falls. Typical of the Fairy are her spiky fingers. But Ashton's own recollections of the Bride's Variation for Fonteyn are most telling of all. It was, he said,

> a very difficult Variation to do which required a tremendous attack and sharpness in her dancing which Margot at that time didn't have ... I used to say to her 'your feet are rather buttery ... too soft' – they didn't have that edge to them.[83]

He uses the word 'edge' again.

In 1988, Fonteyn undertook a reconstruction of the Bride's solo on a dance student in Panama. Her coaching was captured on film as a teaching aid for Nicola Katrak, who was learning the dance for Patricia Foy's film documentary on Fonteyn, and who in turn presented a lecture-demonstration on the solo at the Royal Academy of Dancing's Fonteyn conference in 1999.[84] Another film exists of the solo, shot in 1970 at the Royal Opera House Gala Tribute to Ashton, danced by Jennifer Penney, and including the Coda with the Bridesmaids.[85] But there are numerous stylistic differences here from the Fonteyn/Katrak version and Fonteyn was not involved in this revival. For the *Ashton to Stravinsky* video and the following analysis, the Fonteyn/Katrak sources were central, although the 1970 film was used as the only available source for the ensemble Coda.

In the Panama video, Fonteyn emphasises soft, relaxed arms and their light accent in arabesque. She does not focus on the feet (as Ashton's statement might suggest), but it is crucial that her voicing of counts and foot rhythms stresses the sharp end of the solo's dynamics. She also highlights the stretch of the arm when it is not curved, with the line extended without a break to the fingertips. This is the antithesis of the precisely rounded and placed fifth and first positions of the arms. As Fonteyn teaches it, the solo expresses the extremes between freedom to travel and bend the torso and the containment of body picture over academic, tightly crossed feet. There are obvious movement-style links with *Scènes* in the clear body architecture and staccato dynamics.

Musically and choreographically, the form of the Bride's Solo is:

Introduction	2 bars, in 4/8, 8 dance counts: bars 1–2
Section A	4 bars, 16 dance counts, with varied repeat in the score: bars 3–10
Section B	3+5 bars: bars 11–18
Section C	11 bars: bars 19–29
Recapitulation of Section A	4 bars: bars 30–33
Coda	4 bars: bars 34–37

Ashton meets the musical recapitulation choreographically, but omits the repeat of Section A marked in the musical score at this point. The main theme, forming Section A, is jaunty, with a syncopated, fragmented opening, developing continuity in its second half (see Ex. 4.10). Section B is more legato, with a comma marked in the score to distinguish its 3- and 5-bar units. In Section C, there are metrical shifts between 2/4 and 3/4 (4 and 6 dance counts in a bar respectively). The Coda is a final flourish during which the Bride metaphorically opens a window on to her new world and then turns to finish coyly with her back to the audience.

Ashton's musicality here is typical, led by the melody, which fits its metrical framework quite straightforwardly in this dance. Although the solo does not include the level of musical sophistication of *Scènes*, Ashton, just as in the later work, dissects the rhythm down to the fast semiquaver beat. There are many touches of rhythmic/musical ingenuity within a short time-span; sometimes Ashton responds directly to the musical detail, sometimes he seems to go his own way. In a posé arabesque and plié sequence repeated down the diagonal (Section

Ex. 4.10. *Le Baiser de la fée*, Scene 3, By the Mill, main theme, Bride's solo.

A), the plié is syncopated, given the most time, weighting the offbeat, but it hits the melodic high notes C-sharp and A (bar 2, Ex. 4.10). When the melody repeats, the rise and fall in the steps goes *with* it (the posé on the high notes), adding to the sense of syncopation in what is heard. This is similar to the game of melodic contradiction and reflection that we came across in *Scènes* (see pp. 269, 277-9). At the end of Section A, a decorated pas de bourrée and relevé form an upbeat pattern, counted '*and* 1, 2 and 3 and 4', even though the music does not suggest upbeat phrasing. In Section B, the choreographic phrase structure divides like the music, into 3 bars and then 5, the second phrase an expansion of the first. It begins with the 'Nijinska step' – the arms in a 'balloon shape' and swung up and over the head[86] – and continues into a repeated sequence of runs and two turning changements. However, with this sequence, the choreography develops a new energy and freedom for the dancer to be airborne and travelling, a dynamic change not suggested in the music. As we shall see later, in discussion of *Le Rossignol*, independent dynamic level or contour is typical of Ashton. In Section C (bars 23–27), Ashton mirrors the shifts in the music from 4 dance counts (4/8) in a bar to 6 (3/4), unlike Balanchine who continues in 4s to 'cross' the music at this point (see pp. 236-7).

I have seen several other settings of the Bride's solo on film: three by Balanchine, two versions of the same solo by Kenneth MacMillan (who created his *Baiser* in 1960 for the Royal Ballet as a homage to Ashton[87] and reworked it in 1986), and versions by Nijinska (1928), John Neumeier (Frankfurt Ballet, 1972) and Mark Baldwin (Scottish Ballet, 1996). The style of all but one of these is gentler and more flowing than Ashton's, and they are dressed in soft, longer tutus or skirts to above or below the knee: Baldwin's hard, jazzy neoclassical version is the exception.

The critic Judith Mackrell described MacMillan's movement for the Bride as 'softly curved … lilting … earthbound'.[88] The footwork is always precise, revealing neat pointes, but the steps are less academic than Ashton's, the upper body freer, abandoned – for instance, in the striking initial turn and melt step, nicknamed 'violet crumble'[89] – and the arms liquid with a sense of flow out through the fingers. MacMillan even teases us with a legato unfolding of the leg, low and sustained at the end of Section B, asking for a ritardando – not printed in the score and hardly in Stravinsky style – so that we can fully grasp this special moment.

The Nijinska solo is an oddity. Revived by Irina Nijinska and Nina Youskevitch fifty-four years after it was last performed (in 1936), it was given a public showing and recorded in the New York Public Library in 1990.[90] The vocabulary is formal, but its most striking feature is its multiple turns – fouettés, spinning relevés and pirouettes everywhere, so that all the sections seem to merge into a single identity. There is a strangely asymmetrical approach to repeats. The opening dance phrase is not an introduction, yet it begins during the introductory bars of music, and when we see it again it is shorter and meets a different point in the music (now within Section A, the dance music proper). It is varied yet again in construction and musical relationship during the recapitulation. The tempo of the dance is unusually slow and there are prominent ritardandos. The reconstructed solo is hard to read with its blurred outlines and often indistinct dance beat. It also has nothing to do with the Nijinska musicality of *Noces* or *Les Biches*. Jennifer Somogyi from School of American Ballet danced the solo in a long tutu, although photographs of the original production show the Bride in a short one, her Bridesmaids in longer skirts (the format that Fedorovitch borrowed for Ashton's production).

Especially striking when we survey this group of solos is Ashton's dissection of the pulse into a presto semiquaver unit of time. Neumeier's solo comes closest to his with its little runs and gallops on pointe,[91] but Ashton seeks a much sparkier mode of allegro. As with his *Scènes*, full-grown academic steps, hastily stitched throughout the dance in unpredictable timings and patterns, create a very distinctive dance energy.

The ensemble Coda (one of the Bridesmaids' dances that Dale recalled as precursor to *Scènes*) reflects a similar energy. In reading this from the 1970 Ashton gala film, and reconstructing phrases for *Ashton to Stravinsky*, the music had to be re-synchronised, the dynamics sharpened, and Morris and I brought to the material our knowledge of style from all the evidence that we uncovered.

The eight Bridesmaids open the Coda and are later joined by the Bride. The dance is full of smartly finished pas de chat and needle-sharp grands jetés. From the very opening, clipped, staccato phrase (2/4), there is attention to motor and melody – the pas de chat go with the rising musical gestures and the sissonnes with the bass notes in between, one arm moves upwards in three stages, marionette-style, on the three isolated syncopations, and a series of ballonnés beat the pulse to end the phrase (see Ex. 4.11). Near the end of the dance, there is a series of six accents – three separate (crotchet rests in between), and then three in quick succession – and Ashton marks each one with a clipped pas de chat: it was obviously more important to him to do this here than to maintain the pulse.[92] We see the Fred step here (see p. 277); it gets smaller, like a choreographic diminuendo, before two sharp, loud accents, and the Coda concludes with a group tableau (see Ill. 9). Another musically interesting passage is at [186]: changements at two pulse rates, slow for four of the Bridesmaids and fast for the other four (with circling port de bras, both in the usual direction and in

Ex. 4.11. *Le Baiser de la fée*, Scene 3, By the Mill, opening, Coda after Bride's solo.

Ill. 9. Jennifer Penney as the Bride in *Le Baiser de la fée*, Scene 3, Coda with Bridesmaids (1970 Gala Tribute to Ashton), Royal Ballet.

reverse). They articulate the minim rate and plain crotchet patterns in the score at this point (see Ex. 4.12). The main dance accents every two musical beats are syncopated against the heard musical accents at first, but soon fit like a glove, a happy moment. Stravinsky's irregularity, 'losing' a beat, is responsible for the shift: the choreography just keeps going. But such choreomusical crossing is hardly a feature of the dance as a whole, unlike in Balanchine's setting of the same music.

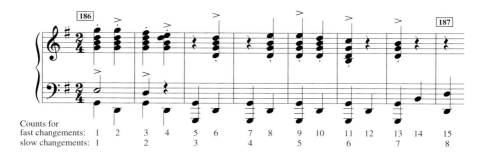

Ex. 4.12. *Le Baiser de la fée*, Scene 3, By the Mill, Coda after Bride's solo.

The only Balanchine Coda that exists in recording comes from his late-career *Divertimento*, although there are two different endings from 1972 and 1974 (see pp. 225-6). In 1972, the whole ballet ended with the Coda, brightly, or relatively so, and Balanchine edited the final section (see p. 227). In the 1974 version, with the Coda ending exactly as Stravinsky wrote it, the ballerina pulls away from her partner, a quiet, dark and 'unfinished' gesture as transition to the final farewell duet.

Up to that point, Balanchine's Coda is replete with phrase units that ride boldly across the musical units. The mode is bracing and motoric, stressing continuity. To Ashton's changement music (at [186]), Balanchine's two groups of corps dancers fold into plain marching up–down piqués, but they go up and down in counterpoint, with the effect of crossing accents and making your eye zigzag sharply from one side of the stage to the other. In the middle of the Coda are two brief solos for the man and woman (see p. 236), respectively phrased in 7s and 5s, again crossing the music. At the end, Balanchine maintains his pulse and momentum through the musical rests, retaining a sense of implacable energy until the final moments of the dance. So Balanchine, as is typical, adds his own extra layer of rhythmic complexity, respects the melodic structure and phrasing far less than Ashton, and allows rare moments of rhythmic harmony to become sudden moments of relief and power.

Again, it is Ashton's sharp stylistic 'edge' and fragmented phrasing that sets him apart from Balanchine, and similarly from MacMillan in his Coda within the full narrative ballet. And it is especially ironic that MacMillan, in a piece that is a homage to Ashton, sees his colleague as more 'romantic' here than Ashton saw himself. Ashton's view of Stravinsky that we witness in *Scènes* and in what little remains of *Baiser* is an embodiment of the cool, hard 1920s, the years of his formative experience of both dance and Stravinsky.

Persephone

'Hardness' and 'cool' are hardly words that spring to mind as apt for *Persephone*, Stravinsky's 1934 score for Ida Rubinstein, which was set by Ashton in 1961. This was the hybrid theatre piece based on the Homeric myth of Persephone and her mother Demeter, the original a collaboration with André Gide as librettist, the director Jacques Copeau, designer André Barsacq and choreographer Kurt Jooss, with Rubinstein herself in the speaking/dancing (miming) title role (see pp. 52-3). It is in three scenes:

The Abduction of Persephone
Persephone in the Underworld
Persephone Reborn

By 1934, Stravinsky's work had moved on and Walsh proposes that 'a more melodious score hardly exists in the repertoire of modernism'.[93] A similar weighting towards lyricism, however, was present in the all-strings *Apollo* of 1928, which marked the shift away from the hard-boiled modernism of the early 1920s. Significantly, *Persephone* quotes the familiar dotted-rhythm string motif from the prologue and apotheosis of this earlier ballet (at [60] and [162]). In Ashton's production, this is most closely associated with Demeter's distress at the loss of her daughter Persephone. And there is a lullaby that Stravinsky tells us was originally composed for Vera, his then mistress.[94] Yet, at the same time, there are contradictions within the score, and Ashton, as we shall see, draws attention to them. Stravinsky's manifesto on abstraction published at the time of the Paris premiere stressed functionalism, emotional restraint, and absence of spectacle and large effect, to the degree that it belies the expressive reality of his own score.[95] Complementary concepts such as gentleness, warmth, serenity, tenderness, sweetness, voluptuousness and humanity readily come to mind, but alongside the contrasting notions of austerity, ritual order, precision, hardness, asceticism and reduction. The piece conveys both intimacy and grandeur.

Maurice Brillant of *L'Aube Musicale* claimed that *Persephone* mixed together the oppositional orchestral effects and feeling states of *Apollo* and *Noces*.[96] Although acknowledging the predominant mood of gentleness, Craft saw the influence of *Noces* in the opening two 'orchestral "tuning" notes', which recall the earlier work 'in pitch and the elimination of preambles'.[97] It is a brutal, arresting beginning. Slow speed then predominates in the piece, as does a quality of timelessness or mobile immobility, through Stravinsky's characteristic devices of ostinato and pedal (sustained notes). But there are effective passages of contrast, such as Mercury's frenetic dance in Scene 2 (from [140]-1) and the merry welcome dances of Scene 3 (from [207]). Opposition is likewise evident between, on the one hand, the female lead who speaks her feelings directly to us and her colleagues on stage, and on the other the tenor Narrator, Eumolpus, who is distanced from events, knowing Persephone's fate, commenting upon, indeed driving the course of events: 'C'est ce que nous raconte Homère ...' Several writers[98] have noted the significance of the central female character to the special tone of this work.

The original 1934 Paris production of *Persephone* was in the manner of a Greek drama, the setting a vast structure of columns and arches containing a smaller Greek temple within, simple, restrained, with minor modifications to situate the story, suggesting flower meadows next to the seashore, the Underworld, and a small hill where Persephone meets her earthly betrothed Demophoon. Upstage was a tall pedestal, from which Eumolpus declaimed. Apart from Persephone, the speaking and dancing roles were separated. A large chorus stood stage right, joined in the last scene by a children's choir brought from Amsterdam. The dancers emerged from the left side of the stage: various named characters – Mercury, Demeter, Triptolemus, The Spirit of Death, who guarded Persephone's tomb – and numerous Nymphs, Hours (who accompanied Mercury), servants of Pluto, Adolescent males and Shades. Craft surmises that, for Stravinsky, Pluto was a 'terrifying presence', the Devil, 'and to have had Pluto sing would have stripped him of his awesomeness and diabolism'.[99] The 'sarabande' music that Ashton and Balanchine later allocated as a dance to Pluto (from [124]+2) Stravinsky gave to the god's servants. Later, Stravinsky maintained that the more characters embodied, the better, including Pluto, to help 'dramatize Gide's undramatic narrative'.[100]

Rubinstein, nearing 50 at this stage of her career, was allocated at least one dance (in Scene 1, [25]+3 to [28]+2), but she seems to have stressed simple, gestural movement or mime and to have played up her statuesque qualities. Of course, she also had to catch her breath for speeches. Jooss's choreography for the dancers in her company referred to received notions of ancient Greek movement, rhythmic evolutions embracing a range of expressive gesture; he taught the company his own modern dance technique, which presumably inflected the style of the movement. L. Franc Scheuer, the critic for *The Dancing Times*, referred to the persistent *Bewegungschore*, alluding to the movement choir culture of Central European modern dance.[101]

It turned out that Jooss's contribution was the most common butt of negative criticism after the *Persephone* premiere – its heaviness and dullness commented upon – but this might well have betrayed the music critics' discomfort with modern dance, and choreographic simplicity could have been appropriate within a complex work of this kind. However, Stravinsky's music was generally admired, with the last scene singled out by many as particularly striking. For quite different reasons, the production received only a handful of performances. Its resource demands, a massive, multi-layered set, a large choir including children, as well as a company of dancers, proved to be a problem that would continue to challenge later choreographers, quite apart from the difficulty of handling a leading role that required someone to mime/dance and speak effectively. *Persephone* is as resource-tricky as *Noces*. But Jooss himself returned to the work in Germany on two further occasions, with productions for Dusseldorf (1955) and Essen (1965).

Ashton faced the problem of Svetlana Beriosova's vocal amplification as his speaking-dancing Persephone. She had a beautiful voice and good French accent, but the microphone that she wore crackled and picked up extraneous sounds, and she pre-recorded her text for the revival six years later. The work was last performed in 1968. It was never the kind of work to be a huge success with audiences, and reviews were very mixed, although Clive Barnes suggested that Ashton had 'unflawed a flawed masterpiece [the music]'.[102] Now it is all but lost except for a silent Edmée Wood film – silent because the accompanying music tape has disappeared – which was used for the following analysis and for the reconstruction of segments for the *Ashton to Stravinsky* video/DVD.[103]

In a press interview before the premiere, which we can piece together from preview articles, Ashton proclaimed that, although 'much of it takes, as it were, a single and apparently simple pattern ... it is the most complex work I have ever attempted'.[104] He also said that he had been thinking about the production for some four or five years and that it would be different from his previous work: 'a more architectural conception, laying stone upon stone'.[105] This suggests that Ashton was attuned to the Stravinsky of the uncompromising neoclassical manifestos, who celebrates the values of solidity, fixity, hardness, anti-flux and anti-impermanence.[106] 'I have tried to make the structure good', added Ashton.[107] A.H. Franks remembered Ashton's musical aim: 'to take into consideration not only the overall impact of the sound, but to work out movement patterns to the pulse which supports the score ...'[108] This would normally go without saying, but we might speculate that the choreographer wanted to make a particular point about pulse here. I shall return to this idea later. We know too that Ashton listened to the 1958 recording of *Persephone* with the composer conducting the New York Philharmonic Orchestra, the only one available at the time;[109] he drew information about the score from his copy of Eric Walter White's 1947 book *Stravinsky: A Critical Survey*, which summarised the libretto and included stage directions agreed between Stravinsky and Gide.[110]

The setting by Nico Ghika for Ashton's production was already complex. There were two stage levels, brilliantly sunny Greek landscapes contrasting with the gloomy rocky chasm of the Underworld in Scene 2, a colourful array of costumes, tunics and robes of varying lengths and styles, and an opulence and radiance absent from the 1934 production. The huge stage cast comprised seventy-one dancers as well as the tenor Eumolpus. The Stravinsky of 1934 might well have found the production too spectacular.[111] Ashton slightly modified the casting to include, most importantly, the figure of Pluto himself (Keith Rosson), not merely his servants representing an unseen god in the shadows – and he could not yet have known that Stravinsky had changed his mind about the presence of this character – also a group of six tall women as Oceanides, and some male attendants to Persephone. Pluto's solo to the 'sarabande' music followed a pas de deux with Beriosova. The pas de deux (from [118]) was Ashton's way of offering a valuable extra dance opportunity for Persephone; apart from this instance, her occasions for dancing are fragmentary and normally shared with the dancing group (see Ill. 10). Alexander Grant took the important role of Mercury, who features regularly through the ballet.

Certainly, it was not the lyrical aspect of Ashton's work that stood out for most

Ill. 10. Svetlana Beriosova as Persephone and Keith Rosson as Pluto in *Persephone*, Scene 2, pas de deux, choreography by Frederick Ashton, Royal Ballet.

reviewers at the premiere. Perhaps encouraged by the choreographer's own comments, the new ballet was perceived as being primarily about harder archi-tectural qualities, and not what was normally associated with Ashton. This is the predominant style of the dancing chorus, who play a major role in the ballet; both their mass and the nature of their movement contribute to these qualities. The reporter for *Time* in the USA summarised:

It proved to be a radical transformation from the gentle, classically-oriented manner of such Ashton successes as *Cinderella* and *Sylvia*. The choreographic style was severe, angular and so stylised that it sometimes seemed Ashton had turned to ancient Greek friezes for his inspiration. The dancers in the corps de ballet frequently were presented in profile, in frieze-like groupings; at other times, they marched flat-footed, with hands on one another's shoulders, or with arms raised and palms held flat ... Few viewers, after they became accustomed to the deliberate jerkiness of the choreography, were bored.[112]

The critic for *The Times* in London voiced Ashton's anti-lyrical approach in rather different terms, emphasising elements of brute forcefulness, as if remembering an earlier Stravinsky:

> *Persephone* has inspired him to a vital and pugnacious originality of invention ... Ashton has looked for the primitive behind the gallic chic ... [This is] a version of *Persephone* which is more Russian than Greek or French, more savage and pagan than classic or Christian.[113]

From the evidence of the silent film, the movement style is predominantly ballet-archaic: as well as two-dimensional 'Greek' movement and frieze, there are many variations on walking and occasional pointe work, particularly for Persephone and her women Friends.[114] In relating the choreography to the music for analytical purposes, the score had to be painstakingly synchronised to the silent film – not in reality (except for those segments reconstructed for *Ashton to Stravinsky*), but within the imagination. This was aided by the piano rehearsal score, which offered detailed information on counts and cues for action, and by comforting clues from reviews as to the frequent harmonisation between dance action and musical detail.

The amount of musical mimicry within the ballet as a whole is surprising, and unusual for Ashton. Visual and aural gestures frequently coincide, with Ashton picking up on Stravinsky's asymmetries. Sometimes there is the mirroring of a sudden, anxious orchestral rumble, flurry or mere chord, or the highlighting of a series of punctuations, which might be quiet and in the bass (as when Persephone emerges from her tomb [221]). Often, dance gestures duplicate a vocal line. In Scene 3, the Friends' emboîtés literally pick out the staccato notes of the choral fragments, and then halt between each one: 'Par-le ... Per-sé-phon-e ... ra-con-te ... Ce que nous ca-chent les hi-vers ...' [243] (see Ex. 4.13). The rest of the corps proceed to 'walk' the following rhythmic fragments flat-foot. Antiphony between choral groups often means antiphony on stage (for instance, at [82], [92] and two bars before [215]), helping us to read as convention the offstage voices as the voices of the dancers whom we see, although Ashton is not always literal in matching genders.

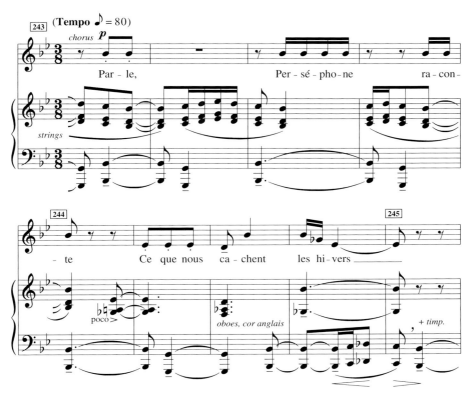

Ex. 4.13. *Persephone,* Scene 3, music for the emboîtés danced by Persephone's Friends.

The tying together of vocal and dance lines often brings words and their meaning into play. The dancers might, for instance, enact the movement of nature indicated in the text. The six Oceanides form the line of a wave during the chorus 'Reste avec nous', and soon the chorus sing 'Vois le soleil qui rit sur l'onde' (at [12]+2). Here, on the raised platform, there is counterpoint to Persephone, her Friends and the walking Nymphs below (three dance lines in all), and the sun shines above them all. The men create surging breakers on the shore as Persephone has a vision of her mother walking on earth 'Sur la plage et des flots imitant la cadence' (at [172]+2). The Nymphs sway to create the effect of the 'brise vagabonde' [16], and the Friends pick flowers to 'Jacynthe, anémone, Safran, Adonide ...' ([32]+2). On other occasions, the dancers mime feeling states and speech. Looking into the narcissus, Persephone observes the Shades in the Underworld, and some of her companions drop to the sound of the word 'triste' while others shield their eyes ([41]+7). Once in the Underworld, Persephone looks again into the narcissus and sees the desolation that she has left behind on earth. The Chorus know that she represents spring – 'Le printemps c'est toi – and the piano rehearsal score reads 'Boys point'. Then, two bars later, for 'Raconte, que vois-tu?' it reads: 'Tell us', and the whole group extend their arms towards her ([159]+2). At other times, the dancers provide a more gener-alised account of feeling, with a vocabulary suggesting sorrow, supplication or sympathy. Thus, one by one, Persephone's Friends show their compassion dur-ing two of her more sustained speeches (Scenes 1 and 3), their gentle bourrées and chaînés fluttering to the gently pulsating flutes and violins (from [41]-1 and [253]+2). The moments of verbal illustration or the matching of contained, abrupt musical gesture bring images and meanings into sharp relief and make them concrete. The mimicry device registers them for us, and we also hear the words more clearly at these points.

The duplication of musical motor pulse has a similar hardening effect, and this is important because walking, which is pure, undiluted pulse, is such a dominant feature of the ballet, and presumably what Ashton meant by a 'single and apparently simple pattern'. It also creates the even, level impression of ritual. There are many kinds of walks, ranging from the sprightly flat-footed march, step—plié, step—plié for Persephone's young nymph attendants in Scene 1, to the more flowing, gentle tread of the Shades in the Underworld, although they develop a spring in their step when they later share the vision of the earthly Demophoon. Sometimes, more than one pulse rate operates simulta-neously, like beat within hyperbeat, or a pulse finds itself within the simplest repeating rhythm pattern, as in the presto short–short–long 'Japanese cha cha step' of Scene 3 [218].

E.C. Mason, reviewing for *Time and Tide*, disliked Ashton's *Persephone* and pro-vided an exaggerated account of its motor style:

> For much of *Persephone*, especially during his aggressive jamboree marches, Ashton seems to be under the delusion that he is working to one of those Stravinsky scores that sound like steam engines going 90 miles an hour.[115]

Ashton would surely have read White's 1947 musical analysis next to his libretto synopsis, in which he suggests that *Persephone* is not as machine-driven as other Stravinsky works. White reflects on the 'swaying ambiguity' of the 'Lullaby of the Shades'. This effect is created by metering the 12-beat phrase not as three bars of 4/4, which is the structure of the vocal and lower string lines, but as alternating 2/4, 3/4, 2/4, 3/4, 2/4, with a syncopated ostinato in a pat-tern of 3/4, 4/4, 5/4 in the violins (see Ex. 4.14).[116] Nevertheless, there is con-sistent pressure of pulse, to which Ashton responds. We might say that he exag-gerates what he hears, and nowhere more so than in the choreography for Mercury and his accompanying Hours. One reviewer referred, disparagingly, to this as 'hop-scotch choreography'.[117] A major motif for Mercury is hopping, to

Ex. 4.14. *Persephone*, Scene 2, 'Lullaby of the Shades'.

a slow beat or in double time, and the Hours borrow this idea as he draws them on to the stage apron at the beginning of Scene 3. In his big solo, his stamps, odd swagger walks and jumps with legs flying out also reveal pulse at its plainest. As an accompaniment, the Hours often form beats as they shift from position to position: 'Clock Ticking' is one of the designations in the rehearsal score [142].

White referred to occasions of 'an aerated style of writing, in which notes and phrases are punctuated by frequent short rests and pauses for breath'.[118] The emboîté passage for Persephone's Friends in Scene 3 is an example (see p. 304). So is the point in Scene 3 when the mass 'bang on hands', beating out ex-clamations of 3-, 5-, 4-, 4-, 4-count units with pauses in between ([216]+2). They demand that the door of Persephone's tomb be opened. The stop–start rhythm also underlies the Friends' dances to the chorus 'Ivresse matinale' (Scene 1, at [23]), which is written in 3/4 but structured as heard into two

Ex. 4.15. *Persephone*, Scene 1, Friends' dance.

phrases of 10 dance counts and five of 8 counts (see Ex. 4.15). The staccato movement matches the heard accents smartly at first. When the music repeats (after Persephone's central solo at [25]+3), extra steps fill out the musical pauses, making the pulse visible during the rests. Here is an example of the jazziness that several reviewers noted in *Persephone*, syncopated rhythms relying on a firm underlying sense of pulse. In a far more pedestrian manner, the male Shades step and gesture their legs brusquely to the rhythms of the chorus 'Les Ombres ne sont pas malheureuses': a series of dotted crotchets (on and off the downbeat), held notes released into lively quavers ([93]+2 – see Ex. 4.16), telling Persephone that their lot is a kind of vacant destiny bereft of humanity. One of the most unusual sections in the ballet is the 'Train' (from [130]+2), when the Shades rally to support Pluto in offering a crown to their new queen of the Underworld. In they come in a kind of stunted march, two parallel lines of alternating men and women from each side of the stage. In fact, they highlight a

Ex. 4.16. *Persephone*, Scene 2, male Shades' dance.

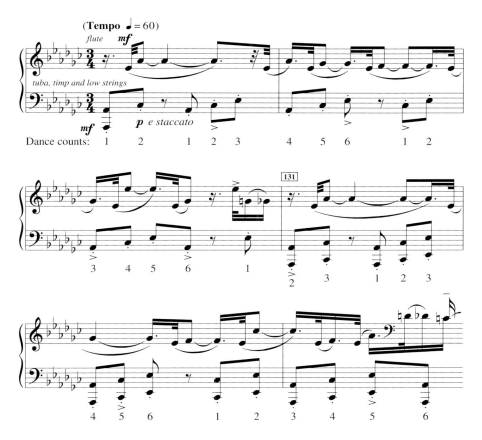

Ex. 4.17. *Persephone*, Scene 2, 'Train'.

sinister ostinato in the bass, a triplet of staccato quavers – A-flat, C-flat, E-flat –
stopping and starting with it as Stravinsky replaces notes with rests at irregular
intervals (see Ex. 4.17). As he does in *Scènes*, Ashton responds to the musical
texture, here, the underpart. Years after the premiere, Stravinsky claimed that
no one had noticed that the two clarinets heard later in this passage 'anticipate
boogie-woogie by a decade'.[119] But perhaps Ashton did.

The 'Train' might be the prime example of the 'angular, quite often choppy'
idiom and 'deliberately bizarre element' in the choreography to which the
Financial Times critic Andrew Porter alluded.[120] It also represents the kind of
mirroring of syncopations that another critic, Noel Goodwin, found problematic:

To me, the musical effect is here sufficient on its own, and calls for a flow of
movement in regular metre to enhance it. By mirroring the dotted rhythms

and displaced accents Ashton seems not only to verge on the banal choreographically, but transmits that back to the music. The hieratic splendour of
myth and ritual becomes momentarily flawed, like scratches appearing on a
golden chalice.[121]

Goodwin may well have had a point, but my alternative reading is that the
motor element highlighted in the piece, whether continuous or stop–start, is a
counter to the rhythmic flaccidity of speeches, the slow tempi and pauses. The
simplicity of means, the walking, is a foil to the complexity and opulence of the
huge production. So there is 'edge' again, and perhaps too a quality of 'camp', a
kind of acidic silliness as a form of irony that evades the danger of sentimentality. The bracing element also counters the manner of Persephone/Beriosova herself, who, even more than the ballerina in *Scènes*, stands out with her own style.
Though powerful, she *is* lyrical, and hers is a generous, luscious, rounded vocabulary that speaks of yearning, sighing and supplication. Time and again she
creates long, unpunctuated lines of movement, against a pulsing corps: she is
constrained into angularity and beat only temporarily in her pas de deux with
Pluto – to what Stravinsky called his 'march-aria'.[122]
    Ashton may well have responded to Stravinsky's especially taut interpretation
of the music in recording and in live performance. Porter reviewed the October
1961 concert at the Royal Festival Hall conducted by the composer:

> All the Royal Ballet seemed to be there on Sunday and no wonder since the
> piece is about to join their repertory. What did they hear? That *Persephone*
> under its composer's baton is a stronger, tougher work than we suspected.
> Fragrant but never fragile. That the flexible rhythms are written into the
> score, which must then be strictly treated. That Stravinsky does not expect his
> performers to add sympathetic colourings of their own to the colours he has
> defined so precisely in his instrumentation.[123]

This was the occasion when Ashton took Beriosova backstage to meet
Stravinsky and, to the composer's approval, she read a passage from the libretto.
He 'really made us feel that we're on our way', she said.[124]
    The hybrid nature of *Persephone* created a stumbling block for some viewers at
the time. People were not used to this kind of spectacle at Covent Garden, although it had been common for years on the continent. Ashton had already
worked with speech when he choreographed Purcell's masque *The Fairy Queen* in
1946. 'I firmly believe in the occasional marriage of the elements of movement,
music and the spoken word', he said.[125] In the same year as Ashton's *Persephone*,
Alfred Rodrigues's choreography to Stravinsky's *Renard* (the premiere) and the

MacMillan/Weill *The Seven Deadly Sins* were seen at the Edinburgh Festival – the term 'total theatre' was now entering popular vocabulary. Yet Ashton's was not as much of a stylised melodrama as many other productions. It was not emphatically hybrid to the degree that the singing chorus appeared on stage, which Stravinsky himself seems to have wanted, and which emphasises the distinction as well as the relationship between singers and dancers, words and movement (with Persephone mediating between).[126]

The *SGD* database contains information on eighteen *Persephone* productions across Europe and the USA. Five of these are German, but more surprising is the strong culture of the work in Italy (as for dancing the opera *Mavra* – see p. 114). There was Janine Charrat's 1956 production in Palermo, then versions by Aurel Milloss in Florence in 1970 and Achim Freyers in Venice in 1994. Margarethe Wallmann, who had staged the piece first in Salzburg in 1955, brought her *Persephone* to Rome in 1956 and Milan in 1966. With Earth and Underworld presented on two stage levels, Wallmann's production might also have been one of the largest of all, like Ashton's. Milloss made a point about preserving the maximum division between aural and visual experience, keeping the chorus hidden and placing his two reciting characters towards the side of the stage.[127]

With its Greek theme, it is hardly surprising that alternatives to ballet style have often been introduced for *Persephone*: as we have seen, Ashton tempered his own style quite radically. More 'natural', earthy styles sometimes seemed appropriate. Jooss was the choreographer who initiated this trend, yet he still choreographed for a ballet company. In 1938, the Tanzgruppe (a modern dance group) of the Bavarian State Theatre in Munich presented a production by Sonia Korty. The design sketches for Wallmann's production (included in the Rome programme) suggest a mixture of barefoot and pointe-work choreography. In 1987, François Raffinot choreographed *Persephone* for the Opéra de Nancy et de Lorraine, working with his baroque dance company Ris et Danceries (on a bill with *Le Rapt de Perséphone*, a commissioned score by André Bon). The Charrat choreography was modern ballet, dressed mainly in all-over tights.

After the Wallmann production of 1955, the dancer-actress Vera Zorina, who was at one time married to Balanchine, became the performer most closely associated with the role of Persephone, in both Europe and the USA. She also enjoyed a close friendship with the composer himself, stemming from her appearance in the 1961 Thomas Andrew production for the Santa Fe Opera Ballet (see p. 61).[128] Zorina choreographed her own production in Minneapolis in 1956. But she also spoke the title role in numerous concert performances, and indeed on the recording that Stravinsky conducted in 1966 (her husband Goddard Lieberson was producer of the famous Columbia series of recordings of

Stravinsky's music). The composer much admired her in this role, describing her as exceptional: 'skilled both as a dancer and *diseuse*, and who is beautiful to look at as well'.[129]

In 1982, Zorina took part in a production that was billed as a collaboration between Balanchine, John Taras and herself and which contributed to the Stravinsky Centenary Celebrations of New York City Ballet. The production was designed by Kermit Love. Balanchine was at this time very unwell (he died a year later) and Zorina recalled that he could not cope with the organisation of the group work. Instead, he 'handed the reins over to John Taras',[130] although he did take charge of the two pas de deux for Pluto and the Spirit of Persephone. This production was not well received and, because of this and all the usual difficulties of staging *Persephone*, it lasted only that single season in the repertory. There is no distinguished choreography either. The movement is often repetitious and textured in the most basic manner, and there are many signs that the production was assembled hastily, within about two weeks before the premiere. Yet, it is illuminating to compare it with the Ashton version as an example of a production with all the singers present on stage.[131]

In the Balanchine production, the singing chorus is hooded and faces the audience in two banks of tiered rows, on both sides of the stage, with a gap through which dancers can pass. Naturally, there is identification with the dancing chorus, but there is also a sense of separation: voices are literally perceived as both outside and speaking through the dancers. At times too, especially when standing (most often in Scene 3), the chorus acquires a dominant presence. Balanchine's *Persephone* is much less choreographed, designed and cast than Ashton's, more like an oratorio with dances as decoration or illustration. Scene 3 is devoid of dancing entirely, save for Zorina's final speech and gestures and a slow farewell: the Nymphs frame her as she is raised aloft upstage by the Shades. Did the trio of collaborators run out of time? A group of boys dressed as choirboys arrives at the opening of this Scene to supplement and give a bright front to the singing group. This increases the sense of Christianised ritual and stills the drama: the story has finished, and now there is a celebration of what can be celebrated (nature on earth has recovered its former glory) and perhaps a confidence to face the more troubled, darker aspects of life. Eumolpus's red priestly raiment matches the under-robe of the choirboys, as if spiritually linking him with them. Thus, the singers are sometimes characters in a drama, sometimes narrators, sometimes oratorio or church choir. Balanchine said that he lit the boys 'from the bottom up ... as if they're candles in church'.[132]

I sense that the Balanchine production drew from a close personal link to the composer. Craft conducted, and those involved seem to have taken into account some of Stravinsky's later, recorded views on the piece and its production. Persephone's role was shared by two performers, as Stravinsky recommended in

Dialogues and a Diary and, probably because of her age, as Zorina too suggested on this occasion.[133] Karin von Aroldingen danced the Spirit of Persephone, alternating on stage with Zorina in the speaking role.

Significantly, the Balanchine production adhered to the principles of melodrama, serving Stravinsky's interest in a non-realistic form of literary theatre, with highlighted divisions between text and movement, and doubled roles. Ashton, on the other hand, took the score as a ballet score, the absence of the chorus on stage allowed space for a larger cast, and there was opportunity for far more exuberant and complex stage activity. Here, we imagine the singing voices as straightforwardly embodied by the dancers on stage. Ashton's distancing effects are different – although Persephone's problematic microphone undoubtedly contributed – and are achieved through a style of dance movement that is often less than 'human'. Contrast this with the New York production, which is in Balanchine's 'romantic' vein, with flowing, languid movement, soft stepping (sometimes across the musical metre, typical of the choreographer) and no pointe work, the dancers' unitards draped with diaphanous cloaks. An example: for the opening chorus 'Reste avec nous', the Nymphs link hands and smoothly entwine, simply stepping on half-pointe once to each crotchet beat. On the other hand, Ashton's young attendants get more done during the same crotchet timespan – step and plié, two separate, jerky actions. Here again is his 'Stravinsky edge', but this time pressed into service against melodious music.

Le Rossignol

Ashton's last Stravinsky setting, the musical fairy tale *Le Rossignol* (1981), was another hybrid work, half opera, half ballet, or, put another way, an opera with a dance line running through it, but it also represented a very different approach to the composer from the earlier works. For a start, Ashton did not choose the score. It was chosen for him, and he contributed to a collaboration in which he did not have prime control. Indeed, he worked on the choreography literally at a distance. He was commissioned by the British director John Dexter, who had planned a Stravinsky triple bill in collaboration with David Hockney at the Metropolitan Opera House, New York, comprising *Le Rossignol*, *Sacre* (with choreography by Jean-Pierre Bonnefous, after Gray Veredon opted out of the project) and *Oedipus Rex*. At this late stage in his life, Ashton conveyed reluctance to undertake new projects, but he eventually agreed to this one.[134]

Rossignol was also a very different kind of Stravinsky, some of it pre-*Firebird*, begun in 1908 and hardly recognisable as Stravinsky in style, the rest of it post-*Sacre*, completed in 1914 (see pp. 33-4). The work, which is about 45 minutes long, was based on Hans Christian Andersen's tale about the beauty and freedom of nature and its healing power and superiority over artifice. Nature is personified by the Nightingale who is taken to the court of the Emperor of China, competes with a Mechanical Nightingale, epitome of artifice, flies away but shows compassion by returning to restore to life the Emperor when he faces death. The three Acts take place respectively at night by the seashore, in a hall in the Emperor's palace, and in the antechambers and bedroom of the Emperor.

Ashton choreographed what might be called his 'dance line' in London, on Natalia Makarova (the Nightingale) and Anthony Dowell (the Fisherman who, delighted and comforted each night by the bird's singing, frames the action within each Act). Ashton never went to New York to see the work in performance – Dowell was in charge of fitting the material into the larger production – although he did see the full work in 1983 when it came to Covent Garden (billed alongside Ravel's *Les Enfants et les Sortilèges*), and possibly too in 1987, when the Paris Opéra Ballet dancers Charles Jude and Claude de Vulpian took over the dancing roles.

Recordings of Ashton's *Rossignol* comprise a London rehearsal directed by the choreographer, stage rehearsal videos of the early New York and Covent Garden productions (all of which are of poor quality), and now the *Ashton to Stravinsky* DVD/video that includes the Fisherman's solos reconstructed by Dowell.[135] Morris and I also saw a revival of the production at the Metropolitan Opera House in 2003, danced by Damian Woetzel and Julie Kent, who had learnt the choreography from the 1981 New York video.[136]

Over the years, *Rossignol* has been seen as a problematic work. This is partly a result of its hybrid genre, its slight action with no dramatic momentum, and hence its reliance on the visual elements of staging. It is also partly a result of the divergence of musical style, ranging from the nature music, the impressionistic shimmering, 'tangled foliage of sonority'[137] of the Fisherman's solos – shades of Rimsky-Korsakov, Wagner and Debussy – to the terse, gestural clatter and mordant dissonance of the later Stravinsky, used to caricature and mechanise the Chinese court culture. Originally, in 1914, Stravinsky believed that the two period styles mapped neatly on to the two aspects of the tale, nature and artifice, although he worked to reprise material in order to unify the overall score, most obviously by bringing back the Fisherman's song at the end of each Act. But his changing feelings about the work betray a shift in his ideas about opera. By 1914, his stance was anti-literary, anti-operatic (see p. 40). Words, Walsh suggests, are primarily 'transportation for the voice', rather than crucial vehicles for meaning.[138] Later, after having completed his first, more traditional kind of opera, *The Rake's Progress* (1951), he complained that much of the earlier work was insufficiently operatic.[139]

In the 1914 production, there were singers 'offstage' in the pit: the Nightingale, represented by a prop on stage (a tiny bird), and the Fisherman, the only role divided between a singer and a dancer. On stage, there were other singing characters and also singing and dancing choruses. The programme lists Characters in Opera and Characters in Ballet. The former included the Emperor, Death, the Kitchenmaid (or Cook) who knows where to find the Nightingale to bring it to court, a High Priest and High Chamberlain, and three Ambassadors of the Emperor of Japan, who bring the rival Mechanical Nightingale as a gift. The Characters in Ballet, over thirty in total, included two Heralds, four warriors, thirteen court ladies, six Mandarins, three men as Monsters, four Youths, a solo female dancer (Fokina II) and the dancer Max Frohman, the onstage Fisherman who appeared with the Nightingale. Reviews tell us little about the contribution of the choreographer Boris Romanov, not even his name (common practice at that time amongst critics, who were mainly music critics), although the long ceremonial procession in Act II was acknowledged as a major dance opportunity.

The designer Alexander Benois, who worked very closely on the production with Stravinsky, conceived the onstage Fisherman as miming the singer's words, which is different from Ashton's much more choreographed approach. During the original, close and enthusiastic collaboration, Stravinsky contributed ideas on the staging: the Entr'acte introduction to Act II at the Emperor's Palace and its crowd chatter behind gauze curtains with Chinese shadow-play effects, the slow, heavy gestures of the Emperor, the moving of curtains and screens.[140] Many reviewers commented on the visual design aspects dominating the production, although, in principle, that need not necessarily have been a problem. Whatever he thought of his own contribution, Stravinsky considered it scenically the most beautiful of his early Diaghilev works.[141] Benois recalled his perceptions in performance, when

> In all the vividness of the fanciful costumery under the enormous dark blue lantern-chandeliers, against a background of white and blue porcelain columns, when from beneath his parasol his Imperial Majesty appeared all glittering with gold and jewels and his assembled subjects all prostrated themselves before him, the effect of it all had a force that I myself did not expect; and for perhaps the first time in my whole theatrical career I had the experience of being touched to the quick by my own creation.[142]

Since the Diaghilev production, directors have tried various ways of handling the visual in relation to words and the weighting between choreography and opera. Even with its pronounced choreographic component, the design aspects of the Dexter/Hockney/Ashton production remained lively, referencing Benois and Diaghilev tradition. Now, the blue and white of willow-pattern tradition, which includes nature representations, were foundation for the whole design. This ranged from the simple Fisherman's home – two cut-out trees and a wave-

Ill. 11. Anthony Dowell as the Fisherman in *Le Rossignol* (the Cook kneeling at his feet), choreography by Frederick Ashton, Royal Opera.

patterned silk panel billowing and rippling like the sea – to the Emperor's grand palace and brilliant procession, with its screens, banners, portable throne, magic animals on litters, sumptuous robes, masked faces, and further masks bobbing and swaying on tall poles held by the chorus. Dowell wore a coolie hat and breeches (see Ill. 11), Makarova a shiny blue all-in-one. Walsh noted the thematic, musically linked use of colour, and that the violence of the reds and golds of the Japanese envoys and their mechanical Nightingale reflected changes in the score.[143] The mechanical bird was a huge, brilliant, bulbous creature with movable head, tail and wings.

The Fisherman and Nightingale on stage had their doubles on view in this production, robed and standing on raised platforms in the pit of the Metropolitan Opera House, watching the stage proceedings and turning round when they sang, presumably in order to be heard more powerfully. At Covent Garden, the singers sat, again clearly on view, at the side of the stage in a box in front of the proscenium. But it is the considerable amplification of the roles of the Nightingale and Fisherman that is the most important point about this production. The Nightingale is a human being rather than a prop and the Fisherman is onstage much more than was originally intended, which involves significant alterations to the story, as well as a major increase in the doubling component within the production. In the original, the Fisherman only appeared in Act I, and his disembodied voice was heard singing offstage (deep in the pit), as if from his

home by the sea, at the ends of both Acts II and III. He never visited the Emper-
or's palace, and became a remote figure. In the Dexter production, he is very
much the supporter and protector of the Nightingale whenever she appears –
her acolyte, part of her world; the original shift between the onstage Fisherman
(seen and heard) and off-stage Fisherman (only heard) was abolished. Dexter's
Fisherman also forms a bond with the Cook, the only other character who knows
the secret magic of the bird (see Ill. 11). The Fisherman becomes the driving
force: the whole experience could be his dream, and about his obsession with
beauty. Indeed, in discussion after coaching James Forbat in his solo material,
Dowell recalled his sense of 'controlling the event',[144] as if he were the power
behind the moving of scenic devices and the storyteller. He embodied the authority and intensity of a magic man.

But the prominence of Dowell was not originally envisaged. Dexter was primarily motivated by the idea of having a real dancer as the Nightingale. Ashton
chose Makarova, a ballerina with a distinguished career in bird roles, and
Makarova needed a partner. Dexter explains:

> One of the earliest notes I sent our choreographer, Frederick Ashton, was that
> the fisherman was available for partnering – mainly because I know Sir Fred's
> delight in complicated lifts. Also, if you want to give an impression of a bird
> moving through the air, you lift.[145]

Dowell was simply the obvious choice as partner: he had worked with Makarova
before, as a member of the Royal Ballet he was very familiar with Ashton's choreography, and he was able to stage the choreography within the New York production.

The only dissenting voice was that of Hockney, who questioned the dramatic
necessity of a dancing Nightingale and preferred an image of the bird – 'a very
plain little bird' – close to the original Andersen story. He felt his point was
proved at a London rehearsal when only Dowell was present, his intensity sufficient to conjure up the image in Hockney's imagination, 'and an awful lot of
people didn't realize something was missing'. Hockney recalls Dexter insisting,
'People pay to come and see Makarova dance. Never mind the story.'[146]

Like Dexter, the critics in the 1980s attended most fervently to Makarova's
contribution, and very positively, apart from a few notable exceptions. Yet I will
suggest that original priorities in the planning stages were overturned by the
stage realisation.

Certainly, the unusually strong presence of *both* dancers contributes to an
important and telling duality between the artificial and the physical in this production. For in this highly stylised staging, where merely simple strides and
wooden gestures represent the motional limits of a pompous court, the presence

of a pair of beings who move with freedom, depth, flow and sensuality is a defining factor both in terms of moral point and the bringing of a 'picture' to life. Originally disembodied characters are now embodied and able to invade and invigorate the world. There is something, too, about mutual possession here, as the singing voice and dancer so clearly interrelate and engage, are perhaps even predatory one upon the other, and at the least show a rapprochement of forces. The solo voice, like a solo musical instrument, also has an important physical power (see p. 182), able to insinuate itself into our darkest and most private spaces. A sense of reciprocal embodiment, the dancer giving something back to, as well as absorbing from, the singer, is especially strong in this *Rossignol*, because of their direct visual engagement, and their sensuality is spectacular within the highly mechanistic surroundings of this particular production. The Dexter production certainly does not support the fascinating but anachronistic reading of *Rossignol* by Daniel Albright: that Stravinsky's heart lay in the Oriental-mechanical rather than in the organic and human, which is the message of the libretto, Nature triumphing over Art 'reversed in the depths of the music' (see p. 105).[147] In emphasising and indeed celebrating the organic and the bodily at the depths of *their* interpretation, Ashton and Dexter overturn any reading of *Rossignol* that gives primacy to the mechanical and to objectification.

Makarova was cast in a series of pas de deux and solos, the latter mainly in Acts II and III, when she sings to the Emperor and brings him back to health. The Nightingale's music is highly decorative coloratura, with additional tweets and embellishments from a solo flute and a melancholic sighing fragment that becomes her motif. Her vocal counterpart sings of nature and a beauty tinged with sadness, in the kind of mystical vocabulary found in Symbolist poetry: about roses that drop diamond tears, sad moonshine, graveyards, dreams and weeping for a beloved. Meanwhile, Makarova expresses the bird, largely through her arms and upper body, in grand beating of wings, tiny flutters and soaring lifts. There are images of trust in Dowell as, for instance, when he strokes her breast, but also demonstrations of a need to escape from bondage. In Act II, she mimes the tears in the Emperor's eyes as he listens to her. In Act III, there is laughter in her music, visualised in chaînés and bourrées, as she tries to cheer the Emperor with images of his beautiful garden. It is easy to spot references to other bird ballets, such as *Swan Lake* and *Firebird*. David Vaughan has noted connections with other Ashton choreography:

… the lifts with petite batterie and the sort of renversée promenade in arabesque that he first used in *The Dream* [1964]; twice, Markarova and Dowell extend opposite legs in a développé à la seconde and bring them down with a little beating movement, recalling a moment in *The Two Pigeons* [1961] …[148]

As regards rapport with music, the phrasing is free and typical of Makarova's personal style, a kind of stretched elasticism within the spans of vocal phrases, driven by emotional impulse, especially so during the solo cadenza passages. Just occasionally, there is a direct response to melodic contour: for example, the dipping and rising lifts to the opening three vocalisms: 'Ah!' [18]–[19]. You cannot contain this bird. Taruskin has written of the Nightingale song:

> Thanks to a massive dose of ornamental passing tones and acciaccaturas [tiny 'crushed-in' grace notes], the music of the artist-bird seems to glide freely (perhaps allegorically) in the chromatic ether, in the lingering [Symbolist] spirit of Mir Iskusstva.[149]

This is also a perfect description of the dancing Nightingale.

Ashton's movement for Makarova is entirely appropriate, but far more memorable and substantial both choreographically and choreomusically is his work with and for Dowell, a dancer far more familiar to him. Indeed, for him, Ashton made some of the most interesting solos that he had ever made for a man, and hence this solo material was revived by Dowell for the *Ashton to Stravinsky* video (danced by Federico Bonelli). It comprises one extended, complex solo at the beginning of the work, immediately establishing the importance of the Fisherman figure, including his 'song' twice, and then solos to the song refrains at the end of each Act, which reveal a process of simplification and reduction. In the last, he simply gestures, searching, listening, takes a formal bow, and then ... 'It's all over'. The vocabulary is barely classical, but neither is it cliché dance chinoiserie; there is just an occasional angular gesture, flexed foot, or hint of folk dance – coaching Bonelli, Dowell refers to a 'Kabuki step' and to an arm movement that should be 'more Javanese'.[150] Many arm moves are particular to the work, such as throwing a net (two arms), drawing the shape of the moon with a finger, a hand flutter to indicate presence of the bird or flicker by the mouth to reflect the magic of her voice.

But the manner in which this vocabulary is delivered is all-important, as is its relation to the music. Dowell immediately establishes a magical authority. When he dances, there is the seamlessness and plasticity for which he is celebrated, but he also plays taut, nervous, suddenly reined in, as if caught up by a moment of major enchantment. We perceive many kinds of freedom and precision here, quite different from other Ashton–Stravinsky, and reflected in aspects of style that have nothing to do with counts and pulse. We observe breath timing, and there are dynamic issues about independence between music and dance, their occasional divergence into two strands or voices, with separate patterns of accent, ebb and flow and, as a result, spots of tension, effects of resistance. Thus, from time to time, straightforward mutual visual/aural embodiment is undermined and put under strain. There are examples of this dance autonomy at the beginning of Act I: the staccato imprints of restless turns to one side and then the other that bring Dowell downstage; a sudden turning jump and sharp heel-first steps that resolve into a descent to the floor and smooth curve forwards and back; then a sudden roll and lightning arrival with hands supporting the body in a taut line followed by a smooth transition into kneeling.

Perhaps the simplicity of the Fisherman's haunting song over the 'tangled foliage of sonority' offered a base from which Ashton felt free to develop his dance fantasy. First, he must surely have asked himself how he was to deal with so many repeats in the score. Musically, the first, extended Fisherman's solo, when he sings of the beauty of the Nightingale's song, is structured like this:

Introduction:[8]
Song   [8]+5
Interlude 1   [10]
Interlude 2   [11]
Song   [13]
Interlude 1   [16]

Then there are the song refrains at the end of each Act, and within each song verse there is still more repetition – two phrases each three bars long, each presented twice:

	a	a	b	b
Bars	3	3	3	3

and phrase *b* contains a repeat within itself (of its initial bar – see Ex. 4.18).

Ex. 4.18. *Le Rossignol*, Act I, Fisherman's song.

Ashton's response is constantly to renew our experience, to articulate different things in the music, not to match its repetitions, not to go for straight symmetry. In the song sections, pulse and rhythm are never far from the choreography – Ashton brings out what is latent in the extremely legato music – but there is dynamic independence again, and once more touches of sharpness, even impatience, in the dance. During the opening song section, the movement steadily increases in amplitude on the repeat of phrase *a*, a series of steps backwards on the diagonal with the working leg drawn into passé and later thrown up to the side with foot flexed. Phrase *b* first time round shows the Fisherman turning and casting his net, twice, matching the musical one-bar repeat, and then he steps and arches back with the turning upwards in the music, as if asking a question. When the song repeats, the first phrase *b* is a variation on the backward-stepping sequence on the diagonal (initially seen to phrase *a* music) – already big movement, but now expanded further still. The sequence ends with a flamboyant pirouette, the leg unfolding into second, and a series of wrist flicks, a lot of movement packed into the relatively quiet close of the musical phrase, and a new intensity not prompted by any change in the music.

We see a touch of the same impatience in the solo that ends Act I, when the Fisherman laments the departure of the Nightingale to the Emperor's palace. He restarts his opening phrase at an earlier point in the music, and consequently has extra time to run upstage before the musical phrase ends. Like the pirouette and wrist flicks that were packed into the opening solo, he packs in a couple of 'extra' steps at the very end of the third phrase (*b*), a last-minute touch of impetuosity.

In the solo that ends Act II, where the Fisherman sings of the Emperor's approaching death (with added musical dissonance at the end), there is a passage of musical crossing during the phrase *b* passage that could be analysed in counts: two sets of 4 (against 3 in the music) for a version of the 'Fred Step' (see p. 277) to one side and then the other; a transition (one count); and then two sets of 5, each a series of steps leading upstage and building to an assemblé. But counts here are irrelevant, even counter-productive. In the revival for *Ashton to Stravinsky*, Dowell taught Bonelli to gauge the 'Fred Step' rhythm from the lilting posé fondu opening. It looks as though the dancer is riding waves: it is relaxed, contemplative, and who can count during that quality of experience? Seen just twice, the step does not set up any sense of metre or regular accentuation, and the pulse is as gentle as it is clear. The sequences that follow are like huge breaths. The second assemblé dissolves into a crouch as the music likewise dissolves into a rhythmless swell.

Rossignol is of course about Dowell as well as Ashton, the dancer as collaborator. Although dynamic discrepancies are common in the larger body of Ashton repertory, it is intriguing to find in *Rossignol* the taut, speedy rhythmic touches that suddenly firm up the adagio in Dowell's other Ashton roles, and yet are remarkably understated. Examples are the sudden 'mad' changements[151] and lightly darting arabesques in his Belyayev solo in *A Month in the Country* (1976),

accents cutting across lyrical music. This dynamic practice is probably the rea-
son why the American dance critic Nancy Goldner considered that Dowell's
Rossignol solos were 'overly fussy and rushed against the music nervously'.[152]
More extreme, the London music critic David Cairns indicated puzzlement

> as to why on earth in ballet the movements of the dancers so often seem to
> pursue a course quite independent of the score, altering significantly at some
> moment when the music is doing nothing in particular, or equally, remaining
> exactly the same regardless of a marked change in tempo or texture.[153]

Goldner and Cairns did not appreciate the expressive significance of space between music and dance, and that this is an aspect of Ashton's choreomusical
style, giving dance the spirit of improvisation, of moving on interior impulse.
Dowell's *Rossignol* solos are a metaphor for the interplay of memory and thought
process, repeating musical reminiscences behind evolving choreography.

Other productions of *Rossignol* represent a range of theatrical approaches.
Alexander Schouvaloff's listing includes several with mention of neither choreography nor dancers, and these have not been represented in the *SGD* database.[154] It is quite possible to perform the piece like a straight opera. When there
has been a choreographic element, sometimes the real Nightingale has been
danced on stage, sometimes not; likewise the Mechanical Nightingale, sometimes danced, sometimes not. The Fisherman has had more or less of a role on
stage and the chorus has been more or less choreographed, according to
whether the staging has been divided into two components, representing respectively opera and ballet. Sometimes the choreographer has been listed as director,
sometimes these roles have been taken by two separate people. Memories of the
original hybrid production have spawned a very fluid approach to staging, a
range of hybridities. Contrasting with Dexter's approach, a version choreographed by John Butler for television (1971) included dance roles for the Fisherman (in Acts I and II), Mechanical Nightingale and Death, and a dancing chorus.[155] Another staged by the film director Jacques Demy for Ballet-Théâtre
Contemporain (1972) was noted for its spare choreographic element by
Françoise Adret, which included work for the corps de ballet, but only one solo
dance role, for the Mechanical Nightingale.[156] Unusually, a production by the
Russian contemporary dance choreographer Tatiana Baganova for the Perm Opera and Ballet (2004) fully integrated the singers into the cryptic, gestural choreographic content of the piece. Thus, the singers (all the named characters)
operated in a close, interactive relationship with the small dance ensemble. This
was a free realisation of the original scenario incorporating the symbol of Yin
and Yang oppositions. Another unusual production was planned, but never realised, by Lincoln Kirstein's Ballet Society. Alongside the premiere of Balanchine's

1947 *Renard, Rossignol* was to be 'danced as a Javanese ballet in the native idiom, arranged by Ratna Mohini'.[157] In the event, Mohini offered a sequence of Javanese Court and Popular Dances.

Of particular note is the 1918 production at the Maryinsky by the experimental theatre director Vsevolod Meyerhold, with designs by Serge Golovine (who had designed Fokine's 1910 *Firebird*), the result of negotiations between Stravinsky and the Maryinsky that had begun in early 1914. 'Stravinsky intended to ask you', Golovine wrote to Meyerhold. The director's approach here was formal and anti-naturalistic with a choreographic orientation, again highlighting the idea of performing doubles, by visually and overtly integrating off-stage manner with onstage performance. The Fisherman, Death and Nightingale singers, carrying their music stands with them, 'commenced their solo at a sign from the conductor, sang while looking at the score and after completing their part would sit (or stand) with an absent facial expression'. The chorus, also static, flanked the stage while silent extras mimed the plot. 'The dead to the dead, the live to the living', Meyerhold described his staging. He also disrupted the convention of a literally invisible Nightingale by having the female singer sitting on view at the start next to the Fisherman, 'unseen' by him as he sings of her enchanting qualities.[158] Thus, perhaps Meyerhold wanted to stress that the real, remarkable body of opera lies in the music, whilst the physical body of the opera singer is 'dead' (invisible): the mime has the 'live', to-be-seen body. Balanchine had a small part in the production, which, he said, gave him useful musical background to choreographing *Le Chant du rossignol* for Diaghilev in 1925.[159]

Diaghilev mounted two productions of *Le Chant du rossignol*, the symphonic poem drawn from Acts II and III of the opera. Both with designs by Matisse, the first production was by Massine in 1920; Balanchine's 1925 sequel introduced the 14-year-old Alicia Markova as the real Nightingale and altered the end of the story so that she dies after bringing the Emperor back to life.[160] Since the Diaghilev period, this shorter score has attracted several well-known choreographers, such as Erich Walter, John Cranko, Aurel Milloss and John Taras. Commissioned to undertake it for the 1972 New York City Ballet Stravinsky Festival, Taras made the point about rushing to tell the story through too little music:

> It has the same problem that most Stravinsky story ballets have – there's never enough time to tell the story, not everything is taken care of, and the story is not very satisfactory.[161]

Hardly surprisingly, the programmatic nature of the music seems to have persuaded most choreographers to take on the challenge of the original scenario, although *Le Chant du rossignol* has still tended towards a 'lavish costume parade'[162] kind of work, rather like the 1914 opera-ballet. An exception is Mark

Baldwin's 1998 setting for his own company, using the piano reduction, just four dancers (three women and one man) and no décor, with the original plot in vestigial form and the performers shifting roles. Bart de Block danced on pointe, representing both real and mechanical nightingales (dressed respectively in red, reminiscent of the Firebird, and black with metallic elements).

* * *

As a version of the opera-ballet, Ashton's *Rossignol* turns out to be one of the most densely choreographed of all, his contribution a memorable and dramatically active component of the whole production. Looked at in context, this work brings us full circle, far removed from other Ashton/Stravinsky conceptions. Even if presented within a highly stylised and 'artificial' production, there is the sensuality and organic flow here that we associate most regularly with the main body of Ashton's work, and which he brought increasingly to the foreground in his later years as a choreographer. Ashton subscribed to Stravinsky's 'cool' in the other three earlier works examined in this chapter, *Scènes de ballet*, *Persephone*, and *Le Baiser de la fée* (as far as we know from the *Baiser* choreography that exists on film). Or at least these works brought to special prominence a tendency within Ashton, so that we can identify through them a particular Ashton–Stravinsky kind of movement. Stravinsky changed the choreographer's movement. Nevertheless, in this last work, using early Stravinsky – the Fisherman's song is a particularly early composition, and atypical – Ashton was able to revise his earlier position. He could glance back towards the ethos of the late nineteenth century and, as a number of musicologists have done in recent years, emphasise and celebrate the lyrically expressive side of the composer. We have also seen how, by comparing Ashton's work with other choreography to the same scores, we can hear and understand Stravinsky's music differently in different contexts, and this will continue to be a focus during the following two chapters.

5

Les Noces: One Score, Many Weddings

Introduction

The first *Les Noces*, with choreography by Nijinska (1923), occupies a unique position within dance/music history. Sourced in Russian peasant wedding ritual, it was an all but lost ballet for thirty years until Nijinska was invited by Frederick Ashton to revive it for the Royal Ballet in 1966, just a few years before her death. The revival met with immediate acclaim, and since then the work has not only become central to the Royal Ballet repertory, but it is also in the broad international repertoire and widely considered a choreographic masterpiece of the twentieth century.

The appeal of *Noces* broadens, as a work held in the same high regard as Balanchine's collaborations with Stravinsky, yet, unlike those, of equal interest to audiences who admire classical ballet and to those who are more sympathetic to modern dance. It is also a company work about collective rather than individual identity, with the focus on ensemble dancing.

Nijinska's *Noces* still looks like no other dance made before or since, way beyond established traditions of movement vocabulary and construction, as if it sprang out of nowhere, and perhaps was so strong that no offshoots from it seemed possible: it was untouchable. It has been called neoclassical because, anticipating Balanchine, Nijinska uses pointe work and offers a reflection upon the medium of dance – movement and the presentation and reworking of a limited number of movement motifs – rather than on the traditional model of narrative through dance. Yet the body attitude is decidedly un-classical, narrow, at the beginning elongated by pointe work so that the dancers, according to Nijinska, 'resemble the saints in Byzantine mosaics',[1] but more often blunted and weighted, with no specific turnout of the legs and the hands held in strange half-clenched fists. As the critic Edwin Denby noted in his vivid description of the movement content, there was a novel earthiness: 'ballet dancers, more familiar with the opposite direction, do these movements with a curious freshness ... the leaps seem higher ... the 'pointes' get a special significance and hardness (almost a form of tapping) ...'[2] New too was the hard, geometrical emphasis of the ballet, with its phalanxes, wedges, pyramids and walls. Horizontal shape is created by the distribution of groups on the stage, vertical shape as frieze by the piling of body upon body (see Ill. 12), culminating in a construction involving the entire ensemble, an image of soaring from a grounded mass, like a cathedral. Denby

Ill. 12. Elizabeth McGorian as the Bride, Sandra Conley and Derek Rencher as the Bride's parents in *Les Noces*, end of Tableau 1, choreography by Bronislava Nijinska, Royal Ballet.

observed that the 'general downward direction [of movement] gives the heaped bodies a sense beyond decoration and gives the conventional pyramid at the end the effect of an heroic extreme, of a real difficulty'.[3] On the other hand, even if the nature of the exertion is unusual, elevation is an important component of Nijinska's choreography and provides a strong counter-emphasis upwards: 'as if the dancers lifted the very ground with them when they jumped'.[4]

Yet one more unusual feature of *Noces*: it is a 'master'-piece by a woman choreographer. After *Sacre*, it was another ballet about female sacrifice, but this time clearly shaped by Nijinska to show the woman's perspective in marriage (even though her Bride barely has a dancing role) – a strong statement for that time, which continues to assert its political power.

Nevertheless, Nijinska's great achievement did not stem the flow of new settings to the score. Quite the opposite. Here was a 'perfect' ballet, but unlike Balanchine's *Apollo* or *Agon*, its presence imposed no restraining order. Indeed, after the 1966 revival, the number of settings has continued to increase exponentially. The 'Stravinsky the Global Dancer' database (*SGD*) reveals a tradition of nearly 70 settings of the score since the original ballet. To be fair, the flow barely got going until the mid-twentieth century, probably because of the difficulties of the score for musicians and listeners and its highly unconventional performance requirements – four grand pianos, percussion, four solo singers and a chorus – expensive to muster, and well beyond the normal musical resource limits of even the biggest ballet companies. Then, through the 1980s and 1990s, we see a significant acceleration in the rate of new productions (at least 33 since 1990), *Noces* by now on a par with the number of new *Firebird* and *Petrushka* productions of the same period. There were no fewer than 4 in 2000. It helped, of course, that a range of recordings of the score became available. Some choreographers have paid homage to Nijinska's original work through stylistic reference and even quotation, most often referencing the unforgettable 'body piles', and, if they have never seen Nijinska's choreography, they have accessed it through photographs. They have paid homage in their own *Noces* – Jiří Kylián (1982), Michael Smuin (1999) and Heinz Spoerli (2006) – and in other Stravinsky works too, in *Firebird* (James Kudelka, 2001) and in *Sacre*, as if seeing Nijinska as the link through to Nijinsky (Richard Alston, 1981, and Javier De Frutos, *Milagros*, 2003).

Why such interest from other choreographers, especially recently? I propose that the nature and premise of the score itself is primarily responsible, its immense rhythmic vitality combined with a Russian-period earthiness that has attracted modern dance as well as ballet choreographers and companies. This is the score that Stravinsky worried over for longer than any other he ever made (see p. 38), working on it, with breaks, from 1914 to 1923 (in 1917 Nijinsky and Massine were potential choreographers[5]). He thus saw it transform itself as he experienced a major shift in his own approach from the so-called Russian-period aesthetic to neoclassicism. Aside from the run on choreographic settings, it has also enjoyed a recent boost in recognition within the field of music. There has been a notable increase in concert performances and in the rate of appearance of new recordings. There has also been especially important research into the Russian ritual sources of the score. Leading the field has been the Russian musicologist Margarita Mazo, opening with her seminal article of 1990, since when she has edited a new edition of the score (2005).[6] Her work has been complemented by that of Richard Taruskin in the 1990s, for whom *Noces* is the acme of Stravinsky's achievement, with Nijinska's production as its most appropriate realisation.[7] Typically, though, Taruskin draws attention to the Janus-faced aspects of the score and their political implications, writing that the

symbols of ideally harmonized existence lend *Svadebka* [*Noces*] both its incomparably compelling aesthetic integrity and its ominously compelling political allure. ... It is precisely the recognition of the danger in the work's allure, the heart of darkness that lurks behind and conditions its gravely joyous affirmations, that so intensifies reaction.[8]

Alluding to Adorno and the tradition of nationalistic totalitarianism (see p. 98), Taruskin goes further to ask us, the audience, to bring to consciousness how we stand in relation to its dark side:

> The tension between nostalgia for the security of community and the obligations of enlightened individualism lives not only in *Svadebka* but in ourselves as, contemplating it, we are emotionally swayed by its potent advocacy of what may appear on rational reflection to be a parlous message. The anxious thrill of moral risk that attends the experience of *Svadebka* is one of the things that has kept it alive, and one of the marks of its creator's fearful potency.[9]

The tradition of *Noces* as a woman's ballet might be an important contributing factor to its rise in profile as a dance score over recent years. More women have set this music than probably any other Stravinsky ballet score, even if this still represents less than a third of the total. The first five productions in the 1920s and 1930s were all by women. There is always the niggling challenge of using the score to question the marriage condition or at least to reflect upon it, and, more than any other Stravinsky score except *Sacre*, *Noces* offers the opportunity for social critique. Was the sudden soaring of production figures in the 1990s (settings by both men and women) possibly a (late) response to the prevailing debates about gender issues and the institution of marriage? Recently too, dance scholars have brought to our attention the proto-feminist consciousness underlying Nijinska's original production and which is likely to have inspired later women choreographers, even if they had not yet seen a performance of her work. Against the political backdrop of early Soviet Russia and the moves at that time towards increased rights for women and a new role for the peasant class, *Noces* is, Sally Banes claims, 'a watershed work, obdurately shifting the terms of the ballet wedding's significance from the male to the female perspective' and the Bride is 'no Other, but a contemporary woman ... With *Les Noces*, the woman's image finally coincides with her social reality.'[10] Lynn Garafola notes as a significant factor that Nijinska's own marriage experience was blighted: separated from her husband (she evicted him when his mistress became pregnant), she was a working woman, responsible at the same time for raising her own two children and caring for an elderly mother. Garafola was also explicit in reading that 'the stabbing pointes, "masculine" in their violence' were a metaphor for 'the drama of sexual penetration'.[11] Nijinska herself, in her article 'Creation of *Les Noces*', written c.1970 after the revival for the Royal Ballet, emphasised the painful aspect of the traditional Russian wedding:

> How can such souls rejoice during their wedding ceremonies: they are deep in other thoughts.

Only the families and guests enjoy themselves.

Although the 'guests' certainly demonstrate a forceful exuberance, this only underlines the unavoidable plight of the peasant woman:

> The young girl knows nothing at all about her future family nor what lies in store for her. Not only will she be subject to her husband, but also to his parents. It is possible that after being loved and cherished by her own kin, she may be nothing more, in her new, rough family, than a useful extra worker, just another pair of hands. The soul of the innocent is in disarray – she is bidding good-bye to her carefree youth and to her loving mother.[12]

Years earlier, Nijinska even described the nature of the peasant wedding as 'of the nature of tragedy'.[13]

The premiere cast of *Noces* comprised Felia Doubrovska (Bride), Nicolai Semenoff (Groom), Lubov Tchernitcheva and Leon Woizikowsky (soloists in the Wedding Feast Tableau 4). The Diaghilev Ballets Russes performance figures for *Noces* are as follows:

1923	8 Paris
1924	6 Paris
1926	4 Paris 7 London [Diaghilev recruited the four composers Georges Auric, Vernon Duke (Vladimir Dukelsky), Francis Poulenc and Vittorio Rieti to play the pianos in London]
1928	5 Paris 4 London[14]

Nijinska later staged the ballet at the Teatro Colón in Buenos Aires (1926),[15] for her own company Théâtre de la Danse Nijinska in Paris (1933) and for de Basil's Ballets Russes in New York (1936). This 1936 production was the first occasion on which Nijinska's daughter Irina assisted her mother with the production; Irina was later to hold the rights in the work and led the staging of productions after Bronislava's death in 1972 until her own death in 1991. It was also the last time that the ballet was seen until the 1966 Royal Ballet revival. Quite apart from the highly unusual and ungainly musical resources required for live performance, Nijinska had no power base, no stable association with a company across the years through which she could sustain the work herself – unsurprising for a woman ballet choreographer during this period. Contrast the Royal Ballet, which has had the right to maintain the work in its own repertory since 1966 and has regularly done so, the longest absences being between the seasons 1984/85 and 1989/90 and later between 1991/92 and 1999/2000.[16] A Benesh score of the work has been made (completed 2001), begun from notes made in 1966 by Christopher Newton, who danced in the original Royal Ballet production and is now responsible for staging the work.[17] The current production still uses as a resource the Edmée Wood rehearsal film of 1967 (with piano accompaniment), an invaluable document stemming from the period of the revival, and with the original Royal Ballet cast: Svetlana Beriosova (Bride), Ray Roberts (Groom), Georgina Parkinson and Anthony Dowell (soloists in the Wedding Feast Tableau 4).[18]

Meanwhile, another performance tradition arose through Irina, stimulated undoubtedly by the acclaim that greeted the 1966 revival, and making use of the Royal's early Benesh scores.[19] This is the version that is now produced around the world. The demand has been considerable over the years, alongside other *Noces* choreographies; the number of companies having been offered the work now totals thirty (see Appendix 6). Although the architecture and relationships between music and movement remain broadly similar across the two performance traditions, this version differs from the Royal Ballet production in many small details of movement and timing. Yet choreographers do make changes, and Bronislava might have altered the choreography or performance manner when she undertook her next (and last) staging in Venice in 1971. Again, Irina assisted her there, and could have noted any changes. Irina also had access to her mother's personal *Noces* materials, which included copious diagrams – floor plans as well as lists of steps.[20]

In my analysis, I intend to be open about differences between the two 'versions' insofar as they affect a choreomusical analysis, rather than judgemental about authenticity, although I indicate what I find most effective, which in turn depends on performance quality and the interpretative stance of the film/videomaker. For the Royal Ballet version, my sources include the Benesh score and 1967 rehearsal film, Newton's piano rehearsal score (which provides counts and outlines the main dance events), and two televised recordings for the BBC by Bob Lockyer (1978) and Ross McGibbon (2001). For the Irina Nijinska version, I have seen video recordings of two Oakland Ballet performances (1981 and 1990) and one by the Paris Opéra Ballet (1990).[21] I admit to my preference for the Lockyer recording, which most accurately captures my image of the ballet from live performance. It communicates the passionate energy and weight of the movement, and the concentration of the effort – as Arlene Croce recalled from seeing the Royal Ballet in 1967, the unforgettable 'combination of wildness and precision'.[22] At the same time it shows us the architecture of the choreography as fully as Lockyer dares for a screen performance, while maintaining an appropriate element of artifice. There are some very distant views, which show us the full stage picture as a floating strip of space, like a kind of constructivist marionette theatre, because the shots were made through glass blocked out at top and bottom by black paint.[23] Above all, from a choreomusical point of view,

Lockyer's version contains remarkably few cuts between shots, and the interactions between music and dance are not obscured.

Other factors are significant when considering the content of *Noces*, not least Nijinska's closeness to her brother's choreography. She had worked with him on the creation of his three early Diaghilev works, *L'Après-midi d'un faune* (1912), *Jeux* (1913) and *Sacre* (1913), had danced as a Nymph in *Faune* (later in the 1922 revival taking her brother's role of the Faun), and had originally been intended as the first Chosen One in *Sacre* (in the end, pregnancy prevented her from performing in the premieres of both *Jeux* and *Sacre* – see p. 422). In *Noces*, we see the frieze style from *Faune* and the relaxed fists from *Jeux*, and from *Sacre* the pose of the women tilting their heads sideways towards hands pressed together, which might have been prompted by Russian icons. From her brother she inherited a radical approach to dance movement and to the dancing body. Like him, too, she had a troubled relationship with Diaghilev and the Ballets Russes and left to return to Russia in 1914, staying there right through the Revolution until, on hearing that Nijinsky was in an asylum, she returned to visit him in Vienna in 1921, and then accepted Diaghilev's invitation to rejoin the Ballets Russes. Once again, after creating seven ballets (including *Renard*) and staging the opera *Mavra*, she left Diaghilev in 1925, rejoining him briefly in 1926.

The seat of the disagreements between Nijinska and Diaghilev was his lack of interest in dance movement and plotless ballet. Her time spent back in Russia was of crucial significance to her progress towards *Noces*. Living and working in Petrograd, Moscow and also Kiev, which had become an important artistic centre, she allied herself to the lively new Russian avant-garde. She was especially attracted to the constructivist movement, which focused on the expressive, utopian potential of geometrical forms and machinery, and collaborated with the artist Alexandra Exter. It is highly likely that she experienced too the multi-body configurations of avant-garde theatre, perhaps the stars or factory complex symbols of the agitprop Blue Blouse troupes and the director Meyerhold's biomechanical exercises, one of which was actually called 'building the pyramid'.[24] Between 1919 and 1921, she ran her own Ecole de Mouvement in Kiev and made a series of short works as experiments in abstract choreography. At the same time, stemming from her period in Moscow in 1917–18, she began work on her treatise 'On Movement and the School of Movement', in which she diminished the centrality of the libretto and concentrated her attentions on movement development and its structuring in space, in time and to music.[25]

Nijinska was able to draw on a musical background, having studied piano, like her brother, at the Imperial Ballet School in St Petersburg. Ashton and Ninette de Valois recalled her ability to analyse music in detail, her counting technique, and that she took along the score of *Noces* 'with the ballet worked out

on it'.[26] In her memoirs, she disapproves of the Dalcroze influence in Nijinsky's *Sacre* (see p. 430), the very close relationship between sight and sound, even though, as Garafola points out, her own school in Kiev had been linked with Dalcroze experimentalism.[27] The Western neoclassical movement of which she was immediately a part on her return from Russia was at odds with his free-body style of training. Yet at the same time, she interrogated music as a sophisticated complement to her choreography and used its forms as a model for her new, non-narrative forms of choreographic construction. In an article in *The Dancing Times* in 1937 she wrote:

> *Noces* was the first work where the libretto was a hidden theme for a pure choreography: it was a choregraphic concerto. [My works in Russia] together with *Noces* and *Biches* ... were the beginning of a long series of ballets in the form of a choregraphic symphony, sonata, étude, or concerto.[28]

The story of the birth of the *Noces* choreography is well known, as told by the choreographer herself: how Diaghilev proposed the commission to Nijinska in 1922 when Stravinsky's final orchestration was not yet finally settled, at which time Natalya Goncharova's designs were heavy, ground-trailing, very colourful and 'sumptuously Russian'. Nijinska was thrilled enough by the music to come up with a clear visual conception:

> [The music] astounded me, overwhelming me with its disturbing rhythm. *Les Noces* seemed to me to be deeply dramatic, interspersed with occasional splashes of joyousness and true feeling of Russia.[29]

But she was not at all persuaded by the movement-unfriendly costumes, and told Diaghilev that she could not choreograph unless they were changed. There is evidence that some kind of work actually began in 1922 – *Noces* rehearsals are mentioned for the period 7–16 April – and contemporary correspondence between Stravinsky and Diaghilev indicates concerns about progress.[30] But Diaghilev replaced the planned premiere with the opera *Mavra* and dropped the project until spring 1923. Nijinska recalls the gist of their next conversation:

> [Diaghilev:] 'We are in the home of the bride-to-be, she is sitting in a big Russian armchair, at the side of the stage, her friends are combing her hair and dressing her braids.'
>
> 'No, Serge Pavlovitch', I cut in, 'the chair's not necessary, the comb is not necessary and the hair-combing even less so.'

Nijinska then sketched the bride with ten feet long braids held by her friends and explained that there would be no combing:

> It will be their dance 'on points' with the bride, that will express the rhythm of braiding.[31]

The final design decision was the plain brown and white work clothes that are indicative of peasant garb. There was also a stark set of screens indicating a variety of interiors, including, in the final scene, a raised platform that is the family anteroom or 'cell' (where we see the Bride and Groom and their parents), leading through a pair of doors to a bedroom beyond. Nijinska's conception was undoubtedly coloured by her experience of the new Russia: 'All the vivid images of the harsh realities of the Revolution were still part of me and filled my whole being.'[32] Yet she wanted such intensity to be contained within the austere formalism of the new Russian avant-garde, and the dance performance manner was highly restrained too, with a complete absence of facial expression. Although Goncharova might have been moving quite independently towards much simpler designs anyway, Nijinska claimed that *Noces* 'was the only ballet in which he [Diaghilev] allowed the choreographer to have a deciding influence over the entire production'.[33]

We will never know for sure whether Nijinska's communications with Stravinsky in 1922 also had an effect upon his final decision about the orchestration. This had gone through numerous more colourful permutations (see p. 38) before the pianos and percussion version that he was later to describe as 'perfectly homogeneous, perfectly impersonal, and perfectly mechanical',[34] but it is not at all unlikely that Nijinska's ideas brought to him relatively late in the creative process had some impact. After all, it was on 18 April 1922 that Stravinsky announced his decision on the orchestration, immediately after Nijinska's scheduled rehearsal period.[35] At Diaghilev's instigation, and possibly because the orchestra pit at the Théâtre de la Gaîté-Lyrique was too small to house the pianos alongside all the other musicians and instruments, performances in Paris had the pianos on opposite sides of the stage (two double Pleyel instruments with two keyboards, one at each end). Reviewers of London performances also mention double pianos, so presumably they were on view there too.[36] Nijinska later dispensed with the piano presence, possibly for practical reasons, but I have come across no evidence that she especially wanted to have any musicians or instruments on view next to her choreography. Watching the 1936 revival, Denby, who had obviously heard about an earlier production, lamented their absence.[37]

At the same time, Stravinsky had entertained his own very different idea of

the staging. 'At first ... Stravinsky was confused and disturbed', Nijinska reminisced to her daughter. 'But Diaghilev had confidence in me. "Let her finish it,
maybe we will be understood twenty years from now ..." he said.'[38] Later, even
though Stravinsky sometimes went into print strongly approving Nijinska's production and her talent as a choreographer (see p. 51), on other occasions he
reminds us of his own earlier conception. In his *Autobiography*, for instance, his
reserved tone betrays disappointment:

> I must say that the stage production of *Les Noces*, though obviously one of
> talent, did not correspond with my original plan. I had pictured to myself
> something quite different.
>
> According to my idea, the spectacle should have been a *divertissement*,
> and that is what I wanted to call it ... Inspired by the same reasons as in
> *L'Histoire d'un Soldat*, I wanted all my instrumental apparatus to be visible side
> by side with the actors or dancers, making it, so to speak, a participant in the
> whole theatrical action. For this reason, I wished to place the orchestra on the
> stage itself, letting the actors move on the space remaining free. The fact that
> the artists in the scene would uniformly wear costumes of a Russian charac-
> ter while the musicians would be in evening dress not only did not embarrass
> me, but, on the contrary, was perfectly in keeping with my idea of a *divertisse-*
> *ment* of the masquerade type.[39]

Quite apart from the presence on stage of all the instrumentalists, not only the
pianists (later, in *Expositions and Developments*, he mentions the 'whole company'
of musicians, which could be read as singers too[40]), the notion of divertissement
and masquerade (and the allusion to *Soldat*) suggests a more colourful, playful
and 'rough' kind of theatricality than Nijinska produced. This notion resonates
with Stravinsky's keen, established interest in anti-realist, mixed-media theatre
(see pp. 31, 35) and not only represents a different kind of theatrical distancing
from the rigorous, stripped-down body stylisation of Nijinska's choreography,
but could also be seen to contradict the description of homogeneity that he later
applied to his own music. We can, on the other hand, observe a link between
what Stravinsky writes here and Goncharova's earlier Russian conception of the
costume designs (she, incidentally, reverted to bold colour and anecdotal detail
in her designs for George Skibine's *Noces* in Aix-en-Provence in 1962). Nor, in
Stravinsky's writings, is there ever any suggestion of real social tragedy or critique.[41] He simply presents the facts of ritual practice, and thus: 'The bride weeps
in the first scene not necessarily because of real sorrow at her prospective loss of
virginity, but because, ritualistically, she *must* weep.'[42]

A handwritten document in the Basle archives, which might once have been
intended to preface the score, demonstrates the composer's very firm views on

the staging: singers in the pit (by implication, as above, everyone else was on stage), all stage directions marked in the score to be scrupulously followed, productions to be free from plot ('intrigue') and Russian folkloric realism. Stravinsky had clear ideas about the design. First there was to be a simple backdrop evoking at the same time a Russian wooden house interior and a village street. Without a break in the action, this would be raised for the final part of the ballet.[43] The full ramifications of this discussion about Stravinsky's theatrical intentions will emerge later.

Texted music: The Noces score

Turning now to the *Noces* score, some preliminaries on its construction are helpful as a base for the later choreomusical analysis of a group of settings. After all, Nijinska herself (and as we shall see, others) undertook detailed analysis of the formal properties of the music (from a piano/vocal reduction) before choreographing any steps. It is also important to consider the text (and the issue of characters who 'speak') alongside the music in interaction with the choreography. But first, as with so many other Stravinsky works, we can talk about *Noces* in terms of block construction (see p. 149). Mazo describes the salient features in the context of *Noces*:

> Each structural block can be repeated exactly, or shifted in musical space (to a different pitch) or in time (to a different beat). It can vary, expand or contract. Each block can be juxtaposed, superimposed or interspersed with other blocks, but it cannot develop into something different as a result of these transfigurations and interactions.[44]

Mazo notes significantly that, in spite of 'structural disjunction', there is an extraordinary sense of coherence in *Noces*, 'an uninterrupted thrust from the first to the last note'[45] that is brought about by the placement and timing of the blocks.

Pieter van den Toorn's dual typology of rhythmic/metrical procedures holds true for *Noces* (see pp. 89–92): Type I based on metrical irregularity, featuring a limited number of rhythmic cells in shifting permutations, Type II based on metrical regularity and including sections of independent rhythmic layers.[46] Metrical regularity usually reflects the presence of an ostinato. However, unlike Type II passages in some other work, for example *Sacre*, ostinatos in *Noces* rarely seem to be in the foreground. They are most often in the bass line of the accompaniment, highly contaminated by the wayward vocal and instrumental lines above, and do not extend over long time-spans to build structural climaxes through the accumulative force of simple repetition. So ostinatos might hardly be registered by the ear as other parts of a texture take precedence, and their style is not to create a hypnotic effect. The machine metaphor is appropriate to *Noces* (see pp. 104-5), but here it is a playful and unpredictable machine that has proved notoriously elusive as regards analysis.

Stravinsky first of all faced the problem of committing himself when barring his written score, especially tricky when different lines are organised independently, and it is generally agreed that the relationship between what is heard and the look of the score is not at all straightforward. The theorists van den Toorn and Gretchen Horlacher have wrestled with the issue of how we make sense of the score's rhythmic complexity, although with different views as to how much we try to hold on to an established metrical framework when faced with disruption (a conservative reading) or allow this sense to be removed by other musical forces such as motivic recurrence or crossing accents conflicting with established metre (a radical reading).[47] I will address issues of rhythmic comprehension later, within the choreomusical analyses, as the addition of a dance element automatically changes the nature of such rhythmic problems. Besides, the fragments of the score analysed in terms of rhythm by these music theorists (van den Toorn selects the opening phrases of the first Tableau, Horlacher the opening of the second) are not always choreographed (they are not, for instance, in the Nijinska production). There has been one valuable attempt at choreomusical analysis of *Noces*, by Jeanne Jaubert, in which she juxtaposes the different 'lines' of aural (heard), choreographic and printed metres in the final scene. However, the weight of her work is on the intricacies of the music rather than the dance, and she had recourse only to the Paris Opéra Ballet recording of the work.[48]

The crucial development with *Noces* (since *Sacre*) was the incorporation of text, and the particular manner of its use, stemming from Stravinsky's 'rejoicing discovery'[49] of 1914 that Russian folk song distorted the spoken stress of words, thus freeing him to give words new value as sounds beyond and separate from their original meaning. He had used this approach in *Renard*, which Nijinska had also choreographed, in 1922. The general style of text setting in *Noces* is syllabic, one note per syllable, almost in the manner of recitation and unusually percussive, drawing attention to rhythm pattern. Stravinsky clearly enjoyed unsettling the rhythms of the texts from time to time, sometimes juxtaposing more than one complex line. It is hardly surprising, then, that any accompanying regularity from ostinatos is easily effaced.

Broadly speaking, the construction of the text follows the structure of the work, which is in two Parts, both building to points of climax, and further divided into four Tableaux, all performed without a break. The church ceremony happens in our imagination between the two Parts:

Part 1:
Tableau 1   At the Bride's House
Tableau 2   At the Bridegroom's House
Tableau 3   The Departure of the Bride

Part 2:
Tableau 4   The Wedding Feast

This structure constitutes Stravinsky's own ordering of events based on selected traditional wedding rituals. Originally, these rituals comprised a drama or
game lasting several days, extending from a matchmaking ceremony to general
feasting and merrymaking.[50] Included in the score are occasional stage directions: for instance, in Tableau 4, references at [114] to the nomination of a
couple to warm the marriage bed for the bride and groom (in the bedroom seen
through doors opening from the 'cell' on the raised platform upstage), the embrace of the newly married couple at [127]-3, and, at [130], the couple led out
through the doors to bed. Mazo refers to the three-pronged conceptual kernel at
the heart of the libretto construction, evident ever since the earliest days of
Stravinsky's work on *Noces*: two parallel plots about bride and groom, based on
the symbols of combing tresses (*kosa*) and curls (*kudri*), merge in the final Part
into the symbol of the marriage bed (*krovat'*).[51] The first part of the traditional
wedding ritual focuses on the Bride, but Mazo points out that Stravinsky went
out of his way to give equal weight to the role of the Groom. She also comments
that the earlier Tableaux juxtapose the ritual genres of lament and song, the
latter predominant in creating the characteristic recitation style of text setting.
The lament sections on the other hand are quite different, slower, and relatively
free in terms of melodic range, flow and syllabic duration:[52] at the opening of the
score, recurring several times, the Bride (Taruskin's Theme A, see p. 343 and Ex.
5.1a); at [21], the Bride and her mother; at [35], the groom's parents (Taruskin's
Theme I); at [82], the mothers of the Bride and Groom (variant of Theme I).
They represent the unusual and very Russian aspect of the wedding ceremony as

Ex. 5.1a. *Les Noces*, Tableau 1, opening lament.

Ex. 5.1b. *Les Noces*, Tableau 4, the lament as song.

Ex. 5.1c. *Les Noces*, Tableau 4, the lament as the Groom's song.

part symbolic funeral, the 'death' of two former selves, an aspect of which Stravinsky was fully aware. But in the fourth Tableau there is no longer a place for lament, and it is significant that the Bride's material from the opening of the work is now transformed into a song: it becomes increasingly important from the middle of the Tableau, just after [114] (see Ex. 5.1b), until, symbolising the new unity of the couple, it becomes the Groom's final song at [133] (see Ex. 5.1c), and then the music of the Coda.

Using this simple symbolic structure of events, Stravinsky created his own text, derived mainly from the Pyotr Vasilyevich Kireyevsky collection of wedding texts, just as he went to traditional sources as basis for his melodic material. The text is deliberately unruly in comparison with the larger semantic structure, the three-pronged conceptual kernel, even though they clearly relate in broad outline. Both levels, detailed and broad, are illuminating as regards choreomusical analysis.

The text avoids any notion of dramatising a wedding or expressing individual feeling, but is instead like a collage of disparate 'found objects' – Stravinsky's aim being to 'present' rather than 'describe'[53] – the linkage between them often unclear. Some statements are near-nonsensical out of their original context, and can be hard to comprehend when more than one is made at a time. The content is both sacred and profane, dealing with both the sacramental solemnity and procreative aspects of the wedding rite. There are blessings and invocations of the saints (mainly the wedding saints Cosmas and Damian), references to the combing of hair, to a conversation between berries, and to swans and geese (all of these symbolic references to the Bride and Groom), and during the Wedding Feast increasing talk about wine and beer and the culmination of the ritual in sex. As Stravinsky put it to Robert Craft years later:

> As a collection of clichés and quotations of typical wedding sayings it [*Noces*] might be compared to one of those scenes in *Ulysses* [James Joyce] in which the reader seems to be overhearing scraps of conversation without the connecting thread of discourse.[54]

Some of the characters are indicated regularly in the score when they speak: the Bride and Bridegroom, whose names are Nastasya Timofeyevna and Fetis Pamfil'yevich, their parents, the friends of the Bride and Groom and the *Druzhko* – a best man who bears some of the characteristics of a jester. However, matters are made extra-complicated in that singers are not always neatly associated with individual characters. Each of them has to take on more than one 'role', and, in any case, as Stravinsky said, they are not meant to represent particular speaking characters, but rather the voices of characters.[55] This might be the reason why he was insistent, at least at first, that the singers should be kept in the pit, disembodied and distanced from immediate association with the dancing characters. The Groom's voice is sung by a duet of bass soloists in Tableau 2 [50] and by just one bass at the end. The Bride's mother is first represented by a tenor in duet with the Bride (represented by a soprano) in Tableau 1 [21], which introduces a gender opposition. Later, in Tableau 3 [83], she is a mezzo-soprano, in duet with the Groom's mother (sung by the soprano);[56] again, she is a mezzo-soprano when she leads her daughter to her son-in-law in Tableau 4 [98]. In Tableau 3, at [67], the Bride is briefly a tenor and then immediately metamorphosed into a soprano and mezzo-soprano duet for two bars – here it is the content of the text that gives the game away, for there is no direction as to who is singing in the score. In Tableau 2, from [35], the lament of the Groom's two parents expands to involve all four solo voices. Sometimes a character is mentioned but never given a singing part: for instance, Palagai, and the couple sent (at [114]) to warm the marriage bed (written into the stage directions). Nijinska would have got used to a level of textual/musical disjunction within *Renard*, but not to this degree of complication.

These are all strategic distancing techniques; yet at the same time, the statements themselves are often highly colourful and, if you can hear them and understand the language in which they are spoken, they contribute significantly to the raucous misrule that reaches its zenith during Tableau 4. There are already a few sung shouts within the first two Tableaux, but in the Wedding Feast there is falsetto whooping, literal shouting (the rhythm pattern specified), the sound of clapping from the stage, first heard during the second part of the women's opening phrase (see p. 371), and two exclamations that are hiatus points, correspondingly treated by Nijinska as breaks in the dance momentum. One of the guests shouts: 'Sing songs!' (one bar before [114], 'acted' by Nijinska's male solo dancer), and later a group of them admire the Bride: 'Nastya black browed!' ([125]-2 – Nijinska's Bride acknowledges the assembled company from her cell above). In this Tableau too there is more than one allusion to drunkenness. While one of the guests shouts to the matchmakers to hand over the Bride to the eagerly awaiting Groom, another sings a verse derived from a traditional song to the Bride's father (originally sung after the marriage contract ceremony): a piece of humour about him selling off his daughter for a drink. The *Noces* text reads:

Oh, drunkard, drunkard! Nastia's father drunk away his child for a goblet of wine, for a goblet of mead![57]

(Nijinska sets a solo for 'two drunks' to these words.) At other points, we hear a tune broken with rests, very much in 'hocket' style (with rests between each note), first as the bass chorus line (at [90]-3), then a bass solo, later taken up by the rest of the chorus. It is another drinking song associated with the conclusion of the marriage contract, about a golden ring and the Bride found by the father of the Groom, who is happy, and lost by the father of the Bride, who is sad.[58] But it could also sound here like a drunk (or drunks) unsteady on his feet or hiccupping. When it returns towards the end of the work, it covers some of the most ribald text of all and here the official English translation covers up the Russian meaning. What became prattle about giving roubles was originally talk about the increased worth of a pregnant woman:

She's now worth a rouble, and when her sides expand, for one like this, two, two [roubles] they'll give.

The last text to the hocket tune has been completely excised from the official English translation – from the chorus, an overt reference to the sex act just before the married couple are led into the bedroom:

Ai, you best men are blind, [don't you see] that the wench girl pushed toward her fellow ... [she] called [him] into the storeroom? You gave us the wench, now give [us] the bed!

In the closing part of the text, what translates literally as 'the male sparrow pairs with the female sparrow' becomes 'the little sparrow makes first his nest, then takes his mate to be with him' in the English translation, and 'my nightly pleasure' becomes 'dearest flower and treasure of mine, fairest flower, sweetest wife'.[59] This information is pertinent because Russian speakers have a very different perception of the work from English speakers listening to the standard English translation (the Royal Ballet originally used the translation and then decided to change to the Russian) or hearing the Russian and not understanding any of the text at all.

As for the relation between text and music and their respective patterns of repetition, Taruskin observes that there are some occasions of stable one-to-one relationship, but more characteristically they 'live separate lives, meeting and parting promiscuously'.[60] This is increasingly the case as the climax of Tableau 4 and of the whole work approaches: indeed, the wild Joycean collage contributes to the climax. Tableau 4 is also the occasion for the most anarchic thematic treatment in the work, with a host of new tunes introduced as non-recurring material alongside material familiar from Part 1. The following plan is a summary using Taruskin's table of musical themes.[61] It demonstrates the pattern of recurrence of musical thematic material, labelled from A to U after Taruskin, with each letter encompassing the variants as well as original versions of the individual themes. This is important as a base for later examination of the interaction with choreographic thematic organisation. The plan does not refer to non-recurring material.

Part 1:
Tableau 1 (to [27])   Themes A–F
Tableau 2 (to [65]-1)   Themes G–L
Tableau 3 (to [87])   Themes C–F (already introduced in Tableau 1), M

Part 2:
Tableau 4 (from [87] to end) Themes A (from Tableau 1), J (from Tableau 2), M (from Tableau 3), N–U

The plan shows that both Tableaux 3 and 4 introduce new thematic material, while also re-absorbing ideas introduced earlier. The use of so many themes from Tableau 1 in Tableau 3, and comparatively few new ones, is consistent with the idea that there is a return to the Bride's House – three of the repeated themes are from the rapidly moving central section of Tableau 1. However, Taruskin points out that the texts to these recurring themes are associated with the Groom from Tableau 2, so there is a mixing device within the score here (music and texts) that symbolises the merging of the 'two rivers'.[62]

Bronislava Nijinska's Les Noces: *The wedding as choreographic concerto*

From the outset, Nijinska subscribed to the notion of an independent but complementary choreographic voice or voices:

> The academic idea of solely imitating the complicated and asymmetrical rhythms and measures in Stravinsky's music, by marking in the dance the strict time of the measure or the fractions, by adapting the pas to them, was not an issue for me, as it seemed not only inapplicable, but also a dancing absurdity.
>
> In bringing several musical measures together into a whole, I was creating a choreographic measure, which, while not necessarily corresponding in its beat to the musical one, responded to the sonorities of the music. For the choreography appeared to me to have its own 'voice', being an independent score within the full score and an integral part of the overall synthesis of the work.[63]

We will later consider in detail how Nijinska's ideas are put into practice. Certainly the notion of an independent beat makes no sense at all in relation to the work itself.[64] The notion that dance bars (measures) are longer than musical bars is an entirely sensible one, given the generally slower progress of dance movement events: the fact that dance counts are normally organised in units of more than one musical bar (in musical terms, hypermeasures) reflects this.

I imagine that Stravinsky and Nijinska might well have discussed the choreomusical approach, even as early as 1922. The composer had joined in theoretical debates of this kind before – for instance, the discussions about rhythmic counterpoint when Massine set *Sacre* in 1920 (see p. 441). We know too that Stravinsky was very hands-on in 1923. Nijinska began rehearsals in Monte Carlo, where the Ballets Russes were based, during his absence, working through the score in chronological order – a letter from him advises her in detail to the point of pedantry about the reprise in Tableau 1.[65] Stravinsky arrived in Monte Carlo to help her engage with the more complex fourth Tableau,[66] and again it is likely that he was closely involved in choreomusical aspects. Some rehearsals used a pianist, but others were conducted to a pianola recording,[67] which must have given the composer assurance that the music would be played as he intended: it also provided a dry, mechanical timbre that could have affected the dynamics of the choreographed movement.

Unsurprisingly, the dancers found the work difficult to learn.[68] But how did they get to grips with the sophisticated choreomusical coordination? There are several accounts to the effect that the dancers learnt the rhythm of the choreography through singing the words as they moved, demonstrating that the text was an integral aspect of rehearsal.[69] Certainly, this makes a lot of sense for the group of nine women dancing the braiding sections in Tableau 1, with its recitation-style vocal line. But, as we shall see, this method does not make sense for all the choreography. As a member of the main ensemble in the 1926 revival, Alicia Markova recalls that Grigoriev wrote down the counts and pinned them on the dancers.[70] Sono Osato, who danced in the 1936 revival, remembers learning from counts on strips of paper that the dancers held in their hands as they rehearsed.[71] Geraldine Morris, who danced in the 1966 Royal Ballet production, remembers that she only got to know the text gradually through hearing it during performance: rehearsals were conducted to piano alone, and the text was never discussed with the dancers.[72]

Returning now to the issue of narrative and text in relation to music, we see that Nijinska responds to the 'merging rivers' technique at the beginning of Tableau 3. Back at the Bride's house, she begins exactly where she left off at the end of Tableau 1, with the first volcanic pyramid of the ballet, the Bride (at the pinnacle) and her Friends, flanked by her parents. Thus, she continues to associate the Bride and her party with particular musical material. Corresponding with the repetition of text associated with the Groom from Tableau 2, we also see at the side two couples from 'outside', all set to initiate the Bridal escort to church, and the two men are the Groom's friends from Tableau 2.

Other than this, Nijinska pursues the unsettling style already established by Stravinsky and maintains an unstable relationship between what we hear (the already independent conceptual entities of text belonging to a particular character and actual voice uttering the text) and what we see on stage. Singing voices sometimes match the characters in action on stage (the Bride, Groom and parents) but often they do not. When the parents lament in Tableau 2, they are present on stage and we may well give them an extra glance as we try to associate solo men's or women's voices with what we see, but our focus is likely to end up on the Groom and his friends rather than on the parents. Solo voices do not necessarily mean solo dancing. Nijinska is inclined to economise on characters. In the same Tableau 2, the *Druzhko* calls upon those present to bless the Groom as he goes on his way, but there is no one at all in Nijinska's cast, nor in Tableau 4, to answer to that name and the choreography progresses regardless. It is the same story with the matchmaker couple in Tableau 4 (at [98]). Towards the end of Tableau 3, at [82], the stage directions tell us that the two mothers enter; there are two corresponding voices, soprano and mezzo-soprano. Nijinska opts out by not having any Groom's mother present at all, which supports her focus on the Bride's story. It is her way of subverting (and thus returning to Russian wedding tradition) Stravinsky's equal weighting of Bride and Groom (see p. 339). In these circumstances, we can accept that two voices mean one person, just as they have already done else-where.

Most of the time, there is a connection between the stage focus and the gender of the singing voices, and when this occurs between a solo voice and a solo dancer, there can be a special effect of heightening that draws attention to the connection, as if, whatever Stravinsky said, the dancer embodies the disembodied voice in the pit with special intensity at that point. This is particularly striking given the inconsistency of such one-to-one association built into the style of the piece. One of the most interesting examples of unstable relationship between what is heard and seen arises with the solo woman in Tableau 4, who, like her opposite number, a solo man, is just one of the guests, with no clear function as a protagonist in the ritual. What becomes her dance motif consists of two little jetés and a flutter of little steps performed as fast as possible, which she first dances to Theme T, several times through after [106], then again to Theme M at [110], both times 'embodying' the soprano voice. Finally, we see her suddenly break out of an ensemble that is now impatient to secure unity, at [124]: the same flutter of steps, again to Theme M, but this time sung by a tenor. The circumstances are strange, perhaps proposed by the connection here between the opening words and the steps: 'My Nastyushka has a quick gait ...' Yet she is no more Natasha (who is up in the cell) than is the male voice singing for her.

Nijinska times the last part of the action differently from the score. She was clearly not interested in bed-warming, possibly because this allusion to an experienced married couple having sex (even imagined, behind closed doors) she saw as out of keeping with her theatrical conception. She also keeps the newly married couple on stage much longer. Stravinsky instructed that they leave for the bedroom at [130], before the Groom's song (as if he addresses her out of our view), and then the curtain begins to fall, 'slowly throughout the following music', until the fifteenth 'bell' chord that marks the end of the work. Nijinska's couple leave at the end of the Groom's song (at [134]+3); she keeps the ensemble moving until the eleventh bell (after the chorus have stopped singing) and the curtain does not start to lower until after the last bell. The question arises: when did Nijinska make her independent decisions on this timing, and did she respect Stravinsky's directions in 1923? Certainly one critic, Henry Malherbe, recalled the animated crowd's continuing exuberance after the departure of the newly-weds – in other words, that the departure happened earlier then than in current productions.[73]

Nijinska also developed her own ideas about thematic organisation – 'Amazingly few movement motives are used', said Denby back in 1936,[74] and David Drew claims that there are only five steps in the piece.[75] When we reach Tableau 4, the music becomes more and more anarchic, bubbling over with new ideas, many of which we never hear a second time, but virtually every dance move looks like something that we *have* seen before. True, the dance moves are assembled into new phrases and, although this is quite rare in *Noces*, just a few of these remain in a stable relationship with their music, always seen next to the same sound. Examples are the opening phrases for the men and women and the hocket material (see pp. 342, 371-2). So we get to know distinctive phrases underlined by musical association, as well as by the already familiar basic movement components of these phrases.

Perhaps the difference between the musical and choreographic approaches is best explained by analogy. The music works from a subterranean language of style, Stravinsky's recognisable take on Russian folk music, and he felt free to burst out of this into multiple thematic/motivic directions, with many apparently new ideas. But Nijinska's thematic tactics are above ground: we get to know her few ideas well, and we take pleasure in seeing just how many things she can do with them. Nijinska adopts Stravinsky's ostinato principle from time to time, the multiple repetition of a single motif, be that sometimes as short as a stamp or a few steps, and there are other occasions when motifs repeat, though not exactly. But Nijinska's ostinatos are foreground moves, unlike those of Stravinsky (see pp. 337-8), and hers do not seek out or visualise any equivalent in the music.

Like Stravinsky, Nijinska thinks architecturally, and in terms of block construction. This can be seen in the geometrical forms created by assembled bodies and their arrangements in horizontal stage space, but also in structures that evolve through time, guided by the beginning and end of musical blocks, with minimal overlap between one block and the next, creating a hard-edged mosaic structure. A level sense of individual movement dynamic operates within discrete blocks, as if the dancers approach their material like a series of facts. Effects of build-up and reduction come not from energy crescendos and diminuendos in individual dance lines, but rather from adding or subtracting numbers of dancers between and occasionally during blocks, and shifting between unison and a complex texture of independent groups. This sounds like a parallel to Stravinsky's procedures, as described by Mazo:

> He creates sound contrasts, build-up and decrease, not so much through changes in dynamics, which are scarce in the score, but rather through the volume, density, and weight of his *matter*, that is, through the number of instruments and voices in any particular block of music, by the register used, and by the density of the contrapuntal layers in the musical texture.[76]

Some of these blocks are passages of task-like, 'untheatrical' action-timing that interrupt the dancing: the business of doing the blessings, for instance, or getting into the multi-body configurations. Nijinska thinks too in terms of layers, just as Stravinsky layers his melodies and ostinatos. There are bodies on top of each other, lines one behind the other, the layering especially clear in horizontal pyramid formations growing from one person in front to a line of six at the back, and when the groups in Tableau 4 operate in counterpoint.

I am loading the scales in favour of Nijinska's rigorously hierarchical approach to structure. Nijinska makes the larger divisions of *Noces* within each Tableau bolder than in Stravinsky's score: it is as if she wants another clear structural division before getting down to the detail of individual episodes and their internal intricacies. Thus we have the blocks of total stillness at the beginning of each of the first three Tableaux, which balance the magnificent one so gradually achieved at the very end of the work. Then, for the long Tableau 4, Nijinska divides the time into large sections demarcated by the arrangement of the ensemble in different spatial formations. Although the collective, or at least one member or two, is always ready to erupt out of any constraining device, those formations are boldly stated (see Ex. 5.2). First, there are two oppositional male–female rectangular blocks side by side upstage (each three lines of six dancers, men stage left and women stage right – see Ill. 13, p. 371). These are soon funnelled into a compact mass of bodies upstage as backdrop to duets and trios (the women lined up at floor level, in front of the men in a huddle above). Then there are two horizontal pyramids, followed by a return to the rectangular blocks, although eventually the male–female opposition disappears.

I would also suggest that, by reintroducing the rectangular blocks from the opening of Tableau 4 at [123], Nijinska clarifies the notion of recapitulation here, prompted by the recurrence of both musical and choreographic thematic material. It is an untidy ABA choreographic structure, but nevertheless much more clearly defined than in Stravinsky's score. It is reinforced by the reawakening of activity in the cell above: the newlyweds coming forward as if to greet the ensemble. Nijinska further strengthens the impression of return by maintaining these rectangular formations for a long time.

In similar fashion, she reinforces a sense of recapitulation in Tableau 1. Taruskin maintains that the reprise of the percussive theme (after the opening lament) marks off in retrospect the passage between [9] and [24] (the dance allegro) as a central section in an ABA form.[77] But Nijinska starts to recapitulate imagery at [18], defining more balanced structural proportions: even though the nine women are now arranged in two lines one behind the other (before, they were all in one line), the re-introduction of bourrées sideways and reengagement of the women in front with the Bride's tresses mark securely the return of the braiding imagery from early in the Tableau. The continuation up to [21] of 'allegro music' (and allegro steps too, at [20]–[21]) hardly subverts this ternary shape.

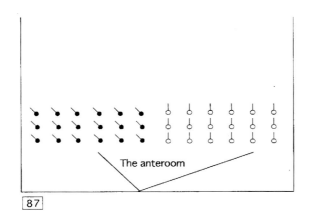

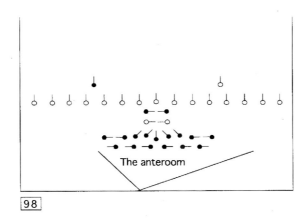

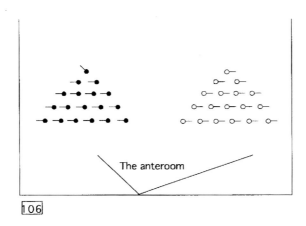

Ex. 5.2. *Les Noces*, Tableau 4, the main ensemble formations as floor plans (Nijinska).

Section A	Alternating pattern of lament (dance sculptures) and percussive, accented theme (braiding with pointe steps, holding tresses)
Section B	[9]: 'Allegro' music and steps
Section A1	[18]: Braiding imagery with tresses returns in the choreography (allegro steps interpolated [20]–[21])
	[21]: Allegro music ends; lament takes over (and dance sculpture)
	[24]: Recapitulation of percussive, accented theme (braiding pointe steps leading to pyramid sculpture)

Similar overlaps and structural overspills happen in Tableau 4, without undermining the sense of larger structure.

Nijinska would probably have been the first to emphasise the motion and drive that she introduces to bring life to her static blocks and architectural arrangements. The dynamic charge across these sectional divisions is at one with the music in building to climaxes at the end of each of the two Parts. In Part 1, the building starts at [53] (in Tableau 2), from a shouting and stamping double line, the regrouping of the full male band; in Part 2 (Tableau 4), it starts from [114], the return of the opening lament theme, when all the solo dancing (save for the eccentric little outburst of the solo woman) has stopped and the guests begin the progress towards mass unity. But Nijinska's play between asymmetry and symmetry also contributes to the final denouement. The quest for stability after pursuing all kinds of instability is a major feature of the choreography as well as of the music: in the structuring of ideas across time, as we shall see, but also in spatial features. To take an example, in the opening Tableau, set in the Bride's house, we see her in the centre of her group of friends on one side of the stage, and her parents on the other. There is one window in the curtain behind the dancers and it is off-centre. Immediately we see asymmetries in terms of size of groups, their placement, and the curtain design. Later, both groups merge by moving sideways into each other, clustering under the window, which has become a kind of off-centre reference point. Finally, there is a moment of huge tension: linked together, the entire ensemble moves to real stage centre, which is stressed for the first time, to form the first pyramid of the ballet, with the Bride ready to be escorted towards a new life (see Ill. 12). The rest of the ballet continues to reinforce this spatial programme, involving too the resolution of opposed male and female presences, forced to mesh within the last Tableau. Here we witness a gradual process of simplification, the confusing contrapuntal hubbub now released into plain unison jumps and walks. The final rationalisation is the 'heroic extreme' of the much-enlarged assemblage of bodies, pure symmetry extending upwards and outwards right across the stage.

Choreomusical detail as rhythmic intrigue

Denby observed that in *Noces* there were 'only the clearest groupings and paths, making the rhythmic subtlety obvious by contrast',[78] and it is to this subtlety, to detail, that I now turn. Again, there are similarities in the manners in which music and dance material are assembled. The common factor is the use of material in a miniature version of block construction, as modules, or short units of two or three notes or two or three moves, that can be re-ordered and reassembled in different ways, but that, as Mazo says, 'cannot develop into something different as a result of these transfigurations and interactions'.[79]

A good musical example of modular/unit construction is the Bride's opening lament of Tableau 1, which is heard over our first view of the dancers, a group sculpture (see Ex. 5.1). It can be analysed as two closely related phrases of respectively four and six bars in length. Both use the device of a firm centre on E, and a falling away from and return to E, a pattern heard twice in the first phrase, three times in the second. The transitions between the Es are never quite the same, the number and arrangement of notes constantly shifting (one, two or three, but always using D and B). Van den Toorn points out the significance of the uneven barring here (varying between 3/8 and 2/8), and the common feature of a D arranged as upbeat to a stressed downbeat on E. When this lament recurs in varied form at [4], the women's choreography articulates the structure, the big phrases, the smaller divisions of fall and return, and even the separate notes (this is a rare example in *Noces* of a move on virtually every note – see Ex. 5.3): during the first phrase, hand to the forehead, bow (D to E, down–up)

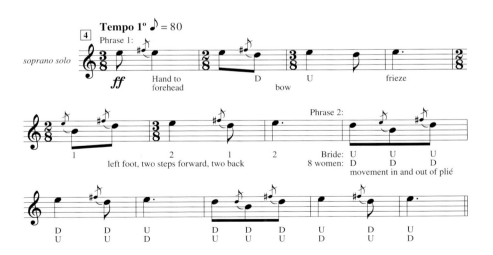

Ex. 5.3. *Les Noces*, Tableau 1, return of lament. D and U refer to the women's 'down' and 'up' movement in the bow and in and out of plié.

and move into a frieze position with the head on the arms, legs in parallel fourth position; steps with the back foot (the left) moving forwards, and then returning to this fourth position; during the second phrase, holding their frieze shape, the women move down into plié and up again in opposition to the Bride, who is the focus in the centre and timed on the last three occasions to show a 'down–up' pattern that accentuates the D to E point of closure.

A good dance example of modular/unit construction[80] is the beginning of the allegro section in the centre of Tableau 1, where material on one quartet of dancers at [9] is answered by that of another quartet at [10], the two groups forming squares in a diagonal stage relationship to each other. Newton says that, as elsewhere in *Noces*, the count structure that the dancers use today is fundamentally the same as the one that Nijinska herself used in 1966.[81] Sitting neatly within the regular 2/4 structure of the music is material that groups the musical bars together into 2- or 3-bar hypermeasures of 4 or 6 dance counts respectively (see p. 15): units A and B alternate to create four phrases (see Ex. 5.4a).

Phrase 1: Unit A, 2 bars, 4 counts: including two heel-taps (with sickle-shaped arms) on counts 2 and 3.
Phrase 2: Unit B, 3 bars, 6 counts: arms down, hands joined in front of the body, a failli step and then the beginning of an assemblé that turns into a

Ex. 5.4a. *Les Noces*, Tableau 1, 'allegro', first women's quartet.

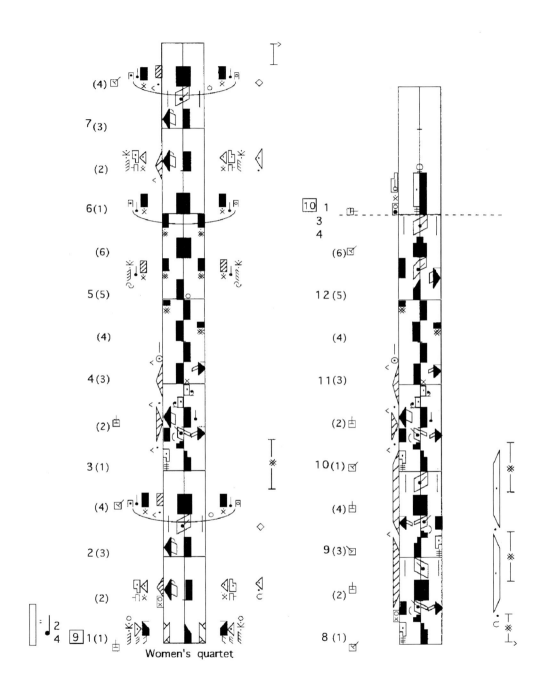

Ex. 5.4a (continued). *Les Noces*, Tableau 1, 'allegro', first women's quartet.

Ex. 5.4b. *Les Noces*, Tableau 1, 'allegro', second women's quartet.

coupé, leading into a step like a pas de bourrée without crossing feet (counts 1–3); a series of rapid steps on the spot ending in a jump with both legs lifted under the body, two feet to two feet ('lifting the ground', see p. 328), the arms now raised above the head (counts 4–6). (Note that Nijinska-style steps are an approximation of classroom steps, without turnout.)

Phrase 3: Unit A repeated, 2 bars, 4 counts: beginning with another jump with legs lifted under the body.

Phrase 4: An elongation of unit B, 5 bars, 10 counts: 4 counts, two failli steps now ending on two feet, a full assemblé; 6 counts, a third failli continuing with rapid steps as before (phrase 2), but the ending this time is a step across and 'full assemblé', looking much more like a repeat of the earlier steps within phrase 4 than the on-the-spot jump with raised legs and arms from phrase 2.

The music here is constructed much more simply than the dance, based on a one-bar ostinato, heard straight or with minor melodic variation, so that the passage can also be read as an irregular assemblage of two very closely related one-bar modules. The interesting point is that the choreography is much more varied than the music, or, put another way, each of the two musical modules has to support more than one kind of dance step. But Nijinska clearly considered the musical organisation: each time you see the same dance step, it is always to the same musical module as before. Nijinska also decided to impart fresh rhythmic interest through her own choreography: although using the same metrical structure as the music, she developed her own rhythmic patterns, and even her own acceleration, forming a miniature dance crescendo within unit B.

At [10], the second quartet of dancers performs units counted as 3+4+4+3, this time constructing a symmetry, the units forming an ABBA structure (see

Ex. 5.4b). The material is clearly related to the first quartet: the new unit A is a slower version of the 'failli, step assemblé' sequence, and the new unit B includes the heel-tap movement, but raised arms are much more prominent in the movement here than before. Choreomusically, the passage is quite different, the relations between music and dance much less tidy. With the tenor solo joined by the bass, then handing over to the female chorus, the music here is barred as 3/4 2/4 2/4 2/4 2/4 5/8. The first two quavers (written as beat 1) sound like an upbeat to a downbeat on the C-sharp (written as beat 2), a fact that is confirmed in the third bar when the C-sharp, in a melodic repeat, *is* written as the downbeat of the bar. But Nijinska had no time for such niceties here, and she ignores the musical thematic organisation, which divides the structure into two distinct parts (four bars for the men, two for the women). Instead, she goes to the barring of the written score: a 3/4 unit A with a clear downbeat on beat 1 (questionable in terms of what is actually heard); two large dance bars or hypermeasures of 4 counts, each striding over a pair of 2/4 bars, BB; and a recapitulation of A, overlapping the end of the 5/8 musical bar in tandem with the new soprano chorus phrase, to take a quaver out of the next musical bar (the equivalent of a bar of 3/4). As we shall see later, Nijinska tends often to go to the look of the musical score as a source: the barring, whether or not we hear the music as it is written. As shown here, however (the overlap at the close), she can also be led by the start, finish and span of a musical phrase. She changes her tactics when it suits. In this ballet, hardly ever do heard, written and danced metres all match.

There are nonetheless instances when music and dance join forces, suddenly and overtly, all of them big, loud moments, such as the bells that end the ballet, when the dancers pull down their arms in a ringing gesture, suggesting that they might be doing the work or helping to create the sound; or the occasional shouts, in Tableau 1 when the women jump at [16] and [17], and in Tableau 2 when the men jump and raise their arms in defiance or exultation at [55] and [59]-1. The men's Tableau demonstrates a one-to-one relation to sound more frequently and forcibly than any other part of the ballet. Kneeling in a half-circle around the Groom (at [36]), each of his friends stamps a foot to a brutal repeating bass chord that creates its own 3/4 metre, eight times in all – the only occasion in *Noces*, apart from the final bells, when the dance articulates a regular musical event or ostinato. Throughout the ballet, walking tends to be rhythmed, on the beat, but in this Tableau, the walking, on the downbeat of the bar particularly, seems to be most pronounced and strident (an example is the pompous route march en masse across the stage towards the father at [58]), as if a kind of forced imposition of authority upon already forceful sound. Is this Nijinska's representation of a male attitude, expressed choreomusically? After all, although much of the vocabulary in *Noces* is shared between men and women, Nijinska does cast differences between the gender groups: a narrower body attitude and occasional softness for the women (depicting oppression and conforming to cultural expectations), more opening of thighs, stamping and punching actions for the men (another set of cultural expectations).

Generally speaking, however, the choreography introduces a marked contrapuntal element to the work – it has its own independent 'voice'. Indeed, there is a great deal of choreomusical shifting in Nijinska's *Noces*, between rhythmic synchrony and counterpoint, structural connection and disconnection, and the nature of these interactions is wide-ranging. Being a fluent reader of music opened Nijinska to many possibilities that would help her in her quest not to 'visualise' or exaggerate components of the music through simple duplication. Yet the one thing that is never contradicted is the basic beat uniting music and dance.

Again, Tableau 1 presents some intriguing examples that set the tone for the whole work. During the opening A section in this ABA form (up to [9] – see pp. 348, 350), the choreography shifts between stillness, a series of striking ensemble sculptures, and dance action during the two 'braiding' sections (at [2] and [7]). All the sculptures frame the Bride symmetrically, with four friends on each side, emphasising the two-dimensional plane. Unfolding gradually through a process of statement and re-statement, from time to time a variant position is added, a new 'picture', whilst a 'picture' that has become familiar is dropped. Several times, we see arms in a shortened Nijinska fifth position overhead. At other times, a group of dancers kneel and crouch low while others place their arms on their exposed backs, chins resting on hands. Near the end, there is the 'eagle', arms extended to the side like a bird of prey, the dancers organised in levels, like a river descending towards the audience, a striking moment that relieves the two-dimensional emphasis. Finally, there is an arrangement of hard arabesques that suggest a blessing or crowning of the Bride.[82] This is how most of the lament music in section A is used, both in its declamatory form and when rhythmed and accompanied by a busy ostinato, and the dancer's timing and performance manner are decidedly untheatrical, task-like. The continuity of the pictures themselves is entirely unpredictable, and likewise there is no association of one particular shape with a particular kind of music.

Contrast the braiding phrases at [2] and [3] (brought back at [7]), where the music (Taruskin's Theme B) and dance operate in a tight rhythmic relationship. The movement, in pathways sideways across the stage (to the left, and then back to the right), consists of bourrées with parallel legs (on all the 5-count units), otherwise stabbing pointes marking each beat with the feet crossing in front and behind (braiding), and percussive accents when the women drop down from pointe and gesture one leg sharply sideways (on each count 1). The dance and musical accents often coincide here, but not always on the downbeat of the bar, especially after [3].

Thus, Nijinska responds to the sound of the score here, not to its written

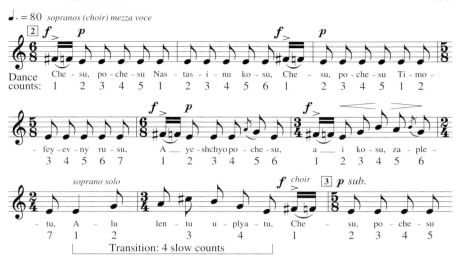

Ex. 5.5. *Les Noces*, Tableau 1, braiding.

metre. But she also adds her own touch of unpredictability, introducing to each pathway a couple of dance accents that are supported by neither musical nor verbal accents. The pattern is as follows (see Ex. 5.5, pp. 357-8), the repeat pathway including an extra 5 dance counts, an asymmetry driven by the score and text:

(A = shared dance/music accent on each count 1)

[2] Stage R to L	Transition for re-arranging the tresses	[3] Stage L to R [4]
5 6 5 7 6 7	4 slow counts	5 6 5 7 5 6 7
A A A A		A A A A

The text accompaniment to the first pathway, showing dance stresses, is:

*Che*su, pochesu *Na*stasinu kosu,   [5+6 counts]
*Che*su, pochesu *Ti*mofeyevny rusu,   [5+7 counts]
A yeshchyo pochesu, *a* i kosu, zapletu,   [6+7 counts]
Alu lentu uplyatu.   [4 slow counts]

[I am combing, I'll keep combing Nastasya's braid,
I am combing, I'll keep combing Timofeyevna's blond [braid],
And again I'll comb [it] and the braid I'll plait,
A crimson ribbon I'll weave in.]

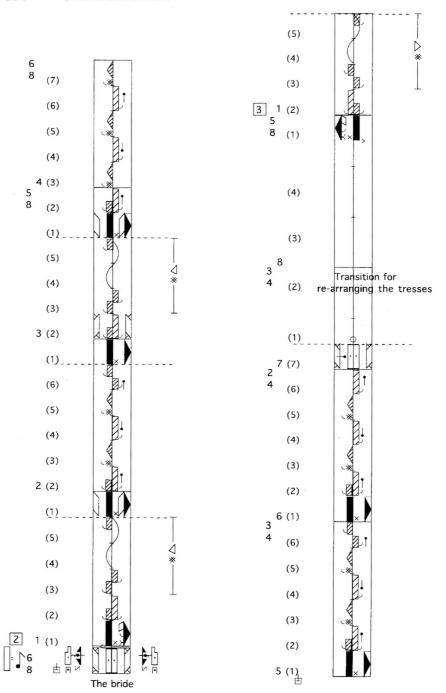

Ex. 5.5 (continued). *Les Noces*, Tableau 1, braiding.

Ex. 5.6. *Les Noces*, Tableau 1, 'allegro', unison group.

After [3], the barring of the musical material shifts, although key verbal stresses still coincide with the downbeat: 'Nast*a*sinu' and 'Timo*f*eyevny'. But Nijinska's choreography responds to the overt musical accents as before, the first of these now scored immediately before the bar-line.

After the asymmetries and unpredictabilities that open the 'allegro' Section B of Tableau 1 (see pp. 348, 350), the Bride's friends form a single unison block behind her. In the passage between [12] and [14], there is a 2/4 ostinato in the bass (G-sharp, F-sharp, and G-sharp, F-sharp an octave lower), but, as so often in *Noces*, this regularity is covered by an irregular foreground in vocal parts that here determine the highly irregular barring (see Ex. 5.6). Newton has described the movement as 'seeming to go on relentlessly regardless of what the music is doing'.[83] Here is one of the longest dance phrases in the entire *Noces*, with no clear repetition structures contained within it. This is possibly the reason for the alternative dance counts in the rehearsal score, arranged in 2s and 4s, but also 8s, 9s and 10s, the large units suggesting that there is a logical manner of memorising material that is not determined by metre. In fact, the movement articulates the ostinato's crotchet beat (though you would hardly ascertain this from what you hear): there is one sharp movement articulating each beat, with hardly any decoration to disturb the plainness, flat-footed steps, isolated arm gestures, and jumps on and around one spot. One very striking moment is the exception, the only break in the relentless flow, in the third bar after [13], a landing on the G in the soprano line (beat 2), and a hold for the beat beginning on the E in the next bar, one crotchet later. Suddenly, the dancers curve over deeply towards the floor, as if the earth sucks them into itself, a giving into weight like a lightning flash of humanity as the motor relaxes for just one second. The effect of heaviness is enhanced as the arms raised before the jump are brought down with it. This striking moment of change is also interesting in that it occurs close to halfway through the dance allegro (the B section of an ABA structure) and thus feels like the centre, the earth centre, of the entire Tableau.

Near the beginning and at the end of Tableau 2 are other vivid examples of counterpoint. Early on, the Groom leads the men in vigorous offbeat stamps (at [31]–[33]), here offbeat in terms of what is heard and seen in the written score, but, because the music shifts into and out of syncopated mode, the stamps shift in their relationship to it, meeting and departing from the musical accents and stressed melody – against, with, against, with, and finally against once more. Keeping the dance stamps steady was enough for Nijinska to ensure choreomusical tension, although she adds an extra edge by shifting her accents from down into the ground to up, with the raised leg, for the later stamps that are decorated with extra steps in between them. Given her behaviour elsewhere, I imagine that she was fully aware of what she was doing. Keep with the dance line and the shifting inflections make you nervous. Newton tells us that this passage is one of the trickiest of all for the dancers, who have to hold their own against the sound of the music.

But it is at the end of Tableau 2 that predictable reinforcements of the music gradually unleash into choreomusical uproar. First, at [59], there is a passage of repeating men's chorus phrases (normally two bars long) with percussion accents marking the start of each phrase. Here, the full male ensemble stand behind the Groom and his father, performing a series of very hard jumps (barely jumps at all) that are like stamps with both feet, ending with a halt on straight legs, downward arm thrusts reinforcing the power of the movement. But the striking feature is the antiphony. The men jump on the downbeats of the bars *between* the musical accents, counter to the music (see Ex. 5.7). The fact that the periodicity does not balance creates extra tautness: after [59], there are shorter gaps between the musical accent and the jump than vice versa, suggesting both uncertainty and impatience.[84] The men are excited.

It is no surprise, then, that these contained two-foot stamps soon (at [61]) break up into a series of 13 regular non-stop jumps of the familiar kind, legs lifted under the body ('lifting the earth'). Then, from [62], the men begin to circle the Groom, accumulating energy through repetition, more of this than at any other point in the choreography; yet at the same time the phrase lengths are irregular. A great deal is achieved through the simplest means in terms of the actual steps: a series of runs interrupted by an occasional huge spring and pounce to the floor (see Ex. 5.8; arms in the 'eagle' position). But you can never predict when these spring-pounces will happen. The count sequence runs as follows, with each spring-pounce timed to occur on the 1 of each group of counts:

3 counts of introductory runs, then: 8 3 6 3 3 6 3 3 6 3 10 3 3

A further rhythmical problem is that, while 3s and multiples of 3 predominate in the choreography, we do not hear the music with it in 3s. Here, with most of the score until the end of the Tableau barred as 6/8, the rhythm is led by the instrumental accompaniment: a 4/4 bass ostinato, a syncopated upper instrumental texture against this (clarifying neither 6/8 nor 4/4), and a series of strong me-

Ex. 5.7. *Les Noces*, Tableau 2, showing alternating men's jumps (J) and musical accents (MA).

Ex. 5.8. *Les Noces*, Tableau 3, piano accompaniment, showing the men's 'spring-pounces' (S-P) and musical accents (MA).

lodic/percussive accents that mark every two (written) bars as a major point of articulation. There are further quirks, ignored by the choreography: one accent a beat early, immediately before [63], and a few bars of varying metre (4/8 at [62]+4, 5/8, 5/8 and 4/8 from [64]-2). The spring-pounces sometimes coincide with the major musical articulations but most often do not. There are 9 musical accents, 13 pounces and only 3 moments of coincidence. This is a long passage, but the effect is one of remarkable uncertainty and growing pressure, with the increasing expectation of, or rather need for, release into stability.

It is noteworthy that, in Irina Nijinska's version of *Noces*, all these spring-pounces are performed straight, *with* the main musical accents. But the dissonance and unpredictability of the Royal Ballet staging adds considerably to the build-up of tension at this point in the ballet. Irina's final series of spring-pounces are additionally laboured because the dancers take much longer in the air before the landing, a full count, such that you have plenty of time to foresee the moment when the downward accents will arrive. Newton recalls that, in 1966, Bronislava was adamant about the particular timing that the Royal Ballet still adhere to; the final section of Tableau 2 was allocated massive rehearsal time.

Unsurprisingly, it is in Tableau 4 that the greatest contrapuntal excitement emerges. Extreme examples are the 'hocket' passages at [91] and [127] (see Ex. 5.9). Newton recalls that Nijinska's choreographic image here had nothing to do with drinking or drunkenness (see p. 342); instead it was about 'searching for the

Ex. 5.9. *Les Noces*, Tableau 4, 'hocket' section (Nijinska and Robbins).

ring', the golden ring mentioned in the text at this point. She certainly adds to the mayhem. The music *sounds* like a series of repeating rhythm patterns in 7/8 metre, but it is *written* in a structure of 4/4+3/4 with the pattern of notes in the 4/4 bar placed *off* the beat and the pattern in the 3/4 bar *on* the beat. In other words, it is written as if the barring indicates a change of tactics. Presumably, Stravinsky wanted performing musicians to sense and project the asymmetry as a kind of 'upbeat/downbeat duplicity',[85] otherwise why else would he have written the passage this way? Nijinska (as shown in the Royal Ballet performance) takes her cue from the writing, not the hearing, but then, unusually, goes entirely her own way. The first 4/4 bar might have prompted her repeating 4-count units, performed by the entire dancing ensemble: either intense crouched-over walking combined with looking straight down to the floor (for the ring), 1, 2, close the front foot back to the other foot 3, hold still 4, or a series of jetés (first, with chest lifted, 1, 2, and then with a drop forward, 3, hold 4). The Bride's simple lilting steps in the cell above reinforce this 4/4. The consequence of the repetition is that the choreographic metre strides boldly across the music, both the 4/4 + 3/4 that we see and the 7/8 that we hear. How do we read this choreomusical strategy? We can read the difficulty of the endeavour and the concentrated effort to find the ring, yet, from the hocketing music, there might also be a hint of drunkenness: ill-fitting steps and a determination to keep steady. Again, like the men's jumps at the end of Tableau 2, the Irina Njinska version of this passage has the dancers fitting the rhythm of the melody pattern with their steps, to much more straightforward, harmonious effect.

There is one example in Tableau 4 where Nijinska sets up, then playfully deconstructs, strong moments of choreomusical reinforcement (see Ex. 5.10). At [94], a pair of shouts 'Oy! lay!' marks the first occasion when the entire mass of men and women join in one thrilling unison block. They all jump to articulate the first shout, and then step forward, raise a fist defiantly and close back to first position during the next. They repeat these moves throughout the passage up to [95]+2, with two jumps instead of one the third time through. Nijinska follows the look of the score, shifting between 2/4 and 3/8: the first move fits the 2/4 bars, accent in the air on count 1, bigger accent on the landing from the jump on count 2 (exactly with the first shout); the second move fits the 3/8 bars, the fist on count 1 and close back to first position on count 3 (the second shout is on count 2, but the overall effect is of choreomusical synchrony); and the dancers count a slow 2 and fast 3 correspondingly. Try the choreography in silence and there is nothing extraordinary, just a touch of irregularity at the double-jump point and with the alternating metres. Put the music to the choreography and the complexity seems extreme: the musical accentuations are irregular and, after initial clear mutual reinforcement (dance moves meeting shouts during the first two bars), the musical support drops out, returns (just one shout), disap-

Ex. 5.10. *Les Noces*, Tableau 4, unison 'Oy!' passage (Nijinska).

pears again, and then comes back, with two shouts again for the final pair of moves. We can presume that Nijinska knew that Stravinsky's barring was only half the story, and again that, by adopting it for her own structure, she could ensure the effect of choreomusical liberation. After all, what we hear is essentially far more important than what is shown in the score.

The next example of choreographic response to the look of the musical score reveals Nijinska's tactics across a larger time-span, from [114] to [122], the point in the fourth Tableau when she begins to draw her ensemble of men and women together as one force. The two groups still occupy separate sides of the stage in two horizontal pyramid formations. In an analysis of the first part of this section ([114]–[117]), Jaubert notes how the antiphonal choral parts elide and shift in relation to each other and in relation to the pianos that maintain the written 3/4 metre (see Ex. 5.11).[86] The chorus take one line, while the soloists introduce a variation of the bridal lament, which starts to 'detonate'[87] at this point in the ballet. The women dancers, meanwhile, hold to the written 3/4 metre and the piano part in 6-count (2-bar) units, bending over to one side, to the other and then engaging in four 'shovel' steps with sickle arms (to each side, counted in pairs, each of which constitutes 6 counts). You notice how the dancers soon seem to lag behind the dominant musical structure, a somewhat laboured effect that draws attention to their effort to push up from the earth, until

Ex. 5.11. *Les Noces*, Tableau 4, women in horizontal pyramid (Nijinska).

coming back into synchronisation with the chorus in the eighth bar. It is as if Nijinska supports choreographically a 'conservative' reading of the music (see p. 338), holding on to the 3/4 metre for longer than we are likely to hear it, and making the effect of conflict seem especially acute. From [115], the lament theme moves into three of the pianos, and both it and the soprano chorus line operate according to irregular periodicity. Now, after a transition, the women start an 'elbow step', a bourrée and drop with the elbow leading the body into a twist, four 3-count units moving to the left, and the same to the right. Nothing in the music confirms the dance rhythm (except the written metre). The women are disconnected, literally, as if mesmerised, moving softly in their own world, or perhaps haunted by the memory of the lament from Tableau 1.

The male band start up at [117], to a bass solo, with a 6-count jumping 'mill step' (two bars of 3/4, the label from the windmill arm movement), but they too seem disconnected, perhaps even more so, again establishing no clear link with the voice, nor with the accompaniment and its polymetrical ostinatos (4/4 against 6/8). (Again, the written 3/4 metre supports the dance but contradicts what you hear.) But their quality is quite different from that of the women, as if they are pushing through treacle, against major resistance, but showing a full determination to 'make the ritual work', and now with clear accentuation of every crotchet beat. They build confidence too, as Nijinska casts them in accumulating layers, led first by the male soloist, who is then joined by the two men immediately behind, and so on until the whole horizontal pyramid is brought into the action. After a sudden interruption at [119] by the familiar opening

Ex. 5.12. *Les Noces*, Tableau 4, 'clap step' (Nijinska).

Ex. 5.13. *Les Noces*, Tableau 4, opening, women's and men's material (Nijinska).

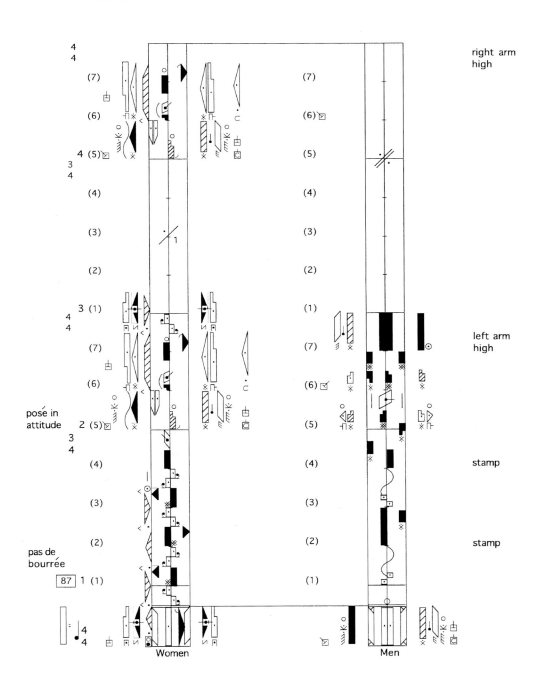

Ex. 5.13 (continued, and on following page). *Les Noces*, Tableau 4, opening, women's and men's material (Nijinska).

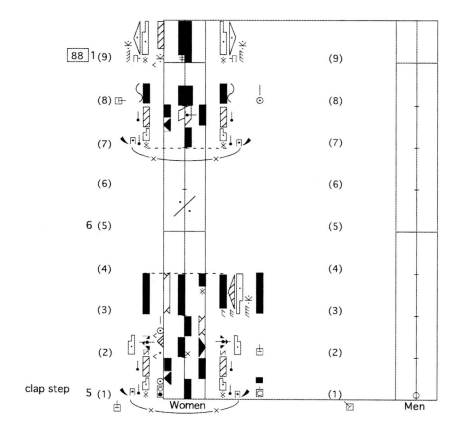

male/female material of the Tableau, the bass solo continues (at [120]), with another building in layers for the men dancers, a phrase of 9 counts, which is repeated within 8 counts, then rounded off with a mill step (6 counts). It is only now, at [121], that what you hear regularly fits the written barring again. There are more shovel steps from the women, and then both sides, male and female groups, join in further elbow steps. Now, these moves have a greater ease and buoyancy in the new context, supported and stabilised by the musical rhythms. The entire ensemble then turn and walk upstage (at [122]), bowed before the family on the platform above. The reconciliation of forces has begun.

Nijinska's tactics across this whole section have been extremely subtle, yet surprisingly simple. She seems to have understood not only that she could be guided by the look of the score as her rhythmic structuring device but also that, by selecting her movement material carefully, the temporary freedom from how the music sounds could turn out to be most effective, moving into a strange 'Other' expressive territory, before returning us to the 'reality' of the Wedding Feast.

Ill. 13. *Les Noces*, opening of Tableau 4, choreography by Bronislava Nijinska, Royal Ballet.

As we have seen, Nijinska engages with musical structure at all levels, from the most broad, the outlines of the whole work, to the very detailed. It is entirely appropriate to consider now how she deals with gradations of accent within the bar itself, the tiniest step patterns. There is the 3-count on-the-spot 'clap step', one of the signature moves from the beginning of Tableau 4 that maintains a stable relationship with its music, repeating with the same music on every occasion that it appears (see Exs. 5.12 and 5.13). It is so named because the first move on count 1 involves throwing the arms up for the hands to meet above the head. The sequence repeats all over again, and then starts, but does not finish, a third time, after which the dancers descend into kneeling (on count 9) and halt. It is in 3/4 time against the written 4/4 musical metre. The complication is that the perceived musical rhythm here shifts from simple to compound time, from 2/8 (or 1/4: a brief moment before the shift to compound time sets in) to 3/8, to 2/8, and then to 4/4 metre (see Ex. 5.12). This internal complication justifies itself in accordance with the written framework by the end of two bars of 4/4.[88]

The immediately preceding material that opens Tableau 4 and also recurs regularly with its music does not conflict with musical metrical structure (see Ex. 5.13). Instead, it shows crossing accents between choreography and music and also between men and women. Here, the dance material is always set up as a contrapuntal texture opposing the male and female ensemble (see Ill. 13). The women perform four pas de bourrée from side to side (counts 1–4), a posé for-wards in attitude with one arm raised over the head (count 5) and a step back with the now familiar heel-tap on count 7. The posé accent marks the musical bar-line (the 3/4 bar that follows a bar of 4/4, the whole read choreographically as one 7-count hypermeasure), but the main musical accent marked as such in the score is on count 3: so Nijinska goes by the barring in the score again.

But the men's jumping, stamping sequence goes for another scheme: it seems to privilege counts 2 and 4 (marked by low stamps) and, at least in some per-formances, count 7 (the final jump on to both feet with one arm raised high overhead). We see the male and female groups countering each other both in the nature of their material and in its moments of accentuation. The raising of arms on counts 5 and 7 contributes to the delineation of these contrapuntal accents. First of all, we see these conflicting arm patterns on the two groups ranged side by side. Later, at [93], the men and women form lines one behind the other and we see the contrapuntal effects through the lines.

Nijinska enjoys the particular intensity achieved here by very quick steps – the semiquaver rate of the women's pas de bourrée, for instance. But this is not only women's style (as is usually the case in ballet footwork): the men also en-gage in on-the-spot bourrées – Newton remembers Nijinska urging, 'Do as many steps as possible', on counts 1 and 3 (also in the decorated stamping in Tableau 2 – see p. 360). (In the Irina Nijinska version, there are just three pas de bourrée for the women, not four, and the men do three slow steps rather than 'as many as possible'.) An especially vivid example of changing pulse rate emerges near the end of Tableau 3 (over a pedal note A, before the lament of the Bride's mother) when the Bride's escort of men and women configures itself into a metaphorical carriage (from [80]): with wheels slowly rolling, a forward and back repeating step pattern (crotchet pulse); bumping, in jumps that cross the 3/4 musical flow (minim pulse); and then racing freely, the same forward and back step pattern in double time (quaver pulse), and looking especially fast because we remember its previous incarnation. Yet Nijinska rhythm is not simply about beat. Subtle varia-tion in the rhythm pattern created by steps and using the framework of beat contributes to the dynamism of her enterprise, inbuilt quality changes as the construction of the steps themselves encourages a brief lift in the body and feel-ing of breath within this rigorous motor style. This is the case with the opening phrases of Tableau 4. Other examples are the rhythm patterns of the women's first allegro steps in Tableau 1, which are fun to speak aloud – the voice naturally wanting to shift in pitch and volume (see pp. 352-4) – and also the excitement of the drop and pause in the centre of this Tableau (see p. 360).

I have drawn attention already to a few discrepancies between the Royal Bal-let and Irina Nijinska versions of *Noces*. Also noticeable is a slightly more relaxed or, put another way, less regimented, attitude to performance in Irina's version, no value judgements intended through this comparison. For instance, in the Irina version, when the two 'drunks' dance a duet in Tableau 4, they 'act' drunk; the Royal Ballet dancers look a trifle off-balance, but their performance manner is straight. There is a striking difference in timing at the end of the work, where bells are rung by arms in response to the musical sound: just after the point of musical articulation in Irina's version, not tightly on the note as in the Royal's. And Irina's final move comes later than in the Royal production, between the 13th and 14th bells (in the Royal production, their final move is *on* the 11th bell). You can literally hear the gentle folding over of the front row of bodies to the floor in Irina's production, a very effective and poignant moment that suddenly allows direct physicality (unmediated by musical presence) to enter the piece. We can ask questions: did these changes emerge through slippage or intention? It is notable that, over time, dance syncopations and rhythmic difficulties are inclined to degenerate, a kind of natural process that choreographers and rehearsal directors allow without always realising either that they have done so or that there is a resultant loss of edge.[89] Yet everything about *Noces* suggests that Nijinska would have watched like a hawk over her rhythmic intentions. On the other hand, she just might have changed her mind herself during her last staging in Venice, for purely artistic reasons, or because the cast could not deal with her rhythmic challenges. Certainly, I much enjoyed the Kirov Ballet performance at Covent Garden in 2003, staged by Howard Sayette. Clement Crisp was captivated by the Russian angle. In his essentialist account, he all but tells us that the performers could do the work so well because they were Russian, in other words, that their Russianness enabled something special to happen:

> The grand interest of *Noces* was to see (and hear) Russian artists in this most Russian of works. The score was superb: four spiffing Kirov Opera soloists, plus chorus and pianists, brought total conviction to the music under Mikhail Agrest's baton – I have never heard it better played in the theatre. And a Russian cast knowing exactly what the sung text meant – this was tremendous ... it is *Les Noces* given with love, understanding and a blazing masterpiece about Holy Russia is honoured.[90]

As we shall see in the ensuing analysis of the work's reception in the 1920s, words do shed an important light on the piece, for those who understand them.

Nijinska meets her audiences

The response to Nijinska's work in Paris and London in the 1920s is revealing. Audiences were enthusiastic in both capitals, and critics generally appreciative, although cooler in London, with both Stravinsky and Nijinska praised and under attack at different times.[91] Drue Fergison points out that many critics compared the new ballet with *Sacre* (the Massine revival was shown during the same 1923 Paris season), referring to the 'new' technological neo-classicism of *Noces* in synthesis with the 'old' exotic primitivism (the old Russian aspect) of *Sacre*.[92] Images of mechanisation and industry were identified across both music and dance: the factory at work, the noise of metal upon metal, the processes of new cinema, the semblance of marionettes in motion. Emile Vuillermoz, for example:

> The only thing he [Stravinsky] needs, in order to create his special pathos, is a solid machine with which to forge lovely accents, a machine to hit, a machine to lash, a machine to fabricate automatic resonances. His genius resides in the organization of the rhythmic panting of this sonorous factory ... On the stage – without decors, and transformed into a vast cinematographic screen – moves a simplified humanity, black and white, as if it came from a projector ... these synthetic marionettes ... One remains forever troubled by the strange accent of humanity possessed by the laments, laughs, and yells that escape from the forge where one sees the great blacksmith Ansermet brandish his menacing fists in order to bend all of his workers on their anvils![93]

The language of a number of writers, who, at this stage, only knew the music 'through' the dance, betrays their sense that the music was the more vibrant and vital of the components, despite its rigorous constraining features. In other words, it had body in it, what Vuillermoz referred to as the 'strange accent of humanity' emerging from the musical forge. Reminiscing on Stravinsky's composition period in Morges, Switzerland, in 1917, Charles-Ferdinand Ramuz, who undertook the French translation of *Noces*, reveals this 'other side' of the score with full force. He knew all about fierce Stravinskian control and rigour, and the composer's current passion for pianola reproduction, and had, like Vuillermoz, employed the metaphor of mechanisation to what he heard from the Morges attic. He described it as like a 'workshop where suddenly machines began to operate in full force as if in emulation – the crankshafts to move, the fly-wheels to revolve, the transmission belts to glide over the shaft-wheels and the gears to engage'. Yet Ramuz also acknowledged the tendency towards disorder and untamed violence, the primitive aspect, reminding the composer of what he later shunned:

> Perhaps you now somewhat regret its impulsiveness, its apparent lack of control ... Perhaps, having placed yourself, in the course of events, under the sign of Apollo, you reproach yourself today for what your music owed to Dionysius ... But I, who have remained more naturalistic than you – or more a disciple of nature – have the privilege of continuing to admire, in memory, the splendid

storm that *Noces* created all one long afternoon, above the little square where the pigeons in their pretty plumage strutted in measured steps.[94]

Again, not responding according to the terms that appealed to Stravinsky in later years, the Soviet critic Boris Asafyev observed the buffoonery and exaggeration in the music that lay alongside its funeral aspect. He also stressed the aspect of *Noces* as fertility ritual with the music of the wedding feast about to 'burst under the onslaught of sensuality'.[95]

Two other émigré Russian writers, André Levinson and Boris de Schloezer, are of great interest in treating the score and dance as separate entities, and in stressing different qualities between what they heard and what they saw. Levinson's criticism appeared first in *Comoedia* and a Russian émigré newspaper, later as part of a compilation article 'Stravinsky and the Dance', published in the American *Theatre Arts Monthly*. He wrote ecstatically about the music, 'so full of vitality and direct power, with its alternating ecstasies and primitive brutalities', while also acknowledging a quality of restraint, an 'intensity without being too colourful'.[96] He celebrated too its mystical properties and Russian aspect:

> It is also informed with the spiritual light of an inner mystery. Every detail of this page of Russian folklore is transfigured by an ineffable emotion. The same rays of light gleam upon the glass of vodka given to the old neighbour at the wedding feast as illuminate the cup of the Holy Grail. The lively movement of the games and the wedding songs comes straight from the soil of Russia.[97]

Most significant of all, he believed in the integral role of the text: 'The words in it are not subordinate to the music.'[98] For him, the sense of difference between music and dance had a lot to do with the textual presence that he understood. On the other hand, Levinson was vitriolic about Nijinska's contribution, seeing it as a 'Marxist' ballet,[99] the product of her association with Soviet and experimental dance culture:

> Mlle. Nijinska brought a hollow image of life, mechanical and bloodless, through her choreography, that reminded one of nothing so much as the athletic stadium or the drill grounds.[100]

The dancers Levinson likened to soldiers and gymnasts. For him, this work lacked the dancing body: it was more like 'electrification applied to ballet'.[101] Most surprising is his perception of a '*mechanical reproduction* of the rhythm', a concept taken from Dalcroze eurhythmics, or rather, from his understanding of this system. As so often in dance circles at the time, Levinson equated the Dalcroze name over-simplistically with exercises in rhythmic duplication of music and beating time in movement. He saw the *Noces* dancers 'walk each note and *tap* each accent with a simultaneous and uniform movement, as if possessed'.[102] As demonstrated in my analysis, this is decidedly not the case in *Noces*. It is hard to imagine that the brilliant but conservative Levinson was so caught up in his opposition to the choreography (and, as a disaffected émigré, to all things Soviet) that for once his perceptual accuracy was diminished. (He had said much the same about Nijinsky's *Sacre* (see p. 430), but in that case, it seems, with more justification.) More likely, the sharp articulation of motor beat throughout Nijinska's work, which was so at odds with his ideal of dance flow, was enough to persuade him of gymnastic activity and mechanical reproduction of rhythm. Levinson was not open to this new kind of dance style or rhythm. As usual, he ended up proclaiming the music self-sufficient and best heard without any dance alongside it (see p. 107).

De Schloezer proved highly appreciative of the choreography as well as remarkably perceptive and forward thinking about what was really going on choreomusically. In a highly insightful article in the Russian publication *Zveno* titled 'On the Occasion of *Les Noces*: A New Form of Synthetic Art', he debated what he saw as a 'new' lack of parallelism between music and the visual aspects of dance and design. He observed that this lack manifested itself in two ways. First he noted dynamic disparity and, although quick to recognise the formalism and abstract leanings of both music and dance, he could not but describe this in terms of feeling and emotional tone:

> The critics wondered: what is the relation between these gloomy, pale colours, these monotonous, almost monk-like costumes and the bright, powerful, driven, dynamic music of Stravinsky? ... An ordinary 'translation', 'embodiment' of music into movement was not found in *Les Noces*. Here is exactly where its idiosyncrasy lies: there is a motion in the music and at the same time, the group on stage, dressed in brown and white moving in front of a grey screen, is calm.

But de Schloezer also recognised a discrepancy at the more detailed level of rhythm. Constrasting Dalcrozian techniques of strict metrical connection, he claimed a new freedom for dance in *Noces* – stretching the point in his enthusiasm – as the choreography engages instead with the larger musical construct. The struggle to articulate such observations is rare in dance (and choreomusical) literature:

> In *Les Noces*, the metrical divisions of dance and music systematically do not coincide, but rhythm gives pulse to the orchestra and charts a trajectory for

the movement. The movement, itself, is constructed by Nijinskaya completely freely, without relation to the music.

The choreography of *Les Noces* is a reflection of the whole musical image in the creative imagination of Nijinskaya. Coming out of that image, Nijinskaya has intuitively conceived an image which is generally connected with the music in its whole, but never coincides in the details.[103]

In *La Nouvelle revue française*, de Schloezer wrote in further detail about the new independence of choreography, noting the impact of this on contemporary audiences:

There is an intimate correlation between dance and music, but not at the level of particularity or detail. This absence of parallelism which sometimes even leads to a kind of discordance, to effects of contradiction, confuses many people who are used to the slavish translation of music through gesture and pose. Nevertheless, there is a link between the two elements, and it is rhythm that creates it ...

Here, in the spirit of experiment, de Schloezer dares to ask for even more independence than Nijinska gives him:

... Nijinska builds her movement construction with a freedom that I would only fault for not reaching its maximum potential. Indeed, the only criticism that I can make of the choreographer is that in a few instances she succumbs to the temptation of literal translation.[104]

If Russians had the advantage of a particular route into the texted *Noces* score that encouraged them to be aware of conceptual disparities between the music and dance, it is interesting that the French critic Michel Georges-Michel was surprised too when confronted with the plain black and white production. In 1919, he had enjoyed a private performance of this 'metallic sun' of a score by Stravinsky: 'He got out of the instrument [the piano] and of himself a strange, exasperated force, each time piercing, in intensity, a new ceiling.' Georges-Michel had a strong impression of the music without the dance. Now that he saw the dance, he spoke of 'costume-characters forming groups reminiscent of Hodler [1853–1918: a Swiss artist known for the spiritual content of his work and its elongation of human figures], excessively Calvinistic, and the Puritans seeming like ridiculous puppets next to Mr. Stravinsky's Greek-style chorus'.[105]

In our own times, the Russian dance historian Maria Ratanova continues to stress contrasts between the music (at least its vocal aspects) and the dance. She suggests that (like the original designs) the libretto Stravinsky concocted demonstrates 'the traditional attributes of the Russian wedding combining tragic and comic features', and that Nijinska went straight to the music, largely ignoring the text. Ratanova interprets Nijinska's contribution (and I add to this her constructivist principles) as being of quite a different order, primarily about 'spiritual upsurge and search ... The choreography of the ballet is a spatial, architectural image, rising through time ... the overwhelming geometry of shapes, the arrangements of human bodies, the construction of volumes and lines serves to create the image of a huge creative effort aimed at overcoming the unavoidable, the transitory.'[106] This accords with what Nijinska herself later said about her work: 'I had wanted a feeling of awe in *Les Noces*, a sense of spiritual striving, of souls revealing themselves.'[107]

Today, however, with the ascendancy of her work as a masterpiece (the 'life' in it now fully recognised), many people have got so used to hearing the *Noces* score through Nijinska that we have been programmed to think her production has to be what Stravinsky intended. For some, hers is not just the best, but the only approach to his score, and it has become increasingly rare for us to conceive of *Noces* without the Nijinska as a guide that limits the potential of the score. So we consider as perfect the match between her austere, monochrome visualisation and the 'homogeneous' black and white and metal musical scoring rendered to us in Stravinsky's prescribed dry manner. But Nijinska, as any choreographer would, invites us to hear the score in 'her' way, erasing from consciousness those aspects, especially textual aspects, that might prompt Stravinsky's masquerade style of theatricality. Anyway, for all we know, perhaps she was secretly glad to be devising a production primarily for non-Russian-speaking non-Russians.

Forgetting that Stravinsky created the score during his period of 'bucolic modernism',[108] the recent stress on the inhuman and impersonal aspects of Stravinsky's score within musicology only adds grist to the mill: narrowing the outlook on the score makes the fit with Nijinska seem even more perfect. Thus, Taruskin praises what he considers Nijinska's complete understanding of Stravinsky's streamlined, 'universal' conception. He takes pleasure in how at one with the composer she is in speaking 'to the utopian that lives within each of us, nostalgic for a past that never was, desirous of a future harmony that can never be achieved within the parameters of what we recognize as human justice'.[109]

Daniel Albright offers a very different account of Stravinsky's suppression of the human subject, suggesting that *Noces* is the composer's ultimate art-machine and that artifice is the antithesis of the natural:

A firm rhythm establishes itself and sweeps all away ... sexuality is intimate with the machine; the peak of the organic and the peak of the inorganic are one and the same.

With a different agenda and led, not by Nijinska's choreography, but by Stravinsky's interest in a *Noces* scoring with pianolas and his story of an in-performance hallucination about playing to an audience of dolls, Albright can even fantasise about 'a wedding night in which mannequins copulate to the pounding of a player-piano'.[110] But it is fascinating that, back in 1923, Vuillermoz had already read the ballet as a statement about us, a metaphor for 'the mechanisation and automatism of society'. He went on to ask: 'In the games of social and religious ritual, are we anything other than obedient marionettes?'[111]

Other weddings

Returning to Stravinsky's masquerade conception with the dancers in Russian costumes and the instrumentalists all on stage in evening dress, we discover that there have been alternatives to Nijinska's approach since the early days, some of these productions clearly prompted by knowledge of Stravinsky's theatrical intentions.

One of these was the first American staging of *Noces* (1929), given under the auspices of the League of Composers, conducted by the celebrated Leopold Stokowski (who also wrote the programme note), with choreography by the former Bolshoi ballerina Elizaveta Anderson-Ivantzova.[112] Aaron Copland was one of the four pianists. The designer was the one-time husband of Vera Stravinsky, Sergey Sudeykin, who, according to his widow Jean Palmer Sudeykina, had initiated a production intended to be totally different from the one that he had seen in Paris.[113] Sudeykin had longstanding connections with Diaghilev's circle, having designed *La Tragédie de Salomé* (Boris Romanov/Florent Schmitt, 1913) and then renewed acquaintance when he emigrated from Russia to Paris with Vera in 1920. He was still in Paris when *Noces* was being discussed in 1922, before leaving for New York later that year, and may well have been privy to information about Stravinsky's original intentions for the work. In 1925, he designed Adolph Bolm's production of *Petrushka* for the Metropolitan Opera House, New York.

The 1929 New York *Noces* was of about the same proportions as the original ballet (thirty dancers), with a pair of matchmakers, two *druzhki* and an old woman in addition to Nijinska's characters. The Russian peasant ritual was explored in more detail. Stokowski's programme note outlined a full scenario containing events from traditional sources: the bride's father drinking wine to seal the wedding contract; barrels of wheat, bread and salt presented as symbols of prosperity; the ceremonies of buying the place next to the Bride; mock whipping of the Bride to indicate her submissiveness; the Bride removing the Groom's shoes; and the presentation of the bridal bedsheet as proof of virginity. This production was in some respects more distant from Stravinsky's image, in others closer to it, than Nijinska's. In the New York production, none of the musicians appeared on stage. Yet, in line with Stravinsky's intentions, it seems, there was no sense of social critique, less tragedy in the New York production – a photograph shows the Bride and Groom smiling – rather the simple acceptance of peasant life and values, and more emphasis on the comic and colourful possibilities of wedding ritual. Olin Downes, the *New York Times* music critic, was enthusiastic about the new production, which he compared with the Nijinska. He described the new choreography as 'lively, perhaps excessively lively …' fitting 'like a glove to the violent and irregular rhythms of Stravinsky's music, and full of grotesque, uncouth and violent primitive movements'.[114] Even if there was more 'plot' content here than Stravinsky might have wished, the manner of the whole production was stylised rather than realist. The movement vocabulary was geometric and angular, dancers evoking mannequins and puppets (which sounds not so different from early descriptions of the Nijinska choreography). Yet, quite unlike the Nijinska, the design was in natural brown-yellow colours, with the Bride and Groom in white. It was also three-dimensional, with bulky, body-encasing costumes, a block-style scenic conception including representations in abstract form of objects from the daily life of the peasantry, and mobile pieces decorated with icons and animal, bird and plant imagery. John Martin, the *New York Times* dance critic, welcomed both productions. Clearly, at that time there was no sense of a masterpiece that set up a special challenge to later choreographers:

> Whether or not there was justice in the accusation that Nijinska's geometric patterning was anemic and devoid of heart, at least it is not applicable to Mme Anderson's. It is extraordinarily interesting to see two women choreographers attack the same work, expressing themselves in approximately parallel syllables, and producing violently antagonistic results which are equally true to a common musical intention.[115]

Once Stravinsky's intentions had been publicised in his *Autobiography*, several *Noces* productions had all the musicians in view on stage. The Brussels production (1936) designed by Stravinsky's son Theodore was one of these, with choreography by Leonid Katchourowsky, but the surprise here was the folkloric emphasis and the colourful picturesque realism that both artists offered. Although Stravinsky was on tour in Argentina at the time of the premiere, it was accepted that he had authorised this approach, which, to many, appeared to be totally at odds with his usual stripped-down, non-realist aesthetic. The highly regarded Hermann Scherchen conducted the orchestra. Reactions were mixed, but Vuillermoz, once he got over the shock of the style, felt that the new staging 'facilitated understanding of the score especially effectively'.[116]

Those responsible for the Zurich production of 1948 (choreography by Hans Macke and designs by Teo Otto) went out of their way to observe the staging description in Stravinsky's *Autobiography*, and letters to Stravinsky from personnel at the Stadttheater underlined this fact.[117] Indeed, they exceeded themselves, assuming that Stravinsky had meant inclusion of the singers on stage as well as the musicians. A photograph shows the four grand pianos and percussion instruments arranged on a raised platform upstage, the singers and conductor in a group stage left. All the musicians are in evening dress and the dancers in Russian style costumes, just as the composer had stipulated.[118]

There is currently no, or at least, very little, information about the nature of many of the other productions listed in the *SGD* database. However, it is possible to note certain trends: such as the prevalence of folk-influenced dance vocabulary, rarely any use of pointework (its inclusion for a section within Maurice Béjart's 1962 *Noces* is highly unusual), a move in later years towards physical theatre movement behaviour, and a range in manner between extreme restraint and unleashed eroticism and violence. The issue of stage musicians continues to be addressed: a preview article on the 2006 production by Heinz Spoerli, for instance, mentions the importance of the visible physicality of musicians, respecting Stravinsky's own view on this too, as cited in his *Autobiography* (see pp. 96-7).[119] Unsurprisingly, most productions have linked Bride and Groom into the dancing group: Nijinska's strategy of keeping them in virtually non-dancing roles has proved exceptional. Jiří Kylián's well-known (and televised) production (choreographed for Nederlands Dans Theater, 1982) sealed the relationship between Bride and Groom with a kiss that cued the start of the musical score.[120] After each has played a central role in Tableaux 1 and 2, they continue to do so with further duet and solo work during the rest of the dance, absorbing, as it were, the substantial anonymous solo roles of Nijinska's Tableau 4. Other productions, like that of Elizaveta Anderson-Ivantzova, have freely included extra characters in the action. It seems to have been in the 1970s that the regular series of small-cast productions began, associated with modern dance rather than ballet companies: those for instance by Lar Lubovitch (1976), Angelin Preljocaj (1989), Kim Brandstrup (1997), each of these for ten dancers, and Javier De Frutos (1997), for five. Aletta Collins cast herself in a solo setting in 2000, before undertaking a mass setting for young people and adults over 50 with the Berlin Philharmonic Orchestra (2006) and a further production for twelve dancers for English National Opera (2007). The impetus behind many of these smaller conceptions was a move away from the old focus on marriage as ancient or distant tradition – arranged, peasant, or otherwise.

Some of those who have continued to explore wedding tradition have referred to Russian heritage: for example, in his 1966 production for La Scala, Milan, Massine included tresses again in the opening scene, but this time many three-rather than two-dimensional multi-body sculptures.[121] There have been further 'Russian' *Noces* productions in the USA: by Lubovitch (1976), who then updated his work in 2001 to give it a Soviet setting – 'the tradition of arranged marriages, practised for generations, has persisted into the 20th century, in spite of the Revolution';[122] and by Ron Cunningham for Sacramento Ballet (1998) – 'uproar, anguish, romantic love and the unpredictable charm of a normal wedding crossed with the volatile Russian temperament'.[123] Béjart gave his production for the Ballet of the 20th Century (1962) an Eastern Russian setting, a distinctly 'oriental' feel, and added two classical-style dancers in white unitards as Visions of the Bride and Groom.[124] Within Russia, there have been at least two productions: first at the Maryinsky by a student at the Vaganova Academy's Department of Choreography, Alexei Miroshnichenko (1997),[125] and then one that has become internationally celebrated, by the modern dance choreographer Tatiana Baganova (1999) for her Provincial Dances Theatre, based in Ekaterinburg. Often the reference to folk heritage in *Noces* has been unspecific. However, there is an interesting example of a production using Korean wedding tradition as a starting point, choreographed by Geungsoo Kim for his own ballet company (2000; revived for the Korea National Ballet Company, 2003).

One of the first productions that we know did not refer specifically to Russian heritage is a surprise: the setting by Merce Cunningham for the Festival of the Creative Arts, Brandeis University (1952), conducted by Leonard Bernstein, the Festival's music director. This also seems to have been one of the first *Noces* settings to emerge from outside the ballet stable. The work was made for a cast of fourteen, and out of keeping with the usual aesthetic of Cunningham, who was then already beginning to experiment with chance and indeterminacy as choreographic devices. The Brandeis work demonstrated none of these techniques. Donald McKayle, a Brandeis student (later a well-known dancer and choreographer) who danced the part of one of the parents, recalls 'big, spatial, leaping movement ... a raw quality, not sophisticated'. A photograph exists of Cunningham as the Groom with a kind of crown on his head in a big jump-lift.[126]

The opening up of the wedding scenario to comment on marriage as a current institution, both inflexible and problematic, seems to have been led by the German Tanztheater choreographer Reinhild Hoffmann in 1980.[127] In her *Hochzeit*, for eight women and eight men, and with the musicians on stage, Hoffmann critiqued the rituals of marriage, presenting a new angle on old customs as if to indicate their continuing power: the brutal cutting of the woman's hair with an axe, the use of ribbons to bind together the couple upon the festive table turned altar or bed. There were striking links with Pina Bausch's *Sacre* (see p. 448): similar costuming (women in white, filmy dresses, men in black trousers and bare chests), the bands of men and women pitted against each other and from whom a female victim is 'chosen' – wedding as sacrificial rite. Marriage as a collective issue, with, not one, but several brides and grooms featured, was a pattern followed by Preljocaj (employing five men and five women) and Stijn Celis (twelve men and twelve women, Les Grands Ballets Canadiens, 2002). Preljocaj toured his work to international acclaim and established the model for an angry, violent physical theatre style of *Noces*, using for all its worth the incisive forcefulness within the score: men (in suits) and women in fraught relationships, and five surrogate brides – life-size dummies in wedding dresses – suggesting both a passive, traditional concept of marriage and cruel destiny when they eventually get hung from up-ended benches.[128] The war between men and women was the topic of more than one of these brutal *Noces* settings: those, for instance, of Mauro Bigonzetti (Compagnia Aterballetto, 2002) and Marie-Claude Pietragalla (Singapore Dance Theatre, 2005). Bigonzetti and his dramaturge Nicola Lusuardi asked: 'The risk is that matrimony can suffocate love by fixing rigorous restrictions. In becoming husband and wife, do lovers accept a fatal contradiction?'[129] Pietragalla used the wedding veil as a symbol of both mystery and imprisonment: 'In this patriarchal society, the woman tries to break away from the weight of tradition.'[130]

Aletta Collins danced a pregnant solo *Noces* that commented on the trappings of weddings, including dancing with a posy, a white dress flying in, and household appliances such as a washing machine and fridge arriving as wedding presents.[131] If this setting has belied all trends, so did Keiko Yagami's athletic version for the K* Chamber Company (Japan, 1993). Although a cross loomed over the proceedings towards the end, this appears to have been essentially an 'abstract' modern dance, the angular, two-dimensional vocabulary possibly linking with Nijinsky tradition.[132] Then there was Javier De Frutos's enigmatically titled *All Visitors Bring Happiness, Some by Coming Some by Going* (Ricochet Dance Company, 1997): the dance communicated threat and brutality as five disturbed individuals (three women, two men) pressed suffering upon one another.[133]

An unusual *Noces* production without dancers was the brainchild of the Bauhaus artist/choreographer Oskar Schlemmer and the conductor Hermann Scherchen. Correspondence between them reveals various plans to produce the work, either at the Dalcroze School in Hellerau (1925), or in Leipzig (1926–7), or in the Albert Hall in London (1927). Schlemmer designed a series of filmed projections to be run alongside the music, but these ideas were never realised, perhaps because of the prohibitive technical costs and difficulties involved.[134] Produced only four years after the monochrome and 'tragic' Nijinska premiere, the designs were decidedly merry, brilliantly multi-coloured and full of event, with doll-like character depictions, religious iconography (a picture of the Madonna with Apostles and angels) and secular representations – for instance, one of the married couple tucked up in bed.

Choreomusically, the *Noces* productions demonstrate a wide range of techniques. There are those that push us towards virtually every accent and detail that the score contains, which is not nearly as interesting as Nijinska's approach. One such production is that by Kylián, both hyperactive and hyperemotional, although it was no mean feat of analytical accuracy to achieve this degree of detailed music visualisation. Emphasising the issue of forced marriage and abuse, Pavel Smok's production for the Prague Chamber Ballet (also 1982) overplayed the final series of bells to add to the horror as the Groom 'used' them to strike his Bride into submission.[135]

Far more interesting is the *Svadebka* by the Russian Baganova, danced to a recording, at least in the performances that I have witnessed, and with imaginative costume designs by Viktoria Mozgovaya. I saw a section from it in a Moscow modern dance festival in 2003, and a rough video of the 2002 performance at the Place Theatre, London. Whether using a cast of six (as in London) or nine (as elsewhere), Baganova made her small group seem like a village crowd. There is a great deal of reference to Russian folk tradition, including tress-cutting (here as the final climax), and mock striking of the Bride (perhaps derived from the old whipping ritual – see p. 379). Yet only the most basic aspect of the original scenario is retained: there is a Bride and Groom, and a Bride's Mother (danced by a man, which introduces an interesting gender tweak), but the Bride and Groom are brought together early on, and at the end there is a Sabre Dancer. Further reference to folk Russia is evident in 'footwork dances', and Garafola has noted the 'strange scurrying figures robed like saints, with the tilted heads of icons and the angular gestures of *lubki* (folk art prints)' that 'seem to spring from collective Russian memory'.[136] But all this is mixed into a wholly contemporary style of movement vocabulary. Well demonstrated in a long phrase through the opening lament, upper bodies carve out generous circles and arcs and plunge into the deepest bows and swoops to the floor, free-wheeling motion articulated by an occasional halt or puncturing staccato gesture.

In Baganova's production, there is no commitment to the demarcation of early scenes in Part 1 of the score by separating men from women. In fact, you would never know from the dance that the score layout is three Tableaux: nothing stops the flow. Baganova introduces a pause of just over two minutes between Parts 1 and 2 of the score – that is her single major structural marker – which she uses for the ritual washing of the Bride's feet amidst wailing women. Important rituals like this happen in the alcoves at the back on either side of a panel bisecting the stage, and here too, amongst an array of props, the arrival of a string of clothes on a line makes the number of people on stage seem larger. As so often in today's modern dance theatre, the structure is episodic, with a mass of event. So there is no major architecture, no semblance of ABA or large exposition and recapitulation structures, but rather a straggle of events, and an ending entirely driven by dramatic timing. Unlike the consolidation of big group energy through dance in the Nijinska, here, ignoring Stravinsky's recapitulations, about half of Tableau 4 (from [120]) is devoted to preparations for the violent denouement, the arrival of the man with the sabre who hands over his weapon to the Groom who cuts the Bride's tress on the high B (screaming out at [132]+2).

Several of the laments are, unsurprisingly, reread to fit Baganova's new 'plot'. Those between Bride and Mother near the end of Tableau 1 (at [21]) and between the two mothers in Tableau 3 (at [82]) become duets for the Bride and Groom. The one between the Groom's parents in Tableau 2 (starting as mezzo-soprano and tenor) is now between the Bride and her Mother (danced by a man, so there is a nicely odd connected-disconnected gender relationship between what we hear and how it is embodied). Contemporary Russian audiences, for whom the work was originally created, would also be in a position to enjoy Baganova's new disjunctions between text and action.

At the detailed level of choreomusical relations, Baganova is remarkably free in her approach, although, because she seems very much at ease with the sharp vitality of the music, any freedom from it never seems to be about incongruence. The musical motor gives the impetus for pulse-based busyness (most often seen in scurry walks and folkish footwork, but occasionally in a few head-judders and hand-beats), but the choreography is nailed to the beat far less frequently than Nijinska's. Baganova finds alternative means of visualising impatient tempi, through the rapid rate of dramatic events. Perhaps the most striking distinction from Nijinska's choreomusicality, a considerable proportion of the body movement is unbroken and legato, with breath and weight. Although it always seems to be racing against time, it nevertheless takes its own time, reconnecting with the music only when it is ready to do so. Interestingly, this breath style seems to seek out the melodic content of the music and make the music sound more legato, in other words it emphasises and nuances aspects of the music that Nijinska does not. It is astonishing, for instance, how the outsize movement to Stravinsky's opening lament phrase suggests a larger range of pitch and more pitch mobility than I actually hear (the material actually confined to B, D and E – see Ex. 5.1a). The only extended instance of 'music visualisation' comes with the entry of the Sabre dancer, a robotic passage across the stage, which is especially eccentric next to the jumpy rhythms of the 'hocket' theme (see p. 363).

There is a two-minute opening without music during which we hear and see someone continually beating a pillow in one of the upstage alcoves, but Baganova's pauses *within* the progress of this score are strictly against Stravinsky intentions and they stop the drive that is one of the most compelling aspects of his score. If the one lasting over two minutes between Parts 1 and 2 works dramatically, another one, about 20 seconds long (at [106]) does not. There is a sharp embrace, a fall to the floor, and then a repeat of the embrace, as if time had stopped. The moment extends the duet possibilities for Bride and Groom, but seems to emerge out of nowhere and to no purpose. Bigonzetti interpolates even more pauses into his work (see p. 383), and to considerably worse effect.

On just a few occasions, choreographers have added extra music to the Stravinsky score. Hoffmann did: the Tanzlieder und Klavierstücke, op. 218b (songs and piano music) by Jürgen Tamchina. Stephan Thoss supplemented the Stravinsky with Arvo Pärt's *Fratres* for violin and piano, in a split-stage account of the contrasting behaviours of two generations of lovers (Stuttgart Ballet, 1994). Henning Paar's *Relitzki* (Ballett Nordhausen, 2000) included music by Dmitri Kabalevsky. The Belgian choreographer Anne Teresa De Keersmaeker goes further than any of these other choreographers with her musical assemblage, as we shall see.

But first we need to take account of the arrival on the market of the Pokrovsky Ensemble's controversial 1994 recording of *Noces*, which raises further questions about the potential theatrical interpretation of Stravinsky's score.[137] A passionately raw, whining and screeching interpretation, it is in itself a radical re-reading of the music. The musician and ethnomusicologist Dmitri Pokrovsky borrowed directly from the oral traditions of villages in south and west Russia, the culture that originally inspired Stravinsky himself, although the composer then shaped and mediated the sources according to his own aesthetic. Pokrovsky's ensemble sings in traditional style, although, for the purposes of the recording, he recreated the instrumental parts on an Apple Macintosh. They also adopt a flexible approach to Stravinsky's divisions between four solo singers and an ensemble, with more than four soloists who emerge from and fold back into the ensemble.[138] Taruskin, naturally, thinks that this 'exotic' rendition 'mutes or at least moderates the vital, disquieting subtext', the 'universal' claims of Stravinsky's music that make it what it really is.[139] But, Taruskin's views apart, for all we know, Stravinsky might have enjoyed the option of a more 'ethnic' reading than he could ever have received in the West. Besides, what was the sound of that Russian church choir brought from Geneva to the Ballets Russes in 1923 (conducted by Vasily Kibalchich)?[140] The Pokrovsky recording has been used to advantage by several choreographers since, among them Javier De Frutos and the choreographers of the next two *Noces* settings chosen here for more detailed analysis, Jerome Robbins (1965, the Pokrovsky used for the 1998 revival) and De Keersmaeker (2002). The Robbins, created for American Ballet Theatre, has since been staged by other companies around the world: the Royal Swedish Ballet (1969), Hamburg Ballet (1976), Finnish National Ballet (1989), Norwegian National Ballet (1990), St Petersburg Ballet (1992) and New York City Ballet (1998). De Keersmaeker's is a far less well-known modern dance version for her Rosas company, nesting within a larger musical and choreographic collage entitled *(but if a look should) April Me*. In contrast with the Nijinska, both are distinctly colourful works in design and dance tone, and for both these choreographers it was their first attempt at a classic ballet score.[141]

Jerome Robbins: Revisiting the composer's intentions

The progress towards Robbins's *Noces* was slow, and he had not seen the Nijinska version before his own premiere. In her biography, Deborah Jowitt outlines his numerous attempts to get the work staged, overlapping with his similar hopes for *Sacre*, some of these prompted by the companies in question, others by himself. Sometimes negotiations carried on for years: for *Noces*, there was La Scala, Milan (in 1953); the Royal Ballet (1953–62); New York City Ballet (1954, Robbins's idea, turned down because Balanchine had no interest in *Noces* or *Sacre* settings for New York City Ballet – see p. 120); the Royal Danish Ballet (1956–60); Juilliard Dance Theatre, New York (1958); Spoleto, Italy (1958 and 1963); before finally, and successfully, American Ballet Theatre.[142] Royal Ballet announcements in spring 1962 listed Colin Davis as prospective conductor and Sean Kenny as designer.[143] Clearly, during those early years, the intention was to respect Stravinsky's wishes about the theatrical conception: the Royal Ballet negotiations ended because Davis and the Royal Opera House would not allow the musicians on stage and the removal of the pianos in and out of the pit during intervals.[144] These negotiations continued through the period when Ninette de Valois was Artistic Director. When Ashton came on the scene in autumn 1963, he set to work to introduce the Nijinska revival instead.

Meanwhile, in December 1959, Robbins had taken himself to see a concert performance in New York's Town Hall with the composer conducting and four star pianists, Aaron Copland (who had been a pianist in the 1929 New York staging – see p. 379), Samuel Barber, Lukas Foss and Roger Sessions. Robbins's description in a letter to the British critic Richard Buckle indicates his interest in the relation between Stravinsky's physical behaviour and the nature of the score:

> Then Stravinsky came on stage, gliding his way past the pianos with wonderful little mincing steps and twisting his body as if fending off blows ... and his conducting was so very wonderful because of his lack of an emotional and over-gesticulating quality; instead one saw the tenacious driving economy.[145]

Robbins, who appears to have enjoyed a friendly relationship with Stravinsky, was extremely anxious to comply with the composer's wishes, not only in terms of the staging but also as regards treatment of musical detail. Twice he wrote to him, on 27 October and 11 November 1953, in preparation for the ill-fated Scala premiere, explaining that he had already undertaken considerable research, inviting his opinions and requesting that the composer check the analysis (1928) by Victor Belyayev, the early Soviet critic.[146] Belyayev had spotted the composer's links with Russian folklore at a time when he was generally considered to have abandoned his roots,[147] and his analysis of *Noces* is the earliest in print. Robbins's musical background served him well in terms of understanding basic musical analysis: he had learnt the piano when young, proving proficient enough to play for Ballet Theatre company classes during the early 1940s. He demonstrated meticulous attention to musical matters, including performance detail, throughout his career.[148] Robbins's second letter to Stravinsky is the more revealing:

> There are so many things I do want to ask you concerning the essential spirit of certain episodes and in general terms the particular qualities and purpose that you as composer were attempting to portray. So what follows are some of the questions that loom most large on the horizon and if you can find the time I would appreciate your advice to any of these problems.
>
> Although they are difficult I seem to manage a good understanding of the first three tableaux. However the last and largest really has me worried. This is where I need most advice as to its approach.

Robbins typed out for Stravinsky Belyayev's analytical diagram of formal and key structure, upon which the composer corrected some of the detail, although hardly in a way that would have shifted the choreographic conception. Robbins was especially intrigued by Stravinsky's play between musical metre and the stress pattern of the text:

> I notice that sometimes you fit and reshift the words to accommodate them within a set metric pattern and at other times you change the time signature to fit the rhythm of the words.

The section in Tableau 1 in which the musical and verbal accents are partly independent from the musical barring (see pp. 356-9), and to which Nijinska set her 'braiding' of the feet, was of particular concern:

> I would be curious to know for instance which way you would like to see it done at No. 2 in your score; would you want the accents to come on the 16th notes, or to have a steady eighth beat running through the whole section with the music making the accents against the pattern.
>
> I have talked with Dubrovska who danced the bride originally and who advises me to do the ballet completely differently.

Robbins was concerned too about the balance between peasant realism and ritual distance:

> To what degree do you see this work in colloquial peasant terms. I know it is a rite and that there is a ritualisation of the happy and sorrowful events of the wedding preparations and ceremonies.

Marc Chagall had been selected as designer for La Scala, and Robbins asked Stravinsky whether he had any further thoughts, as Chagall's work might 'over-burden the dancers and the stage'. At Stravinsky's suggestion, the pair had a meeting about *Noces* in 1953 in California, which was, as Robbins later put it, 'just to let him loose on it, so I could tell what he wanted'.[149] We do not know the details of this meeting, but the choreographer was obviously committed at that point to a theatrical conception that included singers as well as instrumentalists on stage.

In the Robbins archive is material that he typed out from Stravinsky's *Autobiography* and from *Expositions and Developments* (the main Stravinsky sources on *Noces*). Robbins's other research included perusal of the famous early photographs of the Ballets Russes in poses from *Noces* on the roof of the theatre in Monte Carlo. His archive also includes reviews, mostly English and American, one in French by the musicologist Emile Vuillermoz,[150] with most covering the Nijinska production. Amongst the choreographer's notes is a list of productions earlier than his own as well as a variety of choreographic notes and annotated musical scores, the material revealing that Robbins had done his homework thoroughly and had carefully logged his thought processes. Especially interesting is a substantial article written for *The New York Times* shortly before the 1965 American Ballet Theatre premiere. Here, in the original uncut draft of the article, the choreographer shares his vivid impressions of the music and musicianly knowledge of its detail. Like so many others since the 1923 premiere, he is also struck by the machine metaphor embodied in the score:

> The score is monolithic and elegant – barbaric, beautiful and frightening. This description also suits some singular mountain, and trying to climb it is what it feels like to choreograph *Les Noces*. It is as hard and metallic as marble and steel. Its form is stubborn, polished, astonishingly block-like and complete unto itself. It is absolutely unyielding. It cannot be disguised or altered by the choreography. No 'easy' parts happen along. Very few lengths of the same metered bars follow each other. Shifts from 3/4 to 5/8 to 2/4 to 3/8 are the rule and an uninterrupted length of 6/4 is the exception. The dancers must count continuously, unerringly and with unceasing concentration. Their energy in rehearsal has been exhausted as much by using their brains for com-

puters as their muscles for dancing. For once the music starts nothing can stop it. You push a button and this terrifying machine begins to scream, launches into its lamentations, incessant chattering, shocking you with unexpected outbursts and hypnotic murmurings. Still, with its strident shrill pitches, its compulsively repetitive ruts and bumpy shifts, its clanging clanking metallic percussion, a strange and reverent lyricism is aroused. An overpowering tension is created by the simpleness of the material (the wedding) and by the extraordinary, bizarre and inspired means with which Stravinsky has expressed it.[151]

Robbins's *Noces* follows the original scenario and plans, and he shows more attention to textual detail than Nijinska did. Although his programme note reflected Stravinsky's purpose, his account of the scenario weighted more the rough and bawdy, including the warming of the marriage bed by a chosen couple (symbolically – the bed is imaginary), indicating a different conception from Nijinska's. In his 1965 article, he also explained his notion of the personal trauma of the bride and groom 'prepared and offered up in some holy and barbaric rite which must run its course to the end'. Jowitt followed up this idea, reflecting on how 'all elements combine eloquently to intimate how barbarously the social aspects of weddings contrast with the privacy of mating', and on the 'bearish forcefulness in the dancers' torsos that makes the hearty way the celebrators shove the bride and groom together almost shocking'.[152] Thus, the Bride and Groom, major participants throughout the ballet, are frequently manhandled and pushed together like objects by the crowd, but also carried and thrown aloft, given presents, bowed to, and touched as if they have magic properties. At the end, they are spotlit on the rostrum that represents the marriage bed, in a coupling that speaks of terror, discovery, struggle, and finally a sense of desolation as they throw their torsos out and away from each other.

In the original 1965 ballet, all this happened amidst a very busy stage, with all the musicians present, singers included: 26 dancers including 8 soloists (the Bride and Groom, two sets of parents and two matchmakers), 4 pianists, 6 percussionists, 4 solo singers and a chorus of 32, making a total cast of 72. The cover of the May 1965 issue of *Dance Magazine* shows the line-up of singers raised on platforms upstage, the instrumentalists, pianos and percussion below, and then a trio of dancers in the foreground in a Nijinska-derived body sculpture (from Robbins's Tableau 2). Doris Hering described how the usually out-of-view business of performers getting into place became integral and theatrical. Stravinsky might well have enjoyed the artifice:

At the outset, the musicians walked in, bowed, and took their places upstage. So, too, did the singers.

Ill. 14. Alexandra Ansanelli as the Bride in *Les Noces*, Tableau 1, choreography by Jerome Robbins, New York City Ballet.

Then came the dancers. At first they looked small and unimportant, the way dancers often look in opera. They seemed dwarfed by the singers, and more than that, by Oliver Smith's glowing backdrop with its gigantic saints gazing cannily at the mortals below.

The dancers, in two groups, bowed to the singers and to each other. And then the surge began![153]

Benches framed the upstage corners of the dancing space, and the peasant-style costumes after Goncharova by Patricia Zipprodt were now in bright reds, browns, beiges and yellows, and white for the Bride and Groom. American Ballet Theatre continued to present the piece thus, with this massive stage ensemble.[154]

Robbins's work is defined by remarkable imagery, especially for the Bride. In the opening Tableau, she wears tresses as long as those in the Nijinska (see Ill. 14), but here, at one point she is suspended between her friends, the centre of a kind of maypole-dance entwining of braids; at another, reined back as she leads them from the front in a heavy limp; later still, virtually strangled by these fearsome appendages. At other times, she goes sideways in a kind of bourrée, legs open in second position, carving out a huge circle, or, in Tableau 3, like an icon herself, she sits like a statue centre stage in a deep open plié with her white dress stretched taut between her knees.

The community movement style is big and earthy, with energy flung well beyond the extremities of the body. These are high-kicking Broadway peasants who spread their arms and legs and reach to the 'gods' (*Noces* marked Robbins's return to ballet after some years on Broadway). There is also the rough and tumble of acrobatics, even an expressive somersault during the anguished lament of the two mothers in Tableau 3. Robbins used all his commercial theatre experience of dealing with large crowds to create thrilling rivers of motion as well as the striking visual effects of mass huddles and showers of staccato gestures.

Choreomusically, broad rhythms are often in the foreground, led by narrative, encompassing the rush across the stage that marks departures, arrivals and transitions into new confrontations and new ritual behaviour, the spilling-out of old formations to coalesce afresh, and the canon streams across a group or down a line. The mode is essentially fluid, tumultuous and unstoppable: this is not clean-cut, block-style choreographic architecture. Again, led by his narrative, Robbins associates singing voices with characters who, more straightforwardly than Nijinska, 'dance' those voices, the Bride embodying the soprano very clearly in Tableau 1 and again in Tableau 4, where she takes on the line originally given to the anonymous solo woman from amongst the guests. Tableau 3 ends with a conversation between both mothers, as in the score, instead of Nijinska's one. In Tableau 2 (at [35]), Robbins devises a quartet to a passage for four solo voices, and the opening designated for the parents now looks more like that and how it sounds, led by the Groom's mother and father in overlapping statements. In contrast, Nijinska cast this passage as a blessing of the Groom.

We know from Robbins's queries to Stravinsky that he was also deeply interested in the detailed rhythmic component of the score. His solution to the awkward 'braiding' music in Tableau 1 (at [2]) was, after all, to do something quite different from Nijinska, as Doubrovska had advised, and, for the trio backing the Bride, he introduced a big swinging step sideways, followed by a closing of the feet, with a preparatory plié *on* the first musical accent (see Ex. 5.14). The pattern progresses from left to right, left to right (slowing down on the last step), to cut into an extra step right and then left, a bold and unusually elastic movement idea within the work: counted as 6 6 6 5 6 6. Unlike Nijinska, Robbins's tactic here was to follow the look of the score, one step per bar: 6/8 6/8 6/8 5/8 6/8 (=3/4 = 6 dance counts) (see pp. 357-8). Importantly, however, musical accents on downbeats stress the pliés before the first step and the fifth (after the slowing down), structuring the dance phrase into two parts. When the braiding returns at [3], the musical accents have shifted position in relation to the bar-line, but now (and this is like Nijinska), Robbins shifts his phrasing accordingly; the choreography is an almost exact repeat in terms of its synchronisation with the music, again counted as 6 6 6 5 6 6.

Elsewhere, Robbins's choreography is fully pressured by the motor in

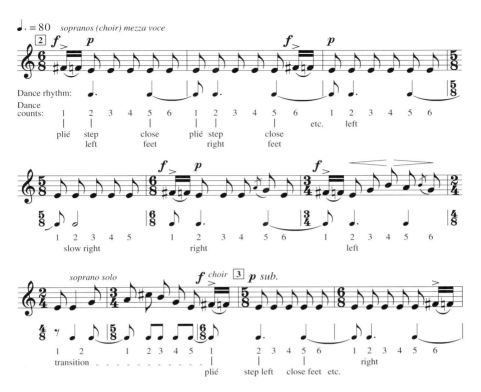

Ex. 5.14. *Les Noces*, Tableau 1, braiding (Robbins).

Stravinsky's music that he admired so much (see p. 106). He shows this plainly and boldly for long stretches, most of the time at a moderate tempo pulse (rarely in smaller time divisions – there is none of the ferocious step-knitting of Nijinska). We see this in movement that references generic folk dance, full-foot marching steps, heel-digs, shunts and bouncing pliés, all of it weighted motion. Some of this is straightforward in terms of the look and sound of the score, such as the beginning of Tableau 4, when four walks and three heel-digs (repeated) reinforce every beat in accordance with the alternating 4/4 and 3/4 musical structure (see Ex. 5.15). But there are other occasions when Robbins elects to cross the musical metre (both what is written and what is heard), most effec- tively a lengthy episode in Tableau 2 from [55] when two parallel lines of dancers conduct a folk-style sideways-walking pattern, with individuals falling off one end of a line to run round and join the other: the pattern is formed of units of 5 and 6 counts (see Ex. 5.16). True to style, all the moves map the crotchet pulse clearly and plainly, but there is a sense of aural–visual disconnection. Another example of crossing occurs in the hocket section of Tableau 4, where two male

Ex. 5.15. *Les Noces*, Tableau 4, unison opening material (Robbins).

Ex. 5.16. *Les Noces*, Tableau 2, double-line dance (Robbins).

soloists lurch and stride across the repeating 4/4+3/4 pattern with an 8-count pattern (not unlike Nijinska's crossing procedure during this passage – see p. 363, Ex. 5.9). The section is labelled 'Drunks' in the score; indeed, again they work against what we hear, Robbins responding to the notion of a drinking song behind this passage.

Occasionally, dance material that fits the written barring clearly works against what we readily hear. The beginning of Tableau 2 (labelled 'First Wedge' in the Labanotation score) offers the best example of this, and is one of the most rhythmically and dynamically charged dance phrases in the entire work (see Ex. 5.17). (Nijinska keeps her dancers still at this point.) Linked in solidarity, each man with a hand on a neighbour's shoulder, the male band (the wedge formation) forces the Groom forwards into the space (metaphorically towards his church wedding) with a series of brutal shoves. The step pattern is bumpy, with moments of holding back, turning sideways, and then sudden bursts, so that each push is a surprise. The structure behind this sophisticated effect is formulaic and

Ex. 5.17. *Les Noces*, Tableau 2, opening (Robbins and De Keersmaeker). Ⓡand Ⓛ designate accented steps right and left into plié, between steps on the toes.

analytically quite simple: the association of particular step patterns with particular metres, in other words, some patterns fit the 5/8 and 7/8 bars, whilst others fit the 3/4 (6/8) bars. Later (at [35]), the steps demonstrate 2/4, with the music, but this is now much more like marking time, going through the motions as an active 'accompaniment': there is a lot of 'step on count 1, close the feet on 2'. All these examples introduce a sense of aural–visual disconnection that contrasts with Robbins's normal choreomusical practice in this ballet.

In summary, the Robbins *Noces* choreography has little of Nijinska's autonomous compulsion, or the light and shade, variety of stress and rhythmic pattern within her work. The opening of Tableau 4 is a good example of the difference in their approaches. Turn the sound off here and we see Robbins's motor ticking away by itself with very little to disrupt, decorate or nuance its unrelenting progress. Sometimes, for limited passages, it works well to leave choreography rhythmically plain when musical rhythms are as complex as they are in *Noces* (and Balanchine clearly understood this – see p. 173). But, after a while, in Robbins's *Noces*, because this technique is used so extensively, and because I find myself reading the dance line for what it is itself and not simply for what it becomes in interaction with the score, I am not persuaded. At those times, my imagination is lured by other strengths: Robbins's remarkable imagery, range of incident and dramatic impetus.

The premiere of Robbins's *Noces* at the New York State Theatre was conducted by his friend Leonard Bernstein (collaborator on *Fancy Free* (1944) and *West Side Story* (1957)). Much was made of the fact that Robbins followed Stravinsky's intentions, and, although there were some detractors, the event was an immediate success and received many ecstatic reviews. Unable to attend the premiere, the composer, his wife and Craft caught up with the work a few weeks later in Chicago. Vera reported 'Big discussion afterward.'[155] Craft recalls that the work 'moved the Stravinskys but also shocked them in that this peasant wedding was set in a vast, rich, and jewel-bedecked church'.[156] Presumably, he was referring to the backdrop of glowing icons. Lillian Libman, Stravinsky's personal manager and press representative at the time, agreed on the Stravinskys' positive reaction, but remembered that Craft objected vehemently to the symbolic consummation of marriage in synchronisation with the 'bells', as 'a commonplace use of the music'.[157]

A year later, Robbins saw Nijinska's production for the first time, performed by the Royal Ballet at the Metropolitan Opera House, sharing the season with his own across the Lincoln Centre Plaza at the New York State Theatre. The productions also shared the same singing chorus, the two male soloists and four pianists. It is noteworthy that, at that time, the Nijinska had not acquired the masterpiece status in the USA that it has now, and some rated the Robbins more highly.

Clive Barnes and Walter Sorell both praised Robbins for complying with the composer's wishes. Barnes evaluated the Nijinska as 'fascinating and disappointing', not as strong as her *Les Biches*; the Robbins 'with all its admitted show-business concessions, is artistically superior'.[158] Sorell found the older version 'somewhat dated today ... [it] shows a simple, gentle approach with many endearing moments'. The Robbins 'is the stronger, more impressive but also slicker version'.[159] But Robbins himself was overwhelmed by what he saw, claiming afterwards that he would not have undertaken a *Noces* had he already known the original.[160] He was moved to write down his impressions: 'I'd been told the wrong things about it', he began, recalling first a famous dance critic: 'dull ... boring ... no choreography ... old-fashioned', and then a musicologist: 'score not used'. He continued:

> It is a work of majestic inspiration. It curiously combines stillness and archaic limitations with overt violence and ecstasy. It is as condensed and ritualized as a Japanese Noh drama ...
>
> Only [Alexandra] Danilova had prepared me for what I was to see. Many years ago when I told her I was considering choreographing *Les Noces* she said immediately – 'oh, its such a *dark* work.'
>
> Well dark and insistent it is – Its enormous power is there but held in ...

His emphasis on the 'dark' quality of her work reveals by contrast the more colourful nature of his own *Noces*. Similarly revealing are his comments on her different musical approach. Because his own work used the music in the more traditional manner of ritual and social dance accompaniment, he perceived a distancing device at work in Nijinska's setting, as if the music possessed a momentum that started up the dance, and then kept going independently after the dance had stopped:

> The ballet seems to happen outside the music. Sections of the score start and later lights come up and the celebrants move – they may stop before the music does and let the score run on – or they – the lights may fade out on the repetitive figure (the men circling the groom) ...[161]

But Robbins does not comment, at least here, on the detail of Nijinska's musicality and rhythmic range.

In 1998, Robbins's acquaintance with the Pokrovsky *Noces* radically altered his conception of his own work. Perhaps he realised that Stravinsky's preferred staging was impractical to resource and make happen, although he was clear that he did not elect to use a recording for financial reasons.[162] As well as foreseeing a much less cluttered stage environment, he must have been aware in turning to this particular recording that he was dealing with a new ethnic colour and raucousness. He had written to Robert Graves about his original piece: 'It's a little athletic, more so than I want it to be, and I think that this is so because of my overzealous attempt to communicate *everything* about what I heard and saw in the music.'[163] Now, he simplified some passages, editing Tableau 4 and fusing some of the counterpoint into unison.[164] It is hard to overestimate the difference between the 1998 revival using the Pokrovsky and the original conception, with two-thirds of those present on stage removed. Garafola lamented the change, for 'without the chorus and musicians onstage, the community that is the ballet's true protagonist is much diminished'. As for the Pokrovsky, she claimed that it 'mutes the original's inner anguish of loss, its piercing cry of pain'.[165] Anna Kisselgoff missed 'the huge sound', but also, without 'the distancing effect that opposes singers in evening dress and dancers in Russian sarafans and laced shoes', this *Noces*, she said, 'has lost some of its ritualistic essence. It has shrunk.'[166] Clearly, for some, a major strength of Robbins's production lay in its adherence to Stravinsky's intentions.

Anne Teresa De Keersmaeker: An April wedding

In her *(but if a look should) April Me*, De Keersmaeker finds even more boisterousness in the Pokrovsky than Robbins does, and a good deal more humour too. Although she had seen and researched the Nijinska version of the choreography, she decided upon an altogether merrier account of a wedding. Save for a meditation (not a lament) at the end of Tableau 3, the whole score is treated as a party, so that what once sounded like nasty whines, shrieks and sneers in the context of Robbins's choreography now become more like naughty gossip, whoops of pleasure and squeals of delight. De Keersmaeker's is also an occasion for the young people: there are no lamenting parents or interfering grown-ups.

In the spirit of her highly collaborative approach to work, De Keersmaeker took up the suggestion of her musical advisor/analyst Georges-Elie Octors to use the Pokrovsky: he had already listened to about eight recordings in the normal 'classical singing' style.[167] Even though De Keersmaeker reads music, Octors created an analysis of the score for her, partly thematic, revealing the recurring melodic material and its variants, but also rhythmic. For the latter, he devised a diagrammatic analysis (an assortment of lines, triangles and oblongs – see Ex. 5.18) as an aide-memoire for each of the dancers as well as for De Keersmaeker, indicating time signatures, metronomic shifts and potential rhythmic difficulties such as: 'be careful, the soprano sings in 2/4 over 6/8' or 'be careful, keep the same tempo'.

De Keersmaeker was intensely interested in the structural possibilities of the

« LES NOCES » 1er Tableau *« La Tresse »*

Cue :
(| | |) Tempo I ♪ = **80**

N°. | | | | | | | | | | | , | | | | | | | | | | | | | | | |

───

Tempo II ♩ = **80** / ♪ = **160** (Doppio più vivo) *« Rideau »*

1 ▢ △ ▢ △ ▢ △ ▢ △ △ △ ▢▢▢
1bis ▢ △ ▢ △ ▢ △ ▢ △ △ △ ▢▢▢
La Mariée ▢▢▢ ▢△

───

Tempo III ♩. = **80** / ♩ = **120** / ♪ = **240** (Ancora più vivo) *« Les amies de noces »*

2 △△ △△ △△ △▢ △△
▢▢▢ ▢▢ ▢▢▢
3 △▢ △△ △△ △△ △△ △△ △▢

───

Tempo I ♪ = **80**

4 | | | | | | | | | | | , | | | | | | | | ,
| | | | | | | | | , | | | | | | | | |

───

Tempo II ♩ = **80** / ♪ = **160** (Doppio più vivo)

5 △ ▢ ▢ △ ▢ △ ▢ △ △ △ ▢▢▢
6 △ ▢ △ ▢ △ ▢ △ △ △ ▢▢▢
La Mariée ▢▢▢ ▢△

───

KEY

| | | = **3/8**

| | = **2/8**

▢ = **2/8**

△ = **3/8**

Ex. 5.18. *Les Noces*, Tableau 1, opening, musical analysis for De Keersmaeker and her dancers by Georges-Elie Octors.

score, and, from the information provided by Octors, she chose which parameters to use choreographically. For instance, in the first three Tableaux there are
very strong and detailed rhythmic, often pulse-based, connections between music and dance, but, as we shall see, they vary greatly in kind, and often De
Keersmaeker did not apply straightforwardly the metrical map that Octors drew
diagrammatically from the score.

Tableau 4 was choreographed quite differently, based on 'theatrical images'
drawn from the improvisation of the Rosas dancers (who are also billed as
creative artists), built into a complex 'contrapuntal framework' following the
larger musical structure. However, it is important that the effect of this kind of
structuring is of a new freedom of movement for dancers and musicians, as at
any party where people get drunk or go a little crazy. In fact, from the very
beginning, the community in Tableau 4 appear to be in a state of happy disorder.
Of course, this switch of tactics matches the shift in the score towards the
raucous and unrestrained. Whereas Nijinska tempers the shift, De Keersmaeker
doubles its effect: drunkenness dances to melody rather than to precise rhythms,
after all.

De Keersmaeker operated boldly in building a construction around her cornerstone ballet score. Her work was not conceived simply as a *Noces*, and, of
course, it does not use the musical title; it has the score setting embedded within
it, as part of an expanded meditation-fantasy on stirrings of life, love and sexuality, loneliness and companionship, and, says the choreographer, spiritual union.[168] This is a full-evening work and marriage is just one, institutionalised,
expression of the many human relationships represented. In her title, De
Keersmaeker refers to E.E. Cummings's sweet-bitter poem 'darling!because my
blood can sing' and its complex collision of feelings:

> – but if a look should april me,
> some thousand million hundred more
> bright worlds than merely by doubting have
> darkly themselves unmade makes love ...
>
> but if a look should april me
> (though such as perfect hope can feel
> only despair completely strikes
> forests of mind, mountains of soul)

She also alludes to the opening of T.S. Eliot's *The Waste Land*: 'April is the
cruellest month'. De Keersmaeker has spoken of the link with the recurring
dualities in her work: between men and women, between rigorous structure and
the irregular and personal. But *April Me* is also about rebuilding from chaos:

'something that had collapsed ...' and 'the image of "many" and the problem of finding one's [own] space'. As for using the *Noces* score:

> It's strange not to do a Stravinsky ... It's really kind of a 'must' ... [It has] a rhythmic complexity I love, which I saw as a challenge, a celebration, a music with words, but words that had no linearity, which was already very modern.[169]

Many other musics surround *Noces*, forming a two-act evening: popular and sacred items from Italy and India, Iannis Xenakis and Morton Feldman, and titles sharing the marriage metaphor: an aria from Mozart's *Marriage of Figaro*, and a specially composed score, *Les Fiançailles* by Thierry De Mey. The set and lighting design were by Jan Versweyveld (assisted by Geert Peymen), costumes by Inge Büscher.

As in much of her other work, the physical presence of musicians was always central to De Keersmaeker's theatrical conception. For the music on either side of *Noces*, the six percussionists of the Ictus ensemble appear on stage and sometimes in the midst of the dance action, and De Keersmaeker decided therefore that they must join in for *Noces*: so, now well beyond Stravinsky's expectations, they turn into dancers alongside the thirteen-strong Rosas team!

There is a noisy opening, with the performing troupe (dancers and musicians) processing through the audience carrying chunks of wood and a refrigerator and singing noisily as they go. Impending domesticity and 'civilisation'? But then, amidst a strange rubble of white planks, they dance, a cool community in blue, bare-chested and -breasted, free, sweatless, sitting on the edge to watch each other, occupying the same metaphorical territory as the musicians upstage. But what is this territory? There are hints that this is a place for children's games, playful competition, the passing of secret messages, the endeavour to follow and match up to a partner's speed and skill, suggestions of tribal ritual with heroic bouts of virtuosity. Always there is a sense of watchfulness and expectancy.

Driving the dancers on is the percussion, thuds and throbs that resonate with somewhere deep in the pelvis at one moment, whilst at others, metallic shrieks pierce the brain. The movement, typical De Keersmaeker/Rosas, looks simple and human in scale – step, hop, jump into squat, a furious, high unfolding of a leg with flexed foot, but invested with eloquent, liquid torsos and lightning heads that drop or shake to impulse the next move. Particularly impressive is the part where the dancers stand high on tables, whipping their sticks to the crash of percussion, commanding their colleagues to halt their dance.

Long and short skirts and different cuts of trousers are not gender-determined any more than the movement is. And, if the half-body nudity unifies and formalises the dancers at the same time as exaggerating the difference between men and women, it could be that this community has not yet reached the crucial stage, or has simply opted out, of the culturally constrained mapping of sexuality on bodies. Yet the critic Raf Geenens has read this scene differently, as 'an exuberant engagement party' including 'a subtle game of seducing and being seduced'.[170]

Suddenly, we see before us a line-up of women in stilettos and knickers, struggling to cover themselves with red towels. We hear the first strain of the Stravinsky, cut off abruptly, and one of the women shouts 'Pause' ('Intermission'). We know that the old world has disappeared. Is the world of Rosas dance theatre, dancers as characters, about to be born?

Lights up for the second half of the evening, and the line of women hoist shocking pink and red dresses up to their behinds and mince side to side. This is Nijinska in reverse, grinning backs turned to us (instead of strait-laced fronts), stilettos attacking the floor (instead of pointe shoes), and a wild Bride (Marta Coronado) performing mayhem somewhere along the line as well as out of it, her white satin dress cut open up the front. If a number of the Rosas dancers are childlike of demeanour, she is most of all – the over-excited schoolkid who loves dressing up. When the music speeds up, the troupe go places, weaving in and out of each other, like the tresses that this section was originally about – still with backs to us.

De Keersmaeker uses the idiosyncratic tone of the Pokrovsky to parody stereotypes of contemporary urban culture – catty, gossiping girls viciously flirtatious before the suited men who generate macho power with their pounding steps, jumps and circle formations. The Groom (Jakub Truszkowski) is half Rosas dancer, half disco king, flash and preening, and so awed by his own prowess and good fortune that he has to be stopped (those fidgety feet too) and dragged away to the wedding by the Bride.

De Keersmaeker retains the original plan of four Tableaux, scenes at the houses of Bride and Groom leading to a wedding feast that brings everyone together. But she goes beyond this. Indeed, she encourages us to examine her creation through the lens of the Nijinska, so often are there parallels between the kinds of formation expressed, and near to the same places in the score: lines, circles, wedges, a wheel effect, and an archway of arms to signal the route to the wedding. At the Groom's house, his best friend wanders about with a comb, referring to the curls mentioned in the text.

So far, so good, and all is in order, just about.... The more striking, therefore, is the shift into the wedding feast. The women and men rush into the space as the music begins and chaos reigns. It is a riot of raucous high spirits, sexual display and playful rebuttal, on the tables, on the floor, drunken totters and collisions, any amount of solo bizarrerie. There are some especially strange goings-on, led

Ill. 15. *Les Noces*, Tableau 4, in *(but if a look should) April Me*, choreography by Anne Teresa De Keersmaeker, Rosas.

by two women, Octors quietly embarking as a dog on all fours, and a colleague driven to shuffle backwards on his behind. The action seems barely controlled by the music, although sometimes the dancers' moves catch a sound whirl and you can spot the tall Russian Igor Shyshko mouthing the words and embodying the wild voice of the text, which seems even wilder when genders of voice and body conflict.

Gradually, from about [129], the ensemble starts to gather into a single mass, a circle around the Bride and Groom (see Ill. 15), a wheel, a line, then several further attempts to settle down and line up, until everyone is finally stilled by the 'Bells' in a circle. Yet this is no firm resolution. The newlyweds end up atop their washing machine, ironic symbol of wedded bliss, and soon the Groom is watching football on television, an ill omen for the future. The aftermath is still more disarray, still more noise, a fractured society through which the Bride rushes, undressed to her knickers, clutching wedding dress and flowers, all by herself, though still giggling. But there is a gradual restoration of calm, the assemblage of all the white planks into one tall tower (an image of rebuilding) and now a new open stage that gives us space to contemplate and wonder.

We realise that the work has all along problematised as well as celebrated bonding and fusion – between music and movement, musician and dancer, man and woman – and, in the abstract terms of dance, counterpoint competes with unison dance material. There is a haunting, magical duet to pianissimo Feldman, in which a woman embodies the physicality of timbre, the moves of the male percussionist mirrored out in the open space. With a quiver of the hand, a flick of the fingers, she 'demonstrates' the tiniest sound. But the 'marriage' does not get anywhere. Now the same woman abducts no less than the Groom and leads him into an absurd duet. Bound cheek to cheek, they dance like Siamese twins, needing, and needing to escape each other, and totally alone. An Indian child's song about the joy of seeing the stars at night reads positively next to this final ambiguous visual image.

Back to *Noces*, and we find that the issues of fusion and counterpoint between men and women and between music and movement are inseparable. Quite differently from Nijinska and Robbins, De Keersmaeker makes her *Noces* a sort of stand-off tease that eases into a meeting ground for separate bands of young women and men, with none of the diversions of family relationships. She is also led by the division between male and female voices in the score to a much greater degree than either of the other two choreographers. The first Tableau is like a hen party, a true girly affair, and it is significant that when the male voices enter at [10] (followed by the return of women's voices for two bars) and then re-enter at [11], the women dancers suddenly halt, move and halt again, as if recognising a male intrusion from 'outside'. This division eases up a little towards the end of Tableau 1 when male and female voices mix, and also during Tableau 2, but it still constitutes the norm and returns again with full force in Tableau 3 when the two bands meet for the first time and size each other up. Into the men's stag party march the women with a confident hip-swinging walk (to the women's chorus), stopping in front of the men to let them gather their defences at [67] (to the tenor solo), after which the women continue start–stop (the men clearly fazed into complete stillness). Married to the solo soprano in eccentric squealing mode, the Bride must burst out at [68]+3 and [69]+5 – always the show-off, she ends up in over-the-top temps levé in arabesque that take her flying across the stage. The climax of the Tableau is antiphonal, the men now fully involved, jumping/singing bands asserting themselves one after the other from [75], then all together from [77], the women off by themselves again at [78] (a unit of 4/8, three steps and a hop, a rare example of crossing the 3/4 written musical metre), joined by the men at [79]+4, and thus onwards together to form the departure archway.

Solo voices are sometimes, but not always, matched by solo dancers, but when they are, as is often the case for the Bride (teamed up with that polyvocal soprano), there is sudden enhancement and a sense of mutual possession. In Tableau 4, the link with musical pulse is less important than with melody and phrase, the improvisation-based choreographic method allowing a new kind of freedom and giving the impression (not the reality) of experiment and chance connections between music and dance. There are a number of voice/dance associations, and a good deal of the liveliness stems from getting us to search out this voiced activity. De Keersmaeker keeps the viewer's eye darting all over the stage to find it, also watching for the links between dancers sharing material, who either operate adjacently or at a distance, divided by the unruly crowd.

There is an especially striking voice/dance association when Shyshko emerges as a kind of party joker given prominent bass roles (chorus and solo) for an extended passage lasting from just before [89] to [106]. He turns up all over the place in the crowd, occasionally linking up with someone else, or they with him: big, mad movement taking him everywhere fast, punctuated by sharp-shock body isolations. Thus, he marks out the hocket rhythms with jerky arms and elbows, plunges floorwards and stamps; he goes even wilder to the bizarre falsetto exclamations, finds himself in the centre and out of sync with his friends during the 'Oys' and then, when a dotty woman totters up to him at [103]-1 (the eccentric soprano newly embodied), he answers (to the bass) with a feigned overwhelm, dropping like a stone to the floor ([103]+3). Between them, the Pokrovsky recording and Shyshko/De Keersmaeker bring out the bass line here far more strongly than in the other two *Noces* analysed. Shyshko is the one cast member who understands all the words, of course, but De Keersmaeker's touch on text is generally light. In her *Noces*, as with many a church service or pop song, people hear words but not necessarily their meanings, which is not such a far cry from Stravinsky's own concept of ritual without real feeling. Even the occasional mouthing of words in Tableau 4 does nothing to undermine this impression.

The tight association of dancers with voices of their own gender only adds to the 'natural', human quality of De Keersmaeker's *Noces*, reflecting a celebration of the wedding participants as normal people through whom we might recognise ourselves. The extended range of body shapes and sizes offered by the musicians also contributes. And just as at many a dance party, the participants are free to talk, giggle, whistle and shout. Although there are characteristic De Keersmaeker forays into dance as opportunities to express individual enjoyment, a surprising amount of the group material is simple walking and jumping, everyday movement crossed with basic dance steps, the kind of thing you recognise from any ceilidh or disco, and 'offstage' behaviour like foot-tapping or bobbing that gets into the groove of beat and offbeat. This 'normal' behaviour is not uncommon in contemporary forms of dance theatre, but what is extraordinary here is the sophisticated use of the everyday and ordinary to form enlivening and unpredictable choreomusical relationships. It is not insignificant that De Keersmaeker once likened her practice here to Baroque dance, with its emphasis on 'the beat of the feet, being anchored in the ground',[171] and, just as in Baroque dance, she shows us the magic that feet can make from different qualities of tread, patterns of impulse and speed of event: high on the toes and fast looks wonderful after sturdy, weighted, full-foot stepping. Such is this magic that she reveals unsuspected disco-jazz potential within Stravinsky/Pokrovsky. So, is there any overt 'music visualisation', emphatic reinforcement of big musical accentuation, in De Keersmaeker's *Noces*? Only occasional shots at it, with the odd gesture and jump, more or less the same amount as in the Nijinska, but here, when everyone jumps (and shouts) to an 'Oy!', there is that happy roughness of unison that all party-dancers understand.

The choreomusical fun begins immediately, at the start of Tableau 1. To the opening lament, the line-up of women, backs turned to us, perform one mincing step (step forwards and close the other foot) at the onset of phrase 1, a second step marking the start of phrase 2 (Octors's rhythm diagram is adhered to by the choreography, a comma marking the division between phrases – see Exs. 5.1a and 5.18). De Keersmaeker is guided by melodic structure, and thus she continues for a while. With the busy ostinato in the bass (at [1] – see Ex. 5.19), the mincing steps accumulate: forwards, backwards, forwards, closing on each accented E, then backwards closing on B, a hold, rather than a move towards the last E (contradictory to expectations), and forwards again during the final chorus bar. On the musical repeat, the step pattern is reversed, beginning with a step backwards. Interweaving during the 'braiding' music at [2], the women glide in a rough approximation of one step per crotchet beat – neither the musical accentuation pattern nor the barring is a determining factor. De Keersmaeker respects the modified repeat of these three passages of music by introducing modified choreographic repetition. For the first passage, repeated at [4], she articulates four phrases instead of two (see Ex. 5.3). The interweaving pattern becomes a point of recapitulation at [21], during the final part of the Tableau.

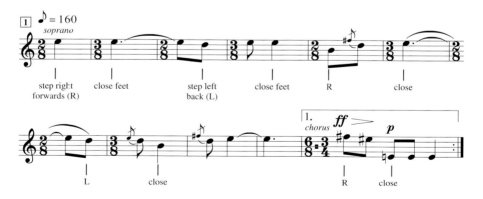

Ex. 5.19. *Les Noces*, Tableau 1, women's movement from [1] (De Keersmaeker).

For much of the dance allegro in Tableau 1, the women just walk about in time, in the pleasurable hip-swinging manner that will be their greeting to the men later, but now they are dressed up for their own hen party in high heels. They crash down from jumps on the big shouts before tossing off their shoes. There is a surprise in the centre, from [12]. A line of stamping stilettos marks out the irregular series of downbeat accents: it looks like a playful statement of defiance, and jazzy. Led here by the voices, whose verbal stresses dictate the beginning of each bar, it is De Keersmaeker's reinforcement of this stress that creates the jazz: 2/8, 3/8, 2/8, 4/8, 2/8, 3/8, 4/8, and so on (for the music, see Ex. 5.6). The effect could hardly be more different from Nijinska's, whose dogged worker peasants merely trod an even pulse throughout this section (see pp. 359-60). We see similar stamping-out of principal beats at [56]+4 in Tableau 2, the men's stag party. A group of men around the edge of the space accompany a group of five in the centre, as in a folk dance. Their pattern is as follows:

4/8	6/8	5/8	5/8	5/8	3/8
stamps on counts 1 and 3	1 and 4	1 and 4	1 and 4	1 and 4	1

Tableau 2 is basically about bravado, the male dancers taking on the more acrobatic role, although there is ample opportunity to celebrate the fine rhythmic skills of the musicians. At the start, all the men are in a huddle stage centre except the Groom and his best friend, who engage in a kind of dance competition in front of and around them. The plan for the group is a series of simple steps down into plié on the accents, otherwise up on the toes, starting on the spot, with arms held firmly by their sides. Each limping or triplet pattern is associated with a bar of 3/4, 5/8 or 7/8, which is rather like Robbins's formulaic approach at this point in the score (see Ex. 5.17):

3/4: **1** 3 5 or **1** 2 3 **4** 5 6 (the accents in **bold**)
5/8: **1** 2 3 **4** 5 or **1** 2 3 4 5
7/8: **1** 2 **3** 4 5 **6** 7

It is interesting that, although the structure fits the barring 3/4, 5/8 and 7/8, the dance accent patterns have a good measure of independence, especially given that the music does not necessarily sound as written. For instance, at [27]+4 we are more likely, in retrospect, to hear the principal downbeat on beat 2 rather than on beat 1, because it is here that the opening motif (from [27]) begins again.[172] By going by the look rather than the sound of the score, like Robbins at this point in the music, De Keersmaeker achieves dance autonomy. The same formation and rhythms recur at [44], lending a sense of architecture to the Tableau through restatement. The men also show 2/4 patterns, with a slow 2-count limp step (from [29]) or step and close the feet (at [35]). Then, from [40], occasional 3/8 bar interpolations introduce a quicker quaver beat to a passage that is essentially framed at crotchet rate. The dancers show the change of pattern assiduously wherever it occurs.

As the musical temperature rises, the men start to jump, ragged versions of Nijinska's 'lifting the ground' jumps (see pp. 328, 354), in question-and-answer dialogue with the Groom and his friend (from [47]). Later, their jumps speed up (as in the Nijinska), finally dissolving at [62] into a circle of big jumping runs (again, as in the Nijinska). True to form, De Keersmaeker does not simply reinforce every musical accent in this final passage. Instead, the men decorate their runs with an occasional hop accompanied by a push back of the working leg, the timing of which has nothing to do with the music. Meanwhile, Octors can be seen gaily skipping around the perimeter tables, lost in his own world. His is a very cheeky, secret touch: a 6/8 pattern that matches what you read in the score (for the music, see Ex. 5.8) but actually hear from no part of it, occasionally modified slightly when he stumbles upon a bar of 4/8 or 5/8.

Throughout this Tableau, the concentration of the men is similar to the kind of attention in any social dance. They show the difficulty of holding on to a part accurately, a determination to keep up with colleagues, and also the fun of a nit-picking exercise in rhythmic precision. Even amusingly pedantic, mind-body exercises are transformed into an enjoyable communal enterprise, with games in circles, line dances, processions and so on. Meanwhile, the soloists enjoy their flights of fancy in unregulated manoeuvres, but these are no more interesting than the big group activity.

In Tableau 3, it is a fine touch when De Keersmaeker engineers her opposing groups of men and women into rhythmic counterpoint. She starts to set this up at [70], when the women modify their hip-swinging walks into hip-swinging triplets (3/4 time, to tenor, then soprano and alto voices). When the basses begin a churchy tune at [71]-2 (first heard as the Mother's tenor line at [21]), the men pull themselves together and slow-walk with it in duple time: their own version of the 'mince': step, close, step, close. 'Careful, here, and at 74', reads Octors's rhythm score, 'the bass chorus sing 2/4 over 3/4', and we see this nicely visualised on stage. It is De Keersmaeker's considerable achievement to make such ordinary step patterns look so lively. Watch the Nijinska and you might never 'hear' this bass line the first time round – I did not – but the second time round it is virtually all that you notice. However, if Nijinska takes church very seriously, De Keersmaeker simply cannot stop the fun that she has set in motion.

Putting *Noces* in the context of the whole of De Keersmaeker's *April me*, I now see it as encapsulating in extreme form the duality between control and freedom that is explored elsewhere during the larger work. Perhaps too, in this broader context, her *Noces* reminds us of our ethnicity in the context of many others, and the effects of cultural conditioning and so-called civilisation– both funny and a touch frightening. De Keersmaeker's *Noces* is a centrepiece in more senses than one.

* * *

If we now put De Keersmaeker's *Noces* in the context of the larger tradition led by Nijinska's example, then from a conservative point of view it is all wrong: set to the controversial Pokrovsky, referencing popular culture quite as much as high art, and more fun than serious in tone. But it is hard not to love it. As for the darker theme that was privileged by Nijinska, De Keersmaeker opts to introduce that in the outer sections around her centrepiece rather than during the course of Stravinsky's score, although we might well be anxious about some of the wedding madness and what people at this party do to themselves and each other. Ironically, within the context of the whole work *April me,* if not for *Noces* in the middle, De Keersmaeker is clearly sympathetic to the mixed-genre theatre that Stravinsky himself had in mind.

Yet, in other respects, there are conceptual links with Nijinska's *Noces*, stronger than the Robbins setting demonstrates, structural and choreomusical in kind. There is the sense of architecture through time: however ragged the unisons and formations, and however many the breakout solos, De Keersmaeker draws the larger outlines within each Tableau boldly and rigorously, and she uses formal recapitulations, however brief, to enable legibility. This is the case even in Tableau 4, where she starts to unify her forces later than Nijinska, perhaps because she has programmed more time to calm the spirits after her *Noces* has finished. There is also the same search for symmetry and stability out of radical asymmetry.

But it is the rhythmic life at the most detailed level and the range of devices used to achieve this that constitute one of the most liberating and dramatic statements of both the Nijinska and De Keersmaeker *Noces*. Even in terms of the much more celebrated Nijinska work, this fact has gone largely unrecognised: the excitement of the independent dance voice that led her to refer to her work as a 'choreographic concerto'. Spatial concerns, the constructivist assemblages, the new movement vocabulary and the social critique have all taken precedence in critical commentary. But it is the choreomusical aspects that generate the unassailable force and unleashed (Dionysian) charge, the 'body' in the work, a feature of the music highlighted through dance, triumphant against the implacable bound-ness and facelessness of its protagonists.

As for the description 'homogeneous' that Stravinsky later applied to his music, it works well in relation to the 'impersonal' and 'mechanical' aspects of the work (both music and dance), but has far less regard for its bodily values. As I have argued, it also sat uneasily against his theatrical conception. The Nijinska tradition of production went along with the musical vision but not the theatrical or textual one. Stravinsky, whether through obstinacy or otherwise, simply ignored the conceptual conflict that he had introduced, acknowledged Nijinska's talent and held fast to his original theatrical preferences. Choreographers since have had choices: to side with the composer or to pay homage to the choreographer – and still at the time of Robbins's *Noces* premiere in 1965, it was the composer who usually won – or a bit of both, or to go it alone. In the end, if we look at the complete chronology, most choreographers seem to have applied themselves to *Noces* as a tradition stemming from Nijinska, be it one that for thirty years (1936–66) was about its absence, the loss of the original choreography, rather than its presence. These are issues that *Noces* has in common with *Le Sacre du printemps*. But they are even more pressing in *Sacre*, and still, to this day, as we see in the final chapter, it is this work, a far more abandoned, 'primitive' affair, that exerts the most power of all over choreographers.

6

Le Sacre du printemps: Icon of a Century

Introduction

There can be no doubt: *Le Sacre du printemps* is the dance score of the twentieth century, if not, indeed, of all time – we need only consider the huge number of settings – and its allure for choreographers has remained strong despite the major challenges of the music. At the beginning of the twenty-first century, *Sacre* clearly retains its position as the most popular score; 181 uses have so far been recorded in the 'Stravinsky the Global Dancer' (*SGD*) database. The numbers expand exponentially: there have been over 90 uses since 1990. The reach is global, demonstrated by settings in over thirty countries worldwide and extending to choreographers who normally shun classical music, let alone Stravinsky. It also extends to a handful of choreographers who keep returning to the score, to try their hand at a new *Sacre*, or a new version of an existing *Sacre*, twice (Uwe Scholz), three times (Michael Clark), four times (Javier De Frutos) or even more (Martine Epoque, Royston Maldoom – see pp. 474, 500). Perhaps the oddest phenomenon is the *Sacre* that uses a fragment of the score, or even none of it at all, but which is still about *Sacre*: the score is there by virtue of its absence, as powerful a presence in the mind as in the realisation. But then, as we shall see, one of the outstanding features of the work is the trail of absence and loss associated with it. In this chapter, I examine why this single score has had such a mighty history within dance and consider just some of the many personalities it has assumed as a result of this history, this unrelenting global demand.

Sacre is a special case on all accounts. It is well known to have suffered the most notorious premiere in history (29 May 1913) and, even if the music was then largely inaudible, people could not fail to notice the overthrow of convention in the spasmodic, bound, grounded, in-turned movement vocabulary. The spectre of that premiere still haunts us, as demonstrated by the highly publicised *Riot at the Rite* television dramatisation (2006).[1] Later 1913 performances revealed the revolution in the score. But, by then, the ballet was gone. Nijinsky married only a few months later (September 1913), at which point he was dismissed from the Ballets Russes by Diaghilev, his former lover, and his ballet suppressed; so it received in all just eight performances – five in Paris, and three more in London (plus one invitation-only dress rehearsal).[2] Until the 1987 reconstruction by Millicent Hodson and Kenneth Archer (responsible respectively

for the choreography and the Nicolay Roerich design element), there was nothing left of the ballet except a memory from which a huge mythology developed: it became both twentieth-century icon and monster.

That mythology lies at the root of the huge *Sacre* production tradition, although it is as well to remember that, for a time, there was little to challenge the force of the original production as memory. The *Sacre* production tradition developed slowly. The First World War curtailed much artistic activity. The piano score was published in 1913, but the orchestral score not until 1921, before then being available only to Pierre Monteux, who conducted the 1913 premiere, and to Sergey Koussevitzky, who conducted the score in Russia (in early 1914) and was also its publisher (at Edition Russe). Diaghilev commissioned Massine to create a second choreography in 1920 (reusing the original Roerich designs; that production continued in the Ballets Russes repertory 1920–24, 1928–9, with 23 performances in total), and then the next setting was by Lasar Galpern in Cologne in 1930. The concert premiere in 1914 proved an outstanding success, but only sporadic concert performances ensued. Walsh claims that, despite its huge notoriety, relatively few had actually heard the score and fewer still had become fully acquainted with it before Leopold Stokowski brought out his dazzling Philadelphia Orchestra recording in 1930.[3] The score was hard to perform and there was concern about further scandal.[4] After that, even though *Sacre* rapidly became a musical classic, its course was still not always without hurdles, and choreographic productions were for a while far fewer than those of *Firebird* and *Petrushka*; just 6 are cited in the database before 1939, as compared with 18 of *Firebird* and 28 of *Petrushka*. In Germany, the score was considered particularly dangerous by the emerging right wing in the 1930s, and thus singled out like *Histoire du soldat* from Stravinsky's other work; it was not performed there at all from 1934 until the end of the Nazi period.[5] On the other hand, the monstrous programme and history behind the *Sacre* score could be useful for marketing. Still, in 1935, for instance, *Time Magazine* in the USA would excite readers with the fear of the music as 'a threat' against institutions, standing for 'all the unnameable horrors of revolutions, murder and rapine'.[6]

Sacre is by far the best-documented score in the *SGD* database, because of the groundwork already carried out by other scholars. Joan Acocella, Lynn Garafola and Jonnie Greene undertook documentation of all productions created up to 1991 (71 choreographers named), with premiere information in their *catalogue raisonné* in *Ballet Review* supplemented by references to literature and visual sources.[7] Since then, Ada d'Adamo has updated their catalogue.[8] Shelley Berg[9] and d'Adamo have both written seminal books comparing numerous productions, and Susan Manning[10] has undertaken a thorough survey of the German *Sacre* tradition. Thus, it has been possible to annotate an unusually high proportion of *Sacre* productions in the database, and to synthesise trends as regards type of setting. The database also holds information on different versions of the score, arrangements of various kinds that are not by the hand of Stravinsky. Those settings to the piano score for four hands, which was the original rehearsal score for Nijinsky's ballet, are found under a separate score heading, and demonstrate a marked increase in popularity in recent years, representing 7 out of the total of 12 documented settings since 2002.

Once the production tradition gets underway and increases in momentum, the database reveals to us a remarkable array of genres: the styles of American and European modern dance, physical theatre, Tanztheater and postmodern Butoh, African dance, Salsa, indeed any number of anti-grace, grounded movement vocabularies, as well as stylistic mixes incorporating ballet (very occasionally pointe work). There have been contemporary as well as historical settings, and a range of cultural contexts. *Sacre* was Stravinsky's prime non-ballet score – we might even call it his modern dance score – with a far larger proportion of non-balletic treatments than any other, which the style of the music itself suggests. Even choreographers from a ballet background have tended to draw from other stylistic sources. In the article accompanying their *Ballet Review* catalogue, Acocella et al. suggest that opera house ballet companies have been grateful for the opportunities that the score presented:

> Under the protective Great-Art mantle of the score, they were permitted, briefly, to lay aside aerialism and give themselves over to heaviness – to the realities of weight and breathing, to graceless postures, to sexual subject matter.[11]

Yet, although it undoubtedly helped market the ballet (or dance), it was not only the Great-Art mantle of the score that appealed to choreographers, but also its dance history aspects, the dance mythology stapled to it – after all, the score was conceived as a ballet. In this respect, Acocella et al. suggest, *Sacre* is a series of 'ideas' if not an actual ballet.[12] These 'ideas' created a challenge that choreographers have both feared and needed to take on, being about the ballet itself as much as about the circumstances associated with it. Reassessment of Nijinsky began in the 1970s with the publication of Richard Buckle's biography and Lincoln Kirstein's *Nijinsky Dancing*,[13] continuing in the 1980s with the 1989 *L'Après-midi d'un faune* as well as *Sacre* reconstruction. It has only fuelled the fascination with 'his' score. There is also the issue of legacy. Testimony to the latter was the 1999 Netherlands Springdance project commissioning a number of artists to create a short work: not another *Sacre*, but nevertheless something inspired by what *Sacre* has come to represent over time, up to the moment of the millennium. Here, it is seen as a revolutionary artistic statement, and the message is positive:

Sacred Solos: *Le Sacre du printemps*; a search for freedom and a new beginning, advocating individual expression uncompromised by society's conventions ... This influence still lingers ...[14]

Tendering darker proposals than the Netherlands Springdance project, Acocella et al. list the 'collection of ideas' associated with *Sacre* as an inheritance from the nineteenth century. They encourage us to see the ballet as referring backwards in time, even to classical ballet itself, and not simply as herald of new developments within twentieth-century modernism or as a symbol of the new machine age in its evocation of what T.S. Eliot called the 'barbaric noises of modern life' (see pp. 104-5).[15] So there is primitivism – 'those things that are least socialized, least civilized – children, peasants, "savages", raw emotion, plain speech – that are closest to truth'; biologism – 'the belief that life is fundamentally its physical facts: birth, death, survival'; sex, and 'the violence with which that force can erupt into life'; apocalyptic beliefs of the turn of the century – 'that Western humanistic culture was coming to an end, combined with a wish that it would come to an end, preferably in a great, orgiastic conflagration;' and of course female sacrifice (a topic that had been important in nineteenth-century ballets such as *Giselle* and *La Sylphide)*.[16] Such ideas in the air in 1913 reflected common concerns across Europe to mend the rift with nature after the problems posed by industrialisation, but also a new image of the primitive, nature and the body as untamed.

At the time of its premiere, the vision through the lens of *Sacre* was predominantly stark. The Russian ballet critic André Levinson summed up the ballet as 'an icy comedy of primeval hysteria'.[17] Unusual for his illuminating and detailed debate of both music and dance, the contemporary French critic Jacques Rivière expanded upon the totally new sociological and biological statement with a compelling account of its lack of moral purpose or compassion. He described a vision of man dominated by something 'more inert, more opaque, more fettered than himself,' a larger society representing a 'terrible indifference', a sea of faces bearing no trace of individuality. He went on:

There is something profoundly blind about this dance ... These beings pose an enormous question. They carry it with them without understanding it, like an animal turning in its cage and never tiring of butting its brow against the bars ... How far away from humanity I was![18]

In his celebrated book *Rites of Spring: The Great War and the Birth of the Modern Age*, the cultural historian Modris Eksteins sees *Sacre* as symptomatic of the origins and catastrophic event of the First World War. Whereas Theodor Adorno linked Stravinsky's music, and especially *Sacre*, to the ethos of Nazism (see p. 98),

Ekstein perceived that the work already held strong resonances in the contemporary German psyche – Germany, 'the modernist nation par excellence' – that led to the 1914–18 war.[19] Audiences could be thrilled by the power and energy of the spectacle as much as shocked by its statement, and that duality, that ambiguity in the work (and also the contradiction between forces of life and death contained within the work) has been the source of fascination ever since its premiere. Furthermore, as much as *Sacre* has also come to speak of freedom and a more positive 'new beginning', that resonance with war has surely connected with the various social and political realities of new *Sacre* choreographers ever since.

The metaphor of sacrifice widened its embrace beyond the original scenario. Choreographers over the century could hardly escape the huge sense of loss to which the circumstances of the premiere gave rise – the sacrifice of the ballet that the public could not appreciate, of the dancers struggling to learn it and perform it in riot conditions, and of the genius choreographer, the supreme ballet revolutionary, misunderstood and abandoned (unlike his composer), and soon to be diagnosed as schizophrenic, signalling the end of his career.

Taking the *Ballet Review* article as my starting point, I propose to illustrate how this 'collection of ideas' infiltrated *Sacre* settings over the century, to indicate further resonances between the original and later versions. At the same time, I do not forget that choreographers still want to make *Sacre* contemporary, drawing from their own experience and finding contemporary significance in its over-arching theme of sacrifice. As the French choreographer Régis Obadia put it in 2003, 'you must get in there and concentrate your vision in order not to be swallowed up by the past, this piece makes you battle with yourself ...'[20]

So what role within the *Sacre* tradition did the 1987 reconstruction play? Certainly, it was big news when it appeared on the Joffrey Ballet in New York, a staging that was televised in 1989.[21] Since then, it has been revived for nine other companies around the world.[22] The Finnish National Ballet, with Zenaida Yanowsky of the Royal Ballet as the Chosen One, danced it in the 2006 *Riot at the Rite* dramatisation. At a conference in New York linked to the premiere in 1987, the philosopher Francis Sparshott mused as to whether, after the return of the 'original', choreographers would still want to create new *Sacres*, and, if so, whether they would now make new versions in relation to a reconstructed 'authentic original', initiating an alternative production tradition.[23] Twenty years later, in August 2007, Yvonne Rainer premiered her 're-vision' of Nijinsky's *Sacre* called *RoS Indexical* (see p. 249), incorporating fragments from the BBC *Riot at the Rite* film of the dance as well as integrating audience reaction from its soundtrack. Yet nothing in principle has changed, rather, increasing numbers of choreographers have been inspired to enter the fray, such as Molissa Fenley, who, moved by the Joffrey production, immediately bought herself a recording with which to begin her own solo choreography (1988 – see p. 476). Referring to the power of the *Sacre* legacy, she remembers that 'the making of the ballet entailed the most visionary feelings I've ever had. I seemed literally to be possessed [Nijinsky and Stravinsky cited as studio presences] throughout the entire time I was creating it.'[24]

What we can perceive as a new phenomenon, however, and one unique to Stravinsky, is the historical slant on *Sacre* as a whole tradition of productions with the score as the main element of continuity, an engine of renewal – permanent regeneration. That is how new choreographers approach their task, and how historians now approach a new production. They reflect less upon a notional original, and more upon a whole history of production, which is a far weightier cause. Hints of it, this new concept of *Sacre*, had emerged earlier, and were undoubtedly fuelled by the reconstruction, after which signal events include: the New York conference (1987); the Acocella et al. chronology (1992); the 1993 film *Les Printemps du Sacre* (featuring, as well as the Nijinsky, five other productions by celebrated choreographers – Mary Wigman (1957), Maurice Béjart (1959), Pina Bausch (1975), Martha Graham (1984) and Mats Ek (1984));[25] a Study Day in May 2002 at Sadler's Wells Theatre (on the occasion of the London premiere of Angelin Preljocaj's *Sacre*, with Hodson as a speaker); and a *Sacre* marathon in Rouen in November 2005 (see pp. 502-3).

There seems to be no strong evidence of an alternative *Sacre* tradition commenting on or relating directly to the 'authentic original'. Do choreographers believe in the reconstruction, or that such a thing is even possible? Rather, are they impressed by what they see? Are the mythologies and fantasies about creation and tradition more exciting, in other words, the primary authenticity?

One thing is certain: the barely programmatic nature of the musical writing has something to do with the number and range of choreographers attracted to it. The published score bears the following series of sub-titles for individual Scenes, but these should not imply that the music tells a story through its 'gestures', in the conventional manner of ballet music:

Part 1 Adoration of the Earth
Introduction
The Augurs of Spring [and] Dances of the Young Girls
Ritual of Abduction
Spring Rounds
Ritual of the Rival Tribes
Procession of the Sage
The Sage
Dance of the Earth

Part 2 The Sacrifice
Introduction
Mystic Circles of the Young Girls
Glorification of the Chosen One
Evocation of the Ancestors
Ritual Action of the Ancestors
Sacrificial Dance (The Chosen One)

Compared with traditional ballet scores, *Firebird* and *Petrushka* included, *Sacre* is open to a wide range of treatments and 'stories', and choreographers were not tied down to passages clearly demarcated for action and mime. Working from evidence that supports Hodson's reconstruction, the 300-year-old woman's early exclamations in Augurs of Spring (at [15], and bars 4, 6 and 7 after [16]), the faltering and kiss of the Earth by the Sage (from [71]) and the selection of the Chosen One (from [102]-1 to [104]) are still occasions of a programmatic kind. Nevertheless, they are merely fragments that barely stop the flow of musical events and can easily be integrated into other kinds of story or, indeed, non-story setting. This aspect of the score was also key to its progress through musicological history, which differs considerably from its dance history. I will now touch on these musicological aspects, because they contribute to my analytical procedures in this chapter. They also go hand in hand with Stravinsky's own developing philosophy of art and changing views on *Sacre*.

Among musicologists, there was a drive to forget the initial conception of the score as a piece for dance. By the 1920s, Stravinsky was already erasing the theatrical past of his score, proclaiming that it was primarily 'an architectonic rather than anecdotal work';[26] later, he was categorical: 'I prefer *Le Sacre* as a concert piece.'[27] Richard Taruskin has linked this propaganda with Stravinsky's developing conservatism – his move from extreme left modernism to the extreme right[28] – and the formalist philosophy famously encapsulated in the composer's *Autobiography:* 'Music is, by its very nature, essentially powerless to express anything at all' (see p. 4).[29] But, specifically in terms of *Sacre*, Taruskin felt that Stravinsky wanted, in the interests of personal gain, to sanitise the work, to conceal its monstrous content or 'prehuman or sub-human reality'[30] (characteristics resonating with the rise of nationalist politics), and to align the work, and himself, within the modernist, formalist, Anglo-American tradition of musicology. But there are other possible reasons. It is painful to admit that the composer was probably made uncomfortable by the implied association with a 'mad' choreographer, and would also have wanted to make the score wholesome for countries where it was considered not merely notorious, but politically dangerous, as in Germany in the 1930s. We could see his reaction too as the result of the disastrous ballet premiere, the poor critical reception that he wanted to forget and the dropping of the ballet from the repertoire. Whatever the case, the upshot of Stravinsky's various statements was the dictum that discussion of the score should concentrate on structure and technical innovation rather than content and context.

So Stravinsky turned his back on the score as a vehicle for choreography and, by doing so, boosted the formalist tradition of musicology. At the same time, his preferences for dance moved far away from Nijinsky's experimentalism towards the tradition of the *danse d'école*, the Petipa tradition that he saw exemplified in the work of Balanchine and that amply met his new criteria for control and order. Taruskin demonstrates that twentieth-century musicology eagerly followed Stravinsky in the move towards decontextualisation of his music, theorising his work according to the tradition of the new, and in terms of musical-technical innovation. After a noisy beginning, the dance content was forgotten, dance and musical traditions went their separate ways, and the reputation of *Sacre* as a purely musical work achieved mythic proportions (of a different kind from within dance) amongst music scholars. For many, it is the crowning symbol of the last century's avant-garde. Taruskin has been of seminal importance in the rereading of Stravinsky's *Sacre* against this formalist tradition, returning to roots and meaning, and acknowledging the dance scholarship (the *Ballet Review* article) that supports his cause.

Yet some of the formalist musical-analytical discourse opens doors for choreomusical analysis, and it would be foolish indeed not to take advantage of its discoveries. How, then, to deal with all that musical literature on *Sacre*, more perhaps than on any other work? I had to make choices. I have concentrated on the analysis that has embraced rhythmic structure and structure-through-time as central concerns, rather than the mass of work focusing on pitch content: for instance, Allen Forte's monograph (1978) on *Sacre*,[31] which concentrates on detailed harmonic organisation, drawing from set theory. The rhythmic-structural theory has already been outlined in Chapter 2 (pp. 88-92), where it served to ground responses to the physicality of Stravinsky's music, and in Chapter 5, as part of the analysis of *Les Noces*. It uses Pieter van den Toorn's dual typology based on metrical irregularity and regularity, both types static in terms of registral and instrumental content, and working within a larger structure of interdependent or discrete blocks.[32] Type I (irregularity) is the most common approach in *Sacre*, but there are several very prominent Type II examples: Augurs of Spring, Spring Rounds, Ritual of the Rival Tribes (its latter part leading into Procession of the Sage), Dance of the Earth and Ritual Action of the Ancestors. With its premise of violent, primitive ritual, making a human sacrifice happen, it is not surprising that there is more extensive, plain repetition and accumulation of energy through repetition than in *Noces*. Van den Toorn's vision intersects with Taruskin's three style principles taken from the Russian musical/

critical tradition, his strategy being to link *Sacre* to its past rather than to any modernist present: immobility (*nepodvizhnost'*, stasis, non-development), sum-of-parts (*drobnost'*, discontinuity or disunification [using the block structure principle]) and simplification (*uproshcheniye*, a stripping-down of means).[33]

It was inevitable that I should examine Pierre Boulez's seminal *Sacre* analysis (1953, revised 1966), in which he claims that the score contains an independent rhythmic structure.[34] Here is a thorough, crystal-clear presentation of arithmetical relationships, the measuring of the number of beats within discrete rhythmic cells, with the labelling of even- and odd-number divisions as rational and irrational, the exposure of retrogrades, changes in pattern or lack of change (mobility and immobility), symmetries, asymmetries and balanced asymmetries. I have drawn occasionally from Boulez's cellular analysis – it is especially useful in demonstrating rhythmic irregularity, but, for choreomusical purposes, it is often more detailed than is appropriate for dance, which tends to operate with larger rhythms and longer individual 'events' than in music (events as individual moves or notes).[35] Besides, I cannot readily hear or feel the music in the manner of the Boulez analysis and have found no evidence that any *Sacre* choreographer has done so either. His work amply demonstrates balance, variety, unity and design, but not the progress of the work. Nor does his formal analysis resonate with any notion of meaning, which is a dimension that I want to include in my analyses.

On the other hand, van den Toorn's book on *Sacre* includes writing on rhythm that is directly useful to my work and does make sense to a dance analyst. He deals with meaning, be it in a somewhat cursory manner (and his analytical language has nothing like the drama of Taruskin's), but, for my *Sacre* project, the real strength of his writing lies in its rationalisation of the energy and continuity of music. He addresses how we actually experience rhythm through time, which I would read as processes of cognitive psychology, as well as learning and education in listening to music. Alongside his typology of rhythmic structure, his analysis of how we perceive metre is especially important to choreomusical discussion of *Sacre*.[36] Van den Toorn understands that we hold patterns, regularities within us, so that we sense disruptions as significant contributing factors to the energy and vitality within Stravinsky's music. Concomitantly, we also seek stability when the music is unstable. I contend that we experience these metrical regularities and irregularities in choreography as much as in music, and that in some *Sacres* (just as in *Noces*) they are a key point of contact between the two media, although I am less ready than van den Toorn to feel regularity as an underlying continuity behind lengthy passages of considerable irregularity (see p. 338).[37] This kind of analysis links readily to a discussion of meaning, particularly to an enquiry into the anxieties raised in possibly every *Sacre* that I know.

Likewise, I especially appreciate the energy within the analysis of Peter Hill (2000), a professional pianist who knows the music from embodiment of the piano reduction.[38] The strength of his book lies not in theoretical depth, but in his persuasive, vivid presentation of how he hears the work through his ears and in his body. In quite a different way from van den Toorn, he describes the progress and drama of the work and his understanding of it as it unfolds through time. This is refreshing and useful to a choreomusical context. As Walsh indicates in his review of Hill's book:

> [Music] analysts tend to look at music as segments of score that are static before their eyes, but performers [and I might add here choreographers too] have always to consider the way that music reaches the ears in time, and *The Rite of Spring* has come down to us, after all, as a concert work with a beginning, a middle and an end and internal continuities that sustain it through the not inconsiderable lapse of more than half-an-hour on the clock.[39]

During the course of my detailed analyses, I also speculate on how choreographers who do not necessarily read music, or at least all the bar-lines and time signatures, seem to hear it as people, not as musicologists – and in this respect, I look at their similarities of approach as well as their differences. *Sacre* choreographers have been largely unaware of Stravinsky's own views and of the views of all those musicologists who wrote in his wake, and many of them have not even conceived of their work in terms of the Scene divisions and titles in the score. But, for ease of comparison and precision in locating moments in the dances described, the musical score titles will be used (alongside score cue points) throughout this chapter.

Vaslav Nijinsky and Leonid Massine: One score puzzle and two early Sacres

The 1987 reconstruction of Nijinsky's *Sacre* on the Joffrey Ballet, New York, is now one of the most widely known settings of the score. Yet there are still questions about how exactly Nijinsky heard Stravinsky's music in terms of theatre and about what his piece really was as a choreomusical entity. Some of the most intriguing questions arise from a four-hand piano score that supposedly contains Stravinsky's choreographic instructions to Nijinsky. The score was sold at Sotheby's in 1967 and then returned to the composer, who promptly summarised the annotations for publication alongside his *Sacre* sketches.[40] Although Stravinsky's published notes on the score have been carefully studied by scholars, the piano score itself, which is housed in the Basle Stravinsky archive, is far less well known.[41] As we shall see, it tells a different story from the published notes, and provokes speculation about the real course of its history. Briefly, in terms of its whereabouts before Stravinsky saw it again in the 1960s: it was given to Diaghilev's patron Misia Sert the day after the premiere – there is a dedication to her on the title page of the score – and returned by her to Diaghilev before Massine's 1920 premiere (apparently to be sold to make money for the new venture). Some time afterwards, and before the Sotheby's auction, it was in the hands of the dancer Anton Dolin, whose name appears on the inside front cover.[42]

As to Stravinsky's opinion of Nijinsky, the rediscovery of the piano score in 1967 and the composer's excitement over this event seem to have marked the turning of the tide. There is the evidence of a remark conveyed by the Bolshoi choreographer Yuri Grigorovitch to Marie Rambert in 1969, that Stravinsky 'had since admitted that it [Nijinsky's choreography] was by far the best rendering of his *Sacre*'.[43] There is also his annotation in Irina Vershinina's 1967 book on his early ballets: she claimed that it was unfair to say that the ballet premiere had been a failure, and Stravinsky added emphatically 'totally [unfair]'.[44]

We need to backtrack through the twists and turns in this sad story. There were the famous rows during the London rehearsals in February 1913, when Stravinsky stamped and banged his fists on the piano, complained about the slow tempi, and without justification treated Nijinsky as if he had no musical sense whatsoever.[45] However, the composer's view of Nijinsky's work at the time of the premiere and in the ensuing months was totally positive, and, in fact, as his *L'Après-midi d'un faune* (1912, Debussy) and his notations of the work demonstrate, Nijinsky was musically very able. He had studied piano at the Imperial Ballet School in St Petersburg and, according to his sister Bronislava Nijinska, 'could play any musical instrument that he came across ... [and] hold perfectly in his memory a piece of music he had heard only a few times'.[46] Stravinsky wrote to his friend the composer Maximilien Steinberg that Nijinsky's *Sacre* choreography was 'incomparable'.[47] He disagreed with an interviewer who considered the choreography alien to the music: 'Nijinsky is an admirable artist ... He is capable of renewing ballet as an art.'[48] Regretting Nijinsky's impending departure from the Diaghilev company, he wrote to Benois: 'The possibility has gone for some time of seeing anything valuable in the field of dance.'[49]

Stravinsky's opinion began to change in 1920 at the time of the Massine version of *Sacre*, when Nijinsky's mental deterioration was widely known, and when it was convenient for the composer to publicise a new version as being better than the original. Now too he could claim that the new version fitted his own new 'architectural', concert reading of his music. Massine

understood it in the spirit of its conception ... Hearing it in concert performance enlightened Massine and, I must confess, also enlightened me as to the new scenic possibilities of my score.

Massine ... from his first hearing, recognised that my music, far from being descriptive, was an 'objective construction'.[50]

But the real damage began with the publication of Stravinsky's *Autobiography* in 1936, when he wrote:

the idea of working with Nijinsky filled me with misgiving ... his ignorance of the most elementary notions of music was flagrant ... What the choreography expressed was a very laboured and barren effort ... [on slowing down the music in order to allow complicated steps] I have never known any [choreographers] who have erred in that respect to the same degree as Nijinsky.[51]

It turned out that Stravinsky's comments about Nijinsky were more disparaging than about anyone else cited in the *Autobiography*. His opinion, probably more than anyone's, fuelled the public doubt about Nijinsky's creative ability (shared by many in the music world) that lasted for years.

As one of her main reconstruction sources, Hodson used Stravinsky's published notes on the Basle piano score, but not the piano score itself, which was only made available to her by Robert Craft after the premiere of her reconstruction in 1987. She also had access to Rambert's copy of the score, upon which, six months after the 1913 premiere, Rambert had written notes based on what Nijinsky had said to her in rehearsals. Dalcroze-trained (see pp. 83, 375), Rambert had been enlisted to help Nijinsky analyse and work with this complex music, and she also danced in his *Sacre*. To supplement these two main score sources, there were five pastels and seventy pencil sketches of moments through the course of the ballet by the artist Valentine Gross, taken from the series of Paris performances; also interviews, memoirs and the reviews of critics writing in Paris and London, who documented images and moments recalled, as well as their opinions. For the Sacrificial Dance, there was a 1967 letter from Nijinska (who was to have been the original Chosen One, but pregnancy prevented this) to the Russian ballet historian Vera Krassovskaya, documenting in great detail the sequence of movement that Nijinsky had made on her, and which was completed for the premiere Chosen One, Maria Piltz.[52] Hodson had to make many difficult decisions when faced with conflicting sources, as well as fill in gaps where information was lacking. This was a fascinating, highly detailed research exercise, a formidable achievement in piecing together countless fragments of information into a whole. About the annotations in the piano score, when she finally saw them, Hodson was clear: 'I found nothing that would have persuaded me to change any details in the reconstruction for the Joffrey Ballet';[53] then in

1996, in the preface to *Nijinsky's Crime Against Grace*, her reconstruction score of *Sacre*: 'they did not alter the information already available'.[54] Hodson's reconstruction score includes a facsimile of Rambert's piano score (with her notes in Russian and in English translation), as well as information from the Stravinsky sources, mostly from his published notes.[55]

The choreographic authenticity of the Hodson and Archer reconstruction, which is now billed as 'after Nijinsky', has already been much discussed and disputed, and I admit that I tend now to the side of the sceptics, although it is highly unlikely that there is any more dance evidence to get us closer to Nijinsky. Hodson and Archer claim that they have 85 per cent of the original *Sacre* in their reconstruction.[56] But art is far too complex to be reduced to percentages and, in this instance, the bulk of the evidence was visual and static, or derived from words and rhythms plotted on a musical score. As the critic Joan Acocella rightly asks, 'How can dance be derived from non-dance evidence?'[57] Even though Nijinska's description of the Sacrificial Dance was exceptionally detailed, it is still not equivalent to dance notation. There is probably an inestimable amount of movement missing that no one will ever get hold of, far less real dance substance than the musical substance of composers' sketches (and their other writing as stylistic model) that has validated the recent reconstruction of works such as Elgar's *Symphony No. 3*. The reconstruction more accurately represents Hodson's undoubted skill and vision as a choreographer inspired by her detailed research into source material.

But the *Sacre* reconstruction certainly raises fascinating musical questions, especially when placed alongside the piano score, and fully justifies analysis from the choreomusical point of view. It is also very popular. Viewing the live event, it would be hard not to be thrilled by the pounding mass of almost fifty performers, the unique introverted and tormented style of their body movement, the contrapuntal group textures, formations and asymmetrical spatial methodology, all wholly innovative for 1913, and the exquisite, radiant Roerich designs (far more readily retrievable than any movement). My main analytical source is the 1989 television recording of the Joffrey Ballet performance, backed up by the dramatisation *Riot at the Rite*, although the latter performance is frequently disrupted by cuts in and out to show the reactions of those watching the 1913 premiere.[58]

Certainly, the overall impression is of choreography that operates very closely to musical detail. When the musical pulse is very clear, we always see it too in the dance, and naturally this is a major contributing factor towards the ritualistic content of the work, where it is customary to think of power being gained through rhythmic repetition. But beyond this, accent patterns and motif organisation are revealed insistently. The famous syncopations of Augurs of Spring (from [13]), made doubly famous as volcanic eruptions in Walt Disney's *Fantasia* (1940), are seen in upper-body and arm gestures differently allocated across the

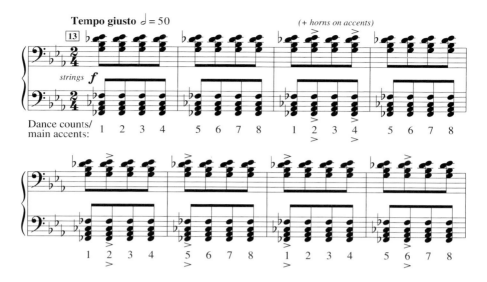

Ex. 6.1. *Le Sacre du printemps*, The Augurs of Spring (Hodson/Nijinsky).

group of men. Their turned-in jumps articulate all eight counts (two bars of four quavers read together as one hypermeasure – see p. 15) and accent the downbeats of each bar, 1 and 5, which are what Stravinsky called in his published notes the 'tonic' accents.[59] The more strongly accented upper-body gestures match the syncopated musical accents precisely (see Ex. 6.1).

Soon the woodwind and brass shriek, and the 300-year-old woman jumps; the bassoons chug and she shuffles and wags her head and arms to and fro. Later, when the irregular series of accents notated in Ex. 6.1 is repeated (called a 'rhythmic' or 'accent theme' by Boulez),[60] the women stamp it out (from [30]+3), and then the other groups show it in gestures and body shifts as they rise from crouching. Later still, the full ensemble perform a fragment of it, punching the air several times at the high-energy conclusion ([34]+4, [35]+4).

Movement motifs are frequently pinned to musical ideas – as in the Glorification, most strikingly a jump to each big whiplash accent in the music (preparation on 1, up on 2 3, land 1 2 – Rambert's counts) and, to the oom-pah pattern that follows, rhythmically matching skipping steps (counted 1 and 2 and etc.) with crouched-over bodies forcing the energy into the earth (see Ex. 6.2). In the Sacrificial Dance, the opening signature material (after the introductory pause bar) is marked by three jumps, up in the air on three consecutive repeating off-the-downbeat chords (see Ill. 16), then, during the tail of three semiquavers that follows, a twist to the right and plié with the arms curving upwards and an arch

Ex. 6.2. *Le Sacre du printemps,* Glorification of the Chosen One, with Marie Rambert's dance counts (Hodson/Nijinsky).

Ill. 16. Yulia Makhalina as the Chosen One in *Le Sacre du printemps*, Sacrificial Dance, reconstruction of Vaslav Nijinsky choreography by Millicent Hodson, Kirov Ballet.

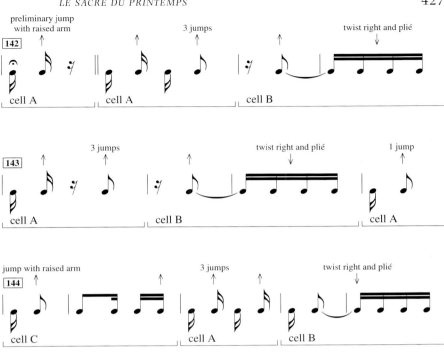

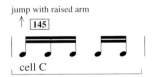

Ex. 6.3. *Le Sacre du printemps*, opening, Sacrificial Dance, diagram of musical cell structure (Boulez) in relation to the Hodson/Nijinsky choreography.

of the torso. The material combines Boulez's cells A and B (see Exs. 6.3 and 2.3a, p. 90).[61] Every time we hear the motif, we see the same movement, give or take a couple of arm variations, with more or fewer jumps depending on the number of repeating chords and minor rhythmic variations in performance. The opening occurrences fit a barring scheme shifting between 3/16, 4/16 and 5/16 (according to the original barring that Nijinsky would have known). Now and again there is a 5-note musical cluster (approximating Boulez's cell C), which is always visualised as a big jump with the right arm shooting up and the body bending side to side, articulating the notes.[62] That familiar opening musical material, which extends into a block of 29 bars, static in registral content but mobile in rhythmic construction, returns three more times in the Sacrificial Dance. The penultimate occurrence is in highly truncated form, the last a modification ('Coda') of the original. I draw the division into structural units from Boulez.[63] The structure is a kind of rondo, but not a straightforward one:

Refrain: Opening passage (based on D) [142]–[149]
Verse 1:   Pedal repeating chords [149]–[167]
Refrain: Repeat (based on C sharp) [167]–[174]
Verse 2:   [174]–[186], divided in the middle by a short reminiscence of the
                Refrain [180]–[181]
Coda Refrain: (based on 'dominant' A): [186] first part; [192] second part, the
                parts defined by cellular structure

The choreographic construction is highly schematic, matching the musical signature material wherever it appears, except when it changes radically (from [192]). Yet it hardly reflects the significant changes in energy and drama in the music: the repeat down a notch (one semitone from D to C sharp), then the ratch up in pitch (to the 'dominant' A), adding tension and renewing energy, a sharpened inflection rather than a restatement of what we hear at the beginning of this final dance. As Hill describes it, the repeat one semitone down at [167] is

a neat solution to Stravinsky's long-term strategy ... a further section at this point in the 'tonic' would rob later climaxes of their force ... [The next flashback, at [174]] is another move in Stravinsky's endgame: it is both a caesura – a momentary catching of the breath from which the storm resumes with even greater fury – and a 'window' which renews contact with the opening music of the 'Sacrificial Dance'. ... [For the last repeat, at [186]] the music suddenly becomes taut, expectant, purposeful – 'vertical', not linear ... now segmented into a pair of short cells.

Then after a 'pinnacle of tension', there is resolution on to a D-centred chord.[64] The choreographic reconstruction seems to stabilise, to iron out such musical effects, although, in theory, the solo dancer could shape her performance to initiate change and build tension through repetition, as a resistance to structured containment, even as critical opposition.[65]

Far less frequently, but nevertheless striking in its coincidence when it does occur, the dancers literally walk or run the pattern of a melody line: each note of the gentle woodwind melody (accompanied by soft trills) that begins and ends Spring Rounds; the short–long and short–short–long of the melody in Mystic Circles of the Young Girls ([100] to [102]-1); and many of the very quick quavers in the Ritual of Abduction.[66] The choreography also proceeds as a series of blocks of material, usually marking changes in musical material and orchestration – for instance, as statement and answer between the asymmetrical groups of men and women (in Ritual of Abduction and the early part of Ritual of the Rival Tribes) – with the dance conventions of gendered musical style and orchestration usually respected, but sometimes as an independent choreographic construction (as in Spring Rounds – see pp. 436-8).

Many of the choreographic principles reflect musical principles. There is the clearly articulated pulse, often staccato, end-stopped in the arms or torso, sometimes to almost robotic effect. But this also reflects the qualities of arrested motion, energy pulled back into the body and machine precision that the critic Rivière perceived.[67] Movement units are brief – a few steps, a couple of jumps – and they usually form simple repeating patterns. Stravinsky demonstrates the same principle of construction, although more sophisticated means of expansion and abbreviation. It is interesting that the identification of dance with musical material leads to a more fragmented composite than the music alone suggests. To take an extreme example, walking on every note seems to separate the notes, to exaggerate their distinction rather than their grouping into a single flowing phrase.

From time to time, Hodson varies her approach, with a brief freeze, a patch of slow-motion combat before the Sage enters, the simulated chaos of over forty simultaneous solos in the Dance of the Earth, or a touch of rhythmic counterpoint (usually suggested by Stravinsky's published notes) where the choreography holds on to an autonomous accent pattern. An especially fine section is Mystic Circles; there is a passage here of highly complex rhythmic counterpoint, a rarity in the reconstruction, that leads to something larger than its constituent parts. The women in their concentric circles sometimes respond to the entry of an instrumental group, but operate in independent rhythmic systems. They dance in units of 5, 3 and 2 counts (from [93]+5 to [97]). The initial flute melody creates the impression of 5/4, or 5-count metre; the accompanying strings are organised in 3/4, or 3-count units. The piano score and Stravinsky's published notes simply indicate 2- and 5-count dance units, without further choreographic detail: there is no mention at all of 3-count units at this point. So it was Hodson's decision to incorporate this extra rhythmic line, perhaps prompted by the pattern in the strings. After a while, Hodson develops her choreography independently of both the sound and look of the score. There are canons and several lines of dance polyphony, arms shooting up at different times across the musical legato in a criss-cross of accents. The multiple strands and constant shifting within the texture create continuity. Detail accumulates into larger-scale motion, and the choreography blooms wonderfully.

But then, a question arises: what kind of choreomusical counterpoint did Nijinsky's choreography include, if any? Was there anything as sophisticated as in Hodson's Mystic Circles? The overwhelming emphasis of observers at the time was on how close the choreography was to the music. This was Stravinsky's line when making comparisons with the Massine version: Nijinsky's work was 'subjected to the tyranny of the bar'.[68] But there are countless other examples – Jean Cocteau, for instance:

> The fault lay in the parallelism of the music and the movements, in their lack of *play*, of counterpoint. Here we had the proof that the same chord often repeated tires the ear less than the frequent repetition of the same gesture tires the eye.[69]

The critic André Levinson perceived the domination of rhythm in the piece as a negative sign, showing the Dalcroze influence. He observed the devices of 'walking the notes' and 'syncopating', and that the *Sacre* dancers

> embody the relative length and force of the sound and the acceleration and slowing of the tempo in the schematic gymnastics of their movement: they bend and straighten their knees, raise and lower their heels, stamp in place, forcefully beating out the accented notes. This is the whole standard pedagogical arsenal of teaching rhythmic gymnastics according to the Jaques–Dalcroze system.[70]

Nijinska remembered following the 'breath' of the music when learning the Sacrificial Dance – in other words, still relating her movement closely to the music, although not counting it in beats as Nijinsky did later, after Rambert's arrival.[71] Some critics noticed other links in *Sacre* between orchestration and the costume colour and arrangement of dancers. For instance, Propert:

> The scarlet groups would instantly dominate the stage in some passage of horns and trumpets, while violins or flutes carried the sense of white or grey ...[72]

The *Times* critic H. Colles commented on the transition passage between the Ritual of Abduction and Spring Rounds:

> the dancers thin out into a straggling line, while the orchestra dwindles to a trill on the flutes; then a little tune begins in the woodwind two octaves apart, and two groups of three people detach themselves from either end of the line to begin a little dance that exactly suits the music.[73]

Emile Vuillermoz made the interesting observation that the Dalcroze approach sometimes meant responding to the look of the score, the underlying metrical structure of strong beats of the bar, which contemporary music often suppressed from hearing through syncopation. The Dalcroze approach thereby contradicted the surface rhythms actually heard:

> When will people realise that Dalcroze students receive a special 'metrical' training? Their aim is to find the strong beats hiding in the melodic underbrush. What good can this do for dancers who have been instructed to visualise modern rhythms that actually contradict the bar-line and will soon want to get rid of it?[74]

The opening of Hodson's Augurs shows both the 'strong' downbeat, with a shunting forwards of the feet, as well as the irregular syncopations (accents in the upper body – see Ex. 6.1).

Colles also observed a new kind of fusion between music and dance: 'a new compound result expressible in terms of rhythm – much as the combination of oxygen and hydrogen produces a totally different compound, water'. Some years ago, I read his notion of a new compound as meaning the product of rhythmic counterpoint between music and dance, but now I do not. Immediately after this statement, Colles's examples are those just quoted, about parallelism, visualizing the flute trill and tune on the woodwind. Only later, without any reference to music at all, does he refer to the 'employment of rhythmical counterpoint in the choral movements'.[75] This now sounds like the innovative amassing of several groups performing different step and rhythm patterns simultaneously, not at all the same thing as choreomusical counterpoint as I, or Stravinsky, would see it. In other words, they were not necessarily creating cross-metres or cross-accents against the music (or indeed against each other).

Yet the Basle piano score and Stravinsky's published notes on the score do suggest choreomusical counterpoint, and we should now examine these sources in more detail.[76] Even though Hodson claimed that the piano score 'did not alter the information already available to her', it is full of contrapuntal rhythmic suggestions and arithmetical ingenuities that do not emerge in the notes and are hence absent from her choreography. Stravinsky admitted in his Preface to the notes that they were merely a summary, by no means the full story, which he rightly admits would have required a facsimile edition: 'I have attempted no more than compendious listing of the accent marks and phrase bracketings ...', adding rather naughtily, 'I do not want to close any avenue to hapless future candidates for what is mysteriously called the Doctor of Philosophy Degree.'[77] The notes were also written quite hurriedly within about a month, between late June and July 1967; at the time, the composer was not in good health, his attention span diminished, and, in July, Craft was away and unable to assist except at weekends.[78]

The annotations on the piano score are often hard to read and contradictory. The composer himself admitted as much:

> I have not been able to decipher all of the rather faint lead pencil annotations, nor can I elucidate all of the legible ones, the contexts themselves in some cases having vanished from my memory.[79]

We need therefore to deconstruct and interpret the score. The instructions, in Russian, include:

- brief notes attached to staves as to who dances and when;
- an occasional movement image, such as 'bell-swing', 'trampling', 'spring', 'heads';
- rhythmic information such as the total number of beats in a section (e.g. 48/4, 48 crotchet beats, though the sums do not always tally accurately with the score);
- big pencilled accents;
- the time signature of dance material;
- brackets indicating how the dance metre falls in relation to the music;
- actual rhythm lines containing precise note values and sometimes extending over several pages at a time.

There are different styles of handwriting, with some musical notes decidedly amateurish, and different pencils have been used, including Stravinsky's familiar blue one. There are also many crossings-out and second attempts at the documentation of rhythms. However, it seems that all of the writing is by Stravinsky himself, except perhaps for some of the rhythm lines in the Sacrificial Dance.[80]

Choreomusical counterpoint comes across most clearly when brackets show dance metre crossing musical metre, and when more detailed dance rhythm lines indicate repeating ostinato structures as well as metrical crossing. Of course, both features, crossing metre and ostinatos, are features that already lie within the musical structure itself. Here, they have been adopted for choreographic purposes. They appear with increasing regularity as the score progresses, most complex of all in the Sacrificial Dance. Stravinsky was clearly fascinated by this discovery:

> I confess that what I do recall … greatly surprises me, especially that I could have envisaged synchronization of music and choreography to such a degree, and expected any choreographer to realize it in 1913. The dance is almost always in counterpoint to the music.[81]

I have extracted a few examples of this kind of rhythmical information for analysis. The brackets sometimes show 'illogical', unconventional metrical crossings: for instance, starting a passage with a downbeat dance accent on a musical upbeat, whereas most crossings of this kind by choreographers (Balanchine, for one) begin in unity, with shared downbeats, relaxing the audience with initial rapport, and then fall out of unity. An example of early downbeat in the dance is the 'women's' musical theme in Ritual of the Rival Tribes, where both music and dance are in 4/4, but the dance bars start one beat before the music (at [60]); the men's brackets beneath show 2/4 grouping within the women's 4/4 (see Ex. 6.4). As this dance metre continues without change while the music includes one bar of 5/4 along the way, when the women's theme recurs, the dance bar begins two beats (rather than one) before the musical barline, at [61]. In the Più Mosso passage in Mystic Circles (at [93]+4), again the dance units (now in an unchanging 5/4 over shifting musical metres) begin one beat before the musical theme begins.

Ex. 6.4. *Le Sacre du printemps*, Ritual of the Rival Tribes, with dance rhythm information, as it appears in the annotated four-hand piano reduction in Basle (*PSS*).

As for the dance rhythm lines, the information in the score is far more comprehensive than it is in the published notes. A 5/8 and 3/4 alternating pattern lasts for virtually the whole of the central section of the Glorification of the Chosen One (from two quaver beats before [111] to the Molto Allargando bar before [117] – see Ex. 6.5). It sits against a constantly changing musical metre and complex rhythms. With a few minor variations along the way, the pattern

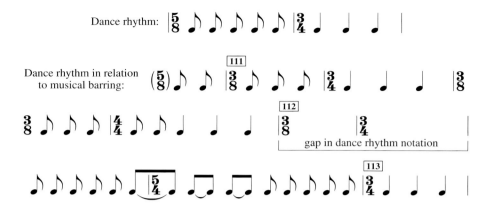

Ex. 6.5. *Le Sacre du printemps*, Glorification of the Chosen One, dance rhythm line (Basle piano score).

repeats, and when the crotchets stride awkwardly over the bar-line of the music they are written as two tied quavers. This is a notation that would be extremely difficult to realise in practice, given the complexity of the musical rhythms and the choreomusical counterpoint, especially as dancers in 1913 were far less rhythmically skilled than they are today. But the published notes just mention a 5/8 + 3/4 unit and no more detail as to the time values of steps. In the Ritual Action of the Ancestors, there is a 7/4 line from [131] to [134], then 3/4 until [135] (see Ex. 6.6a). Again, the pattern itself is not shown in the published notes. Stravinsky did, however, get into print the full pattern from [138]-1, taken from a sheet of paper inserted into the score: the rhythm of a contrapuntal canon between women and men that crosses the music (see Ex. 6.6b).

In the Sacrificial Dance, the earliest rhythm lines written into the score are the easiest to decipher. The first of these occurs during Verse 1 (from [149]),

Ex. 6.6a. *Le Sacre du printemps*, Ritual Action of the Ancestors, two dance rhythm lines (Basle piano score).

Ex. 6.6b. *Le Sacre du printemps*, Ritual Action of the Ancestors, a third dance rhythm line, as it appears in the Basle piano score.

which is based on a series of stuttering chords, each repeating like a pedal, but forming an irregular rhythmic pattern. For the Chosen One, from [149] to [152]+1, there is a 5/8 and 6/8 ostinato (again, no time values are given in the published notes – see Ex. 6.7a). From [153]-1 to [158]+2 (second quaver) and from [162] (second quaver) to [167], the repeating pattern is 7/8 7/8 6/8 (3/4) (see Ex. 6.7b). From the repeat of the Refrain [167] onwards, the score annotations are especially complex and with numerous crossings out, such that Stravinsky gave up completely on information about the rhythm lines in his published notes.

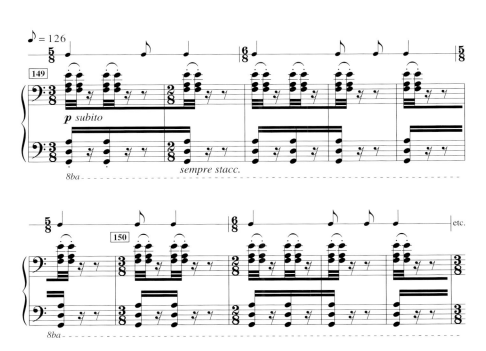

Ex. 6.7a. *Le Sacre du printemps*, Sacrificial Dance, Verse 1, with the dance rhythm line as it appears in the Basle piano score.

Ex. 6.7b. *Le Sacre du printemps*, Sacrificial Dance, Verse 1, a second dance rhythm line (Basle piano score).

Hodson's choreography does not include any of the rhythm lines documented in the score. In the Ritual Action of the Ancestors, her basic dance beat (quaver rate) is twice as fast as suggested by the rhythm lines. In her Sacrificial Dance, it is the circle of Ancestors who provide the real rhythm during Verse 1 (from [149]), not the Chosen One, and their steps are not in counterpoint, but mark exactly the irregular rhythm of the repeating 'pedal' chords. Still, how could Hodson have known the full detail from the published notes anyway? The two bars of 7/8 and one of 6/8 indicated in the notes from [153]-1 Hodson translated into the Chosen One's fast stamping and beating of hands against her knees, not showing the actual rhythm line, but strangely not coordinated with the music's quaver beat either,[82] and placed later than indicated (from [154]).

To add to the mayhem, Stravinsky's published notes contradict the piano score on several occasions, and the mode of documentation is sometimes downright bizarre. For instance, for Augurs, note 7 reads:

2 ms. of 22: 'No one moves during these two measures.'

I assume that this means two bars after [22], but the bracket in the score starts two bars before [22] and extends over 3 bars. Note 8 reads:

5 ms. before 22, second quarter-beat: 'They must start here.'

In the score, this indication appears two bars after [22]. Read notes 7 and 8 together and they appear to be documenting events in reverse order, but, of course, according to the score they are not. Note 6 tells us:

12 ms. before 22: 'The old woman.'

Here, Stravinsky could just as well have given the cue [21]. These are just examples; but there is one instance in the work where Stravinsky's published notes are spectacularly misleading, a passage in Spring Rounds from [53] to [54]. This is where Hodson was persuaded to expand the division of the stage activity into five groups according to bars of shifting time signatures. The breakdown of the passage, drawing from Hodson's published notes,[83] is shown in Table 5, the counts indicating when the dancers move.

Table 5. *Le Sacre du printemps*, Spring Rounds, group counterpoint.

The layout of the music:

1	2	3	4	5	6	7	8	9	10	11
4/4	4/4	4/4	5/4	4/4	3/4	4/4	4/4	3/4	4/4	4/4

First unit: Young women (blue) – Dropping the upper body to the floor and then slowly unfolding.
1, 2, 3, 4 for each bar of 4/4 (bars 1, 2, 3, 5, 7, 8, 10)

Second unit: Adolescents (red) – The same movement as the women in blue.
–, 2, 3, 4/ 1 (following bar) of bars of 4/4 (bars 1, 2, 3, 5, 7, 8, 10)
(leaving the first beat as a rest, thus in syncopation with the women in blue)

Third unit: Women (purple, with tall hats) – Two high steps forwards.
–, 2, 3 of each bar of 3/4 (bars 6, 9)
(no one moves on the first beat of each bar of 3/4, creating a rest here)

Fourth unit: Young People and Young Men.
–, –, –, –, (and) 5 (and) of the 5/4 bar (bar 4) and
–, –, –, (and) 4 (and) of two bars of 4/4 (bars 8 and 10)
(in her piano score, Rambert marked these bars for the men's percussive, syncopated plunge forward)

Fifth unit: Adolescents – Accents, pulling the arms alternately upwards and down towards the floor.
1, –, –, – of each bar of 4/4 (bars 1, 2, 3, 5, 7, 8, 10)

Unison: All (bar 11)

This rhythmic arrangement creates a very striking stage picture, breaking up the flow of the choreography across the groups, while the music retains independent continuity. Hodson took her cue from Stravinsky's note and music example for [53]+5: 'the second group [of dancers] is assigned to a phrase of four quarters [crotchets], and the third group to a phrase of two quarters' (see Ex. 6.8a). This description corresponds precisely with the activity of her second and third groups. The composer said that he found this passage 'extremely interesting', although he admitted that he found the rhythms of the other groups 'too complex to describe'.[84] But the piano score tells me of just three groups, labelled

Ex. 6.8a. *Le Sacre du printemps,* Spring Rounds, Stravinsky's music example accompanying his published notes on the Basle piano score.

I, II, and III, each assigned a line parallel to the musical staves; group II performs numbered phrases 1–4 that start to be taken up, as in canon, by group III (see Ex. 6.8b). There is an additional 4-beat syncopated pattern (messy, notated across more than one line and with crossings-out, but most likely group I material) that recurs regularly every two bars, and therefore has to cross the musical metre when it shifts from 4/4 to 5/4 to 3/4: one more example of simple choreomusical counterpoint. This is quite a different interpretation from Hodson's. It is hardly possible to interpret the piano score in the manner of Hodson's reconstruction, but then, she was, after all, working at one stage removed, interpreting an interpretation, Stravinsky's own idiosyncratic reading of his piano score.

Perhaps the crucial point at the end of this analysis is that the contrapuntal rhythmic detail in the piano score does not sound at all like the style of Dalcroze Nijinsky or the 'breath' style of his Sacrificial Dance. It is also hard to believe that if such strange contrapuntal goings-on had happened in 1913, they did not excite attention. Indeed, I have never yet seen a dance with the degree of choreomusical counterpoint that is indicated in this score.

Nevertheless, despite the contradictions within the score and the further contradictions that it has given rise to in the reconstruction, it is important to consider it in detail: after all, it indicates a vision of a choreographed *Sacre.* But now we might ask, whose vision? Or how many visions? To all appearances, the markings on the score look like a series of ideas jotted down, sometimes altered, sometimes the job done very methodically (those ostinatos stretching for pages), sometimes less so. Perhaps they are instructions, or sketches of ideas, or a record betraying that the writer had difficulty getting the information down correctly, or a mixture of these scenarios developed over time. Yet Stravinsky takes responsibility for everything as being his directives to Nijinsky.

Even given the composer's dominant personality in theatrical situations, it is hard to believe that this is the full truth. Conveying this kind of rhythmic detail is not normal practice for composers, including Stravinsky. But, if we were to give him the benefit of the doubt, considering the exceptional circumstances in which *Sacre* was created, why do the annotations look so messy and uncertain and appear in different styles of writing? There is also the puzzle over when Nijinsky could have had access to the printed piano score. The score was officially published on 21 May 1913, only a few days before the premiere,[85] so somehow Stravinsky must have got hold of a pre-publication copy if any directives

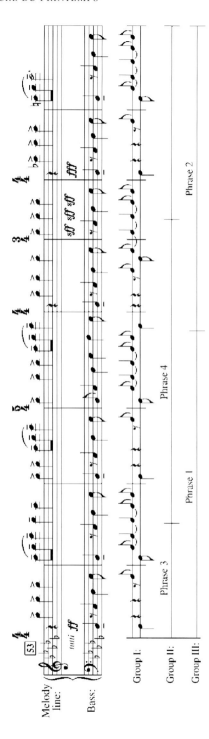

Ex. 6.8b. *Le Sacre du printemps,* Spring Rounds, diagram drawn from Basle piano score, showing dance group II continuing, with phrases 3 and 4, and group III starting, with phrases 1 and 2.

were to be useful to Nijinsky. Was one ready when he choreographed the Sacrificial Dance on Nijinska? Apparently not. In her memoirs, Nijinska remembers the rehearsal pianist transposing from a sketch of the orchestral score.[86] Nijinsky sent a curious telegram to Stravinsky in late March 1913, only two months before the premiere: he had completed Act I and requested that the piano score of 'the sacred dance' be dispatched immediately.[87] Whether Nijinsky is asking here for the piano score for the whole of Part 2 or for just the Sacrificial Dance is uncertain, but what is very clear is that he could not have had the complete piano score with the annotations to hand!

Neither Nijinska nor Rambert mentions seeing this kind of contrapuntal information when Nijinsky was choreographing. Furthermore, there is no suggestion that Nijinska's solo had radically changed by the time Piltz performed it – quite the reverse (see p. 422). In the only part of Rambert's score where she provides a sustained series of counts, the Glorification of the Chosen One, she counts musically, avoiding the touches of rhythmic crossing prescribed in the Basle piano score. After the premiere of Nijinsky's *Sacre*, the piano score was given to Misia Sert and returned to Diaghilev in 1920. We might now entertain the possibility that at least some of these annotations stem from a later period.

Massine's 1920 *Sacre* is an obvious target for enquiry, and a body of evidence from a variety of sources confirms its rhythmic aspects. This was choreography of similar scale to the Nijinsky, likewise noteworthy for showing dancing groups (five) in counterpoint with each other, and it re-used Roerich's flamboyant original designs. But major differences were the absence of the extreme physical introversion of the original, and the reduction of narrative and character content: no ancient woman, no Sage or kiss of the Earth, no elders wearing animal masks. Instead, Massine offered a more abstract account of male and female bands interacting, opposing each other, occasionally dissolving into unison, and eventually becoming audience and accompaniment to the Chosen One. Here is evidence of the 'objective construction' that Stravinsky welcomed. Massine revived the work on several occasions: for instance, in 1930, in New York, when Martha Graham danced the Chosen One; in 1948, for La Scala, Milan (with new but equally colourful costumes by Roerich); and a final version in 1973 for the Teatro Comunale in Florence. Here, Massine's assistant was Susanna Della Pietra, who has since staged the Florence version for the ballet companies in Nice (1994) and Bordeaux (2007).

In an interview at the time of the 1920 premiere, Stravinsky enthusiastically explained Massine's new musical process:

> Massine does not follow the music note by note or bar by bar. Quite the contrary, he battles against the metre, but keeps exactly to the rhythm. I will give you an example. Here is one bar of four, then one of five beats: Massine might

make his dancers do three threes, which corresponds and adds up to exactly the same total, but goes better under the music than a note-by-note transference, which was the fault of the old choreography. And he starts up this battle, this slowing down or quickening, whether for two or twenty bars, but always falls back into accord with the section as a whole.[88]

Does this not sound like the principle behind the rhythm lines in the Basle piano score? Many years later, Massine recalled that he had been at pains to avoid Nijinsky's mistakes and, when they discussed the new production over the summer, he had suggested to the composer: 'I can throw a bridge over certain pages of your score and do my own rhythms.'[89] So he attempted

> a counterpoint in emphasis between it [the score] and the choreography, and while Stravinsky played selected passages from the score on the piano I demonstrated my idea. Stravinsky approved and urged me to begin work at once.[90]

Might the rhythmic principles have been written into the score around this time? When later, in his *Autobiography*, Stravinsky had changed his mind and decided that Massine's version had 'something forced and artificial about it',[91] his description of the rhythmic technique remained the same as in 1920.

Massine's practice was highly unusual at the time, but it had a history. In 1919, he had written a short manifesto in which he claimed that the 'correspondence between dancing and music ... can be defined as a certain counterpoint to the musical design created by the composer'.[92] Then, according to the writer Boris Kochno, Diaghilev's secretary, there was counterpoint in his setting of Stravinsky's *Le Chant du rossignol* premiered not long before *Sacre*, in February 1920. To some, probably because they had not seen this choreomusical technique in action before, the dancers appeared unmusical and poorly rehearsed.[93] Now people *were* noticing strange contrapuntal goings-on.

At the time of Massine's *Sacre* premiere (meanwhile, his *Pulcinella* had been premiered in May), Levinson remembered what had been impressive about Nijinsky's production. 'Whereas his dancers were tormented by rhythm, Massine's had such a relaxed relationship to the measure that it too often felt as if there was no metre at all.'[94] Perhaps his comment betrays the difficulties with rhythmic precision that the dancers experienced. Sergey Grigoriev, the *régisseur* of the Ballets Russes, also read the counterpoint in Massine's version, but rather differently: 'It was as if Massine paid greater heed to the complicated rhythms than to meaning. The result was something mechanical ...'[95]

Both the very rough and hard-to-read silent film that exists of the 1948 La Scala Milan revival and the Bordeaux revival of Massine's *Sacre* strongly support the argument that the principles recorded in Stravinsky's piano score are

Massine's.[96] A glance at his Sacrificial Dance shows that there are again repeating asymmetrical rhythm patterns underlying the steps of the Chosen One, and the notes that Massine made on his orchestral score during the 1973 revival for the Teatro Comunale in Florence appear to confirm the earlier film evidence.[97]

The solo is structured as a series of dance units functioning like ostinatos, although, unlike in Hodson's Nijinsky reconstruction, there is no regular repetition of steps in association with the musical Refrain. In the long first Verse, for instance, from [149], there is a 7/8 (7-count) pattern, a sideways shunt with the right foot swinging out and then kicking back in to confirm the rhythm (see Ex. 6.9a). The Chosen One shows this step unit twice; the men seated on the floor surrounding her then punch out the same rhythm, after which she performs her step unit three more times. This is followed by a rocking, twisting step in 7 counts that is also extended into an 8-count unit (approximately from [153] to [156] – see Ex. 6.9b). Then, from [162] to [165], there is another 7/8 (7-count) pattern, a variant of the shunt now enlarged into jumps, performed five times (see Ex. 6.9c).

These patterns differ from those in the Basle piano score (see Exs. 6.7a and b), although Massine's first 7/8 pattern at [149] (Ex. 6.9a) matches the one in the Basle score at [153]-1 (Ex. 6.7b). But Massine was well known for making choreographic changes – for instance, between 1920 and the 1930 New York version of *Sacre* and between the 1948 and 1973 Italian revivals.[98] The significant fact is that he used the same rhythmic principle in 1948 (and 1973) as in the piano score. Supporting the Massine case, Lydia Sokolova, his first Chosen One, remembered learning repeating step rhythm patterns, and also the difficulty of remembering the number of repeats of each step and performing counter to what she heard, 'but by ignoring the sound and keeping straight on, I eventually met the music on a given beat followed by a tacit bar'.[99] She also remembered dancing full-out virtually all the time during the Sacrificial Dance,

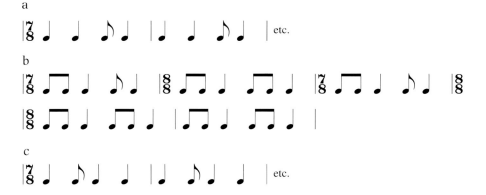

Ex. 6.9a–c. *Le Sacre du printemps*, Sacrificial Dance, Verse 1, three dance rhythm lines (Massine).

unlike Maria Piltz, whom she saw in the original *Sacre*.[100] This is in accordance with the piano score documenting rhythmically patterned dancing of this kind for virtually the whole of Verse 1, whereas Hodson's Chosen One hardly dances at all during this passage. Looking beyond the Sacrificial Dance, the Massine work, at least as it comes down to us today, is far less detailed in response to musical rhythm patterns and accentuations than the Nijinsky. It shows us the steady metres more boldly when we hear them in the score. This is the approach, for instance, to Augurs of Spring, which respects the 2-bar hypermeasures but duplicates none of the famous syncopations. However, we may well ask why the Sacrificial Dance provides the only example of the more complex contrapuntal annotations in the piano score. There are occasional cross-rhythms elsewhere, but no other examples of autonomous dance ostinatos. Were many of the latter merely ideas, shared and perhaps initiated by both choreographer and composer, flights of imagination that were never physically realised? Did some of these complexities disappear as Massine revised the work?

In the final analysis, I think that Hodson was absolutely right to be sparing with counterpoint in her Nijinsky reconstruction and to act according to the bulk of her evidence. But we might now ask whether there was reason to use any of the rhythmic information from Stravinsky's published notes. We might also ask whether indeed Stravinsky would have changed his opinion of Nijinsky, his famous recanting of the late 1960s, had he felt less secure that the annotations in the original piano score belonged to the 1913 premiere.

The puzzling piano score has in its own way added to the *Sacre* mythology and is yet another example of absence (of information and, to some degree, physical realisation). Consider Hodson's Spring Rounds: a Nijinsky reconstruction based on Stravinsky notes that are already a poor reflection, a distortion, of markings on a piano score that might have had little to do with Nijinsky in the first place! Ultimately, the score is best seen as a multi-faceted vision, a reflection of choreographic speculation, and not least documentation of a highly intricate rhythmic architecture that would have been a counting nightmare.

Hodson is not the only choreographer to have used Stravinsky's published notes as a Nijinsky source. So too did John Taras (1972), Richard Alston (1981) and Jean-Pierre Bonnefous (1981). The notes are an intriguing starting point for a choreographer interested in getting inside the workings of the *Sacre* score and in weaving a dance strand in and around the musical counterpoint and rhythms. Likewise, scholars interested in the dance component of the original *Sacre* production have been ready believers in Stravinsky's published notes, without having had an opportunity to look at what the original piano score really says – for instance, the musicologists Nicholas Cook, Jann Pasler and Volker Scherliess and the dance historian Shelley Berg.[101] A facsimile of the piano score would now be a very welcome addition to the published Stravinsky literature.

Maurice Béjart: Sacre as universal pop ballet

Mention *Sacre* today and, after Nijinsky, two choreographers are by far the most frequently cited as the exemplars of the tradition: Maurice Béjart and Pina Bausch. Created respectively in 1959 and 1975, their two *Sacres* have had far-reaching international impact; indeed, they have achieved 'classic' status.

Béjart's *Sacre* was the first ever to achieve international success, toured from the 1960s on his phenomenally popular Ballet of the 20th Century, staged on numerous companies around the world, and still in the repertory today. Although critics have been divided, some concerned that Béjart's work lived off a kind of false modernity through its shock value, vulgarity and simplistic choreographic techniques, there is no question that he reached a new, young ballet audience. With *Sacre* as a leading repertory item, he represented the contemporary ethos. It is interesting too that Balanchine, who, whatever he really thought (see p. 120), used to claim that *Sacre* was unchoreographable, nevertheless cited Béjart's as 'the best anyone has done';[102] perhaps too it is the best ballet that Béjart has ever made. Certainly, it was the first 'pop ballet', the beginning of a new genre, as Berg describes:

> the progenitor of a style of ballet using monumental scores, hordes of dancers [like the Nijinsky, Béjart used about fifty dancers in his *Sacre*], an eclectic, athletic hybrid movement style that is a mixture of ballet, 'modern' jazz and some form of 'ethnic' dance, combined with pared down sets and minimal costumes.[103]

Béjart's *Sacre* also initiated a kind of mainstream response to Stravinsky's monumental score. He prompted a large number of works in the new genre, and it is probably this kind of *Sacre* that Alston once derided as an 'all-out primitive bash',[104] referring to what he distinctly did not want for his own 1981 chamber setting (see pp. 478-9). Choreographers absorbed actual movement ideas from Béjart too. The 'African' wide-legged stance with low centre of gravity, the mass huddle, the raising-up of the soloist(s) in the centre of the mass, the women straddled around the waists of their partners – all these ideas became clichés in later, sexually charged *Sacres*.

Béjart was invited to create the new work while still early in his career, by the forward-thinking Maurice Huisman, Director of the Théâtre Royal de la

Monnaie in Brussels. He began work never having seen any other *Sacre*, hardly surprising at that time. But he was fascinated by the figure of Nijinsky and had recently learnt parts of the original *Sacre* from his teacher Nicholas Zverev, who had danced in the Diaghilev production.[105]

For his own setting, Béjart broke away radically from the 'tragic' scenario, devising instead a fertility ritual that celebrated the sexual union of a chosen woman with a chosen man. Several of the 'ideas' cited by Acocella, Garafola and Greene (see p. 413) are clearly embedded here, although the dark element of sacrifice has given way to a statement of unity. There is no victim. Béjart weights the visceral thrill in the music, the positive exploitation of sexuality, rather than the theme of death, and, as his programme note suggests, he mixes this with a generalised spirituality: 'Human love, in its physical aspects, symbolizes the act by which the divinity creates the Cosmos and the joy the divinity thereby derives.'

Béjart opens up to choreography the Introductions to both Parts 1 and 2 of the score,[106] which were originally played with the curtain down. His Part 1 is for men only; from them, one is chosen. It is a brutal initiation: 'he' is the one who falls to the floor at the end of the score section labelled Ritual of Abduction (although the score labels no longer make any sense in relation to this choreography) and, after his solo in Spring Rounds (backed by the male group), he is kicked and pulled by the hair. The men commence the action in their own space, but later a bright light shining on them from offstage alerts them to a world beyond, inhabited by women. They depart frog-jumping in single file. In Part 2, we are in the women's territory, which the men invade to eleven strategic hammered chords (during one bar of 11/4, at [103]+2). Already chosen from amongst the women at the start of Part 2, 'she' has her solo during the Ritual Action of the Ancestors. Then there is the union of man and woman in the Sacrificial Dance, accompanied by mass bands from both sides.

Béjart's *Sacre* is led by conventional masculinity, stereotypical notions of men as strong and aggressive, and Deborah Jowitt's compelling description of his usual movement characteristics can surely be charged to them: 'a kind of voluptuous forcefulness, a pressurized, high-protein muscularity'.[107] The women, on the other hand, behave more softly and decoratively. But the cast also represent 'all men' and 'all women', as Béjart removed specific ethnological reference in favour of the more global reach, the ideal of unity, that typified a certain thinking in the 1960s. In his programme note, he explained:

At a time when the borders that divide the human spirit are gradually crumbling, we must begin to speak in terms of the culture of all mankind. Let us avoid folklore that is not universal and only retain the essential forces of mankind which are the same all over the world and throughout all periods of history.

Béjart's *Sacre* is also inclusive in demonstrating an erotic 'primitivism' with roots close to nature. There are allusions to plant life and to sex, when the women lie round the chosen woman, in Béjart's words, 'their arms and legs thrown wide apart, lifting their pelvises like buds that are about to open'[108] (to each hit of the cymbal, at [80], [81] and [82]). Like animals, the men spring on all fours or in a wide second position, their hands held like paws, or they clash like angry stags. During their respective solos, the chosen pair hover low, arms extended sideways like great birds of prey.

Béjart tells us that he worked at length with the orchestral score.[109] Clearly, its nature allowed him considerable freedom to devise an independent scenario, yet he still took a broad view and ignored some obvious musical connotations. The places marked for lyricism (and thus for women) in Part 1 had to be overridden. In Augurs of Spring, the piano rehearsal score (but significantly not the orchestral score) indicates the entry of the young women at two bars before [27]: they are set to dance to a flute theme over a shimmering accompaniment. Here, Béjart's two male couples simply continue in fighting mood, thrusting a heel towards a partner, or jumping sharply into a spread-leg lift, and the music is quiet enough to let us hear their feet hitting the ground. My perception of Stravinsky's music changes within this new environment: what is irrelevant is erased from consciousness. When, at the end of Spring Rounds, we hear a gentle woodwind line accompanied by soft trills, we watch two men pulling the chosen man by the hair and pushing him to the floor. The visual drama continues despite the music, which means that we hear the woodwind line far less clearly than when it is literally printed out by the feet in Hodson's *Sacre* (see p. 428). Yet the trills seem to acquire a touch of menace in this context: innocent and mysterious in the Hodson, they now sound like a mocking titter. Béjart used the same technique of forceful choreography overriding gentle music in the Lullaby of his *Firebird* (see p. 137).

A contrasting example is Béjart's treatment of the 11/4 bar in Part 2, which was originally like a separate moment in the dance, the terrifying moment confirming the selection of the victim. In Béjart's version, it signals the invasion of the men, a strange hopping on each chord in crouched bird-of-prey position with the working leg pinned across the supporting knee, but now clearly linked to the Glorification of the Chosen One: the hops continue through the oom-pah bars (see pp. 424-5) that follow. Hill has observed that the 11/4 bar is 'an integral idea within the dance [he means the music for the dance] and not just a preparatory gesture' and describes its impact as if 'to drum a pulse into our minds'.[110] Here, according to Hill's reading, Béjart seems to be following the musical implications, more closely than he would have done if he had followed the original scenario.

The hopping in the Glorification, the pulsating springs in Augurs and frog-jump exit at the end of Dance of the Earth all demonstrate Béjart's emphasis on a big, plain beat that enables the body to engage fully with the earth (at crotchet rate in Augurs, for instance, as written in the score). The shorter beat that is far more prominent in Hodson's reconstruction, such as in the opening jumps to the quaver notes in Augurs, and also in Kenneth MacMillan's *Sacre* (1962), engenders a much lighter attitude towards weight. But then, the whole approach in Béjart's *Sacre* is broad-scale and bold, appropriate to a statement that is fundamentally about affirmative power. Together with brute physicality, there is spectacle, projection towards the audience from the start, extrovert full-body gesticulations breaking out of ground-hugging pulsations, sculptural poses of both single and grouped bodies, and simple, powerful textures: big unison ensembles and soloist(s) against mass. In the Sacrificial Dance, the climax is a statement of confidence drawn from a series of striking mass unison poses that start on the floor and move into lifts; the succession quickens until everyone rushes into the famous photo huddle, reaching to the ecstatic pair aloft in their midst. Dance motifs are not nailed to musical motifs as consistently as in Hodson's reconstruction, but this is in keeping with Béjart's story of growth towards a celebratory climax. Repetition leads to exhaustion, the darker story, and Béjart wants none of this. There is a feeling of agency, male agency at least, in Béjart's *Sacre*, to create dance beat rather than simply to respond to the pressure of Stravinsky's musical beat.

In keeping with his broad, positivist vision, Béjart does not burrow into the musical texture for syncopations or strike out with independent cross-rhythms: his rhythmic approach is clear-cut and clean, although occasionally the dancers ride like a huge tidal wave over the score in service of the drama. One rare moment of counterpoint with musical rhythm is the men's frog-jump exit at the end of Part 1 (two beats per jump, against three in the musical bar), but the dance effect here is so strong that we might well begin to hear the music through the dance anyway, and a stronger sense of 2/4 than of 3/4.

Béjart not only altered the scenario of the original *Sacre*, but also demonstrated that the dramatic shape of the choreomusical composite could be different from the shape of the music alone. Some choreographers who have adhered more closely to the original scenario have followed his lead in this respect, by shifting the detail of the familiar events in relation to the score. 'Tocsin 3' is the moment when the victim is chosen and it comes with the additional stipulation that the Chosen One should then hold still until her Sacrificial Dance (according to stage directions in the piano score, at [102]). ('Tocsin' is Hill's term for the three sinister accents that lead up to and include this moment of selection.[111]) MacMillan moved back the moment of selection from the third to the first 'tocsin' and added solo material for his Chosen One during the Ritual Action of the Ancestors (as Béjart does), winding her up, as it were, before the Sacrificial

Dance.[112] Martha Graham (1984) staged the moment of choice even earlier, halfway through Part 1, including a ritual binding with rope by a young, charismatic Shaman (replacing the ancient Sage) during the Dance of the Earth.[113] Her Chosen One, too, begins her solo during the Ancestors' Dance, observed by the Shaman, carrying on into the Sacrificial Dance, when the ensemble returns to reinforce the drive towards her death. So Graham's *Sacre* starts the personal drama very early, making it more central, prolonging the private anguish and the crescendo towards oblivion.

Pina Bausch: The real body in Sacre

In her *Das Frühlingsopfer* (1975), Pina Bausch brings us back to the ideas within the original scenario of *Sacre*. In the programme note that accompanied the premiere, she wrote:

> Here one sees the original libretto as if viewed from afar: the adoration of the earth, the veneration of the forces of nature, the glorification of life at the beginning of spring; the angst of the sacrificial victim in the face of death, the power that radiates from the executor of the group will (the oldest or the wise one or the chief); the relentlessness of the group that is damned to sacrifice in order to live; finally the breaking out of the forces of nature within us and around us (the spring); and not least the purpose that the living give to the sacrifice and that the sacrificial victim gives to those who survive.[114]

There is a victim, the moment of choosing her happens at the 'right' place in the score, after which, just as Stravinsky stipulated, she does not dance until her designated final solo. There is also abduction and rape, rival tribes (men and women), and a man who takes responsibility as chief or leader.

Yet the premiere programme note does not hint at what is so new about this *Sacre*. There are no named characters in Bausch's *Sacre* – nor does the programme name the woman and man who dance the victim and male leader – there are no specific cultural clues, no ancestors, no colourful costumes – just black trousers (chests bare) for the men and flimsy flesh-coloured shoulder-strap dresses for the women – and place is simply defined by a floor strewn with brown peat and prepared right in front of us before the dance begins (no curtain down). A blood-red cloth is a key feature of the work, symbolising the sacrifice. One of the women can be seen lying on it at the start, in touch with the earth; later it is thrown in fear from one woman to another; the leader lies on it, which is both a sexual act and a signal that the moment of selection is imminent; and it finally emerges as the dress that marks out by its colour the Chosen One. But this paring-down of scenario and character information only underscores the key

theme of this *Sacre*: 'the antagonism between the sexes and the resultant alienation of the individuals',[115] and, perhaps for the first time, the clear critical focus
on the position of women as social victims.

Bausch's critical stance led her away from the tradition of *Sacre* as a
presentational statement that foregrounds picture-making and visceral thrill.
Her *Sacre* shows us the body in a state of collapse, out of control. Her Chosen One
stumbles, barely able to hold herself upright, let alone in a still position. We have
the impression that we are looking at real, unstyled bodies here, doing real physical work. The convulsions, tics, spasms and shivers have been identified as signals of hysteria, fundamental physical symptoms unmediated by thought or by
intention to shape the movement into the symbol of an idea.[116]

How dancers feel doing this dance contributes to what they communicate to
their audience. My own overriding impression from trying out some of the
rhythmic moves is of discomfort and disorientation, the head flung and dropped,
leading to off-balance and a blurred sense of direction, especially acute given the
frightening speed of much of the action. At a 2006 Hamburg conference focusing on Bausch's *Sacre*, Gitta Barthel, who danced with Bausch in the 1980s,
spoke about a 'lived' ritual. This had been broken only by the final applause of
the audience, which provoked a 'feeling of shame' in her: it was as if she had
been witness to a death and the audience had applauded her for this terrible
event.[117] A dancer in the Paris Opéra production of 1997 told *The New York
Times*: 'It's not something I can express in words. It's more the feeling of things
that have passed through the body. But I have no doubt that this has been one of
the primordial experiences of my seventeen years at the Paris Opéra Ballet.'[118]

Bausch's *Sacre* has been a regular item in the repertory of her own company
Tanztheater Wuppertal ever since its premiere, reaching a wide audience
through international touring. The Paris production is the only instance to date
when she has staged the work on a company other than her own. *Sacre* is also
one of her earliest works, and indeed the earliest of all still to be in the repertory.
This is especially significant given that, as an 'all-dance' piece, it contrasts markedly with the dance theatre works that have typified her output ever since: collage structures of props, scenery, speech, and selections from a range of musical
and movement styles.

Sacre was Bausch's own idea, and originally situated within a Stravinsky
evening, after two other Bausch premieres. These were *Wind von West* (to the
Cantata, with its references to the 'sacrifice' of Christ) – another work about
alienation, here, people struggling to make contact and searching for love and
inner peace – and *Der zweite Frühling* (the Second Spring, to a selection of short
pieces – see pp. 145-6), about an elderly couple musing on their pasts. Hence
both the gender and Stravinskian content of *Sacre* were highlighted during the
programme as a whole. This was an important period for discussion of gender,

with the women's movement a recent development, internationally recognised and unstoppable. As for the *Sacre* tradition in Germany, Béjart's production had toured there triumphantly during the 1960s, after which appeared the large-scale productions of Erich Walter (Dusseldorf, 1970), John Neumeier (Frankfurt, 1972) and Glen Tetley (Munich, 1974). In West Germany, these were also times of political unrest and urban terrorism (Red Army Faction activities), and Bausch was deeply disturbed by the brutality and climate of fear.[119] Perhaps too she might have been aware of that 'other' reading by Adorno of Stravinsky's music, and especially of *Sacre*, his bitter account of the totalitarian tendencies within that score. Certainly her stance within her own production does not deny this possibility.[120]

Although the following analysis treats Bausch's *Sacre* as stage choreography, my central source was the 1978 film for television by Pit Weyrich, the only publicly available recording of the work. Looking at this film before watching a live performance was enough to establish the Bausch production as the most intensely moving and powerful of those seen, offering too an apparently endless flow of new choreographic and choreomusical ideas, amply able to sustain itself after many viewings. The film is noteworthy for its lack of editing: there is just one cut, and consequently no interference with the rhythmic relationships between the music and dance. It is a remarkable account of the physical energy of the performers, especially as the cameraman, who turns into our eye, moves with the performers. Such long takes increase the effect of the power of the gaze, as the camera roams. It underlines the victimisation in Bausch's *Sacre*.[121]

Yet inevitably some of the stage choreography is missing from the screen, and we need to speculate through the film in an attempt to reach the stage version. In 2006, I saw a live performance at the Cirque Royale in Brussels, the event greatly enhanced by the presence of the orchestra of the Théâtre Royal de la Monnaie (conducted by Zigmunt Kowalski), an integral theatrical component ranged in front of the dancing space. The live performance revealed a generally higher level of lighting than the film and also confirmed what was missing from screen. There were no surprises, although a clearer spatial architecture emerged along with a new element of claustrophobia: the performers, once on stage, never leave, even though they sometimes turn their backs and group together in a tight corner. The number of dancers has varied over the years between twenty-four and thirty-two, which is the current figure.

Not the least remarkable feature of Bausch's *Sacre* is its musicality, and again, this makes the work stand out as very different from her other current repertory. Mention Bausch, and we would now never think of music-based work, although there are other early works that are just this: for instance, her choreography to the Bacchanale from Wagner's *Tannhäuser* (1972), her Mahler evening (1974) and her production of Gluck's opera *Orpheus und Eurydike* (1975). But what is most astonishing is her entirely original and sophisticated choreomusical approach to the *Sacre* score, despite the fact that she does not read music. Bausch's process was to note the score subtitles, to come to rehearsal having worked out all the movement on her own body and to listen to numerous orchestral recordings.[122] In the end, she chose the famous 1969 recording by Boulez with the Cleveland Orchestra,[123] which she has used ever since, in rehearsal and performance, and conductors are expected to model their interpretations on this recording when there is live orchestral accompaniment. Now, as in 1975, Bausch is musically very precise when rehearsing the piece.

First we should take the 'view from afar' and consider the basic fact of the size of the *Sacre* score. Bausch makes a virtue of its colossal forces, perceiving it as something to be reckoned with, and as outside the world of the dance: not just complicit with the tribe against the victim (as Adorno would say, although unfairly charging Stravinsky as tribe leader – see p. 98), but 'outside' all of them. Bausch clearly signals this from the start, as her dancers listen to and look out towards something clearly beyond their immediate space. As the piece progresses, they are increasingly burdened by sound – which shows in their bodies – swept up by its power, then gradually beaten down and exhausted by it. It is as if the music gets to the inside of them, taking over from human agency. Only by the end of Part 2, the Sacrifice, are the mob (by now in unison) and music complicit, against the Chosen One. But the music is not just physically outside; it is also outside in the sense of representing the power and burden of the past, of so many other *Sacres*.

On structuring dance material

Turning now to detail, before undertaking a choreomusical analysis it is instructive to consider how Bausch structures dance material. A mosaic of motifs rides across the entire piece, symbolising the identity of the person within a community, as these motifs are shared, transferred, personalised, added to, left incomplete, or, in the Sacrificial Dance, shattered. The dance as a whole demonstrates extraordinary economy and variety in its application of a limited number of movement ideas. It is surprising how many of them are shared across men and women, but, unless shown in unison, they are normally nuanced quite differently: the men extrovert, foregrounding straight lines and angles, the women expressing more circular shapes and a narrower body image, in movement that refers constantly back to the womb.

Augurs of Spring provides good examples of motivic development and transfer of ideas from women to men. The women's opening unit of movement becomes a key dance motif, from [13] (see Ex. 6.10). It lasts two bars, then repeats, and consequently Bausch, like Hodson, groups the musical bars into pairs here – hypermeasures. We count the beats as 1 2 3 4 (which are Bausch's own counts –

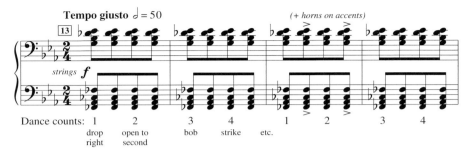

Ex. 6.10. *Le Sacre du printemps*, The Augurs of Spring, opening, women's key dance motif (Bausch).

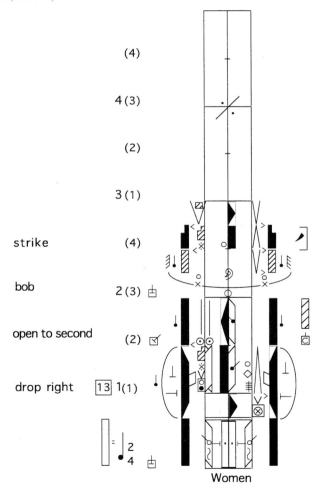

Ex. 6.10 (continued). *Le Sacre du printemps*, The Augurs of Spring, opening, women's key dance motif (Bausch).

unlike Hodson's counts 1–8)[124] as opposed to 1 2 1 2, which would follow the musical barring:

- A step to the right, drawing in the left leg, the upper body and head dropping over the knees, hands crossed over the thighs, count 1;
- The left leg opens to second position plié and the dancer looks upwards, hands reaching down in opposition, count 2;
- The dancer bobs in the same position, count 3;
- Hands are clasped above the head in preparation for the main dynamic accent on count 4, a striking action down the front of the body, pulling the torso and head down with it.

It is important not to overplay the framework of beats and dance counts here; use of breath, the human element, in conjunction with the pull of gravity, is also crucial to the style.

The final striking action, which is the most memorable image here, becomes the culminating movement in the first male solo. He is the first man to dance (from [23], 4 bars, 8 dance counts), to the upward-rushing gestures of the violins (see Ex. 6.11):

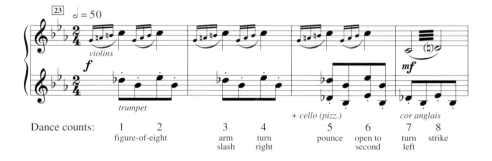

Ex. 6.11. *Le Sacre du printemps*, The Augurs of Spring, man's solo (Bausch).

- He turns towards the audience into a 'figure-of-eight' (see Ill. 17),[125] one arm sweeping up and over into an under-curve, his body pulling back towards it so that the focus is upwards in the opposite direction, the leg on the same side bent and raised across the supporting leg (counts 1-2);
- He makes a slashing motion with his right arm across to the left (count 3), turns to the right (count 4), and pounces towards the floor on the right diagonal (count 5);
- An opening of the right leg to second position plié turns him towards up

Ill. 17. *Le Sacre du printemps*, Ritual of the Rival Tribes (Barbara Passow with red cloth), choreography by Pina Bausch, Tanztheater Wuppertal.

stage (count 6), and finally, after a left turn, he makes the big striking action down the front of the body with hands clasped (count 8).

Watching this solo, you might well recognise the pounce and opening to second, which were also seeded by earlier movement performed by the women. An 8-count unit from [19] showed these moves (on counts 2 and 3 – see p. 462). But whereas the women imbued these moves with an underlying sense of desperation – giving into weight, flinging their heads down, then up and back, and concluding the striking action with a release of energy – the man, moving ag-

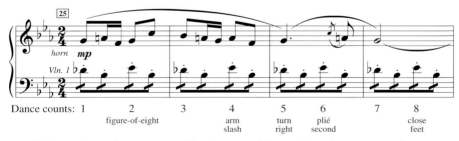

Ex. 6.12. *Le Sacre du printemps*, The Augurs of Spring, men's quartet to horn tune (Bausch).

gressively and at much greater speed, emphasises precision and strength, body weight held, with no noticeable head movement, and the strike is a smart chop, a 'bound flow' ending, motion stopped abruptly.

The follow-up to the man's solo phrase ([24]-1) demonstrates one of the characteristic ways in which Bausch manipulates material in *Sacre*. This second phrase lasts 5 counts (5 beats), continuing after the support of the violins has disappeared, a kind of repeat of what went before, but all that is left is the figure-of-eight, the left turn and the chop (on count/beat 5). Later, to a 'suave' horn tune at [25],[126] the longest musical unit so far in Augurs, a quartet of men perform a slower, more legato account of familiar moves, lasting 4 bars (8 counts): figure-of-eight, arm slash, right turn, sink into second position plié and close the feet together (see Ex. 6.12). Notably, Bausch absorbs musical principles of construction but uses them choreographically on her own terms, adding her own layer over the music; in other words, she does not duplicate musical structure in the manner of music visualisation. Here, whether consciously or not, she adopts the musical strategy of contraction and dissection (as well as extension) of units and also a range of periodicity (unit lengths of usually between one and four bars, 2 to 8 counts).

One of the most striking passages in Augurs is at ([28]+5), where a broad cantabile theme for trumpets that re-emerges in Spring Rounds dominates the multi-layered musical texture. Bausch responds with legato movement, visualising the cantabile, but without following the organisation of the musical theme. We can analyse the music as three units, each beginning in similar, but not identical, fashion, and divided into five smaller units (14 bars in total), asymmetrical and unpredictable, typical of Stravinsky, as follows (see Ex. 6.13, pp. 456-7):

Reading from [28]+5 as bar 1:
a Bars 1–6: 4+2, with bar 5 sounding as much like the end of the previous unit as the beginning of a new one.
b Bars 7–11: 3+2, the previous opening unit (bars 1–4) now truncated with just one bar of repeated B-flats.
c Bars 12–14: 3 bars, the opening unit now commencing with a rest. The unit concludes with an arbitrary cut-off, one block of material giving way abruptly to the next.

Bausch largely ignores the detail of the music, except for re-starting her material in bar 13 (after a transition bar 12) in delayed response to the musical repeat. Instead, for the entire group save one solo woman out front who repeats the key 'bob/strike' motif that opens Augurs (and another holding the red cloth), she weaves together the longest phrase of material that we ever see in *Sacre* (11 bars); part of it recurs to different music within Spring Rounds, Mystic Circles and

Ex. 6.13. *Le Sacre du printemps*, The Augurs of Spring, 'Big Phrase' (Bausch).

Ritual Action of the Ancestors. This 'Big Phrase' begins again like the man's solo: figure-of-eight, arm slash, right turn (bars 1–2); then it continues differently, punctuated by staccato pulses of the arms (they end crossed over folk-style), followed by a plié (bar 6), a little run backwards on the toes (bars 7–8), and a fold into the Augurs motif, briefly in unison with the woman out front (4 dance counts, bars 9–10). Then the main group of dancers step back into a kneel, like a massive yawn that links without a break into the figure-of-eight and the choreographic repeat (bar 13). This much-abbreviated repeat (just two bars) ends with a clap. Everything about this phrase seems special: length, legato, expanse of movement, the first sight of a surging unison mass. Its seed lies in the quartet of men and the new continuity and breath of their earlier 4-bar musical phrase (at [25]).

The figure-of-eight often signals an unusually close relationship between movement and sound, its pulling, sweeping characteristics and upward focus complementing cantabile, legato quality and rise in pitch. In such instances, we seem to hear the music with special clarity. In the Ritual of the Rival Tribes, the women use the figure-of-eight to initiate a soft, gentle statement (to theme B, [60] – see Ex. 6.4) that opposes the strident fussiness of the men (to theme A, [57]+3 – see Ex. 6.14). This is the clearest example of gender differentiation through orchestration in the whole of Bausch's *Sacre* (Evocation of the Ancestors is another example): women dance to woodwind and strings, and men to brass. Here, also unusually, Bausch matches passages of changing periodicity in

Ex. 6.14. *Le Sacre du printemps*, Ritual of the Rival Tribes, Theme A.

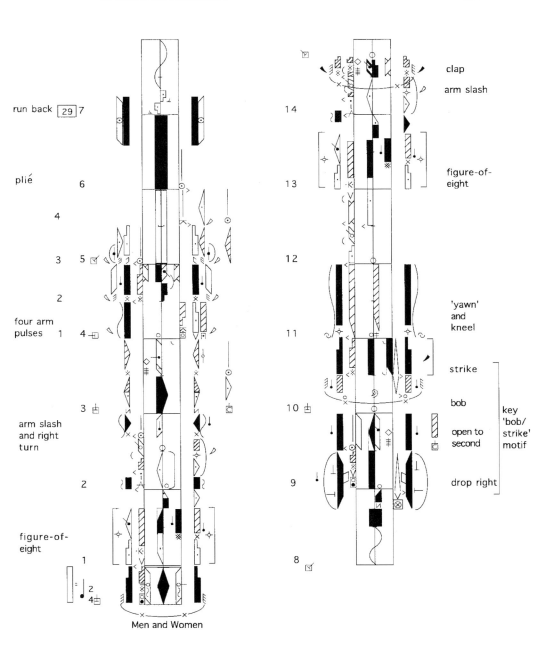

Ex. 6.13 (continued). *Le Sacre du printemps,* The Augurs of Spring, 'Big Phrase' (Bausch).

the music by responding to these changes in her choreography, at [60] and [61]. There is time to enjoy the relationship here, and shared repetition highlights the point. The figure-of-eight sings, with the opening rise in pitch. The second move is a plié in second position with arms circling up the sides and down the front of the body, and the third a turn with the circular motion continuing on through the arms. Depending on the length of the musical units, Bausch speeds up the dance material, or shortens it from three to two moves, and the figure-of-eight 'matches' the melodic contour of the opening musical motif with increasing frequency (see Ex. 6.15). Neither Hodson nor Béjart draws particular attention to this musical theme, but Bausch's emphatic treatment is appropriate to her particular context, where the women's easing into melody seems to confirm their bonding in sorrow and pain, or to reiterate a plea for compassionate behaviour.

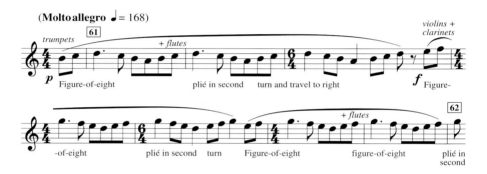

Ex. 6.15. *Le Sacre du printemps*, Ritual of the Rival Tribes, Theme B, women's material (Bausch).

There are further examples of structuring principles shared between music and dance. First, there is a tendency for material (especially the women's) to open out from and return to the body in a manner analogous to Stravinsky's phrases that wind around a central point or note. Then there is the device of ostinato, the unit of repeating material, and its recontextualisation through layering, sometimes several voices interacting as they operate simultaneously, sometimes more than one ostinato juxtaposed. Compared with the Hodson and Béjart *Sacres*, Bausch's choreography demonstrates a far more sustained use of the ostinato principle. But then, her work shows a far greater commitment to the intricacies of the musical score as a stepping-stone for independent as well as complementary choreographic development.

Rhythmic strategies

Returning again to the 'view from afar', as Bausch's *Sacre* progresses, we witness the battle lines being redrawn, from confrontation between bands of men and women to the pitting of a mixed mob against the Chosen One. We also see more use of the body as a non-dancing body, one that huddles together with others for protection (the women before the moment of selection) or to gain power (the men), one that watches and moves through space only in order to watch better, a hysterical body that, in the struggle to dance again, self-destructs. Alongside these dramatic developments, Bausch devises a structure of sharply contrasting attitudes towards rhythm. On the one hand, there is a regularity with highly predictable features, driven by an often thunderous pulse (which might be stopped, cut off, at any point, as with Stravinsky's block forms); on the other, its opposite, a state of diffusion, messiness, disarray. It is the highly regularised rhythmic sections that constitute the trajectory of power through her *Sacre*, pressing towards the event of annihilation, most strikingly in Augurs of Spring, the end of Ritual of the Rival Tribes (which leads into the Procession of the Sage), in the central section of Glorification of the Chosen One, and during the Ritual Action of the Ancestors. Passages like this come and go but, even if the actual time allocated to them is surprisingly brief, they dominate with their presence. Respite only reinforces the power of their reappearance, until, in the Sacrificial Dance, pulse turns into a taunting agent, a presence that always warns of absence, an absence that threatens presence. Bausch emphasises rhythmic contrast as two polarities far more than Stravinsky does in the score alone, taking advantage of the driving tendency within the music and exaggerating it when she chooses to use it, to make a composite statement with especially sharp outlines.

But the beginning of Bausch's *Sacre* is diffusion and disarray, and likewise the second beginning in Part 2. Like Béjart, Bausch chose to choreograph the Introductions to Parts 1 and 2, but, unlike him, she conceived both as women's music, and as a series of solos or independent dance voices. Individuals sometimes start up out of the crowd or rush across the space to make a statement. Out of this emerge accumulations of energy that draw the women closer into canons and unisons, the latter most prominent in Part 2. Pulse is relatively quiet, and during these Introductions we listen more to timbre and pitch contour: the woodwind in Part 1 conjuring up the calls of nature, the stronger string presence in Part 2 adding a story of sorrow and pain. The women seem like a visual equivalent to the musical babble that develops at the end of Part 1. Sometimes an instrumental line appears to attach itself to one of the women, insinuate itself and then be possessed: for instance, the lively curves of an oboe line and shrill answering clarinet embodied within rippling, snaking movement ([9]–[10]), and then the repeat of the clarinet motif acclaiming the image of a dress lifted over a woman's face to expose the front of her body (at [10]+2). When we see the dress image elsewhere, it is 'heard' quite differently, as process, the act of raising it, at [1]+2 and, in conjunction with mounting chord pressure, at the beginning of Part 2. Body and sound readily 'sop up' qualities from each other (see pp. 9-10) at particular moments that achieve sudden focus. There is a wonderful moment early on when a woman rises on her toes to a confident oboe line (at [5]), her body and arms opening bravely to the sound, and soon afterwards we pick out the low stutters on the bass clarinet echoed by her feet as she stumbles forward and back.

Perhaps the most significant feature of these introductory women's passages is the fluidity of the choreomusical relationship, movements coinciding with, echoing and anticipating sound. 'It' is 'outside' them, it calls them, although they have a way of making it part of their own personal speech (as they do in Ritual of the Rival Tribes –see p. 458), embodying it, engaging in a dialogue, or even occasionally leading it. The first woman to move stretches slowly over the red cloth in silence before the score even begins, sensually, as if dissolved into herself, and soon another rushes into our vision ahead of a melody line, already in a state of anxiety. The women are not yet controlled by sound. They have a measure of autonomy or agency. The Part 2 Introduction is more of an occasion for anguished contemplation of the past, remembering through movement, whilst a new motif on muted trumpets at [85]-1 (needless to say, not embodied) warns of the impending terror. By then, the music has begun to assume more control.

In other contexts where pulse is more pronounced in the score, Bausch tends to respond in one of two ways. The first is to choreograph without counts and to coordinate movement and music through listening, often with the instruction to do something as fast as possible and to finish on a given musical cue. Sometimes, musical accent patterns are extremely irregular, and the shock of an accent is embodied in a physical shriek, the body in reflex mode, gesture or jump as automatic response, like being shot from a gun. Take, for instance, the action of the first woman in Augurs to pick up the red cloth. Using the music's rhythmic motif (from [30]+3 – see p. 424), six irregularly spaced accents cast as punctuating chords, the cloth is jerked sharply into her body, four times, then thrust out to the extremity of reach on the last two accents. We then suffer a series of aftershock accents, now entirely freed from the musical texture, as the cloth is thrown in terror from one dancer to another. But there are other occasions when the music is far more regular, as in the Dance of the Earth (a section called 'Chaos' by Bausch). This begins with initial panic during which the dancers choose between four movements and which one to do where and when. Then, a long 3/4 ostinato passage begins in the bass, but the crowd just run and clutch at each other, blindly out of control.

Elsewhere, in her second mode of response, Bausch does use counts, and responds to metrical regularity within the music, and to irregularity referring back to its basis in metrical regularity, absorbing these musical principles into her choreography. I now want to focus on this aspect, as it indicates in extreme form the controlling capacity of the music, operating as it were outside this dance 'community'.

A working machine

My first example is Augurs of Spring. The music is written in 2/4, which is set up as an ostinato D-flat, B-flat, E-flat, B-flat in the transition passage at the end of the Introduction, when the women wait to begin dancing ([13]-7). Then we feel a downbeat 'one' in both music and dance, and the famous irregularly accented big chords begin (see Exs. 6.1 and 6.10). But there are soon passages where this sense of musical downbeat is less clear and we are unsettled. Thus, at the start of Augurs, we feel security, a regular 2/4 already established; we continue to feel it despite the shifting accents (of the rhythmic motif) occurring regularly on the offbeat. Then by about the sixth bar after [13], when the accents begin to shift to the onbeat, we begin to have doubts. Van den Toorn explains:

> Onbeats become indistinguishable from offbeats and, in terms of both the metre and pulse, the listener becomes 'lost'. So, too, in establishing and then disrupting these familiar crutches, their automatic, background character breaks down and they are momentarily thrust to the surface of musical consciousness.[127]

At [14], the D-flat, B-flat, E-flat, B-flat ostinato reappears and restores the sense of 2/4. The second disruption is more unsettling still (from [15]), as different instrumental voices branch out like exclamations and then with the added confusion of a 3/4 ostinato in the bass line. After a while, the repeating Augurs chords return (at [18]), and with them a brief sense of stability, yet their irregular accents now continue for much longer than before, and our sense of 2/4 is soon suspended, or at least reduced, until the end of the first Section of this dance (at [22]).

I will analyse Augurs in two Sections. There is a clear break at the end of Section 1. Section 2 involves more of the orchestra, layers of instruments and rhythms piling up, energy accumulating through pattern repetition and resulting in a climax. Only the women dance Section 1; the men join them for Section 2. The structural layout of Section 1 is as follows:

[13]-7	Transition: 'waiting'		
1 [13]	Key 'bob/strike' motif	4-count unit	x 8
2 [15]	Diagonal pathway	4-count unit	x 9
3 [18]	Turning upstage and back	4-count unit	x 4
4 [19]	Turning upstage and back	8-count unit (expansion of 3)	x 5 (last time 7 counts)
5 [21]+3, beat 2	Key dance motif (recapitulation)	4-count unit	x 4 (until [22]-2)

In Section 1, from time to time, we hear a solo instrument and see one of the women break out of the group accordingly. But let us focus here on the group. We feel the same downbeat 1 in the dance as in the music at the start, but this is not the only dance accent. There are other, dynamic accents, independent from those in the music: unlike Hodson/Nijinsky and scores of other choreographers, Bausch makes no attempt to bring out the rhythmic motif created by the irregular musical accents at this point. The first unit of movement, the key 'bob/strike' motif (lasting 4 counts/4 beats, 2 bars, from [13] – see pp. 451-3) is performed here like an ostinato, eight times in succession, and the strike is an example of independent dynamic accent. With all the repeats, there is plenty of time to register the movement, before an abrupt gear-shift. Bausch uses Stravinsky's procedures of immobility and abrupt discontinuity, ostinatos and block construction, but on her own terms and to her own expressive purpose: her own length of ostinato, her own block construction.

When the music first begins to sound metrically insecure (by about the sixth bar), the pattern in the dance is already established, and security continues within the dance through its repeating motif. The second dance unit is closely related to the first, and again in 4 counts (from [15] to [18]), concluding with the same big dance accent (the striking action) on count 4, but it travels down the diagonal and is shown nine times. Again, the choreography preserves the continuity when the music becomes rhythmically less certain, although in the *Sacre* film, this sense diminishes when the camera moves off the group.

From [18], there is another 4-count unit (performed four times), including the same dropping of the body and head, but turning upstage and back; and then, from [19], an 8-count unit turning upstage and back twice and performed five times (it is in fact the previous movement expanded with a new beginning – 4 extra counts – see p. 454). The step on count 1 of the 8-count unit has a lift to it, creating a fresh kind of accent, but this is a longer, more complex unit of material than the others, and we may well lose a secure sense of choreographic metre by the end of this passage, especially as our sense of musical metre is also weak at this point. How we sense regular periodicity may of course depend on how well we know the dance, and on whether we have kept our attention on the group or let it go to the breakout solos. As part of my own methodology, I deliberately took a break from viewing to get back to a position of naivety, of not 'anticipating' what was going to happen. Finally, the opening 4-count motif returns (at [21]+3, beat 2), at which point it is hard indeed to spot that the main dance (dynamic) accents have now moved from beat 2 to beat 1 of the musical bar.

Thus, Bausch creates her own rhythmic layer and modifies her own accent patterns. Interacting with the music, she presents her own version of security and insecurity, which is quite different from the effect of the music alone. Metrically speaking, we might call her reading 'conservative', because she never actively disrupts the sense of 2/4, despite her cross-accents. As much as we still hear Stravinsky's rhythmic dynamism, I would suggest that the power of the visual rhythm is, at least until [19], strong enough to settle us metrically where the music unsettles us. But by doing this, Bausch also makes us hear the music differently. So, to recapitulate, as much as the music is perceived as an 'outside', powerful force, Bausch can also interact with and change our perceptions of it. Some aspects of it might indeed, through mutual highlighting, become especially powerful.

On that point, as much as we experience real body sweat, toil, dishevelled hair, dirt, we might now consider that Bausch's Augurs is also an anti-body, anti-Subject (the human Subject) construction: mass as army or conscripted bodies or machine. This is established from the start as a position statement, the women bunched close together in a phalanx: unison movement, unison facings, largely on the spot, or hardly travelling at all. We recall that the machine was a very important feature of early twentieth-century art (see pp. 104-5) and certainly important to Stravinsky, whether embodied in the puppet Petrushka, the pianola, or his strict motor rhythms. In Bausch's Sacre, there is the excruciating tension between the image of the machine and the signs of humanity spilling out at every turn, through breath, convulsion and collapse.[128]

Bausch more than articulates the machine element that is already in the music – indeed, more than any other Sacre choreographer I know, she exaggerates the giant turbines at work in this score. We have a heightened awareness of Stravinsky's motor pulse because she shows that pulse so emphatically. But she also emphasises plain ostinato repetition more starkly than Stravinsky, which is of course a Bausch choreographic signature that extends well beyond her Sacre. One single idea goes on for a long time, underlined by mass unison; there is little to complicate the rhythmic canvas at this stage of Augurs. There are also moments of sudden lightness in the dance movement, such as the lift up and back on count 1 in the 8-count unit. The downward drive is not yet all-consuming. And there is a sense of freedom from musical accentuations, which is important at this point in the narrative.

In Section 2 of Augurs, from [27]-2, we see one of the women start up the machine again, recapitulating the opening motif, which is by now very familiar. A dance texture develops: several rhythmic voices, female group, male group, and solo woman, so that we see two, then briefly three, layers of arm accents all occurring at different times. Bausch borrows the principle of musical layers here, but again takes the principle on her own terms, not visualising any particular layer in the music. The succession of arms shooting upwards counterpoints the weight of the down accents that follow.

Later, from [31] to the end of the Scene, there is another layered effect in both score and choreography. In the score, the texture expands to a multi-voiced full orchestra of cyclical repetitions, offset by a syncopated bass line. There is a crescendo to climax and, in Hill's vivid description, 'the orchestra is gripped in a ritual of highly charged panting (the sexual implication is inescapable, surely intended) capped by whooping horns'.[129] Now, the men usurp the space, edging down a long diagonal with a repeating 8-count (4-bar) phrase (performed 8 times), and the women in 4-count (2-bar) units resort to the periphery.[130]

Through the power of the visual, Bausch subtly modifies our sense of shape during the second Section of Augurs. The Big Phrase at [28]+5 to [30] (see pp. 455-7) is in fact a mini-climax with a remarkable 'still' centre point, developing from multiple layers into mass unison, and even more remarkable in that the shifts in texture arrive effortlessly and in totally unpredictable fashion. For just two bars (4 counts), a wonderful moment, the male and female groups are in unison with the solo woman out front, all dancing the 4-count 'bob/strike' motif ([29]+3 – see Ex. 6.13). This impressive moment of harmony coincides most effectively with a thickening of the orchestral texture and an increase in volume. The group then slide away into their own material again, back to solo/accompaniment texture. Contrast the Hodson approach, which does not acknowledge this passage (from [28]+5) at all, indeed allows it to be especially quiet, and the tactics of Béjart who has all his men shuffle into position, so that the mass dancing merely confirms what we already predicted. Significantly, in *Fantasia*, Disney made the point at [28]+5 by shifting suddenly from boiling lava to a static image, a massive mountain dominating the screen. Driven by her particular agenda, Bausch's process of setting up this passage is long and gradual, notably avoiding use of the orchestra as a conventional gender signal. She chose not to allocate to the women the flute theme that Stravinsky scored for 'les Adolescentes' (at [27]). Instead, we hardly notice the gentle sound: Bausch sets to work on the textural overlays and plans for the longer-term future.

Soon, in *Sacre*, the music seems to take greater command in channelling the energy on stage. But, before examining the passage where the Ritual of the Rival Tribes leads without a break into the Procession of the Sage, we might first look back and consider how Bausch sets up this next 'machine'. Again, in her own way, she uses principles suggested in the score. At [64] in the Ritual of the Rival Tribes, a new theme C enters the score, on the tuba (see Ex. 6.16), overlapping with the women's continuing theme B (see Ex. 6.15). Originally, it was meant to signal the arrival of the Sage, and it leads seamlessly into his Procession at [67]. Theme C is in 4/4 time and counterpointed after two bars by a bass-drum line

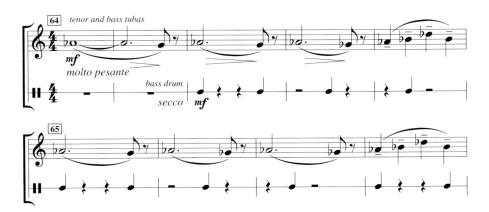

Ex. 6.16. *Le Sacre du printemps*, Ritual of the Rival Tribes, Theme C.

marking 3/4: together they turn out to be Bausch's next 'machine music'. Theme B drops out by [66], and much of the orchestra with it, leaving a very spare texture, soon after which the orchestral accumulation towards the second climax of the work commences, towards what was originally the moment when the Sage kissed the earth. Bausch adopts for herself the musical strategy of over-lap, but she introduces her machine movement much earlier than the music suggests, well before the arrival of tuba theme C. It is an arm phrase for the women, characterised by an elbow pulling sharply into the body, and a swing driving downwards, grouped as 3 x 3 counts/beats. Initially, this phrase alter-nates with their movement to theme B. We first glimpse it at [63]+2 (the women at that point fighting to hold their own against the men's movement and music), then it takes over entirely by itself, a repeating ostinato at [64], eleven bars before the musical texture drops to its own all-time low (bassoons, horns, tubas, drum, and moderate dynamics). At [66], when this low is reached, the women sud-denly seem very exposed.

By introducing her machine image in the choreography so early, Bausch is able to make the ostinato last for a very long time – so long, indeed, that we start to ask questions. Just how much longer will these wretched women do this? Will they ever be allowed to stop? We might even read the elbow movement as self-inflicted violence. Is it only the music that drives them? Who has agency here?[131] There are far more ostinato repetitions than in Augurs, seventeen plus an extra elbow pull from [64] to [71], and the phrase alternates with theme B twice before that. It is also significant that Bausch's phrase traces the 3/4 drumbeat thud, which gives the movement an edge as if the elbow action is a stomach punch – Bausch is one of only two choreographers I know who finds that drumbeat and highlights it choreographically – the other is Marie Chouinard, who uses it for half as long in a solo progression across the stage (see pp. 476-7). The women are pinned down by the drum, trapped and brutalised like a herd of animals. This is a dramatic strategy that gives huge power to Bausch's machine metaphor. Having found what she wants, she ignores the host of musical irregularities elsewhere in the texture that continue until [70], not only the distinctive rhythmic patterns of the different layers, but also the shifting periodicity of the tuba theme and horn motif, the latter creating unsettling on- and offbeat displacements.[132] Bausch goes for plain, stark impact.

When [70] is reached, the men start to dance the outline of a brazen, square trumpet ostinato, an incisive arm-slash marking the opening interval, and, unlike the women, with no sense of being beaten down. Here are layers again in both dance and music, the women still moving in 3s, the men in 8s (performing their phrase six times), all of them now visualising specific rhythmic layers in the music, which is, at this point, like the choreography, totally regular in its cyclical repetitions. The dancers are determined by sound pattern. Again, there is climax through repetition, which can only be halted by being literally cut off. I read that the women's pulse is literally dominated here, crushed by the rest of the music (including the men's music) during this brutal climax, a metaphor in musical terms for the narrative content of the work – we can see it but can hardly hear it. Returning to the concept of interaction, the possibility of mutual highlighting between media, Bausch makes us hear better the least emphatic layer in the score and, in this unusual context, we also hear that it is overpowered.

So how does the by now controlling capacity of the music progress during the second Part of *Sacre*, the Sacrifice? I suggest that the machine component becomes increasingly streamlined, with fewer and fewer cross-accents and cross-rhythms. The dance rhythm is now at its plainest and most pared-down, just as the dance texture is simplified, now just full ensemble (men and women in unison), and the male leader operating with the Chosen One. Much of Ritual Action of the Ancestors can be heard as plain four-square, or at least Bausch lets us hear it this way. She sets to the music either stillness or rhythmless walking or, at the two climaxes, the mass machine in action again. The first build to climax is an accumulation of dance material from the past, nearly all from Augurs, but on this occasion not just one ostinato repeated many times. Instead, each idea is repeated just a few times, before the onset of a new one. The dance metre is as clear as it has ever been (I count it in 4s, equal to 4 musical beats), with all the material timed so that the big accents are consonant with the music, on count 1: nothing is wayward any more. At [134], the Big Phrase from [28]+5 comes back, now tightened up with all breath removed, a movement on nearly every count. For the dancers, it is simply a matter of getting the movement accomplished on time, and, if necessary, forcing the pace. We feel the difference in effect, the choreography now completely absorbed into musical structure. Bausch achieves her second climax (at [138]) very simply, a stark image: the forces gather into a throbbing mob that inches forward, a vicious bounce added to every step.

The Sacrificial Dance

In the Sacrificial Dance, any notion of periodicity or regularity is constantly alluded to and lost. There is no musical ostinato here. Furthermore, during the Refrain material, the unit of beat operates at sub-tactus level, defined by the tiny semiquaver, a time unit shorter than what we normally physically understand as pulse. Irregularity at this level, so that no firm beat, let alone regular metre, can be sensed, is especially disruptive.[133] Bausch highlights the slipperiness in the score with a veritable breakdown in dance terms.

But first, it is important that this is such spare choreography (compared with, for instance, the Sacrificial Dance of Béjart and Hodson), and the least legible, formally crystallised part of Bausch's *Sacre*; it is a summary of community experience, a crazy assemblage of movement recollections, much reduced, sketched, barely there. The Chosen One goes along with a musical phrase, then it pulls her up short, and she stumbles, freezes or falls to the ground. The end is predicted from the start, an anticipatory fall (in the upbeat 'pause' bar to this dance), after which she picks herself up and immediately launches herself into the tempest. A key motif that returns again and again is the convulsion, single or double, both with the music and independent of it. Already familiar from earlier in *Sacre*, the movement ends with hands on thighs or clasped and shooting down between the knees. In different guises and degrees of clarity, it appears at the start of all the Refrain passages, and at the end of the whole dance it alternates with its opposite, a desperate reach with both arms, a final exertion or gasp strengthened by the new visual link with the male leader. He lies on the ground behind her, arms likewise raised parallel, but for the entirety of this dance.

As for pulse, I suggest that Verse 1 (see p. 428 and Ex. 6.7a), with its long span of irregularly spaced chords, is, in Bausch's hands, metaphor for a machine that now only functions in disrepair, in jerks and shudders – in other words, a metaphor for regularity or stability destroyed. We can find a crotchet pulse, but it happens within the silences as much as on particular chords, and is unable to form any higher-level regularity as metre. Later, there are only odd occasions when something more stable seems to emerge, just a couple of suggestions of duple time. Stravinsky saw the onset of the Sacrificial Dance as a significant moment of shift in his score. He once used the image of a 'driving rod' setting the 'rhythmic machine' of *Sacre* in motion, but considered the Chosen One's dance as 'excentrique' and 'outside the piece': it is what happens when the machine stops working and death takes over from life.[134] Probably without realising the connection, Bausch seems to have captured that image in her choreography with remarkable accuracy.

How does the Chosen One relate to what she hears? She clutches at what she can, but, for this dance, it is especially instructive to compare different perform-ance interpretations, to go beyond the 1978 film (with Malou Airaudo as the Chosen One), because what is perceived as something to clutch on to and the manner of the clutch vary considerably. The issue is dynamic and subtle rather than structural. There have been numerous Chosen Ones during Bausch's *Sacre* history, and a visit to the Wuppertal company archive allowed me to see seven more on company video from different periods and a film of Bausch rehearsing Kyomi Ichida in 1987.[135] Apparently, there is notionally a correct version of the solo (described through diagrams and word notes in a company 'black book')[136] and, from evidence extending to the present, this seems to be based on Marlis Alt's original performance. Yet 'natural' changes are understood to happen in the act of performance – how could a dance be alive without that capacity to live and risk in the moment? – indeed the two recordings of Alt herself already show variation. There is also the obstacle in performance of working through the stage peat, which creates its own pressures on and difficulties for feet and legs. I will concentrate on two interpretations of the music that 'speak' differently, the familiar film performance of Airaudo and that of Alt, for whom the role was created.

Airaudo seems to grasp the beat during the two clearest passages of duple time, both in Verse 2. First, she is forced into the elbow and arm-swing phrase (from [177], the onset of a repeating pedal note D, on violins and D trumpet), a much weakened account of the original (4 times); her attachment to what sounds like the syncopated beat 2 of a 2/4 bar gives the movement a limping quality (see Ex. 6.17). (In fact, her movement occurs on the written downbeat, in the middle of each D pedal note.) Later, she rushes forward and back, throwing her arms around her body in exasperation (from [184]-2, 6 times). Like many choreographers, Bausch draws out the musical repetition at these points in the score. (In his positivist account, Béjart magnifies these beats even further, his full ensemble eagerly following the leading couple in driving them home, fully moti-

Ex. 6.17. *Le Sacre du printemps*, Sacrificial Dance, D pedal in Verse 2.

vated and engaged, rather than pressured.[137]) Certainly, at these points, we begin to lose Stravinsky's image of a machine that has stopped working. Elsewhere, however, Airaudo's dance is like a struggle to obey, to match up to the command of chaotic sound that drags her energy into action and exhausts her in the process. Her behaviour is tragic reaction; she is repeatedly doomed to failure and hardly stands a chance.

Just before the end of *Sacre*, regular beat tries to reassert itself one last time, but the two rhythm lines in the score are out of phase. Soon after [198], as Hill writes: 'The effect of the bass is to move in even quavers, a semiquaver "out" with the upper line which likewise could be heard as regular, with a consistent quaver pulse ...' (see Ex. 6.18). The effect is ever more insistent, until they are forced back together in the 'climactic downbeat whack' at [201].[138] Airaudo seems to

Ex. 6.18. *Le Sacre du printemps*, Sacrificial Dance, final part of Coda.

make a colossal effort to be with one or other of the rhythmic lines, by now rooted to one spot and one facing direction in a series of massive spasms that ultimately fail as life is punched out of her. The big whack at [201] is the trigger for her to reach out to be saved one last time; then she crashes flat to the ground. The music cruelly clinches the deed with a final whack after her collapse, and so at last does the man's horribly impassive act of closure as he folds his arms down across his chest. Music specialists have often worried about the end of this huge score, how to end something so massive, so challenging, with so many crisis points along the way.[139] Bausch's profoundly economical solution demonstrates that theatre can help, and it works powerfully in all performances that I have seen.

Yet, seeing Alt's performance late on during the analytical process, after Airaudo's, came as a shock. There was not only a wholly different presence, but quite as surprising was my sudden awareness of much more musical detail, especially rhythmic and dynamic detail. Far more of the movement was precisely attached to note patterns, for Alt had exceptional ability both to move at light-ning speed (to keep with the music by dancing 'as fast as possible') and to stop on a sixpence, to be precise in timing and yet look out of control. I am convinced that she gave something back to the music, so that it in turn seemed sharper and larger in scale, somehow wrenched apart, yet at the same time never at the expense of its unnerving continuity. Examples:

- her arm and elbow gestures, zigzagging like a wicked knife, dissect into individual notes those units that Boulez labelled cell C (see Ex. 2.3a);
- she isolates a big chord by flinging her right leg to the side and her body in opposition, as if ripping herself in two;
- the dizzy, circling flourishes that climax Verse 1 are highlighted by a phrase of arm-circles – down in front of her, over the head, scooping her into a turn – you do not 'hear' this in other performances (which are so different as to suggest that the basic choreography has changed).

Of course, the music wins – it shoves and hurls her brutally – she tires, but Alt is nothing if not a brave fighter. She even slightly anticipates musical impulse at the start, in her determination not to fail, to create maximum ritual power, which makes it even more horrifying when she loses the battle in a final wild rush of uncontrollable hysteria. Musicality is a major contributor to Alt's extreme statement of resistance as the Chosen One, to her heroism.

It turns out that, whereas Airaudo and a number of other women seem to have stressed aggressive determination leading to exhaustion in the Sacrificial Dance, Alt had a wholly different way of looking at what she was doing. She describes the dance as 'like a gift so that life can continue, spring can come up ... I was dancing because of love [for my community]. I fought too at the beginning, but then I gave up ... I wanted to die.'[140] She identifies a specific moment when she relinquished her own self as a positive act, when, after circling her arms feverishly to the orchestral roar, she opens them wide and rushes down the stage diagonal, as if embracing her future (Verse 2, [175]–[176]): 'I started to live, but I [also] gave up life – very paradoxical!' The reading that the solo is primarily about woman's grim terror and despair needs to be revisited.

Alt's reading also had implications for her relations with music, 'at one with it', thrilled by its power, propelled by it to stumble, also believing that it helped her by giving her energy: it sustained her. And thus she appears to dance 'on top of' the music, but never in the sense of 'Mickey-Mousing', fiercely connected to it, almost triumphant about this rapport. She recalls that the choreography developed during an intense working process in the confines of Bausch's 'office' (the choreographer providing movement ideas that were then shaped through dialogue) and through performance. The notion of giving to her community was Alt's own. I imagine that the subtleties of musicality were hers, too.

Returning finally to the larger picture of *Sacre*, we have seen that Bausch is one of many choreographers to take advantage of the driving beat in Stravinsky's score. The difference with Bausch is the degree to which she exaggerates this musical presence, using the symbol of the machine as an agent of oppression, and pointing this up within a context that also reveals the opposite tendency towards chaos and devastation – where there is no beat, a loss of structure, a kind of staged illegibility. At the same time, it is fascinating to see that, in devising her own line through *Sacre* and pursuing a choreomusical policy that is definitely not about straightforward visualisation or duplication, she took off from so many suggestions that lie within the score itself, and from what she heard with an exceptionally acute ear, not from looking at the score.

This draws me back to the point about legacy, as I watch each *Sacre* through every other, at least notionally. I can now trouble that idea of Bausch's stage community being overpowered by sound, and the concomitant idea of sound as an 'outside' force, in which respect Bausch's *Sacre* has been a model for many that followed. Even if she broke sharply from the tradition of Béjart, could her *Sacre* not be another kind of spectacle? Her version now looks big. Mass unison becomes impressive, even when expressing pain, and the staging of a real body, undertaking real work and reaching a state of real exhaustion, is now a stylistic convention. Now that I consider Bausch's *Sacre* in the context of almost two hundred others, I cannot help but see it in 'spectacular' terms, more perhaps than I might have done in the 1970s, and especially as the number of performers has increased: a certain intimacy that the original production had is now lost. Sheer numbers say a lot. Bausch's *Sacre* is still miraculous, but perhaps after all an opera house ballet, still part of the old tradition, as much as it looks to the future.

A century of tradition

The production tradition of *Sacre* includes not only settings that draw from the models of Nijinsky, Béjart and Bausch, but also some that go in quite different directions. This production history is not straightforward; there are a number of overlapping trends and approaches to the score. It also extends beyond the orchestral score to encompass the four-hand piano *Sacre* and other arrangements.

Most choreographers have maintained the original 'tragic' scenario of the sacrifice of a Chosen One. Some, however, have extended the theme of sacrifice to embrace more generalised suffering and destruction, or, rather than portraying some archaic or exotic event, have elected to work within a more contemporary reality. Thus, some choreographers have stressed apocalyptic themes, holocaust and annihilation. One example was John Neumeier's 1972 production for the Frankfurt Ballet, which, partly prompted by the assassination of the Israeli athletes at the Munich Olympics, emphasised the degeneration of a society into chaos, alongside images of mass copulation.[141] In his 1990 *Sacre*, Horst Müller (Nuremberg Ballet) packed twenty dancers into a restricted space evoking a bunker. Susan Manning asks:

> Did Müller's production point toward the danger of nuclear holocaust? Or did his *Sacre*, which had its premiere several months after the Berlin Wall had fallen, refer not to the tension between East and West, but rather to the danger of environmental annihilation after Chernobyl?[142]

Other settings resonating with a local political context have used sacrifice as the prompt towards a positive outcome within the work itself. In Chile (*The Vindication of Spring*, Santiago, 1987), Patricio Bunster's chosen woman, personified as Spring, was tortured (sacrificed) by a Death figure, but then rescued during an uprising, life 'germinated' as result.[143] The first Soviet *Sacre*, by Natalia Kasatkina and Vladimir Vasilyov (1965), portrayed the emptiness of religion through the vehicle of a love story involving a shepherd (the proletarian hero) and a girl who is sacrificed to a totem god. In anguish, he plunges a dagger into the totem; without the expected punishment, the falsity of the god is revealed (see pp. 127-8).[144]

Other choreographers have revised the gender content of the original scenario. Mary Wigman (Ballet of the Städtische Oper Berlin, 1957) increased the role of women beyond the Chosen One, introducing a group of female Elders who initiate her into the secrets of the ritual and stand by her until the very end.[145] There has been a series of male victims, with several further examples from Germany. The first was the 1937 Cologne production by Lasar Galpern, cast as a symbolic struggle between the seasons, with the male Winter Devil defeated by women representing spring; then Glen Tetley's version for the Bavarian State Opera Ballet, Munich (1974), in which the Chosen Boy was like a Christ figure, suffering, killed and reborn with the spring; and Irene Schneider's version (1988), a feminist project in which three women representing the phases of the moon drove the ritual.[146] In 1997, the Russian contemporary dance choreographer Yevgeny Panfilov created an all-male urban *Sacre* for the Kirov Ballet.[147] Arranged marriage has also been staged, by Mats Ek (Cullberg Ballet, Sweden, 1984) within a traditional Japanese samurai family,[148] and Motaz Kabbani (Montreal, 2003) within an Arabic cultural setting (see p. 500).

The expressive range of *Sacre* has opened up considerably in recent years. Consider, for instance, the swiftly shifting mood-content of Javier De Frutos's highly acclaimed *The Palace Does Not Forgive* (London, 1994), about being an outsider, a Venezuelan living in London, a gay man raised as a Catholic: 'solitude, religion, sexuality ... I was using my body as a medium for getting them out. I was the sacrificial virgin, but I was questioning all the way why I had to participate in this ritual.'[149] In gold lurex dress (and nothing beneath), moving down a narrow corridor flanked by spectators and with 'altars' at each end, he seemed at various times angry, aggressive, passionate, self-mocking and flirtatious. It was a *Sacre* about confronting himself and the world.

A rapid Internet search has revealed further surprises, such as Michael Sakamoto's *The Rite of Spring, etc.* (Los Angeles, 2004), which incorporated comedy alongside frenetic dance, Butoh movement, melodrama and dream imagery, as well as having popular music excerpts interspersed through the piano score. It showed four characters 'sacrificing' their normal psychological defences – arrogant actor, idealistic monk, absurd harlequin and free spirit.[150] Then there was the half-burlesque extravaganza by Julie Atlas Muz (Dance Theater Workshop, New York, 2004), inspired by the story of JonBenet Ramsey (the murdered child beauty queen), carrying overtones of sexual violence as well as monstrous bad behaviour – 'dildo-unicorns, pageant-goers without underpants and a mastur-batory take on the traditional bourrée'.[151] It used an arrangement of Stravinsky's score for three guitars and drums. Obviously, some choreographers feel that, after this length of time and all the weight of heritage, they can afford to ease up on the original programme.

Most other settings have been more or less abstract, perhaps containing references to violence or suffering, whilst a few *Sacres* have indicated a primary concern with formal structure. An early *Sacre* clearly in line with formalist Stravinsky propaganda is the next recorded in *SGD* after the Béjart: the 1960 production in San Francisco by Joseph Marks (aka Jamake Highwater, later exponent of American Indian dance forms). His programme note stressed that the music is 'essentially an abstract composition' and likewise that this was essentially 'an abstract dance, echoing the Stravinsky concept wherever possible and giving meticulous attention to the musical idiom and emotional expression of the music as an entity of itself'.[152] Stravinsky could not have asked for more sympathetic intentions!

In 1974, in the programme note for his Dutch National Ballet production, Hans van Manen quoted from the revisionist Stravinsky: 'There is no plot, nor a reason why there should be one.'[153] The statement comes from the time of Massine's *Sacre* (1920), but makes far more sense in the context of van Manen's work, which had no specific story or setting, although, as is characteristic of this choreographer, there were strong overtones of feelings and eroticism. The same year, in New York, Joyce Trisler produced what was essentially a suite-like abstraction emphasising dance movement, and based in the style of Lester Horton. The final section was essentially a group dance.[154] The Chinese-born choreographer Shen Wei (New York, 2003) set his plotless *Sacre* to the piano score and used thirteen dancers as soloists engaging in multidirectional motion and occasionally teaming up into unison groups. Although this setting referred to the broad sweep of the music and its shifts between relative calm and nervous fury, it also picked out more detail than most others: the flurries of notes and trills transferred into complex multi-jointed motion, falls and rolls, and scurrying transitions. The choreographer himself created the floor painting.[155]

This discussion has already raised the issue of size of production. The mass tradition of *Sacres* continued apace over the last century, and it still does, choreographers thrilling their audiences by virtue of the physical power of huge forces. Perhaps the biggest *Sacre* of all, however, was the one in Berlin (2003) for some 250 schoolchildren from twenty-five different cultural backgrounds. Choreographed by Royston Maldoom, it was presented in the huge Treptow Arena in collaboration with Simon Rattle and the Berlin Philharmonic Orchestra.[156] This was one in a series of *Sacres* by Maldoom that began in 1989 with a setting for a London youth group, representing a fresh take on the score. Maldoom's work is as much to do with the practical experience of young people on stage as about a theatre experience for us as spectators. Most of those with whom he has worked have come from deprived backgrounds, and some have been street children. They have learnt about themselves, their personalities and physical identities, through collaboration and concentrated effort and, in Berlin, have done so alongside a world-class orchestra. Maldoom's *Sacres* have been staged in places as diverse as Ethiopia, Peru and Northern Ireland, as well as Germany and Britain, all carrying common elements, but with a programme flexible to change for different performing contexts.

Unsurprisingly, the Berlin Philharmonic production has attracted the most attention, especially because it was the subject of a highly acclaimed and widely shown film, *Rhythm is it!* (2004), which took audiences through the process of preparing this *Sacre*.[157] The production drew ideas from the original scenario, themes of ancestry and nature, including a figure who represents greater age and wisdom (here a Priestess). Maldoom awakened children to the existence of oppression through several examples of sacrifice: in Augurs of Spring, a woman who personifies a hunted deer; in Mystic Circles, a group of very young children who are threatened and from whom one is selected to be strung from a pole like a hunting trophy (during Evocation of the Ancestors); finally, the principal chosen girl as victim. For the audience, the commitment and energy that radiates from this production was deeply inspiring. Most of the participants were totally new to dance, and the fact that they operated without the mask of a dance style or training was especially refreshing: like the small black boy running in a huge circle to the crescendo in the centre of Dance of the Earth, dipping one arm down and up as if carving out a wave (from [75] in the score). Despite his size, his personal moment had magnitude: a run for the thrill of it and for life.

Rattle had apparently wanted for a long time to do a *Sacre* with children. Why *Sacre*? 'For me it is full of energy, one of the most powerful pieces that have ever been written. This piece of music immediately takes hold of your whole body and it feels as if it is emerging from the depths of the earth.'[158] The dance participants were not so sure at first. 'Stravinsky isn't what you'd call modern ... I really don't have a feeling for it.' [Philipp] 'I played the music to lots of people, but nobody liked it ... But a good friend and I figured we could use it for sampling ... There are some really cool passages.' [Martin] Yet, gradually, through rehearsal, imaginations were sparked, and moving to *Sacre* became a voyage of discovery: 'You feel like living inside the music now ...' [Gerry] 'I experience myself differently ... Everything is different.' [Martin] This has to be one of the most far-reaching *Sacres* of our time, and perhaps one of the most educationally important for its performers. In Germany, it led to the introduction of dance for the first time into the curriculum of a number of schools, the popularity of the film documentary playing a key role.

Yet alongside acclaim for the project, concerns were voiced about the strong discipline-based, goal-oriented approach which, although needed in order to get the show together on time, militated against student-based learning. Faced with a method of directing students that was far from her own, one of the teachers, Miriam Pech, says during the film: 'On the one hand, we understand his [Maldoom's] artistic goals, his approach, his way of demanding and pushing and treating them as artists. On the other hand, we see that they've all reached their limit and really can't go on.' The choice of *Sacre* is important: a 'dangerous' work that became a metaphor for the learning process itself. It raised diverse identity issues and engendered strong personal feelings: about loss of self within a group, fear of crowd control, mob power (its thrills and horrors), as well as the experience of collaboration and the phenomenon of being literally moved by sound.

At the opposite end of the size spectrum, Joseph Marks's abstract production had a cast of just five women dancers. Unusually small for its time, it anticipated one of the most striking trends in *Sacre* treatment of the late twentieth and early twenty-first centuries. Choreographers have recognised the monster that Stravinsky made. Over the century, the scale of orchestral forces has been a problem for choreographers, either to match up to them or at least to negotiate some kind of power relationship with them, and indeed some decided that the score was too colossal to bear choreography, however large the cast. But more recently, choreographers (usually from outside opera house institutions) have made a virtue of that unmatchable power, with the music clearly read as a force 'outside' the dance, the dancers making contact with something beyond their space or reach. A small number of performers on stage has been part of the purpose. The convention of mass response thus undermined, the audience now engage with individuals, personalities confronting something much larger than themselves.

The American Molissa Fenley made her solo *State of Darkness* (Sesto Fiorentino, 1988) to reflect the broad drama of the music and the fear she felt it contained (the plotless option was no longer unusual by this time), while also drawing from animal and nature imagery. She explained her unclothed torso: 'I wanted to work with a lot of very subtle quivering movements such as a deer would make – this frightened, quivering thing – and I couldn't do that wearing a top.'[159] But her version seemed also to be a celebration of human power, a huge endurance test for this dynamo dancer, and perhaps, too, recognition of Nijinsky's individual creative achievement (she said she had felt his presence in the dance studio – see p. 416). At the end, as she moved from darkness into light, to stand, gazing boldly at the audience, the orchestra allowed Fenley's Chosen One to become superhuman.

A version from the French Canadian choreographer Marie Chouinard (Ottawa, 1993) looked at the solo form in a different way, more as an opportunity for eight onstage individuals, often moving in independent spotlights. According to Chouinard, there is no linear progression in this *Sacre*, '... no cause and result, there is only simultaneity', and there is no theme of destruction: 'It is as if I was dealing with the very moment in which the first germ of life appears. The performance is the analysis of this moment.'[160] Expressing physicality as passion, the dancers are anonymised in body tights, occasionally with horns, claws or quills added – like Fenley, drawing from nature, often moving more like animals and plants than humans. They refer to the two-dimensional imagery associated with Nijinsky (*L'Après-midi d'un faune*), while communicating bodily depth, sometimes in a trancelike state, breathing audibly, sometimes bursting with pent-up energy. In a different way from Fenley, Chouinard's dancers rise to the challenge of the music. From their power in isolation, we are made to believe that just one body is more than able to match its force.

Many other small-scale *Sacres* present the power of music as punishing. In Daniel Léveillé's setting to the piano score (Montreal, 1982), four dancers moved solo as if 'after the bomb', representing the 'craziness that happens at the end of the world'.[161] Co-choreographed with the Russian Seasons Dance Ensemble, Min Tanaka's *Sacre* (Moscow, 1998) stemmed from Butoh tradition, which is predicated upon a notion of self-sacrifice, relinquishing the ego in order to reach a new spirituality.[162] Here, music is a power above the stage action, dominating the ritual. The score is a life force struggling to be born, its opening phrase heard over and over before the rest is released. The community of twelve men and women move through simple repetitive sequences, expressing struggle and loss of control, their outbursts of energy ending inevitably in hopeless collapse. They look upwards to the sound and listen to its call, moved by it, compelled to match up to it; unable to get into its rhythmic groove, they succumb to exhaustion. The music continues implacably, an overt symbol of oppression.

Certain similar qualities imbue the internationally acclaimed solo *Hunt* (Venice Dance Biennale, 2002) by the Finnish choreographer Tero Saarinen, who, initially a classical ballet dancer, later studied Butoh and modern dance. The Saarinen Company information booklet indicates that *Hunt*, made 'in the information age', represents 'inner conflicts ... [between] the hunter and the hunted, good and evil, masculinity and femininity'.[163] There are references to *The Dying Swan* (Fokine, 1907) in a recurring broken-wing motif. Again, there is a sense of the music occupying surrounding space, and in Part 1 an air of experiment as Saarinen listens, meditates, opens up to and absorbs sound according to his own terms – a deep physical experience. Saarinen is hardly with the music in the sense of its rhythms or presentational aspects; indeed, often he moves after the musical stimulus.

At the start of Part 2, a huge, stiff white skirt descends from the sky like a spacecraft.[164] Saarinen rises into it and, at this point, the element of intrusive force increases in parallel with the music's power. Saarinen has become 'the hunted'. There are moments now when the motor drives him, but, even more invasive, after a plunge into darkness, a moving projection by the multimedia artist Marita Liulia, showing Saarinen's own dancing body and using the musical rhythms, spreads like a wild virus from his face across his entire apparatus. Technology takes over the motor, subsuming his identity, threatening oblivion, and the last part of the Sacrificial Dance becomes increasingly dark – to the slow beats of a strobe – the music by now much more of a driving force. There is a final glimpse of the possibility of escape, with Saarinen caught by the strobe in the midst of a jump towards freedom and light (or perhaps to death). The ending is ambiguous. So his *Sacre* questions both received ideas of embodying the musical rhythmic content as dance music and the victim's inevitable collapse. It resists what we know best.

Choosing the four-hand piano (rehearsal) version of the score automatically enables distance from the mainstream *Sacre* tradition. It is not simply a matter of employing a reduced accompaniment to 'match' a chamber cast on stage, an obvious solution for small dance groups seeking live accompaniment and needing something more portable than an orchestra. The piano scoring creates a different piece of music. Sometimes the emphasis within a musical texture is different and sometimes the separate voices are less clear. Performance interpretation plays a role, but the piano sound is already more homogeneous than the orchestra; what was once a fortissimo orchestral tutti may now seem like a perfectly normal accompaniment for just one dancer. But it is especially interesting that the cantabile theme for trumpets at [28]+5 (which accompanied Bausch's Big Phrase – see pp. 455-7) is far less impressive on the piano, here a low-volume tune that sidles in, no louder or more prominent than the music that precedes it. This is perhaps the reason why Hodson (prompted by the published notes drawn from the early piano rehearsal score) responds so quietly to this passage: Nijinsky's *Sacre* was, after all, created to the piano score.

Some of Stravinsky's rhythmic layering is absent from the piano score, because four hands cannot manage the full complexity of the orchestral texture. Perhaps the most significant differences between versions occur in the Procession of the Sage, where the 3/4 drumbeat that Bausch 'discovered' (see pp. 465-6; here a low chord cluster) disappears early from the piano score, at [68].[165] Later, at [70], the striking, sharply outlined trumpet ostinato, to which Bausch's men stamped and gestured violently, cannot be found at all. Repetition with a change of orchestral scoring has often meant a change of dancer, even a change of gender. On the piano, there is no such suggestion. The piano can also suggest monochrome imagery, as it did for Shen Wei's stripped-down black, grey and white interpretation, and for Alston's 1981 production for Ballet Rambert, which referred to the icy Russian winter.[166] With the piano as an essentially percussive instrument, a quality that Stravinsky himself eagerly accepted (see p. 138), the legato of strings and wind gives way to a more articulate surface: played Stravinsky style, the piano can even sound mechanistic, tinny or brittle.

The number of *Sacre* settings to piano has increased markedly in recent years, but not just to Stravinsky's four-hand original. Recently popular is Fazil Say's solo version, a double-track recording merging his own performances of each two-hand part, on Yamaha Disklavier (2000). Accompanying Shen Wei live in 2003, Say supplemented his electronically produced metallic sound with some prepared-piano plucking.[167] Motaz Kabbani and Michael Sakamoto have also used Say's recording. In his *Milagros* for the Royal New Zealand Ballet (2003), his fourth setting of *Sacre*, de Frutos used the pianola recording of the score, for which Stravinsky himself had supervised the programming of the piano rolls. This enhanced level of dehumanisation appropriately underscored the spare, formal and repressive elements within De Frutos's construction: for six men and six women in long white dresses, a cruel ritual that pitted explosions of desire and violence against harsh sexual constraint. The choreographer enjoyed the exceptional speed of the pianola version and the fact that, in this version, 'the dancers can feel bigger than the music. The rite is coming from them, not from the orchestra.'[168] But there are other 'straight' uses of the piano, for instance, a four-piano version by Maarten Bon used by Ed Wubbe in a plotless setting (Rotterdam, 1996), when an inclined wall-mirror reflected and multiplied the movement of the pianists (onstage) and dancers.[169] Sometimes, choreographers have preferred to use two pianos for the four-hand score, rather than only one – for instance, Paul Taylor (1980), and Uwe Scholz in his solo *Sacre* (2003).

Again, using the piano score, in *Dream Driven* (New York, 1985), Rebecca Kelly opted for a radically new theme, a young woman's struggle with alcoholism. The story was told mostly in flashback, but ended in hospital, a detox scene in which she surrenders to the figures of her past. Introducing a complex cluster of characters – including woman/patient, doctor, husband, lover, crazy inmate, party woman, career woman, young girl dreaming – the dance was also about female victimisation. Writing about the 2000 revival, Lynn Garafola described how Kelly's 'protagonists are stripped and sent to madhouses, surrounded by creatures of nightmare, violated by half-naked men ... always unable to escape'.[170] Tom Schilling titled his setting *Die Probe* (*The Rehearsal*, East Berlin, 1985), another reason to use the piano score, recalling its original purpose: he showed two rival ballerinas, first in a studio, then, confronting danger in an empty, timeless space, drawing together in their suffering.[171]

Paul Taylor's piano Sacre: A Rite *rehearsal and detective story*

Perhaps the most celebrated use of the piano score, subtitled 'The Rehearsal', is the one by Paul Taylor created in 1980, the first use of the piano version currently identified in *SGD*. It is also a fascinating choreomusical enterprise. Before 1980, Taylor's only experience of *Sacre* settings had been Disney's *Fantasia* (seen as a child) and live performances of the ballets by Béjart and Tetley.[172] But he had used the score as the musical basis for rehearsals of *Scudorama* in 1963, before the completion of its commissioned electronic score by Clarence Jackson.[173]

Aside from the rehearsal connotations, Taylor felt that 'the rhythms sound clearer' in the piano version.[174] The construction of the music in blocks within larger Scenes suited the style of his narrative, a cartoon detective story (set c. 1930) comprising a litter of events of different kinds: 'Nothing [in the music] goes on for terribly long at a time,' he said, 'and there's a lot of variation in tempo and in texture.'[175] First, the plot, as neatly summarised by the critic Alan M. Kriegsman:

> ... it begins with the warm-ups of a dance class, presided over by a blankly imperious Rehearsal Mistress (Bettie de Jong) in a cossack outfit. What the troup 'rehearses' is a plot out of Fu Manchu or some other pennydreadful whodunit, involving a Private Eye (Christopher Gillis), a Girl with babe-in-arms (Ruth Andrien), an Oriental Crook (Elie Chaib), his Stooge (Lila York) and his Mistress (Monica Morris), with the 'corps de ballet' depicting henchmen, cops, and 'bar maidens'.
>
> The central action concerns the kidnapping of the infant, the jailing of the private dick, his escape and retrieval of the child, and a satirical stage-strewn-with-corpses ending that leaves only one cast member – the Girl – still 'alive'. The coda returns us to the dance classroom, with the Rehearsal Mistress looming ominously over the drained, supine figures of her charges.[176]

As Angela Kane has pointed out, unlike in most other *Sacres*, Taylor's plot 'tends to focus on the actions of individual characters rather than a ritual-driven, homogeneous group'.[177] There are just twelve dancers, all of whom appear at some point as named characters, whilst the detective and rehearsal 'stories' interweave throughout. Another element incorporated into the piece was the movement style of Nijinsky, a tribute to the past. Here again, the two-dimensional, twisted-body style was taken from Nijinsky's *Faune*. Taylor had also seen photographs of the original *Sacre*, and absorbed from them the principles of 'bound' movement and angularity, so that the energy always returns to the core of the body rather than giving the illusion of expanding beyond physical possibility.

'Irreverent Rite' was the title of Kriegsman's article, whilst Anna Kisselgoff and Octavio Roca called Taylor's work an 'anti-*Sacre*', and Arlene Croce thought it 'too cheerful, too impersonally efficient to be disturbing'.[178] All of them loved it. Yet, with the twist at the end, we confront the horror full on, powerfully reminded of the original 'tragedy'. As Berg suggests: 'The ritual murders which Taylor depicts are more numerous, calculated and chilling ... Taylor seems to be saying that the drive to destruction of modern man is more terrifying in its indiscriminate victimization of innocent and guilty alike.'[179] Taylor's work is also unsettling because it seems on the surface to be highly ambiguous, disturbing because it both seems to 'enjoy', by sending up, social breakdown and to register how awful that breakdown is. How can anyone assume such polarised positions simultaneously? The media encourages us to do so all the time. Taylor, for whom contemporary social violence is a regular concern, as are 'the corruptive influences of popular culture and media stereotypes',[180] unmasks that fact. The wonder of the work is that all these component parts, which expand our imaginations over a broad canvas, are constrained within a very economical framework: a spare set and designs by John Rawlings, a cluster of small props (handbag, money, the baby as a doll), a ladder that is both a dancer's barre and a drinking bar, a fence for a jail cell, a dressing table, costumes in white, grey and black with an occasional splash of red (blood), as well as the 'reduced' piano score.

Sources for analysis are the television broadcast of the work (1981) and the Labanotation score (1979–86).[181] I used the four-hand piano recording by Benjamin Frith and the music analyst Peter Hill as my principal musical recording.[182] The pianists featured in the television broadcast are Donald York and Michael Ford.

Taylor's main dance events connect with Stravinsky's score as follows:

Part 1: Adoration of the Earth

Introduction	Two scenes: Rehearsal, and meeting of Private Eye and Girl with baby
The Augurs of Spring [and] Dances of the Young Girls	Bar dance
Ritual of Abduction	Raid and kidnapping of baby by Crook's Mistress
Spring Rounds	Rehearsal Mistress and Crook's Mistress in mirror pantomime; the Crook brings jewels to the Mistress
Ritual of the Rival Tribes	Duet: Crook and Mistress
Procession of the Sage	Rehearsal Mistress pays dancers

| Dance of the Earth | Duet: Rehearsal dancers, which becomes double duet when the Crook and Mistress join them |

Part 2: The Sacrifice

Introduction	Dream duet: Private Eye (in jail) and Girl
Mystic Circles of the Young Girls	Private Eye's jail break; Rehearsal Mistress and Crook's Mistress in second mirror pantomime
Glorification of the Chosen One	Fight between Private Eye and three Policemen
Evocation of the Ancestors	Meeting of Private Eye and Girl in the park with the rescued baby
Ritual Action of the Ancestors	The Killing, with 'Garland' trio of women as interlude
Sacrificial Dance	Solo (Girl); Ensemble

It is worth noting that Taylor does not read music, which he considers an advantage: 'It does force me to listen very hard, and I think that can be a benefit.'[183] Does this lack of reading affect his approach to the music? Taylor felt free to partition the score in a fresh way, led by the demands of his scenario. There is no break between the two Parts (no real pause at all), and many of the original Scenes divide into sub-scenes or episodes featuring different protagonists and furthering the action. Yet there are some connections with the score subtitles: there is an abduction (of the baby) in the Ritual of Abduction; the Crook and his Mistress have such a combative relationship that they become the 'Rival Tribes'; and there is without doubt a Sacrificial Dance at the right time by a solo Girl. Most sections of the work contain mime as well as dance, the two modes brilliantly intertwined. There are just three real 'dances'. The first, to the Dance of the Earth, continues the strife theme between Crook and Mistress, but is now led by two 'rehearsal' dancers, with the other pair in their shade, an eruption of angry energy that is also a consolidation, drawing on familiar movement material. Then there is a love duet during the Introduction to Part 2 of the score, the Private Eye's dream, tender and quiet by contrast with the Dance of the Earth. Taylor creates a new dramatic shape with an all-dance 'centre', violent exclamation followed by a rare glimpse of humanity. Finally, there is the Sacrificial Dance itself.

The development of events also affects the shape of individual Scenes of the score. For instance, there is less sense of major accumulation at the end of Augurs of Spring (the Bar Dance) than in the other *Sacres* analysed, and more continuity instead. The Scene is cut off early, as argument breaks out and three men don caps as policemen preparing to sort out the trouble. Similarly, the Procession of the Sage and Dance of the Earth end with the dancers leaving the stage at the final climax. Taylor prepares for the next action, rather than trapping the accumulated energy within the confines of the stage.

An especially interesting example that invites us to compare Bausch's contrasting treatment of the same music (in the orchestral version) is the Ritual Action of the Ancestors. Taylor subdivides the Scene into several episodes. It begins just after the family have been reunited – Private Eye, Girl and baby (Evocation of the Ancestors) – and most of the movement is mixed dance-mime:

[129] The Crook's Stooge enters intent on killing the baby.
[131] The Rehearsal Mistress enters with three 'rehearsal women' and a garland of flowers, a strange interruption 'outside' the main thriller plot.
[132] The trio dance around the Rehearsal Mistress, referring to the tradition of the three Graces and Greek-style dancing.
[134] The Crook suddenly arrives and dances alone. FIRST MUSICAL CLIMAX
[135] He is joined by his Stooge and, in the last four bars of this episode, by one of the Henchmen, gathering power and confidence.
[138] They hide as two Policemen dance. SECOND MUSICAL CLIMAX
[139] The characters kill each other in turn, seven individuals in total, plus the baby last of all, leaving only the Rehearsal Mistress and the Girl.

Bausch starts her menacing mass 'machine' at [132], with, admittedly, an increase in volume from the orchestra to support her (whereas the piano score merely indicates *piano* and *tranquillo*). She builds steadily to the Big Phrase climax at [134] (see p. 467), the dancers pressing on in inexorable fashion, spreading forwards and sideways to occupy more and more space, looming up behind the Chosen One and the leader who sustains her prior to her dance of doom. Then there is respite before an even larger climax, the throbbing mass inching forwards, at [138]. Taylor develops tension from a range of disparate events and character groupings, with stop-start dynamic shifts and many more twists and turns. The killing of the baby is a shock upbeat to the Sacrificial Dance. It happens within a musical silence, the unlikely action of the dying Stooge jabbing the baby behind her head. After 'all that', people titter in disbelief at what they have witnessed – at least, they do on the television broadcast.

In reverse, the Sacrificial Dance turns into a large statement using the full cast resources to achieve its effect. Taylor divides it into two distinct halves, the solo and then an ensemble dance – the only real mass dance in the piece, dominating until a final glimpse of the Girl, who is the last to fall to the ground.

Given that dance can confer specific meanings upon, or transfer attributes to, music (which is a site for the negotiation of meaning – see p. 8), here the piano scoring not only evokes the notorious rehearsals of Nijinsky's ballet, but also the percussively driven American modern dance class. Its mechanistic potential is

highlighted by the dance rhythmic content. As is often the case, the transference of attributes works both ways. The piano in turn underscores the dance: the acid trills in Spring Rounds (at [51]) underline the shaking of stolen jewellery and seem to become nastier by association, and the infernal rattle over aggressive chords in Ritual Action of the Ancestors bolsters the Policemen's dance at [138], their final thrust of determination before the killing starts. The piano calmly supports the love duet (Introduction, Part 2), but, like the couple, it is glassy, never too sentimental, never too sweet.

As well as finding the rhythms 'clearer' in the piano score, Taylor claimed that *Sacre* was 'one of the easiest things to dance to I've ever done ... [because] the basic tempo is not fluctuating, and once you get the basic beat, then it's easy'.[184] This point is especially revealing, because Taylor's choreography is indeed more consistently beat-driven than any other *Sacre* that I know. Croce expresses this vividly as an expressive device, drawn from the particularities of the piano score:

> Stravinsky exposed its pistons and gears, and it's this mechanistic aspect of the music that Taylor responds to. He hears the ticktock ostinato that winds up those massive charging rhythms – hears it as the music of automatons chugging to their doom in a deterministic universe.[185]

Taylor's characters operate like automatons in two ways. It shows in their reaction, or rather lack of reaction, to horrific events and their emotionless, thoughtless return to routine behaviour. But it also shows in their embodiment of rhythm and their body language. They attach themselves fiercely to the score in plain walking, running and gestural sequences, and often within hard duple-time patterns of repetitive motion, series of jumped lifts up and down (1 2, 1 2 etc.), rocks back and forth, twists side to side. There is a good measure of 'Mickey-Mousing' too, matching accentuations drawing attention to themselves as a mechanically applied device.

The nature of the body work drives this rhythmic style, with the movement stopped in angular designs, cardboard-cutout style, and motion into a design often marking a pulse or accent in the music. The two-dimensional shape of one leg forward, the other back, arms raised in opposition to the legs and angular flexion everywhere you look, is the theme image of the whole work, whether upright or tilted (see Ill. 18). Taylor takes full advantage of rhythmic potential in the air with movement that has neither the uplift of ballet nor the groundedness of some styles of modern dance: bodies with apparently neutral weight indicate the height of a jump or lift as a clear design in space and as a clear rhythmic moment. Add the piston-style repetitive motion and the somersault lifts that turn bodies into cartwheels, and the transformation of characters into 'noisy' machinery is complete.

Ill. 18. Lisa Viola as the Girl in *Le Sacre du printemps (The Rehearsal)*, Sacrificial Dance, choreography by Paul Taylor, Paul Taylor Dance Company.

It is crucial that there is little relief from this rhythmic style. Only the Girl gives us a glimpse of a better world, and even then just occasionally. She still makes plenty of 'pictures', but also softens as she gives her weight to her man – which in turn gives 'body' back to the music – and as she rocks her baby in scooping, shifting steps from side to side. In Augurs, significantly, she assumes for herself what was originally the 4-bar legato horn (men – see Ex. 6.12) and then flute (women) theme. Equally significantly, in the Ritual of the Rival Tribes at [60], the Mistress assumes the 'women's music' (theme B) just once (see Ex. 6.4), to mime the same baby-rocking, showing that she yearns for the baby far more than for the Crook's stolen jewels. Then, the autopilot combative relationship with the Crook subsumes all. To the next, more extended passage of 'women's music' (at [61]; see Ex. 6.15) – the piano timbre admittedly more gender-neutral than the original orchestration – Taylor has devised a remarkable progress for the Mistress and Crook across the stage, a repeating 3-count unit of mutual sparring, blows and avoidance of blows (crossing the musical metre).

Even during the fluid Introduction to Part 1, Taylor is eager to start up his motor. The musical Scene is divided into four dance episodes:

- the Private Eye (in front of a scrim, [1]);
- a group warming up for rehearsal, roll-ups, pliés and stretches, several activities happening simultaneously (behind the scrim, [1]+4);
- back to the Private Eye (at [4]), who is visited by his Girl and then leaves with her;
- back again to the rehearsal, where warming-up has now accelerated into allegro and jumping, and rehearsal props are exchanged ([7]+3).

When there is no pulse readily available in the music, the dancers make their own. Warm-ups provide an obvious opportunity, but there is an absurd argument between the Private Eye and Girl out front (from [5]), who drop one after the other into a kneel (the Girl) or a splat fall (the Private Eye), a repeating sequence that between them creates a bold, slow pulse, and there is also to-and-fro action, an altercation between a couple of the rehearsal dancers over a red bag [9]. A musical ostinato starts up at [7]: usually I barely notice it, and I have never seen it choreographed, but perhaps the piano score makes it more pronounced. Taylor celebrates its steady, fast pulse, introducing it on the lead couple for their cakewalk departure [7], later allocating it to the rehearsal dancers for classroom jumps and jogs: the Laban score at [7]+3 indicates that they should appear mechanical in the manner of automatons.

This early exposition of different pulse rates sets the style for the whole of Taylor's *Sacre*, and indeed we seem to experience the fast pulse more often and with more definition during his work than we do from the music alone. This happens early on in Augurs, patterns of stepping forward and back (4 moves), with a heavy shunt on two feet to start [13], marking the quavers: Taylor does not visualise the famous cross-accents here. Even when the bigger crotchet beat is announced as the couples rock to and fro and the women fly at their partners in stomach bumps (at [14]+5), the group constantly returns to the quaver rate. You see it in the sprightly running, in the men's steps as they promenade or lift the women (or at least they seem to try to move that quickly), and in Taylor's favourite bouncing jumps, two feet to two feet (flexed feet in the air, one leg forward, the other back, the theme image again), when beat is perceived both on the up and on the down.

There are times when the beat imprinted on our consciousness is even faster than this. One example is the triplet quavers in the Dance of the Earth, when the men hold their partners under the armpits and rush them forwards like juddering wheelbarrows. There are countless instances, too, of small stuttering runs that seem to analyse the structure rather than show the overall effect of trills and tremolos. Perhaps because we are geared from the beginning to spot the rhythmic fit between music and dance, we notice such minute articulations, and as a kind of temporal fragmentation that engenders mental, if not physical, strain. Pulse sends us a little mad, too.

Dissection of the principal musical beat happens in the most unlikely places, when the music barely supports the progress of the story. There are two parallel passages in Spring Rounds and Mystic Circles when the Rehearsal Mistress and Crook's Mistress sit opposite each other at an invisible dressing-table mirror – the one becomes mirror for the other. They mime staccato against legato music: a bit of baby-bouncing on the knees (see Ex. 6.19), then baby-patting, nose-powdering and deodorant-applying – spots of brisk, rhythmic activity that keep us feeling sprightly when the music does not. Possibly to speed the dramatic pace when things are beginning to hot up, Taylor takes the Mystic Circles music much faster than Stravinsky's metronome indication (crotchet = 80 and 108 as opposed to the scored 60 and 80).

Ex. 6.19. *Le Sacre du printemps*, Spring Rounds, in four-hand piano reduction (Taylor).

Often Taylor shows simultaneous dance lines proceeding at different pulse rates and the relationship between big and small beat. Perhaps as relief, drawing upon his established choreomusical behaviour elsewhere, Taylor introduces moments of metrical crossing – 3s against 4s in the music, or 2s against 3s, again drawing attention to beat – but these are sporadic spice rather than stylistic substance in his *Sacre*. In the Dance of the Earth, several moments in rapid succession develop dance (or rather choreomusical) momentum highly effectively. Here, the 3/4 musical ostinato sustained throughout enables steady accumulation to musical climax, but Taylor plays both with and against it. At [73]+4, the rehearsal couple engage in a jumping contest – a 3-count unit labelled 'jumping bean' that fits the musical metre, although it did not when we first saw it in Augurs, at [19]+6 – then they push themselves forward and back one after the other, 'me, you, me, you'-style (a step in a 2-count crossing rhythm). Later, to the crescendo from [75], there is a long series of cartwheel lifts, the Crook and his rotating Mistress now working in canon with the rehearsal couple, each lift marking the 3/4 bar. Finally, more jumping and forward and back alternations (3s and 2s) precede a dazzling, bouncing exit (a 4-count unit), the women's springs enlarged by an extra heave from their partners.

In the Glorification of the Chosen One, Taylor exploits to the full Stravinsky's play between offbeat and onbeat (or weak and strong beats). This is the exceptionally irregular Scene when big whipping musical gestures alternate with a heavily pulsed *oom*-pah figure that takes over for a large part of the central section and itself highlights the on-offbeat dichotomy (see Ex. 6.2, bar 3). The oom-pah underscores the confrontation between the Private Eye and three Policemen. It is complicated by a reverse form, 'oom-*pah*-oom-*pah*' [109] (see Ex. 6.20), when the upper chords take on greater weight than before and could suggest a metrical shift to the ear: they now sound like onbeats rather than offbeats.

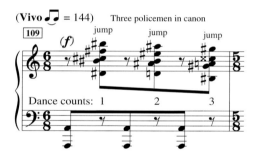

Ex. 6.20. *Le Sacre du printemps*, Glorification of the Chosen One, in piano reduction, fast jumps landing on offbeat counts (Taylor).

Taylor offers various rhythmic permutations. First, during the famous 11/4 bar of repeating chords (see p. 445), the Private Eye alternates with the Policemen jumping and pawing the ground, in rapid canon one chord apart. Then, for a while, the choreography carries on confirming the crotchet beat, which is marked by the bass chords. But then, to the reverse 'oom-*pah*' figure at [109], the Policemen jump towards the Private Eye, one after another in rapid canon, pointing fingers of blame, with stressed landing 'down' on the offbeat upper chords. The Private Eye's response continues this rhythmic approach. Soon, at [113]-1, we see the same trio in canon again, followed by a bouncing jump exit with landings still hitting the offbeat upper chords. The Private Eye continues this pattern when he re-enters at [114].

Normal dance rhythm is for the 'down' of a change of weight to coincide with the musical onbeat, which is what we had become accustomed to here at the beginning of the Glorification Scene. So, at the start of the new arrangement, we feel a slight jolt and a measure of insecurity. Has the onbeat accent of the music shifted one quaver out in relation to the established metre, with the upper chords? Or does the landing on the upper chords make it *seem* as if the musical onbeat has shifted, through 'sopping up' accents from the dance? Or is it just the dance that has shifted, the landing on the musical offbeat now, in syncopation against the music?

Yes and no to each of these questions. The 'natural' dance counts (confirmed by the Laban score) are half a beat out from the musical beats. In truth, we are disoriented, as we cannot favour either of the two rhythmic lines during this procedure, or the up, or the down. Everything could be an onbeat and the intensity of that impression is sometimes unnerving. Later, at [115], the Private Eye adds to the mayhem with four big bouncing jumps taking twice as long, up in the air accenting the first (offbeat) upper chord of the bar so that the major dance accent now seems to be at the apex of the jump, with the landing on the second (offbeat) chord, in effect creating a minim hyperbeat, and still totally at odds with the musical bar-line and written beat structure (see Ex. 6.21). The outcome of all this is major anxiety combined with mechanical precision, an absurd pairing for this point in the story, taking its cue from the extreme musical syncopation. Hardly is a pattern established than it is subverted, and soon we too, like the dancers, feel that we barely touch base (the ground).

The Sacrificial Dance takes this on-offbeat theme even further, but first, there is the Girl's solo, which is a shock. As Croce put it: 'We have so completely forgotten the music's historic connections that we're jolted when Taylor reminds us of

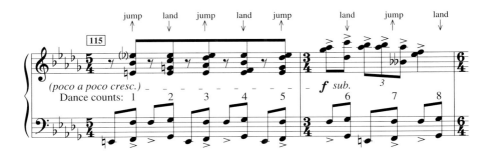

Ex. 6.21. *Le Sacre du printemps*, Glorification of the Chosen One, in piano reduction, slow jumps using offbeat counts (Taylor).

them.'[186] Yet it is also the nature of the dance and its relation to music that jolt us. They are of a totally different order from anything that we have witnessed so far. If the Girl has represented all that is gentle and good until this point, she is now driven and distraught, a fighter. She flings her fists heavenwards, plunges to the ground, stomps impatiently, convulses, in a body-wrenching torrent of three-dimensional movement that sets her hair and skirt flying. Finally, here is a dance that is literally hard to read. Apart from a repeat of the whole Refrain dance to the repeat of the musical Refrain (see p. 428), which at early viewings we are hardly likely to notice, there is an ever-onward rush of material, with minimum repetition – and, if ideas are familiar from the past, they are now deranged in execution. The Girl's relationship with the musical structure is a strange mixture of terrifying tautness and headstrong craziness, recognising the real body and its fight against gravity. Croce again:

> It's a real twister, filled with irregular phrases none of which accord with the music's irregularity and all of which must be attacked at the highest energy level. Andrien dances in a delirium of precision – between the bar lines, so to speak – and maintains unwavering rhythmic accuracy: a marvellous performance.[187]

The second half of the Sacrificial Dance could hardly be more different, and it gains strength from the contrast: it covers Verse 2 and the Coda Refrain. The Girl is now grounded and rolling in anguish from side to side across the stage. The scrim behind her is raised and we see the full cast in rehearsal mode, a dance studio mirror behind them, and more than ever like automata: piston pliés and arm lifts, flexed-foot jumps and grands battements, all at an absurd speed, a crazy callisthenic account of a dance class that mindlessly overpowers the woman in front. If there are still some spots of cross-metre in relation to the music here, the main rhythmic statement is that pulse (and duple metre) is back, and offbeat/onbeat duplicity (and up/down) is back too when the dancers break off into one-beat-apart canons and counterpoint. In Verse 2, the passages that sound like 2/4 (from [177] and [181] – see pp. 468-9) further exaggerate the dancers' hectic beats, but in the Coda Refrain, Taylor choreographs a fully discernible pulse despite the music and its constant evasion of regularity. No other end of a Sacrificial Dance is machine-driven to this extent.

Who would have thought of the music this way? Recall Taylor's claim: 'The basic tempo is not fluctuating, and once you get the basic beat, then it's easy.'[188] The fact is that, in true Stravinsky style, the tiny semiquaver sub-tactus remains totally exact, so Taylor can build his own bigger beat from it (quaver rate) and command his dancers to march on implacably, now invading the territory of the woman in front. If their beat at some points hits the unstressed moments in the music, simple mathematics guarantees that it will synchronise again later, and it is the dance beats that dominate, the visual over the aural, 121 of them in total (counted at the quaver rate). At the same time, by not reading the score himself, Taylor was untroubled by the frightening irregularities that hit the eye. The end of the Sacrificial Dance is the death of the mass machine, a regimented unison collapse, followed by the Girl seconds later. Like an answer to the dead baby falling as upbeat to the Sacrificial Dance, the curtain (another machine) and the music have the last word, its 'drop' meeting the final 'bang'.[189]

Again, I have emphasised the machine metaphor in Taylor's dance, but his is of quite a different order from Bausch's machine, the difference between 'tick-tock' toy and army tank, and without her contradictory human spillage, breath and disarray. His also carries on working for longer, beyond Stravinsky's intentions too (see p. 468), until the very end of the score. But is there too much machine here for its own good? After a while, suffering from a sort of cerebral repetitive stress syndrome, I stopped rhythmic viewing in order to remind myself of the marvellous theatricality of this dance. Certainly, part of Taylor's project is to make the score more one-dimensional, to suit his one-dimensional human characterisations. I am quite sure that he hears far more in the score than he shows us, but decides what he wants us to hear alongside his particular dance, and that happens to be a stripped-down version of what Adorno and Gelsey Kirkland heard in Stravinsky's music (see pp. 100, 106). If the composer once said of Balanchine that what he wanted more than anything else was a motor impulse (see p. 106), he could well have said the same about the Taylor of *Sacre*, but this time without irony.

Sacre *and the performative*

With a surfeit of *Sacres* currently on the market or activated by historical debate, the challenge of commanding attention and still using this score has never been bigger. We now move into a field of work that is less theatrical in the usual sense of the word, but that encompasses a performative approach and deals with the issue of motor in an entirely different way. Here, performers in front of an audience perform 'themselves', although, as we shall see, the concept of self also has its problems.

Both Raimund Hoghe and Jérôme Bel situate themselves within this choreographic tradition. The new work is political and insists on the presence of the dancer and on the dancer with a performative body that has not assumed a dancerly identity in any conventional theatrical sense. There is also a shift in the definition of choreography from being about 'dance' to being about 'the movement of ideas'[190] and having an alignment with the visual arts, especially the minimalist movement, and performance or live art rather than dance tradition.

Yet, at the same time, the approaches of Hoghe and Bel to the performance paradigm are radically different; indeed, we could be talking here about two distinct traditions of work. Hoghe is aligned to the European Tanztheater tradition (he was Bausch's dramaturge for ten years), which continues to work with the idea of the body expressing an interior state. Bel's work, on the other hand, is concerned with the body as a contested site, allied to the notion of self as fundamentally non-unitary and incoherent. He is part of the European Konzept Tanz movement, which recognises in turn the precedent of the New York Judson Dance Theater of the 1960s (which brought together postmodern artists such as Yvonne Rainer, Steve Paxton and Trisha Brown). His work is also informed by post-structural theorists, particularly Roland Barthes and Jacques Derrida.

Hoghe's *Sacre – The Rite of Spring* (2004) is for two men, Lorenzo De Brabandere and Hoghe himself, and it is important that they look so different from each other. De Brabandere is a young man, tall, athletic, in T-shirt, tracksuit bottoms and trainers; Hoghe is in middle years, small, in black shirt and trousers, and, as he puts it in one of his programmes, his torso has grown in ways 'that do not comply with the norm'.[191] But even though he has made an issue of his physique in other work, here it is just one facet of his being, alongside many others.[192] It is important that the performers meet on the same terms. Their movement is straightforward, repetitive, easy to read. At the start, we see the pair lying on stage at right angles, on their stomachs, one pair of ankles locked over the other. Hoghe lifts his lower legs, which means that he also lifts his partner's legs. This is just one of many recurring movement images or tasks that we see during the piece. Some are static: a lean in towards the partner, flat hand against flat hand, weight against weight, one hand, two hands. No stage manner is put on – Hoghe often settles himself and pulls his shirt down after a big move: he does not disguise the disarray. Some of the later movement is excruciating to watch. To the thunderous 11/4 bar, and then on into Glorification, De Brabandere lies back on his hands and walks on all fours, like a strange animal constructed upside down and in reverse. Hoghe embarks on a juddering, stuttering robotic walk of tiny steps and shuffles. A threatening presence, De Brabandere approaches Hoghe with remarkable ease and backs off. Later, with soles of feet in contact, Hoghe on his back, his partner seated, both squirm across the stage, an image of terrible struggle, and they do not get very far.

Like all Hoghe's work, his *Sacre* is a kind of ritual. There is a particular intensity of attention, so that the piece becomes a sort of manifesto for the two men, and for us. The critic Gerald Siegmund explains that the connection with ritual originates in a

> time-consuming attention to detail. Every step and gesture are meticulously articulated by a performer who is completely absorbed in what he does. He

appears calm and composed, already neutral, displaying no emotions while performing. Rigidly he adheres to a fixed sequence of steps and gestures whose rules are not to be altered, or the act performed might lose its magical power.[193]

There is the studied use of a few props in a bare performance space: an olive tree in an upstage corner, a piece of red Japanese paper, a small glass trough of water (see Ill. 19). Distance and stage placement are crucial. Sometimes the pair break apart suddenly to separate sides or corners of the stage and prepare for the next task. They print the stage with moments, images etched in the memory that belong to precise locations. But, at the same time, this is a ritual without the presence of gods, as Siegmund has observed: 'a ritual in reverse, a ritual that is so far removed from a ceremony that it touches it again from the other side'.[194]

Hoghe chose the Stravinsky score because it both underlines the element of ritual and carries a history. He explains that his *Sacre* is partly about remembering, and it contains images from other *Sacres*, most obviously the Bausch, which is suggested by the red paper (as opposed to cloth) introduced for the Sacrificial Dance.[195] Stravinsky's recorded words are heard framing the piece and they rein-

Ill. 19. Lorenzo De Brabandere and Raimund Hoghe in *Sacre – The Rite of Spring*, Sacrificial Dance, choreography by Raimund Hoghe.

force this notion of remembering or absence, as distance from the past and distance between creator and score. At the beginning, the composer, then (in 1965) in his eighties, sits in the Théâtre des Champs-Elysées recalling the scandalous opening night in 1913. At the end (again in 1965), he is in the house in Clarens, Switzerland, where he wrote *Sacre*, and we hear him talking about making the work as if it was out of his control: 'I heard and I wrote what I heard. I was the vessel through which *Le Sacre* passed.'[196]

Hoghe suggests that he and De Brabandere are likewise 'vessels', and insists: 'We are not creators ... [our objective was] not to be impressive and make big, complicated movement. The music is stronger than people.' Although the piece bears the past within it, there is a new take on the original scenario. Hoghe's statement is about two people working together, sharing a difficult process and, if there is confrontation, there is just as much mutual understanding and protection. As he explained to Rosita Boisseau of *Le Monde*: 'I had Pina's *Sacre* in my mind and wanted to do a version that was far away from any notion of victimisation. The idea of protecting someone else, of becoming neither prey nor predator, presented itself. It was no longer a question of sexuality but of love. The music cleanses the mind as much as the suffering is boundless.'[197] There is also a determination not to be overcome: 'We have to finish the ritual,' they seem to say. 'We will not be sacrificed.'

Several moments galvanise the attention. To Dance of the Earth, De Brabandere runs in panic from spot to spot, from one home to another. Hoghe stands upstage centre, resting an elbow in the opposite hand, moving the lower part of his arm like a very slow metronome. Upstage centre is the power spot. He is like a shaman. During the Sacrificial Dance, Hoghe goes back to his power position and circles his arms, marking each circle with a passing slap of the thighs, while De Brabandere runs the stage perimeter, leaping high and pouncing to the floor each time that he passes his partner. The last view is of them lying apart, fingers dipped into the glass trough, linked through the water that flows between, yet not actually linked – a connection to the past. End of ritual.

Stravinsky's characteristic moments of rupture or cut-off (see pp. 88-9) are made visual by the pair tearing themselves apart, abruptly breaking off a task – though sometimes, just as suddenly, the music gives meaning to a task. In Augurs of Spring, they stand at a distance, arms raised vertically, a full-body greeting enlarged by the cantabile trumpet theme that Bausch herself used to such purpose (the Big Phrase). During the final 'gunshots' of the Ritual of Abduction, they do the same with one raised arm and the image becomes confrontational, dangerous. Later on, the sheer force of the music seems to subsume them, to sweep them up into its power. Yet there is an almost total lack of attention to detailed musical structure and rhythms. By conventional standards, this could be seen as a perverse use of such a score, yet if you accept Hoghe's performative approach, it makes a lot of sense. Hoghe's economical staging gives us space to contemplate the performers as human beings like us, not dancing beings, and he tells us that we can all face the challenge of this monumental aural presence that is also a profound (visual) absence, a memory.

Jérôme Bel's work that uses *Sacre* is called *Jérôme Bel* (1995) and is not really a *Sacre* at all. Or is it? It seems appropriate to expand further upon its musical perspective, to add to the existing perceptive writings about the work and link it to the dance tradition of *Sacre*. At the foundation of Bel's work is the critique or unmasking of strategies of representation, the notion of the unified self or subjectivity that is the lie or fantasy of modernism. This has been projected both through role-playing at the heart of theatre as illusion and by author-choreographers who set their dancers in motion according to their own image. Bel takes the issue of representation into the conceptual field of mind/body, language/corporeality games. In a 1999 text, he claimed that 'there is no such thing as a single subject or a central focus (a "you" and a "me")' and proceeded to cite thirty-three names as identities that were part of his own identity at the moment of writing: author Samuel Beckett, theorist Peggy Phelan, fellow conceptual choreographer Xavier Le Roy, Madame Bovary, Diana Ross, Ballet Frankfurt (William Forsythe's company) ... and 'yourself'.[198] As André Lepecki writes:

> The subjectivity and the body Bel proposes are clearly not monads or self-mirroring singularities, but packs, open collectives, continuous processes of unfolding, multiplicities.[199]

It is no surprise, then, that several of Bel's pieces have been concerned with authorship, and he is upfront about this in naming a work after himself, thereby underlining his controlling absence – he never appears – as well as asking who the author really is.[200] Furthermore, the performative as opposed to dancerly body is already inscribed for Bel; the concept of performing the self, for the people who are on stage, is already complicated. But the removal of theatrical overlay in a theatrical situation (a venue with a box office and all the marketing paraphernalia surrounding the event) only underlines the point about inscription.

Bel explains that, in *Jérôme Bel*, he wanted

> to find a kind of 'zero point of literature' for dance. I wanted to avoid two things: the erotic body and the perfectly muscular body, the body as warrior. Sex and power: in our entire culture – not only in dance – these stand for the two most dominating representations of the body. And I have examined the body, the primary instrument of dance, in a way that denies it its usual signs.[201]

In this piece of about fifty minutes, four naked people, representing a range of ages and builds, demonstrate the four basic principles of dance: the body, in a bare space, lit (an older woman, Gisèle Tremey, holds a light bulb – that is the extent of the illumination), and with music, the *Sacre* score. But *Sacre* is not rendered in any familiar fashion: here it is sung by another woman, Yseult Roch.[202] The first task of Tremey and Roch is to chalk up on the back wall names of people who they are not and who are of the opposite sex. This only magnifies the problem of their own identity at this stage: Thomas Edison (by Tremey), Stravinsky, Igor (by Roch). Then the other two performers, Claire Haenni and Frédéric Seguette, write their own names and various statistics pertaining to their identity: age, size, weight and phone numbers (which suggests how we might begin to think about Tremey and Roch in relation to their chalked-up names). But then Haenni and Seguette become bodies slowly and quietly examining bodies, folds of skin, blemishes, painting themselves with lipstick – writing, drawing lines that segment the body, marking the spots on their skin. Haenni writes on her leg, 'Christian Dior'. Seguette handles his genitals shamelessly as if they have a status no different from any other body part, but don't they? – the music is *Sacre*, isn't it? Towards the end, both of them calmly urinate on the floor.

The reduction is absurd: the basic space, the lighting, the untheatrical timing of task-like activity, the matter-of-fact performance of the taboo, but perhaps most of all the lack of dance as we know it. Billed as choreography, we seek it out and find only its foundations. At the same time, we are reminded of our own construction by language, how we too are encoded by names, the media, industry. By association, we reflect upon how dancers are inscribed by our own projections of beauty, 'sacrificed' by us, and, once we remove such expectations, we can focus on issues relating to our own inscription. The spectator shifts from being 'voyeur' to 'accomplice', to 'feel at ease with the body's nudity on stage, and therefore feel at ease with his own body, too'.[203] The slow timing and small space allow us to contemplate sensuality, to develop a physical rapport with the performers and to let their identities flow into ours. Already, concepts such as 'voyeur' and 'sacrifice' resonate with *Sacre* tradition, even as they are strangely, and humorously, nuanced in these idiosyncratic circumstances.

But the main point about *Jérôme Bel* is that it is never just one thing. So often, it can be read at cross-purposes, and thoughts about it can ricochet in many directions. The writing of Stravinsky's name on the wall accentuates the distance between author (composer) and his work, and what the work has become. On the one hand, Stravinsky too is reduced, minimalised. He is a mere cipher – especially as his name is reversed like an academic reference. He is somewhere else, like Bel the choreographer. In this minimal rendition, the Great Art music is as theatrically reduced as everything else, the huge force, primitivism and eroticism drained from it, and the thousands of bodies driven by it over the century stilled. On the other hand, reduction celebrates connotations that have become stale through over-exposure in conventional large-scale ventures. That is the paradox. The work is and is not what it is. But it is another instance of connotational connection and disconnection, with conceptual fields in head-long confrontation (see pp. 9, 11). For Bel, the authority of Stravinsky is recognised through reduction and denial: the naming is all-important, doubly empowered by large, public writing, and, as Lepecki says, it 'overdetermines' presence.[204] And academic-style naming? That places him in the super-league. At the same time, the physicality of Stravinsky is spectacularly renewed. It is hard to think of a more literally corporeal *Sacre*, emerging from the body itself, from one body, Roch, who has 'become' the name she chalked up at the start. Hers is a tour de force of deep and surface sounds, emanating from stomach cavity, throat, tongue, lips. Accents are spat out and there is both lyricism and speech-like song. Somehow, she manages to articulate both upper and lower parts of the Glorification texture. Organic production on full view.

In a witty manoeuvre, after Roch has sung through to the end of the Sacrificial Dance, the performers use the urine (the bodily) to erase the chalked-up names, the power, except for the letters that spell out 'Eric chante Sting'. Then a man called Eric, fully dressed, ends the piece with another sign, singing as instructed Sting's 'An Englishman in New York'. Thus, writes Lepecki, 'The body is the primary agent for the transformation of language,' resulting in 'a new performance, a new body, a new performative, a new beginning, a new song ...'[205]

In one important respect, Bel's work is aligned to Hoghe's, and to Saarinen's (see pp. 477-8), for that matter. All of them, in their very different ways, deny the rhythmic motor of the score as a dance motor or even an impulse for movement. Lepecki has described the modernist project of choreography in terms of an ideological blindness: 'the self-enclosure of subjectivity within representation as an entrapment in spectacular compulsive mobility ... Choreography is a necessary technology for an agitated subjectivity that can only find its ontological grounding as a perpetual being-toward-movement.'[206] Returning to *Sacre*, I now find useful Carol Brown's observation, that 'not using the score to motorise the dance'[207] is an important means of challenging dance's traditional assumptions about the kinaesthetic. The presence of such a powerful motor alongside what these choreographers do only magnifies the point.

Arrangements and collage constructions

Increasingly since the late 1980s, Stravinsky has found himself truncated, manipulated and subject to collage conditions and, more than for any other score, the identity of *Sacre* has expanded through its use in arrangement and next to other music. But the *SGD* database exposes a couple of early instances of radical selection from *Sacre*, and of the placement of chosen items in contexts entirely at odds with Stravinsky's original intentions. There is the 1958 *Troika* by the Soviet choreographer Leonid Jacobson, created for his ballet company Choreographic Miniatures before Stravinsky's music was fully rehabilitated in the USSR. But the way he used the music, Augurs of Spring, cleverly distracts from its dangerous origins. A film of the work shows a happy Russian snow scene, a coachman playing at driving three women like horses.[208] They folk-step and flirt, topple over and become increasingly unruly, and then leave the way they arrived. Jacobson had the score edited to suit his purposes (by Boris Kravtchenko), beginning at [18] and continuing up to the Ritual of Abduction [37], at which point there is a specially ordered recapitulation from [18] to [22] (the end of Part 1). Treated this way, I felt that I was listening to *Petrushka*. All innocence and jollity, the piece is a fascinating illustration of how music can assume a very different identity when its visual context is altered. Perhaps at that time, many listeners within Soviet culture would have been unused to or unaware of the more familiar connotations of this musical excerpt and hence untouched by the conceptual conflict that Jacobson had introduced. In New York, using the Glorification of the Chosen One and Evocation of the Ancestors in a collage with other musical material, Sophie Maslow based her *The Gentleman from Cracow* (1966) on a story about a devil who visits a Jewish village in Poland and takes as his bride a girl who turns out to be Lilith in disguise. But here, Clive Barnes of *The New York Times* registered a complaint about such use of music, also mentioning that 'a drum-roll had been inserted into its mutely protesting middle'.[209]

Nowadays, it is hardly possible to use *Sacre* innocently. A mere whiff, and connotations from the *Sacre* tradition burst forth. Often, the spectre of Nijinsky has been evoked. The Japanese choreographer Saburo Teshigawara began *Dah-dah-sko-dah-dah* (1991) with multiple anxious images of the dancer in a solo to a saxophone and piano arrangement of sections from *Sacre*.[210] This set the scene for a 'noise dance piece' about urban industrial brutality. In his autobiographical 'dance musical' *Dream Analysis* (1998), the American Mark Dendy incorporated the Sacrificial Dance into a 'coming out' apotheosis. Dressed as Judy Garland, Eric (Dendy's alter ego) was the Chosen One 'surrounded by menacing savages with long, flopping prosthetic phalluses'.[211] Nijinsky and his 'split half' featured among the characters in the piece. Dietmar Seyffert's *Clown Gottes* (Berlin, 1990) prefaced the full *Sacre* with a collage that included the Danse Russe from *Petrushka*: the work referred to various aspects of Nijinsky's career, including the experience of insanity.[212] In Britain, Michael Clark's *Modern Masterpiece* (1992, later retitled *Mmm ...*) again used the whole *Sacre* score but referred to the energy and shock values of its tradition through a punk aesthetic, juxtaposing the score with music by the Sex Pistols and Pil. The piece was for four dancers, with appearances by Clark's mother Bessie and the flamboyant designer/performance artist Leigh Bowery.[213] It was reworked and expanded for twelve dancers in autumn 2006, again with a punk prologue before the interval (and Barbra Streisand singing 'Send in the Clowns'). Using the piano version of *Sacre*, Clark continued the theme of defiant humour and sexual charge projected through his own brand of twisted classicism.

A recent trend is to 'sample' from the Stravinsky score, to take recognisable gestures and patterns from the music and manipulate them within a new soundscape. One acclaimed example is *Sacre Material* by Christine Gaigg (Vienna, 2000, revived 2006), a work that interwove brief Stravinsky fragments (for instance, from Spring Rounds, Glorification, Ritual Action of the Ancestors and the Sacrificial Dance) into a percussion score by Max Nagl. An analysis of the original *Sacre* in terms of 'the social reality of today,' referencing its poses and stylistic principles, the work was performed by three women testing their 'physical and psychic limits', each occupying a separate stage and exposed to a mobile audience.[214] There is also *Beauté Plastique* by Etant Donné (Rouen, 2005), which deconstructed the notion of female beauty to highlight the fictions to which women are expected to conform: another example of female sacrifice posited in feminist terms.[215] Two women posed, often awkwardly, and put on faces in a highly self-conscious manner. The most striking image was a stage full of Barbie dolls in lines of seven by nine (two empty spaces being left for the performers), dolls that later featured on film, manically jumping and waving arms to manipulations (by Hubert Michel) of Stravinsky's Sacrificial Dance. Bits of *Sacre* had been extracted according to the chronological order of the original, so the continuity of the complete score (and memories of the original scenario) could be grasped, whilst the static 'moment form' of what had been selected was exaggerated. The fragments heard were always those that exhibit mechanical repetition, here extended to frightening proportions: for example, the chords in Augurs (but not the irregular accents) or in Verse 1 of the Sacrificial Dance, hammered out again and again without respite. This was a brutal, reductive account of Stravinsky, but, most effectively, it reinforced one of the score's strongest tendencies, Adorno's worst nightmare. Collage and sampling techniques exert their power because *Sacre* already has such a strong hold upon our imaginations.

Marking identity in a global dance economy

One of the outstanding developments of the last twenty years is the greatly enlarged cultural spread of *Sacre* settings. I have already considered the particular political/cultural issues surrounding the production and reception of *Sacre* in Germany and Russia (see pp. 125, 128), and the *Sacre* performance figures for Germany still seem to be the highest internationally, but the *SGD* database reveals further interesting clusters of activity rooted in particular countries or communities within countries.

Perhaps in situations where identity is a major political issue a proliferation of *Sacres* is likely, as in Canada, which has hosted at least nine new productions. The big productions come from the English-speaking sector, the smaller and arguably more questioning from Francophone Canada (including Chouinard's 1993 production – see pp. 476-7). Remarkably, Martine Epoque, a choreographer who is currently professor at the University of Quebec in Montreal, has turned to the score seven times since 1986, mainly reworking the same choreography and theme (the renewal of a people after rebellion against dictatorship). Her 1987 version was the first to use the music in performance, yet she had already made *YUL* (1986), which was based on the rhythmic structure of the Augurs of Spring and Spring Rounds, and which she thought strong enough to sustain itself without the presence of the score. Her most recent *Sacre* (to be completed in 2008) will be 'an ode to our planet', a digital exploration as a plea to humankind for the protection of our environment.[216] The Syrian-born, and now Canadian-based, Motaz Kabbani produced a *Sacre* with strong cultural reference for Le Festival du monde arabe de Montréal (2003). A publicity statement describes how he transposed this dance 'about life' for five women 'onto the traditional and intimate setting of the Hammam, or bath, where a virgin is being prepared for an arranged marriage. The theme of this work is water, traditionally a sacred element and purification symbol for several peoples.' Indicating that his *Sacre* was not specifically Islamic in theme, Kabbani introduced other traditional features such as black burqas and the vocabulary of belly dancing; he also drew parallels between his own position and that of Stravinsky and Nijinsky as immigrants adding their own Russian traditions to a culture other than their own.[217] The critic Philip Szporer suggested that the work raised issues about the conflicting demands of traditional and contemporary culture and 'coming to terms with one's sexuality and sensual awakening'.[218] Kabbani used the piano arrangement by Fazil Say (see p. 479), but included additional layering by Dino Giancola, Charmaine Leblanc and Kia Tabassian. From time to time we hear Middle Eastern strains superimposed upon Stravinsky, with vocalisation, strings, percussion, even lively syncopations inserted into the Ritual Action of the Ancestors.

Clearly it is no longer enough to read *Sacre* within the confines of Western cultural traditions. Lester Horton was possibly the earliest choreographer to identify specific non-Russian (and non-Western) reference in his 1937 'American Indian' *Sacre*, but many other *Sacres* have alluded to a kind of universal concept of erotic 'primitivism' and ritual: after all, Béjart made the principle international. Yet, whereas some choreographers have used 'primitivism' and cultural reference cosmetically for colour and excitement, many recently have used *Sacre* more critically as a vehicle for reflection on their own specific cultural background, knowing that the music carries political weight and bears the tradition of being an important life statement. Often it is a question of the diasporas speaking, artists working both outside and within their country of origin, and some of these are international travellers transporting their work, even the premiere, to countries in which they are not necessarily based. But who knows how many producers now keen to promote 'fusion' and 'cross-cultural' projects have nudged some of these choreographers towards *Sacre?*

In 1997, there was the big Australian *Rites* production of Stephen Page, which was televised, and broadcast by the BBC the following year.[219] This was a collaboration between Australian Ballet and Bangarra Dance Theatre, alluding to the sacrifice of a young man but in an Australian aboriginal/Kouri setting, in six sections referring to the elements of nature as well as to cultural roots: Awakening, Earth, Wind, Fire, Water, Dreaming. Amongst the large cast was a presiding Shaman figure from the Kouri community, Djakapurra Munyarryun. In 2000, *Sacre* was staged by Bartabas on the Zingaro troupe of horses and dancers, part of the evening-length *Triptyk*, followed by settings of Pierre Boulez's *Dialogue de l'ombre* and Stravinsky's *Symphony of Psalms*. Zingaro publicity indicated Bartabas's interest in a 'mix of world cultures'. This *Sacre* incorporated a group of Kalaripayatt dancers from Kerala, India, who specialise in an ancient form of martial arts; to the Sacrificial Dance, one of them dances for his life, threatened by the circling horses and their riders, finally falling to the earth exhausted.[220]

The number of Japanese *Sacres* during the 1990s is especially interesting, many of them stemming from Butoh tradition, all by choreographers working outside ballet, and some premiered outside Japan (such as Teshigawara's 1999 setting for the Bavarian State Opera Ballet, Munich). Several of these settings have opened up questions about women's experience. In 1995, a project entitled 'Three Rites of Spring' featured the women choreographers Sakiko Oshima, Tomoko Ehara and Akiko Kitamura. For five women dancers, in contemporary day clothes, Oshima's feminist interpretation for her H Art Chaos company represented sacrifice as an outcome of violence and hostility in today's world. Ehara's setting (premiered earlier in 1990) stressed the sacrifice of childhood and innocence to time and experience as she assumed the look of an old woman.[221] The male Butoh choreographer Min Tanaka staged a series of *Sacres* between 1989 and 1998, including one in Paris (1990); yet only the last, the end-of-the-century version for the Russian Seasons Dance Ensemble of Moscow, actually used Stravinsky's score (see p. 477). All were depictions of an ancient rural community, the first an open-air production in Japan (in Hakushu Village, the Shirasu Summer Festival) influenced by the performance persona of

Nijinsky. It is interesting that, undoubtedly because of the title, audience members might have heard, or wanted to hear, fragments of the score within Minoru Noguchi's improvisational 'noise' accompaniment, although Tanaka himself has denied its presence.[222] Another Butoh choreographer Carlotta Ikeda premiered her *Haru no Saïten – un sacre du printemps* for six women in Paris (1999). Here, there is just fleeting reference to the *Sacre* score: most of the music is by Alain Mahé. Ikeda has spoken of 'wanting to keep detached from Stravinsky in order to get closer to the Japanese *Sacre* experience, which brings together chaos, eros and cosmos. I seek to go beyond sex in order to attain self-effacement, a kind of pure experience.'[223] Yet, such is the power of the very title *Sacre* that, in all these productions, even when literally absent, Stravinsky's presence was undeniable.

Ikeda's *Sacre* contributed to an extraordinary *Sacre* year in France in 2005. There was such an abundance of performances and cultural mix that it provoked the article by Boisseau in *Le Monde* for which she interviewed Hoghe. In it she surveyed the production profile (or rather the French experience) of the work as a dance piece, and the promise of the year to come: nine pieces mentioned in all, as well as the three 'classics' of Nijinsky, Béjart and Bausch. The *Sacres* to be shown in France in 2005 were:

Raimund Hoghe:	(premiered Brussels, 2004) Festival 'C'est de la danse contemporaine', Centre de Développement Chorégraphique de Toulouse, 7 and 8 February.
Heddy Maalem:	(premiered Lyons, 2004) Festival les Presqu'îles de danse, La Ferme du Buisson, Noisiel, 12–13 February; Les Hivernales d'Avignon, 18 February; Opéra-Comédie, Montpellier, 12 March.
Carlotta Ikeda:	(premiered Paris, 1999) Les Hivernales d'Avignon, 15 February.
Georges Momboye:	(premiered 2005) Biennale de danse du Val-de-Marne, 9–12 and 19–20 March.
Régis Obadia:	(premiered Moscow, 2003) Théâtre d'Arcachon, 2 and 24 September.

Boisseau also mentioned the *Sacres* of the French Canadian Marie Chouinard (Ottawa, 1993) and of Angelin Preljocaj (Berlin, 2001), both of which had been seen in France in recent years; Sylvie Guillermin's piece to the Fazil Say piano recording (France, 2003); and the Israeli Emanuel Gat's version (France, 2004), which uses slippery salsa as its community language – yet another recent *Sacre* that dances around, rather than to, Stravinsky's motor rhythms.[224] At the point of writing, Boisseau could not have foreseen the 'Marathon Sacre du printemps' day in Rouen (13 November 2005), which included the premiere of *Beauté*

Plastique alongside performances by Hoghe, Momboye and Saarinen. Here, as elsewhere during this exceptional year, *Sacre* performances were supplemented by debates and films. This schedule is also fascinating as an indication of the place of these *Sacres* within the larger scheme of things, the international touring schedule. Several of these works originated in France and then travelled abroad, while others moved in the opposite direction. For 2005, at least, it is as if France became something of a hub for this particular dance score.

Momboye and Maalem are both choreographers from French-speaking Africa who moved to France. Published interviews stress that both choreographers were intent on expressing the African experience, convinced that Stravinsky's music was appropriate to realising this. There was one precedent of a French *Sacre* with African reference, the 1997 *Réveil* by Elsa Wolliaston: of African and American parentage, she emigrated to France in 1969.[225]

Hitherto unfamiliar with Stravinsky's music, Momboye was commissioned by Michel Caserta to open the Biennale du Val-de-Marne, and rapidly became immersed in *Sacre*'s dual evocation of the positive aspect of birth/renewal and the destruction of life forces. Aiming to convey the suffering of women and children in Africa, he also felt that the sacrifice of the Chosen One related to his personal history. Born into an Ivory Coast family that respected traditional masking and religious customs, with his father converting to Islam, Momboye felt the need to leave behind his family heritage and move in an alternative direction.[226]

For Maalem, the son of an Algerian father and French mother, Stravinsky's score recalled the drums that he heard in his youth. But the idea of creating a *Sacre* originated in a visit to Lagos, Nigeria, where he found a parallel to the score in the mixture of vibrant modernity with extreme misery and despair: 'Lagos gave me a feeling of the end of the world like Stravinsky's music is for me a contradiction between giving life and then killing it.'[227] Confronting his own marked situation within French colonial history, his own broken heritage, he wanted to offer audiences a truer, less reductive perspective of African dance identity than was usual in France.[228] In his *Sacre*, Stravinsky is framed by and intercut with film footage and a sound track of urban Lagos (by Benoît Dervaux and Benoît De Clerck respectively) and, even though there is a Chosen One, the dance reflects broadly on the notion of sacrifice and on the cycle of night and day, as a symbol of death and rebirth. Maalem's fourteen young dancers came from Benin, Mali, Senegal and Nigeria, as well as two from France (who were born in Africa and the West Indies), all versed in traditional rather than contemporary dance styles.

* * *

Our needs change, dance changes, and so do our perceptions of music. The 'all-out primitive bash' Sacre[229] is no longer current; it has grown tired. Clearly too, we have gone far beyond the formalist musicological tradition that dominated the twentieth century, and which Stravinsky notably supported. Indeed, it seems that dance led this blast into the future, and the number of dance Sacres continues to increase as new ways of celebrating the power of Stravinsky's score have emerged, an impressive number of them noteworthy.

Stravinsky's score continues to expand into new semantic fields. The recently much enlarged cultural reach of Sacre speaks of a new pluralism of tradition and of identity issues faced across the world. Today the score is rapidly becoming 'world music', an established fixture within the global arena, and new dance settings foreground the fact that it can belong to all of us, past and present, near to and far away from our own roots. Looking back, for almost a hundred years something elemental and of fundamental human concern has been read into this special score, whether that be about sacrifice as an act of oppression or the urgent need for change towards a more positive future.

But it is important that issues of rhythm and motor have also been a central concern across Sacre tradition. In the early days, the difficulty and complication of this new music was a talking point, its irregularities appearing to offer a virtually impossible challenge to Ballets Russes dancers and their audiences. Then, along the way, Bausch exaggerated to frightening proportions what was regular, and, on a smaller scale, Taylor found Sacre 'one of the easiest things to dance to I've ever done'. Today, Maalem mentions that his dancers were perturbed by the 'binary' emphasis of Stravinsky's rhythms and that they needed to create a counterpoint to this.[230] So, at the beginning of the twenty-first century, we find an African-French group anxious to combat a perceived rigidity in at least some of Stravinsky's music. Indeed, by this time, the Stravinsky machine had acquired a kind of cliché status, the phenomenon of the 'driving rod' exaggerated, simplified and 'over-determined' to such a degree that Yvonne Rainer, in her Agon setting, seemed to interrogate it through a witty mix of subversion and reinforcement. But a number of scores and score treatments addressed in this book (such as Symphonies of Wind Instruments and Mark Morris's Frisson), have had little or nothing to do with this machine. Sacre, with its colossal status, has been largely responsible for these exaggerations.

Sacre is also exceptional because of its huge force, its lengthy accumulations of energy and the reinforcement of its tenacious rhythmic repetition with massive orchestral sound. It is symbolic of a terrifying power. So, in recent years, as we have seen, still other choreographers have staged a critical resistance to the notion of a machine in the music that sets the body in motion and usurps its authority – witness the Butoh-influenced settings, and those of Hoghe and Bel. For them, the score offers other opportunities that are anything but about celebrating the notorious Stravinsky rhythm. Rather, in actively denying that rhythm, they stress it as a problem. But what other composer could these choreographers have chosen, and what other score? The most celebrated composer, the most celebrated dance score of the twentieth century: there is none better to make the point about power through a choreographer's calculated act of negation. And *Sacre* is the score with the most notorious past and the greatest weight of history, both a musical history and a history of dance productions.

As for Stravinsky himself, although he clearly extended existing notions of *musique dansante*, he could never have envisaged the further extension, even radical rewriting, of his principles through dance. This rewriting has been prompted by the full range of his music, both what he intended for dance and what he did not, but still, most of all, by *Sacre*. Perhaps here lies the most exciting and important aspect of his dance legacy: the persistent flow of re-visions, the constant regeneration of ideas that still move us, literally, into the future.

Appendix 1

Stravinsky's Dance Scores: A Chronology[1]

The following list includes scores that were conceived for dance or were premiered as hybrid works with a dance component. The scores are listed in the order of their completion.

The Firebird, fairy-story ballet in 2 scenes, for orchestra, 1909–10. First performance: Paris, June 25, 1910, Ballets Russes. Conception: Fokine. Choreography: Fokine

Petrushka, burlesque in 4 scenes, for orchestra, 1910–11. First performance: Paris, June 13, 1911, Ballets Russes. Conception: Stravinsky and Benois. Choreography: Fokine

Le Sacre du printemps, scenes of pagan Russia in 2 parts, for orchestra, 1911–13. First performance: Paris, May 29, 1913, Ballets Russes. Conception: Stravinsky and Nicolay Roerich. Choreography: Nijinsky

Le Rossignol, musical fairy tale (opera) in 3 acts, 1908–9, 1913–14. First performance (as opera staged with dance): Paris, May 26, 1914, Ballets Russes. Conception: Stravinsky and Stepan Mitusov. Choreography: Boris Romanov

Renard, burlesque in song and dance, for 2 tenors, 2 basses and small orchestra, 1915–16. First performance: Paris, May 18, 1922, Ballets Russes. Conception: Stravinsky. Choreography: Nijinska

Le Chant du rossignol, symphonic poem and ballet in 1 act, for orchestra, 1917 (arranged from *Le Rossignol*, Acts II and III). First performance: December 6, 1919 (concert), February 2, 1920 (ballet), Paris, Ballets Russes. Conception derived directly from *Le Rossignol*. Choreography: Massine

Histoire du soldat, to be read, played and danced, in 2 parts, for 7 players, 1918. First performance: Lausanne, September 28, 1918, ad hoc theatre group. Conception: Stravinsky and Ramuz. Choreography: George and Lyudmila Pitoëff

Pulcinella, ballet in 1 act, for solo voices and chamber orchestra, 1919–20. First performance: Paris, May 15, 1920, Ballets Russes. Conception: Massine. Choreography: Massine

Les Noces, Russian choreographic scenes, in 4 scenes, for solo voices, chorus, 4 pianos and percussion, 1914–19, 1921–3. First performance: Paris, June 13, 1923, Ballets Russes. Conception: Stravinsky. Choreography: Nijinska

Apollon musagète, ballet in 2 scenes, for string orchestra, 1927–8. First performance: Washington, April 27, 1928, ad hoc ballet company. Conception: Stravinsky. Choreography: Adolph Bolm

Le Baiser de la fée, ballet in 4 scenes, for orchestra, 1928. First performance: Paris, Ballets Rubinstein, November 27, 1928. Conception: Benois and Stravinsky. Choreography: Nijinska

Persephone, melodrama in 3 scenes, for speaker, solo tenor, chorus and orchestra, 1933–4. First performance: Paris, April 30, 1934, Ballets Rubinstein. Conception: André Gide and Stravinsky. Choreography: Kurt Jooss

Jeu de cartes, ballet in 3 deals, 1935–6. First performance: New York, April 27, 1937, American Ballet. Conception: Stravinsky and Nikita Malayev. Choreography: George Balanchine

Circus Polka, for piano, 1941–2 (arr. David Raksin for circus band, 1942). First performance: New York, April 9, 1942, as 'The Ballet of the Elephants', Ringling Brothers and Barnum & Bailey's Circus. Conception: George Balanchine. Choreography: George Balanchine

Scènes de ballet, for orchestra, 1944. First performance: Philadelphia, November 27, 1944, Billy Rose revue, The Seven Lively Arts. Conception: Stravinsky and Dolin. Choreography: Anton Dolin

Orpheus, ballet in 3 scenes, 1946–7. First performance, New York, April 28, 1948, Ballet Society. Conception: Balanchine and Stravinsky. Choreography: George Balanchine

Agon, ballet for 12 dancers, 1953–7. First performance (concert), June 17, 1957, (ballet) New York, December 1, 1957, New York City Ballet (private charity performance, November 27). Conception: Stravinsky. Choreography: George Balanchine

The Flood, musical play for solo speakers and singers, chorus and orchestra, 1961–2. First telecast performance as *Noah and the Flood*, CBS TV (USA), June 14, 1962, New York City Ballet. Conception: Stravinsky and Craft. Choreography: George Balanchine

Stravinsky's orchestral arrangements of other composers' music

Chopin, two pieces for *Les Sylphides* (1909), *Nocturne in A-flat*, op. 32, no. 2; *Grand Valse brillante in E-flat*, op. 18: Paris, June 2, 1909, Ballets Russes

Grieg, *Kobold*, op, 71, no. 3: St Petersburg, February 20, 1910, a solo for Nijinsky

Tchaikovsky, re-orchestration of *The Sleeping Beauty* (1921), Variation d'Aurore and Entr'acte (Act II): London, November 2, 1921; a re-orchestration of the 'Bluebird' pas de deux from *Beauty* (1941): New York, February, 1941, Ballet Theatre

NOTE
1. Score subtitles and descriptions have been taken from the lists in Stephen Walsh's two-volume biography: *Igor Stravinsky: A Creative Spring* (London: Jonathan Cape, 2000), pp. 543–9; *Stravinsky: The Second Exile: France and America, 1934–1971* (New York: Alfred A. Knopf, 2006), pp. 573–6.

Appendix 2

Stravinsky's Attendance at Dance Events: A Partial Listing

The following listing is based primarily on programmes and other documentation of Stravinsky's activities housed in the Paul Sacher Stiftung, Basle (*PSS*), supported by programmes in the Jerome Robbins Dance Division of The New York Public Library for the Performing Arts (*NYPL*). Other sources are:

- Vera Stravinsky's diaries, from 1922, the year after she met Stravinsky, through to his death in 1971, except for the years 1925, 1932–7 and 1939 (the originals in the *PSS* and the published version in Robert Craft, ed., *Dearest Bubushkin: The Correspondence of Vera and Igor Stravinsky, 1921–1954, with Excerpts from Vera Stravinsky's Diaries, 1922–1971*, trans. Lucia Davidova (*DB*; London: Thames and Hudson, 1985))
- Robert Craft's diary-based publications *Stravinsky: Chronicle of a Friendship* (Nashville & London: Vanderbilt University Press, 1994) and *An Improbable Life* (Nashville & London: Vanderbilt University Press, 2002)
- Richard Buckle's biography *Diaghilev* (London: Weidenfeld and Nicolson, 1979)
- Stephen Walsh's two-volume Stravinsky biography.

The chronology by Nicole Wild of the Diaghilev Ballets Russes Paris seasons has also been used: in Martine Kahane and Wild, *Les Ballets Russes à l'Opéra* (Paris: Hazan/Bibliothèque Nationale, 1992).

The listing of attendance is partial, covering documented attendance at dance events, although it includes dates when Stravinsky was living and working close to his ballet associates. On such occasions, depending on the seasonal timing, he is likely to have attended further performances (e.g. in Paris during the seasons of the Ballets Russes or in New York in the proximity of Balanchine, his companies and other dance activity). Between 1910 and 1929, for instance, Stravinsky saw virtually the entire repertory of the Ballets Russes. Stravinsky's appearances as a conductor are shown, usually of one ballet on a programme, unless otherwise indicated. On these occasions, it is highly uncertain whether he saw the other items on a programme, but I have listed these items because the programme context in which Stravinsky's ballets appeared is informative. Except for a few instances that are especially noteworthy, the chronology does not include Stravinsky's attendance at rehearsals of his own ballets.

A note on Stravinsky's early association with dance: he recalls that ballet was an important part of his life as a child, that he saw Pavlova in St Petersburg, c.1905/06 and that at the age of seven or eight he saw *The Sleeping Beauty* (premiered 1890). The choreographer Petipa was a friend of his father. [1]

1910
Stravinsky [IS] in Paris with Diaghilev's Ballets Russes, c. June 7 to late June, c. July 7–10
June 25 *Carnaval*, Fokine/Schumann, *The Firebird*, Fokine, premiere, *Les Orientales*, various choreographers/composers, including Grieg arrangement by Stravinsky, *Polovtsian Dances* from *Prince Igor*, Fokine/Borodin, Opéra, Paris
July 7 *The Firebird*, Opéra, Paris

1911
IS in Monte Carlo with Ballets Russes, early to late April
IS in Rome with Ballets Russes, c. May 9 to end of May
May 14 opening of season *Le Pavillon d'Armide*, Fokine/Tcherepnin, *Les Sylphides*, Fokine/orchestrated Chopin (two pieces by IS), *Polovtsian Dances*, Teatro Costanzi, Rome
IS in Paris with Ballets Russes, for all four performances of *Petrushka*
June 13, 15–17 *Petrushka*, Fokine, premiere, *Le Spectre de la rose*, Fokine/Weber arr. Berlioz, *Scheherazade*, Fokine/Rimsky-Korsakov, Théâtre du Châtelet, Paris

1912
IS in Monte Carlo with Ballets Russes, rehearsing c. April 14 to end of April/early May
IS in Paris with Ballets Russes, mid-May to second week of June
May 29 *L'Après-midi d'un faune*, Nijinsky/Debussy, premiere, *The Firebird*, *Le Spectre de la rose*, *Thamar*, Fokine/Balakirev, Théâtre du Châtelet, Paris
June 8 *Daphnis and Chloe*, Fokine/Ravel, premiere, *L'Après-midi d'un faune*, *Le Spectre de la rose*, *Scheherazade*, Théâtre du Châtelet, Paris
IS in Berlin with Ballets Russes, November 21 to c. December 11
November 21 *The Firebird*, Berlin
December 4 *Petrushka*, Berlin

1913
IS in Budapest and Vienna with Ballets Russes, January 4–15
January 4 *The Firebird*, Budapest
January 15 *Petrushka*, Vienna
IS in London with Ballets Russes, until mid-February
February 4 *Petrushka*, Covent Garden, London
IS in Paris with Ballets Russes, from May 13, illness preventing attendance after June 2
May 15 *The Firebird*, *Jeux*, Nijinsky/Debussy, premiere, *Scheherazade*, Théâtre des Champs-Elysées, Paris
May 29 *Les Sylphides*, *Le Sacre du printemps*, Nijinsky, premiere, *Le Spectre de la rose*, *Polovtsian Dances*, Théâtre des Champs-Elysées, Paris
June 2 *Les Sylphides*, *Le Sacre du printemps*, *Scheherazade*, Théâtre des Champs-Elysées, Paris

1914

IS in Paris with Ballets Russes, mid-May to late May, leaving after one or two performances of *Le Rossignol*

May 26 *Le Rossignol*, Boris Romanov, premiere, *Le Coq d'or*, Fokine/Rimsky-Korsakov, Opéra, Paris

IS in London with Ballets Russes, for approximately a week from June 15

June 18 *Le Rossignol*, *Midas*, Fokine/Steinberg, Theatre Royal, Drury Lane, London

1915

December 29 *Scheherazade*, **conducted** *The Firebird*, Fokine, 'Bluebird' pas de deux from *The Sleeping Beauty*, *Soleil de nuit*, Massine/Rimsky-Korsakov, *Polovtsian Dances*, Diaghilev Ballets Russes, Opéra, Paris (**first conducting for ballet**)

1916

IS in Madrid with Ballets Russes, c. May 21, for season beginning May 26, ending June 9

May 26 *The Firebird*

May 31 *The Firebird*

June 6 *Petrushka*

June 9 *Petrushka*

1917

IS in Rome with Ballets Russes, from April 5, with company to Naples, leaving c. April 22

April 12 *Fireworks*, Balla (a 'happening'), Teatro Costanzi, Rome

April 17–22 *Las Meninas*, Massine/Fauré, *Soleil de nuit*, *The Good-Humoured Ladies*, Massine/Scarlatti arr. Tommasini, two performances attended at Teatro San Carlo, Naples

1918

September 28 *Histoire du soldat*, George and Ludmilla Pitoëff, premiere, Théâtre Municipal, Lausanne

1920

IS in Paris with Ballets Russes, late January to mid-February

February 2 *Thamar*, *Le Chant du rossignol*, Massine, premiere, *Contes Russes*, Massine/Liadov, Opéra, Paris

IS in Monte Carlo with Ballets Russes, brief visit mid-April, in Paris, May 7 to c. May 27

May 15 *Contes Russes*, *Pulcinella*, Massine, premiere, *Soleil de nuit*, Opéra, Paris

December 15 *Les Sylphides*, *Le Sacre du printemps*, Massine, premiere, *The Three Cornered Hat*, Massine/de Falla, Ballets Russes, Opéra, Paris

1921

IS in Madrid with Ballets Russes, c. March 16 to mid-April

conducted *Petrushka*, Madrid (one performance)

IS in Paris with Ballets Russes and attended short season at Théâtre de la Gaîté-Lyrique, mid-May

IS in London with Ballets Russes, June 7 to mid-June, returned to France, then in London June 27 to early July

June 27 *Le Sacre du printemps*, Prince's Theatre, London

IS in London with Ballets Russes, late October into first week of November

November 2 *The Sleeping Princess*, Petipa/Tchaikovsky (two sections re-orchestrated by IS), premiere, Alhambra Theatre, London

1922

IS in Monte Carlo with Ballets Russes, late April to c. May 7, for *Renard* rehearsals with Nijinska

April 29 evening ballet performance, Monte Carlo

IS in Paris with Ballets Russes, from May 18 to mid-June

May 18 opening of season *Carnaval*, *Aurora's Wedding* (from *The Sleeping Beauty*), *Renard*, Nijinska, premiere, *Polovtsian Dances*, Opéra, Paris

June 3 *Le Sacre du printemps*, *Mavra*, Nijinska (direction), premiere, *Petrushka*, Stravinsky Evening, Opéra, Paris

1923

IS in Monte Carlo with Ballets Russes, early April to mid-May, for *Les Noces* rehearsals with Nijinska

April 17 opening of season *Carnaval*, *Aurora's Wedding*, *Scheherazade*, Théâtre de Monte Carlo

IS in Paris with Ballets Russes, mid-June to June 30, end of season, staying on until early July

June 13 *Polovtsian Dances*, *Petrushka*, *Les Noces*, Nijinska, premiere, Théâtre de la Gaîté-Lyrique, Paris

June 30 *Aurora's Wedding*, Versailles Fête

August 16 *Triadic Ballet*, Oskar Schlemmer, Bauhaus, Weimar

August 19 *Histoire du soldat*, choreographer unknown (Frankfurt production), Bauhaus, Nationaltheater, Weimar

1924

April 24 *Histoire du soldat*, George and Lyudmila Pitoëff, Théâtre Bériza, Paris

IS in Paris with Ballets Russes, late May to June

May 26 opening of season *Les Tentations de la bergère*, Nijinska/Montéclair, **conducted** *Les Noces*, *Les Biches*, Nijinska/Poulenc, Théâtre des Champs-Elysées, Paris

June 4 *Les Fâcheux*, Massine/Auric, *Les Noces*, *Petrushka*, Théâtre des Champs-Elysées, Paris

June 11 *Les Noces*, *Les Biches*, *Polovtsian Dances*, Théâtre des Champs-Elysées, Paris

June 13 *Une Education manquée*, Chabrier (opera), *Les Fâcheux*, *Le Sacre du printemps*, Théâtre des Champs-Elysées, Paris

1925

March 13 *Petrushka*, Bolm after Fokine, Metropolitan Opera House, New York

April 28 *The Soldier's Tale*, Georgi Kroll, Teatro d'Arte di Pirandello, Rome

IS in Paris with Ballets Russes, June 15–20

June 15 opening of season *Pulcinella, Zephyre et Flore*, Massine/Dukelsky, *La Boutique fantasque*, Massine/Rossini, arr. Respighi, Théâtre de la Gaîté-Lyrique, Paris
June 17 *Le Chant du rossignol*, Balanchine, premiere, *Les Matelots*, Massine/Auric, premiere, *Les Biches*, Théâtre de la Gaîté-Lyrique, Paris
December 6 **conducted** *Petrushka*, Fokine, Royal Theatre, Copenhagen

1926

May 9 **conducted** *Petrushka*, premiere, Boris Romanov, La Scala, Milan
May 12 and 16 **conducted** *Petrushka*, Romanov, La Scala, Milan
IS in Paris late May with Ballets Russes, May 18 to June 11, attending numerous performances
IS in London for 3 days during week of July 7–11, and saw *Les Noces*

1927

IS in Paris with Ballets Russes, May 3 to June 11, end of season
May 27 opening of season *Le Triomphe de Neptune*, Balanchine/Berners, *La Chatte*, Balanchine/Sauguet, *The Firebird*, Théâtre Sarah-Bernhardt, Paris
May 30 *The Firebird*, **conducted** *Oedipus Rex*, Stravinsky Evening, Théâtre Sarah-Bernhardt, Paris
June 2 *The Firebird*, **conducted** *Oedipus Rex*, *Mercure*, Massine/Satie, premiere, Théâtre Sarah-Bernhardt, Paris
June 11 *Le Pas d'acier*, Massine/Prokofiev, *The Firebird*, *Mercure*, *Polovtsian Dances*, Théâtre Sarah-Bernhardt, Paris
IS in London with Ballets Russes, c. June 19–28
June 27 **conducted** *Petrushka*, Fokine, *Pulcinella*, *The Firebird*, Ballets Russes, Prince's Theatre, London

1928

February 25 *Petrushka*, Max Terpis, Staatsoper, Berlin
IS in Monte Carlo with Ballets Russes, for a few days at the beginning of March and beginning of April, for discussions about *Apollo*
IS in Paris with Ballets Russes June 6, beginning of season, conducting full run of performances of *Apollo*
June 12 *Pulcinella*, **conducted** *Apollo*, Balanchine, premiere, *Barabau*, Balanchine/Rieti, Théâtre de Sarah-Bernhardt, Paris
June 13 *Ode*, Massine/Nabokov, **conducted** *Apollo*, *La Chatte*, *Polovtsian Dances*, Théâtre de Sarah-Bernhardt, Paris
June 14 *Le Pas d'acier*, **conducted** *Apollo*, *Barabau*, Théâtre de Sarah-Bernhardt, Paris
June 19 *Pulcinella*, **conducted** *Apollo*, *The Firebird*, Stravinsky Festival, Théâtre de Sarah-Bernhardt, Paris
June 21 *Le Pas d'acier*, *La Chatte*, **conducted** *Apollo*, *Soleil de nuit*, Théâtre de Sarah-Bernhardt, Paris
June 23 *La Chatte*, **conducted** *Apollo*, *L'Après-midi d'un faune*, *Soleil de nuit*, Théâtre de Sarah-Bernhardt, Paris
IS in London with Ballets Russes, June 25 to end of June

June 25 **conducted** *Apollo*, *Cimarosiana*, Massine/Cimarosa, *The Firebird*, His Majesty's Theatre, London

November 27 *Les Noces de Psyché et de l'Amour*, Nijinska/Bach arr. Honegger, premiere, **conducted** *Le Baiser de la fée*, Nijinska, premiere, *Boléro*, Nijinska/Ravel, Ballets Ida Rubinstein, Opéra, Paris

December 4 **conducted** *Le Baiser de la fée*, Ballets Ida Rubinstein, Opéra, Paris

December 7 *Le Baiser de la fée*, *Les Noces de Psyché et de l'Amour*, *Boléro*, *Nocturne*, Nijinska/Borodin, *La Princesse Cygne* (from *Tsar Saltan*) Nijinska/Rimsky-Korsakov, Ballets Ida Rubinstein, Théâtre de la Monnaie, Brussels

1929

IS in Paris with Ballets Russes, from May 13, for just over 3 weeks

May 19 *Prodigal Son*, Balanchine/Prokofiev, rehearsal

May 20 *Prodigal Son*, preview

May 21 opening of season *Les Fâcheux*, **conducted** *Renard*, Lifar, premiere, *Prodigal Son*, premiere, *Polovtsian Dances*, Théâtre Sarah-Bernhardt, Paris

1930

May 28 **conducted** *Histoire du soldat*, dir. Abraham van der Vies, Stadsschouwburg, Amsterdam

1931

February 16 *Prélude Dominical*, Lifar/Ropartz, premiere, *L'Orchestre en liberté*, Lifar/Sauveplane, premiere, Opéra, Paris

1933

June 7 *Mozartiana*, Tchaikovsky, premiere, *Les Songes*, Milhaud, premiere, *The Seven Deadly Sins*, Weill, premiere, all-Balanchine programme, Les Ballets 1933, Théâtre des Champs-Elysées, Paris

1934

April 30, May 4, 9 **conducted** *Persephone*, Jooss, premiere, *Diane de Poitiers*, Fokine/Ibert, *La Valse*, Nijinska/Ravel, Ballets Ida Rubinstein, Opéra, Paris

1935

March 10 all-Balanchine programme, American Ballet, Adelphi Theatre, New York

March 21 *The Firebird*, Fokine, Monte Carlo Ballet Russe, Majestic Theatre, New York

1936

May 7, 10 **conducted both** *The Firebird* **and** *Petrushka*, Fokine, Teatro Colón, Buenos Aires

May 14 **conducted full programme**, *The Firebird*, *Petrushka*, *Le Baiser de la fée*, Nijinska, Teatro Colón, Buenos Aires

May 26 **conducted both** *Petrushka* **and** *The Firebird*, Teatro Colón company, Montevideo

November 28 *Madrigale*, Romanov/Rieti, *Pulcinella*, Romanov, Teatro Quirinetta, Rome

1937

March 12, 13 **conducted** *Petrushka Suite*, Theodore Kosloff after Fokine, Kosloff Ballet, Los Angeles

April 27, 28 **conducted full programme,** *Apollo*, *The Card Party*, Balanchine, premiere, *Le Baiser de la fée*, Balanchine, premiere, Stravinsky Festival, American Ballet, Metropolitan Opera House, New York

1939

May 21 **conducted** *Petrushka*, Fokine, Ballet Russe de Monte Carlo, Teatro Comunale, Florence

1940

August 27 **conducted** *Firebird Suite*, Bolm, Adolf Bolm Ballet, Hollywood Bowl, Los Angeles

October 12 *Fantasia*, animation film, Disney

October 16 *Scuola di ballo*, Massine/Boccherini orch. Françaix, *Symphonie Fantastique*, Massine/Berlioz, *Graduation Ball*, Lichine/Johann Strauss, arr. Dorati, Original Ballet Russe, Philharmonic Auditorium, Los Angeles

October 17 *Paganini*, Fokine/Rachmaninov, *Le Coq d'or*, Original Ballet Russe, Philharmonic Auditorium, Los Angeles

November 10 *Les Sylphides*, *Peter and the Wolf*, Bolm/Prokofiev, *Jardin aux lilas*, Tudor/Chausson, Ballet Theatre, Chicago

November 15 *Jardin aux lilas*, *Swan Lake* (one-act version), Petipa and Ivanov/Tchaikovsky, rehearsal, Ballet Theatre, Chicago

IS in New York, November 26 to December 13

December 2, *Les Sylphides*, *Prodigal Son*, Lichine/Prokofiev, *Graduation Ball*, Original Ballet Russe, Fifty-First Street Theatre, New York

December 9 *Cabin in the Sky*, Balanchine in collaboration with Katherine Dunham/Vernon Duke (musical comedy), Martin Beck Theatre, New York

IS in New York, December 22 to January 3, 1941, January 9–12, January 19 to February 6

1941

January 22 *Cotillon*, Balanchine/Chabrier, **conducted** *Balustrade* (to IS's *Violin Concerto*), Balanchine, premiere, *Aurora's Wedding*, Original Ballet Russe, New York

January 24 *Swan Lake* (one-act version), **conducted** *Balustrade*, *Scheherazade*, Original Ballet Russe, New York

August 9 Balanchine Preview, Los Angeles

November 18 Fred Astaire film

1942

February 11 *Serenade*, Balanchine/Tchaikovsky, *Nutcracker*, Ivanov/Tchaikovsky, *Gaîté Parisienne*, Massine/Offenbach arr. Rosenthal, Ballet Russe de Monte Carlo, Los Angeles

December 5 *Rodeo*, de Mille/Copland, *The Snow Maiden*, Nijinska/Glazunov, Ballet Russe de Monte Carlo, Los Angeles

1943

January 26 *Pillar of Fire*, Tudor/Schoenberg, Ballet Theatre, San Francisco
January 27 **conducted** *Petrushka*, Fokine, Ballet Theatre, San Francisco Opera House
February 8 **conducted** *Petrushka*, Ballet Theatre, Philharmonic Auditorium, Los Angeles
IS in New York with Ballet Theatre, March 31 to May 10
April 1 opening of season *Swan Lake Act I*, *Pillar of Fire*, *Bluebeard*, Fokine/Offenbach arr. Dorati, Metropolitan Opera House, New York
April 2 **conducted** *Petrushka*, *Les Sylphides*, *Pas de Quatre*, Keith Lester/Pugni, arr. Leighton Lucas, *Gala Performance*, Tudor/Prokofiev, Metropolitan Opera House, New York
April 10 *Billy the Kid*, Loring/Copland, *Romeo and Juliet*, Tudor/Delius, *Helen of Troy*, Lichine/Offenbach arr. Rosenthal, Metropolitan Opera House, New York
April 12 **conducted** *Petrushka*, Metropolitan Opera House, New York
April 25 **conducted** *Apollo*, Metropolitan Opera House, New York
April 26 **conducted** *Petrushka*, Metropolitan Opera House, New York
May 9 **conducted** *Apollo*, Metropolitan Opera House, New York
July 13 **conducted** *Petrushka*, Ballet Theatre, Los Angeles
July 17 **conducted** *Petrushka*, Ballet Theatre, Los Angeles

1944

June 30 Balanchine rehearsal, probably *Song of Norway*, Grieg, arr. Wright and Forrest (operetta), Los Angeles
August 12 and 31 **conducted** *Petrushka*, Ballet Theatre, Hollywood Bowl, Los Angeles
December 1 *Les Sylphides*, *Danses Concertantes*, Balanchine, *Gaîté Parisienne*, Ballet Russe de Monte Carlo, Philharmonic Auditorium, Los Angeles
December 5 *Le Bourgeois Gentilhomme*, Balanchine/Richard Strauss, *Danses Concertantes*, *Ballet Imperial*, Tchaikovsky (Balanchine Festival), Ballet Russe de Monte Carlo, Philharmonic Auditorium, Los Angeles
December 6 *Scheherazade*, **conducted** *Danses Concertantes*, *The Red Poppy*, Igor Schwezoff/Glière, arr. Arthur Cohn, Ballet Russe de Monte Carlo, Philharmonic Auditorium, Los Angeles[2]

1945

IS in New York, January 27 to February 26
February 22 *Danses Concertantes*, Ballet Russe de Monte Carlo, New York
November 30 opening of season *Comedia Balletica*, Bolender (to exerpts from *Pulcinella*) Ballet Russe de Monte Carlo, Los Angeles

1946

IS in New York, January 19 to February 18
February 17 *Les Sylphides*, **conducted** *Le Baiser de la fée*, Balanchine, *Gaîté Parisienne*, Ballet Russe de Monte Carlo, City Center, New York
IS in New York, December 6 to January 16, 1947 (including side-trips out of New York)
December 18 *Divertimento*, Balanchine/Haieff, rehearsal, Ballet Society

1947

January 13 and 14 *Pastorela* (ballet-opera), Lew Christensen and José Fernandez/ Paul Bowles, *Javanese Court and Popular Dances*, arr. Colin McPhee, *Witch* and *Litany*, Iris Mabry/Ralph Gilbert, *Renard*, Balanchine, premiere, *Divertimento*, Balanchine/ Haieff, premiere, Ballet Society, Hunter College Playhouse, New York
IS in New York, April 23 to May 1
April 30 *Apollo*, *Pillar of Fire*, *Pas de Quatre*, Keith Lester/Pugni, arr. Leighton Lucas, *Fancy Free*, Robbins/Bernstein, Ballet Theatre, City Center of Music and Drama, New York
August 7 *Nutcracker*, *Rodeo*, Ballet Russe de Monte Carlo, Hollywood Bowl, Los Angeles

1948

IS in New York, April 5 to May 4
April 20 *Theme and Variations*, Balanchine/Tchaikovsky (Balanchine conducting), *Shadow of the Wind*, Tudor/Mahler, *Interplay*, Robbins/Gould, Ballet Theatre, Metropolitan Opera House, New York
April 27 **conducted** *Apollo*, *Petrushka*, Ballet Theatre, Metropolitan Opera House, New York
April 28 *Elegie*, *Renard*, **conducted** *Orpheus*, premiere, *Symphonie Concertante*, Mozart, all-Balanchine programme, Ballet Society, City Center of Music and Drama, New York

1949

IS in New York, February 3–4 and 15–28
June 16 **conducted** *Story of a Soldier*, dir. Henry Schnitzler/Antonia Cobos, Royce Hall, UCLA, Los Angeles Music Festival
November 25 Ballet Nègre, Los Angeles

1950

IS in New York, February 18 to March 18, attending New York City Ballet, returning late March to end of April
February 21 *The Guests*, Robbins/Blitzstein, **conducted** *Firebird*, Balanchine, *Symphony in C*, Balanchine/Bizet, City Center, New York
February 22 *Symphonie Concertante*, *Divertimento*, **conducted** *Orpheus*, *Bourrée Fantasque*, Chabrier, all-Balanchine evening, City Center, New York
February 23 *Mother Goose Suite*, Bolender/Ravel, *Prodigal Son*, Balanchine/Prokofiev, *Symphony in C*, City Center, New York
February 26 *Concerto Barocco*, Balanchine/Bach, *The Age of Anxiety*, Robbins/Bernstein, premiere, *Symphony in C*, City Center, New York
March 2 *Symphonie Concertante*, *Illuminations*, Ashton/Britten, premiere, *Firebird*, City Center, New York
March 3 *Serenade*, Tchaikovsky, *Pas de Deux Romantique*, Weber, *Prodigal Son*, *Bourrée Fantasque*, all-Balanchine evening, City Center, New York
March 9 *Mother Goose Suite*, *Jones Beach*, Balanchine/Jurriaan Andriessen, premiere, *Orpheus*, City Center, New York

1951

IS in New York, November 22 to December 27, and saw many ballets, including *Swan Lake* (one-act version), *La Valse*, Ravel, and *Tyl Ulenspiegel*, Richard Strauss (all Balanchine premieres)

November 25, *The Card Game*, Balanchine, **conducted** *Le Baiser de la fée*, *The Cage*, Robbins, *Apollo*, Stravinsky Evening, New York City Ballet, City Center, New York

1952

IS in New York, April 23–28

May 14 **conducted** *Orpheus*, New York City Ballet, Théâtre des Champs-Elysées, L'Oeuvre du XXe siècle, Paris

May 19 **conducted** *Oedipus Rex* (Jean Cocteau production), Théâtre des Champs-Elysées, L'Oeuvre du XXe siècle, Paris

IS in New York, December 15 to March 11, 1953

1953

January 1 *Picnic at Tintagel*, Ashton/Bax, *Metamorphoses*, Balanchine/Hindemith, *Scotch Symphony*, Balanchine/Mendelssohn, *The Pied Piper*, Robbins/pipe music, New York City Ballet, City Center, New York

January 2 *Tyl Ulenspiegel*, *The Cage*, *Concertino*, Balanchine/Francaix, *Symphony in C*, New York City Ballet, City Center, New York

February 14 *The Rake's Progress*, stage direction Balanchine, premiere, Metropolitan Opera House, New York

February 19 *The Rake's Progress*, Metropolitan Opera House, New York

February 21 'City Center Show', New York

IS in New York, April 28 to May 2

December 9 *Swan Lake*, Sadler's Wells Ballet, Los Angeles

December 12 *The Sleeping Beauty*, Sadler's Wells Ballet, Los Angeles

December 15 *Sylvia*, Ashton/Delibes, Sadler's Wells Ballet, Los Angeles

IS in New York end of December to February 3, 1954

1954

IS in New York, March 25 to April 1

April 1 *Kismet*, choreography by Jack Cole (musical), New York

July 12 *Con Amore*, Lew Christensen/Rossini, *La Valse*, Balanchine/Ravel, *Sylvia Pas de Deux*, Balanchine/Delibes, *Fanfare*, Robbins/Britten, New York City Ballet, Greek Theatre, Los Angeles

October 25 *Les Sylphides*, **conducted** *Petrushka*, *Napoli*, Bournonville/various composers, London Festival Ballet, Chicago

October 26 *Swan Lake* (one-act version), **conducted** *Petrushka*, *La Esmeralda Act 2*, Perrot/Pugni, London Festival Ballet, Chicago

December 7 **conducted** *Petrushka*, London Festival Ballet, San Francisco

December 11 **conducted** *Petrushka*, London Festival Ballet, San Francisco

December 25 **conducted** *Petrushka*, London Festival Ballet, Shrine Auditorium, Los Angeles

1955

January 1 **conducted** *Petrushka*, London Festival Ballet, Shrine Auditorium, Los Angeles

IS in New York, January 21–26

January 24 *House of Flowers*, Balanchine/Arlen (musical comedy), New York

IS in New York, December 12 to January 11, 1956

1956

IS in New York, June 19–27

September 18 *Serenade*, *The Duel*, William Dollar/Raffaello de Banfield, *Pas de Deux*, Balanchine/Glazunov, *Bourrée Fantasque*, New York City Ballet, Teatro La Fenice, Venice

IS in New York, December 21 to January 23, 1957

1957

IS in New York, July 23 to August 1 and November 6–14

November 10 *Agon*, Balanchine, rehearsal, New York City Ballet

1958

IS in New York, July 23–29

1959

IS in New York, December to January 21, 1960

1960

IS attending New York City Ballet

January 19 *Agon*, *Seven Deadly Sins*, Weill, *Pas de Dix*, Glazunov, *Night Shadow*, Rieti, all-Balanchine evening, City Center, New York

December 11 mat. *Liebeslieder Walzer*, Balanchine/Brahms, *Jazz Concert* (*Creation of the World*, Bolender/Milhaud, *Ragtime*, Balanchine, *Les Biches*, Moncion/Poulenc, *Ebony Concerto*, Taras), City Center, New York, and/or

eve. *Swan Lake*, *The Still Point*, Bolender/Debussy, *Jazz Concert*, City Center, New York

IS in New York, December 7 to January 9, 1961

1961

July 19 **conducted** *Persephone*, Thomas Andrew, Santa Fe Opera, Santa Fe

IS in New York, August 24 to September 1

September 29 **conducted** *Persephone*, Theater des Westens, Berlin

First week in October **conducted** *Persephone*, Belgrade

October 18 **conducted** *Histoire du soldat*, dir. Michel de Lutry, Stadttheater, Zurich

1962

IS in New York, January 23 to February 3, after which several other short visits

February 1 *A Midsummer Night's Dream*, Balanchine/Mendelssohn, New York City Ballet, City Center, New York

May 2 opening of 'Stravinsky and the Dance' exhibition, Wildenstein Gallery, New York

June 23 (open rehearsal), 24–28 (performances), *Orpheus*, *Agon*, and **conducted** *Apollo*, (80th birthday celebrations), Hamburg Opera, Hamburg

August 1 **conducted** *Renard,* Andrew, Santa Fe Opera, Santa Fe
August 8 and 10 *Persephone,* Andrew, Santa Fe Opera, Santa Fe
September 25 *Orpheus,* Boyarsky, *Petrushka,* Fokine, *The Firebird,* Fokine, Maly Theatre, Leningrad

1963

April 5 *Movements for Piano and Orchestra,* Balanchine, rehearsal, New York City Ballet
April 30, May 4 *The Flood,* Peter van Dijk, Hamburg Opera, Hamburg
May 7 *Le Sacre du printemps,* Imre Eck, Budapest State Opera Ballet, Budapest
June 24, 27, 28 *The Flood,* Peter van Dijk, La Scala, Milan
IS in New York, September 9–17 and November 26 to February 5, 1964
December 6 *Fanfare,* Robbins, *Donizetti Variations,* Balanchine, *Movements for Piano and Orchestra, Stars and Stripes,* Balanchine/Sousa, New York City Ballet, City Center, New York

1964

IS attending New York City Ballet
January 25 mat. *The Four Temperaments,* Hindemith, *Meditation,* Tchaikovsky, *Firebird,* all-Balanchine programme, City Center, New York, or
eve. *Bugaku,* Mayuzumi, *Divertimento No. 15,* Mozart, *Agon, Stars and Stripes,* all-Balanchine programme, City Center, New York
January 26 mat. *Concerto Barocco, Episodes,* Webern, *Tarantella,* Gottschalk, *Firebird,* all-Balanchine programme, or
eve. *The Four Temperaments, Raymonda Variations,* Glazunov, *Waltz-Scherzo,* Tchaikovsky, *Gounod Symphony,* all-Balanchine programme, City Center, New York
October 4 *Serenade, Piège de lumière,* Taras/Damase, *Pas de deux* (Tchaikovsky), *La Valse,* all-Balanchine programme, New York State Theater, New York
IS made five additional short visits to New York during the year, also November 22 to January 11, 1965

1965

April 19 *Les Noces,* Robbins, Ballet Theatre, Chicago
IS in New York, April 20 to May 1
May 24 *Le Sacre du printemps,* Alfred Rodrigues, Warsaw Opera Ballet, Teatr Wielki, Warsaw
Early September, **conducted** *Apollo* for televising of Balanchine's ballet, Norddeutscher Rundfunk Television, Hamburg
IS in New York, June 13–18 and September 15 to October 10
September 30 *Don Quixote,* Balanchine/Nabokov, New York City Ballet, New York State Theatre, New York
IS in New York, December 10 to January 18, 1966

1966

IS made four additional short visits to New York in 1966, also September 18 to October 12
July 15 *Ragtime,* Balanchine, Philharmonic Hall, New York

December 10 Ukrainian Dance Company, Los Angeles

1967
IS in New York, January 1–12 and May 18–31

1968
IS in New York, September 8–24 and November 14–18
November 8 *Le Sacre du printemps*, Béjart, Ballet du XXe siècle, Opéra, Paris

1969
April 7 Diaghilev Exhibition, Los Angeles County Museum
IS in New York, April 20 to July 9, and September 15 moved to New York from Los Angeles

NOTES
1. Stravinsky and Robert Craft, *Memories and Commentaries* (London: Faber and Faber, 1960), pp. 31–2.
2. Charles M. Joseph reports that Stravinsky attended many performances of *Danses Concertantes* when it was programmed in Los Angeles. Stravinsky told a newspaper reporter in 1949 that he had seen it 'recently' (it left the repertory after the 1947–8 season): Hubert Roussel, 'Houston Jinx Lets Up on Stravinsky,' *Houston Post*, January 26, 1949.

Appendix 3

Selected Statements by Stravinsky Relating to Dance: A Chronology

This chronology traces changes in Stravinsky's dance aesthetics and attitude towards dance, and includes selected relevant comments on opera and film as hybrid forms. Most of the composer's specific comments on particular dances have been omitted, many of these having been incorporated within the main text of the book. The chronology includes some paraphrased material.

July 21, 1911: Letter to Vladimir Rimsky-Korsakov, son of the composer

I love ballet and am more interested in it than in anything else. And this is not just an idle enthusiasm, but a serious and profound enjoyment of scenic spectacle – of the art of animated form [zhivaya plastika] ... If a Michelangelo were alive today, I thought, looking at his frescoes in the Sistine Chapel, the only thing his genius would recognize and accept would be the choreography that is being reborn today. Everything else that takes place on the stage he would doubtless call a miserable farce. For the only form of scenic art that sets itself, as its cornerstone, the tasks of beauty, and nothing else, is ballet. And the only goal Michelangelo pursued was visible beauty ...

(... you have said that ballet is lower than opera, while for me all art is equal – there are not higher and lower arts, there are different forms of art – if you place one below another, it only proves that the plastic arts are less dear to you than another form of art – or else simply a thing you can do without), you dream only of artistic productions of existing operas, not giving any thought to the fact that opera is a spectacle, and a spectacle, at that, with an obligation to be artistic, and, consequently, as such, ought to have its own self-sufficient value – just as captivating gestures and movements in dance – which for some reason you place lower than recitative – are valuable, when they are created by the fantasy of a ballet master's talent, just as music, divorced from spectacle [is valuable]. These are not mere applied arts – it is a union of arts, the one strengthening and supplementing the other ...

... I think that if you would attend the ballet regularly (artistic ballet, of course), you would see that this 'lower form' brings you incomparably more artistic joy than any operatic performance (even the operas with your favourite music), a joy I have been experiencing now for over a year and which I would so like to infect you all with and share with you. It is the joy of discovering a whole new continent. Its development will take lots of work – there's much in store![1]

September 27, 1912: *Peterburgskaya gazeta*

Opera does not attract me at all. What interests me is choreographic drama, the only form in which I see any movement forward, without trying to foretell its future direction. Opera is falsehood pretending to be truth, while I need falsehood that pretends to be falsehood. Opera is a competition with nature.[2]

February 13, 1913: 'Musical Revolutionary: M. Stravinsky on his Dislike of Opera,' *Daily Mail* [London]

I dislike opera. Music can be married to gesture or to words – not both without bigamy. That is why the artistic basis of opera is wrong and why Wagner sounds at his best in the concert-room. In any case, opera is in a backwater. What operas have been written since *Parsifal*? Only two that count – *Electra* and Debussy's *Pelléas*.

February 16, 1913: '*Petrouschka* Composer on London Audiences: Mr Igor Stravinsky Talks of Russian Dancing and of the New Ballet in Preparation for Covent Garden,' *London Budget*

As a Russian, I may be permitted to say that the Russian ballet has influenced the dancing art of the other nations. Again I must refrain from comparisons, but there is something about the colour and animation of the Russian ballet which never fails to arouse interest. Eventually Moscow will be the artistic centre of Europe as it is now the artistic centre of Russia. One cannot tell why the Russians are able to achieve these great things in music and dancing. My people may be the interesting blend of the Orient and the Occident, and this fusion is good for art.

June, 1914: in interview with M.D. Calvocoressi, 'M. Igor Stravinsky's Opera: *The Nightingale*,' *The Musical Times*

I can write music to words, viz., songs; or music to action, viz., ballets. But the cooperation of music, words and action is a thing that daily becomes more inadmissible to my mind. And even if I should finish *The Nightingale*, I do not think that I shall ever attempt to write another work of that kind.[3]

September 24, 1914: Romain Rolland recalls meeting Stravinsky in his diary, *Journal des années de guerre*

He [Stravinsky] agrees that theatrical performance, such as it is today, diminishes the music, reduces the emotion or motion expressed, enclosing these within too precise a character image. However, there is value in performance through gesture and movement (a kind of rhythmic gymnastics, but more artistic than those of Dalcroze), broad, generous, sweeping lines in motion. He resents designs and costumes that are too rich and too individual, that detract from the spirit of musical emotion. The painter seems to him to be the musician's enemy. The Wagnerian dream of the artwork in which all the arts would join together is mistaken, he said. Where there is music, it must be sovereign! It is not possible to have two masters at the same time. Suppress colour! Colour is too powerful; it is a kingdom in itself, a music of its own. 'Colour is an inspiration for me to write music,' says Stravinsky. 'But when the music is written, it must be self-sufficient, it is its own colour. We should just keep lighting (which should be more varied than up till now and should follow the modulations of the sound), gestures and rhythms.'[4]

July 3, 1921: 'Interview with Stravinsky,' *The Observer* [London]

I have never tried, in my stage works, to make the music illustrate the action, or the action the music; I have always endeavoured to find an architectural basis of connection. I produce 'music itself'. Whenever 'music itself' is not the aim, music suffers ...

I have always felt the same. I have never made 'applied music' of any kind. Even in the early days, in the *Firebird*, I was concerned with a purely *musical* composition. The only forms which are worth anything are those which flow (*découler*) from the musical material itself ...

In the *Rite of Spring*, for instance, the pretext of the pre-historic birth of spring, has suggested to me the construction of the work that I have called *The Rite of Spring*. The 'pretext' I choose is but a pretext, like the painter's pretext for painting. If anyone objects, and prefers anecdote to a simple musical monument, they are surely in their mental infancy.

The *Rite* exists as a piece of music, first and last. Two different choreographies have been adapted to it, the earlier by Nijinsky, the later by Massine. The choreographic construction of Nijinsky, being of great plastic beauty, was, however, subjected to the tyranny of the bar; that of Massine is based on phrases each composed of several bars. This is the sense in which is conceived the free connection of the choreographical construction with the musical construction.

November 4, 1921: 'A Tchaikovsky Revival: M. Stravinsky on his Music. *The Sleeping Beauty,' The Times*

Tchaikovsky had a great admiration for the classical art of the ballet of petit pas. It should be remembered that he had an enormous formal imagination. That is what has made the ballet the parent of all the ballets that have come after, and that too, is why I have been so enthusiastic about the production. Of the forces brought together to carry out that production it is difficult for me to speak objectively. In the first place, because I love the ballet so well; and in the second place, because I am really one of the family.

July 8, 1923: 'Stravinsky "Not Revolutionary": Composer of *Les Noces* denies it himself: Hates Progress: Says Music is no longer Servant of the Ballet,' *Evening Standard* [London]

I wrote *Les Noces* ten years ago because I wished to give expression to an idea. Since the time of Tschaikowsky the relation of ballet and music has changed. Before that master's time, the composer was the servant of the ballet. He was ordered to write a series of numbers to fit in with the dancing. Now a ballet composer writes a composition to which the dancers must apply their art. It is their work to fit in their dances and their art.

The time will come when the much criticised modern ballets will be regarded as the classics are to-day. We have simply made a step in a new direction, or shall we say made a new variation on an old theme.

Everyone who studies ballet knows that the base of the ballet has never changed, only the expression. The classic formula remains although modern institutions are introduced. The only thing that matters are [*sic*] the relative importance of value and art.

The art which has the most value will live and that which has less will die.

Sometimes a theme has value for the moment and when people have lost interest or time has dulled memory, it ceases to be.

The great thing, therefore, in these so-called innovations in ballet and ballet music is to obtain something which has a lasting value in its relation to art.

It has often seemed to me that those who talk much of the ballet are too often carried away with the spectacular things and pleasing details. Surely it is better to get at the motive of the composer or the choreographer.

January 10, 1924: in interview with Guy Davenel, 'Un grand musicien à Anvers: ce que nous dit Igor Stravinsky,' *Le Matin* [Antwerp]

[Asked if his ballets lose something in concert, Stravinsky replied:]

Nothing, Sir. All my works are conceived symphonically and according to a virtually classical initial framework. Note, for instance, that I selected particular episodes from *Petrushka* and arranged them as the three traditional movements of the Sonata. [author's translation]

January 21, 1924: in interview with Joe van Cottom, 'Dans le train avec Igor Stravinsky,' *Comoedia*

Wagner is certainly not a real musician; he was always involved in theatre, which turned out to be an obstacle to musical ideas, the development of which was hindered by his narrative drive and philosophy. Each time he was tempted to write pure music, he came a cropper. Any good boxer can, in certain circumstances, lose a match, but if he loses several times in succession, he would have to admit clear inferiority. The public beg for double pleasure to the ear and eyes at the Opéra, without the extra fatigue of following a plot that gives them the creeps. [author's translation]

January 6, 1925: 'Igor Stravinsky Not a Modernist,' *The New York Times*

The ballets are also effective in concert ... *Petrushka*, for example, might be compared to a sonata, with its succession of movements, allegro, adagio, scherzo. The music as danced loses in two respects; for the author it is an alien métier, while for the public it diverts attention from the ear to the easier impressions of the eye.

January 6, 1925: F.D. Perkins, 'Stravinsky Aids Modern Music, but Detests It,' *Tribune* [New York]

[Perkins reports on Stravinsky's press conference:]

While not a few of his works are originally ballets, he explained that the music was complete in itself, a form, not a picture. With a ballet something is taken from the intensity of the music; the eye is always more impressionable. Mr Stravinsky expressed no preference among his own works. 'A composer is always interested in what he is doing now,' he said.

January 10, 1925: Henrietta Malkiel, 'Modernists Have Ruined Modern Music, Stravinsky Says,' *Musical America*

[Malkiel reports on Stravinsky's press conference:]

His ballets, Stravinsky says, are more effective in concert than on the stage. The *Sacre du printemps* is beautiful on the stage. There are two versions, one more exquisite than the other, by Nijinsky and Massine. But it is not music that is written to accompany a stage picture. It is an entity in itself. You can see that by the way it sounds in a concert hall. Of course the music loses when it is given with the ballet. The eye gets impressions more easily than the ear. Either the music detracts from your enjoyment of the ballet or the ballet from your absorption in the music. And then, ballets are not the perfect instruments that orchestras are. There is not the exact coordination between the movement and the music that is essential if it is to be an artistic achievement.[5]

1926, recalled October 27, 1927: Michel Georges-Michel, *Excelsior*

[Georges-Michel reports:]

Last year Diaghilev had asked Stravinsky for a new work, and the composer told him that he would not write a ballet because ballet is the anathema of Christ. And he gave him the oratorio *Oedipus Rex*.

May 27, 1930: *Le Vingtième Siècle*

Having been neglected for so long, it is only natural that rhythm in music and dance should now be in the forefront.[6]

1932: typescript statement for *Candide*, PSS interviews file

Not being part of the expressionist movement in music, I think that the role of the latter is not to convey the meaning of a play or of its text, nor to create the 'atmosphere' of a performance. One should instead ask what principle operates in a collaboration between musical flow and theatrical action. According to the principle of independence of the one from the other, here is my response. Each true art is necessarily canonical, possessing its own laws which drive and govern it. As this principle applies to all stage performance (theatre), I find no logical reason why it should not be applied just the same to all screen performance (cinema). [author's translation]

February 22, 1934: 'Stravinsky and his Music,' *Manchester Guardian*

Assuredly I believe that ballet will live and grow. The dance is as old as man and as young as man. It did not die with the Russian ballet. It is an essential, a dramatic part of the life of the theatre. But there is not a great deal of good ballet music. Either it is sunk in the dance or it is irrelevant to it as a rule. Music and dance should be a true marriage of separate arts, a partnership, not a dictatorship of the one over the other. Ballet music should have an independent existence. Too often it is tied to the theatrical spectacle ...

I believe that music has a most important part to play in the art of the cinema, which is a separate artform, only the cinema does not yet recognise the fact. Just as drama plus music made opera, so film plus music will make – what? I do not know, but I feel sure it will be something vital to us, something new.

June 6, 1935: in interview with Marie A. Levinson, 'Igor Strawinski: globe-trotter et homme de lettres,' *Candide*

We were saturated in classicism at the time [before Fokine's innovations]. I return to classical principles today with double the fervour. André Levinson [father of Marie, Russian dance critic and strong advocate of classicism] led the way. I consider Petipa the greatest of all artists, founder of a choreographic 'canon' without rival. Already, in my *Apollon-Musagète*, when, at Diaghilev's request, I had to explain the plot, I described something that did not require any explanation. The ballet is a work without intrigue, self-sufficient; it's there that lies the true key to the mystery of Terpsichore ...

[On the question of relationships between music and dance:]

What are the common elements that unite and separate them? Indeed, this is an important question: impossible to tackle it in five seconds. Allow me to restrict myself to saying that in my opinion there should be no subservience on either side, but a harmonious relationship, an ideal synthesis.

Let's talk about the struggle between musician and choreographer, the case of the admirable Nijinsky.

I wouldn't repeat for anything in the world the choreographic experience of *Le Sacre du printemps* that Diaghilev entrusted to this wonderful dancer. I described in my book [the first part of the *Autobiography*] the torture of such a collaboration; I insist that, despite a certain gift of plastic imagination, Nijinsky was in the end only a magnificent dancer, a splendid interpreter. Creativity was absolutely not his strength. [author's translation]

1936: *Autobiography*

[On *Le Chant du rossignol*:]

I reached the conclusion – very regretfully, since I was the author of many works for the theatre – that a perfect rendering can be achieved only in the concert hall, because the stage presents a combination of several elements upon which the music has often to depend, so that it cannot rely upon the exclusive consideration which it receives at a concert ...

... It was a real joy to me to take part in this creation [*The Sleeping Beauty*], not only for love of Tchaikovsky but also because of my profound admiration for classical ballet, which in its very essence, by the beauty of its *ordonnance* and the aristocratic austerity of its forms so closely corresponds with my conception of art. For here, in classical dancing, I see the triumph of studied conception over vagueness, of the rule over the arbitrary or order over the haphazard. I am thus brought face to face with the eternal conflict in art between the Apollonian and Dionysian principles. The latter assumes ecstasy to be the final goal – that is to say the losing of oneself – whereas art demands above all the full consciousness of the artist. There can, therefore, be no doubt as to my choice between the two. And if I appreciate so highly the value of classical ballet, it is not simply a matter of taste on my part, but because I see exactly in it the perfect expression of the Apollonian principle...

... The evolution of the classical dance and its problems now seem much more real to me, and touch me more closely than the distant aesthetics of Fokine ...

... When, in my admiration for the beauty of line in classical dancing, I dreamed of a ballet of this kind, I had specially in my thoughts what is known as the 'white ballet', in which to my mind the very essence of this art reveals itself in all its purity. I found that the absence of many-coloured effects and of all superfluities produced a wonderful freshness. This inspired me to write music of an analogous character [*Apollo*].[7]

June 30, 1936: Letter to Balanchine

[On the preparation of *Jeu de cartes*]:

I have never before composed ballet music without knowing the subject beforehand or having done a preliminary examination of the sequence of episodes of action, consistency, and structure. This is absolutely essential for the general musical structure ... My ballet has a definite and fully intelligible subject with some light intrigue.[8]

March 22, 1937: Alfred Frankenstein, 'Just Where is Stravinsky?', *San Francisco Chronicle*

[On a prospective film project:]

I shall not compose music in accompaniment to a photoplay. The story and the setting and all the rest will be written around the music, and the music will be composed in terms of the sound film. Thus the whole production will be conceived as a unit. I am not able at the present time to reveal the theme of the picture, but it will not be a Russian folk story.

May, 1937: André Frank, 'Igor Stravinsky va composer pour le cinema,' *L'Intransigeant*

I think the moment has arrived when music must stop being an accompaniment to film. It can, at times, provide the subject, underline the scenario, give sense to a cinematic work and undoubtedly even be its inspiration.

March 3, 1938: 'Histoire d'un ballet: une idée dans un fiacre,' *Le Jour*

Why did I compose *Jeu de cartes*? Simply because it had been a long time since I had written for ballet, and written something that was primarily destined to be danced. A work in which the saltatory element, the act of dancing, would be respected.

Into dance one can introduce movements of all kinds, on condition that what I would call the 'canons' of the dance or, if you prefer, its immutable laws, are respected. Now, choreographers who respect these principles have become rare.

I have therefore created a ballet that is truly about dancing. I wanted it to have as little narrative as possible, and a subject that can be easily grasped by the least experienced members of the public.

I therefore chose the game of cards! [author's translation]

June 3, 1938: French radio broadcast in response to questions from Georges Auric, *PSS* interviews file

Whatever the destination of a musical work – whether it be made for the theatre, for concert performance or for cinema – it must above all have intrinsic value, an existence of its own, its own *raison d'être* … That's why my first anxiety when I write for the theatre is to make certain that the music has an autonomous existence and thus to guard it from the danger of subjecting itself to the demands of the other theatrical components. As for my later scores, they are entirely conceived and constructed as complete musical entities, independent of their scenic destination. And it is for that reason that I attach as much importance to their concert performance as to their presentation on stage. [author's translation]

January 7, 1941: Carter Brooke Jones, 'Stravinsky Rehearses Symphony with Football Player's Energy,' *The Evening Star* [Washington]

It's too much … to train both the ballet and the orchestra to do it properly.

January 7, 1941: G.D.G., 'Stravinsky Bares Aversion to Canned Music on Radio,' *Times-Herald*

You will notice … that music for the ballet usually is indifferently performed. That is because there are too few rehearsals …

March, 1945: Marcel Valois, 'Chronique musicale: Avec Igor Stravinsky,' [Montreal] *PSS* interview file (no newspaper name given)

[At the Montreal press conference, Stravinsky said:]

[I want] to return to the classical dance in all its beauty and purity. These Ballet Scenes [*Scènes de ballet*] are in the nature of music that would be composed today if the classical ballet dominated as it did at that time.

April, 1945: Francis A. Coleman, 'A Talk with Igor Stravinsky,' *Dance*

[Coleman reports on Stravinsky's Montreal press conference. Stravinsky said:]
'Ballet is the purest form of theatrical art!'

Opera, as a mode of expression does not interest him, despite his own experiments in this form, and the music drama of Wagner leaves him cold. On the contrary, he appreciates the work of earlier Italian operatic composers.[9]

September, 1946: 'Igor Stravinsky on Film Music, as Told to Ingolf Dahl,' *Musical Digest*

What is the function of music in moving pictures? What, you ask, are the particular problems involved in music for the screen? I can answer both questions briefly. And I must answer them bluntly. There are no musical problems in the film. And there is only one real function of film music – namely, to feed the composer! In all frankness I find it impossible to talk to film people about music because we have no common meeting ground; their primitive and childish concept of music is not my concept. They have the mistaken notion that music, in 'helping' and 'explaining' the cinematic shadow-play, could be regarded under artistic considerations. It cannot be.

Do not misunderstand me. I realize that music is an indispensable adjunct to the sound film. It has got to bridge holes; it has got to fill the emptiness of the screen and supply the loudspeakers with more or less pleasant sounds. The film could not get along without it, just as I myself could not get along without having the empty spaces of my living-room walls covered with wall paper. But you would not ask me, would you, to regard my wall paper as I would regard painting, or apply aesthetic standards to it?

Misconceptions arise at the very outset of such a discussion when it is asserted that music will help the drama by underlining and describing the characters and the action. Well, that is precisely the same fallacy which has so disastrously affected the true opera through the 'Musikdrama'. Music explains nothing; music underlines nothing. When it attempts to explain, to narrate, or to underline something, the effect is both embarrassing and harmful.

What, for example, is 'sad' music? There is no sad music, there are only conventions to which part of the western world has unthinkingly become accustomed through repeated associations. These conventions tell us that Allegro stands for rushing action, Adagio for tragedy, suspension harmonies for sentimental feeling, etc. I do not like to base premises on wrong deductions, and these conventions are far removed from the essential core of music.

And – to ask a question myself – why take film music seriously? The film people admit themselves that at its most satisfactory it should not be heard as such. Here I agree. I believe that it should not hinder or hurt the action and that it should fill its wallpaper function by having the same relationship to the drama that restaurant music has to the conversation at the individual restaurant table. Or that somebody's piano playing in my living-room has to the book I am reading.

The orchestral sounds in films, then, would be like a perfume which is indefinable there. But let it be clearly understood that such perfume 'explains' nothing; and, moreover, I can not accept it as music. Mozart once said: 'Music is there to delight us, that is its calling.' In other words, music is too high an art to be a servant to other arts; it is too high to be absorbed only by the subconscious mind of the spectator, if it still wants to be considered as music.

Furthermore, the fact that some good composers have composed for the screen does not alter these basic considerations. Decent composers will offer the films decent pages of background score; they will supply more 'listenable' sounds than other composers; but even they are subject to the basic rules of the film which, of course, are primarily commercial. The film makers know that they need music, but they prefer music which is not very new. When, for commercial reasons, they employ a composer of repute they want him to write this kind of 'not very new' music – which, of course, results in nothing but musical disaster.

I have been asked whether my own music, written for the ballet and the stage, would not be comparable in its dramatic connotation to music in the films. It cannot be compared at all. The days of *Petrouchka* are long past, and whatever few elements of realistic description can be found in its pages fail to be representative of my thinking now. My music expresses nothing of realistic character, and neither does the dance. The ballet consists of movements which have their own aesthetic and logic, and if one of those movements should happen to be a visualization of the words 'I

Love You', then this reference to the external world would play the same role in the dance (and in my music) that a guitar in a Picasso still-life would play: something of the world is caught as pretext or clothing for the inherent abstraction. Dancers have nothing to narrate and neither has my music. Even in older ballets like *Giselle*, descriptiveness has been removed – by virtue of its naiveté, its unpretentious traditionalism and its simplicity – to a level of objectivity and pure art-play.

My music for the stage, then, never tries to 'explain' the action, but rather it lives side by side with the visual movement, happily married to it, as one individual to another. In *Scènes de Ballet* the dramatic action was given by an evolution of plastic problems, and both dance and music had to be constructed on the architectural feeling for contrast and similarity.

The danger in the visualization of music on the screen – and a very real danger it is – is that the film has always tried to 'describe' the music. That is absurd. When Balanchine did a choreography to my *Danses Concertantes* (originally written as a piece of concert music) he approached the problem architecturally and not descriptively. And his success was extraordinary for one great reason: he went to the roots of the musical form, of the *jeu musical*, and recreated it in forms of movements. Only if the films should ever adopt an attitude of this kind is it possible that a satisfying and interesting art form would result.

The dramatic impact of my *Histoire du Soldat* has been cited by various critics. There, too, the result was achieved, not by trying to write music which, in the background, tried to explain the dramatic action, or to carry the action forward descriptively, the procedure followed in the cinema. Rather was it the simultaneity of stage, narration, and music which was the object, resulting in the dramatic power of the whole. Put music and drama together as individual entities, put them together and let them alone, without compelling one to try to 'explain' and to react to the other. To borrow a term from chemistry: my ideal is the chemical *reaction*, where a new entity, a third body, results from uniting two different but equally important elements, music and drama; it is not the chemical *mixture* where, as in the films, to the preordained whole just the ingredient of music is added, resulting in nothing either new or creative. The entire working methods of dramatic film exemplify this ...

... If I am asked whether the dissemination of good concert music in the cinema will help to create a more understanding mass audience, I can only answer that here again we must beware of dangerous misconceptions. My first premise is that good music must be heard by and for itself, and not with the crutch of any visual medium. If you start to explain the 'meaning' of music you are on the wrong path. Such absurd 'meanings' will invariably be established by the image, if only through automatic association. That is an extreme disservice to music. Listeners will never be able to hear music by and for itself, but only for what it represents under the given circumstances and given instructions. Music can be useful, I repeat, only when it is taken for itself. It has to play its own role if it is to be understood at all. And for music to be useful to the individual we must above all teach the self-sufficiency of music, and you will agree that the cinema is a poor place for that! Even under the best conditions it is impossible for the human brain to follow the ear and the eye at the same time... [10]

July 26, 1948: 'Master Mechanic,' *Time*

[Stravinsky refuses to write for film:]

I cannot submit myself to their rules and laws. Practical restrictions I have always welcomed; psychological restrictions, no! They say to me, 'Create atmosphere' ... I am ashamed. I blush. I am absolutely incompetent to create atmosphere. I say to them, 'You must create the atmosphere from what I write.' I cannot artificate [*sic*].

March 26, 1949: W. H. Hadden Squire, 'Concerts in London,' *Christian Science Monitor*

My music for the stage ... never tries to 'explain' the action, but rather it lives side by side with the visual movement, happily married to it, as one individual to another.

October 15, 1949: Stravinsky's response to questions about *Orpheus* posed by RCA's Allan Kayes, typescript in *PSS*

We decided also the exact length of the music or rather the exact duration of each movement ... A thing much more important in a ballet than in any other dramatic form. Precision of timing and the physical capabilities of the dancers are primary factors which I have always considered in constructing the proportions of my ballets.[11]

January 30, 1954: Ed Brooks, '"Dancing Symphony": Next Stravinsky Composing Aim,' *Times-Picayune* [New Orleans]

Movements of all sorts may be introduced into the dance, but on the condition that the canons of the dance and its immutable laws are respected... Well, choreographers who respect these principles have become rare.

1960: *Memories and Commentaries*

Choreography as I conceive it must realize its own form ...[12]

NOTES

1. Richard Taruskin, *Stravinsky and the Russian Traditions: A Biography of the Works through 'Mavra'* (*SRT*; Oxford: Oxford University Press, 1996), pp. 973–4; trans. from L.S. Dyachkova, ed., *I.F. Stravinsky: Stat'i i materiali* (Moscow: Sovetskiy Kompozitor, 1973), pp. 459–62.

2. *SRT*, p. 982 (Taruskin's translation).

3. M.D. Calvocoressi, *The Musical Times*, 55 (June, 1914), p. 372.

4. Romain Rolland, *Journal des années de guerre* (Paris: Editions Albin Michel, 1952), pp. 59–60 (author's translation).

5. Henrietta Malkiel, 'Modernists have Ruined Modern Music, Stravinsky Says,' *Musical America*, January 10, 1925, p. 9.

6. Stravinsky quoted in Vera Stravinsky and Craft, *Stravinsky in Pictures and Documents* (New York: Simon & Schuster, 1978), p. 203.

7. Stravinsky, *An Autobiography* [1936] (London: Calder & Boyars, 1975), pp. 84, 99–100, 130, 135.

8. Robert Craft, ed., *Stravinsky, Selected Correspondence*, II (London: Faber and Faber, 1984), p. 315.

9. Francis A. Coleman, 'A Talk with Igor Stravinsky,' *Dance* (April, 1945), p. 14.

10. 'Igor Stravinsky on film music, as told to Ingolf Dahl,' *Musical Digest*, (September, 1946), reprinted *Cinema* (June, 1947) and currently on the web: www.filmmusicsociety.org/news_events/features/newsprint.php.

For further comments by Stravinsky on film and television, see Stravinsky and Robert Craft, *Dialogues and a Diary* (London: Faber and Faber, 1968), pp. 79–80 [working notes on *The Flood*]; Craft, *Stravinsky: The Chronicle of a Friendship* (London: Victor Gollancz, 1972), p. 308.

11. Charles M. Joseph, *Stravinsky and Balanchine: A Journey of Invention* (New Haven & London: Yale University Press, 2002), p. 190.

12. Stravinsky and Robert Craft, *Memories and Commentaries* (London: Faber and Faber, 1960), p. 37. For the full statement, see p. 69.

Appendix 4

The American Ballet/New York City Ballet Stravinsky Festivals, 1937, 1972, 1982

The ballets listed below are by Balanchine, unless otherwise indicated.

The last two Stravinsky Festivals included concert performance of a few scores: in 1972, *Fanfare for a New Theater*, *Greeting Prelude* (*Happy Birthday*) – Stravinsky's arrangement for Pierre Monteux, *Fireworks* and *The Faun and the Shepherdess*; in 1982, again *Fanfare for a New Theater* and *Fireworks*. *Symphony of Psalms* ended the 1972 Festival with the dancers seated at the side of and behind the singers. The 1982 closing night included Stravinsky's setting of the poem about the Last Judgement, *Zvezdoliki*.

April 27 and 28, 1937 – Metropolitan Opera, New York
Apollo, The Card Party, Le Baiser de la fée

June 18–25, 1972 – New York State Theater
June 18:
Fanfare for a New Theater, *Greeting Prelude* (Happy Birthday), *Fireworks*, *Sonata*,* *Scherzo Fantastique* (Robbins),* *Symphony in Three Movements*,* *Violin Concerto*,* *Firebird* (Balanchine and Robbins)
June 20:
Symphony in E Flat (John Clifford),* *The Cage* (Robbins), *Concerto for Piano and Winds* (John Taras),* *Danses Concertantes**
June 21:
Octuor (Richard Tanner),* *Serenade in A* (Todd Bolender), *The Faun and the Shepherdess*, *Divertimento from 'Le Baiser de la fée'*,* *Ebony Concerto* (Taras), *Scherzo à la Russe*,* *Circus Polka* (Robbins)*
June 22:
Scènes de Ballet (Taras),* *Duo Concertant*,* *The Song of the Nightingale* (Taras),* *Capriccio for Piano and Orchestra* (*Rubies*)
June 23:
Concerto for Two Solo Pianos (Tanner), *Piano-Rag-Music* (Bolender),* *Ode* (Lorca Massine),* *Dumbarton Oaks* (Robbins),* *Pulcinella* (Balanchine and Robbins)*
June 24:
Apollo, Orpheus, Agon
June 25:
Choral Variations on Bach's 'Von Himmel hoch',* *Monumentum pro Gesualdo, Movements for Piano and Orchestra, Requiem Canticles* (Robbins),* *Symphony of Psalms*

June 10–19, 1982 – New York State Theater

June 10:

Circus Polka, Fireworks, Tango, Piano-Rag-Music* (Peter Martins),* Duo Concertant, Pastorale* (Jacques d'Amboise),* Ca*priccio for Piano and Orchestra (Rubies), Concerto for Piano and Winds* (Taras),* Symphony in Three Movements*

June 11:

Noah and the Flood, Suite from 'Histoire du Soldat'* (Martins), *Eight Easy Pieces* (Martins), *Violin Concerto*

June 12 (matinée):

Noah and the Flood, Monumentum/Movements, Pastorale, Serenade en La, Symphony in Three Movements

June 12 (evening):

Divertimento from 'Le Baiser de la fée', Scherzo à la Russe, Norwegian Moods (Lew Christensen), *Concerto for Piano and Winds, Agon*

June 13 (matinée):

Circus Polka, Fireworks, Monumentum/Movements, Piano-Rag-Music, Elégie, Tango, Concerto for Two Solo Pianos* (Martins),* Noah and the Flood*

June 13 (evening):

Noah and the Flood, Concerto for Piano and Winds, The Cage, Agon

June 15:

Divertimento from 'Le Baiser de la fée', The Cage, Monumentum/Movements, Pastorale, Serenade in La, Symphony in Three Movements

June 16:

Orpheus, Four Chamber Works (Robbins)*, Capriccio for Piano and Orchestra (Rubies)*

June 17:

Suite from 'Histoire du Soldat', Four Chamber Works, Divertimento from 'Le Baiser de la fée'

June 18:

Zvezdoliki, Apollo, Persephone (Balanchine, Taras and Vera Zorina)*, Symphony in Three Movements*

June 19 (matinée):

Orpheus, Four Chamber Works, Apollo

June 19 (evening)

Orpheus, Persephone, Agon

*= premiere

The premiere of Balanchine's *Variations* was scheduled for the June 13 matinée, but was postponed until July 2, 1982.

Appendix 5

Balanchine's Stravinsky: A Chronology

1. The Stravinsky–Balanchine ballets[1]
* designates that the ballet is still in repertory.

Ragtime	1918/1922	performed in Petrograd
Pulcinella	1920/1924	rehearsed but not performed
Le Chant du rossignol	1917/June 17, 1925	Ballets Russes
*Apollon Musagète** (later titled *Apollo*)	1928/June 12, 1928	Ballets Russes
The Card Party	1936/April 27, 1937	American Ballet (commissioned score – ballet also called *The Card Game* and *Poker Game*, original score title *Jeu de cartes*)
Le Baiser de la fée	1928/April 27, 1937	American Ballet
Balustrade	1931/January 22, 1941	Original Ballet Russe (to *Concerto in D for Violin*)
The Ballet of the Elephants	1942/April 9, 1942	Ringling Brothers and Barnum & Bailey's Circus (commissioned score – *Circus Polka*, arranged for circus band by David Raksin)
Danses Concertantes	1942/September 10, 1944	Ballet Russe de Monte Carlo
Circus Polka	1942/November 5, 1945	School of American Ballet
Elégie	1944/November 5, 1945	School of American Ballet
Renard	1916/January 13, 1947	Ballet Society

*Orpheus**	1947/April 28, 1948	Ballet Society (commissioned score)
*Firebird**	1945/November 27, 1949	New York City Ballet (1945 *Suite* drawing from 1910 full ballet score)
The Rake's Progress (opera direction)	1951/February 14, 1953	Metropolitan Opera
*Agon** (commissioned score)	1957/December 1, 1957[2]	New York City Ballet
*Monumentum pro Gesualdo**	1960/November 16, 1960	New York City Ballet
Ragtime I	1918/December 7, 1960	New York City Ballet
Noah and the Flood	1962/June 14, 1962	New York City Ballet (commission for television)
*Movements for Piano and Orchestra**	1959/April 9, 1963	New York City Ballet
Variations	1965/March 31, 1966	New York City Ballet (to *Variations Aldous Huxley in Memoriam*)
Elégie	1944/July 15, 1966	New York City Ballet (first danced in concert)
Ragtime II	1918/July 15, 1966	New York City Ballet (first danced in concert)
*Rubies** (central section from *Jewels*)	1929/April 13, 1967	New York City Ballet (to *Capriccio for Piano and Orchestra*)
Requiem Canticles	1966/May 2, 1968	New York City Ballet
Sonata	1904/June 18, 1972	New York City Ballet (Scherzo movement)
*Symphony in Three Movements**	1945/June 18, 1972	New York City Ballet

Violin Concerto (later titled *Stravinsky Violin Concerto*)*	1931/June 18, 1972	New York City Ballet
*Danses Concertantes**	1942/June 20, 1972	New York City Ballet
*Divertimento from 'Le Baiser de la fée'**	1934/June 21, 1972	New York City Ballet (drawing from 1928 full ballet score)
*Scherzo à la Russe**	1944/June 21, 1972	New York City Ballet
*Duo Concertant**	1932/June 22, 1972	New York City Ballet
Pulcinella (with Jerome Robbins)	1920/June 23, 1972	New York City Ballet
Choral Variations on Bach's 'Von Himmel hoch'	1956/June 25, 1972	New York City Ballet
Tango	1953/June 10, 1982	New York City Ballet (1953 orchestration using 1940 piano solo)
Noah and the Flood	1962/June 11, 1982	New York City Ballet
Elégie	1944/June 13, 1982	New York City Ballet
Persephone (with John Taras and Vera Zorina)	1934/June 18, 1982	New York City Ballet
Variations for Orchestra	1965/July 2, 1982	New York City Ballet (to *Variations Aldous Huxley in Memoriam*)

2. Balanchine's Stravinsky transcriptions for piano
Violin Concerto in D, Aria I
Choral Variations on Bach's 'Von Himmel hoch'
Monumentum pro Gesualdo
Three Pieces for String Quartet, first movement (never choreographed)
Scènes de ballet (never choreographed)
Symphony in E-flat (begun, never choreographed)

NOTES
1. This chronology does not include details of Balanchine's many revisions of his ballets, but major re-workings are shown as independent ballets in the list.
2. There was a preview performance of *Agon* on November 27, 1957.

Appendix 6

Stagings of Bronislava Nijinska's Les Noces

1923 premiere, Ballets Russes, Théâtre de la Gaîté-Lyrique, Paris, France
1926 Teatro Colón, Buenos Aires, Argentina
1933 Théâtre de la Danse Nijinska, Paris, France
1936 Col. W. de Basil's Ballets Russes, Metropolitan Opera, New York, USA
1966 Royal Ballet, Covent Garden, London, UK
1971 Teatro La Fenice, Venice, Italy
1974 Stuttgart Ballet, Stuttgart, Germany
1976 Paris Opéra Ballet, Paris, France
1981 Oakland Ballet, California, USA
1984 SUNY Purchase University Dance Corps, New York, USA
1985 Eliot Feld Ballet, New York, USA
1985 Pittsburgh Ballet, Pittsburgh, USA
1987 Compania Nacional de Danza, Mexico City, Mexico
1987 Les Grands Ballets Canadiens, Montreal, Canada
1988 Vienna State Opera Ballet, Vienna, Austria
1988 Washington Ballet, Washington D.C., USA
1989 Joffrey Ballet, Dorothy Chandler Pavilion, Los Angeles, USA
1989 Dance Theatre of Harlem, New York, USA
1991 National Institute for the Arts, Taipei, Taiwan
1991 Dutch National Ballet, Amsterdam, Netherlands
1994 Companhia Nacional de Bailado, Lisbon, Portugal
1995 Mussorgsky (Maly) Theatre of Opera and Ballet, St Petersburg, Russia
1996 Ballet of the Teatro Municipal, Rio de Janeiro, Brazil
1996 Ballet of the Deutsche Oper, Berlin, Germany
1997 Ballet du Nord, France
1997 Ballet National de Nancy et de Lorraine, France
1998 Tokyo Ballet, Tokyo, Japan
2003 Kirov Ballet, Maryinsky Theatre, St Petersburg, Russia
2006 Boston Ballet, Boston, USA
2007 Ballet de l'Opéra National de Bordeaux, France

The chronology does not include revivals of *Noces* stagings on the companies listed. I am greatly indebted to Natalie Raetz for providing me with a detailed list of stagings, supported by information from Howard Sayette.

Notes

Sources appearing in abbreviated form

Aut   Igor Stravinsky, *An Autobiography* [1936], London: Calder & Boyars, 1975
DB   Robert Craft, ed., *Dearest Bubushkin: The Correspondence of Vera and Igor Stravinsky, 1921–1954, with Excerpts from Vera Stravinsky's Diaries, 1922–1971*, trans. Lucia Davidova, London: Thames and Hudson, 1985
Dial   Igor Stravinsky and Robert Craft, *Dialogues and a Diary*, London: Faber and Faber, 1968
Expo   Igor Stravinsky and Robert Craft, *Expositions and Developments*, London: Faber and Faber, 1962
ISCS   Stephen Walsh, *Igor Stravinsky: A Creative Spring*, London: Jonathan Cape, 2000
Mem   Igor Stravinsky and Robert Craft, *Memories and Commentaries*, London: Faber and Faber, 1960
SB   Charles M. Joseph, *Stravinsky and Balanchine: A Journey of Invention*, New Haven & London: Yale University Press, 2002
SGD   Stephanie Jordan and Larraine Nicholas, 'Stravinsky the Global Dancer' [Internet database chronology], www.roehampton.ac.uk/stravinsky, 2003 (ongoing project)
SPD   Vera Stravinsky and Robert Craft, *Stravinsky in Pictures and Documents*, New York: Simon & Schuster, 1978
SRT   Richard Taruskin, *Stravinsky and the Russian Traditions: A Biography of the Works through 'Mavra'*, 2 vols, Oxford: Oxford University Press, 1996
SSCI   Robert Craft, ed., *Stravinsky: Selected Correspondence*, I, London: Faber and Faber, 1982
SSCII   Robert Craft, ed., *Stravinsky: Selected Correspondence*, II, London: Faber and Faber, 1984
SSCIII   Robert Craft, ed., *Stravinsky: Selected Correspondence*, III, London: Faber and Faber, 1985
SSE   Stephen Walsh, *Stravinsky: The Second Exile: France and America, 1934–1971*, New York: Alfred A. Knopf, 2006

Other abbreviations

PSS   Paul Sacher Stiftung, Basle
HTC   Harvard Theatre Collection, Houghton Library, Harvard University

Introduction

1. Stephanie Jordan and Larraine Nicholas, 'Stravinsky the Global Dancer' (*SGD*), Internet database, www.roehampton.ac.uk/stravinsky, 2003 (ongoing project).

2. Igor Stravinsky and Robert Craft, *Expositions and Developments* (*Expo*; London: Faber & Faber, 1962), p. 133.

3. Richard Buckle, *Diaghilev* (London: Weidenfeld and Nicolson, 1979); Lynn Garafola, *Diaghilev's Ballets Russes* (New York & Oxford: Oxford University Press, 1989); Garafola and Nancy Van Norman Baer, eds, *The Ballets Russes and Its World* (New Haven & London: Yale University Press, 1999); Charles M. Joseph, *Stravinsky and Balanchine: A Journey of Invention* (*SB*; New Haven & London: Yale University Press, 2002).

4. Modern dance is the term used in this book (and in *SGD*) for Western dance traditions outside ballet, as an umbrella term covering contemporary dance, postmodern dance, Tanztheater and Ausdruckstanz. However, these other terms are specified where appropriate.

5. Linda J. Tomko, 'Considering Causation and Conditions of Possibility', in *Rethinking Dance History: A Reader*, ed. Alexandra Carter (London & New York: Routledge, 2004), p. 90. Tomko draws from Michel Foucault, *The Order of Things: An Archaeology of the Human Sciences* [1966] (New York: Vintage Books, 1973). See also Linda Hutcheon, *The Politics of Postmodernism* (London: Routledge, 1989), p. 66. Carter's reader, led by her own Chapters 1 and 2, is a valuable exposition of current issues in historiography as applied to dance.

6. Stravinsky, *An Autobiography* [1936] (Aut; London: Calder & Boyars, 1975), pp. 53–4.

7. *Expo*, p. 101.

8. Stephen Walsh, *Igor Stravinsky: A Creative Spring* (*ISCS*; London: Jonathan Cape, 2000), pp. 375–76; Stravinsky, 'Some Ideas About My Octuor', *The Arts* (Brooklyn), January, 1924, pp. 4–6; reprinted in White, *Stravinsky: The Composer and his Works*, pp. 574–77.

9. Clip from CBS 'News Special' (1965) incorporated in *Once at a border...*, film documentary on Stravinsky directed by Tony Palmer, London Weekend Television, 1982. Supplementary information, including Palmer's full script and details of his film source material, is housed in files in the Paul Sacher Stiftung, Basle (*PSS*).

10. Richard Taruskin, *Stravinsky and the Russian Traditions: A Biography of the Works through 'Mavra'* (*SRT*; Oxford: Oxford University Press, 1996); *Stravinsky: The Second Exile: France and America, 1934–1971* (*SSE*; New York: Alfred A. Knopf, 2006); *ISCS*; *SB*.

11. Jonathan Cross, ed., *The Cambridge Companion to Stravinsky* (Cambridge: Cambridge University Press, 2003).

12. Robert Craft, ed., *Stravinsky: Selected Correspondence*, 3 vols. (London: Faber and Faber, 1982, 1984, 1985).

13. *SSE*, pp. 1, 25, 368, 421–2, 497.

14. Robert Craft, ed., *Dearest Bubushkin: The Correspondence of Vera and Igor Stravinsky, 1921–1954, with Excerpts from Vera Stravinsky's Diaries, 1922–1971*, trans. Lucia Davidova (*DB*; London: Thames and Hudson, 1985); see *SSE*, p. 597, note 16.

15. Stephanie Jordan, *Music Dances: Balanchine Choreographs Stravinsky* (New York: George Balanchine Foundation, 2002) and, with Geraldine Morris, *Ashton to Stravinsky: A Study of Four Ballets with Choreography by Frederick Ashton* (London: Dance Books, 2004).

16. Robynn J.Stilwell, 'Stravinsky and Balanchine: A Musical-Choreographic Analysis of *Agon*', unpublished PhD dissertation, University of Michigan, 1994; Julia Phillips Randel, *Dancing with Stravinsky: Balanchine, 'Agon', 'Movements for Piano and Orchestra', and the Language of Classical Ballet*, unpublished PhD dissertation, Harvard University, 2004; Andrew Wachtel, ed., *'Petrushka': Sources and Contexts* (Evanston, Illinois: Northwestern University Press, 1998).

17. Simon Morrison and Stephanie Jordan, eds, 'Sound Moves' [issue], *The Opera Quarterly {Performance+Theory+History}*, 22/1 (Winter, 2006).

18. See, for instance:
   • the contributions by Rachel Duerden, Beth Genné, Christian Matjias, Simon Morrison, Kimiko Okamoto and Marian Smith in the Proceedings of *Sound Moves: An International Conference on Music and Dance*, Roehampton University, 2005, www.roehampton.ac.uk/soundmoves/proceedings.htm
   • Rebecca Harris-Warrick and Carol G. Marsh, *Musical Theatre at the Court of Louis XIV: Le Mariage de la Grosse Cathos* (Cambridge & New York: Cambridge University Press, 1994)
   • Marian Smith, *Ballet and Opera in the Age of 'Giselle'* (Princeton, New Jersey: Princeton University Press, 2000)
   • Roland John Wiley, *Tchaikovsky's Ballets* (Oxford: Clarendon Press, 1985)
   • Inger Damsholt, 'Mark Morris, Mickey Mouse, and Choreomusical Polemic', 'Sound Moves' (see note 17), pp. 4–21
   • Rachel Duerden, *The Choreography of Antony Tudor* (Madison & Teaneck: Farleigh Dickinson Press/London: Associated University Presses, 2003)
   • Deborah Mawer, *The Ballets of Maurice Ravel: Creation and Interpretation* (Aldershot, Hants, & Burlington, Vermont: Ashgate, 2006)
   • Simon Morrison, 'Shostakovich as Industrial Saboteur: Observations on *The Bolt*', in Laurel Fay, ed., *Shostakovich and His World* (Princeton: Princeton University Press, 2004), pp. 117–61, and 'The Origins of *Daphnis et Chloé* (1912)', *19th-Century Music*, 28/1 (Summer, 2004), pp. 50–76
   • Stephen D. Press, *Prokofiev's Ballets for Diaghilev* (Aldershot, Hants & Burlington, Vermont: Ashgate, 2006)
   • Barbara White, '"As if they didn't hear the music", Or: How I Learned to Stop Worrying and Love Mickey Mouse', 'Sound Moves' (see note 17), pp. 65–89.

19. Stephanie Jordan, *Moving Music: Dialogues with Music in Twentieth-Century Ballet* (London: Dance Books, 2000).

20. Claudia Gorbman, 'Narrative Film Music', *Yale French Studies*, 60 (1980), p. 189.

21. Hanns Eisler and Theodor W. Adorno, *Composing for the Films* (London: Dennis Dobson, 1947), p. 70. Note that Adorno's role was uncredited in the original English edition; see Philip Rosen, 'Adorno and Film Music: Theoretical Notes on Composing for the Films', *Yale French Studies*, 60 (1980), pp. 157–82.

22. Gorbman, 'Narrative Film Music', pp. 189–90.

23. Kathryn Kalinak, *Settling the Score: Music and the Classical Hollywood Film* (Madison, Wisconsin: University of Wisconsin Press, 1992), pp. 29–31. On the issue of counterpoint within film, see

also Michel Chion, *Audio-Vision: Sound on Screen* [1990], ed. and trans. Gorbman (New York: Columbia University Press, 1994), pp. 35–9.

24. Nicholas Cook, *Analysing Musical Multimedia* (Oxford: Oxford University Press, 1998), p. 70. See also Cook, 'Theorizing Musical Meaning', *Music Theory Spectrum*, 23/2 (October, 2001), pp. 170–95.

25. George Lakoff and Mark Johnson, *Metaphors We Live By* (Chicago: University of Chicago Press, 1980), p. 142.

26. Mark Turner and Gilles Fauconnier, 'Conceptual Integration and Formal Expression', *Journal of Metaphor and Symbolic Activity*, 10 (1995), pp. 183–203; Fauconnier and Turner, *The Way We Think: Conceptual Blending and the Mind's Hidden Complexities* (New York: Basic Books, 2002).

27. Lawrence M. Zbikowski, 'Music Theory, Multimedia, and the Construction of Meaning', *Intégral*, 16/17 (2002/2003), pp. 251–68; Zbikowski, *Conceptualizing Music: Cognitive Structure, Theory, and Analysis* (Oxford & New York: Oxford University Press, 2002).

28. Cook, *Analysing Musical Multimedia*, p. 98; see pp. 98–108 for a full discussion of Cook's analytical model.

29. Ibid., p. 103.

30. Ibid., p. 182.

31. Cook borrows the term 'sopping up' from Lawrence E. Marks, *The Unity of the Senses: Interrelations Among the Modalities* (New York: Academic Press, 1978), p. 78.

32. Cook, *Analysing Musical Multimedia*, pp. 180–81.

33. Doris Humphrey, *The Art of Making Dances* (New York & Toronto: Rinehart, 1959), p. 80.

34. Daniel Albright, *Stravinsky: The Music Box and the Nightingale* (New York: Gordon and Breach, 1989).

35. Daniel Albright, *Untwisting the Serpent: Modernism in Music, Literature, and Other Arts* (Chicago & London: University of Chicago Press, 2000), pp. 7, 28–9.

36. Ibid., p. 7.

37. White, '"As if they didn't hear the music"....', p. 69.

38. Ibid., pp. 81–2.

39. Eisler and Adorno, *Composing for the Films*, pp. 59–61; Jacques Attali, *Noise: The Political Economy of Music*, trans. Brian Massumi (Minneapolis: University of Minnesota Press, 1985), p. 6.

40. White, '"As if they didn't hear the music"....', p. 73.

41. Raina Katzarova, 'Sur un phénomène concernant le manque de coïncidence entre la figure chorégraphique et la phrase mélodique', *International Folk Music Journal*, 12 (1960), p. 69; Felix Hoerburger, 'On Relationships between Music and Movement in Folk Dancing', *International Folk Music Journal*, 12 (1960), p. 70; György Martin, 'Considérations sur l'analyse des relations entre la danse et la musique de danse populaires', *Studia Musicologica*, 7/1–4 (1965), pp. 333–4; Ernő Pésovár, 'Three Round Verbunks', *Dance Studies*, 1 (1976), p. 50.

42. Duerden, 'Dancing in the Imagined Space of Music', *Dance Research*, 25/1 (Summer, 2007), p. 77.

43. Andrew Imbrie, 'Extra Measures and Metrical Ambiguity in Beethoven', in Alan Tyson, ed., *Beethoven Studies* (New York: Norton, 1973), pp. 45–66; Fred Lerdahl and Ray Jackendoff, *A Generative Theory of Tonal Music* (Cambridge, Mass: MIT Press, 1981); Pieter C. van den Toorn, *The Music of Igor Stravinsky* (New Haven: Yale University Press, 1983); van den Toorn, *Stravinsky and 'The Rite of Spring': The Beginnings of a Musical Language* (Berkeley & Los Angeles: University of California Press, 1987), pp. 57–114; Gretchen Horlacher, 'Metric Irregularity in *Les Noces*: The Problem of Periodicity', *Journal of Music Theory*, 39/2 (Fall, 1995), pp. 285–309.

44. One of the outcomes of this project was the analytical video *Ashton to Stravinsky: A Study of Four Ballets*.

45. Jordan, *Moving Music*, pp. 73–89. See also Jordan, 'Music as a Structural Basis in the Choreography of Doris Humphrey', unpublished PhD dissertation, University of London, Goldsmiths College, 1986.

Chapter 1

1. Margarita Mazo, ed., *Igor Stravinsky: 'Les Noces' Study Score* (London: Chester Music, 2005), in 'Igor Stravinsky's *Les Noces*, the Rite of Passage', [Preface], p. xii, and note 36; translated from Vladimir Derzhanovsky, 'The Latest Compositions by Igor Stravinsky', in the section 'News from Abroad', *Muzïka*, 219 (April 18, 1915), pp. 262–3. (The journal date here represents the Russian (Old Style) as opposed to Western (New Style) calendar. The Western calendar date would be May 1, 1915. I will use the Russian calendar for other early Russian sources in this book – publications and letters.)

2. Mazo, *Igor Stravinsky*, p. v, and note 4; translated from letter from Stravinsky to Nikolay Struve, April 6, 1919, Paul Sacher Stiftung, Basle (*PSS*), *La Copie des lettres*, pp. 136–46.

3. Letter from Stravinsky to Otto Kling, November 23, 1919, *PSS*, *La Copie des lettres*, p. 201.

4. Stravinsky quoted in Philippe Parès, 'Pendant une répétition de *Noces* d'Igor Stravinsky', *Les Feuilles critiques* (May–June, 1923), clipping held in *PSS* [no page number].

5. Stravinsky, *An Autobiography* [1936] (*Aut*; London: Calder & Boyars, 1975), p. 106.

6. Lynn Garafola, ed. and trans., 'The Diaries of Marius Petipa', *Studies in Dance History*, 3/1 (Spring, 1992).

7. Stravinsky and Robert Craft, *Expositions and Developments* (*Expo*; London: Faber and Faber, 1962), p. 113.

8. Stephen Walsh, *Stravinsky: Oedipus Rex* (Cambridge: Cambridge University Press, 1993), pp. 2, 26, the point made first in Walsh, *The Music of Stravinsky* (London: Routledge, 1988); Richard Taruskin, *Stravinsky and the Russian Traditions: A Biography of the Works through 'Mavra'* (*SRT*; Oxford: Oxford University Press, 1996), pp. 1579–80; Walsh, *Igor Stravinsky: A Creative Spring* (*ISCS*; London: Jonathan Cape, 2000), p. 346.

9. Scott Messing, *Neoclassicism in Music: From the Genesis of the Concept through the Schoenberg/ Stravinsky Polemic* (Ann Arbor: UMI Research Press, 1988), p. 129; from Boris de Schloezer, *Revue contemporaine*, February 1, 1923, p. 257.

10. See especially *SRT* and *ISCS*, note 8.

11. Charles M. Joseph, *Stravinsky and Balanchine: A Journey of Invention* (*SB*; New Haven & London: Yale University Press, 2002).

12. Stravinsky and Craft, *Memories and Commentaries* (*Mem*; London: Faber and Faber, 1960), p. 31.

13. Ibid., p. 32.

14. *ISCS*, p. 28.

15. Prince Peter Lieven, *The Birth of Ballets-Russes*, trans. L. Zarine (London: George Allen and Unwin, 1936), p. 56; see *SRT*, pp. 535–6.

16. Garafola, 'The Diaries of Marius Petipa.'

17. Dated Paris, October 1, 1921, translated by Edwin Evans for publication in *The Times* (October 18, 1921) and the ballet programme; reprinted in Eric Walter White, *Stravinsky: The Composer and his Works* (London: Faber and Faber, 1979), pp. 573–4.

18. Roland John Wiley, *Tchaikovsky's Ballets* (Oxford: Oxford University Press, 1985), pp. 120–31.

19. Alexander Benois, *Reminiscences of the Russian Ballet*, trans. Mary Britnieva (London: Putnam, 1941), p. 246.

20. Ibid., pp. 370–71.

21. *SRT*, pp. 528–35, 1042.

22. *SRT*, pp. 540–41; translated in condensed form from Benois, 'Beseda o balete [Colloquy on Ballet]', in Vsevolod Meyerhold et al., *Teatr* (St Petersburg: Shipovnik, 1908), pp. 103–4.

23. Joan Ross Acocella, 'The Reception of Diaghilev's Ballets Russes by Artists and Intellectuals in Paris and London, 1904–1914', unpublished dissertation, Rutgers University, 1984, p. 138.

24. Lynn Garafola, *Diaghilev's Ballets Russes* (Oxford: Oxford University Press, 1989), p. 25. This book is referred to here as a seminal scholarly source on the Ballets Russes.

25. Valeriy Bryusov, 'Unnecessary Truth', in Michael Green, ed. and trans., *The Russian Symbolist Theater: An Anthology of Plays and Critical Texts* (Ann Arbor: Ardis, 1986).

26. Garafola, *Diaghilev's Ballets Russes*, pp. 20–21.

27. Vsevolod Meyerhold, 'The Stylized Theatre', in Edward Braun, ed. and trans., *Meyerhold on Theatre* (New York: Hill and Wang, 1969), pp. 62–3.

28. Stravinsky met Craig in Rome in 1917 and was impressed by the puppets that the artist showed to him: Stravinsky and Craft, *Dialogues and a Diary* [1963] (*Dial*; London: Faber and Faber, 1968), p. 24.

29. *Expo*, p. 27.

30. *SRT*, pp. 371–2.

31. Garafola, *Diaghilev's Ballets Russes*, pp. 30–31.

32. Ibid., p. 54.

33. *ISCS*, p. 200; see also Craft, ed., *Stravinsky: Selected Correspondence*, II (*SSCII*; London: Faber and Faber, 1984), pp. 8–9, note 13.

34. *ISCS*, pp. 307, 262.

35. *SB*, pp. 53–4.

36. *ISCS*, p. 134.

37. Typescript programme notes (1927) for Aeolian Company piano rolls of *Firebird*, *PSS*.

38. *SRT*, p. 587.

39. *SB*, p. 39; many of the corrections are reproduced in Charles Joseph's *Stravinsky and the Piano* (Ann Arbor: UMI Research Press, 1983).

40. Letter from Stravinsky to his mother Anna Stravinsky, March 17, 1912, translated in *SRT*, p. 970; from L.S. Dyachkova, ed., *I.F. Stravinsky: Stat'i i materialï* (Moscow: Sovetskiy Kompozitor, 1973), pp. 467–8.

41. Michel Fokine, *Memoirs of a Ballet Master*, trans. Vitale Fokine, ed. Anatole Chujoy (London: Constable, 1961), pp. 187–90.

42. *SRT*, p. 673.

43. Andrew Wachtel, 'The Ballet's Libretto', in Wachtel, ed., *'Petrushka': Sources and Contexts* (Evanston, Illinois: Northwestern University Press, 1998), p. 36.

44. *Mem*, p. 34; see also Daniel Albright, *Stravinsky: The Music Box and the Nightingale* (New York: Gordon and Breach, 1989), pp. 11–12.

45. Letter from Stravinsky to Benois, February 3, 1911, translated in Wachtel, ed., *'Petrushka': Sources and Contexts*, p. 134; from L.S. Dyachkova, ed., *I.F. Stravinsky: Stat'i i materialï*. However, in the light of the letter's later concerns about having to write more linking music, Walsh maintains that this letter has been regularly mistranslated, as if Benois disagreed with Stravinsky on this matter. If they had disagreed, there would have been no musical problem and no need to write more linking music. See *ISCS*, p. 588, note 31.

46. Janet Kennedy, 'Shrovetide Revelry: Alexandre Benois's Contribution to *Petrushka*', in Wachtel, ed., *'Petrushka': Sources and Contexts*, p. 65; John Bowlt, *The Silver Age* (Newtonville, Mass.: Oriental Research Partners, 1979), p. 196.

47. *ISCS*, p. 167.

48. *ISCS*, p. 171.

49. Meyerhold, 'The Stylized Theatre', p. 62.

50. *SRT*, p. 982; translated from M. Dvinsky, 'U Igorya Stravinskogo', *Birzhevïye vedomosti*, September 25, 1912.

51. *SRT*, p. 981; translated from 'Teatral', *Peterburgskiy listok*, September 27, 1912.

52. *SRT*, p. 865.

53. Joan Acocella, Lynn Garafola and Jonnie Greene, '*The Rite of Spring* Considered as a Nineteenth-Century Ballet', *Ballet Review*, 20/2 (Summer, 1992), pp. 68–71.

54. Garafola, *Diaghilev's Ballets Russes*, Appendix B, pp. 393–8.

55. *SRT*, p. 1087. Taruskin here cites the subtitle of the descendant ballet *Pulcinella*.

56. Letter from Alexander Sanin to Stravinsky, February 17, 1913, translated in *SSCII*, p. 198.

57. *SRT*, p. 1070; translated from Sergey Volkonsky, '"Zolotoy petushok" v postanovke S.P. Dyagileva', *Rech'*, 135 (1914).

58. *SRT*, p. 1071; translated from N. Minsky, 'Soyedineniye iskusstv: pis'mo iz Parizha', *Utro Rossii*, May 24, 1914. See also a review by Daniel Chennevière [Dane Rudhyar] recommending split-level action and abstract choreographic drama as an alternative to traditional opera, in *Montjoie!*, 2/4–6 (April–June, 1914), p. 22, translated in *SRT*, p. 1076.

59. *SRT*, p. 1071.

60. Letter from Benois to Stravinsky, January 14, 1914, in Vera Stravinsky and Craft, *Stravinsky in Pictures and Documents* (*SPD*; New York: Simon & Schuster, 1978), p. 116.

61. Letter from Stravinsky to Benois, July 30, 1913, in *SPD*, p. 114.

62. Virgil Thomson, 'Stravinsky's Operas' [1974], in *A Virgil Thomson Reader* (Boston: Houghton Mifflin, 1981), p. 505.

63. Margaret Crosland, ed. *Cocteau's World: An Anthology of Writings by Jean Cocteau* (London: Peter Owen, 1972), p. 326.

64. *Expo*, p. 91.

65. Letter from Stravinsky to Misia Sert, July 24, 1916, in A. Gold and R. Fizdale, *Misia* (New York: Alfred A. Knopf, 1980), pp. 175–6.

66. Letter from Ansermet to Stravinsky, August 12, 1916, translated in *ISCS*, p. 268; from Claude Tappolet, ed. *Correspondance Ansermet–Strawinsky* (1914–67), I (Geneva: Georg, 1990), pp. 52–3.

67. *Expo*, p. 121.

68. *SRT*, pp. 1206–7.

69. *SRT*, pp. 1237–46.

70. *ISCS*, p. 259.

71. White, *Stravinsky: The Choreographer and his Works*, p. 240.

72. *ISCS*, p. 243.

73. The translation comes from the liner notes of the CD *Igor Stravinsky 1882–1971, Ballets* –

Vol. 1, Sony Classical, 1991.

74. Daniel Albright, *Untwisting the Serpent: Modernism in Music, Literature, and Other Arts* (Chicago: University of Chicago Press, 2000), pp. 57–8.

75 André Schaeffner, 'Une nouvelle forme dramatique: Les chanteurs dans la "fosse"', *Revue Musicale*, 6/1 (November 1, 1924), p. 23.

76. Boris Asafyev, *A Book about Stravinsky* [1929], trans. Richard F. French (Ann Arbor: UMI Research Press, 1982), p. 162; *SRT*, p. 1292.

77. Elliott Carter, 'Stravinsky: A Composer's Memorial', *Perspectives of New Music*, 9/2–10/1 (1971), p. 4.

78. *SRT*, p. 1245.

79. Walsh, *Stravinsky: Oedipus Rex*, p. 15.

80. Albright, *Untwisting the Serpent*, p. 59.

81. Mazo, *Igor Stravinsky*, p. vii.

82. Ibid., pp. x–xvii. Mazo refutes Stravinsky's later recollections that the earliest instrumentation was for a large 'super-*Sacre*' orchestra: see Stravinsky and Craft, *Retrospectives and Conclusions* (New York: Alfred A. Knopf, 1969), p. 118.

83. Mazo, *Igor Stravinsky*, pp. xiv–xv.

84. The term comes from Peter Brook, *The Empty Space* (London: Pelican, 1972). Jonathan Cross has usefully categorised Stravinsky's theatre works according to Brook's notions of rough and holy theatre, depending on whether they allude to the traditions of popular or ritual theatre – the dualism between Meyerhold's Blok and Maeterlinck settings – but he recognises many overlaps between the two categories, and there is a less satisfactory case to be made for linking the more abstract ballets of his later career to these categories, such as *Apollo, Jeu de cartes* and *Agon*: 'Stravinsky's Theatres', in Cross, ed., *The Cambridge Companion to Stravinsky* (Cambridge: Cambridge University Press, 2003), pp. 137–48.

85. Joan Evans, '"Diabolus triumphans": Stravinsky's *Histoire du soldat* in Weimar and Nazi Germany', in John Daverio and John Ogasapian, eds, *Varieties of Musicology: Essays for Murray Lefkowitz* (Warren, Mich.: Harmonie Park Press, 1999), pp. 177–8.

86. *ISCS*, p. 287.

87. *ISCS*, p. 290.

88. Letter from Stravinsky to Vladimir Rimsky-Korsakov, July 21, 1911, translated in *SRT*, pp. 972–4; from L.S. Dyachkova, ed., *I.F. Stravinsky: Stat'i i materialï* (Moscow: Sovetskiy Kompozitor, 1973), pp. 459–62.

89. 'Musical Revolutionary: M. Stravinsky on his Dislike of Opera', *London Daily Mail*, February 13, 1913 [no author given].

90. *SRT*, p. 982; translated from 'Teatral', 'U kompozitora I.F. Stravinskogo', *Peterburgskaya gazeta*, September 27, 1912. See also Michel-Dmitri Calvocoressi, 'M. Igor Stravinsky's Opera: *The Nightingale*', *Musical Times*, 55 (June, 1914), p. 372.

91. Romain Rolland, *Journal des années de guerre (1914–1919)* (Paris: Editions Albin Michel, 1952), pp. 59–60, entry for September 26, 1914 (author's translation).

92. Letter from Stravinsky to Benois of June 8, 1912, *ISCS*, p. 181; from Viktor Varunts, ed., *I.F. Stravinsky: Perepiska s russkimi korrespondentami. Materialï k biografii*, I (Moscow: Kompozitor, 1997), pp. 337–9.

93. Letter from Stravinsky to Benois, July 24, 1914, translated in *ISCS*, p. 241; from Russian Museum, St Petersburg.

94. Garafola, *Diaghilev's Ballets Russes*, p. 98.

95. The quotation is from the published score preface.

96. *Dial*, p. 27.

97. Letter from Stravinsky to Cocteau, April 2, 1952, *PSS* Cocteau correspondence; Craft, ed., *Stravinsky: Selected Correspondence*, I (*SSCI*; London: Faber and Faber, 1982), p. 117.

98. *Dial*, p. 25. Three dancers were listed in the programme and seven tableaux vivants: 1. La Peste à Thèbes 2. Tristesse d'Athéna 3. Les Oracles 4. Le Sphinx 5. Complexe d'Oedipe 6. La Tête de Jocaste 7. Oedipe aveugle et ses filles.

99. *ISCS*, pp. 349–50.

100. *Expo*, p. 112.

101. White, *Stravinsky: The Composer and his Works*, p. 98.

102. The term 'time travelling' comes from Constant Lambert, *Music Ho! A Study of Music in Decline* [1934] (London: Faber and Faber, 1966), pp. 71–8.

103. *Mem*, p. 42.

104. Stravinsky, 'Some Ideas About My Octuor', *The Arts* (Brooklyn), January, 1924, pp. 4–6; reprinted in White, *Stravinsky: The Composer and his Works*, pp. 574–7.

105. Jacques Maritain, *Art et scolastique* (Paris: Art Catholique, 1920).

106. *ISCS*, pp. 378–9.

107. *SRT*, p. 1615.

108. See also Walsh, *Stravinsky: Oedipus Rex*, pp. 2, 24–7; Louis Andriessen and Elmer Schönberger, *The Apollonian Clockwork: On Stravinsky*, trans. Jeff Hamburg (Oxford & New York: Oxford University Press, 1989), pp. 18–20. Andriessen's analogy between Stravinsky's neoclassicism and Magritte's *La Condition humaine* (1934) is useful in indicating the varying power relationships between original source and Stravinsky's neoclassical product; *Baiser*, for instance, is an example where the source (Tchaikovsky) is exceptionally strong. Walsh suggests that the *Concerto for Two Solo Pianos* (1935) initiated a new phase in Stravinsky's work when questions of borrowed style became less important: *Stravinsky: The Second Exile: France and America, 1934–1971* (*SSE*; New York: Alfred A. Knopf, 2006), p. 28.

109. André Schaeffner, 'Une nouvelle forme dramatique', p. 20, referring to the 1923–4 programme for the Vieux-Colombier.

110. Schaeffner, p. 33 (author's translation).

111. *ISCS*, p. 500.

112. Diaghilev in interview with Michel Georges-Michel, 'Une nouvelle oeuvre d'un grand musicien d'aujourd'hui: *L'Apollon* d'Igor Stravinsky et les concepts inédits du compositeur', *Excelsior*, October 27, 1927.

113. Nicolas Nabokov, 'Stravinsky and the Drama', in Minna Lederman, ed., *Stravinsky in the Theatre* [1949] (New York: Da Capo Press, 1975), pp. 109–10.

114. *ISCS*, pp. 376, 486–7, 489.

115. 'Interview with Stravinsky', *The Observer*, July 3, 1921.

116. Henrietta Malkiel, 'Modernists Have Ruined Modern Music, Stravinsky Says', *Musical America*, January 10, 1925, p. 9.

117. He was already clear in 1912 that the ballet score *Petrushka* was also suitable as a concert work: see letter to the Russian editor Vladimir Derzhanovsky, June 18, 1912, *SSCI*, p. 43. See also a series of reviews of a concert performance of *Orpheus*, written by American critics in 1949, all maintaining that the score needed stage action: Olin Downes, 'Stravinsky Leads Own Works Here', *The New York Times*, February 17, 1949; Harriett Johnson, 'Music: The Two Stravinskys with Boston Symphony', *The New York Post*, February 17, 1949; Robert Sabin, 'Igor Stravinsky Conducts Boston Symphony in Own Works', *Musical America*, March, 1949, p. 44.

118. Emile Jaques-Dalcroze, 'Chronique musicale', *Tribune de Genève*, February 8, 1917.

119. *Aut*, pp. 30, 100.

120. Letter from Stravinsky to Balanchine, November 22, 1935, *SPD*, p. 275.

121. George Balanchine, 'The Dance Element in Stravinsky's Music' [1947], in Minna Lederman, ed., *Stravinsky in the Theatre*, p. 81.

122. Nicolas Nabokov, *Old Friends and New Music* (Boston: Little, Brown, 1951), p. 104.

123. Charles M. Joseph, *Stravinsky Inside Out* (New Haven & London: Yale University Press, 2001), p. 47.

124. *SB*, pp. 81, 83, 85. Soulima Stravinsky, the composer's son, recalled early meetings about *Apollo* in France: see Joseph, 'Diaghilev and Stravinsky', in Lynn Garafola and Nancy Van Norman Baer, eds, *The Ballets Russes and its World* (New Haven & London: Yale University Press, 1999), p. 199. Walsh is far more reticent about the notion of collaboration between Balanchine and Stravinsky, in other words, any influence that Balanchine may have had on the composer.

125. *ISCS*, p. 451.

126. Letter to Ernest Ansermet, January 4, 1929, *SSCI*, p. 195.

127. *Aut*, p. 147.

128. Letter from Stravinsky to his publisher Gavril G. Païchadze, October 17, 1928, translated in *SPD*, p. 285.

129. Letter from Stravinsky to his publisher Gavril G. Païchadze, October 20, 1928, using the translation from Russian into English in the Ida Rubinstein correspondence files, *PSS*. For an account of Stravinsky's work with Rubinstein, see Lynn Garafola, 'Igor Stravinsky and Ida Rubinstein', *Ballet Review* (Summer, 2004), pp. 84–94.

130. Letter from Stravinsky to Païchadze, October 27, 1928, translated in *SPD*, p. 285.

131. *Aut*, p. 148.

132. *Mem*, p. 40. See also his praise for *Renard* in *Aut*, p. 102.

133. Telegram from Nijinska to Stravinsky from the Teatro Colón, Buenos Aires, November 6, 1926, *PSS*.

134. *Aut*, p. 106; *Expo*, pp. 117–8.

135. Examples of such hybrid spectacles for Rubinstein's pre-war company were *Le Martyre de*

Saint Sébastien (1911: d'Annunzio, Debussy, Fokine) and *Hélène de Sparte* (1912: Emile Verhaeren, Déodat de Séverac, dir. Alexander Sanin), and, for the company that she ran in the late 1920s and early 1930s, *Amphion* (1931: Valéry, Honegger, Massine).

136. Vera Stravinsky, Rita McCaffrey and Craft, *Igor and Vera Stravinsky: A Photograph Album, 1921 to 1971* (London: Thames and Hudson, 1982), p. 23; translated from *Pesti Hirlap*, c. March 29, 1933.

137. *Dial*, p. 38.

138. *ISCS*, p. 530.

139. Ibid.

140. Telegram of September 1, 1933, in Craft, ed., *Stravinsky: Selected Correspondence*, III (*SSCIII*, London: Faber and Faber, 1985), p. 480, note 4 (in Appendix B: '*Perséphone*: The Evolution of the Libretto'). Years later, Stravinsky decided that Balanchine and the neo-romantic surrealist Tchelitcheff would have been the ideal collaborative team: *Dial*, p. 37.

141. *ISCS*, pp. 527–8 and p. 662, note 51.

142. 'Igor Stravinsky nous parle de *Perséphone*', *Excelsior*, April 29, 1934, and May 1, 1934 (incomplete form, with a paragraph omitted in the first print reinserted); reprinted in White, *Stravinsky: The Composer and his Works*, pp. 579–81.

143. *Aut*, p. 173.

144. *Dial*, p. 36.

145. Contact with Boris Romanov continued, which is just one instance of Stravinsky supporting colleagues from the Diaghilev days in his later career. He proposed Romanov to undertake *Sacre* in Buenos Aires in 1932 (letter of February 14, 1932, to Païchadze, *PSS* correspondence and documents file for 1932; *SSCII*, pp. 204–5.) In 1954, he advised the President of the Birmingham Civic Ballet, Miss Gage Bush, that Romanov would be the most competent person to help with the staging of Fokine's *Firebird* (letter of July 23, 1954, *PSS* correspondence and documents files for 1954).

146. Vera's diary is held in the *PSS*. The entry for August 16, 1922, mentions *Triadic Ballet*, although the published version of the diary simply reads, 'Ballet in the evening': Craft, ed., *Dearest Bubushkin: The Correspondence of Vera and Igor Stravinsky, 1921–1954, with Excerpts from Vera Stravinsky's Diaries, 1922–1971*, trans. Lucia Davidova (*DB*; London: Thames and Hudson, 1985), p. 18.

147. *ISCS*, pp. 463–4.

148. Letter of November 16, 1931, *PSS* correspondence and documents file for 1931.

149. Letter from Vera Stravinsky to the Marions, Stravinsky's daughter Milène and her husband, December 8, 1951, *DB*, p. 155.

150. *SB*, p. 180; Joseph, *Stravinsky Inside Out*, p. 52.

151. *DB*, entry for May 4, 1955, p. 179; see also Craft, *An Improbable Life: Memoirs by Robert Craft* (Nashville: Vanderbilt University Press, 2002), p. 170.

152. Julie Kavanagh, *Secret Muses: The Life of Frederick Ashton* (London: Faber and Faber, 1996), p. 355.

153. Letter from Stravinsky to Arthur Gibson, February 5, 1956, *PSS* Chester correspondence.

154. Craft, *Stravinsky: The Chronicle of a Friendship* (2nd, expanded edition; Nashville and London: Vanderbilt University Press, 1994), p. 456.

155. *BS*, pp. 157–8.

156. *BS*, pp. 178–82, 188.

157. Letter from Stravinsky to Lucia Chase, July 14, 1947, *PSS* Chase correspondence.

158. The row score is dated March 5, 1965, *PSS* Chase correspondence.

159. Joseph, *Stravinsky Inside Out*, p. 185; from outtake housed in the *PSS*. The 1965 CBS film was produced by David Oppenheim.

160. Transcript of interview with representative from Columbia Broadcasting Systems, New York, 1946, clipping in *PSS* Interview file.

161. Original Vera Stravinsky diaries consulted, *PSS*; see *DB*, entries for November 10, 1940, p. 117, and January 26, 1943, p. 127.

162. Nancy Goldner, *The Stravinsky Festival of the New York City Ballet* (New York: The Eakins Press, 1973), p. 232.

163. Craft, *Stravinsky: The Chronicle of a Friendship* (London: Victor Gollancz, 1972), entry for June 11, 1966, p. 292.

164. Mario Bois, *Près de Strawinsky* (Paris: Marval, 1996), pp. 73–9.

165. Letter from Stravinsky to Rufina Ampenoff, September 3, 1968, *PSS* Boosey & Hawkes (B&H) correspondence.

166. Bois, *Près de Strawinsky*, p. 78. Vera went to see *Sacre* again in Brooklyn (January 26, 1971)

and reported in her diary that it was disastrous (*DB*, p. 237).

167. *Pulcinella* programme, *PSS* correspondence and documents for 1920, under *Pulcinella*.

168. The *DB* entry is incorrect (p. 168). Programmes support Craft's corrected account in *An Improbable Life*, p. 160.

169. Walter Terry, 'The Dancer's Composer', *The Saturday Review*, May 29, 1971, p. 43.

170. Paul Horgan, *Encounters with Stravinsky: A Personal Record* (Middletown, Conn.: Wesleyan University Press, 1989), pp. 206–7.

171. Joseph, *SB*, p. 372; the reference is a letter from John Crosby to Balanchine, March 2, 1962, housed in the George Balanchine Archive, Harvard Theatre Collection (*HTC*), Houghton Library, Harvard University.

172. John Crosby, 'Stravinsky and the Santa Fe Opera', programme of the 1962 Santa Fe Opera Festival, p. 5.

173. *SB*, p. 404, note 2; see also *SSE*, pp. 373–4.

174. Walsh references Craft's evidence on *Renard* but notes that Todd Bolender, who danced the Fox, denied Stravinsky's presence at rehearsals: *SSE*, pp. 197–8 and 613, note 45.

175. *DB*, entry for February 16, 1940, p. 111.

176. Wayne D. Shirley, 'For Martha', *Ballet Review*, 27/4 (Winter, 1999), p. 84. I am grateful to Henrietta Bannerman for drawing my attention to this article.

177. Nabokov, 'Stravinsky and the Drama', p. 108.

178. Walsh plays down the collaborative relationship; see earlier note 124.

179. Lincoln Kirstein, 'Working with Stravinsky', in Lederman, ed., *Stravinsky in the Theatre*, p. 139.

180. Ibid., pp. 138–9.

181. *SB*, pp. 202, 205.

182. Letter from Kirstein to Stravinsky, August 23, 1950, *PSS* Kirstein correspondence; *SSCI*, pp. 276–7, note 16.

183. Letter from Stravinsky to Robert Graff, August 2, 1959, *PSS* Graff correspondence; *SSE*, pp. 408–9.

184. Joseph, *Stravinsky Inside Out*, pp. 144–5 (the whole of Chapter 5 is devoted to *The Flood*); *BS*, p. 284; letter from Stravinsky to Rolf Liebermann, January 29, 1961, *PSS* Liebermann correspondence; Arthur Todd, 'What Went Wrong?' *Dance Magazine*, 36 (August, 1962), p. 39.

185. Letter from Stravinsky and Balanchine to Graff, April 5, 1962, *PSS* Graff correspondence; Joseph, *Stravinsky Inside Out*, p. 152.

186. *Dial*, p. 79.

187. Interestingly, in 1967, Stravinsky did allow his work to be used as mood music for a United Airlines travel film celebrating the USA, with *Firebird* as background to images of the Great West, *Apollo* to the monuments of Washington: Craft, *Stravinsky: The Chronicle of a Friendship* (1972), p. 308; Lillian Libman, *And Music at the Close* (London: Macmillan, 1972), pp. 176–7.

188. Stravinsky quoted in Marcel Valois, 'Chronique musicale; Avec Igor Stravinsky', Montreal, March, 1945, clipping in *PSS* interview file (no newspaper name given).

189. Stravinsky quoted in Ed Brooks, '"Dancing Symphony": Next Stravinsky Composing Aim', *Times-Picayune*, New Orleans, January 30, 1954.

190. 'Igor Stravinsky on Film Music as told to Ingolf Dahl', *Cinema* (June, 1947), p. 8; reprint of interview first published in *The Musical Digest* (September, 1946).

191. *Mem*, p. 37.

192. Letter from Stravinsky to Leonid Massine, June 20, 1937, replying to Massine's letter, June 17, *PSS* Massine correspondence; *SSE*, pp. 66–7.

193. Letter from Stravinsky to Ernest Voigt, March 19, 1942, *SSCIII*, p. 279; see also *SSE*, p. 139.

194. Annotation in letter from Massine to Stravinsky, March 23, 1962, *PSS* Massine correspondence.

195. The proposal came to Stravinsky from Boris Mouravieff, Vice-President of the International Guild of Culture, University of Geneva, January 30, 1957, *PSS* correspondence and documents for 1957.

196. Letter from Eugene Berman to Stravinsky, February 7, 1946, *PSS*. Walsh notes, from a letter that Stravinsky wrote to his son Theodore (April 4, 1946), that Stravinsky started to work on the *Medea* project, but it was called off because his terms were not met: *SSE*, p. 612, note 11.

197. Letter from Stravinsky to David Adams, September 26, 1952, *PSS* B&H correspondence. Correspondence on the matter ended the following October.

198. Letter from Michael Powell to Stravinsky, January 5, 1953; Stravinsky indicated his plans in a letter to Ernst Roth, January 16, 1953, *PSS* B&H correspondence.

199. Letter from Arnold Weissberger to Stravinsky, May 5, 1966, *PSS* Weissberger correspondence.

200. Letter from Kirstein to Stravinsky, May 7, 1946, *PSS* Kirstein correspondence.

201. *BS*, p. 187; letter from Kirstein to Stravinsky's lawyer Aaron Shapiro, June 7, 1946, *PSS* Kirstein correspondence.

202. Letter from Ralph Hawkes to Stravinsky, October 29, 1947, *PSS* B&H correspondence.

203. Letter from Hawkes to Stravinsky, October 10, 1947, *PSS* B&H correspondence.

204. Letter from Stravinsky to Hawkes, October 13, 1947, *PSS* B&H correspondence.

205. Letter from Stravinsky to Bruno Zirato, March 25, 1947, *PSS* correspondence and documents for 1947.

206. Letter from Lucia Chase to Stravinsky, March 8, 1948, and Stravinsky's reply, March 10, *PSS* Chase correspondence.

207. *SB*, p. 189.

208. Cable from Roth to Stravinsky, December 27, 1957, *PSS* B&H correspondence.

209. Letter from Stravinsky to Roth, December 28, 1957, *PSS* B&H correspondence.

210. Letter from Stravinsky to Roth, January 11, 1958, *PSS* B&H correspondence.

211. Letter from Stravinsky to Hawkes, July 4, 1947, *PSS* B&H correspondence.

212. Letter from Gretl Urban to Stravinsky, August 13, 1945, and handwritten notes of his ensuing telephone conversation with Urban, August 20, *PSS* Associated Music Publishers correspondence (author's translation).

213. Letter from Stravinsky to Urban, August 24, 1945, *PSS* Associated Music Publishers correspondence (author's translation).

214. *PSS*, Leeds Music Corporation correspondence of the 1950s and early 1960s.

215. Letters from Stravinsky to Rufina Ampenoff, May 9, 1966, *PSS* B&H correspondence.

216. Correspondence between Betty Bean and Stravinsky, October–December, 1950, *PSS* B&H correspondence.

217. Letter from Vittorio Rieti to Stravinsky, October 27, 1945, *PSS* Rieti correspondence.

218. Letter from Sapiro to Lucia Chase, May 6, 1946, *PSS* correspondence and documents for 1928, under *Apollo*.

219 Letter from Ellen M. Bywater (Executive Secretary of Ballet Theatre) to Sapiro, May 11, 1946, *PSS* correspondence and documents for 1928, under *Apollo*.

220. Letter from Stravinsky to Leonid Massine, August 27, 1946, *PSS* Massine correspondence.

221. Letter from Ampenoff to Stravinsky relaying London Festival Ballet's request, August 13, 1963, and Stravinsky's reply, August 17, *PSS* B&H correspondence.

222. Letter from Jerome Robbins to Stravinsky, February 23, 1960, and Stravinsky's reply, February 25, *PSS* Robbins correspondence.

223 White, *Stravinsky: The Composer and his Works*, p. 547. Stravinsky earned himself a fee of $500 for the arrangement and royalties for each performance; see letter from the composer to Richard Pleasant, February 3, 1941, *PSS* Chase correspondence.

224. Letter from Stravinsky to Pleasant, February 4, 1941, *PSS* Chase correspondence.

225. Letter from David Diamond to Stravinsky, September 8, 1944, *PSS* correspondence and documents for 1942, under *Danses Concertantes*.

226. Stravinsky quoted in Hubert Roussel, 'Houston Jinx Lets Up on Stravinsky', *Houston Post*, January 26, 1949.

227. Letter from Maurice Abravanel to Eric Walter White, February 28, 1981, pp. 3–5, in John Schuster-Craig, 'Stravinsky's *Scènes de ballet* and Billy Rose's *The Seven Lively Arts*: The Abravanel Account', in Susan Parisi, ed., *Music in the Theater, Church, and Villa: Essays in Honor of Robert Lamar Weaver and Norma Wright Weaver* (Warren, MI: Harmonie Park Press, 2000), p. 288.

228. Stravinsky quoted in *L'Intransigeant*, March 5, 1938; also see letter to his publisher Wilhelm Strecker, January 24, 1938, *SSCII*, p. 322.

229. *DB*, letter from Vera to Stravinsky, May 12, 1954.

230. Letter from Adams to Stravinsky's secretary André Marion, July 30, 1952, *PSS* B&H correspondence.

231. *ISCS*, pp. 272–3. See also Pierre Lalo's review of the ballet, 'La Musique', *Feuilleton du temps*, January 22, 1917. Diaghilev had already thought of using *Fireworks* in 1912, *ISCS*, p. 184.

232. 'Ragtime Ballet Quarrel', *Evening News* [London], April 3, 1922.

233. Letter from Stravinsky to Comte Etienne de Beaumont, February, 1924, *PSS* de Beaumont correspondence.

234. See Stephanie Jordan, *Moving Music: Dialogues with Music in Twentieth-Century Ballet* (London: Dance Books, 2000), pp. 10–15.

235. Letter from Stravinsky to Serge Lifar, August 2, 1930, summarised in the catalogue for the exhibition and auction *Music and Ballet: Including the Papers of Serge Lifar* (London: Sotheby's, 2002), p. 134.

236. Letter from Rieti to Stravinsky, September 13, 1947, and Stravinsky's reply, September 25, *PSS* Rieti correspondence.

237. Letter from Stravinsky to Kirstein, September 25, 1953, *PSS* Kirstein correspondence.

238. Letter from Stravinsky to Kirstein, September 25, 1953, *PSS* Kirstein correspondence; *SSCI*, p. 288.

239. Letter from Stravinsky to Nabokov, February 9, 1952, *PSS* Nabokov correspondence.

240. Telegram from Stravinsky to Sapiro, February 24, 1947, *PSS* Robbins correspondence. Deborah Jowitt records that, the year before, he had staged a duet called *Afterthought* to the *Five Easy Pieces* (the original piano pieces later orchestrated as the *Suites*) at a benefit for the Greater New York Committee for Russian Relief. Jowitt, *Jerome Robbins: His Life, His Theater, His Dance* (New York: Simon & Schuster, 2004), p. 125. The benefit performance took place May 2, 1946.

241. Letter from Robbins to Stravinsky, January 7, 1956, in the Jerome Robbins archive, Jerome Robbins Dance Division of the New York Public Library for the Performing Arts. At one point, there was a suggestion that Robbins would stage *Symphony in Three Movements* for the New York City Ballet's 1972 Stravinsky Festival, but Balanchine took the score instead: Nancy Goldner, *The Stravinsky Festival of the New York City Ballet* (New York: The Eakins Press, 1973), p. 234.

242. Letter from Kirstein to Stravinsky, June 25, 1951, *PSS* Kirstein correspondence; *SSCI*, p. 283.

243. Letter [from Jessica Williams] to Stravinsky, September 23, 1952, and Stravinsky's reply September 27, *PSS* correspondence and documents for 1929, under *Capriccio*.

244. *SB*, p. 162.

245. *SB*, p. 171; from interview in *Intellectual Digest*, June 1972.

246. Balanchine quoted in Dale Harris, 'Balanchine: Working with Stravinsky', *Ballet Review*, 10/2 (Summer, 1982), p. 21.

247. *PSS* correspondence and documents for 1942, under *Danses Concertantes*. The notes were sent to a radio announcer before the premiere of the ballet and were included in a letter to the publisher Hugo Winter, June 4, 1944, *PSS* Associated Music Publishers correspondence; *SSCIII*, p. 295.

248. *SB*, p. 172.

249. Letter from Stravinsky to Kirstein, September 9, 1953, *PSS* Kirstein correspondence; *SSCI*, p. 287.

250. Stravinsky quoted in Ed Brooks, '"Dancing Symphony": Next Stravinsky Composing Aim'.

251. Cable from Stravinsky to Ampenoff, April 26, 1962, and Stravinsky's handwritten note for return cable, *PSS* B&H correspondence.

252. Bois indicates, with regard to the choreographers Milko Sparemblek and Mischa Van Hoecke, that it was easier to get formal permission to set *Symphony of Psalms* after the composer's death in 1971, *Près de Strawinsky*, pp. 76–7. In fact, even though a programme note on Nault dates his *Symphony of Psalms* premiere as 1969, some sources date it as 1971 or 1972.

253. Letter from Stravinsky to Lederman, September 1, 1947, *PSS* correspondence and documents for 1947.

Chapter 2

1. W.K. Wimsatt and Monroe Beardsley, 'The Intentional Fallacy' [1954], in Joseph Margolis, ed., *Philosophy Looks at the Arts: Contemporary Readings in Aesthetics* (Philadelphia: Temple University Press, 1978), pp. 293–306.

2. Arthur C. Danto, *The Transfiguration of the Commonplace* (Cambridge, Massachusetts: Harvard University Press, 1981).

3. I am indebted to the advice of Bonnie Rowell on the philosophical issues involved here; see Rowell, *An Investigation into the Critical Analysis of Postmodern Dances*, unpublished PhD dissertation, University of Surrey, Roehampton, 2003.

4. Phyllida Lloyd quoted in 'Interpreting or Remaking the Text? A Cross-Arts Panel', (scribe: Henrietta Bannerman) in Stephanie Jordan, ed., *Preservation Politics: Dance Revived, Reconstructed, Remade* (London: Dance Books, 2000), p. 117. It is illuminating to note the acceptance of and excitement generated by the folk-style performance of *Noces* introduced by the Pokrovsky ensemble and recorded in 1994 (Nonesuch), which some would argue vehemently contradicts Stravinsky's performance principles (see p. 386).

5. Hanns Eisler [and Theodor W. Adorno], *Composing for the Films* (London: Dennis Dobson, 1947), pp. 77–8.

6. Nancy Goldner, *The Stravinsky Festival of the New York City Ballet* (New York: Eakins Press, 1973), p. 14.

7. Roland John Wiley, 'Reflections on Tchaikovsky', *The Dancing Times*, 80 (May, 1990), p. 801; see also Wiley, *Tchaikovsky's Ballets* (Oxford: Clarendon Press, 1985), pp. 5–9.

8. Nicolas Nabokov, 'Stravinsky Now', *Partisan Review*, 11 (1944), p. 332.

9. Richard Taruskin, *Stravinsky and the Russian Traditions: A Biography of the Works through 'Mavra'* (*SRT*; Oxford: Oxford University Press, 1996), pp. 958–61.

10. *SRT*, p. 963; translated from Irina Vershinina, *Ranniye baleti Stravinskogo* (Moscow: Nauka, 1967), p. 180.

11. Pierre Boulez, 'Stravinsky Remains' [analysis of *Le Sacre du printemps*, 1953, revised 1966], in *Stocktakings from an Apprenticeship*, trans. Stephen Walsh (Oxford: Clarendon Press, 1991), p. 96.

12. Pieter C. van den Toorn, *Stravinsky and 'The Rite of Spring': The Beginnings of a Musical Language* (Berkeley & Los Angeles: University of California Press, 1987), pp. 99–100.

13. For further discussion of the principle of construction in blocks or as the 'sum-of- parts', see *SRT*, pp. 955–6, 1451–2. Taruskin maintains that this kind of construction peaked during the Swiss years, in such works as the second of the *Three Pieces for String Quartet* (1914) and the *Symphonies of Wind Instruments* (1920), *SRT*, p. 1451. See also the seminal article, using different terminology, by Edward T. Cone, 'Stravinsky: The Progress of a Method', *Perspectives of New Music*, 1/1 (Fall, 1962), pp. 18–26.

14. *SRT*, p. 957.

15. Louis Danz, 'Stravinsky – Reflections on the Purport of his Work', *Pacific Coast Musician*, February 16, 1935.

16. Roger Shattuck, 'The Devil's Dance: Stravinsky's Corporal Imagination', in Jann Pasler, ed., *Confronting Stravinsky: Man, Musician, and Modernist* (Berkeley: University of California Press, 1986), pp. 82–8.

17. Robert Craft, ed., *Stravinsky: Selected Correspondence*, III (*SSCIII*; London: Faber and Faber, 1985), p. 43.

18. Craft, *Stravinsky: Chronicle of a Friendship* (London: Victor Gollancz, 1972), p. 60.

19. Stravinsky, *An Autobiography* [1936] (*Aut*; London: Calder & Boyars, 1975), p. 82.

20. See photographs of Stravinsky exercising in 1924, in Vera Stravinsky and Craft, *Stravinsky in Pictures and Documents* (*SPD*; New York: Simon & Schuster, 1978), p. 298; and displaying his muscular physique in 1925, in Craft, ed., *Stravinsky: Selected Correspondence*, I (*SSCI*; London: Faber and Faber, 1982), opposite p. 242.

21. Balanchine quoted in Goldner, *The Stravinsky Festival of the New York City Ballet*, p. 33; from *Newsday*, June 11, 1972.

22. Nicolas Nabokov, 'Igor Stravinsky', *Atlantic Monthly* (November, 1949), p. 22.

23. *SPD*, p. 302; translated from unidentified newspaper cutting from Vienna, 1926.

24. Elliott Carter, 'Igor Stravinsky, 1882–1971' [1971], in Else Stone and Kurt Stone, eds, *The Writings of Elliott Carter* (Bloomington: University of Indiana, 1977), pp. 301–02.

25. Carter, *Flawed Words and Stubborn Sounds: A Conversation with Elliott Carter* (New York: W.W. Norton, 1971), p. 56.

26. Eric Walter White, *Stravinsky: The Composer and his Works* (London & Boston: Faber and Faber, 1979), p. 564.

27. *SPD*, p. 325; translated from *Le Soir* [Brussels], January 15, 1924.

28. Stephen Walsh, *Igor Stravinsky: A Creative Spring* (*ISCS*; London: Jonathan Cape, 2000), p. 463; translated from unidentified cutting in Paul Sacher Stiftung, Basle (*PSS*).

29. Armand Pierhal, 'Les Revues étrangères', *Les Nouvelles littéraires*, June 24, 1933, *PSS* (author's translation).

30. *ISCS*, p. 384; translated from E. Closson, in *L'Indépendance belge*, January 17, 1924.

31. This 1965 recording of the 1945 *Firebird Suite* is included on 'The Firebird & *Les Noces*' [Royal Ballet], BBC Classical Music Production in association with Opus Arte, BBC Worldwide, 2001. The *Apollo* recording is included in the documentary 'A Stravinsky Portrait', directed by Richard Leacock and Rolf Liebermann, Norddeutscher Rundfunk Television, Hamburg, 1966.

32. Transcription from outtake of Tony Palmer's documentary *Once at a Border...* (London Weekend Television, 1982), Blue Folder, *PSS*, p. 110.

33. Concert at the Wigmore Hall, London, October 29, 2004.

34. *Aut*, p. 72. As well as having reservations about passive listening, Stravinsky was also concerned about recordings not conforming to his principles of execution, *Aut*, pp. 150–54.

35. Theodor W. Adorno, *Philosophy of Modern Music* [1949], trans. Anne G. Mitchell and Wesley V. Bloomster (London: Sheed & Ward, 1973).

36. See, in particular, Max Paddison, *Adorno's Aesthetics of Music* (Cambridge: Cambridge University Press, 1993); Paddison, 'Stravinsky as Devil: Adorno's Three Critiques', in Jonathan Cross, ed., *The Cambridge Companion to Stravinsky* (Cambridge: Cambridge University Press, 2003), pp.

192–202.

37. Paddison, *Adorno, Modernism and Mass Culture: Essays on Critical Theory and Music* (London: Kahn & Averill, 2004), p. 50.

38. Adorno, 'Die stabilisierte Musik' [1928], in Rolf Tiedemann, ed., *Gesammelte Schriften*, 18 (Frankfurt/Main: Suhrkamp Verlag, 1984), pp. 721–8; 'Zur gesellschaftlichen Lage der Music' [1932], in *Gesammelte Schriften*, 18, pp. 729–77; English version: 'On the Social Situation of Music', trans. Wesley Bloomster, *Telos*, 35 (Spring, 1978), pp. 128–64.

39. For an analysis of Stravinsky's political stance, see *ISCS*, pp. 519–22.

40. Paddison, 'Stravinsky as Devil...', p. 200.

41. Adorno, *Philosophy of Modern Music*, p. 147.

42. Adorno, 'Stravinsky: A Dialectical Portrait' [1962], in *Quasi una Fantasia: Essays on Modern Music*, trans. Rodney Livingstone (London, New York: Verso, 1992), p. 148.

43. Ibid., p. 173; see also Paddison, *Adorno's Aesthetics of Music*, pp. 269–70, and 'Stravinsky as Devil', p. 202. I am grateful to Paddison for his advice in interview, December 3, 2005.

44. For instance, Jonathan Cross writes: 'A distance from one's materials does not necessarily mean indifference to the subject matter, nor does it mean the abandonment of a free self': *The Stravinsky Legacy* (Cambridge: Cambridge University Press, 1998), p. 14. See also Milan Kundera, *Testaments Betrayed*, trans. Linda Asher (London: Faber and Faber, 1996), pp. 57–98.

45. Richard Taruskin, 'Stravinsky and the Subhuman: A Myth of the Twentieth Century: *The Rite of Spring*, the Tradition of the New, and "The Music Itself"; Notes on *Svadebka*', in Taruskin, *Defining Russia Musically: Historical and Hermeneutical Essays* (Princeton: Princeton University Press, 1997), pp. 360–467.

46. Cross, *The Stravinsky Legacy*, pp. 233–4.

47. Adorno, *Philosophy of Modern Music*, pp. 175–6.

48. Ibid., pp. 193–7.

49. Ibid., p. 178.

50. Ibid., p. 200.

51. Ibid., p. 212.

52. Paddison, 'Stravinsky as Devil...', p. 193.

53. Adorno, *Philosophy of Modern Music*, pp. 155, 159, 167, 190, 194, 200, 202.

54. Cecil Gray, *A Survey of Contemporary Music* (London: Oxford University Press, 1924), pp. 139, 142–3. Pieter C. van den Toorn discusses the stances of Adorno, Gray and Lambert in *Stravinsky and 'The Rite of Spring': The Beginnings of a Musical Language*, pp. 57–63.

55. Constant Lambert, *Music Ho!* [1934] (London: Faber and Faber, 1966), p. 51.

56. Ibid., pp. 75, 89, 91.

57. Ibid., p. 92.

58. Ibid., pp. 71–8.

59. Gelsey Kirkland, *Dancing on my Grave: An Autobiography* (London: Hamish Hamilton, 1987), p. 68.

60. Boris Asafyev, *A Book About Stravinsky* [1929], trans. Richard French (Ann Arbor: UMI Research Press, 1982), p. 126.

61. Ibid., p. 98.

62. *SRT*, p. 1237.

63. Asafyev, *A Book About Stravinsky*, p. 97.

64. Suzanne Farrell, with Toni Bentley, *Holding on to the Air: An Autobiography* (New York: Summit Books, 1990), p. 152.

65. Ibid., p. 205.

66. For instance, Felia Doubrovska, Tanaquil Le Clercq and Melissa Hayden, all quoted in Walter Terry, 'The Dancer's Composer', *Saturday Review*, May 29, 1971, pp. 42, 43 and 59.

67. Siobhan Davies, speaking at 'The Great Balloon' debate, BBC Radio 3 interview, January 1, 2005. This was a debate to decide the greatest composer; Davies proposed Stravinsky.

68. Davies, email communication with the author, January 10, 2007.

69. Transcription from outtake of Tony Palmer's documentary *Once at a Border...*, Blue Folder, *PSS*, p. 222.

70. Ibid., Grey Folder, p. 68.

71. T.S. Eliot quoted in Lyndall Gordon, *Eliot's Early Years* (Oxford: Oxford University Press, 1977), p. 108.

72. Daniel Albright, *Stravinsky: The Music Box and the Nightingale* (New York: Gordon and Breach, 1989), p. 4.

73. Ibid., p. 15.

74. Ibid., p. 22.

75. Ibid., p. 27.

76. George Balanchine, 'Marginal Notes on the Dance', in Walter Sorell, ed., *The Dance has Many Faces* [1951] (Chicago: a capella Books, 1992), p. 42.

77. Balanchine quoted in Louis Botto, *Intellectual Digest* (June, 1972), in Selma Jeanne Cohen, ed., *Dance as a Theatre Art* (New York: Dodd, Mead, 1974), p. 190.

78. Balanchine, 'The Dance Element in Stravinsky's Music' [1947], in Minna Lederman, ed., *Stravinsky in the Theatre* [1949] (New York: Da Capo Press, 1975), p. 81.

79. Stravinsky and Craft, *Themes and Episodes* (New York: Alfred A. Knopf, 1966), p. 25. This sentence was altered in Igor Stravinsky, *Themes and Conclusions* (London: Faber and Faber, 1972), p. 34: '[Balanchine] always tells me that he needs a motor impulse, not a *pas de deux*.'

80. Jerome Robbins quoted in Rosemarie Tauris, 'Two Masters Met – A Double Whammy', *Time*, July 3, 1972.

81. Kirkland, *Dancing on my Grave: An Autobiography*, p. 84.

82. Balanchine, 'The Dance Element in Stravinsky's Music', p. 75.

83. *SRT*, p. 768; from Nikolai D. Kashkin, 'Teatr i musïka', *Russkoye slovo*, January 20, 1915.

84. André Levinson, 'Stravinsky and the Dance' [1923], in Joan Acocella and Lynn Garafola, eds, *Dance Writings from Paris in the Twenties* (Hanover & London: Wesleyan University Press, 1991), p. 37. Fokine likewise considered some of Stravinsky's music lacking in 'danceabiliy' (see p. 30).

85. André Levinson, *Ballet Old and New* [1918], trans. Susan Cook Summer (New York: Dance Horizons, 1982), p. 74.

86. Levinson, 'Stravinsky and the Dance', p. 38.

87. Levinson, 'Stravinsky and the Dance', p. 41.

88. Levinson, *Ballet Old and New*, pp. 73–4.

89. The establishment of the database was an AHRB grant-aided project (May 2001–October 2002).

90. Alexander Schouvaloff and Victor Borovsky, *Stravinsky on Stage* (London: Stainer & Bell, 1982).

91. For instance, there are letters from Rufina Ampenoff to Stravinsky indicating that companies were using Stravinsky scores – *Sacre*, *Petrushka*, *Firebird* and *Histoire du soldat* (at the Bolshoi) – were about to do the same with *Pulcinella* (at the Kirov), and were in the habit of copying materials for use in Russia and other Eastern bloc countries, without any payment: January 30 and March 4, 1964. A Soviet Information Service Bulletin documents the Bolshoi programmes, January 20, 1975, *PSS* Boosey & Hawkes (B&H) correspondence.

92. Choreographers are not permitted to break up scores in order to interpolate other music, but they can use other music before or after a score has been played, or use sections rather than the whole of a score, like a single movement from a work. They are not permitted to use scores in arrangement or altered in any way, although a slightly reduced orchestration of *Sacre* (by Jonathan McPhee) can be used by ballet companies touring theatres with small pits.

93. In preparing this discussion of copyright issues, I am especially grateful for help from Tony Pool, Andrew Kemp and Claudine Murphy at Boosey & Hawkes, email communication, April 5, 2006, and from Carolyn Fuller of Music Sales, telephone communication, March 28, 2007.

94. According to the database, Italy has staged an unusually large proportion of hybrid, texted works within its overall Stravinsky output.

95. DVD entitled *Igor Stravinsky: Oedipus Rex*, staging and film direction by Julie Taymor, Peter Gelb Production, CAMA Video/NHK, 1992.

96. Philippe Verrièle, 'Profusion irrévérente: cohérence et déférence', *Les Saisons de la danse* (December, 1995), p. 13.

97. See letters from Stravinsky to Alexander Siloti, April 6, 1915, and from B.P. Jurgenson to Stravinsky, April 15, 1915, in Craft, ed., *Stravinsky: Selected Correspondence*, II (*SSCII*; London: Faber and Faber, 1984), pp. 213, 225–6.

98. Edwin Denby report from Rome quoted in Walter Terry, 'Winner of Guggenheim Award Discusses Rome, Milan Ballets', *The New York Herald Tribune*, June 13, 1948.

99. Richard Alston, for instance, before deciding on *Three Movements from Petrushka*, sought a Stravinsky work that had not been 'done definitively': interview with the author, April 27, 2000.

100. Alfio Agostini, 'Aurelio M. Milloss', trans. Mariel Dolfini, *L'Avant-Scène: Ballet/Danse*, 3 (August–October, 1980), pp. 60–61. See also Patrizia Veroli, 'The Choreography of Aurel Milloss, Part Four: Catalogue', *Dance Chronicle*, 14/1 (1994), p. 79.

101. Jerome Robbins wanted to choreograph *Noces* and *Sacre*, knowing that Balanchine would never choreograph them: Deborah Jowitt, *Jerome Robbins: His Life, His Theater, His Dance* (New York: Simon & Schuster, 2004), p. 360.

102. The main sources on these Diaghilev Ballets Russes descendants are Jack Anderson, *The One*

and Only: The Ballet Russe de Monte Carlo (London: Dance Books, 1981); Kathrine Sorley-Walker, *De Basil's Ballets Russes* (London: Hutchinson, 1982).

103. Sorley-Walker, *De Basil's Ballets Russes*, p. 69.

104. Jonathan Cott interview [1978] in *Portrait of Mr B* (New York: The Viking Press, 1984), p. 134; Balanchine quoted in Anna Kisselgoff, 'Balanchine: Champion of Stravinsky's Work', *The New York Times*, April 24, 1982.

105. Stephen Walsh, *Stravinsky: Oedipus Rex* (Cambridge: Cambridge University Press, 1993), p. 73.

106. White, *Stravinsky: The Composer and his Works*, p. 114.

107. William Glock, 'Stravinsky Conducts', *The New Statesman* (December 20, 1958).

108. Dyneley Hussey, 'The Tragedy of Stravinsky', *The Dancing Times*, 36 (September, 1946), pp. 617–18.

109. Stravinsky and Craft, *Expositions and Developments* (London: Faber and Faber, 1962), p. 111.

110. Richard Buckle, 'Stravinsky Fills the Bill', *The Sunday Times*, February 4, 1962.

111. Pamela M. Potter, *Most German of the Arts* (New Haven & London: Yale University Press, 1998), p. 4; from Hans Joachim Moser, *Geschichte der deutschen Musik*, III (Stuttgart: Cotta, 1923), pp. 467, 469–70.

112. I am indebted to Stephen Walsh for confirming this point, email communication, April 15, 2003. He suggests that the German commitment to Stravinsky might have begun as early as the 1912 Berlin performances. The composer's first non-Russian publisher was Schott. It should also be acknowledged here that German musical culture is unusually receptive generally to new work from abroad.

113. Clive Barnes, 'Summit Meeting', *Dance and Dancers* (August, 1963), p. 27.

114. Joan Evans, '"Diabolus triumphans": Stravinsky's *Histoire du soldat* in Weimar and Nazi Germany', in John Daverio and John Ogasapian, eds, *Varieties of Musicology: Essays for Murray Lefkowitz* (Warren, Mich.: Harmonie Park Press, 1999), p. 175. This 1923 production is not yet in the *SGD* database because the name of the person responsible for the dance element has not been found.

115. Fred K. Prieberg, *Musik im NS-Staat* (Frankfurt: Fischer Taschenbuch Verlag, 1982), p. 54.

116. *SPD*, p. 641.

117. See Valerie Preston-Dunlop, *Rudolf Laban: An Extraordinary Life* (London: Dance Books, 1998), pp. 68–9, 149; Lillian Karina and Marion Kant, *Hitler's Dancers: German Modern Dance and the Third Reich* [1999], trans. Jonathan Steinberg (New York & Oxford: Berghahn Books, 2003), pp. 14–16.

118. For discussion of the work of Yvonne Georgi and Kreutzberg in the opera houses of Hanover and Leipzig, see Brigitta Weber and Regina Brauer respectively in Frank-Manuel Peter, ed., *Der Tänzer Harald Kreutzberg* (Cologne: Edition Hentrich/Deutsches Tanzarchiv Köln, 1997), pp. 23–63.

119. Joan Evans, 'Stravinsky's Music in Hitler's Germany', *Journal of the American Musicological Society*, 56/3 (Fall, 2003), pp. 525–94; see also Evans, 'Diabolus triumphans', pp. 179–89; Evans, 'Die Rezeption der Musik Igor Strawinskys in Hitlerdeutschland', *Archiv für Musikwissenschaft*, 55/2 (1998), pp. 91–109.

120. Evans, 'Stravinsky's Music in Hitler's Germany', p. 557.

121. Stravinsky and Craft, *Themes and Episodes*, pp. 34–5; emphasis added.

122. Letter from Strecker to Stravinsky, July 19, 1937, *PSS*, translated in Evans, 'Stravinsky's Music...', p. 559.

123. Evans, 'Diabolus triumphans', p. 179.

124. Letter from Strecker to Stravinsky, October 21, 1937, *PSS*, translated in Evans, 'Stravinsky's Music...', p. 559.

125. Elizabeth Souritz, *Soviet Choreographers in the 1920s*, trans. Lynn Visson, ed. with additional trans., Sally Banes (Durham & London: Duke University Press, 1990), pp. 262–6, 289–301.

126. Mary Grace Swift, *The Art of the Dance in the USSR* (Notre Dame, Ind.: University of Notre Dame Press, 1968), pp. 301–03.

127. Boris Schwarz, *Music and Musical Life in Soviet Russia* (Bloomington: Indiana University Press, 1983), p. 75.

128. Ibid., p. 95.

129. Marion Kant's letter to Susan Manning, November 22, 1991, quoted in Manning, 'German Rites Revisited: An Addendum to a History of *Le Sacre du printemps* on the German Stage', *Dance Chronicle*, 16/1 (1993), p. 118.

130. I am indebted here to Lucie Rozmankova for her research on my behalf, using the archive of the National Theatre, Brno, as well as Internet sources.

131. I am indebted to Chae-hyeon Kim, Professor, School of Dance, Korea National University for

the information provided on South Korean usage of Stravinsky.

132. Brian Macdonald discusses and rehearses *Firebird* in 'Harkness Ballet: Triple Exposure', directed by Ivan Curry, produced by Judith Pearlman, WNET-TV/13, New York, January 2, 1968, housed in the Jerome Robbins Dance Division of the New York Public Library for the Performing Arts (*NYPL*).

133. Anna Greta Stahle, 'Stockholm...', *Dance News* (January, 1973), p. 9.

134. Oleg Kerensky quoted in George Balanchine and Francis Mason, *Balanchine's Festival of Ballet* (London: W.H. Allen, 1978), pp. 243–4.

135. Irene Lidova, 'Festive Dancing', *Dance and Dancers* (November, 1983), p. 39; Horst Koegler, 'Invasion of the Extraterrestrials', *Ballett International*, 6/3 (March, 1983), p. 42.

136. Leipzig Ballet company video of Uwe Scholz's *Firebird*, May 26, 1996.

137. James Kudelka, *Firebird*, directed by Barbara Willis Sweete, produced by Rhombus Media, Channel 4, December 25, 2003.

138. Glen Tetley, *Ildfuglen* [*Firebird*], Royal Danish Ballet, directed by Thomas Grimm, Danmarks Radio/RM Arts production, BBC Dance International, November 18, 1983.

139. Bettina Schulte, 'Feuervogels Mondfahrt', *Badische Zeitung*, May 19, 2003.

140. Publicity letter on *Feuervogel* distributed by Kalasri, 2004.

141. Jennifer Weber, email communication with the author, August 11 and 14, 2006; see also Decadancetheatre publicity, www.decadancetheatre.com. Another example of *Firebird* use in collage was Sally Potter's *Wheat* (London, 1975), which repeated the opening bars of the music a number of times. Oscar Araiz incorporated 'le cri de Vaslav' ('Petrushka's cry') in a collage score for *Misia* (Geneva, 1987), a work about the Diaghilev patron Misia Sert, featuring Nijinsky as one of the characters (see *SGD*).

142. Patricia Stöckemann, *Kurt Jooss und das Tanztheater: Etwas ganz Neues muss nun entstehen* (Munich: Kieser, 2001), p. 143. Harald Kreutzberg also created a *Petrushka* with Yvonne Georgi as the dancer wearing long pantaloon trousers and sandals (not the standard ballerina image). Frank-Manuel Peter, ed., *Der Tänzer Harald Kreutzberg*, p. 60 [photograph].

143. Mary Clarke, 'Vinogradov's *Petrushka*: A Scottish/Kirov Link', *The Dancing Times*, 79 (June, 1989), p. 851.

144. Maggie Foyer, 'Stravinsky in Gothenburg', *Dance Europe*, 15 (April/May, 1998), p. 42.

145. Alice Lewisohn Crowley, *The Neighborhood Playhouse: Leaves from a Theatre Scrapbook* (New York: Theatre Arts Books, 1959), pp. 41–3. Linda Tomko dates this *Petrushka* as 1916, but the Diaghilev Ballets Russes first night in the USA was as early as January 17, 1916: see Tomko, *Dancing Class: Gender, Ethnicity, and Social Divides in American Dance, 1890–1920* (Bloomington, Ind: Indiana University Press, 1999), p. 114.

146. Gerda Alexander and Hanz Groll, eds, *Tänzerin, Choreographin, Pädagogin Rosalia Chladek* (Vienna: OBV Pädagogischer Verlag, 1995); John Martin, 'The Dance: In Austria', *The New York Times*, September 25, 1932.

147. Paul Taylor Dance Company video of *Le Grand Puppetier* (2004).

148. Charles D. Isaacson, 'Dance Events Reviewed', *The Dance Magazine* (November, 1931), p. 69.

149. Joan Acocella, 'Van Grona and His First American Negro Ballet', *Dance Magazine*, 56 (March, 1982), pp. 22–4, 30–32.

150. John Martin, 'The Dance: Negro Art', *The New York Times*, November 7, 1937.

151. It is likely that a number of entries recorded as using the full ballet score may in fact use a *Suite* instead, but there is currently no information to confirm this.

152. Charles M. Joseph, *Stravinsky and Balanchine: A Journey of Invention* (*SB*; New Haven & London: Yale University Press, 2002), p. 180.

153. Letter from Irving Deakin (on behalf of Sol Hurok) to Stravinsky, April 20, 1945, *PSS* Adolph Bolm correspondence.

154. Balanchine quoted in Nancy Reynolds, *Repertory in Review: 40 Years of the New York City Ballet* (New York: The Dial Press, 1977), p. 98.

155. Robert Garis, *Following Balanchine* (New Haven & London: Yale University Press, 1995), p. 95.

156. Balanchine, *Firebird* pas de deux, *From Silence to Sound*, video directed and produced by Ron Honsa, Pensa Communications [using the silent film shot at Jacob's Pillow, directed by Carol Lynn (1951)], 1995, *NYPL*. I also used Tallchief's critique of the musical synchronisation here, on the video *Maria Tallchief on 'Firebird': pas de deux and 'Sylvia': pas de deux*, c. 1995, *NYPL*.

157. Jim McDowell, 'Kaleidoscope', *Dance Magazine*, 55 (December, 1981), p. 58.

158. Jeannette Andersen, 'A New Firebird in Munich', *The Dancing Times*, 86 (March, 1996), p. 541.

159. Béjart quoted in Balanchine and Mason, *Balanchine's Festival of Ballet*, p. 243; from inter-

view in *The New Yorker*, February 6, 1971.

160. Information on Béjart's choreography for the Ballet of the 20th Century taken from *Invitation to the Dance: The Firebird*, directed by Rudolf Kufner, BBC, September 9, 1980.

161. Artur Rubinstein, *My Many Years* (New York: Alfred A. Knopf, 1980), pp. 101–02.

162. Stravinsky, 'Quelques Confidences sur la musique' [1935], in White, *Stravinsky: The Composer and his Works*, Appendix A, p. 584.

163. Rubinstein, *My Many Years*, p. 102.

164. John Percival, 'Neumeier's Dream and Other Fantasies in Hamburg', *Dance and Dancers* (October, 1977), p. 27. In a full *Petrushka* in Hamburg (1982), Neumeier presented a skeleton account of the original tale, focusing on the power struggle between a magician figure and two creatures of his imagination, the latter finally set free.

165. Richard Alston in interview with the author, April 27, 2000. The piece was originally entitled *Three Movements from Petrushka*.

166. There is also reference to Alston's setting of *The Rite of Spring* (1981), where again he used the piano score (for four hands).

167. Richard Alston Dance Company videos of Darshan Singh Bhuller (The Place, December 1, 1994) and Ben Ash (Queen Elizabeth Hall, March 11, 1999), in *Movements from Petrushka*.

168. *SRT*, pp. 664–9.

169. Stephanie Jordan, *Striding Out: Aspects of Contemporary and New Dance in Britain* (London: Dance Books, 1992), pp. 105–130.

170. Stravinsky, programme note for the 1946 premiere of *Symphony in Three Movements*, quoted in White, *Stravinsky: The Composer and his Works*, p. 430.

171. Stravinsky and Craft, *Dialogues and a Diary* [1963] (*Dial*; London: Faber and Faber, 1968), pp. 50–52.

172. Patrizia Veroli, 'The Choreography of Aurel Milloss, Part Four: Catalogue', p. 79.

173. Edward Thorpe, *Kenneth MacMillan: The Man and his Ballets* (London: Hamish Hamilton, 1985), p. 102.

174. Leipzig Ballet company video of Uwe Scholz's *Symphony in Three Movements*.

175. Christine Rodes, 'Le Ballet de l'Opéra de Lyon: Stravinski: l'inconsistance', *Pour la danse* (February, 1983), p. 38.

176. Jowitt, *Jerome Robbins*, pp. 187–90.

177. Private archive video of Hans van Manen's *Tilt*, Nederlands Dance Theater, Part 1, January 24, 1972, Part 2, February 26, 1972.

178. Stephanie Jordan, 'Small Talk', *The New Statesman*, August 3, 1984.

179. Programme of *Vision*, NYPL.

180. Stravinsky and Craft, *Memories and Commentaries* (*Mem*; London: Faber and Faber, 1960), p. 95.

181. White, *Stravinsky: The Composer and his Works*, p. 233.

182. Amy Lowell, 'Stravinsky Three Pieces *Grotesques*, for String Quartet', in *The Complete Poetical Works of Amy Lowell* (Boston: Houghton Mifflin, 1955), p. 148.

183. *SSCI*, p. 407; from notes accompanying performances by the London Philharmonic Quartet, February–April, 1919.

184. *SRT*, p. 1468.

185. White, *Stravinsky: The Composer and his Works*, p. 263.

186. For background on Marie Marchowksy and an analysis of the dance element, see Naomi Jackson, *Converging Movements: Modern Dance and Jewish Culture at the 92nd Street Y* (Hanover & London: Wesleyan University Press, 2000), pp. 151–5.

187. Marie Marchowsky, *After Toulouse-Lautrec*, film, c.1952, NYPL.

188. Videos of James Waring's *Arena*: in rehearsal, Manhattan Festival Ballet, c. 1967, and included in *Dances by James Waring*, Judson Dance Theater Workshop, 1978, NYPL.

189. Michael Mao in interview with the author, September 14, 2006.

190. Tanztheater Wuppertal video of *Der zweite Frühling*, c.1975.

191. Marianne Kielian-Gilbert, 'The Rhythms of Form: Correspondence and Analogy in Stravinsky's Designs', *Music Theory Spectrum*, 9 (1987), pp. 42–66.

192. Mark Morris in interview with the author, November 18, 2005. Morris provided information on the creative process behind *Candleflowerdance*, and all quotes relating to the piece stem from this interview.

193. Steven Beck in interview with the author, November 18, 2005. Information on the choreography of *Candleflowerdance* has been taken from the Mark Morris Dance Group video of the performance at Birmingham Hippodrome, October 26, 2005, as well as live performances seen in London and Woking in October and November, 2005.

194. Morris quoted in David Jays, 'To Think about Posterity is a Big Stupid Mistake', *Dance Gazette* (2006), p. 33.

195. Stephanie Jordan, 'Second Stride', *The Dancing Times*, 72 (August, 1982), p. 824.

196. Jonathan Cross, *The Stravinsky Legacy*, p. 80.

197. Boris de Schloezer, *Revue contemporaine*, February 1, 1923, p. 257.

198. *ISCS*, p. 317.

199. Edward T. Cone, 'Stravinsky: The Progress of a Method', pp. 18–26.

200. Alexander Rehding, 'Towards a "Logic of Discontinuity" in Stravinsky's *Symphonies of Wind Instruments*: Hasty, Kramer and Straus Reconsidered', *Music Analysis*, 17/1 (1998), pp. 48, 61.

201. Lázló Somfai, '*Symphonies of Wind Instruments* (1920). Observations of Stravinsky's Organic Construction', *Studia Musicologica Academiae Scientarum Hungaricae*, 14 (1972), pp. 355–83; Jonathan D. Kramer, 'Discontinuity and Proportion in the Music of Stravinsky', in Jann Pasler, ed., *Confronting Stravinsky: Man, Musician, and Modernist*, pp. 174–94; Rehding, 'Towards a "Logic of Discontinuity".' For summaries of analyses of the *Symphonies*, see *SRT*, p. 1487, note 63, and Cross, *The Stravinsky Legacy*, pp. 26–8.

202. Stravinsky, 'Some Ideas About My Octuor', *The Arts* (Brooklyn), January, 1924, pp. 4–6.

203. Scott Messing, *Neoclassicism in Music: From the Genesis of the Concept through the Schoenberg/Stravinsky Polemic* (Ann Arbor: UMI Research Press, 1988), p. 130; translated from Boris de Schloezer, *Revue contemporaine*, February 1, 1923.

204. *ISCS*, pp. 366–7; translated from *Zveno*, June 25, 1923. Walsh also references de Schloezer, *Nouvelle revue française*, 21 (1923), p. 247.

205. White, *Stravinsky: The Composer and his Works*, pp. 293–4.

206. Stravinsky [1924] quoted in Deems Taylor, *Of Men and Music* (New York: Simon & Schuster, 1937), pp. 89–90.

207. *Aut*, p. 95.

208. *SRT*, pp. 1488–9, 1493.

209. Arnold Whittall, 'Stravinsky in Context', in Jonathan Cross, ed., *The Cambridge Companion to Stravinsky*, p. 50.

210. Information on the creative process behind *Frisson* came from Morris in interview with the author, February 14, 2005. Sources for analysis were Mark Morris Dance Group videos of performances at Dance Theater Workshop, New York, December 15, 1985, and Théâtre Royal de la Monnaie, Brussels, December, 1988.

211. Rehding, 'Towards a "Logic of Discontinuity",' p. 60.

212. Jonathan Kramer, *The Time of Music* (New York: Schirmer Books, 1988), p. 283.

213. The timing from the Monnaie video has been described here; it is different from that of the Dance Theater Workshop video, but Morris was particularly insistent that the Monnaie performance should be scrutinised.

214. Matjaz Faric, *Clone*, video produced by Plesni Teater Ljubljana, 1997, *NYPL*.

215. North Carolina Dance Theatre video of Alvin Ailey's *Myth*, 1972, *NYPL*.

216. Paul Sanasardo, *Rotaring: The Stravinsky Dance Circus*, Batsheva Dance Company, produced by Israeli Television, c. 1979, *NYPL*.

217. University of Michigan School of Music, University Dance Company video of Peter Sparling's *The Second Space*, February 5, 2004.

218. The source of information was the performance of Anne Teresa De Keersmaeker's *D'un soir un jour* at Sadler's Wells Theatre, London, October 16, 2006.

Chapter 3

1. Nancy Goldner, 'Stravinsky and Balanchine' [review of Charles M. Joseph's *Stravinsky and Balanchine*], *Raritan*, 23 (Summer, 2003), pp. 124–5, 127–8.

2. Nancy Goldner, *The Stravinsky Festival of the New York City Ballet* (New York: The Eakins Press, 1973).

3. Balanchine quoted in Richard Buckle, *George Balanchine: Ballet Master*, in collaboration with John Taras (London: Hamish Hamilton, 1988), p. 80.

4. Apart from the *Symphony in E flat*, all the transcriptions mentioned are housed in the George Balanchine Archive, Harvard Theatre Collection (*HTC*), Houghton Library, Harvard University. Balanchine did not identify the *String Quartet* movement as a Stravinsky work. Charles M. Joseph identified it as such: a facsimile appears in *Stravinsky and Balanchine: A Journey of Invention* (*SB*; New Haven & London: Yale University Press, 2002), p. 22. Goldner indicates that Balanchine began the Symphony transcription in summer, 1971: *The Stravinsky Festival of the New York City Ballet*, p. 229.

5. Stephanie Jordan, *Moving Music: Dialogues with Music in Twentieth-Century Ballet* (London:

Dance Books, 2000), pp. 189, 266.

6. George Balanchine, 'Marginal Notes on the Dance', in Walter Sorell, ed., *The Dance Has Many Faces* [1951] (Chicago: a capella Books, 1992), p. 42.

7. Quoted in 'Balanchine: An Interview by Ivan Nabokov and Elizabeth Carmichael', *Horizon* (January, 1961), p. 47.

8. Balanchine quoted in *The Guardian*, June 20, 1963.

9. Balanchine, 'The Dance Element in Stravinsky's Music' [1947], in Minna Lederman, ed., *Stravinsky in the Theatre* [1949] (New York: Da Capo Press, 1975), pp. 75–6.

10. Stravinsky and Robert Craft, *Themes and Episodes* (New York: Alfred A. Knopf, 1966), p. 25. Elsewhere, Craft clarifies that Stravinsky asked him to write this passage about *Movements* on his behalf: *An Improbable Life* (Nashville: Vanderbilt University Press, 2002), p. 268. There are in fact three versions in print, with minor, but sometimes interesting, distinctions between them, the third appearing in Stravinsky, *Themes and Conclusions* (London: Faber and Faber, 1972), p. 34. The following extract from the first paragraph of the 2002 version contains a specific example from the work: 'Balanchine began by identifying familiar hallmarks of my style, of which I myself became conscious only through his eyes and ears ... I watched him fastening on the tiniest repeated rhythmic figure (bars 155–56).'

11. Stravinsky and Craft, *Themes and Episodes*, p. 24.

12. Robert Garis, *Following Balanchine* (New Haven & London: Yale University Press, 1995), p. 83. Garis outlines his argument in the chapter 'Balanchine and Stravinsky', pp. 67–89.

13. Ibid., p. 79.

14. Letter from Lincoln Kirstein to Stravinsky, August 31, 1953, Paul Sacher Stiftung (*PSS*), Kirstein correspondence; Craft, ed., *Stravinsky: Selected Correspondence*, I (*SSCI*; London: Faber and Faber, 1984), p. 287.

15. Craft, *Stravinsky: The Chronicle of a Friendship 1948–1971* (London: Gollancz, 1972), p. 346, note 1. Stephen Walsh notes that this information was removed from the 1994 edition of the book: *Stravinsky: The Second Exile: France and America, 1934–1971* (*SSE*; New York: Alfred A. Knopf, 2006), p. 670, note 44.

16. Arlene Croce, 'The Spelling of *Agon*', *The New Yorker*, July 12, 1993, p. 87.

17. Craft, *The Moment of Existence* (Nashville & London: Vanderbilt University Press, 1996), pp. 281–2.

18. Balanchine and Francis Mason, *Balanchine's New Complete Stories of the Great Ballets* (Garden City, N.Y.: Doubleday, 1968), pp. 275–6.

19. John Martin, *The New York Times*, January 21, 1954.

20. Letter from Nicolas Nabokov to Stravinsky, July 2, 1958, *PSS* Nabokov correspondence; Craft, ed., *Stravinsky: Selected Correspondence*, II (*SSCII*; London: Faber and Faber, 1984), p. 401.

21. *SB*, p. 411, note 41; Balanchine and Stravinsky are seen discussing the score of the *Variations* during Tony Palmer's film documentary *Once at a border...* (London Weekend Television, 1982), a clip from material originally shot for *Portrait of Stravinsky*, directed and produced by David Oppenheim, CBS, 1966.

22. There are photographs of Balanchine and Stravinsky discussing *Requiem Canticles* in Arnold Newman and Craft, *Bravo Stravinsky* (Cleveland & New York: World Publishing Company, 1967).

23. The *Lulu Suite* transcription is housed in the *HTC*, see earlier note 4.

24. Craft, ed., *Dearest Bubushkin: The Correspondence of Vera and Igor Stravinsky, 1921–1954, with Excerpts from Vera Stravinsky's Diaries, 1922–1971*, trans. Lucia Davidova (*DB*; London: Thames and Hudson, 1985), p. 194.

25. Croce, 'Balanchine's Girls: The Making of a Style', *Harper's Magazine*, April, 1971, in Croce, *After-images* (New York: Vintage Books, 1979), p. 418.

26. Kirstein, *Movement and Metaphor: Four Centuries of Ballet* (London: Pitman Publishing, 1971), p. 242.

27. Suzanne Farrell quoted in Robert Tracy, *Balanchine's Ballerinas* (New York: Linden Press/ Simon & Schuster, 1983), p. 158.

28. Garis, *Following Balanchine*, p. 77.

29. William Weslow quoted in Francis Mason, *I Remember Balanchine* (New York: Doubleday, 1991), p. 321; Croce, 'Enigma Variations', *The New Yorker*, May 21, 1979, in Croce, *Going to the Dance* (New York: Alfred A. Knopf, 1982), p. 181.

30. Croce, 'Enigma Variations', p. 181.

31. Craft, *Down a Path of Wonder: Memoirs of Stravinsky, Schoenberg and Other Cultural Figures* (London: Naxos Books, 2006), p. 142.

32. Kirstein, *Thirty Years: Lincoln Kirstein's The New York City Ballet* (London: Adam and Charles Black, 1979), p. 215.

33. Letter from Nicolas Nabokov to Stravinsky, June 27, 1951, *PSS* Nabokov correspondence; *SSCII*, p. 381. Denis Dabbadie writes that Balanchine had proposed choreographing *Sacre* in Russia very early in his career, before joining Diaghilev, but the Maryinsky Theatre did not support his idea: 'Un Printemps véritablement sacré', *L'Avant-Scène: Ballet/Danse*, 3 (August–October, 1980), p. 97.

34. *SB*, p. 367, note 10. Kirstein also mentions that, after the 1972 Stravinsky Festival, Balanchine 'felt he might one day arrange the piece' for the two-piano reduction: *Nijinsky Dancing* (London: Thames and Hudson, 1975), p. 143.

35. Craft, 'The Rite: Counterpoint and Choreography', *The Musical Times* (April, 1988), p. 171.

36. Out-take from *Portrait of Stravinsky*, produced and directed by David Oppenheim, CBS, 1966, *PSS*.

37. Doris Hering, 'The Human Element: American Ballet Theatre's Triumphant 25th Anniversary Season at New York State Theater', *Dance Magazine*, 39 (May, 1965), p. 42.

38. Balanchine quoted in Anna Kisselgoff, 'Balanchine: Champion of Stravinsky's Work', *The New York Times*, April 24, 1982.

39. *SSE*, pp. 142, 157–8.

40. Suzanne Farrell discussing *Movements* on the analytical video *Music Dances: Balanchine Choreographs Stravinsky*, conceived, written and narrated by Stephanie Jordan (New York: The Balanchine Foundation, 2002).

41. Boris de Schloezer, 'Chronique musicale', *Nouvelle revue française*, 31 (July 1, 1928), p. 108.

42. Balanchine, 'The Dance Element in Stravinsky's Music', p. 84.

43. Stephen Walsh, *Igor Stravinsky: A Creative Spring* (ISCS; London: Jonathan Cape, 2000), p. 451.

44. Edwin Denby, 'Apollo', *The New York Herald Tribune*, October 28, 1945, in Denby, *Dance Writings*, ed. Robert Cornfield and William Mackay (London: Dance Books, 1986), p. 334.

45. Kirstein, *Thirty Years: Lincoln Kirstein's The New York City Ballet*, p. 135.

46. Three video recordings were used in the analysis of *Apollo*: *Balanchine and Stravinsky: 'Apollon Musagète'* (led by Jacques d'Amboise and Suzanne Farrell), produced by Richard Leacock and Rolf Liebermann, BBC, August 27, 1967, using the recording from *A Stravinsky Portrait*, Norddeutscher Rundfunk Television, Hamburg, 1966; *Stravinsky and Balanchine: Genius Has a Birthday!* (led by Peter Martins and Suzanne Farrell), directed by Emile Ardolino, produced by Barbara Horgan and John Goberman, WNET/New York, 1982; *Baryshnikov Dances Balanchine* (led by Mikhail Baryshnikov and Christine Dunham), directed by Thomas Grimm, produced by Judy Kinberg and Grimm, executive producer Jac Venza, co-production WNET/New York and Danmarks Radio, 1988.

47. Kirstein, *Movement and Metaphor: Four Centuries of Ballet*, p. 227.

48. *SB*, p. 104.

49. Croce, 'New from the Muses', *The New Yorker*, September 11, 1978, in *Going to the Dance*, p. 116.

50. Stravinsky and Craft, *Dialogues and a Diary* [1963] (*Dial*; London: Faber and Faber, 1968), p. 33.

51. Suki Schorer quoted in Nancy Reynolds, *Repertory in Review* (New York: The Dial Press, 1977), p. 49.

52. Croce, 'Repertory Dead and Alive', *The New Yorker*, February 19, 1979, in *Going to the Dance*, p. 155.

53. Balanchine and Mason, *Balanchine's Festival of Ballet* (London: W.H. Allen, 1978), p. 403.

54. Stravinsky quoted in Nicolas Nabokov, *Old Friends and New Music* (London: Hamish Hamilton, 1951), p. 155.

55. Edwin Denby quoted in Croce, 'Repertory Dead and Alive', p. 156.

56. Stravinsky referred to the symphony as war music in its first programme note (1946), although Balanchine claims that he knew nothing of these origins until after the premiere of his ballet: Balanchine and Mason, *Balanchine's Festival of Ballet*, p. 628.

57. This passage from *Stravinsky Violin Concerto* is included in the analytical video *Music Dances: Balanchine Choreographs Stravinsky*. A number of other passages discussed in this chapter are also illustrated and discussed during this video (from *Rubies*, *Duo Concertant*, *Danses Concertantes*, *Stravinsky Violin Concerto*, *Agon*, *Movements for Piano and Orchestra*, and *Divertimento from 'Le Baiser de la fée'*).

58. Jordan, *Moving Music*, pp. 167–73.

59. See the discussion of *Rubies* in Jordan, *Moving Music*, pp. 169–70.

60. Balanchine quoted in the *Cincinatti Enquirer*, June 18, 1972: see Goldner, *The Stravinsky Festival of the New York City Ballet*, p. 35. Balanchine had made a similar comment about non-interference with music when undertaking *Noah and the Flood*: quoted in Arthur Todd, '*Noah and The Flood*', *Dance and Dancers* (July, 1962), p. 12.

61. Anna Kisselgoff, 'Balanchine Revival and a Birthday', *The New York Times*, May 6, 1989; Deborah Jowitt, *Jerome Robbins: His Life, His Theater, His Dance* (New York: Simon & Schuster, 2004), p. 493.

62. Stravinsky and Craft, *Themes and Episodes*, p. 45; see also the later edition of the discussion of *Danses Concertantes* in *Themes and Conclusions*, p. 51.

63. John Cage, 'Grace and Clarity', *Dance Observer*, November, 1944, in Cage, *Silence* (London: Marion Boyars, 1968), p. 90.

64. Denby, 'Balanchine's *Danses Concertantes*', *The New York Herald Tribune*, September 17, 1944, in *Dance Writings*, p. 241.

65. Tobi Tobias, 'Born Yesterday', *New York Magazine*, May 22, 1989.

66. My sources for analysis of *Danses Concertantes* were New York City Ballet company videos: 1972 (without sound), January 16, 1990, and June 25 (evening), 1993.

67. For a discussion of this theoretical point, see Jordan, *Moving Music*, p. 287.

68. Karin von Aroldingen quoted in Mason, *I Remember Balanchine*, p. 500. Goldner reports on the rehearsal time allocation for a number of ballets that were presented in the 1972 Festival: *The Stravinsky Festival of the New York City Ballet*, p. 243. Balanchine also told Walter Terry that *Violin Concerto* was his best 1972 ballet, quoted in 'Stravinsky Ballets Revisited', *Saturday Review*, August 19, 1972.

69. Denby, 'A Note on Balanchine's Present Style', *Dance Index* (February–March, 1945), in *Dance Writings*, p. 413.

70. The two New York City Ballet television recordings used in the analysis of *Stravinsky Violin Concerto* were: directed by Merrill Brockway, produced by Emile Ardolino, Dance in America, WNET/New York, 1977; directed by Hugo Niebeling, RM Productions, ZDF, 1973. I also used the Labanotation score by Leslie Rotman, based on stagings by Karin von Aroldingen (New York: Dance Notation Bureau, 1987). In his programme note for the Royal Ballet's 2006 revival of *Stravinsky Violin Concerto*, Alastair Macaulay has made a number of insightful observations about the relationship between *Balustrade* and the current setting of the *Violin Concerto*. I also observed silent film fragments of *Balustrade*, excerpts of two performances and a rehearsal by the Original Ballet Russe, filmed by Laird Goldsborough, c. 1941, housed in the Jerome Robbins Dance Division of the New York Public Library for the Performing Arts (*NYPL*).

71. Garis, *Following Balanchine*, p. 211.

72. *SB*, pp. 339–40.

73. Garis, *Following Balanchine*, p. 210.

74. The first of these wide-spanning chords opens each of the four movements. According to the violinist Samuel Dushkin, Stravinsky called it the 'passport' to his concerto: 'Working with Stravinsky', in Edwin Corle, ed., *Igor Stravinsky* (New York: Duell, Sloan and Pearce, 1949), p. 182.

75. *SB*, pp. 342–3. Charles Joseph learnt the story behind Aria II from the film-maker Tony Palmer, who had interviewed Dushkin's wife Louise for his documentary on Stravinsky. Presumably having heard the same story from within the New York City Ballet community, Edward Villella confirmed it at the conference 'From the Mariinsky to Manhattan: George Balanchine and the Transformation of American Dance', University of Michigan, November 1, 2003.

76. *SB*, p. 343.

77. Peter Martins, *Far From Denmark* (Boston: Little, Brown, 1982), p. 61.

78. Balanchine quoted in Jonathan Cott, 'Two Talks with George Balanchine' [1982], in *Portrait of Mr. B* (New York: Viking Press, 1984), p. 135.

79. Martins, *Far From Denmark*, p. 61.

80. Macaulay, programme note for the Royal Ballet's 2006 revival of *Stravinsky Violin Concerto*; Goldner, 'Curtain Up', *Dance Now*, 15/3 (Autumn, 2006), pp. 57–9.

81. Croce, 'Free and More than Equal', *The New Yorker*, February 24, 1975, in *After-images*, p. 126.

82. Croce, 'Echo Chamber Music', *The New Yorker*, February 20, 1978, in *Going to the Dance*, p. 60.

83. Lynne Rogers, 'Stravinsky's Break with Contrapuntal Tradition: A Sketch Study', *The Journal of Musicology*, 13/4 (Fall, 1995), p. 478.

84. *SB*, p. 333.

85. Markings added to the piano score accompanying the Labanotation score reveal Balanchine's licence at these two points.

86. Balanchine quoted in Cott, 'Two Talks with George Balanchine', p. 135.

87. Jordan, *Moving Music*, p. 167.

88. See Chapters 9–11 of *SB*, pp. 211–76.

89. Julia Phillips Randel, *Dancing with Stravinsky: Balanchine, 'Agon', 'Movements for Piano and Orchestra', and the Language of Classical Ballet*, unpublished PhD dissertation, Harvard University,

2004.

90. Denby, 'Three Sides of *Agon*', *Evergreen Review* (Winter, 1959), in *Dance Writings*, p. 460.

91. Ibid., p. 464.

92. Ibid., p. 461.

93. For Stravinsky's preference, see *SB*, p. 224; Craft indicated his preference in *World Magazine* (August 15, 1972), in Goldner, *The Stravinsky Festival of the New York City Ballet*, p. 211.

94. *Suzanne Farrell coaching principal roles from 'Monumentum pro Gesualdo' and 'Movements for Piano and Orchestra'* [2001], The George Balanchine Foundation Interpreters Archive (*GBF*), New York, 2007.

95. *SSE*, pp. 417–8, 523.

96. Bernard Taper, *Balanchine: A Biography* (New York & London: Collier/Macmillan, 1974), p. 262.

97. Reynolds, *Repertory in Review*, p. 221; from Donal J. Henahan, *The Chicago Tribune*, August 8, 1963.

98. Walter Terry, 'Dance: New York City Ballet', *The New York Herald Tribune*, April 10, 1963.

99. Reynolds, *Repertory in Review*, p. 220; from *The Times*, September 8, 1965.

100. Randel, *Dancing with Stravinsky*, p. 159.

101. Jennifer Dunning, 'Dance: The City Ballet in Two by Balanchine', *The New York Times*, May 21, 1985.

102. Stravinsky and Craft, *Themes and Episodes*, pp. 24–5.

103. Balanchine quoted in Suki Schorer, with Russell Lee, *Suki Schorer on Balanchine Technique* (New York: Alfred A. Knopf, 1999), p. 383.

104. Stravinsky and Craft, *Memories and Commentaries* (*Mem*; London: Faber and Faber, 1960), p. 106.

105. *SSE*, p. 381.

106. Stravinsky wished to have the pause before each interlude: Stravinsky and Craft, *Themes and Episodes*, p. 25. The interludes are also prefaced by the same metronome marking as the movements that follow.

107. Kirstein, *Thirty Years*, p. 179.

108. Christoph Neidhöfer, 'From Simple to Complex: A Sketch-Based Study of Stravinsky's Compositional Strategies in *Movements for Piano and Orchestra*', Canadian University Music Society Conference, Toronto, November 5, 2000, p. 3.

109. Pieter C. van den Toorn, *The Music of Igor Stravinsky* (New Haven: Yale University Press, 1983), pp. 428–9, where van den Toorn also provides a useful summary of the stylistic and technical developments in Stravinsky's late serial works. I am also indebted to Christoph Neidhöfer for sharing with me his full serial analysis of the *Movements* and his unpublished MA dissertation *Analysearbeit im Fach Komposition/Musiktheorie über die Movements for Piano and Orchestra von Igor Strawinsky*, Musik-Akademie der Stadt Basel, 1991.

110. Garis, *Following Balanchine*, p. 159.

111. Balanchine and Mason, *Balanchine's Festival of Ballet*, p. 370.

112. Schorer reported to me that Balanchine had told her this: interview, September 17, 1991.

113. Randel, *Dancing with Stravinsky*, p. 176.

114. Balanchine quoted in Cott, 'Two Talks with George Balanchine', p. 136.

115. Randel, *Dancing with Stravinsky*, pp. 175–6.

116. Joseph N. Straus, *Stravinsky's Late Music* (Cambridge: Cambridge University Press, 2001), pp. 124–30; Neidhöfer, 'From Simple to Complex'; Douglas Rust, 'Stravinsky's Twelve-Tone Loom: Composition and Precomposition in *Movements*', *Music Theory Spectrum*, 16/1 (Spring, 1994), pp. 62–76.

117. *DB*, p. 194.

118. Edward T. Cone, 'Stravinsky: The Progress of a Method', *Perspectives of New Music*, 1/1 (Fall, 1962), p. 26.

119. In more detail, my sources for analysis of *Movements* were: studio rehearsal film with piano accompaniment (1963), *NYPL*; telecast of performance given on Lincoln Center Day, CBS Television, September 22, 1963; New York City Ballet company videos, with Farrell and Sean Lavery, June 13, 1982, with Heather Watts and Jock Soto, January 6, 1993, and with Helene Alexopoulos and Lindsay Fischer, May 27, 1993; Dutch National Ballet company video, including *Monumentum*, December 11, 1984; *Suzanne Farrell coaching principal roles from 'Monumentum pro Gesualdo' and 'Movements for Piano and Orchestra'* [2001], *GBF*, 2007. Jurg Lanzrein's 1973 Benesh score is housed in *HTC*, and the piano score in the New York City Ballet company archive.

120. Farrell, with Toni Bentley, *Holding On to the Air: An Autobiography* (New York: Summit Books, 1990), p. 79.

121. Farrell in interview with the author, March 3, 2007. Unless otherwise identified, the information that Farrell provided on *Movements* stems from this interview.

122. Farrell, with Toni Bentley, *Holding On to the Air*, p. 78.

123. Farrell in interview with Joan Acocella and Nancy Reynolds, September 16, 2001, for the 2007 *GBF* video of *Monumentum* and *Movements*.

124. In *Monumentum*, there are a couple of previews of the *Movements* style of vocabulary: the line of women in arabesque penchée, who then flex their raised feet, and at the end, their slow descent to splits, before their knees soften into the final sitting position.

125. Stravinsky and Craft, *Themes and Episodes*, p. 24.

126. Edward T. Cone, 'Stravinsky: The Progress of a Method', p. 26.

127. Video sources reveal discrepancies at this point. Farrell's first solo phrase regularly ends on count 5, but the man's solo and the duet show some leeway between finishing on count 4 or 5. The Benesh score suggests that all the phrases should end on count 5.

128. For instance, during the exposition of Movement 1, the soloists punctuate the flute phrase with rapid, isolated movements when the piano is silent: Randel, *Dancing with Stravinsky*, pp. 176–7.

129. See earlier note 10.

130. Richard Moredock in interview with the author, September 19, 1991.

131. 'An Interview with Gordon Boelzner', *Ballet Review*, 3/4 (1970), p. 57.

132. Denby, 'In the Abstract', *New York City Ballet Souvenir Program*, 1959–60, in *Dance Writings*, pp. 467–8.

133. *Dial*, p. 76.

134. David Vaughan (chronicle and commentary), and Melissa Harris, ed., *Merce Cunningham: Fifty Years* (New York: Aperture, 1997), pp. 39–43, 52–3.

135. Le Clercq quoted in Reynolds, *Repertory in Review*, p. 80.

136. Farrell in interview with Acocella and Reynolds.

137. Croce, 'Balanchine's Girls: The Making of a Style', p. 418.

138. *SB*, pp. 299–300.

139. R.P. Blackmur, 'The Swan in Zurich' [1958], in Roger Copeland and Marshall Cohen, eds, *What is Dance?* (Oxford: Oxford University Press), p. 357.

140. Farrell in interview with Acocella and Reynolds.

141. Randel, *Dancing with Stravinsky*, pp. 159, 178–9.

142. Ibid., pp. 184–7, 213–14 and 218.

143. Farrell speaking on *Music Dances: Balanchine Choreographs Stravinsky*.

144. D'Amboise, Lincoln Center Day telecast.

145. Farrell, with Bentley, *Holding On to the Air*, p. 78.

146. Stravinsky and Craft, *Themes and Episodes*, p. 25.

147. Croce, 'Balanchine's Girls: The Making of a Style', p. 418.

148. *Stravinsky, An Autobiography* [1936] (*Aut*; London: Calder & Boyars, 1975), p. 147.

149. *Choreography by George Balanchine: A Catalogue of Works* (New York: Viking, 1984), p. 138.

150. Lynn Garafola, 'Stravinsky and Ida Rubinstein', *Ballet Review* (Summer, 2004), pp. 89–90: referring to Alexander Benois's letter to Nijinska, September 9, 1928, Nijinska Papers, Library of Congress; Stravinsky's remarks on his sketches for the ballet, *PSS*; and André Levinson, 'Les Ballets de Mme Ida Rubinstein: *Le Baiser de la fée*; La Chorégraphie', *Comoedia*, December 1, 1928, p. 2. For a discussion of Nijinska's *Baiser*, alongside other settings, see David Vaughan, '*Le Baiser de la fée*: Nijinska, Ashton, Balanchine', in Vaughan and John V. Chapman, eds, *Looking at Ballet: Ashton and Balanchine, 1926–1936*, *Studies in Dance History*, 3/2 (Fall, 1992), pp. 1–8.

151. Bernard Haggin, *Ballet Chronicle* (New York: Horizon Press, c. 1970), p. 21.

152. For a discussion of different endings performed by the Ballet Russe de Monte Carlo, see Frederic Franklin in Arthur Mitchell, Franklin, Lisa Attles, Francis Mason, 'NYCB and DTH: Anniversary Reflections', *Ballet Review*, 22/3 (Fall, 1994), pp. 20–21.

153. Minna Lederman, 'With the Dancers', *Modern Music*, 23/2 (Spring, 1946), pp. 137–8.

154. Lynn Seymour, with Paul Gardner, *Lynn* (London: Granada, 1984), pp. 122, 124.

155. Birmingham Royal Ballet company video of James Kudelka's *Le Baiser de la fée*, September 26, 1996.

156. Jean-Pierre Pastori, 'Suisse', *Les Saisons de la danse*, 133 (April, 1981), pp. 49–50; Michel Perret, 'Suisse: Bâle [et] Genève', *Pour la danse*, 69 (April, 1981), p. 39.

157. Information on John Neumeier's *Baiser* taken from the programme note for the 1974 American Ballet Theatre production, which includes a historical note by Olga Maynard; Horst Koegler, 'News from Germany', *Dance Magazine*, 46 (March, 1972), p. 99; Tobi Tobias, ' A Point of View...', *Dance Magazine*, 48 (October, 1974), p. 52.

158. Anna Kisselgoff, 'Ballet: *Baiser de la fée*', *The New York Times*, July 20, 1974.

159. Marie-Françoise Christout, *Maurice Béjart* (Paris: Editions Chiron, 1988), p. 168; William Como, 'The New Theatricality', *Dance Magazine*, 60 (January, 1986), p. 60.

160. Scottish Ballet company video of Mark Baldwin's *Ae Fond Kiss*, April 5, 1996.

161. Croce, 'Blind Fate', *The New Yorker*, December 2, 1974, in *After-images*, pp. 101–02. My discussion of *Baiser* was first published in *Dance Chronicle*, 29/1 (2006) pp. 1–16, developed from a paper given at the conference 'From the Mariinsky to Manhattan', October 31, 2003.

162. Croce, 'Blind Fate', p. 101.

163. In more detail, my sources for analysis of *Baiser* were, in the *NYPL*: Pas de deux for Bride and Young Man/Groom and Bride's Solo, with Tanaquil Le Clercq and Frederic Franklin, silent film by Carol Lynn shot at Jacob's Pillow Dance Festival, 1951, with piano accompaniment added for the production *From Silence to Sound*, 1996; Pas de deux for Gypsy and Young Man/Groom, with Maria Tallchief and Frederic Franklin, silent film by Ann Barzel shot at Chicago Opera House, 1947; reconstructions of the Pas de deux for Bride and Young Man/Groom and for Gypsy and Young Man/Groom by Frederic Franklin, with Maria Tallchief and Vida Brown, 1996–7, George Balanchine Archive of Lost Choreography, New York. I also used my analytical video documentary, *Moving Music: Balanchine Choreographs Stravinsky* (New York: George Balanchine Foundation, 2002), which includes the man's solo from *Divertimento from 'Le Baiser de la fée'* performed by Peter Boal; New York City Ballet company videos of *Divertimento*, with Patricia McBride and Helgi Tomasson, November 23, 1984, and with Nichol Hlinka and Peter Boal, June 10, 1993; a video of Tomasson coaching the man's solo from *Divertimento* in 2003, *GBF* (forthcoming).

164. For a discussion of Balanchine's editing of musical scores, see Jordan, *Moving Music*, pp. 124–5.

165. The music credit in *Choreography by George Balanchine: A Catalogue of Works* reads: 'excerpts from *Divertimento*, concert suite, 1934, and the full-length ballet, *Le Baiser de la fée*, 1928'; p. 260.

166. Croce, 'Blind Fate', p. 102.

167. For a discussion of *Scotch Symphony*, see Jordan, *Moving Music*, p. 149.

168. Goldner, *The Stravinsky Festival of the New York City Ballet*, pp. 110–11.

169. Paul Gellen, 'The Stravinsky Festival', *Ballet Review*, 4/3 (1972), p. 16.

170. For a detailed exposition of Stravinsky's borrowings in *Baiser*, see Lawrence Morton, 'Stravinsky and Tchaikovsky' [1962], in Paul Henry Lang, ed., *Stravinsky: A New Appraisal of His Work* (New York: W.W. Norton, 1963), pp. 47–60.

171. David Brown, *Tchaikovsky: A Biographical and Critical Study* (London: Gollancz, 1992), IV, p. 152.

172. Video of Tomasson coaching the man's solo from *Divertimento from 'Le Baiser de la fée'* in 2003, *GBF* (forthcoming).

173. Stravinsky himself notes the link with Carabosse, in Stravinsky and Craft, *Expositions and Developments* (*Expo*; London: Faber and Faber, 1962), p. 84.

174. Video of Tomasson coaching the man's solo from *Divertimento from 'Le Baiser de la fée'* in 2003, *GBF* (forthcoming).

175. Goldner, *The Stravinsky Festival of the New York City Ballet*, p. 112.

176. For full references on the films of the 1951 performance of the Bride's solo by Tanaquil Le Clercq and of the reconstruction of the Bride's solo by Frederic Franklin in 1996–7, see note 163.

177. Patricia McBride quoted in Reynolds, *Repertory in Review*, p. 296.

178. Croce, 'Bounty', *The New Yorker*, August 10, 1981, in *Going to the Dance*, p. 405.

179. Croce, 'Blind Fate', p. 100.

180. Naima Prevots, *Dance for Export: Cultural Diplomacy and the Cold War* (Hanover & London: Wesleyan University Press, 1998), pp. 7–22.

181. For a detailed discussion of *L'Oeuvre du XXe siècle* and its political implications, from which my own summary has been derived, see Mark Carroll, *Music and Ideology in Cold War Europe* (Cambridge: Cambridge University Press, 2003).

182. *Choreography by George Balanchine: A Catalogue of Works*, p. 35. This source has been used for all data relating to New York City Ballet tours and stagings of Balanchine works on other companies, together with the current Balanchine Trust database of Balanchine stagings. An updated on-line version of the Balanchine catalogue is scheduled to be released in January 2008.

183. Reynolds, *Repertory in Review*, pp. 47–8. As well as the stagings on European companies mentioned, others date from the 1940s, on companies in the USA, Cuba and South America.

184. Susan A. Manning, *Ecstasy and the Demon: Feminism and Nationalism in the Dances of Mary Wigman* (Berkeley, Los Angeles & London: University of California Press, 1993), p. 247.

185. Jochen Schmidt, 'From *Swan Lake* to the Weed Garden: The Development of Ballet and Dance Theatre in the Federal Republic of Germany since 1967', in Manfred Linke, ed., *Theater/Theatre*, 1967–1982 (Berlin: International Theatre Institute, 1983), p. 77.

186. Prevots, pp. 20–21.

187. Hamburg was also the city where Balanchine's *Apollo* was filmed for television with Farrell as Terpsichore (Norddeutscher Rundfunk Television, 1966, directed by Richard Leacock and Rolf Liebermann). In 1973, Balanchine took the New York City Ballet to Berlin for RM productions to film fifteen of his ballets.

188. Letter from Rolf Liebermann to Stravinsky, December 9, 1961, *PSS* Liebermann correspondence.

189. Of course, there are more productions that the database does not yet cover. For instance, there was one by Robert Mayer in Kassel, during the time when he led the ballet company there (1959–70). No precise date is given by Horst Koegler, *Friedrichs Ballettlexikon* (Hanover: Friedrich Verlag, 1972), p. 383. Another production by Lothar Höfgen was seen in Basle in 1968 but premiered some time earlier, probably in Karlsruhe, where Höfgen was ballet master (1966–9). I am indebted to Marianne Forster for providing this information.

190. I am indebted to the Czech scholar Vladimir Vasut for providing me with initial information about this, fax communication, February 17, 2003, also to Lucie Rozmankova, for her research on my behalf, using the archive of the National Theatre, Brno, as well as Internet sources. The two photographs of the Máša Cveji čová *Apollo* are published in *Divadelní list*, 17 (March 29, 1933).

191. Charles M. Joseph, *Stravinsky Inside Out* (New Haven & London: Yale University Press, 2001), p. 60.

192. Françoise Adret, telephone communication with the author, March 29, 2003.

193. Robin Grove, email communication with the author, January 6, 2003.

194. *Apollo* [and] *Orpheus*, NHK-Television Tokyo, 1972, *NYPL*.

195. Horst Koegler, 'Three German *Agons*', *Dance Magazine*, 32 (November, 1958), p. 62. There were also plans for early productions outside Germany, at La Scala, Milan, and in Zurich (letter from Ernst Roth of Boosey & Hawkes to Stravinsky, January 6, and reply January 11, 1958, *PSS*); these too did not materialise. Testimony to the importance of the European premiere (Krüger choreography) is the mass of newspaper and journal articles prompted by it. Yet the piece lasted only one season (13 performances). I am indebted to Margret Schild, librarian at the Theatermuseum der Landeshauptstadt Düsseldorf, for providing this information. In Berlin, Gsovsky's *Agon* was given 19 performances, lasting until the 1960/61 season. I am indebted to Karin Heckermann of the Deutsche Oper Berlin for providing this information.

196. Koegler, 'Three German *Agons*', p. 38.

197. Peter Williams paraphrases Ansermet here, '*Agon* – Décor', *Dance and Dancers* (October, 1958), p. 11.

198. Clement Crisp, 'Stravinsky's *Agon*', *The Financial Times*, August 21, 1958.

199. J.B., 'A Londres *Agon* de Stravinsky transfiguré par la représentation scénique', *Arts*, November 25, 1958 (author's translation).

200. Clive Barnes, '*Agon*', *Dance and Dancers* (October, 1958), p. 8.

201. 'Stravinsky Performance a Fiasco', *Glasgow Herald*, September 8, 1958.

202. Ann Nugent, email communication with the author, May 22, 2003.

203. Information from programme in Boosey & Hawkes archive (New York offices).

204. Erik Aschengren, 'News from Denmark: winter 1967', *Dance Magazine*, 41 (March 1967), p. 92.

205. Chrissie Parrott, email communication with the author, April 14, 2003. Parrott was taken through the score by composer-pianist Roger Smalley and purposely avoided seeing the Balanchine work before creating her own version. See also Lee Christofis, 'Reviews: Putting Flesh on Bone', *Dance Australia* (August/September, 1993), pp. 50–51.

206. David Hough, 'Move Aside Balanchine!' *Dance Australia*, 67 (June/July, 1993), p. 9.

207. I have not counted here as an *Agon* production *The Sleep of Reason* (1992) by Sasha Spielvogel, which took as its theme the artist Goya and also used music by de Falla. Information from publicity for *The Sleep of Reason*, *NYPL*. Whether it used the whole Stravinsky score is not yet known.

208. Anna Kisselgoff, 'The Dance: Murray Louis At the Joyce', *The New York Times*, November 3, 1982. Video of Louis's *A Stravinsky Montage* [with *Porcelain Dialogues*] from a performance at the Joyce Theatre, New York, April 20, 1986, *NYPL*.

209. Helmut Scheier, 'New Ballet Director in Hagen: Jean-Jacques Vidal Stages his *Le Sacre du printemps*', *Ballett International/Tanz Aktuell* (May, 1997), p. 61.

210. Michael Clark, *O* (1994), video directed by Sophie Fiennes, 1994. I attended live performances of the two versions of *O* at the Brixton Academy, London, in 1994 and at the Barbican Theatre, London, November 2, 2006. See also Sophie Constanti, 'The Power of Pelvic Thrust', *The Guardian*, May 9, 1994; Judith Mackrell, 'Messenger from the Gods', *The Independent*, June 23, 1994; Nadine Meisner, 'Clark is Letter Perfect', *The Times*, May 10, 1994.

211. Liz Roche, *Sweet Apollo*, DVD, 2006; further information taken from programme material.

212. I am grateful to Ann Nugent for providing factual information on Forsythe's *Eidos:Telos* in interview with the author, January 14, 2007. The programme reproduced part of the score of Stravinsky's Apotheosis alongside the new, manipulated account by Willems.

213. Deborah Jowitt, 'Does He Mean You Know What?' *Village Voice*, December 21, 1982.

214. Gordon quoted in Jennifer Dunning, 'David Gordon's Dance Ironies', *The New York Times*, December 12, 1982. For a discussion of Gordon's approach to music, see Joyce Morgenroth, *Speaking of Dance: Twelve Contemporary Choreographers On Their Craft* (New York: Routledge, 2004), pp. 49–53.

215. David Gordon, *Trying Times*, performed by David Gordon/Pick Up Company, videotaped by Video D from performance at Dance Theater Workshop, December 17, 1982, NYPL.

216. Sources for analysis of Yvonne Rainer's *AG Indexical, with a little help from H.M.* were videos/DVDs of performances at Dance Theater Workshop, New York, April 20, 22 and 23, 2006.

217. Rainer, *Work 1961–73* (Halifax: The Press of the Nova Scotia College of Art and Design, 1974), p. 111. This speech was an accompaniment to *Performance Demonstration* (1968). Douglas Crimp has written about the important role of music in Rainer's work in 'Yvonne Rainer, Muciz Lover', *Grey Room*, 22 (Winter, 2005), pp. 48–67.

218. Rainer, talking with Clarinda MacLow, 'AG Indexical, with a little help from H.M.', March 4, 2006, www.movementresearch.org/publishing/cc/interview/rainer1.html

219. Rainer, email communication with the author, October 16, 2006. Unless otherwise indicated, quoted comments stem from this email. I am also grateful to Rainer for helping me with factual details about the work.

220. Balanchine's actual words are: 'The ballet is a purely female thing; it is a woman, a garden of beautiful flowers, and man is the gardener': quoted in *By George Balanchine* (New York: San Marco Press, 1984), p. 16.

221. Rainer, talking with Clarinda MacLow.

222. Taisha Paggett, a UCLA student, had performed this material with Rainer in Los Angeles, whilst Rainer was a scholar-in-residence at the Getty Research Institute, 2005.

223. Rainer, talking with Clarinda MacLow. Whelan is a New York City Ballet soloist well known for dancing this solo; she appears in it on the video *Music Dances*.

224. Rainer, talking with Clarinda MacLow.

225. Crimp, 'Yvonne Rainer, Muciz Lover', pp. 61, 63.

Chapter 4

1. Ashton quoted in Julie Kavanagh, *Secret Muses: The Life of Frederick Ashton* (London: Faber and Faber, 1996), p. 355.

2. Ashton, 'The Production of a Ballet', unpublished notes for a broadcast (1948), copy housed in the Ashton archive, Royal Opera House, Covent Garden.

3. Ashton quoted in Hans-Theodor Wohlfahrt, 'Ashton's Last Interview', *Dance Now*, 5/1 (Spring, 1996), p. 30.

4. Kavanagh, *Secret Muses*, p. 103.

5. Kavanagh, *Secret Muses*, pp. 373, 357–78.

6. A.H. Franks, 'Ashton, Stravinsky, Gide –', *The Dancing Times*, 51 (December, 1961), p. 142.

7. 'The Camargo Society', *The Dancing Times*, 21(October, 1931), p. 6.

8. Constant Lambert's evaluation of Stravinsky is clarified in *Music Ho! A Study of Music in Decline* [1934] (London: Faber and Faber, 1966).

9. Robert Irving in interview with Tobi Tobias, Oral History Project transcript, housed in the Jerome Robbins Dance Division of the New York Public Library (NYPL), July–December, 1976, p. 59. De Valois had used Stravinsky on one occasion herself in *Les Trois Graces*, a trio divertissement at the Royal Court Theatre, November 26, 1928. The programme does not tell us what score she used: Kathrine Sorley Walker, *Ninette de Valois: Idealist Without Illusions* (London: Hamish Hamilton, 1987), p. 244.

10. Lambert, *Music Ho!*, p. 102.

11. Ashton quoted in Gillian Widdicombe, 'A Guru of the Ballet', *The Observer*, August 21, 1983.

12. Letter from Ralph Hawkes, the music publisher (Boosey & Hawkes) to Stravinsky, January 7, 1948, reporting on a meeting with Ashton the night before and indicating the original plan for Balanchine to produce *Orpheus* at Covent Garden. The letter is housed in the Paul Sacher Stiftung (PSS), B&H correspondence.

13. Anton Dolin, *Autobiography* (London: Oldbourne, 1960), p. 163.

14. Vera Stravinsky and Robert Craft, *Stravinsky in Pictures and Documents* (SPD; New York:

Simon & Schuster, 1978), p. 376. Correspondence between Gretl Urban of Associated Music Publishers and Stravinsky confirms Chase's intention to stage the ballet during the 1946–7 season: letters dated September 1 and 4, 1947, *PSS* Associated Music Publishers correspondence.

15. Letter from Lincoln Kirstein to Stravinsky, October 16, 1947, *PSS* Kirstein correspondence.

16. Letter from Stravinsky to Kirstein, September 15, 1950, *PSS* Kirstein correspondence.

17. Letter from Eugene Berman to Stravinsky, March 15, 1950, *PSS* Berman correspondence.

18. Soulima's admiration is also recorded in a letter from Ashton to Dick Beard, quoted in Kavanagh, *Secret Muses*, p. 357.

19. Letter from Stravinsky to Kirstein, August 28, 1953, *PSS* Kirstein correspondence.

20. Michael Somes testified to this, according to David Vaughan, *Frederick Ashton and His Ballets* (London: Adam & Charles Black, 1977), p. 222. I would suggest that Ashton had help from a trained musician, possibly the conductor Geoffrey Corbett who arranged the score for piano. According to Pauline Clayden he frequently attended early rehearsals: interview with the author, April 10, 1999.

21. Recording dating from February 5, 1945, Columbia 11997/8-D in set X245.

22. Letter from Hawkes to Stravinsky, April 24, 1947 and response, May 11, 1947, *PSS* B&H correspondence.

23. *Orpheus* awaited Balanchine's setting. The only other work that Stravinsky composed in 1947 was an unpublished 'Little Canon' to mark the birthday of Nadia Boulanger.

24. Housed in the Royal Ballet Video Archive, Royal Opera House.

25. The piano score arrangement is housed in the Music Library and the Benesh scores in the Royal Ballet Archive at the Royal Opera House. The Royal Ballet score by Faith Worth dates from 1960, but it has been updated over the years with revivals of the ballet, and there are numerous later annotations. There is also a 2002 score by Martin Safstrom and Eva Lundstrom derived from the Royal Swedish Ballet staging by Malin Thomas.

26. Excerpts from *Scènes* were revived especially for Stephanie Jordan and Geraldine Morris, *Ashton to Stravinsky: A Study of Four Ballets with Choreography by Frederick Ashton* (London: Dance Books, 2004): the two ballerina Variations, Danses II and a number of other fragments are discussed within the current text.

27. Stravinsky and Craft, *Dialogues and a Diary* [1963] (*Dial*; London: Faber and Faber, 1968), pp. 49–50.

28. Desmond Shawe-Taylor, *The New Statesman and Nation*, June 5, 1954.

29. Lawrence Morton, 'Incongruity and Faith', in Edwin Corle, ed., *Igor Stravinsky* (New York: Duell, Sloane and Pearce, 1949), pp. 194–5.

30. Dolin, *Autobiography*, p. 156; *SPD*, p. 374.

31. *SPD*, p. 374.

32. Letter from Stravinsky to Hugo Winter, June 27, 1944, in Craft, ed., *Stravinsky: Selected Correspondence*, III (*SSCIII*; London: Faber and Faber), p. 296.

33. Edwin Denby, '*Scene* [sic] *de Ballet* at Billy Rose's', *The New York Herald Tribune*, December 24, 1944.

34. Letter from Mercedes de Acosta to Vera Stravinsky, December 15, 1944, *PSS*.

35. *Dial*, p. 49.

36. Denby, '*Scene de Ballet* at Billy Rose's'.

37. The description is taken from Richard Taruskin's exposition of the Stravinsky aesthetic, 'The Pastness of the Present and the Presence of the Past', in Nicholas Kenyon, ed., *Authenticity and Early Music: A Symposium* (Oxford: Oxford University Press, 1988), p. 186.

38. José Ortega y Gasset, *The Dehumanization of Art and Other Essays on Art, Culture and Literature*, trans. Helene Weyl (Princeton: Princeton University Press, 1968), p. 47.

39. André Boucourechliev, *Igor Stravinsky* (Librairie Arthème Fayard, 1982), p. 279.

40. Richard Buckle, *The Adventures of a Ballet Critic* (London: Cresset Press, 1953), pp. 99–100.

41. P.J.S. Richardson [The Sitter Out], *The Dancing Times*, 38 (April, 1948), p. 348.

42. Philip Hope-Wallace, *Time and Tide*, February 21, 1948.

43. Letter from Ashton to Richard Beard, quoted in Kavanagh, *Secret Muses*, p. 356.

44. Jennifer Dunning, 'The Man Behind Ballet's Ashton Touch', *The New York Times*, June 26, 1981.

45. Letter from Hans Werner Henze to Ashton, quoted in Kavanagh, *Secret Muses*, pp. 357, 425.

46. Alastair Macaulay, 'To Stravinsky', *The Dancing Times*, 74 (August, 1984), p. 922.

47. I am grateful to Macaulay for drawing my attention to this in his lecture 'The Dance Theatre of Frederick Ashton' for *The Ashton Exchange* seminar series at the Royal Opera House, November 18, 2004.

48. Macaulay, 'To Stravinsky', p. 922.

49. *Dial*, p. 50.

50. *Dial*, p. 49.

51. Antoinette Sibley in a lecture-demonstration at the conference 'Following Sir Fred's Steps: A Conference Celebrating Ashton's Work', Roehampton Institute London, November 12, 1994.

52. Indication at [30] in Corbett's piano arrangement of Stravinsky's score.

53. Joan Acocella, 'Life Steps: The Frederick Ashton Centennial', *The New Yorker*, August 2, 2004, p. 85.

54. Buckle, *The Adventures of a Ballet Critic*, p. 110.

55. I am indebted to Pauline Clayden for copying her diagrams of this passage, preserved by her since the creation of the ballet. David Vaughan has observed the kinship between *Scènes* and Merce Cunningham's spatial procedures, equalising the territories of the stage and opening up new directional possibilities: 'Birthday Offering', *Ballet News* (October, 1979), p. 11. I would suggest a special relationship here with Cunningham's *Torse* (1977), a work that devised directions according to chance with the stage as an imaginary grid of eight by eight squares.

56. *Dial*, p. 49.

57. See Morris on *Ashton to Stravinsky* for further analysis of the movement vocabulary.

58. Edward T. Cone, 'Stravinsky: The Progress of a Method', *Perspectives of New Music*, 1/1 (Fall, 1962), pp. 19–20.

59. *Dial*, p. 49.

60. The form of the Variation is discussed further by Geraldine Morris in 'Processing a Research Process', *Dance Now*, 14/1 (Spring, 2005), p. 94.

61. Ashton, 'The Production of a Ballet.'

62. Hans Werner Henze, *Ondine: Diary of a Ballet* [1959], trans. Daniel Pashley (London: Dance Books, 2003), p. 62.

63. The influence of Nijinska's groupings on Ashton has already been noted, for instance, by Vaughan, *Frederick Ashton and His Ballets*, pp. 52–3 and 162.

64. Information from reviews of the Sadler's Wells Ballet 1948 European tour housed in the Royal Ballet Archive, Royal Opera House.

65. Sadler's Wells Ballet press release for March–April, 1949, *NYPL*.

66. Ashton initiated another design change early on, removal of a very ornate second set by André Beaurepaire. The Dutch National Ballet production (excerpts of which are included in *Ashton to Stravinsky*) includes the set that was removed from the Royal Ballet production.

67. Nancy Reynolds, *Repertory in Review: 40 Years of the New York City Ballet* (New York: The Dial Press, 1977), p. 297.

68. Jack Anderson, 'A Hard-Headed Miracle: New York City Ballet Concludes its Spring Season with a History-Making Stravinsky Festival', *Dance Magazine*, 46 (September, 1972), p. 26.

69. Clive Barnes, 'Dance: Salute to Master', *The New York Times*, April 9, 1972.

70. Barnes, 'Ballet: Seconds at Stravinsky Feast', *The New York Times*, June 23, 1972.

71. New York City Ballet company video of Christopher Wheeldon's *Scènes de ballet*, February 18, 2000.

72. The videotapes containing *Scènes* are entitled *Pittsburgh Ballet Theatre* and date from 1972, one a recording of a performance, April 1, 1972, *NYPL*.

73. Barnes, 'Dance: Salute to Master', *The New York Times*, April 9, 1972.

74. Private archive video of Hans van Manen's *Ballet Scenes*, directed by Wilbert Bank, NOS TV, November 5, 1986.

75. Leipzig Ballet company video of Uwe Scholz's *Scènes de ballet*, May 26, 1996.

76. The main sources for the ballet are Vaughan, *Frederick Ashton and His Ballets*, pp. 124–30 and H.S. Sibthorp (c. 1941), *The Vic-Wells Ballet 1931–1940*, unpublished manuscript housed in the Theatre Museum, London.

77. Vaughan, *Frederick Ashton and His Ballets*, p. 127.

78. Ibid.

79. Ashton, '*Baiser de la Fée*', *The Old Vic and Sadler's Wells Magazine*, 2/27 (November, 1935), p. 2.

80. Kavanagh, *Secret Muses*, pp. 173–4.

81. Ashton, '*Baiser de la Fée*'.

82. Photographs by Gordon Anthony in Vaughan, *Frederick Ashton and His Ballets*, p. 129, and by J.W. Debenham, in Keith Money, *Fonteyn: The Making of a Legend* (New York: Reynal, 1974), p. 33.

83. Ashton speaking on *Margot Fonteyn: A Tribute*, documentary directed and produced by Patricia Foy, Antelope/Aurora Production for Reiner Moritz Associates and Channel Four Television, 1989. He made the same point to Jann Parry, BBC Radio 3, January 3, 1992, as quoted in Meredith Daneman, *Margot Fonteyn* (London: Viking, 2004), p. 94.

84. The Panama film was made by Patricia Foy as preparation for her television documentary *Margot Fonteyn: A Tribute*. A video of Nicola Katrak's lecture-demonstration on the Bride's solo for

the 1999 Fonteyn conference is housed in the Royal Academy of Dancing library. The *Ashton to Stravinsky* DVD/video includes versions of the Bride's Variation, by Ashton, MacMillan and Balanchine, as well as fragments from the Coda to Ashton's Bride's solo. For a further detailed analysis of the Bride's solo, concentrating on movement style, see Geraldine Morris, 'Ashton and MacMillan in Fairyland: Contrasting Styles in *Le Baiser de la fée*', *Dance Chronicle*, 29/2 (Autumn, 2006), pp. 133–59.

85. The film of the 1970 Gala Tribute to Ashton is housed in the Royal Ballet Video Archive, Royal Opera House.

86. The descriptive terms stem from Katrak's 1999 lecture-demonstration.

87. Lynn Seymour, with Paul Gardner, *Lynn: The Autobiography of Lynn Seymour* (London: Granada, 1984), p. 124. Two Royal Ballet Archive videos were examined: an Edmée Wood film with Lynn Seymour, Donald McCleary and Svetlana Beriosova (c. 1960) and a recording of the revival led by Maria Almeida, Jonathan Cope and Fiona Chadwick (c. 1986).

88. Judith Mackrell, 'Fairy Tales', *Dance Theatre Journal*, 4/4 (Winter, 1986), p. 11.

89. Seymour, *Lynn*, p. 123.

90. Lecture-demonstration on Nijinska's Bride's Solo, videotaped for the Jerome Robbins Archive by Penny Ward/Video, November 10, 1990, *NYPL*.

91. The solo was danced by Nathalie Perriraz during the Prix de Lausanne 1984, a recording of the broadcast by Télévision Suisse Romande, *NYPL*.

92. David Vaughan notes that the style of steps punctuated by pauses also appeared in the 'Bells' section in *Apparitions* (1936, Liszt), email communication with the author, March 15, 2007; see Vaughan, *Frederick Ashton and His Ballets*, p. 137, information from interview with Margaret Dale.

93. Stephen Walsh, *Igor Stravinsky: A Creative Spring* (*ISCS*; London: Jonathan Cape, 2000), p. 534.

94. *Dial*, p. 38.

95. Stravinsky, 'M. Igor Strawinsky nous parle de *Perséphone*', *Excelsior*, May 1, 1934.

96. Maurice Brillant, 'Les Fêtes dansées de Mme Ida Rubinstein', *L'Aube Musicale*, May 2, 1934.

97. *SSCIII*, p. 477, note 4.

98. For instance, Wilfrid Mellers, *The Masks of Orpheus: Seven Stages in the Story of European Music* (Manchester: Manchester University Press, 1987), p. 161; Craft, 'Music and Words', in Minna Lederman, ed., *Stravinsky in the Theatre* [1949] (New York: Da Capo Press, 1975), p. 97.

99. *SSCIII*, p. 475.

100. *Dial*, p. 37.

101. L. Franc Scheuer, 'The Rubinstein Ballets', *The Dancing Times*, 24 (June, 1934), p. 244.

102. Clive Barnes, '*Persephone*', *Dance and Dancers* (January, 1962), p. 9.

103. The *Ashton to Stravinsky* DVD/video includes the Scene I dance for Persephone and her friends, the pas de deux for Persephone and Pluto (Scene 2) and fragments of corps de ballet material. The silent Edmée Wood film is housed in the Royal Ballet Video Archive, Royal Opera House.

104. A.H. Franks, 'Ashton, Stravinsky, Gide –', *The Dancing Times*, 51 (December, 1961), p. 142.

105. 'Stravinsky Sets a Problem with *Persephone*', *The Times*, December 5, 1961.

106. See Stravinsky, *The Poetics of Music* (Cambridge: Harvard University Press, 1947), pp. 41, 43; Taruskin, 'The Pastness of the Present and the Presence of the Past', pp. 165–6.

107. Ashton quoted in 'Dying a Little to Live a Little', [no author given], *Topic*, December 9, 1961.

108. Franks, 'Ashton, Stravinsky, Gide –', p. 142.

109. Stravinsky, *Persephone*, New York Philharmonic Orchestra, Columbia ML5196 LP, 1958 (with Vera Zorina as Persephone).

110. Eric Walter White, *Stravinsky: A Critical Survey* (London: John Lehmann, 1947), pp. 142–9. Ashton's library, which contained this book, is now housed in the Royal Ballet School archive.

111. Although he never saw Ashton's *Persephone*, Stravinsky would undoubtedly have heard details of the production. Isaiah Berlin wrote positively about the work from London in a letter to Craft (December 28, 1961), quoted in *An Improbable Life* (Nashville: Vanderbilt University Press, 2002), p. 229.

112. [no author given], *Time*, December 22, 1961.

113. 'A Masterpiece Salved After Shelving', *The Times*, December 13, 1961.

114. For a more detailed analysis of the movement content of *Persephone*, see Geraldine Morris, '*Persephone*: Ashton's Rite of Spring', *Dance Research*, 24/1 (Summer, 2006), pp. 21–36.

115. E.C. Mason, 'Accents from Russia', *Time and Tide*, December 21, 1961.

116. White, *Stravinsky: A Critical Survey*, p. 147.

117. Richard Last, 'A Goddess "Flops" on a Date', *Daily Herald*, December 13, 1961.

118. White, *Stravinsky: A Critical Survey*, p. 147.

119. *Dial*, p. 38.

120. Andrew Porter, 'Royal Opera House: *Persephone*', *The Financial Times*, December 13, 1961.

121. Noel Goodwin, '*Persephone*: Music', *Dance and Dancers* (January, 1962), p. 11.

122. *Dial*, p. 36.

123. Andrew Porter, '*Persephone*', *The Financial Times*, October 31, 1961.

124. Kavanagh, *Secret Muses*, p. 462.

125. Franks, 'Ashton, Stravinsky, Gide –', p. 142.

126. He seems to have wanted this visibility of the chorus at the same time as it 'should stand apart from and remain outside the action', *Dial*, p. 37.

127. Milloss programme note quoted in Patrizia Veroli, 'The Choreography of Aurel Milloss, Part Three: 1967–1988', *Dance Chronicle*, 13/3 (1990–91), p. 373.

128. Vera Zorina, *Zorina* (New York: Farrar Straus Giroux, 1986), p. 240.

129. *Dial*, p. 37.

130. Zorina, *Zorina*, pp. 299–300.

131. The source for analysis is the recording of a 1982 performance of *Persephone*, directed by Emile Ardolino, produced by Judy Kinberg, Great Performances/Dance in America, PBS, February 14, 1983.

132. Balanchine quoted in Jonathan Cott, 'Two Talks with George Balanchine' [1982], in *Portrait of Mr. B* (New York: Viking Press, 1984), p. 143.

133. Zorina, *Zorina*, p. 299.

134. Interview with Jane Hermann, November 10, 2003. Hermann, then coordinator of special programmes at the Metropolitan Opera House, New York, acted as go-between to secure Ashton's collaboration in the opera project.

135. The *Ashton to Stravinsky* DVD/video comprises all four of the Fisherman's solos. The Royal Opera and Metropolitan Opera videos are housed in their company archives in the Royal Opera House, London, and in New York respectively.

136. Damian Woetzel in interview with Geraldine Morris and the author, October 24, 2003.

137 *ISCS*, p. 123.

138. Ibid., p. 125.

139. Stravinsky and Craft, *Memories and Commentaries* (*Mem*; London: Faber and Faber, 1960), p. 131, note 1.

140. *SPD*, pp. 114, 118–19.

141. *Mem*, p. 132.

142. Richard Taruskin, *Stravinsky and the Russian Traditions: A Biography of the Works Through 'Mavra'* (*SRT*; Oxford: Oxford University Press, 1996), p. 1106; translated from Benois, *Moi vospominaniya*, II (Moscow: Nauka, 1980), p. 536.

143. Walsh, 'A double bull's eye', *The Observer*, September 25, 1983.

144. Lecture-demonstration given by Dowell at Roehampton University, November 11, 2004.

145. John Dexter, 'Hockney at the Met', in Martin L. Friedman, ed., *Hockney Paints the Stage* (London: Thames & Hudson, 1983), p. 138.

146. David Hockney quoted in Robert Tracy, 'David Hockney', *Dance Ink* (Spring, 1992), p. 29.

147. Daniel Albright, *Stravinsky: The Music Box and the Nightingale* (New York: Gordon and Breach, 1989), p. 22; see also Albright, *Untwisting the Serpent: Modernism in Music, Literature, and Other Arts* (Chicago: The University of Chicago Press, 2000), pp. 57–8.

148. David Vaughan, 'Reviews: VII', *Dance Magazine*, 56 (March 1982), p. 104.

149. *SRT*, p. 1104.

150. Dowell in rehearsal at the Royal Ballet School, White Lodge, April 5, 2004.

151. Dowell in interview with the author, June 8, 1993.

152. Nancy Goldner, 'Reviews: Stravinsky Bill', *Dance News* (January, 1982), p. 3.

153. David Cairns, 'The Snares of Simplicity', *The Sunday Times*, September 25, 1983.

154. Alexander Schouvaloff and Victor Borovsky, *Stravinsky on Stage* (London: Stainer & Bell, 1982), pp. 80–82.

155. The broadcast programme *Stravinsky Remembered* contains John Butler's setting of *Le Rossignol*, WNET/13, November 22, 1971, *NYPL*.

156. John Percival and Marie-Françoise Christout, 'Stravinsky Celebrated in Paris', *Dance and Dancers* (June, 1972), pp. 28–32, 54.

157. A note in the Ballet Society programme, November 20, 1947, *NYPL*.

158. Konstantin Rudnitsky, *Meyerhold, the Director* [1969], trans. George Petrov, ed. Sydney Schultze (Ann Arbor: Ardis, 1981), pp. 250–51. Rudnitsky's Golovine quotation is taken from a letter to Meyerhold, July 7, 1918. He also draws information from a review by N. Malkov, 'Solovei Igoria Stravinskogo', *Teatr i iskusstvo*, 20–21 (1918), pp. 213–14.

159. Balanchine quoted in Simon Volkov, *Balanchine's Tchaikovsky* (New York: Simon and

Schuster, 1985), pp. 165–6.

160. Kenneth Archer and Millicent Hodson, 'To Catch a Nightingale', *Dance Now*, 8/4 (Winter, 1999–2000), p. 10.

161. Reynolds, *Repertory in Review*, p. 300.

162. Ibid., p. 299.

Chapter 5

1. Boris Kochno, *Diaghilev and the Ballets Russes* (New York & Evanston: Harper & Row, 1970), p. 189.

2. Edwin Denby, 'Nijinska's *Noces*', *Modern Music* (May–June, 1936), in Denby, *Dance Writings*, ed. Robert Cornfield and William Mackay (London: Dance Books, 1986), p. 37.

3. Ibid.

4. Brendan McCarthy, 'Kirov Ballet: *Les Noces*', *ballet.magazine* (August, 2003), www.ballet.co.uk

5. Bronislava Nijinska, 'Creation of *Les Noces*', trans. and introduced by Jean M. Serafetinides and Irina Nijinska, *Dance Magazine*, 48 (December, 1974), p. 58. Written in Russian a few years after the 1966 revival for The Royal Ballet, an adapted French version of this article was published in Tatiana Loguine, ed. *Gontcharova et Larionov* (Paris: Editions Klincksieck, 1971). I have not yet been able to access the Russian original of this article.

6. Margarita Mazo, 'Stravinsky's *Les Noces* and Russian Village Wedding Ritual', *Journal of the American Musicological Society*, 43 (1990), pp. 99–142; *Igor Stravinsky: 'Les Noces' Study Score*, ed. Mazo (London: Chester Music, 2005).

7. Richard Taruskin, 'Stravinsky and the Subhuman: A Myth of the Twentieth Century: *The Rite of Spring*, the Tradition of the New, and "The Music Itself"', in Taruskin, *Defining Russia Musically: Historical and Hermeneutical Essays* (Princeton: Princeton University Press, 1997), p. 461; Taruskin, *Stravinsky and the Russian Traditions: A Biography of the Works Through 'Mavra'* (*SRT*; Oxford: Oxford University Press, 1996), p. 1419.

8. Taruskin, 'Stravinsky and the Subhuman', pp. 448 and 461.

9. Ibid., p. 391.

10. Sally Banes, *Dancing Women: Female Bodies on Stage* (London & New York: Routledge, 1998), pp. 120–21.

11. Lynn Garafola, *Diaghilev's Ballets Russes* (New York & Oxford: Oxford University Press, 1989), p. 128.

12. Nijinska, 'Creation of *Les Noces*', p. 59.

13. Nijinska quoted in John Martin, 'The Dance: Revival of Nijinska's *Les Noces*', *The New York Times*, May 3, 1936.

14. Programme information, confirmed in the record books of the Diaghilev Ballets Russes *régisseur* Sergey Grigoriev, Harvard Theatre Collection, Houghton Library, Harvard University (*HTC*).

15. Telegram from Nijinska to Stravinsky from the Teatro Colón, Buenos Aires, November 6, 1926, Paul Sacher Stiftung, Basle (*PSS*).

16. Dates in repertory have been taken from Robert M. J. Kimber, *Ballet Chronicles*, e-book, www.sylphide.demon.co.uk – I am very grateful to Kimber for assisting me in accessing his material.

17. *Les Noces* Benesh score, notated by Christopher Newton, Elizabeth Cunliffe and Harriet Castor (2001), housed in the Royal Ballet collection of Benesh scores, Royal Opera House, Covent Garden. The image-based titles of steps used in this analysis (which are titles developed by the Royal Ballet, not from Nijinska herself) are taken from this score and the accompanying piano rehearsal score.

18. The film by Edmée Wood is housed in the Royal Ballet Video Archive, Royal Opera House.

19. Andrea Grodsky Huber, 'A Conversation with Irina Nijinska', *Ballet Review*, 20/1 (1992), p. 43.

20. Ibid. *HTC* houses a photocopy example of Nijinska's notation of a short section from Tableau 1.

21. In more detail, sources for analysis of the Royal Ballet 'version' of *Les Noces* were: *Dance Month: Les Noces*, directed by Bob Lockyer, produced by John Selwyn Gilbert and Rodney Greenberg, BBC, May 13, 1978; *The Firebird and Les Noces: The Royal Ballet*, directed by Ross MacGibbon, produced by Bob Lockyer, BBC Opus Arte Productions, DVD, 2001. Sources for analysis of Irina Nijinska's 'version' of *Les Noces* were: *Les Noces*, Oakland Ballet, directed by Jerome Schnur, produced by Frederick J. Maroth, Educational Media Associates, 1981; *Les Noces*, Oakland Ballet, videotaped in rehearsal by Jay Millard, for the Dance Collection of The New York Public Library, 1990; *Paris Dances Diaghilev*, Paris Opéra Ballet, directed by Colin Nears, co-produced by NVC Arts and La Sept in association with the Arts and Entertainment Network, Elektra Nonesuch Dance

Collection, 1990.

All notated dance information has been taken from the Royal Ballet *Noces* production, unless otherwise indicated, using score as well as video sources. In music/dance examples, I have barred dance rhythm information according to my reading of the dance structure, which sometimes differs from the musical structure.

22. Arlene Croce, *The New Yorker*, July 17, 1989.

23. Bob Lockyer in interview with the author, January 13, 2004.

24. Garafola, *Diaghilev's Ballets Russes*, p. 126.

25. Nijinska, 'On Movement and the School of Movement', in Nancy Van Norman Baer, *Bronislava Nijinska: A Dancer's Legacy* (San Francisco: Fine Arts Museum of San Francisco, 1986), pp. 85–8; Nijinska, 'Reflections About the Production of *Les Biches* and *Hamlet* in Markova–Dolin Ballets', trans. Lydia Lopokova, *The Dancing Times*, 27 (February, 1937), pp. 617–18.

26. Ninette de Valois, 'Modern Choreography: II', *The Dancing Times*, 23 (February, 1933), p. 550; Drue Fergison also indicates that Nijinska's scores in the Nijinska Archive (now in the Library of Congress, Washington) contain the kind of detailed annotations that demonstrate sound musical knowledge: in Fergison, '*Les Noces*: A Microhistory of the Paris 1923 Production', unpublished PhD dissertation, Duke University, 1995, p. 49.

27. Nijinska, *Early Memoirs*, trans. and ed. Irina Nijinska and Jean Rawlinson (London & Boston: Faber and Faber, 1981), pp. 450–52, 457; Lynn Garafola, 'Forgotten Interlude: Eurhythmic Dancers at the Paris Opéra', *Dance Research*, 13/1 (Summer, 1995), p. 77.

28. Nijinska, 'Reflections...', p. 618.

29. Nijinska, 'Creation of *Les Noces*', p. 59.

30. Fergison, 'Bringing *Les Noces* to the Stage', in Lynn Garafola and Nancy Van Norman Baer, eds, *The Ballets Russes and Its World* (New Haven & London: Yale University Press, 1999), p. 172 and p. 371, note 10; Fergison, '*Les Noces*: A Microhistory of the Paris 1923 Production', p. 84. This indication of 1922 rehearsals is at odds with Nijinska's recollections that no work on *Noces* was begun until spring, 1923, in Nijinska, 'Creation of *Les Noces*', p. 59.

31. Nijinska, 'Creation of *Les Noces*', p. 59.

32. Ibid.

33. Ibid.; see also Stephen Weinstock, 'Goncharova, Nijinska and Stravinsky: The Evolution of *Les Noces*', *Dance Magazine*, 55 (April, 1981), pp. 70–75.

34. Stravinsky and Robert Craft, *Expositions and Developments* (*Expo*; London: Faber and Faber, 1962), p. 118.

35. Cable from Stravinsky to Ernest Ansermet, April 18, 1922, in Claude Tappolet, ed., *Correspondance Ansermet–Stravinsky* (1914–67), II (Geneva: Georg, 1991), p. 8.

36. Noted in *The Times*, June 15, 1926 and *The Observer*, June 20, 1926; see Nesta Macdonald, *Diaghilev Observed by Critics in England and the United States 1911–1929* (New York: Dance Horizons, 1975), pp. 325, 328.

37. Edwin Denby, 'Nijinska's *Noces*', p. 38.

38. Nijinska, 'Creation of *Les Noces*', p. 61 (in the postscript).

39. Stravinsky, *An Autobiography* [1936] (*Aut*; London: Calder & Boyars, 1975), p. 106.

40. *Expo*, pp. 117–18.

41. Lawrence Sullivan, '*Les Noces*: the American Premiere', *Dance Research Journal*, 14/1&2 (1981–2), p. 7.

42. *Expo*, p. 116.

43. Handwritten document by Stravinsky, in Correspondence and Documents on *Les Noces* (1923), PSS.

44. Mazo, Preface to *Igor Stravinsky: 'Les Noces' Study Score*, p. xvii.

45. Ibid.

46. Pieter C. van den Toorn, *The Music of Igor Stravinsky* (New Haven: Yale University Press, 1983), p. 177.

47. Ibid.; Gretchen Horlacher, 'Metric Irregularity in *Les Noces*: The Problem of Periodicity', *Journal of Music Theory*, 39/2 (Fall, 1995), pp. 285–309. See also van den Toorn, *Stravinsky and 'The Rite of Spring': The Beginnings of a Musical Language* (University of California Press: Berkeley & Los Angeles, 1987), pp. 67, 71–9; van den Toorn, 'Stravinsky, *Les Noces* (*Svadebka*), and the Prohibition Against Expressive Timing', *The Journal of Musicology*, 20/2 (2003), pp. 285–304. The concept of conservative and radical readings stems from Andrew Imbrie, 'Extra Measures and Metrical Ambiguity in Beethoven', in Alan Tyson, ed., *Beethoven Studies* (New York: Norton, 1973), pp. 45–66.

48. Jeanne Jaubert, 'Some Ideas about Meter in the Fourth Tableau of Stravinsky's *Les Noces*, or Stravinsky, Nijinska, and Particle Physics', *The Musical Quarterly*, 83/2 (Summer, 1999), pp. 205–26.

49. *Expo*, p. 121.

50. Arthur Comegno, 'Introduction', in Roberta Reeder and Comegno, 'Stravinsky's *Les Noces*', *Dance Research Journal*, 18/2 (Winter, 1986–7), pp. 33–4.

51. Mazo, Preface, p. ix.

52. Mazo, Preface, pp. ix–x.

53. *Expo*, p. 115.

54. Ibid.

55. Ibid; see also Mazo, 'Stravinsky's *Les Noces* and Russian Village Wedding Ritual', pp. 120–21.

56. Taruskin assumes from literary sources that the two mothers are meant thus to be associated with the voices, but they share the opening material, hence the distinction is blurred, *SRT*, pp. 1431–2.

57. The alternative English translations from the Russian that I have used for my analysis are by Reeder and Comegno, in 'Stravinsky's *Les Noces*', pp. 38–53.

58. *SRT*, p. 1433.

59. The official English translation is copyright Chester Music.

60. *SRT*, p. 1348.

61. Ibid., pp. 1423–40.

62. Ibid., p. 1352.

63. Nijinska, 'Creation of *Les Noces*', p. 61.

64. The issue of independent beat is avoided in the translation drawn from the French adaptation of Nijinska's article: 'By uniting several musical bars into a single one, I made a choreographic bar which, if it did not always match the original exactly, submitted always to the sonorities of the music': in Nijinska, 'The Creation of *Les Noces*', trans. into English from the French version of Nijinska's article in *Gontcharova et Larionov*, ed. Tatiana Loguine, in Clement Crisp and Mary Clarke, *Making a Ballet* (New York: Macmillan, 1974), p. 132.

65. Stravinsky's letter to Nijinska, March 27, 1923 is translated and analysed in Fergison, '*Les Noces*', pp. 47–9; from the Nijinska Archive, Library of Congress.

66. Nijinska, 'Creation of *Les Noces*', p. 59.

67. Fergison, '*Les Noces*', pp. 53–4; she quotes Serge Lifar's account of the use of the pianola in *Noces*, in *Ma Vie: From Kiev to Kiev*, trans. James Holman Mason (London: Hutchinson, 1965), p. 30. Alicia Markova remembered that a pianola was also used in rehearsals of *Le Chant du rossignol* (Balanchine, 1925): see Charles M. Joseph, 'Diaghilev and Stravinsky', in Garafola and Van Norman Baer, eds, *The Ballets Russes and Its World*, p. 206. Joseph references the Markova interview that was an out-take from Tony Palmer's documentary *Once at a Border...*, London Weekend Television, 1982.

68. Felia Doubrovska (the original Bride) and Alicia Markova quoted in Walter Terry, 'The Dancer's Composer', *Saturday Review*, May 29, 1971, p. 42; Serge Lifar, *Serge Diaghilev: His Life, His Work, His Legend: An Intimate Biography* (London: Putnam, 1940), p. 355; S. L. Grigoriev, *The Diaghilev Ballet, 1909–1929*, trans. and ed. Vera Bowen (London: Constable, 1953), p. 185.

69. Doubrovska quoted in Terry, 'The Dancer's Composer', p. 42, also in conversation with Robbins, who confirmed her point in a letter to Stravinsky, November 11, 1953, The Jerome Robbins Papers, housed in the Jerome Robbins Dance Division of the New York Public Library for the Performing Arts (*NYPL*); Millicent Hodson reporting from a meeting with Irina Nijinska and quoted in Brendan McCarthy, '*Les Noces* Then and Now'; Alexandra Danilova, *Choura: The Memoirs of Alexandra Danilova* (London: Dance Books, 1987), p. 76.

70. Markova quoted in Walter Terry, 'The Dancer's Composer', p. 42.

71. Sono Osato, *Distant Dances* (New York: Alfred A. Knopf, 1980), p. 99.

72. Geraldine Morris in interview with the author, June 19, 2006.

73. Henry Malherbe, 'Chronique Musicale: A la Gaîté-Lyrique', *Le Temps*, June 20, 1923, trans. Fergison, '*Les Noces*', p. 432. After seeing a performance of *Noces* in London in 1972, Craft claimed in his memoirs that Nijinska had changed her choreography (the mothers' lament and the ending): *An Improbable Life* (Nashville: Vanderbilt University Press, 2002), p. 308. However, although he might well have suspected this after an examination of the score, Craft does not provide evidence that the original production was as written in the score.

74. Denby, 'Nijinska's *Noces*', p. 37.

75. David Drew, 'Nijinska's World', on the DVD *The Firebird and Les Noces: The Royal Ballet*.

76. Mazo, Preface to *Igor Stravinsky: 'Les Noces' Study Score*, p. xvi.

77. *SRT*, p. 1350.

78. Denby, 'Nijinska's *Noces*', p. 37.

79. Mazo, Preface, p. xvii.

80. Christopher Newton outlined the modular structure of this passage in a lecture-demonstration on *Noces* with dancers from The Royal Ballet, at *Sound Moves: An International Conference on*

Music and Dance, Roehampton University, November 6, 2005.

81. Newton in interview with the author, August 17, 2006. I am indebted to Newton for clarifying a number of points about process and movement detail that are referred to during my analysis.

82. Irina Nijinska explains that arms stretched towards the head symbolise the sun's rays, the sun symbolising new life after the long Russian winter: Huber, 'A Conversation with Irina Nijinska', p. 58.

83. Newton, lecture-demonstration, *Sound Moves*.

84. Stravinsky puts most accents on the after-beat, perhaps to engender extra tension in the performer.

85. Pieter C. van den Toorn, *The Music of Igor Stravinsky*, p. 143.

86. Jaubert, 'Some Ideas about Meter in the Fourth Tableau of Stravinsky's *Les Noces...*', pp. 219–22.

87. *SRT*, p. 1353.

88. Jaubert, 'Some Ideas about Meter...', pp. 209–10.

89. Questions have already been raised about the musicality of the 1990 revival by Irina Nijinska and Nina Youskevitch of the Bride's solo from Bronislava Nijinska's *Le Baiser de la fée* (see p. 296).

90. Clement Crisp, 'Diaghilev Triple Bill/Kirov Ballet', *The Financial Times*, July 30, 2003.

91. Sources include the full press previews and reviews for the Paris premiere compiled (with translations) by Fergison, '*Les Noces*', pp. 355–469; a summary of the London coverage in Nesta Macdonald, *Diaghilev Observed by Critics in England and the United States 1911–1929*, pp. 322–9.

92. Fergison, 'Bringing *Les Noces* to the Stage', p. 185.

93. Emile Vuillermoz, 'Premières. Ballets Russes: *Noces*, d'Igor Strawinsky', *Excelsior* (June 18, 1923), trans. Fergison, '*Les Noces*', pp. 413–14.

94. C.F. Ramuz, 'Souvenir of Switzerland – 1917' [1946, trans. Dollie Pierre Chareau], in Minna Lederman, ed., *Stravinsky in the Theatre* [1949] (New York: Da Capo Press, 1975), pp. 33, 37.

95. Boris Asafyev, *A Book About Stravinsky* [1929], trans. Richard French (Ann Arbor: UMI Research Press, 1982), pp. 130, 153.

96. André Levinson, 'Ballets Russes: *Les Noces*', unidentified Russian émigré newspaper and date, trans. Penka Kouneva, in Fergison, '*Les Noces*', p. 453, held in the Nijinska Archive, Library of Congress.

97. Levinson, 'Stravinsky and the Dance' [1924], in *André Levinson on Dance: Writings from Paris in the Twenties*, ed. Joan Acocella and Lynn Garafola (Hanover & London: Wesleyan University Press, 1991), p. 41.

98. Levinson, 'Ballets Russes: *Les Noces*', p. 454.

99. Ibid., p. 455.

100. Levinson, 'Stravinsky and the Dance', p. 41. For the link between Nijinska's Kiev school and Dalcroze eurhythmics, see Lynn Garafola, 'Forgotten Interlude: Eurhythmic Dancers at the Paris Opéra', p. 77.

101. Levinson, 'Ballets Russes: *Les Noces*', p. 455.

102. Levinson, 'Les Ballets Russes à la Gaîté-Lyrique. *Noces*. Ballet de M. Igor Stravinski', *Comoedia*, June 16, 1923, trans. Fergison, '*Les Noces*', p. 390.

103. Boris de Schloezer, 'On the Occasion of *Les Noces*: A New Form of Synthetic Art', *Zveno*, 24, undated, trans. Penka Kouneva, in Fergison, '*Les Noces*', pp. 451–2.

104. De Schloezer, 'La Saison musicale', *La Nouvelle revue française*, August 1, 1923, p. 247 (author's translation).

105. Michel Georges-Michel, 'Les Ballets Russes à la Comédie-Française', *L'Eclair*, June 16, 1923 (author's translation, with the assistance of Pat Corcoran). Mazo confirms that the private hearing took place in 1919 at Georges-Michel's apartment, Preface to *Igor Stravinsky: 'Les Noces' Study Score*, p. xv, note 45.

106. Maria Ratanova, Introduction to the Russian edition of Nijinska's memoirs, sent to the author in English translation: 'Bronislava Nijinskaya: v teni legendy o brate', in Bronislava Nijinskaya, *Rannije vospominaniia*, I (Moscow: Artist. Rezhissior. Teatr (A.R.T.), 1999), pp. 5–61.

107. Nijinska quoted in *Nijinska, A Legend in Dance*, directed and produced by Linda Schaller, KQED/San Francisco, 1989. The spiritual and mystical content of *Noces* was confirmed by Irina Nijinska, in Huber, 'A Conversation with Irina Nijinska', p. 59.

108. Stephen Walsh, *Igor Stravinsky: A Creative Spring* (*ISCS*; London: Jonathan Cape, 2000), p. 366.

109. Taruskin, 'Stravinsky and the Subhuman', p. 461.

110. Daniel Albright, *Stravinsky: The Music Box and the Nightingale* (New York: Gordon & Breach, 1989), p. 27.

111. Vuillermoz, 'Chroniques et notes: la musique en France et à l'étranger: *Noces* – Igor

Strawinski', *Revue musicale* (August, 1923), p. 71 (author's translation).

112. For an analysis of this staging, which was used as the basis of my description, see Sullivan, 'Les Noces: The American premiere', pp. 3–14.

113. Ibid., p. 8; from Jean Palmer Sudeykina, in interview with Sullivan, June 5, 1981.

114. Olin Downes, 'Composers League in Unique Programme', *The New York Times*, April 26, 1929.

115. John Martin, 'The Dance: Stravinsky', *The New York Times*, April 21, 1929.

116. Emile Vuillermoz, extract from review in *Excelsior* quoted in 'Le Retentissement à l'étranger: Ce qu'écrit la presse étrangère', *Les Beaux Arts*, 6/209 (June 12, 1936), p. 22 (author's translation). See also, in the same journal issue, an extract from the review in *Vendredi* by de Schloezer, p. 24, and Gille Anthelme, 'Les Ballets de M. Katchourowsky', p. 16.

117. Letters to Stravinsky from the Stadttheater, Zurich: from Zimmermann, Artistic Director, June 12, 1948, and Victor Reinshagen, Kapellmeister, June 20, 1948, Correspondence and Documents on *Noces*, *PSS*.

118. Minna Lederman, ed., *Stravinsky in the Theatre*, photograph, p. 109.

119. Julia Wehren, 'Rhythmisch, exotisch, romantisch', February 14, 2006, www.dansesuisse.ch/news – see also *Aut*, p. 72.

120. Jiří Kylián, *Svadebka* (*Les Noces*), directed by Hans Hulscher, NOS TV & RM Arts, 1984.

121. Leonid Massine, *Les Noces*, silent film of rehearsal, La Scala, Milan, 1966, *NYPL*.

122. Lar Lubovitch Dance Company, programme note, 2001.

123. William Glackin, 'Sacramento Ballet', *Dance Magazine*, 72 (June, 1998), pp. 78–9.

124. Clive Barnes, 'Clive Barnes at the Paris Opéra: Les Noces', *Dance and Dancers* (July, 1965), pp. 20–21.

125. Igor Stupnikov, 'Letter from St. Petersburg', *The Dancing Times*, 87 (September, 1997), p. 1099.

126. David Vaughan (chronicle and commentary), and Melissa Harris, ed., *Merce Cunningham: Fifty Years* (New York: Aperture, 1997), pp. 64–5. A programme for this performance is housed in the *HTC*.

127. *Reinhild Hoffmann*, directed by Barbara Schlicht and Axel Bornkessel, produced by TBF-Bonn for Inter Nationes, 1982, *NYPL*.

128. Gay Morris, 'Two Programmes in Paris', *The Dancing Times*, 83 (August, 1993), p. 1070; Anna Kisselgoff, 'Review/Dance; A French Company's Version of *Noces*', *The New York Times*, June 22, 1991; Kisselgoff, 'Dance Review: An Erotic Dream for Seamier Times', *The New York Times*, July 3, 1995.

129. Compagnia Aterballetto, programme note, 2005.

130. Marie Claude Pietragalla, programme note, www.singaporedancetheatre.com, 2005.

131. Elizabeth Old, 'An Unlikely Two and a Stravinsky Trio', *Dance Europe* (November, 2000), p. 54.

132. Keiko Yagami, *Les Noces*, video, February 4, 1995, *NYPL*.

133. Javier De Frutos, *All Visitors Bring Happiness, Some by Coming Some by Going*, Ricochet Dance Company, DVD, 1997. In 2007, De Frutos used the *Noces* score again, in *Los Picadores*, Phoenix Dance Theatre (a setting for six dancers).

134. *Oskar Schlemmer: Les Noces* [exhibition catalogue] (Lugano: Fabbri Editori, 1988), p. 105.

135. *Prague Chamber Ballet*, choreography by Pavel Smok, including *Les Noces*, directed by Sergio Genni, produced by Carlos Piccardi, Radiotelevisione della Svizzera Italiana, c. 1980–82.

136. Garafola, 'Diaghilev in Perm', *The Nation*, November 24, 2003, p. 30.

137. *Les Noces*, Pokrovsky Ensemble, Elektra Nonesuch, 1994.

138. Liner notes for the Pokrovsky Ensemble recording. During performances 1994–6, the Ensemble incorporated a folk-style dance component within their *Noces* performances: Maria Nefedova of the Ensemble in interview with the author, March 25, 2007.

139. Taruskin, 'Stravinsky and the Subhuman', p. 463.

140. Fergison, 'Bringing *Les Noces* to the Stage', pp. 168–9.

141. My sources for analysis of Jerome Robbins's *Noces* were: American Ballet Theatre rehearsal film (silent, in rehearsal), Kroll Productions, 1967, *NYPL*; New York City Ballet performance (in wide and close shot), May 20, 1998, *NYPL*; Labanotation score notated by Muriel Topaz and Lucy Venable (1966–78), Dance Notation Bureau, New York, as taught by James Moore to American Ballet Theatre in 1966 and 1969 under the personal supervision of Robbins; Moore's scores of dance counts, Jerome Robbins Papers, *NYPL*. I also saw a performance of the work during the 1999 New York City Ballet Stravinsky Festival. My sources for analysis of Anne Teresa De Keersmaeker's *Noces* were: Rosas company DVD of performance, February 11, 2003, and two live performances in Ghent, Belgium (2003).

142. Deborah Jowitt, *Jerome Robbins: His Life, His Theater, His Dance* (New York: Simon & Schuster, 2004), pp. 360–63.

143. Sean Kenny later designed the *Noces* production for the Royal Swedish Ballet (1969).

144. Jowitt, *Jerome Robbins*, p. 362.

145. Draft of a letter from Robbins to Richard Buckle, n.d., quoted in Jowitt, *Jerome Robbins*, p. 362. Jowitt suggests that the draft may have been written late October, 1959, p. 566, note to p. 362.

146. Letters from Robbins to Stravinsky, October 27 and November 11, 1953, Jerome Robbins Papers, *NYPL*.

147. Victor Beliaev [Belyayev], *Igor Stravinsky's 'Les Noces': An Outline*, trans. S.W. Pring (London: Oxford University Press, 1928), pp. 4–5.

148. Jowitt, *Jerome Robbins*, pp. 12, 59; Stephanie Jordan, *Moving Music: Dialogues with Music in Twentieth-Century Ballet* (London: Dance Books, 2000), pp. 89–91.

149. Robbins quoted in Jennifer Dunning, 'A Rarely Seen Romp through a Stravinsky Classic', *The New York Times*, May 17, 1998.

150. Vuillermoz, 'Chroniques et notes: la musique en France et à l'étranger: Les Théâtres Lyriques: *Noces*: Igor Strawinski', pp. 68–72.

151. Robbins, typescript article on *Noces*, March 19, 1965, Jerome Robbins Papers, *NYPL*. The edited version of the article appeared as 'Robbins on *Les Noces*', *The New York Times*, March 28, 1965.

152. Jowitt, 'Back, again, to ballet', *The New York Times Magazine*, December 8, 1974, p. 100.

153. Doris Hering, 'The Human Element', *Dance Magazine*, 39 (May, 1965), p. 42.

154. For the 1969 Swedish revival, the musicians were out of sight in the pit: John Percival, 'Stockholm: The Royal Swedish Ballet at the Royal Opera House, Stockholm', *Dance and Dancers* (September, 1970), p. 47.

155. Craft, ed., *Dearest Bubushkin: The Correspondence of Vera and Igor Stravinsky, 1921–1954, with Excerpts from Vera Stravinsky's Diaries, 1922–1971*, trans. Lucia Davidova (*DB*; London: Thames and Hudson, 1985), p. 216.

156. Craft, *An Improbable Life*, p. 282.

157. Lillian Libman, *And Music at the Close: Stravinsky's Last Years* (London & Basingstoke: Macmillan, 1972), p. 306.

158. Clive Barnes, 'Dance: Nijinska's *Les Noces* Returns', *The New York Times*, May 7, 1967.

159. Walter Sorell, *Journal-Bulletin*, undated and without further reference information, in Royal Ballet clippings file, *NYPL*.

160. Dunning, 'A Rarely Seen Romp through a Stravinsky Classic'.

161. Robbins, handwritten notes after seeing Nijinska's *Noces*, Jerome Robbins Papers, *NYPL*.

162. See, for instance, Lynn Garafola, 'New York City Ballet: New York State Theater: *Les Noces*', *Dance Magazine*, 72 (September, 1998), p. 108.

163. Letter from Robbins to Robert Graves, April 25, 1967, quoted in Jowitt, *Jerome Robbins*, p. 366.

164. Jowitt, *Jerome Robbins*, p. 512.

165. Garafola, 'New York City Ballet', p. 108.

166. Anna Kisselgoff, '*Les Noces* with a Muted Stravinsky', *The New York Times*, May 22, 1998.

167. Georges-Elie Octors in interview with the author, February 12, 2003, and Anne Teresa De Keersmaeker, email communication, August 14, 2006. All information on working process is taken from these sources, unless otherwise stated.

168. Claire Diez, article on *(but if a look should) April me* for Rosas website, www.rosas.be/Rosas/april.html

169. De Keersmaeker quoted in *Dance Notes*, directed by Michel Follin, produced by Pierre-Olivier Bardet and Jacques-Henri Bronckart, Idéale Audience and Versus Production in co-production with ARTE France and RTBF, 2002. De Keersmaeker has also used Stravinsky's *Symphonies of Wind Instruments* and *Fireworks* in *D'un soir un jour* (2006): see p. 157.

170. Raf Geenens, article on *(but if a look should) April me* from the *Monnaie Magazine* for Rosas website, www.rosas.be/Rosas/april.asp

171. De Keersmaeker quoted in Diez, see note 168.

172. Horlacher, 'Metric Irregularity in *Les Noces*', p. 299.

Chapter 6

1. *Riot at The Rite*, written by Kevin Elyot, directed by Andy Wilson, BBC2, March 11, 2006.

2. Bronislava Nijinska suggests that, even before Nijinsky's marriage, Diaghilev had doubts that he could afford to risk Nijinsky's avant-garde choreography any more: Nijinska, *Early Memoirs*, trans. and ed. Irina Nijinska and Jean Rawlinson (London & Boston: Faber and Faber, 1981), p. 473.

3. Stephen Walsh, [Review of Jonathan Cross, *The Stravinsky Legacy*], *Music Analysis*, 19/2 (2000), p. 282.

4. François Lesure mentions the 'scandal' in Vienna (1925) and that some members of the audience left the concert hall in Philadelphia (1928): Lesure, ed., *Igor Stravinsky, 'Le Sacre du printemps': Dossier de Presse* (Geneva: Edition Minkoff, 1980), p. 7.

5. Joan Evans, 'Stravinsky's Music in Hitler's Germany', *Journal of the American Musicological Society*, 56/3 (2003), pp. 535, 540–41; see also Evans, '"Diabolus triumphans": Stravinsky's *Histoire du soldat* in Weimar and Nazi Germany', in John Daverio and John Ogasapian, eds, *Varieties of Musicology: Essays for Murray Lefkowitz* (Warren, Mich.: Harmonie Park Press, 1999), pp. 175–85.

6. Charles M. Joseph, quoting from *Time Magazine* in *Stravinsky Inside Out* (New Haven & London: Yale University Press, 2001), p. 15.

7. Joan Acocella, Lynn Garafola and Jonnie Greene, 'The Rite of Spring Considered as a Nineteenth-Century Ballet' and 'Catalogue Raisonné', *Ballet Review*, 20/2 (Summer, 1992), pp. 68–100.

8. Ada d'Adamo, *Danzare il Rito: 'Le Sacre du Printemps' attraverso il Novecento* (Rome: Bulzoni Editore, 1999).

9. Shelley Berg, *'Le Sacre du printemps': Seven Productions from Nijinsky to Martha Graham* (Ann Arbor: UMI Research Press), 1988.

10. Susan Manning, 'German *Rites*: A History of *Le Sacre du printemps* on the German Stage', *Dance Chronicle*, 14/2 (1991), pp. 129–58; 'German *Rites* Revisited: An Addendum to a History of *Le Sacre du printemps* on the German Stage', *Dance Chronicle*, 16/1 (1993), pp. 115–20.

11. Acocella et al., *'The Rite of Spring* Considered as a Nineteenth-Century Ballet', p. 71.

12. Ibid., p. 68.

13. Richard Buckle, *Nijinsky* (New York: Simon and Schuster, 1971); Lincoln Kirstein, *Nijinsky Dancing* (New York: Alfred A. Knopf, 1975).

14. Website for Springdance Festival, advertising a series of solos at the Akademietheater, Amsterdam, April 25, 1999.

15. T.S. Eliot quoted in Lyndall Gordon, *Eliot's Early Years* (Oxford: Oxford University Press, 1977), p. 108.

16. Acocella et al., *'The Rite of Spring* Considered as a Nineteenth-Century Ballet', pp. 68–71.

17. Richard Taruskin, 'Stravinsky and the Subhuman: A Myth of the Twentieth Century: *The Rite of Spring*, the Tradition of the New, and "The Music Itself"', in Taruskin, *Defining Russia Musically: Historical and Hermeneutical Essays* (Princeton: Princeton University Press, 1997), p. 386; translated from André Levinson, 'Russkiy balet v Parizhe', *Rech'*, June 3, 1913.

18. Jacques Rivière, *'Le Sacre du printemps'*, *Nouvelle revue française*, November, 1913, in Lesure, ed., *Igor Stravinsky, 'Le Sacre du printemps': Dossier de Presse*, pp. 47–8 (author's translation).

19. Modris Eksteins, *Rites of Spring: The Great War and the Birth of the Modern Age* (Boston & New York: Houghton Mifflin, 1989), p. xvi.

20. Régis Obadia quoted in Rosita Boisseau, 'Les Chorégraphes multiplient les *Sacre du printemps*', *Le Monde*, February 6, 2005.

21. 'The Search for Nijinsky's *Rite of Spring*', directed and produced by Thomas Grimm and Judy Kinberg, WNET/New York and Danmarks Radio, 1989.

22. The nine other companies that have performed the *Sacre* reconstruction are: Paris Opéra Ballet (1991), Finnish National Ballet (1994), Companhia Nacional de Bailado, Lisbon (1994), Zurich Ballet (1995), Ballet of the Teatro Municipal, Rio de Janeiro (1996), Rome Opera Ballet (2001), Kirov Ballet, St Petersburg (2003), Birmingham Royal Ballet (2005), Hyogo Performing Arts Centre Ballet, Japan (2005). I am grateful to Millicent Hodson for providing this information.

23. Francis Sparshott, 'The Big Questions' panel, chaired by Sally Banes at 'The Rite of Spring at Seventy-Five', Dance Critics Association and Dance Collection Conference, New York Public Library for the Performing Arts, Lincoln Center, 1987.

24. Molissa Fenley quoted in John Gruen, 'Molissa Fenley: A Separate Voice', *Dance Magazine*, 61 (May, 1991), p. 41.

25. *Les Printemps du Sacre*, conception and direction, Jacques Malaterre and Brigitte Hernandez, produced by Josette Affergan, Telmondis, La Sept-Arte (Paris), 1993.

26. Michel Georges-Michel, 'Les deux *Sacres du printemps*', *Comoedia*, December 11, 1920, in Lesure, ed., *Igor Stravinsky, 'Le Sacre du printemps': Dossier de Presse*, p. 53.

27. Igor Stravinsky and Robert Craft, *Expositions and Developments* (*Expo*; London: Faber and Faber, 1962), p. 144. Yet Stravinsky showed interest in the possibility of a *Sacre* production with Balanchine (see pp. 167-8) and was certainly interested in the prospect of a Robbins setting before turning down the request to use a reduced orchestration (see p. 75).

28. Richard Taruskin, *Stravinsky and the Russian Traditions: A Biography of the Works Through*

'Mavra' (SRT; Oxford: Oxford University Press, 1996), p. 1515.

29. Stravinsky, An Autobiography [1936] (Aut; London: Calder & Boyars, 1975), p. 53.

30. Taruskin, 'Stravinsky and the Subhuman', p. 379.

31. Allen Forte, The Harmonic Organization of 'The Rite of Spring' (New Haven: Yale University Press, 1978).

32. Pieter C. van den Toorn, Stravinsky and 'The Rite of Spring': The Beginnings of a Musical Language (Berkeley & Los Angeles: University of California Press, 1987), pp. 97–101; van den Toorn, The Music of Igor Stravinsky (New Haven: Yale University Press, 1983), pp. 137–43, 204–51.

33. SRT, pp. 951–6, 1449–62.

34. Pierre Boulez, 'Stravinsky Remains' [analysis of The Rite of Spring, 1953, revised 1966], in Boulez, Stocktakings from an Apprenticeship, trans. Stephen Walsh (Oxford: Clarendon Press, 1991), pp. 55–110.

35. Stephanie Jordan, Moving Music: Dialogues with Music in Twentieth-Century Ballet (London: Dance Books, 2000), p. 79.

36. In SRT, Taruskin estimated van den Toorn's discussion of Stravinsky's metrics as the most thorough to date, p. 961.

37. Van den Toorn, Stravinsky and 'The Rite of Spring', pp. 66–7, 113. His view is that it is only through a 'conservative' reading, invoking our tendency to seek out and then hold on to established metre for as long as possible, that insight can be gained into the nature of Stravinsky's disruptions. As regards reading metre, the terms 'radical' and 'conservative' were introduced by Andrew Imbrie, 'Extra Measures and Metrical Ambiguity in Beethoven', in Alan Tyson, ed., Beethoven Studies (New York: Norton, 1973), pp. 45–66. See also Eliot Ghofur Woodruff, 'Metrical Phase Shifts in Stravinsky's The Rite of Spring', Music Theory Online, 12/1 (February, 2006); Chapter 5, p. 9.

38. Peter Hill, Stravinsky: 'The Rite of Spring' (Cambridge: Cambridge University Press, 2000).

39. Walsh, [Review of Peter Hill, Stravinsky: 'The Rite of Spring'], Music & Letters, 83/1 (2002), p. 143.

40. Stravinsky, The Rite of Spring: Sketches 1911–1913 (London: Boosey & Hawkes, 1969), Appendix III, pp. 35–43.

41. An article by Craft on the piano score provided a noteworthy beginning to the analytical process: 'The Rite: Counterpoint and Choreography', The Musical Times (April, 1988), pp. 171–6. See also Jörg Rothkamm, 'Choreomusikalisch konzipiert? Neues zur Beziehung von Musik und Choreographie in Stravinskys/Nijinskys Le Sacre du Printemps', in Silke Leopold and Dorothea Redepenning, eds, Kongressbericht zur Jahrestagung der Gesellschaft für Musikwissenschaft, Theater um Mozart, Heidelberg University, October 4–7, 2006 (proceedings forthcoming). Both these sources include examples from the Basle piano score in facsimile. A number of these examples are included in transcribed form within my own chapter.

42. Stravinsky, The Rite of Spring: Sketches 1911–1913, p. 35; Vera Stravinsky and Craft, Stravinsky in Pictures and Documents (SPD; New York: Simon & Schuster, 1978), pp. 515, 656.

43. Marie Rambert, Quicksilver: An Autobiography (London: Macmillan, 1972), p. 59.

44. Irina Vershinina, Ranniye baletï Stravinskogo (Moscow: Nauka, 1967), p. 140, Stravinsky's annotation on the copy housed in the PSS.

45. Rambert, Quicksilver, pp. 58–9; Nijinska, Early Memoirs, p. 458.

46. Nijinska, Early Memoirs, pp. 122, 444.

47. Letter from Stravinsky to Maximilien Steinberg, July 3, 1913, translated in SPD, p. 102.

48. Stravinsky quoted in Henri Postel du Mas, 'Un Entretien avec M. Stravinsky', Gil Blas, June 4, 1913 (author's translation).

49. Letter from Stravinsky to Benois, October 3, 1913, translated in ISCS, p. 219.

50. Michel Georges-Michel, 'Ballets Russes...les deux Sacre du Printemps', Comoedia, December 14, 1920, in Lesure, ed., Igor Stravinsky, 'Le Sacre du printemps': Dossier de Presse, p. 53 (author's translation).

51. Aut, pp. 40, 48.

52. Maria Piltz corroborated the contents of Nijinska's letter in conversation with Krassovskaya: Millicent Hodson, 'Sacre: Searching for Nijinsky's Chosen One', Ballet Review, 15/3 (Fall, 1987), p. 63.

53. Millicent Hodson, 'Puzzles chorégraphiques: reconstitution du Sacre de Nijinsky', in 'Le Sacre du printemps' de Nijinsky (Paris: Editions Cicero et Théâtre des Champs-Elysées, 1990), p. 47.

54. Millicent Hodson, Nijinsky's Crime Against Grace: Reconstruction Score of the Original Choreography for 'Le Sacre du Printemps' (Stuyvesant, New York: Pendragon Press, 1996), p. xxi. See also Hodson, 'Sacre: Searching for Nijinsky's Chosen One', (p. 59), where she indicates that 'I may add movements for the extra accents.'

55. My sources on Hodson's working processes are the reconstruction score and 'Puzzles

chorégraphiques', also a video recording of Hodson's lecture-demonstration at the *Preservation Politics* conference, University of Surrey, Roehampton, November 8–9, 1997. I am also grateful to Hodson for her interview with me, March 31, 1995.

56. Hodson and Kenneth Archer follow the suggestion originally made by Robert Joffrey who commissioned their reconstruction: Archer and Hodson, 'Confronting Oblivion: Keynote Address and Lecture Demonstration on Reconstructing Ballets', in Stephanie Jordan, ed., *Preservation Politics: Dance Revived Reconstructed Remade* (London: Dance Books, 2000), p. 2.

57. Joan Acocella, 'The Lost Nijinsky: Is It Possible to Reconstruct a Forgotten Ballet?' *The New Yorker*, May 7, 2001.

58. See notes 1 and 21. I have also seen live performances of the ballet by the Paris Opéra Ballet, Kirov Ballet and Birmingham Royal Ballet, and a Birmingham Royal Ballet company video.

59. Stravinsky, *The Rite of Spring: Sketches 1911–1913*, p. 36.

60. Boulez, 'Stravinsky Remains', p. 68.

61. Ibid., pp. 95–6.

62. Hodson, *Nijinsky's Crime Against Grace*, p. 168.

63. Boulez, 'Stravinsky Remains', pp. 94–103.

64. Hill, *Stravinsky: 'The Rite of Spring'*, pp. 87–8.

65. For an alternative view of the Sacrificial Dance as choreography and performance, see Tamara Levitz, 'The Chosen One's Choice', in Andrew Dell'Antonio, ed., *Beyond Structural Listening? Postmodern Modes of Hearing* (Berkeley, Los Angeles & London: University of California Press, 2004), pp. 70–108.

66. A few additional steps break up the long notes in Mystic Circles, but the general effect is of matching music and dance rhythm patterns.

67. Jacques Rivière, '*Le Sacre du printemps*', pp. 42–8.

68. 'Interview with Stravinsky', *The Observer*, July 3, 1921, in Lesure, ed. *Igor Stravinsky, 'Le Sacre du printemps': Dossier de Presse*, p. 77. See also Michel Georges-Michel, 'Ballets Russes...les deux *Sacre du Printemps*', p. 53.

69. Jean Cocteau, '*Le Sacre du printemps*', in Minna Lederman, ed., *Stravinsky in the Theatre* [1949] (New York: Da Capo Press, 1975), p. 18, trans. Louise Varèse from *Le Coq et L'Arlequin* (Paris: Editions de la Sirène, 1918).

70. André Levinson, *Ballet Old and New* [1918], trans. Susan Cook Summer (New York: Dance Horizons, 1982), p. 55.

71. Nijinska, *Early Memoirs*, p. 450.

72. W.A. Propert, *The Russian Ballet in Western Europe, 1909–1920* (London: Bodley Head, 1921), p. 79.

73. H.C. Colles, 'The Fusion of Music and Dancing: *Le Sacre du Printemps*', *The Times*, July 16, 1913, in Lesure, ed., *Igor Stravinsky, 'Le Sacre du printemps': Dossier de Presse*, p. 67. On the point of 'matching' orchestration, see also Cyril Beaumont, *Bookseller at the Ballet: Memoirs 1891 to 1929* (London: C.W. Beaumont, 1975), p. 137.

74. Emile Vuillermoz, 'La Saison russe au Théâtre des Champs-Elysées', *Revue musicale* S.I.M., June 15, 1913 (author's translation).

75. The feature of choral groups in counterpoint is also mentioned by Beaumont, *Bookseller at the Ballet*, p. 137.

76. I first discussed the piano score and its relation to the *Sacre* reconstruction in a seminar at the Paul Sacher Stiftung, Basle: 'Writings on Stravinsky's *Rite*: Choreographic Tales from a Rehearsal Score', December 11, 2001.

77. Stravinsky, *The Rite of Spring: Sketches 1911–1913*, pp. 35–6.

78. Correspondence between Stravinsky and Rufina Ampenoff at Boosey & Hawkes indicates that the score was to be sent airmail to Stravinsky (June 14, 1967) and the final draft of the annotations was received July 24, Paul Sacher Stiftung, Basle (*PSS*) B&H correspondence. The notes were translated into French and German, for foreign-language editions of the *Sacre* sketches. For a discussion of Stravinsky's state of health, see Stephen Walsh, *Igor Stravinsky: A Creative Spring* (*ISCS*; London: Jonathan Cape, 2000), pp. 531–2. For details of Craft's activity at this time, see Craft, ed., *Dearest Bubushkin: The Correspondence of Vera and Igor Stravinsky, 1921–1954, with Excerpts from Vera Stravinsky's Diaries, 1922–1971*, trans. Lucia Davidova (*DB*; London: Thames and Hudson, 1985), p. 223.

79. Stravinsky, *The Rite of Spring: Sketches 1911–1913*, p. 35.

80. I am indebted to Margarita Mazo, the distinguished *Noces* specialist who is well acquainted with Stravinsky's writing from this period, for sharing her view on the handwriting in this score.

81. Stravinsky, *The Rite of Spring: Sketches 1911–1913*, p. 35.

82. Hodson, *Nijinsky's Crime Against Grace*, pp. 173–4.

83. Hodson, 'Puzzles chorégraphiques', p. 67.

84. Stravinsky, *The Rite of Spring: Sketches 1911–1913*, p. 38.

85. Louis Cyr, '*Le Sacre du printemps': petite histoire d'une grande partition*, in François Lesure, ed., *Stravinsky: études et témoignages* (Paris: Jean-Claude Lattès, 1982), p. 114. Cyr took the date from the Editions Russes catalogue of this period, which gives exact dates of publication.

86. Nijinska, *Early Memoirs*, p. 449. The November 1912 date that Nijinska gives for the Sacrificial Dance choreography is under dispute. See Levitz, 'The Chosen One's Choice', p. 103, note 55. However, the differences of opinion do not alter my argument.

87. Telegram from Nijinsky to Stravinsky, March 23, 1913, *PSS* Nijinsky correspondence. I am grateful to Dorinda Offord and Maria Ratanova for helping me with the translation from the Russian. It seems highly unlikely that Stravinsky's 'directives' would have been transferred on to the piano score from some other earlier source, because of the effort involved and also because of the mixture of writing styles and confusions still evident in the piano score.

88. Stravinsky quoted in Michel Georges-Michel, 'Ballets Russes...les deux *Sacre du Printemps'*, p. 53 (author's translation).

89. Leonid Massine quoted in Barry Hyams, 'Dance: Another Spring for Stravinsky's Revolutionary Rite', *The Los Angeles Times*, May 29, 1977, p. 66.

90. Massine, *My Life in Ballet*, ed. Phyllis Hartnoll and Robert Rubens (London: Macmillan, 1968), p. 152.

91. *Aut*, p. 92.

92. Massine, 'On Choreography and a New School of Dancing', *Drama*, 1/3 (1919), p. 70.

93. Boris Kochno, *Diaghilev and the Ballets Russes*, trans. Adrienne Foulke (New York & Evanston: Harper & Row, 1970), p. 138.

94. André Levinson, 'Les deux *Sacres'*, June 5, 1922, in *La Danse au théâtre: esthétique et actualité melées* (Paris: Librairie Bloud & Gay, 1924), p. 57 (author's translation).

95. Serge L. Grigoriev, *The Diaghilev Ballet, 1909–1929* [1953] (London: Penguin, 1960), p. 71.

96. Massine, *Le Sacre du printemps*, video recording from silent rehearsal film, La Scala, Milan, 1948, housed in the Jerome Robbins Dance Division of the New York Public Library for the Performing Arts (*NYPL*). I saw live performances of the Ballet de L'Opéra National de Bordeaux production of Massine's *Sacre*, March 28 and 29, 2007. Ballet master Eric Quilleré and Chosen One Emmuelle Grizot offered valuable information about rhythmic structure in interview, March 29, 2007.

97. I am grateful to Susanna Della Pietra for providing me with the annotated copy of the Dance of the Earth and Sacrificial Dance from Massine's orchestral score (used for the 1973 revival).

98. Berg, '*Le Sacre du printemps'*, p. 81; Susanna Della Pietra informed me that Massine choreographed a new Dance of the Earth and made small changes in Spring Rounds for the 1973 revival: email communications, May 18 and June 8, 2006.

99. Lydia Sokolova, *Dancing for Diaghilev*, ed. Richard Buckle (San Francisco: Mercury House, 1960), p. 160.

100. Ibid., p. 43.

101. Nicholas Cook, *Analysing Multimedia* (Oxford: Oxford University Press, 1998), Chapter 5 [on the *Sacre* sequence in Disney's *Fantasia*, pp. 174–214]; Jann Pasler, 'The Choreography for *The Rite of Spring*: Stravinsky's Visualization of Music', *Dance Magazine*, 55 (April, 1981), pp. 66–9; Volker Scherliess, *Igor Stravinsky: Le Sacre du printemps, Meisterwerke der Musik*, 35 (Munich: Wilhelm Fink, 1982), pp. 30–31.

102. Jonathan Cott, 'Two Talks with George Balanchine' [1982], in *Portrait of Mr. B* (New York: Viking Press, 1984), p. 138.

103. Berg, '*Le Sacre du printemps'*, p. 89. Berg is used here as a seminal background source on the Béjart *Sacre*.

104. Richard Alston quoted in Jennifer Dunning, 'Britain's Oldest Ballet Troupe on Tour', *The New York Times*, October 10, 1982, p. 32.

105. Béjart quoted in Olga Maynard, 'Maurice Béjart: On the Creative Process', *Dance Magazine*, 47 (February, 1973), p. 58A. The choreographic information from Zverev (and from Marie Rambert) emerged in Béjart's *Nijinsky, Clown of God* (1972).

106. The film source for analysis of the Béjart work was *Le Sacre du printemps*, Ballet of the 20th Century, produced by Artium Summa, Brussels, 1970, *NYPL*.

107. Deborah Jowitt, 'The Hybrid: Very Showy, Will Root in Any Soil', *Dance Calendar*, May, 1975, in Jowitt, *Dance Beat: Selected Views and Reviews, 1967–1976* (New York & Basle: Marcel Dekker, 1977), pp. 64–6.

108. Berg, '*Le Sacre du printemps'*, p. 94; translated from Béjart, *Un Instant dans la vie d'autrui* (France: Flammarion, 1979), p. 134.

109. Radio interview with Béjart, WQXR, New York, March 22, 1977, *NYPL*.

110. Hill, *Stravinsky: 'The Rite of Spring'*, pp. 56, 81.

111. Ibid., p. 77.

112. Perhaps because of this, and because of the later, rapid succession of movement events, MacMillan opted to give the Chosen One a pause during the Sacrificial Dance.

113. The analytical source was a rehearsal of Graham's *Rite*, in *Martha Graham at Work, 1984–1987*, video, c. 1989, NYPL.

114. Programme note quoted in and translated by Susan Manning, 'German *Rites*: A History of *Le Sacre du printemps* on the German Stage' (1991), p. 146.

115. Norbert Servos, *Pina Bausch-Wuppertal Dance Theater, or, The Art of Training a Goldfish*, trans. Patricia Stadié (Cologne: Ballett-Bühnen Verlag, 1984), p. 31.

116. Mark Franko draws from the nineteenth-century associations between dance and hysteria in 'Bausch and the Symptom', in Gabriele Brandstetter and Gabriele Klein, eds, 'Methoden der Tanzwissenschaft: Modellanalysen zu Pina Bauschs *Sacre du Printemps*', *TanzScripte*, IV, 2007, pp. 253–64. This volume (accompanied by DVD examples) comprises papers given at the conference 'Movement in Transmission: Methods in Dance Research', Hamburg, January 27–8, 2006.

117. Gitta Barthel, speaking at the conference 'Movement in Transmission: Methods in Dance Research', January 28, 2006.

118. Barbara Newman, 'Pina Bausch in Frankfurt and Paris', *The Dancing Times*, 87 (September, 1997), p. 1070.

119. Ann Daly, 'Mellower Now, A Resolute Romantic Keeps Trying' [1999], in Daly, *Critical Gestures: Writings on Dance and Culture* (Middletown, Conn.: Wesleyan University Press, 2002), p. 31.

120. Even though Adorno was less regularly read in Germany in the decade that followed his death in 1969, he was still part of the intellectual environment, witness the important writings that emerged during the 1970s: Max Paddison, *Adorno's Aesthetics of Music* (Cambridge: Cambridge University Press, 1993), p. 11.

121. Bausch, *Das Frühlingsopfer*, directed by Pit Weyrich, ZDF, 1978. Apparently, Bausch was all set for an 'edited' production, but settled for the all-through rehearsal shoot, which was originally intended just to 'give us a sense of it before we have to chop it up in bits': Chris de Marigny and Barbara Newman, 'Progressive Programming' [interview with Michael Kustow], in Stephanie Jordan and Dave Allen, eds, *Parallel Lines: Media Representations of Dance* (London: John Libbey, 1993), p. 97.

122. Barbara Hampel and Ed Kortlandt in interview with the author, October 19, 2006. Hampel and Kortlandt, former members of Tanztheater Wuppertal and now rehearsal/teaching staff, provided most of my details about Bausch's working process.

123. Pierre Boulez, *Le Sacre du printemps*, The Cleveland Orchestra, CBS Records, 1969.

124. Gitta Barthel confirmed that Bausch's dance counts matched my own at this point, but also noted that in other parts of her *Sacre* there are no dance counts and that the instruction was then to move 'as fast as possible.' Barthel was speaking at the conference 'Movement in Transmission', January 27, 2006.

125. I use the label 'figure-of-eight' here, because the movement resembles the one with this name that is part of the codified Kurt Jooss technique/style in which Bausch trained. I am grateful to Ana Sanchez-Colberg for providing this information, email communication, May 8, 2006.

126. Hill, *Stravinsky: 'The Rite of Spring'*, p. 65.

127. Van den Toorn, *Stravinsky and 'The Rite of Spring'*, p. 69.

128. In terms of the balance between individualism and mass power, it is perhaps significant that the Bausch *Sacre* performance style was heavier, more grounded and less uniform in the 1970s and 1980s than it is today.

129. Hill, *Stravinsky: 'The Rite of Spring'*, p. 66.

130. Here again, the film cameraman makes a choice and cuts out the full rhythmic texture, some of the machine effect. The camera focuses on the 'free' individual outbursts, and we have to look behind the screening.

131. The issues of self-infliction and agency arose in response to my paper 'Stravinsky and the Choreomusical Gesture', presented at the conference 'Music and Gesture II', Royal Northern College of Music, Manchester, July 21, 2006.

132. Van den Toorn, *Stravinsky and 'The Rite of Spring'*, pp. 104–08.

133. Ibid., pp. 63–4.

134. Valérie Dufour, *Strawinsky à Bruxelles* (Brussels: Académie Royale de Belgique, 2003), p. 153; from Stravinsky quoted in Paul Collaer, 'Actuel: Paul Collaer à propos d'Igor Strawinsky', interview by Jean-Louis Jacques and Marcel Doisy, Archives R.T.B.F. broadcast, March 3, 1971.

135. The dancers ranged from Marlis Alt, the first Chosen One, and Malou Airaudo, both captured on film in the 1970s, to Beatrice Libonati, Jo Ann Endicott, Monika Sagon, Kyomi Ichida, then

to two current dancers in the role, Ruth Amarante and Ditta Jasifi. The rehearsal film was *Pina Bausch – Kyomi Ichida – Probe Sacre*, directed by Angelika Kaczmarek, produced by Herbert Rach, L'ARCHE Editeur, Paris, 1992. All these recordings are housed in the Tanztheater Wuppertal archive.

136. Interview with Barbara Hampel and Ed Kortlandt.

137. Béjart's dancers respond to the repeating high D pedal notes, from [181], a little earlier than Bausch's second response to the suggested 2/4 metre.

138. Hill, *Stravinsky: 'The Rite of Spring'*, p. 59.

139. Ibid., pp. 88–9; *SRT*, p. 965.

140. Marlis Alt in interview with the author, October 30, 2006.

141. Antoine Livio, 'Le 'Sacre' consacrant John Neumeier', *L'Avant-Scène: Ballet/danse*, 3 (August–October, 1980), p. 102; Manning, 'German *Rites*', pp. 144–5.

142. Manning, 'German *Rites*', p. 152.

143. Acocella et al., '*The Rite of Spring* Considered as a Nineteenth-Century Ballet', p. 76; Hans Ehrmann, 'Santiago', *Dance Magazine*, 72 (February, 1998), pp. 29, 84. This was a new version of Bunster's original setting, *Uka-Ara* (1964).

144. Berg, '*Le Sacre du printemps*', pp. 107–08.

145. Manning, *Ecstasy and the Demon: Feminism and Nationalism in the Dances of Mary Wigman* (Berkeley, Los Angeles & London: University of California Press, 1993), p. 236.

146. Manning, 'German *Rites*', pp. 133–5, 145, 151–2.

147. Larissa Barykina, 'The Unruly One: Panfilov's *Sacre* in St. Petersburg', *Ballett International/Tanz Aktuell* (December, 1997), p. 61.

148. The Mats Ek ballet is illustrated and discussed in the film *Les Printemps du Sacre*.

149. Judith Mackrell, 'The Rite Stuff', *The Guardian*, April 14, 2004. See also Josephine Leask, 'History–Identity–Sexuality', *Ballett International/Tanz Aktuell*, (January, 1995), p. 39; Ann Nugent, 'Opening Out the Umbrella', *Dance Now*, 3/4 (Winter, 1994), pp. 25–6.

150. Website publicity: www.michaelsakamoto.com/rite.html. See also Donna Perlmutter, 'Season for Breaking the Rules', *The Los Angeles Times*, March 18, 2004.

151. Katherine Keithley, 'What Grows in Spring's Green Grass', *Offoffoff Dance*, April 16, 2004, www.offoffoff.com/dance/2004/brooksmuz.php.

152. Programme for Joseph Marks's *The Rite of Spring*, NYPL.

153. John Percival, 'Plotless *Rite*', *Dance and Dancers* (August, 1974), pp. 26–9; the quotation used came from Michel Georges-Michel, 'Ballets Russes...les deux *Sacre du Printemps*', p. 53.

154. Joyce Trisler, *Le Sacre du printemps*, video of performance at Joyce Theater, New York, March 19, 1986, NYPL.

155. Shen Wei, *Rite of Spring* and *Folding*, DVD of performance at Lincoln Center Festival, produced by Shen Wei Dance Arts, July, 2003.

156. When Daniel Barenboim was conductor of the Berlin Philharmonic Orchestra, he had initiated a *Sacre* (2001) by Angelin Preljocaj.

157. 'Rhythm Is It!', documentary directed by Thomas Grube and Enrique Sanchez Lansch, produced by Boomtown Media, 2004; Grube and Lansch also undertook a film of the full choreography of *Sacre*, video housed in the archive of the Berlin Philharmonic Orchestra.

158. Sir Simon Rattle quoted in John Green, 'Rhythm Is It!', www.rhythmisit.com

159. Fenley quoted in Gruen, 'Molissa Fenley: A Separate Voice', p. 41. The work is recorded in *Splash Festival*, video of work by Fenley, 1988, NYPL.

160. Marie Chouinard quoted in publicity for Budapest Autumn Festival, 1999; see also Linda Howe-Beck, 'Quebec Quests', *Dance Magazine*, 68 (January, 1994), pp. 112–14; Karen Dacko, 'Deliverance', *Dance Magazine*, 69 (April, 1995), pp. 84–5. Chouinard's *Sacre* included additional noise music by Rober Racine. The work is part of the TV documentary *Die Erschaffung des Lebens*, directed/produced by Eva-Maria Wittke and Mechthild Lange, NDR-Fernsehen, 1994.

161. Paula Citron, 'The Well-Choreographed Montreal Dance Explosion', *Performing Arts in Canada*, 19/1 (Summer, 1982), p. 42.

162. Min Tanaka, *The Rite of Spring*, Vagabond Video, directed by Min Tanaka, co-produced by Kazue Kobata and Alexandra Korneva, 1998, NYPL.

163. Tero Saarinen, *Westward Ho!–Wavelengths–Hunt*, promotional video (and accompanying information booklet) of Tero Saarinen Company, directed by Ilmo Lintonen, Minus Movie, 2006.

164. Donald Hutera, 'Brief Reviews: Tero Saarinen', *Dance Europe*, 56 (October, 2002), p. 56.

165. The original piano score shows percussion lines beneath the piano parts, perhaps as a potential addition.

166. Berg, '*Le Sacre du printemps*', p. 129.

167. Anna Kisselgoff, 'A Breakout for the *Rite*', *The New York Times*, July 25, 2003.

168. Judith Mackrell, 'The Rite Stuff'. The programme note indicates that *Milagros* is the Spanish word for 'miracles and votive offerings left at churches or shrines'. The recording used was by Rex Lawson as the player pianist, Innovative Music Productions, 1991.

169. The dance is noted on the website of Scapino Ballet, www.scapinoballet.nl

170. Lynn Garafola, 'Idioms Merge in Moderns: Rebecca Kelly Ballet', *Dance Magazine*, 74 (September, 2000), p. 99. See also *Dream Driven*, video directed and produced by Linda Lewett, c. 1987, NYPL.

171. Manning, 'German *Rites*', p. 150.

172. Angela Kane, 'Paul Taylor's Choreography: In the Public Domain', unpublished PhD dissertation, University of Kent at Canterbury, London Contemporary Dance School, 2000, p. 203. For full discussions of Taylor's *Sacre*, see Kane, pp. 200–05, and Berg, '*Le Sacre du printemps*', pp. 109–23.

173. Kane, 'Paul Taylor's Choreography', p. 200. Kane also mentions that a passage to Spring Rounds, called the Bar Dance, is phrased just as it was to the equivalent music in the original *Scudorama* (from Bettie de Jong interview with Rita Felciano during the conference 'Last Looks and First Words', at the Yerba Buena Center for the Arts, San Francisco, April 11, 1999).

174. Taylor quoted in Katherine Teck, *Music for Dance: Reflections on a Collaborative Art* (New York, Westport, Conn. & London: Greenwood Press, 1989), p. 9.

175. Taylor quoted in Holly Brubach, 'Talking about Dance: Paul Taylor's *Rite of Spring* – America's Native-Son Choreographer Takes on Stravinsky's Toughest Score', *Vogue*, April, 1980.

176. Alan M. Kriegsman, 'Irreverent *Rite*', *The Washington Post*, January 16, 1980.

177. Kane, 'Paul Taylor's Choreography', p. 205.

178. Anna Kisselgoff, 'Taylor Presents *Rite of Spring* Premiere', *The New York Times*, April 17, 1980; Octavio Roca, 'Paul Taylor's Enigmatic *Spring*', *San Francisco Chronicle*, April 9, 1999; Arlene Croce, '*Le Sacre* without Ceremony', *The New Yorker*, May 19, 1980, in Croce, *Going to the Dance* (New York: Alfred A. Knopf, 1982), p. 271.

179. Berg, '*Le Sacre du printemps*', p. 123.

180. Kane, 'Paul Taylor's Choreography', p. 200.

181. 'Paul Taylor: Two Landmark Dances', directed by Emile Ardolino, produced by Ardolino and Judy Kinberg, WNET/Thirteen in association with the University of North Carolina Center for Public Television, 1981; Labanotation score of Taylor's *Sacre*, notated by Janet Moekle, 1979–86 (New York: Dance Notation Bureau, 1986). The score remains in unfinished form. Part 1 extends up until [25]+3 during the Augurs of Spring; the whole of Part 2 is notated in draft.

182. Stravinsky, *Music for Four Hands*, played by Benjamin Frith and Peter Hill, Naxos, 8.553386, 1996.

183. Taylor quoted in Teck, *Music for Dance: Reflections on a Collaborative Art*, p. 174.

184. Ibid., p. 10.

185. Arlene Croce, '*Le Sacre* without Ceremony', p. 271.

186. Ibid.

187. Ibid.

188. Taylor quoted in Teck, *Music for Dance: Reflections on a Collaborative Art*, p. 10.

189. Taylor described the ending of *Sacre* as 'bang bang bang dribble dribble dribble bang', in Holly Brubach, 'Talking about Dance: Paul Taylor's *Rite of Spring*'. I am very grateful for information on rhythmic synchronisation provided by Taylor, Bettie de Jong, Michael Trusnovec and Richard Chen See, at the Paul Taylor Dance Company studios, New York, September 12, 2006.

190. Carol Brown, email communication with the author, July 17, 2006. I am indebted to Brown for her dialogue with me about my performative examples of *Sacre*.

191. Programme statement quoted in Ramsay Burt, 'Another Dream' [review], February 2, 2005, http://forum.criticaldance.com

192. Raimund Hoghe, *Sacre – The Rite of Spring*, DVD of premiere performance, 2004. My analysis is also informed by a live performance at the Théâtre de la Bastille, Paris, January 15, 2005.

193. Gerald Siegmund, 'Raimund Hoghe and the Art of Ritual Substitution', lecture at Kaaitheater, January 26, 2004, http://kulturserver-nrw.de/home/rhoghe/en/en_lecture.html

194. Ibid.

195. Hoghe in interview with the author, May 7, 2005. This interview is the source of other quotations from Hoghe, unless otherwise indicated.

196. Stravinsky quoted on *The Essential Igor Stravinsky*, Sony Classical 89910, 2003. In the introduction to the CD, John McClure refers to the 1965 visit to Europe from which these sound clips were taken. The reference to being a 'vessel' is also found in *Expo*, pp. 147–8.

197. Hoghe quoted in Boisseau, 'Les Chorégraphes multiplient les *Sacre du printemps*'.

198. Jérôme Bel, 'I am the (W)Hole Between Their Two Apartments', *Ballett International/Tanz*

Aktuell Yearbook (1999), p. 36.

199. André Lepecki, *Exhausting Dance: Performance and the Politics of Movement* (New York & London: Routledge, 2006), p. 50.

200. Ibid., p. 54.

201. Bel quoted in Siegmund, 'In the Realm of Signs: Jérôme Bel', *Ballett International/Tanz Aktuell* (April, 1998), p. 36.

202. *Jérôme Bel*, filmed by Luciana Fina, DVD, produced by R. B. Jérôme Bel (Paris), 1999. I refer to the original cast of performers in my text.

203. Siegmund, 'In the Realm of Signs: Jérôme Bel', p. 37. With regard to the 'voyeur' concept, consider the very different ironic *Sacre* by Patrick Roger (1986), in which the spectators are seated on stage watching three members of Compagnie Ecchymose discussing and showing items of professional sacrifice, their own bruises and injuries. Protected voyeurs of traditional *Sacres*, the audience had now to look at itself looking. For one critic, this work resolved the ambiguity of the original work (music and choreography), which 'cherche la communion avec le spectateur tout en lui imposant une distanciation de fait': Alain Foix, 'Patrick Roger', *Pour la danse* (February, 1987), p. 20.

204. Lepecki, *Exhausting Dance: Performance and the Politics of Movement*, p. 49.

205. Ibid., pp. 56–7. Xavier Le Roy, also part of the Konzept Tanz movement, used Simon Rattle's movements, when conducting *Sacre*, as the basis of his solo *Sacre*, premiered June 27, 2007.

206. Ibid., p. 58. The concept of 'being-toward-movement' is taken from Peter Sloterdijk, *La Mobilisation infinie* (Paris: Christian Bourgeois Editeurs, 2000), p. 36.

207. Brown, email communication with the author, July 17, 2006.

208. Leonid Jacobson's *Troika* is included in *Khoreograficheskie miniatiury*, directed by M. Sheinin, Lenfilm Studios production, 1960, *NYPL*. See also Denis Dabbadie, 'Un Printemps véritablement sacré', *L'Avant-Scène: Ballet/danse*, 3 (August–October, 1980), p. 97.

209. Clive Barnes, 'Dance: Ballets for Hanukkah Festival', *The New York Times*, December 6, 1966.

210. Saburo Teshigawara, *Dah-dah-sko-dah-dah*, video, produced by Karas/Kei Miyata, 1991, *NYPL*.

211. Daniel Jacobson, 'Peeling Our Eyes', *Ballet Review*, 26/2 (summer, 1998), p. 80.

212. Manning, 'German *Rites*' (1991), pp. 152–3.

213. Live performance of Michael Clark's *Mmm...* viewed at The Roundhouse, London, June 27, 1992. See also Clement Crisp, 'Michael Clark Dance Company', *The Dancing Times*, 82 (August, 1992), p. 1044. I saw a live performance of the second version of this work at the Barbican Theatre, London, October 28, 2006.

214. Programme note for Christine Gaigg's *Sacre Material*, supported by Gaigg/2nd Nature company video (2000).

215. Live performance of *Beauté Plastique* viewed at The Place Theatre, London, February 11, 2006.

216. Information provided by Martine Epoque, email communication with the author, April 28, 2006.

217. Information on Motaz Kabbani's *Sacre* from interviews/previews: Aline Apostolska, 'Un Sacre aux parfums d'Orient', *La Presse Montréal*, October, 2003 [no day given]; Frédérique Doyon, 'Un Sacre du printemps arabe', *Le Devoir*, October 31, 2003. The work was also viewed on a company video recording (2003).

218. Philip Szporer, 'A Middle Eastern Take on *Le Sacre*', *The Dance Current*, www.thedancecurrent.com

219. Stephen Page, *Rites*, directed by Peter Butler, Australian Broadcast Corporation, 1998, later broadcast on BBC2, Summer Dance, August 15, 1998.

220. The Zingaro *Sacre* is included in *Triptyk* (conducted by Pierre Boulez), production director Philippe Worms, ARTE France/KM/Zingaro/France 3/Equidia, 2000. An Internet search also reveals a *Sacre* setting *Spirit Land* by Ileana Citaristi, an Italian-born, Orissi-based Odissi dancer-choreographer: it is about oppression and injustice, hope in the midst of despair, premiered in Kuala Lumpur (2003), and inspired by the work of the Malaysian poet Usman Awang, http://narthaki.com/info/reviews/rev129.html

221. Akiko Tachiki, 'Absolute *Sacre*', *Ballett International/Tanz Aktuell* (November, 1999), p. 25.

222. I sensed allusion to Augurs of Spring in the section of the 1989 work included in *Butoh: Body on the Edge of Crisis*, documentary directed and produced by Michael Blackwood in association with Westdeutscher Rundfunk, BBC TV, YLE/NOS/BRT, SVT1/DR/ORF, 1990.

223. Carlotta Ikeda quoted in Boisseau, 'Les Chorégraphes multiplient les *Sacre du printemps*'.

224. Ibid. (Boisseau). I saw a performance of Emanuel Gat's *Rite of Spring* in the Woking Dance Festival, March 20, 2007.

225. Antonin Jefferson, 'Entretien avec Elsa Wolliaston', www.moulinette.com/sites-archive/tcd/e-wollias.htm

226. 'Entretien: Georges Momboye', www.journal-laterrasse.com/dossier_ds_biennal.htm; Boisseau, 'Les Chorégraphes multiplient les *Sacre du printemps*'.

227. Boisseau, 'Les Chorégraphes multiplient les *Sacre du printemps*'.

228. Interview with Heddy Maalem, promotional DVD, 2006, and company DVD of *Le Sacre du printemps*, 2003.

229. Richard Alston quoted in Jennifer Dunning, 'Britain's Oldest Ballet Troupe on Tour', p. 32.

230. Maalem quoted in Bernadette Bonis, 'Bande-annonce: avant-premières; Heddy Maalem aux Francophonies: Un *Sacre du printemps* africain', *Danser* (September, 2005), pp. 66–7.

Selected bibliography

Acocella, Joan, Lynn Garafola and Jonnie Greene, 'The Rite of Spring Considered as a Nineteenth-Century Ballet' and 'Catalogue Raisonné', Ballet Review, 20/2 (Summer, 1992), pp. 68–100

Berg, Shelley, 'Le Sacre du printemps': Seven Productions from Nijinsky to Martha Graham, Ann Arbor: UMI Research Press, 1988

Carr, Maureen, Multiple Masks: Neoclassicism in Stravinsky's Works on Greek Subjects, Lincoln: University of Nebraska Press, 2002

Cross, Jonathan, The Stravinsky Legacy, Cambridge: Cambridge University Press, 1998

Cross, Jonathan, ed., The Cambridge Companion to Stravinsky, Cambridge: Cambridge University Press, 2003

D'Adamo, Ada, Danzare il Rito: 'Le Sacre du Printemps' attraverso il Novecento, Rome: Bulzoni Editore, 1999

Garafola, Lynn, Diaghilev's Ballets Russes, New York & Oxford: Oxford University Press, 1989

Garafola, Lynn and Nancy Van Norman Baer, eds, The Ballets Russes and Its World, New Haven & London: Yale University Press, 1999

Goldner, Nancy, The Stravinsky Festival of the New York City Ballet, New York: Eakins Press, 1974

Jordan, Stephanie, Moving Music: Dialogues with Music in Twentieth-Century Ballet, London: Dance Books, 2000

Joseph, Charles M., Stravinsky Inside Out, New Haven & London: Yale University Press, 2001

Joseph, Charles M., Stravinsky and Balanchine: A Journey of Invention, New Haven & London: Yale University Press, 2002

Lederman, Minna, ed., Stravinsky in the Theatre [1949], New York: Da Capo Press, 1975

Pasler, Jann, ed., Confronting Stravinsky: Man, Musician, and Modernist, Berkeley: University of California Press, 1986

Reynolds, Nancy, Repertory in Review: 40 Years of the New York City Ballet, New York: The Dial Press, 1977

Schouvaloff, Alexander and Victor Borovsky, Stravinsky on Stage, London: Stainer & Bell, 1982

Stravinsky and the Dance: A Survey of Ballet Productions, New York: New York Public Library, 1962

Stravinsky, Igor, *An Autobiography* [1936], London: Calder & Boyars, 1975

Stravinsky, Vera, and Robert Craft, *Stravinsky in Pictures and Documents*, New York: Simon & Schuster, 1978

Taruskin, Richard, *Stravinsky and the Russian Traditions: A Biography of the Works through 'Mavra'*, 2 vols, Oxford: Oxford University Press, 1996

Taruskin, Richard, *Defining Russia Musically: Historical and Hermeneutical Essays*, Princeton: Princeton University Press, 1997

Van den Toorn, Pieter C., *The Music of Igor Stravinsky*, New Haven: Yale University Press, 1983

Van den Toorn, Pieter C., *Stravinsky and 'The Rite of Spring': The Beginnings of a Musical Language*, Berkeley & Los Angeles: University of California Press, 1987

Walsh, Stephen, *Stravinsky: Oedipus Rex*, Cambridge: Cambridge University Press, 1993

Walsh, Stephen, *Igor Stravinsky: A Creative Spring*, London: Jonathan Cape, 2000

Walsh, Stephen, *Stravinsky: The Second Exile: France and America, 1934–1971*, New York: Alfred A. Knopf, 2006

White, Eric Walter, *Stravinsky: The Composer and his Works*, London: Faber and Faber, 1979

Other sources

Jordan, Stephanie, *Music Dances: Balanchine Choreographs Stravinsky* [analytical documentary video conceived, written and narrated by Jordan], New York: The George Balanchine Foundation, 2002

Jordan, Stephanie and Geraldine Morris, *Ashton to Stravinsky: A Study of Four Ballets with Choreography by Frederick Ashton* [analytical documentary video/DVD], London: Dance Books, 2004

Jordan, Stephanie and Larraine Nicholas, 'Stravinsky the Global Dancer' [Internet database chronology], www.roehampton.ac.uk/stravinsky, 2003 (ongoing project)

NB Theoretical, methodological sources are indicated in the notes to the Introduction.

Permissions acknowledgements

Associated Music Publishers: Excerpts from Stravinsky/AMP correspondence. Used by Permission of Associated Music Publishers, Inc.

Boosey & Hawkes Music Publishers: Excerpts from Stravinsky/Boosey & Hawkes correspondence. Reprinted by permission of Boosey & Hawkes Music Publishers Ltd.

Edinburgh University Press: material from articles by Stephanie Jordan originally published in *Dance Research* (Summer, 2000 and Summer, 2004), used here in expanded and modified form.

Drue Fergison: Excerpts from translations in Fergison, '*Les Noces*: A Microhistory of the Paris 1923 Production', unpublished PhD dissertation, Duke University, 1995. Reprinted by permission of Drue Fergison.

The Literary Executor of the Lincoln Kirstein Papers and Copyrights: letter by Lincoln Kirstein of 31 August 1953, copyright 1953 by Lincoln Kirstein with the rights transferred to the New York Public Library (Astor, Lenox and Tilden Foundations).

Oxford University Press: Excerpts from *Stravinsky and the Russian Traditions* by Richard Taruskin (1996). Reprinted by permission of Oxford University Press.

Natalie Raetz: Excerpts from 'Creation of *Les Noces*' by Bronislava Nijinska, *Dance Magazine* (1999). Reprinted by permission of Natalie Raetz on behalf of the Nijinska Estate.

The Robbins Rights Trust: Excerpts from correspondence and other unpublished material from the Jerome Robbins Papers. Used by permission of The Robbins Rights Trust.

The Paul Sacher Stiftung: Excerpts from various unpublished documents. Reprinted by permission of the Paul Sacher Stiftung.

John Stravinsky: Excerpts from Stravinsky material. Reprinted by permission of John Stravinsky on behalf of the Stravinsky Estate.

Stephen Walsh: Excerpts from *Igor Stravinsky: A Creative Spring* and *Stravinsky: The Second Exile* (London: Jonathan Cape, 2000 and 2006) by Stephen Walsh. Reprinted by permission of Professor Stephen Walsh.

Music credits

Stravinsky score examples reproduced by permission of Boosey & Hawkes Music Publishers Ltd:

Le Sacre du printemps
© Copyright 1912, 1921 by Hawkes & Son (London) Ltd
Excentrique from *Quatre Etudes*
© Copyright 1930 by Hawkes & Son (London) Ltd
Revised version © Copyright 1971 by Boosey & Hawkes Music Publishers Ltd
Serenade in A
© Copyright 1926 by Hawkes & Son (London) Ltd
Symphonies of Wind Instruments
© Copyright 1926 by Hawkes & Son (London) Ltd
Movements for Piano and Orchestra
© Copyright 1960 by Hawkes & Son (London) Ltd
Le Baiser de la fée
© Copyright 1928 by Hawkes & Son (London) Ltd
Revised version © Copyright 1952 by Hawkes & Son (London) Ltd
US copyright renewed
Persephone
© Copyright 1934 by Hawkes & Son (London) Ltd
Revision version © Copyright 1950 by Hawkes & Son (London) Ltd
US copyright renewed
Le Rossignol
© Copyright 1914 by Hawkes & Son (London) Ltd

Other Stravinsky score examples

Violin Concerto
© 1931 Schott Music GmbH & Co. KG, Mainz, Germany, worldwide rights except the United Kingdom, Ireland, Australia, Canada, South Africa and all so-called reversionary rights territories where the copyright © 1996 is held jointly by Schott Music GmbH & Co. KG, Mainz, Germany, and Chester Music Ltd.

Scènes de ballet
© 1945, Schott Music GmbH & Co. KG, Mainz, Germany, worldwide rights except North and South America and Israel and the United Kingdom, Ireland, Australia, South Africa and all so-called reversionary rights territories where the copyright © 1996 is held jointly by Schott Music GmbH & Co. KG, Mainz, Germany, and Chester Music Ltd.

Danses Concertantes
© 1971 Schott Music GmbH & Co. KG, Mainz, Germany, worldwide rights except the United Kingdom, Ireland, Australia, Canada, South Africa and all so-called

Choreography credits

Choreomusical analysis of the Balanchine repertory published by permission of The George Balanchine Trust.

Ashton choreography and *Les Noces* examples used with permission of Anthony Russell-Roberts of The Royal Ballet.

Examples from Pina Bausch's *Das Frühlingsopfer* used and notated with permission of Tanztheater Wuppertal.

Illustration credits

Illustrations 2 and 18: Photographs by Lois Greenfield

Illustrations 3, 4, 5 and 14: Photographs by Paul Kolnik. Illustrations 3, 4 and 5: © The George Balanchine Trust

Illustration 6: Photograph by Julieta Cervantes

Illustrations 7, 8, 9, 11, 12 and 13: Photographs by Leslie E. Spatt

Illustration 10: Photograph by Houston Rogers, reproduced by kind permission of the Victoria and Albert Museum

Illustration 15: Photograph by Herman Sorgeloos

Illustration 16: Photograph by Dee Conway

Illustration 17: Photograph by Gert Weigelt

Illustration 19: Photograph by Rosa Frank

Index